DATE DUE

DEMCO 38-296

GREAT EVENTS FROM HISTORY
NORTH AMERICAN SERIES

GREAT EVENTS FROM HISTORY
NORTH AMERICAN SERIES

Revised Edition

Volume 1
15,000 B.C. – 1819

Edited by
FRANK N. MAGILL

Associate Editor
JOHN L. LOOS

Managing Editor, Revised Edition
CHRISTINA J. MOOSE

Salem Press, Inc.
Pasadena, California   Englewood Cliffs, N.J.

Editor in Chief: Dawn P. Dawson
Managing Editor: Christina J. Moose
Acquisitions Editor: Mark Rehn
Manuscript Editor: Irene Struthers
Research Supervisor: Jeffry Jensen
Research Assistant: Irene McDermott
Photograph Editor: Valerie Krein
Proofreading Supervisor: Yasmine A. Cordoba
Map Design and Page Layout: James Hutson
Data Entry: William Zimmerman

Library of Congress Cataloging-in-Publication Data

Great events from history : North American series / edited by Frank N. Magill ; associate editor, John L. Loos.
— Rev. ed.
    p. cm.
Includes bibliographical references (p.) and index.
ISBN 0-89356-429-X (set). — ISBN 0-89356-430-3 (vol. 1)
1. North America—History. 2. United States—History. I. Magill, Frank Northen, 1907-   . II. Loos, John L.
E45.G74   1997
970—dc21
                                          96-39165
                                            CIP

First Printing

CONTENTS

LIST OF MAPS

Note to the Revised Edition

Great Events from History: North American Series, Revised Edition combines original entries from Magill's *Great Events from History: American Series* (1975) with selected entries from *Great Events from History: Worldwide Twentieth Century Series* (1980) and 325 completely new entries. The new edition thus broadens the original publication's focus on U.S. history through 1975 to cover North American history through 1996. Supplementing the text are 146 photographs and 56 maps illustrating many of the key events. The result is this substantially updated and expanded *Revised Edition*, consisting of 202 illustrations and 665 articles on significant occurrences in the history of both the United States and Canada, along with highlights from Mexican and Caribbean history.

The contents of the *Revised Edition* include nearly all of the articles in the *American Series*: 298 of the original 336 topics are here, along with 42 topics germane to North American history from the *Worldwide Twentieth Century Series*. All information—dates, personages, categorization of events—was scrutinized, updated, and where necessary corrected by historians and other experts to ensure accuracy and currency. Each article's "Pertinent Literature" and "Additional Recommended Readings" sections were replaced by a more current annotated bibliography, entitled "Additional Reading," in which readers will find the best of both classic and recent publications for in-depth study.

In addition to the 340 articles updated from the original publications, 325 new articles have been commissioned to provide coverage of events from Canadian, as well as highlights from Mexican and Caribbean, history; key events in the history of the ethnically and racially diverse North American peoples, from Native Americans and African Americans to Latino and Asian Americans; events in North America's history of civil (including women's) rights; and important social, political, and economic milestones omitted from the original edition. Finally, two decades of history since the original publication dictated addition of 60 of the most important political, legal, economic, and scientific developments since 1975, from Canada's Human Rights Act through détente with the former Soviet Union to the rise of North American terrorism and the sudden growth of the Internet. As a result, nearly half of the *Revised Edition* consists of entirely new material written expressly for the current publication.

Revision and updating extended to the articles' format as well as to the table of contents. Each article retains the same basic ready-reference listings, including event, year, locale, and principal personages ("Key Figures"). In the *Revised Edition*, the editors have preceded each event's title with the year, in boldface, for ease in locating events that fall within a specified chronological period. Following the title, the editors have added a capsule summary identifying the significance of the event in the context of North American history. A more precise "Date" line for each event was researched in order to add the exact month and day, as well as the year, of the event wherever appropriate. Finally, the top matter adds a list of "Categories," replacing the old "Type of Event" with a listing of *all* categories to which the event is pertinent, from "African American history" through "Immigration" to "Wars, Uprisings, and Civil Unrest."

As in the original publication, the text consists of a "Summary of Event" which rehearses the event itself and presents its impact. Depending on the event, this body of the article ranges from 1,000 to 1,200 words in length. In the case of the 340 updated entries, academicians in the fields of history, economics, and political science have reviewed the summaries' accuracy, have added material to correct or update the facts presented, and have reconsidered each event's impact in the light of new research during the years since 1975. The 325 new entries have likewise undergone editorial review for factual accuracy. Finally, the text of all articles has undergone a review for objectivity: Although history can never be impervious to viewpoint and interpretation, bias in both content and language has been strictly monitored in favor of reportorial presentation of the event and its impact, rather than interpretation. To the extent that interpretations do appear, it is the editors' hope that the broad range of academicians who have revised, updated, and newly written these articles—as well as the broad range of topics, nearly double in number from that of the original edition—will, in the aggregate, provide the emphasis on fact befitting a reference publication.

Each article's text ends with the signature of its author—or, in the case of updated entries, authors. Aesthetics dictated this positioning of the byline; the contributing authors were also responsible for compiling the bibliographies that appear at the ends of the articles.

The articles' end matter consists of two elements: the annotated bibliography of "Additional Readings," consisting of approximately five sources for further study with brief notes regarding their usefulness; and a listing of cross-references headed "See also." These "See also" cross-references list related events covered in the *Revised Edition*. The cross-reference format begins with the event's year, followed by its title, to enable the reader to flip quickly to the event, whose heading includes the same information, boldfaced and in the same order.

Additional aids to accessing the information in these volumes exist in the form of two lists appearing at the end of each volume: a permuted index, entitled the Key Word Index, which lists titles by every key word appearing in them; and a Category List, listing each article in each of the thirty-one different categories to which it is pertinent. A count of entries in these categories reveals the following distribution: African American History is a major focus of 76 entries; Asian American History, 24; Business and Labor, 60; Canadian History, 67; Civil Rights, 84; Communications, 15; Court Cases, 31; Cultural and Intellectual History, 25;

Diplomacy and International Relations, 68; Economics, 90; Education, 27; Environment, 9; Expansion and Land Acquisition, 68; Exploration and Discovery, 28; Government and Politics, 122; Health and Medicine, 12; Immigration, 33; Jewish American History, 2; Latino American History, 48; Laws and Acts, 106; Native American History, 97; Organizations and Institutions, 55; Prehistory and Ancient Cultures, 10; Religion, 28; Science and Technology, 51; Settlements, 19; Social Reform, 29; Transportation, 20; Treaties and Agreements, 34; Wars, Uprisings, and Civil Unrest, 135; and Women's Issues, 43. Clearly the emphasis here is on social, political, and economic history; the significant number of intellectual, artistic, and scientific events covered reflects the extension of their impact beyond their immediate disciplines to the sociopolitical development of North America.

Two more reference tools will be found at the end of Volume 4: the Personages Index, listing all key figures and other personages who are listed in the articles' top matter *or* who receive significant discussion in the text; and the Subject Index, which lists all events, movements, acts, personages, terms, works, tribes, battles, treaties, locales, and concepts that receive significant textual discussion or that appear in contexts that cast further light on them.

The editors wish to thank the 293 contributors—historians, political scientists, economists, sociologists, and scientists—who prepared the material that appears in this publication. These academicians have provided not only their expertise but also their judgment in extracting the most important issues and facts for inclusion, as well as in updating their predecessors' work responsibly and seamlessly. A list of contributors to both the first edition and the *Revised Edition* can be found in the opening pages of Volume 1.

C.J.M.

PREFACE TO THE FIRST EDITION

The three-volume American Series of *Great Events from History* begins with the arrival of the Indians, the first Americans, from Asia and ends with the first manned lunar landing in 1969. Between these two noteworthy happenings, 336 additional events are studied in depth through the scholarly literature they have inspired. The two other three-volume sections of the overall work, the Ancient and Medieval Series and the Modern European Series, contain 336 events each. Thus the nine-volume set contains 1,010 events, each with its own coverage of relevant literature.

Unlike the other two series, which simply pick up a continuum at a given point (4000 B.C. or A.D. 1469) and proceed to follow along with an ongoing social development, the American Series, starting with the fourth article, enables one to examine the beginning and development of a brand-new society from point zero—a societal *tabula rasa*, so to speak. Furthermore, this development may be examined through contemporary sources not flawed by myth and information gaps, as well as through scholarly retrospect. Nowhere in human history has such an opportunity on so large a scale presented itself, where the record is there without guesswork—the social development as clear as an ant colony behind glass. It is a remarkable story that unfolds.

Shortly after Columbus landed, the Old World began to explore the New, then slowly fill it with its own restless masses. The open space, the freedom to expand, led men to resent restrictions placed by the Old World, safe at home and unable to understand the challenge and fulfillment of the frontier. Soon the new men began to think seriously in terms of liberty and the rights to live as they pleased, with no king and no nobility over them to thwart their aspirations. Thus began the building of a social organism so original and, despite some human failings, so successful that it is emulated in altered forms in many parts of the world today.

A glance through the chronological list of events will reveal the pattern of the remarkable story that unfolded as the incipient Republic sought to enhance its new concept in political democracy. From the beginning, in the eyes of these political innovators vigilance and broad participation in government were vital to liberty. Indeed, self-government was deemed so essential that the First General Assembly of Virginia was called only twelve years after the initial settlement of Jamestown.

The 1600's were a period of colonial settlement and growth but there was time for consideration of civilizing influences too. Massachusetts passed a compulsory school law in 1647 and Maryland insisted on religious freedom for all its people by the Act of Toleration in 1649. By 1734 freedom of the press had been established in the courts, a concept that later found its way into the new Constitution.

Having left the ways of the Old World far behind, the new men now found oppression from that source intolerable. If liberty must be purchased with the sword, so be it. Beginning with the Stamp Act crisis in 1765, a dozen articles in this work record the key events leading up to Cornwallis' surrender and the end of British rule in the American colonies.

Out of this conflict a new nation emerged whose people were now committed more than ever to the principles of individual liberty and equal justice under the law. Dedicated leaders soon devised a Constitution by which to be governed, a living instrument that could be changed with changing conditions and that would assure rule by laws, not men.

The new nation's growth was spectacular. Soon Slater's spinning mill, Whitney's cotton gin, and McCormick's reaper would herald the modest beginnings of the greatest industrial power the world has ever known.

This was a unique social unit, a nation whose great energy was fed by waves of immigrants, each adding new vigor to the society. The receding frontier was tamed time after time as it shifted westward, each group bringing with it the church and the school. This was a people who advanced the highly civilized and unheard-of proposal of buying land from France—and later

Russia—instead of warring for it. Yet at times they were tough and deadly. The fratricide of 1861-1865 was one of the bloodiest wars in history though it was slow to develop. Fifteen events over a period of thirty years leading up to the war are examined here.

Following the war and Reconstruction, the nation knew a period of great economic growth and by the end of the nineteenth century—hardly more than a century after its founding—had become a world power. The twentieth century has seen this position of leadership expand, sometimes to the despair of those who yearn for the chance to withdraw. It is not likely, however, that the great and diverse people who tamed much of the North American continent and now have their eyes on space will soon lose their sense of spiritual leadership, their energy, their curiosity, or their desire to master the greatest frontier of all—the deep mystery of life and nature.

The articles in this work consist of four sections: (1) Quick reference material at the beginning showing type of event, time, locale, and principal personages involved if applicable; (2) Summary of Event, a "journalistic" account of the occurrence describing the basic facts of what took place and some of the causes and effects; (3) Pertinent Literature, wherein two original essay-reviews of scholarly works written about the event are presented; and (4) Additional Recommended Reading, which lists and annotates several other works that the student or researcher might profitably examine if he is interested in an in-depth study of the event. Works reviewed in Item (3) are usually books though sometimes scholarly articles are reported on instead. An effort has been made to select for review works of divergent viewpoints, especially if the event under consideration is controversial. The critical evaluations presented in Items (2) and (3) provide a review of the immediate and long-range effects of an occurrence and should enable the reader to view objectively the forces that sparked the event.

The primary objective of the editors has been to present an individual discussion and analysis of more than one thousand significant happenings whose consequences have changed the course of history in the Western world. *Great Events from History* is not a compilation of reprinted historical material; all the material it contains was newly written expressly for this set by some one hundred and fifty history professors and scholars from more than fifty campuses throughout the United States. These contributing professors and scholars have brought their special knowledge and skill to the task of writing the capsule summaries of events and the individual evaluations of the two thousand appropriate works that are reviewed. They have made their articles accurate in reporting facts, scholarly but not dull, clear and not technical without cause, and interpretive in the presentation of the central ideas advanced in the books being reviewed. Reports of the events themselves average eight hundred to one thousand words in length while individual reviews of the literature run about six or eight hundred words each. Events are presented in chronological order in the text.

At the beginning of each volume there appears a chronological list of events for that volume. Volume three includes these six indexes: Alphabetical List of Events, Key Word Index of Events, Category Index for Type of Event, an alphabetized listing of Principal Personages, a listing by author of the Pertinent Literature Reviewed, and a listing by author of the Literature for Additional Recommended Reading. Since, unlike book titles, not all events lend themselves to a specific title universally applied, as do "Battle of . . ." or "Establishment of . . ." articles, the Key Word index should enable the user to locate many events more readily than would an alphabetical index of events whose first word was arbitrarily assigned by the editors.

The two indexes of historical literature provide a reading list of thousands of titles and thousands of authors whose works are pertinent to at least one of the events under examination. Such extensive coverage of the literature of the discipline offers a convenient source for in-depth research by the student, and for course development and class assignments by the instructor.

The three score contributors to the American Series are listed elsewhere in this volume along with their academic affiliations. My sincere appreciation goes to these professors and scholars and to the researchers and assistants whose efforts were so important to the completion of the work. I am especially indebted to Mr. Robert Edward Ostermeyer of the Graduate School, Department of History, University of Southern California, for his invaluable assistance with the project. All of us hope that the work will be useful and stimulating to those whose interest lies in the fascinating field of American history. FRANK N. MAGILL

INTRODUCTION TO THE FIRST EDITION

History may be defined in a number of different ways. One useful definition is that it is a body of knowledge concerning the past which has been generally accepted by scholars. Of all that has been thought and done by man, only an infinitesimal part has been made a matter of record, and only a small fraction of that record has been examined and evaluated by qualified experts. From the records which they have investigated, these scholars have selected certain facts which they have decided are of sufficient importance to be considered historical facts, to be used in their accounts of the past. Thus the history of the United States is made up of those facts which historians have concluded are significant in understanding this nation's past. While there is naturally not complete agreement on every historical fact, the disagreement among historians is less about the facts than it is about their relative importance and what they mean.

The particular historical facts which should be emphasized and the way in which they should be interpreted change from time to time, for every generation looks to the past for answers to questions which seem to be of special relevance to it. Today, for example, the American people are especially concerned about matters of women's rights, race, and ecology. Historians are, therefore, studying this country's past with particular reference to the roles and activities of women, blacks, and Indians and to the manner in which the people have used the nation's natural resources and treated the environment down through the years. Each historian, furthermore, studies the past in terms of his own education, experience, and philosophy of life, and his writing reflects these influences in greater or less degree.

In this work the history of the United States is viewed in terms of certain facts, or "great events," which stand out on the historical landscape as having been of extraordinary importance. The three volumes contain 336 such events. What constitutes a "great event" has, of course, been a matter of editorial judgment with which our readers are bound to have some disagreement. The events included here have not been chosen with any particular interpretation of American history in mind. The work has no special theme or thesis to present. It does not try to glorify the American past or to denigrate it. It does not view American history as having been characterized mainly by consensus or by conflict. It considers no single aspect of history as basically more important than another.

In making their selection the editors have taken a broad view of the American past. They have been careful to cover the entire span of American history, including even prehistory, from the migration to America of the Indians, the first human beings to inhabit this continent, to man's first successful landing on an extra-terrestrial body, the moon. They have included major events from all kinds of history—political, economic, social, military, diplomatic, religious, literary, and artistic. Geographically, the events which they have chosen embrace all sections, or regions, of the United States. Since ours is and has been principally a secular society which has produced little in the way of organized philosophy or abstract thought, religious and philosophical events do not figure prominently in this list of great events. By the same token, because this country represents a highly successful political experiment and has been favored by great natural wealth which its people have developed and exploited with unusual resourcefulness and energy, political and economic events loom large in the editors' selection. Although Americans have always considered themselves to be a peace-loving people, wars have been important in their history, and a significant number of events are, therefore, related to wars, and especially the Civil War and World War II. Reflecting the popular concern with the nation's recent past, one-third of all the events fall within the twentieth century.

These events were written by fifty-eight historians. The summaries are generally straightforward accounts of the events placed in their proper historical settings. The books which the authors have chosen to review not only contain full and accurate treatments of the subject, but they are often distinctive for their literary quality and/or the interpretation which they give the event. Some of the volumes are rather old, but they are still authoritative and have not been superseded by more modern studies. The editors have for the most part had a particular volume reviewed for only one event. They have deliberately included reviews of some of the great classics of American historiography, like volumes from Francis Parkman's *France and England in North America* and Charles M. Andrews' *The Colonial Period of American History*. Three historical works are considered to be so important that their publication constitutes three of the great events included in this study. Whenever an event is the subject of varying, or conflicting, interpretations, the editors have had reviewed books which present those differing interpretations.

As is true of events themselves, there may well be some disagreement on the part of our readers with the selection of books reviewed for a particular event or listed in the additional recommended reading. The books from which the editors could choose were much greater for some events than for others, because some events of American history have attracted the interest of historians more than others. There are, for example, relatively few good books on the founding of most colonies, while there are many excellent works on all aspects of the Civil War; and much more has been written about some Presidential elections than about others. It can fairly be stated that, altogether, the summaries and book reviews contained in these three volumes constitute a comprehensive survey of American history.

The editor offers his thanks to the contributors to this work and to a small group of graduate students at Louisiana State University whose assistance was most valuable.

JOHN L. LOOS
Professor of History
Louisiana State University

CONTRIBUTORS TO THE FIRST EDITION

(Affiliations are current as of publication of first edition.)

J. Stewart Alverson
University of Tennessee

Stephen E. Ambrose
Louisiana State University, New Orleans

David L. Ammerman
Florida State University

Paul Ashin
Stanford University

Robert A. Becker
Louisiana State University, Baton Rouge

Meredith William Berg
Valparaiso University

Warren M. Billings
Louisiana State University, New Orleans

James J. Bolner
Louisiana State University, Baton Rouge

Jack L. Calbert
Indiana University

Ronald J. Cima
Library of Congress

John G. Clark
University of Kansas

Michael D. Clark
Louisiana State University, New Orleans

Terrill J. Clements
University of Nebraska at Omaha

Sidney L. Cohen
Louisiana State University, Baton Rouge

Richard H. Collin
Louisiana State University, New Orleans

William J. Cooper, Jr.
Louisiana State University, Baton Rouge

Charles E. Cottle
University of Wisconsin

David H. Culbert
Louisiana State University, Baton Rouge

Merle O. Davis
Louisiana State University, Baton Rouge

John H. DeBerry
Memphis State University

E. Gene DeFelice
Purdue University

Tyler Deierhoi
University of Tennessee

Daniel D. DiPiazza
University of Wisconsin

Fredrick J. Dobney
St. Louis University

Maurice T. Dominguez
Tulane University

John Duffy
University of Maryland

Robert F. Erickson
Southern Illinois University

Cecil L. Eubanks
Louisiana State University, Baton Rouge

Elizabeth Fee
The Johns Hopkins University

James E. Fickle
Memphis State University

James F. Findlay, Jr.
University of Rhode Island

George J. Fleming
Calumet College

George Q. Flynn
University of Miami

Jonathan M. Furdek
Purdue University

John C. Gardner
Louisiana State University, Baton Rouge

Don R. Gerlach
University of Akron

Manfred Grote
Purdue University

William I. Hair
Florida State University

R. Don Higginbotham
University of North Carolina at Chapel Hill

Donald Holley
University of Arkansas at Monticello

W. Turrentine Jackson
University of California at Davis

Charles W. Johnson
University of Tennessee

Burton Kaufman
Louisiana State University, New Orleans

Jeffrey Kimball
Miami University, Oxford, Ohio

John L. Loos
Louisiana State University, Baton Rouge

Anne C. Loveland
Louisiana State University, Baton Rouge

Frank N. Magill
University of Southern California

Russell Magnaghi
Northern Michigan University

Edward J. Maguire
St. Louis University

Rex O. Mooney
Louisiana State University, Baton Rouge

Burl L. Noggle
Louisiana State University, Baton Rouge

Doris F. Pierce
Purdue University

Mark A. Plummer
Illinois State University

Francis P. Prucha
Marquette University

Anne C. Raymer
Independent Scholar

John D. Raymer
Purdue University

Germaine M. Reed
Georgia Institute of Technology

Merl E. Reed
Georgia State University

William L. Richter
Cameron College

Karl A. Roider
Louisiana State University, Baton Rouge

Courtney B. Ross
Louisiana State University, Baton Rouge

Richard H. Sander
Woodstock Institute

Margaret S. Schoon
Purdue University

Terry L. Seip
Louisiana State University, Baton Rouge

Gustav L. Seligman
North Texas State University

Thomas M. Smith
University of Oklahoma

Ronald N. Spector
Office of the Chief of Military History

Leon Stein
Roosevelt University

Emory M. Thomas
University of Georgia

Anne Trotter
Memphis State University

William M. Tuttle
University of Kansas

Jonathan G. Utley
University of Tennessee

Bennett H. Wall
Tulane University

Major L. Wilson
Memphis State University

Theodore A. Wilson
University of Kansas

Edward A. Zivich
Calumet College

CONTRIBUTORS TO THE REVISED EDITION

Wayne Ackerson
Salisbury State University

Richard Adler
University of Michigan—Dearborn

Craig W. Allin
Cornell College

William Allison
Bowling Green State University

Thomas L. Altherr
Metropolitan State College of Denver

Mary Welek Atwell
Radford University

Bryan Aubrey
Independent Scholar

James A. Baer
Northern Virginia Community College

Sue Bailey
Tennessee Technological University

Mary Pat Balkus
Radford University

Carole A. Barrett
University of Mary

Paul Barton-Kriese
Indiana University East

Richard A. Bennett
Southern College of Technology

Alvin K. Benson
Brigham Young University

Milton Berman
University of Rochester

Nicholas Birns
The New School for Social Research

Kent Blaser
Wayne State College

Pegge A. Bochynski
Indepenent Scholar

Steve D. Boilard
Western Kentucky University

Suzanne Riffle Boyce
Independent Scholar

Daniel A. Brown
California State University, Fullerton

Kendall W. Brown
Brigham Young University

Stephanie Brzuzy
Arizona State University

Mary Louise Buley-Meissner
University of Wisconsin—Milwaukee

Edmund J. Campion
University of Tennessee

Byron D. Cannon
University of Utah

Richard K. Caputo
Barry University

Kathleen Carroll
Southern Illinois University

Lawrence I. Clark
Independent Scholar

David Coffey
Texas Christian University

James J. Cooke
University of Mississippi

David A. Crain
South Dakota State University

Stephen Cresswell
West Virginia Wesleyan College

Norma Crews
Independent Scholar

Laura A. Croghan
College of William and Mary

Edward R. Crowther
Adams State College

LouAnn Faris Culley
Kansas State University

Sudipta Das
Southern University at New Orleans

Jane Davis
Fordham University

Bruce J. DeHart
Pembroke State University

Judith Boyce DeMark
Northern Michigan University

M. Casey Diana
University of Illinois

Stephen B. Dobrow
Fairleigh Dickinson University

Paul E. Doutrich
York College of Pennsylvania

T. W. Dreier
Portland State University

Joyce Duncan
East Tennessee State University

Steven I. Dutch
University of Wisconsin—Green Bay

Jodella K. Dyreson
Weber State University

Jennifer Eastman
Clark University

Craig M. Eckert
Eastern Illinois University

Robert P. Ellis
Worcester State College

John L. Farbo
University of Idaho

James D. Farmer
Virginia Commonwealth University

Randall Fegley
Pennsylvania State University

Anne-Marie E. Ferngren
Western Washington University

John W. Fiero
University of Southwestern Louisiana

Brian L. Fife
Ball State University

Michael Shaw Findlay
California State University, Chico

David G. Fisher
Lycoming College

Michael S. Fitzgerald
Pikeville College

George J. Flynn
State University of New York—Plattsburgh

Rory Flynn
Independent Scholar

John C. Fredriksen
Salem State College

Gregory Freeland
California Lutheran University

C. George Fry
Lutheran College

Jane M. Gilliland
Butler County Community College

Nancy M. Gordon
Independent Scholar

Robert F. Gorman
Southwest Texas State University

Lewis L. Gould
University of Texas, Austin

Kelley Graham
Franklin College of Indiana

Mary M. Graham
York College of Pennsylvania

Gretchen L. Green
Rockhurst College

Michael Haas
University of Hawaii at Manoa

Irwin Halfond
McKendree College

Susan E. Hamilton
University of Hawaii at Hilo

B. Carmon Hardy
California State University, Fullerton

Stanley Harrold
South Carolina State University

Fred R. van Hartesveldt
Fort Valley State College

James Hayes-Bohanan
University of Arizona

Pamela Hayes-Bohanan
McAllen Memorial Library

Peter B. Heller
Manhattan College

Thomas E. Helm
Western Illinois University

Arthur W. Helweg
Western Michigan University

Mark C. Herman
Edison Community College

Kay Hively
Independent Scholar

Russell Hively
Independent Scholar

Carl W. Hoagstrom
Ohio Northern University

Ronald W. Howard
Mississippi College

Richard Hudson
Mercy College

William E. Huntzicker
University of Minnesota

John Jacob
Northwestern University

Robert Jacobs
Central Washington University

Duncan R. Jamieson
Ashland University

Kristine Kleptach Jamieson
Ashland University

Joseph C. Jastrzembski
University of Texas at El Paso

Robert L. Jenkins
Mississippi State University

Albert C. Jensen
Central Florida Community College

K. Sue Jewell
Ohio State University

Jeffrey A. Joens
Florida International University

Bruce E. Johansen
University of Nebraska at Omaha

Jane Anderson Jones
Manatee Community College

Sally J. Kenney
University of Minnesota

Melvin Kulbicki
York College of Pennsylvania

Jeri Kurtzleben
University of Northern Iowa

Philip E. Lampe
Incarnate Word College

Linda Rochell Lane
Tuskegee University

Lisa Langenbach
Middle Tennessee State University

Ralph L. Langenheim, Jr.
University of Illinois

Sharon L. Larson
University of Nebraska—Lincoln

Abraham D. Lavender
Florida International University

Joseph Edward Lee
Winthrop University

Van M. Leslie
Union College

Gregory A. Levitt
University of New Orleans

Edward J. Lordan
Villanova University

David C. Lukowitz
Hamline University

Judith N. McArthur
University of Houston—Victoria

William M. McBride
U.S. Naval Academy

Sandra C. McClain
Georgia Southern University

Grace McEntee
Appalachian State University

Paul D. Mageli
Independent Scholar

Bill Manikas
Gaston College

Barry Mann
Independent Scholar

Nancy Farm Mannikko
Independent Scholar

Kimberly Manning
Victorville Valley College

Chogollah Maroufi
California State University, Los Angeles

Daniel J. Meissner
University of Wisconsin—Madison

Maurice Melton
Andrew College

Diane P. Michelfelder
*California Polytechnic State University,
San Luis Obispo*

Elizabeth J. Miles
Independent Scholar

Ken Millen-Penn
Fairmont State College

Liesel Ashley Miller
Mississippi State University

Gordon R. Mork
Purdue University

Michael J. Mullin
Augustana College

Michele Mock Murton
Indiana University of Pennsylvania

Bert M. Mutersbaugh
Eastern Kentucky University

Vidya Nadkarni
University of San Diego

Joseph L. Nogee
University of Houston

Charles H. O'Brien
Western Illinois University

O. A. Ogunseitan
University of California, Irvine

Gary A. Olson
San Bernardino Valley College

William A. Paquette
Tidewater Community College

Craig S. Pascoe
University of Tennessee, Knoxville

Darryl Paulson
University of South Florida

P. Ann Peake
East Tennessee State University

Thomas R. Peake
King College

William E. Pemberton
University of Wisconsin—La Crosse

Marilyn Elizabeth Perry
Independent Scholar

Nis Petersen
Jersey City State College

Erika E. Pilver
Westfield State College

Julio César Pino
Kent State University

George R. Plitnik
Frostburg State University

Marjorie Podolsky
Penn State University—Erie

John Powell
Penn State University—Erie

Victoria Price
Lamar University

R. Kent Rasmussen
Independent Scholar

Eugene L. Rasor
Emory & Henry College

William G. Ratliff
Georgia Southern University

E. A. Reed
Baylor University

Betty Richardson
*Southern Illinois University—
Edwardsville*

Edward J. Rielly
Saint Joseph's College (Maine)

Janice G. Rienerth
Appalachian State University

Ernest G. Rigney, Jr.
College of Charleston

Claire J. Robinson
Independent Scholar

Peggy Waltzer Rosefeldt
Independent Scholar

John Alan Ross
Eastern Washington University

Mary Ellen Rowe
Central Missouri State University

Joseph R. Rudolph, Jr.
Towson State University

Dorothy C. Salem
Cuyahoga Community College

Vicki A. Sanders
Paine College

Richard Sax
Madonna University

Glenn Schiffman
Independent Scholar

Helmut J. Schmeller
Fort Hays State University

John Richard Schrock
Emporia State University

Larry Schweikart
University of Dayton

Rose Secrest
Independent Scholar

Donald C. Simmons, Jr.
Troy State University

Gary Scott Smith
Grove City College

Christy Jo Snider
Purdue University

Sandra K. Stanley
California State University, Northridge

Glenn Ellen Starr
Appalachian State University

David L. Sterling
University of Cincinnati

Pamela R. Stern
Independent Scholar

Ruby L. Stoner
*Penn State University
College of Technology*

Geralyn Strecker
Ball State University

Leslie Stricker
Park College

Irene Struthers
Independent Scholar

Taylor Stults
Muskingum College

Glenn L. Swygart
Tennessee Temple University

Stephen G. Sylvester
Montana State University—Northern

James Tackach
Roger Williams University

Robert D. Talbott
University of Northern Iowa

Stephen Wallace Taylor
University of Tennessee

Susan M. Taylor
Indiana University, South Bend

Emily Teipe
Fullerton College

Ann Thompson
Independent Scholar

Gale M. Thompson
Delta College

Vincent Michael Thur
Wenatchee Valley College

Leslie V. Tischauser
Prairie State College

Brian G. Tobin
Lassen College

Frank Towers
Clarion University

Kenneth William Townsend
Coastal Carolina University

Paul B. Trescott
Southern Illinois University

Spencer C. Tucker
Texas Christian University

Robert D. Ubriaco, Jr.
University of Illinois

Jiu-Hwa Lo Upshur
Eastern Michigan University

Mary E. Virginia
Independent Scholar

Thomas J. Edward Walker
*Penn State University
    College of Technology*

Deborah D. Wallin
Skagit Valley College

William E. Watson
Drexel University

Jessica Weiss
University of California, Berkeley

Marcia J. Weiss
Point Park College

Winifred O. Whelan
St. Bonaventure University

D. Anthony White
Sonoma State University

Richard Whitworth
Ball State University

Edwin G. Wiggins
Webb Institute

Raymond Wilson
Fort Hays State University

Sharon K. Wilson
Fort Hays State University

John D. Windhausen
Saint Anselm College

Michael Witkoski
Independent Scholar

Cynthia Gwynne Yaudes
Indiana University of Pennsylvania

Clifton K. Yearley
State University of New York—Buffalo

GREAT EVENTS FROM HISTORY
NORTH AMERICAN SERIES

15,000 B.C. ■ BERING STRAIT MIGRATIONS: the first humans arrive in the Western Hemisphere

DATE: Beginning c. 15,000 B.C.
LOCALE: Bering Strait, between Siberia and Alaska
CATEGORIES: Native American history; Prehistory and ancient cultures

SUMMARY OF EVENT. About two million years ago, for reasons not entirely understood, Earth's temperature began to fall. In the north, more snow fell in winter than melted in summer, and great sheets of ice formed on the landmasses. These glaciers went through a series of advances and retreats—sliding forward under the influence of gravity and melting back under warmer climatic conditions.

At the same time, a group of primates (monkeys, apes, and their relatives) was evolving in Africa. The group of interest had already developed the ability to walk on their hind limbs rather than on four feet, thus freeing the forelimbs for functions other than locomotion. Climatic change had initiated a drying trend in Africa, replacing rain forests with grasslands and savannas. Several species of the two-legged primate group had successfully invaded the grassland environment and spread throughout Africa. Well into the ice age, late-developing species migrated north into Europe and Asia, using tools, animal skins, and especially fire to cope with the cold. Some members of one species, today called *Homo sapiens* (literally, "wise human"), eventually moved into frigid Siberian environments.

Eastern Siberia and western Alaska were not covered by glaciers, even at the height of glacial advance. Although the climate in these unglaciated regions was cold, a number of large mammal species (mammoths, mastodons, giant bison, and others) had invaded the northern environment ahead of the humans. The newcomers probably used many food sources, but they became especially skilled at hunting the large animals.

Tremendous amounts of water were required to build the continental glaciers. That water came primarily from the most abundant source of water on the planet, the oceans. As a result, each advance and retreat of the glaciers was accompanied by dramatic changes in sea level—the sea rose as glaciers melted, and fell with each glacial advance. Today, only about fifty miles of water separate Siberia from Alaska across the Bering Strait. The Bering Strait is less than two hundred feet deep, and the adjacent parts of the Chukchi and Bering seas are not much deeper. Because of this, a strip of Bering Strait and adjacent sea floor one thousand miles wide became dry land whenever extensive glaciation occurred. Along with adjacent parts of Siberia and Alaska, this region is called Beringia. When the glaciers were in full retreat, the Bering Strait reformed, splitting Beringia and placing a barrier between the two continents.

The sea level rose and fell throughout glacial times, and the connection between Alaska and Siberia was established and broken repeatedly. Various land organisms crossed the bridge when it was available, but exchange between the continents was blocked when it was inundated. Mammoths, mastodons, camels, horses, and many other species of animals and plants crossed throughout the ice age, but humans probably did not reach northeastern Siberia until the most recent glacial advance.

In North America, the last glacier (the Wisconsin) advanced until approximately sixty thousand years ago, at which time it began a retreat called the "mid-Wisconsin interglacial." Fewer than thirty thousand years ago, it began its final advance (the late Wisconsin glaciation) followed by its most recent retreat, which began eighteen thousand years ago. It was during or after the mid-Wisconsin interglacial that humans from Siberia made their way across Beringia into North America.

This migration was not a directed, purposeful movement to a new continent. It is unlikely that the first Americans had any sense of their role in history or the nature of continents. The migration probably was the simple result of growing populations expanding into new regions, perhaps drawn by the presence of herds of the large mammals they were so adept at hunting.

The populations continued to expand throughout Alaska and adjacent Canada but were restricted from much of Canada by two major glacial masses. The Laurentide ice sheet covered most of Canada and much of the northern United States, from the east coast to the Rocky Mountains. The second mass of ice resulted from the coalescence of a number of mountain glaciers into a single glacial complex, the Cordilleran glacier located between the Rockies and the coastal mountain ranges.

During glacial advance, the two ice masses probably met and blocked the migrants' route south. However, when the glaciers melted, a corridor opened between them. The migrants moved south through Mexico and Central America, and on to the tip of South America. As the most recent glacial retreat continued, the first Americans expanded their range into all parts of Canada as well.

Anthropologists and archaeologists call these first Americans (or their immediate descendants) Paleo-Indians. Many details of relationship and pathways of descent are not known, but the Paleo-Indian culture gave rise to another widespread culture, called the Archaic, around 7000 B.C. Approximately two thousand years ago, the Archaic culture began to give way to the mound-building culture of eastern North America (the Adena, Hopewell, and Mississippian), the agricultural groups of the southwestern deserts (the Hohokam, Mogollon, and Anasazi), and other cultures. Some time before A.D. 1500, these prehistoric cultures gave rise to the Native American tribes that were later displaced by European settlement. A similar sequence of cultural replacement took place in Mexico and Central and South America, culminating in the Inca, Aztec, and Mayan civilizations decimated by the Spanish conquistadores in the 1500's.

One of the most vituperative arguments in the history of science centers on the question of when the first Americans arrived. A few students of the question argue for dates earlier

BERING STRAIT MIGRATIONS

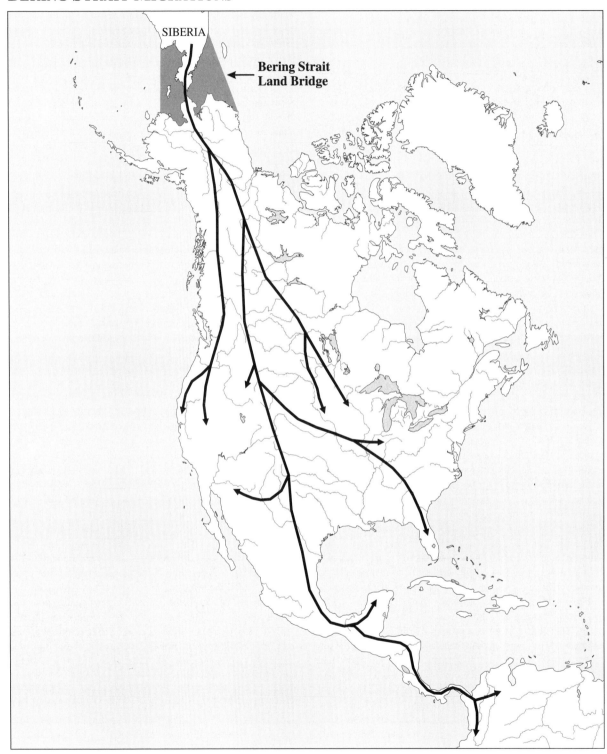

As early as 15,000 B.C., during a period when the huge ice sheet covering the top half of North America had retreated, indigenous peoples from Siberia began to make their way across a land bridge that today is the Bering Strait. Eventually, traveling between glaciers, they reached eastern, central, and southern North America and Mesoamerica.

than the mid-Wisconsin interglacial, many argue for entry times more than thirty thousand years ago (during the mid-Wisconsin interglacial), but most favor a time somewhat more than twelve thousand years ago (during the Wisconsin glacier's retreat).

The basis for the most popular position is the absence of strong evidence for earlier human occupation of the continent. The widespread occurrence of a particular type of spear point found at archaeological sites all over North America, sites determined to be between 11,500 and 10,500 years old, is the first irrefutable and extensive evidence of such occupation. These sites constitute the first recognized North American Paleo-Indian culture, now called the Clovis culture because it was established on the basis of finds in Blackwater Draw near Clovis, New Mexico. Because the culture was so widespread, archaeologists assume that Native Americans must have been on the continent some time before the Clovis dates. Some believe that a thousand years is enough time for the first immigrants to have spread from Beringia to Tierra del Fuego and throughout both continents; others think a longer time was required.

Evidence based on Native American languages, tooth anatomy, and genetics suggests that there were at least three migrations of different Siberian peoples into North America. The first group of migrants gave rise to most Native American groups. One of the later migrant groups was ancestral to the Navajo, Apache, and some western Canadian tribes; the Eskimo (Inuit) and Aleut peoples derived from the other group. Each migration probably involved movement of many subgroups through an extended time period. Some archaeologists believe that marine travelers, along the coast or across open seas, may have contributed to the colonization as well.

The timing and details of the colonization of North America are unsettled, but most archaeologists agree on its basic character. Northern Asiatic people crossed Beringia into North America some time before twelve thousand years ago and spread fairly rapidly throughout North and South America. These people, with possible contributions from later (and earlier) immigrants, developed into the multitude of Native American groups present when Europeans "discovered" the continents. Ancestors of the Native Americans who met the European explorers and colonists some five hundred years ago had occupied the Americas for more than twelve thousand years.

—Carl W. Hoagstrom

ADDITIONAL READING:

Dillehay, Tom D., and David J. Meltzer. *The First Americans: Search and Research.* Boca Raton, Fla.: Chemical Rubber Company Press, 1991. A set of papers written to explore and encourage exploration of the total context of migrations into North America. Illustrations, reference lists.

Dixon, E. James. *Quest for the Origins of the First Americans.* Albuquerque: University of New Mexico Press, 1993. An archaeologist discusses the first Americans in the context of his own research. Illustrations, index, bibliography.

Fagan, Brian M. *Ancient North America: The Archaeology of a Continent.* Rev. ed. New York: Thames and Hudson, 1995. A consideration of the first Americans in the context of North American archaeology. Illustrations, index, bibliography.

Fladmark, Knut R. "Getting One's Berings." *Natural History* 95, no. 11 (November, 1986): 8-19. The first of thirteen articles on the peopling of North America published in *Natural History* between November, 1986, and January, 1988. Illustrations.

Thomas, David Hurst. *Exploring Ancient Native America: An Archaeological Guide.* New York: Macmillan, 1994. An outline of Native American prehistory and a guide to accessible sites. Illustrations, index, appendix of sites to visit, bibliography.

SEE ALSO: 1500 B.C., Olmec Civilization; 700 B.C., Ohio Mound Builders; 300 B.C., Hohokam Culture; A.D. 200, Mayan Civilization; A.D. 200, Anasazi Civilization; A.D. 700, Zapotec Civilization; A.D. 750, Mogollon Culture.

1500 B.C. ■ OLMEC CIVILIZATION: *one of the earliest advanced civilizations on the North American continent*

DATE: 1500-300 B.C.
LOCALE: Southern Mexico
CATEGORIES: Native American history; Prehistory and ancient cultures

SUMMARY OF EVENT. Olmec civilization is considered to be one of the oldest civilizations of native North America. Recognition and identification of Olmec culture are based exclusively on archaeological evidence, since no direct descendants of Olmec civilization have ever been identified. The Olmec heartland included the present Mexican states of Veracruz, Tabasco, and Chiapas, along the southern and western edge of the Gulf of Mexico, but Olmec influence extended across most of southern Mexico and northern Central America. The term "Olmec" is drawn from the Aztec language Nahuatl and loosely translates as "the rubber people," in reference to the production of rubber in the Olmec heartland.

Evidence of Olmec culture first appears about 1500 B.C. in the state of Tabasco. The area consists of flat, swampy coastal floodplains crossed by rivers draining from highland mountains to the south into the Gulf of Mexico to the north. Seasonal flooding and the lush tropical environment permitted the development of agriculture and the exploitation of domesticated plants, particularly corn, which led to the development of sedentary societies and advanced forms of social and political organization.

At sites such as San Lorenzo Tenochtitlán, the Olmec constructed large earthen platforms more than 3,000 feet long, 1,000 feet wide, and 150 feet high, upon which were erected ritual and ceremonial structures of stone and more perishable materials such as wood or plaster. These platform complexes served several purposes, including residences for elite Olmec families and rulers, gathering places for public ceremonies, and burial sites for Olmec royalty. At the site of La Venta, the Olmec constructed conical pyramids in the center of their platform complexes, perhaps meant to imitate mountains or volcanoes not found in the immediate Olmec area. The earthen platforms consisted of layers of worked colored stone laid out in large plazas and covered with as many as a dozen sequential layers of sand and earth piled one on top of the other to construct the platforms. The complexity suggests that the process of construction was as important as the final structure.

Platforms were engineered and constructed to control water flow throughout the structure. Elaborate drainage systems, composed of sections of carved stone, channeled water throughout the platforms, diverting it for waste runoff and public hygiene and creating decorative and sacred ponds and streams of fresh water within the platform complexes. The scale and complexity of the earthen platforms, along with the evidence of extensive farming and agriculture, suggest that several thousand people may have used or occupied the sites at one time. At least ten large-scale Olmec sites have been identified in the Olmec heartland. Advanced systems of political organization must have been in place to enable the assembly and management of the workforce necessary to construct such elaborate complexes. It is also significant that the Olmec created their buildings and monuments without the wheel, domesticated animals, or metal tools, none of which was used by any Mesoamerican peoples.

Most information regarding Olmec culture that does not come from their architecture is drawn from their remaining artworks. Although the Olmec probably created a wide variety of art forms, such as paintings and textiles, most of these forms have not survived in the archaeological record. What has survived in great abundance is Olmec stone sculpture, and the remaining carved stone images convey a great deal of information about Olmec beliefs. The Olmec were extremely adept at working very hard types of stone, particularly volcanic basalt and jade, neither of which occurs naturally near the Olmec heartland sites. Large basalt boulders, some more than ten feet tall and weighing several tons, were transported as much as sixty miles from volcanic mountain ranges such as the Tuxtla mountains; sacred green jade was imported from areas of western Mexico or eastern Guatemala and Belize.

The basalt boulders were carved into a variety of shapes, usually human but occasionally representing animals or mythological deities, probably originally intended to be displayed in the open plazas of the earthen platforms. Many of the large carved boulders were intentionally defaced or broken and buried within the platforms during Olmec times, suggesting that either the Olmec or a foreign people symbolically killed the sculptures before abandoning the sites.

One of the most common types of boulder sculptures is a series of human heads carved in a lifelike, naturalistic style. Although the specific identity of the subjects is not clear, evidence suggests that the heads portray either former Olmec rulers or defeated enemies. Facial features vary noticeably from one head to the next, suggesting individualized depictions, and each wears a distinctively different type of skullcap or helmet. The caps may represent royal headdress or a type of headgear worn by participants in a ball game similar to modern-day soccer. The losers of this game, which was played on stone, I-shaped courts throughout ancient Mesoamerica, were ritually sacrificed, usually by decapitation. Portions of the ball game may have developed in the Olmec heartland, since that is the source of the rubber used for the ball itself. Regardless of the specific identity of the stone heads, the size and degree of naturalism attest the Olmec sculptors' ability to manipulate large, hard stone for artistic purposes. Smaller stone objects, such as jewelry, ritual implements, and burial offerings, were carved from other hard stones, including jade. The color green was probably considered sacred, and jade was much valued by all pre-Columbian societies. Humans and animals were common subjects, and implements such as ax heads were frequently formed in the shape of humans, suggesting a spiritual tie between the function of the object and its symbolic imagery.

Olmec art reveals much about Olmec political and religious beliefs. Olmec sites were probably governed by elite royal families and kings. Warriors and human prisoners are frequently depicted in Olmec sculpture, suggesting that the Olmec practiced formalized warfare and related forms of human sacrifice. They worshiped a pantheon of natural spirits, chief among which were powerful animals such as the cayman or alligator, the eagle, the shark, and, perhaps most important, the jaguar. The Olmec were similar to most Native American cultures in that the most important religious figures in Olmec society were the shamans, or curers, who were believed to be able to change into animal forms at will and communicate directly with the supernatural world. Olmec sculpture frequently depicts shamans in the act of such transformations.

Between 1000 and 300 B.C., Olmec influence stretched far beyond the Olmec heartland. Carved jade and ceramics in Olmec style have been found in central and far west Mexico, and Olmec-style rock carvings, paintings, and earthen platforms occur in areas south of Mexico City. Large Olmec-style carved boulders and upright stones occur along the southern Pacific coast of Guatemala and El Salvador during this period, and Olmec ceramics are found as far east as eastern Guatemala and Belize. The evidence suggests that the Olmec were interacting with a large number of non-Olmec cultures throughout the area at this time. After 500 B.C., early examples of hieroglyphic writing, similar to the later hieroglyphic writing of the Maya, appear in a few isolated examples of Olmec art, but these cases are rare, and Olmec civilization appears to have declined before the writing system was fully exploited.

After 300 B.C., Olmec culture disappears from the archaeological record. Several later Mesoamerican cultures, particularly the Maya of Guatemala and the Yucatan peninsula, inherited and continued many aspects of Olmec style and culture, and the Maya, in fact, seem to have considered the Olmec as their divine ancestors.
—*James D. Farmer*

ADDITIONAL READING:

Benson, Elizabeth P., ed. *The Olmec and Their Neighbors: Essays in Memory of Matthew W. Stirling*. Washington, D.C.: Dumbarton Oaks Research Library and Collections, Trustees for Harvard University, 1981. Collected papers focusing on shared artistic influences between Olmec and neighboring or later Mesoamerican cultures.

Coe, Michael D. *America's First Civilization*. New York: American Heritage, 1968. One of the earliest comprehensive treatments of Olmec art and culture. Coe was the first scholar to interpret Olmec culture as the precursor to later, more widely known Mesoamerican cultures such as the Maya.

Coe, Michael D., and Richard A. Diehl. *In the Land of the Olmec*. Austin: University of Texas Press, 1980. Extensive report of archaeological investigations at the Olmec site of San Lorenzo Tenochtitlán between 1966 and 1968. Includes numerous detailed maps and line drawings and illustrations of stone monuments from the site.

Pina Chan, Roman. *The Olmec: Mother Culture of Mesoamerica*. Translated by Warren McManus. New York: Rizzoli International Publications, 1989. Well-illustrated volume of Olmec art. Presents a thorough summary of Olmec art, archaeology, and culture by a noted Mexican and pre-Columbian scholar.

Sharer, Robert J., and David C. Grove, eds. *Regional Perspectives on the Olmec*. New York: Cambridge University Press, 1989. Discusses Olmec culture in the broader context of greater Mesoamerica. Scholarly treatment of Olmec cultural interaction with other pre-Columbian cultures.

Stuart, George S. "New Light on the Olmec." *National Geographic* 184, no. 5 (November, 1993): 88-115. Discusses revised and up-to-date interpretations of Olmec culture and art, including previously undocumented monuments and controversial translations of Olmec hieroglyphic writing. Includes artists' reproductions of Olmec lifeways.

SEE ALSO: A.D. 200, Mayan Civilization; A.D. 700, Zapotec Civilization.

700 B.C. ■ OHIO MOUND BUILDERS: *the earliest "architects" in North America built elaborate burial sites*

DATE: 700 B.C.-A.D. 500
LOCALE: Valleys and tributaries of the Ohio River
CATEGORIES: Native American history; Prehistory and ancient cultures

SUMMARY OF EVENT. When a large number of human-made burial mounds were found in the Ohio River drainage and other parts of eastern North America in the nineteenth century, the ancestors of native North Americans seemed an unlikely source for their grandeur, at least to the European mind. Various non-Indian Mound Builders were hypothesized: the lost tribes of Israel, the Vikings, and other Old World groups. This oversight of Native Americans is surprising, given the high culture developed by the Native Americans in Mexico and Peru. In fact, other hypotheses suggested that the Mound Builders were an offshoot of, or ancestral to, these Middle American cultures. Few explanations allowed for a relationship to North American Indians. Late in the nineteenth century, however, careful studies by the Smithsonian Institution's Bureau of Ethnology demonstrated that the mounds were built by ancestors of the historic North American tribes.

How did the builders of such elaborate structures, presumably sedentary agriculturalists of high culture, develop? How did they give rise to the more mobile, and seemingly less highly cultured, natives encountered by the pioneers? These questions cannot be answered definitively, but much is known about the Mound Builders, and reasonable hypotheses for their origin and relationship to the historic Indian tribes have been developed.

Most evidence suggests that the original natives of North and South America were members of Siberian tribes that crossed the Bering Strait from Siberia to Alaska some time after fifteen thousand years ago. This was during the early stages of the last glacial retreat, when the Bering Strait was dry land. These tribes were big-game hunters who moved south into North, Central, and South America as the ice sheets melted. These people, called Paleo-Indians, moved into the eastern part of North America and came to live in sparse, wide-ranging populations in the forests that developed there after the glacier melted.

Archaeologists recognize a second Native American culture, the Archaic, beginning about eight thousand years ago. Directly descended from Paleo-Indians, the Archaic Indians are thought to have given rise to the Mound Builders around 700 B.C. Some late Archaic woodland groups buried their dead in small, natural hills, and a few built small burial mounds, the presumed progenitors of the more elaborate burial mounds built by the Woodland Indians. The larger burial mounds are widespread throughout eastern North America but are centered in the Ohio River drainage.

The earliest of the Ohio River Mound Builders are called Adena Indians and are thought to have lived between 700 B.C. and A.D. 200. Their culture is characterized by the development of fiber-tempered pottery, domestication of several kinds of native plants, and the development of elaborate rituals and practices for burying their dead, including the mounds in which they were buried. They also worked stone to make pipes and various ornaments. In addition to cultivating plants, they gathered wild plant products and hunted available animals. They used a spear-throwing device called an "atlatl" (developed by Archaic or late Paleo-Indians) to produce greater flight speed in their spears. They added burials to individual mounds through time, and were more sedentary than their Archaic predecessors. There is evidence that trading networks developed between the Adena people and contemporaneous American Indian cultures.

The Adena gave rise to the Hopewell Indian culture, which was also centered in the valleys of the Ohio River and its tributaries. The Ohio Hopewell culture is recognized from

This monitor frog effigy pipe was produced by the Hopewell Indian culture near present-day Ross County, Ohio. (Photograph courtesy of National Museum of the American Indian, Smithsonian Institution)

around 100 B.C. until about A.D. 400 or 500. The Hopewell tradition is characterized by advanced pottery production and stoneworking, more intensive cultivation of native plants, some cultivation of corn (*Zea mays*, ultimately obtained from Mexico), and more elaborate funeral procedures and burial mounds.

Although corn was grown by the Hopewell people, it was not the staple it became in Middle American and Mississippian cultures. Instead, corn seemed to be grown more for symbolic and religious ceremonies. There is some anthropological evidence that the Hopewell people's more diversified diet, based on the cultivation of several native plant species and supplemented by hunting and gathering, produced a healthier population than did the corn-intensive diet of the Mississippians.

The Hopewell Indians also developed vast, nearly continentwide, trading networks. This trade may have been associated with another cultural development that differentiates the Hopewell from the Adena. Researchers have hypothesized that some Hopewell men obtained privileged positions in society due to their trading skill and trade contacts. These men were buried with more elaborate material goods and in larger and more complex mounds than were other members of the population. As a result, Hopewell burials suggest a class structure not seen in the more egalitarian Adena burials.

Adena and Hopewell mounds were built by people carrying baskets full of dirt from a source region, called a borrow pit, and depositing the dirt on the growing mound. Large mounds with many burials were built in stages, with one set of burials superposed upon an earlier group. Many artifacts, presumably prized possessions and tools needed for the next life, were buried with the dead. More of these are found in Hopewell burials than in Adena burials. The Hopewell differentiation of class, and contrasting Adena egalitarianism, are hypothesized on the basis of such artifacts and specific conditions of the burials.

Hopewell characteristics are all elaborations of Adena characteristics. It is impossible to determine the point in time at which the Adena culture ended and the Hopewell began; instead, there is a lengthy transition period. Clearly, the Hopewell tradition is a continuation of the Adena culture.

The Hopewell culture peaked in the Ohio River Valley around A.D. 200, and their mound-building activities, at least, disappeared between A.D. 400 and 500. Numerous hypotheses have been proposed for the decline of Hopewellian peoples, at least as Mound Builders. The theories range from an environmental catastrophe, brought on by larger population concentrations and intensive agriculture, to changes in trade balances that brought an end to the Hopewell people's strategic central position between the northern and southern and between the eastern and western sources of raw materials and finished goods.

The last North American mound-building culture, the Mississippian, was centered along the Mississippi River, at Cahokia, where East St. Louis, Illinois, now stands. It developed around A.D. 700 and flourished until after 1500. Adena and Hopewell mounds were primarily burial mounds, but many Mississippian mounds were platforms upon which temples, houses, and other structures were built. Many scholars believe that these Mississippian Mound Builders were descendants of the Hopewell, through intermediaries who, for unknown reasons, abandoned mound-building activities. Many also believe that the Mississippians were directly ancestral to the Cherokee, Sioux, and other historic American Indian tribes. Some researchers posit that Hopewellians were ancestral to the Iroquois.

The Ohio Mound Builders maintained a developing culture for more than a millennium and played a central role in North American prehistory for much of that time. Their descendants gave rise to the prehistoric Mississippian culture and to historic Indian tribes. In addition, North American archaeology traces its professional roots to the exploration of their mounds.

—*Carl W. Hoagstrom*

ADDITIONAL READING:

Fagan, Brian M. "The Eastern Woodlands." In *Ancient North America: The Archeology of a Continent.* 2d ed. New York: Thames and Hudson, 1995. Describes the Mound Builders and their place in prehistory. Chapter 2 gives a brief history of the European Mound Builder hypothesis. Illustrations, maps, index, bibliography.

Shaffer, Lynda Norene. *Native Americans Before 1492: The Moundbuilding Centers of the Eastern Woodlands.* Armonk, N.Y.: M. E. Sharpe, 1992. Explores Mound Builder cultures and the interactions and interrelationships between those cultures and other Native American cultures. Illustrations, maps, index, bibliography.

Silverberg, Robert. *The Mound Builders.* Athens: Ohio University Press, 1970. Discusses the European-Mound-Builder-race hypothesis and its demise. Also describes the American Indian Mound Builder cultures. Illustrations, maps, index, bibliography.

Snow, Dean R. "The Nations of the Eastern Woodlands." In *The Archaeology of North America.* New York: Chelsea House, 1989. Outlines the prehistory of the Mound Builders. Chapter 1 covers the Mound Builder mystery and its importance in American archaeology. Illustrations, maps, index, glossary, bibliography.

Thomas, Cyrus. *Report on the Mound Explorations of the Bureau of Ethnology.* 1894. Reprint. Washington, D.C.: Smithsonian Institution Press, 1985. Describes the Bureau of Ethnology's mound work. The introduction to the 1985 edition adds historical perspective. Illustrations, maps, index.

Webb, William S., and Charles E. Snow. *The Adena People.* Knoxville: University of Tennessee Press, 1974. Descriptions of the mounds, pottery, pipes, and other artifacts of the Adena and Hopewell people. Illustrations, maps, index, bibliography.

Woodward, Susan L., and Jerry N. McDonald. *Indian Mounds of the Middle Ohio Valley: A Guide to Adena and Hopewell Sites.* Blacksburg, Va.: McDonald and Woodward, 1986. A guide to Adena and Hopewell sites that can be visited by the public. Illustrations, maps, index, lists of pertinent topographic maps and publications.

SEE ALSO: 15,000 B.C., Bering Strait Migrations; A.D. 750, Mississippian Culture.

300 B.C. ■ HOHOKAM CULTURE: *adapting to the desert environment, these ancestors of the modern Pimi and Papago established agricultural settlements and irrigation systems*

DATE: 300 B.C.-A.D. 1400
LOCALE: Southern Arizona

CATEGORIES: Native American history; Prehistory and ancient cultures

SUMMARY OF EVENT. One of four prehistoric cultures in the Southwest, the Hohokam people, ancestors of the modern Pimi and Papago, lived in the fertile valleys of the Salt and Gila Rivers in what is today southern Arizona. Artifacts show that this seemingly bleak region, the Arizona-Sonora Desert, was home to the Hohokam for more than seventeen hundred years, but archaeologists are not certain where they originated. Were they descendants of the earlier Cochise people, who hunted and gathered in the same desert area, or did they migrate from Mexico? Much of their cultural history suggests a Mesoamerican influence; however, this could have been acquired through the extensive trade routes established by the Hohokam.

Development of Hohokam culture occurred in four phases: Pioneer, 300 B.C.-A.D. 500; Colonial, A.D. 500-900; Sedentary, A.D. 900-1100; and Classic, A.D. 1100-1400. The Hohokam culture was similar to the desert cultures of the Anasazi, Hakataya, and Mogollon, but a major difference was their complex irrigation system. Evidence from the Pioneer phase shows that the Hohokam lived in pit houses and began the cultivation of corn in their small villages. Floodplains along the rivers were rich with silt deposited from spring rains and snowmelt from nearby mountains. The earliest irrigation was probably achieved by directing the floodwaters.

About 300 B.C., during the Pioneer phase, the village of Skoaquick, or Snaketown, was founded on the north bank of the Gila River. The first canal was build there to divert river water to irrigate fields as far as three miles away. Early canals were shallow but very wide. Later, using technology from Mexico, the Hohokam built narrow, deep canals with many branches and lined them with clay to channel water more than thirty miles. Gates made of woven grass mats controlled the flow from large dams throughout the canal system. Archaeological evidence suggests that construction of the canals was done by men using digging sticks and stone hoes. Earth was carried away in baskets by women and was probably used in building their pyramid ceremonial platforms.

Continual maintenance was needed to keep the canals open after floods or thunderstorms, but this full-time technology provided a reliable subsistence for the Hohokam and supported a denser population. Instead of harvesting crops from the natural habitat, the Hohokam successfully brought agriculture into their villages to develop a stable farming society in which the men tended the fields instead of hunting.

As domesticated corn moved northward from Mexico, it evolved into a new type with a floury kernel more easily crushed when dry. The Hohokam harvested their domestic corn and prepared it by traditional desert-culture methods of sun-drying, parching in baskets with coals, and grinding dried kernels. Storage in large pits kept their surplus food secure for several years. The plentiful food supply allowed time for the creation of art, including shell carving, loom weaving, and pottery making. Images of Kokopelli, the humpbacked flute player, a fertility god believed to assure a good harvest, frequently decorated the pottery. Epic poems carried Hohokam cultural history through many generations.

The archaeological record shows that the Hohokam had no weapons; their bows, arrows, and spears were used for hunting deer, rabbits, and other small game to supplement their crops. Deerskins and rabbit fur were used for ponchos, robes, and blankets. Cotton shirts and breechcloths were typical outfits for men, and apron-skirts of shredded fiber were worn by women. Both wore sandals of woven fiber and wickerwork. Other Hohokam artifacts include stone and clay pipes, cane cigarettes, noseplugs, wooden spoons, flutes, and prayer sticks. Stick and ring games, guessing games, gambling bones, and dice were also part of Hohokam culture.

Petroglyphs, pot shards, pyramids, and pit houses tell the story of Hohokam contact with Mexico. In addition to pottery and domestic crops, which by A.D. 600 included cotton, the Colonial phase shows the use of astronomy to calculate planting dates. Narrower, deeper canals were dug to control evaporation, ball courts were built for ceremonial use, and images of the feathered serpent were used in ceremonial art.

In the Sedentary phase, a smaller area of the desert was occupied by the Hohokam. Greater development occurred in the material culture, which showed more influence from Mexico: red-on-buff pottery, copper bells, turquoise mosaics, iron-pyrite mirrors, textiles, and bright-feathered macaws as pets in homes. During this period, Hohokam artists began the process of etching. The earliest people in the Western world to master the craft, they devised a method of covering the shells with pitch, carving the design, then dipping shells in the acidic juice of the saguaro cactus fruit. Along with salt, these shells were highly prized for exchange on the extensive trade route.

During the Classic phase, the Salados (a branch of the Anasazi people) moved into Hohokam territory, bringing a new architecture of multistory adobe houses. They introduced other varieties of corn, as well as beans and squash, and brought basketry, the newest art form. Always peaceful people, the Hohokam coexisted with the Salados, who assisted with the building of canals. By A.D. 1350, the complex network extended more than 150 miles. Of great importance to the Hohokam were the new songs and ceremonies brought by the Salado, for these kept the world in balance and assured a life of abundance and harmony.

As early as 300 B.C., Snaketown had been the year-round site of a village of about fifty families who relied on the production of domestic crops. It remained the center of Hohokam culture for fifteen hundred years. During the expansive period, more than one hundred pit houses covered the three-hundred-acre site. A highly developed social organization was needed to oversee the large population, produce abundant food, and maintain the network of canals. As their culture evolved from the Pioneer through the Classic phase, Hohokam social organization had shifted from small bands to tribes to chiefdoms to states.

In the early fifteenth century, the Hohokam abandoned Snaketown and other settlements, possibly because of a long period of drought. In the nineteenth century, Mormon farmers used part of the network of canals skillfully engineered almost two thousand years earlier. Continuing the legacy, a canal at Snaketown near present-day Phoenix was reconstructed in the twentieth century to divert water from the Salt River.

The ancient Hohokam spoke Uto-Aztecan, one of the seven Southwest language families, which also included Hopi, Pima, Yaqui-Mayo, and Huichol. In the Piman language, the term "Hohokam" translates as "the vanished ones." Myths and songs about the mysterious desert whirlwinds are found in Piman culture, inherited from their Hohokam ancestors. Perhaps the whirlwinds hold the secret of the vanished ones.

—*Gale M. Thompson*

ADDITIONAL READING:

Ortiz, Alfonso, ed. *Southwest*. Vol. 9 in *Handbook of North American Indians*, edited by William C. Sturtevant. Washington, D.C.: Smithsonian Institution, 1979.

_____. *Southwest*. Vol. 10 in *Handbook of North American Indians*, edited by William C. Sturtevant. Washington, D.C.: Smithsonian Institution, 1983. These two volumes in the Smithsonian's multivolume history cover both the Pueblo (volume 9) and non-Pueblo (volume 10) peoples of the Southwest. Maps, photographs, illustrations, bibliographies, indexes.

Taylor, Colin, and William C. Sturtevant, eds. *The Native Americans: The Indigenous People of North America*. New York: Smithmark, 1991. Native American culture and lifestyle in nine culture areas, from the Arctic to the Southwest. Includes twenty-eight photographic spreads showing more than a thousand artifacts, dating from 1860 to 1920; 250 archival photographs, maps, and color plates, dating from 1850 to 1940; bibliography; catalog of artifacts; and index.

Thomas, David Hurst. *Exploring Ancient Native America: An Archeological Guide*. New York: Macmillan, 1994. Overview of Native American cultures and the evolution of numerous Native American civilizations. References more than four hundred accessible sites in North America. Discusses new scientific data from burial mounds, petroglyphs, artifacts, and celestial observations. Photographs, drawings, maps, and index.

Underhill, Ruth M. *Red Man's America: A History of Indians in the United States*. Chicago: University of Chicago Press, 1953. Concise volume surveying origins, history, and definitive accounts of social customs, material culture, religion, and mythology. Written from the perspective of the first peoples of North America. Illustrations, maps, notes, extensive bibliography, and index.

Waldman, Carl. *Atlas of the North American Indian*. New York: Facts On File, 1985. Comprehensive coverage of prehistory, including Hohokam. Appendix lists chronology of North American Indian history, pre-contact and post-contact locations, reservations, place names, museums, and archaeological sites in the United States and Canada. Maps and illustrations.

SEE ALSO: A.D. 200, Anasazi Civilization; A.D. 750, Mogollon Culture.

A.D. 200 ■ MAYAN CIVILIZATION: *these Mesoamericans contributed profound achievements in art, mathematics, astronomy, and architecture*

DATE: A.D. 200-900
LOCALE: Mesoamerica
CATEGORIES: Latino American history; Native American history; Prehistory and ancient cultures
SUMMARY OF EVENT. Mayan history is divided into three periods: Preclassic (2000 B.C.-A.D. 200), Classic (A.D. 200-900), and Postclassic (A.D. 900 to the Spanish conquest). The Maya lived in an area that included the present-day Mexican states of Chiapas, Tabasco, Campeche, Yucatan, and Quintana Roo, in addition to the countries of Belize, Guatemala, Honduras, and El Salvador. Scholars who study the Maya have divided the entire region into three subregions: the southern subregion of Guatemala highlands and the Pacific coast; the central subregion of northern Guatemala, its adjacent lowlands, and the Petén region; and the northern subregion of the Yucatan peninsula. The highland areas of southern Guatemala and Chiapas flourished during the late Preclassic period; lowland areas in the Petén region reached their height during the Classic period; and the area in the Yucatan Peninsula prospered in the late Classic and Postclassic periods.

The end of the Preclassic period and the beginning of the Classic period, when the Maya flourished, had formerly been defined by the appearance of vaulted stone architecture, monumental inscriptions, and polychrome pottery. However, subsequent finds have revealed that each of these traits appeared at different times during the Terminal Preclassic. Consequently the "official" end of the Preclassic period and beginning of the Classic period has been changed from A.D. 300 to 250 or 200. During the late Preclassic period, writing, mathematics, architecture, astronomy, and calendars were used, but these were all more fully developed in the Classic period.

A few city-states, such as El Mirador and Kaminaljuyu, developed in the Preclassic period, but it was the Classic period that witnessed the rise of the larger, more advanced city-states for which the Maya are known. One of the earliest and largest of the Classic-period centers was Tikal, located in the Petén region of Guatemala. It covered a six-square-mile area, contained more than three thousand constructions, and had an estimated forty thousand inhabitants. One pyramid, 224 feet high, is the tallest pre-Columbian edifice in America. Copán, which was in Honduras, 250 miles southeast of Tikal, may have been a scientific center specializing in astronomy. Although the Maya did not have telescopes, jade tubes were used, which helped to concentrate their vision on selected celestial bodies. Their knowledge of astronomy was such that they not only had an accurate calendar of 365 days but also were able to predict solar and lunar eclipses, as well as the movement of Venus.

Palenque, in Chiapas, Mexico, had an aqueduct to direct water from a nearby stream to the center of the city and contained a building called the Palace, which was 228 feet long and 180 feet deep, with a four-story tower with an internal stairway. Perhaps its most famous feature is the tomb of the ruler Pacal, who died in 683 after ruling for sixty-eight years. The lid of the sarcophagus was a five-ton, twelve-foot slab of limestone carved with a bas-relief image of the ruler as he entered the jaws of death in the underworld. Palenque also is special for the fact that two women ruled before Pacal assumed the throne.

Bonampak, also located in Chiapas, is best known for its Temple of Frescoes. The frescoes depict many activities and scenes of daily life not represented elsewhere. Some of these representations have helped scholars to realize that the Maya were not the peaceful people they once were believed to be.

Other important centers in the Yucatan peninsula, such as Chichén Itzá, began in the Classic period but continued to flourish in the Postclassic period under the influence of the Toltecs, who invaded Mayan territory in the tenth century. Some of the aforementioned centers had previously experienced a foreign influence early in the Classic period. In the fifth century, Teotihuacán, which was located in the central basin of Mexico, began to spread its influence throughout southern Mesoamerica, including the Mayan cities of Kaminaljuyu, Copán, and Tikal. This influence ended in the eighth century, and there has been speculation that this was a factor in the demise of the Classic period at the end of the ninth century.

The Classic period was characterized by the construction of impressive structures, often one on top of the other. Either existing structures were demolished and the material was used in the new construction, or a new and larger structure enveloped the older one. Buildings were typically covered with stucco. If it was an important structure, the date would be recorded and the event would be celebrated with a religious ceremony that included bloodletting.

Some of the main features of Mayan architecture were large, flat-topped stone pyramids with steps that led to a temple decorated with tiled pediments known as "roof combs"; buildings covered with bas-reliefs; jutting corbeled arches or vaults; ballcourts; large public squares or plazas; and stelae, altars, and monoliths inscribed with names, dates, and important events. A major feature of the large ceremonial centers was the formal plaza lined by public buildings. Much of this was made possible by the Mayan practice of cementing the cut stones together. They had perfected the use of mortar, plaster, and stucco.

Society was highly stratified. At the top was an elite who ruled and enjoyed special privileges. It was the function of the common people to provide not only necessities but also luxuries for the elite. There were probably a number of strata between the royal family and the common farmers, based on birth or occupation, which may have been hereditary. Each city-state had its own ruling dynasty, which is believed to have been by patrilineal primogeniture accessible to others only through marriage. The inequality of treatment did not end with death; while the nobility were buried in tombs, the peasants were buried under the floor in their homes.

ANCIENT CIVILIZATIONS OF THE SOUTHWEST AND MESOAMERICA

Religion was of central importance to Mayan culture. Myriad gods controlled everything and therefore had to be consulted and appeased constantly. Mayan religious concerns encouraged the development of astronomy and mathematics. Each day and number had its patron deity. When a child was born, a priest would predict its future with the aid of astrological charts and books. Each day and each moment was governed by a different god. Depending on the exact day and time of its birth, a child would owe a special devotion to the ascendant deity throughout its lifetime. Religious ceremonies were of the utmost importance. An important aspect of some religious ceremonies was the practice of shedding human blood. Bloodletting took the form of human sacrifices—either of enemies or possibly of devout martyrs—and nonfatal self-immolation. The latter seems to have been a common practice, which entailed the piercing of the tongue, lips, earlobes, or penis. The blood was sometimes dripped onto paper strips that then were burned. In addition to giving nurture and praise to the gods, the Maya believed contact could be made with gods or deceased ancestors by the letting of blood.

The Classic period was marked by competition and conflict. There was an extensive system of short- and long-distance trade, not only among the Maya but with other indigenous peoples as well. Economic success brought growth and prosperity to the many city-states, but it also brought increased competition for territory and power. Warfare was a frequent outcome. Some of the conquered rivals provided sacrificial victims to satisfy the gods; others were beheaded, with the heads possibly used as trophies. During this period, Tikal was defeated by Caracol, which later was defeated by Dos Pilas. Thus fortunes changed for communities and individuals alike.

The end of the classic Mayan civilization was both swift and mysterious. Numerous theories attempt to explain the rather sudden and widespread demise of the prosperous lowland Mayan communities. Undoubtedly, there were both internal and external causes. The former may have included environmental degradation, overpopulation relative to the food supply, disease and malnutrition, a revolution of peasants against the elite, and decay of the artistic, political, and intellectual superstructure of society. Invasion and economic collapse due to changes in other parts of Mesoamerica are possible external causes. While the southern past of the Mayan civilization was undergoing collapse and depopulation, the centers in northern Yucatan continued to prosper and some southward immigration occurred to fill the vacuum. The succeeding Postclassic period, which witnessed the dominance of the Yucatan area, continued until the Spanish conquest in the mid-sixteenth century. —*Philip E. Lampe*

ADDITIONAL READING:

Carrasco, David. *Religions of Mesoamerica*. San Francisco: Harper & Row, 1990. Includes chapters on Mayan religion and closely related practices.

Hammond, Norman. *Ancient Maya Civilization*. New Brunswick, N.J.: Rutgers University Press, 1982. Good synthesis of available data, with scholars' theories and interpretations.

Henderson, John. *The World of the Ancient Maya*. Ithaca, N.Y.: Cornell University Press, 1981. Examines Mayan culture from the earliest settlements through the period of Spanish conquest.

Ivanoff, Pierre. *Maya Monuments of Civilization*. New York: Madison Square Press, 1973. Photographs and brief text on many important sites.

Landa, Diego de. *Yucatan Before and After the Conquest*. Translated by William Gates. New York: Dover, 1978. Historical explanation of manuscript by Landa, which is the source of much of the information available on Mayan history and culture.

SEE ALSO: 1500 B.C., Olmec Civilization; A.D. 700, Zapotec Civilization; 1428, Aztec Empire.

A.D. 200 ■ ANASAZI CIVILIZATION: *this Basket Maker civilization of the Southwest*

emerged, advanced architecture and agriculture, and then vanished

DATE: A.D. 200-1250
LOCALE: Four Corners area of New Mexico, Arizona, Utah, and Colorado
CATEGORIES: Native American history; Prehistory and ancient cultures
SUMMARY OF EVENT. The Anasazi, believed to be descendants of ancient Desert Archaic people, are the best known of the Southwest prehistoric cultures. Different groups of Anasazi spoke at least six languages, which were not mutually understood. The term "Anasazi" derives from an English-language corruption of a Navajo term, Anaasa'zi, which describes the many stone ruins of the Four Corners region and may mean "ancient ones," "enemies of the ancient ones," or "ancient enemy."

The earliest Anasazi are known as the Basket Makers because of their extraordinary skill in basketry. These early people were indistinctive initially, with a few cave sites and rock shelters along the San Juan River and open sites in the Rio Grande Valley. Inhabitants of these early villages planted maize and squash, a skill learned from their ancestors, but also hunted and foraged.

The villages, perhaps occupied seasonally, comprised a few pit houses: low, circular houses dug into the ground, approximately seven feet across. Stone slabs were used for some houses. Upper walls and roofs of many dwellings were made of wood and adobe or wattle and daub. The houses had fire pits and were entered by ladders placed in the smokehole of the roof. Tunnellike side entries faced the east. Larger pit houses were for ceremonial use. Smaller slab-lined structures were used for storing food. Baskets (some woven tightly enough for cooking), sandals, and other articles were of high caliber, highly stylized with geometric motifs. These designs gave rise to later Anasazi pottery painting traditions. Anasazi rock art of the period illustrates humans with broad shoulders, trapezoid-shaped bodies, and very large hands and feet. Elaborate headdresses, hair ornaments, necklaces, earrings, and sashes adorn the figures. Found near the villages, the art appears to have been part of community life.

As the Basket Maker Anasazi population grew and their territory expanded, their villages became larger. Almost all had ritual rooms, which the later Hopi called "kivas." Pit houses became deeper, more complex, and spacious. Earth-covered wooden roofs were supported by four posts with crossbeams. Some houses were dome-shaped. Storage bins, benches, a central fire pit, and a draft deflector between the fire and the ventilator shaft were found in many dwellings. Roof or side entrances were retained.

Within the village were many outdoor work and cooking areas. Slab-lined storage buildings and ramadas—roofed, open-walled structures shading work and living areas—were built on the surface. Some kivas were modified houses, but many were larger, some thirty-five feet across. Excavated holes called *sipapu* were dug near the center of the floor in many homes and in most kivas. Turquoise or other offerings were placed in the *sipapu*, the opening to the underworld from which people emerged.

Farming became increasingly important to the Anasazi. To ensure successful crops, check dams and devices were used in fields near villages. By A.D. 600, beans, introduced from Mexico, were cultivated. By A.D. 700, cotton, the bow and arrow, and stone tools were used generally. Maize was ground on large stone mortars using two-handed grinding stones.

Basketry, sandalmaking, and weaving also became increasingly elaborate. Feathers and rabbit fur were woven into robes. Pottery making developed as both an occupation and a basis for trade. Pots were used for rituals, storing food and water, and cooking and serving food.

The quantity and variety of rock art increased. Rock art was near or in villages, on mesa boulders, near hunting trails, or in other open locations. Subjects included birds, animals, hunting scenes, and figures playing the flute. Human handprints covered some cliff walls in massed profusion. Home, village, and the kiva were the focus of community life, which endeavored to encourage and ensure agricultural prosperity.

The Pueblo period of the Anasazi began about A.D. 700. Villages varied in size from small complexes to those with more than a hundred dwellings. Architecture gradually developed into rectangular surface buildings of dry masonry or stone and adobe that followed a linear arrangement with multiroom units. Buildings usually faced a plaza located to the south or southeast. One or more kivas were built in the plaza. Kiva architecture included an encircling bench attached to the wall, roof support poles, a central fire pit, a ventilator shaft, and a *sipapu*. The kiva was entered by ladder through a roof opening that also allowed smoke to escape. Jars, bowls, and ladles were frequent forms for pottery. Turkeys and dogs were domesticated. Infants were bound to cradle boards so that the child could be near the mother. By A.D. 900, trade activities and movement of the people had engendered a certain amount of cultural uniformity, although some local differences occurred in agriculture, architecture, and pottery.

The Anasazi realized their cultural apogee between 1000 and 1300. The building of Chaco Canyon, the cliff houses of Mesa Verde, and the ruins of Kayenta date from this time. Many communities of this period and virtually all of the Chaco-style "great houses" were planned or renovated into single, self-enclosed structures. New rooms were attached to older ones.

Restored ruins of the Cliff Palace at Mesa Verde, Colorado, built by the Anasazi civilization c. 1100. Cliff Palace numbered about two hundred rooms with twenty-three kivas, underground circular rooms for ritual ceremonies. (Photo by Jesse L. Nusbaum. Courtesy Museum of New Mexico)

Linear units grew into L-shapes when a room was added at the end of a row to enclose space. L-shapes became U's and U's turned into rectangles. If a village grew or became old enough, the public space of the plaza was enclosed. "great kivas" were usually built in the Chaco plazas in addition to smaller ones. Rooms were organized into units of two or three, with a doorway facing the plaza. Ladders led to upper-level units.

The Chaco Canyon district included nine great houses and eighteen great kivas within an eight-mile area. Families occupied suites of rooms in the great houses. Other rooms were for storage, turkey pens, trash, or sometimes burial chambers. Anasazi ate stews of meat, corn mush, squash, and wild vegetables and cornmeal cakes.

Beginning about 1050, the Chaco Anasazi built a complex of twelve elaborate towns that became their religious, political, and commercial center. Grandest of all the great houses was Pueblo Bonito, a five-story D-shaped structure with eight hundred rooms and thirty-seven kivas, covering three acres. It took 150 years before the planned village of Pueblo Bonito realized the conceptions of the original designers.

Skilled as astronomers, the Anasazi built celestial observatories on clifftops. Of these, Fajada Butte is the most famous. Three stone slabs lean against a vertical cliff face on which two spiral petroglyphs are carved. Each day before noon, sun daggers fall through the slabs onto the spirals in different places and, depending on the time of year, mark the solstices and equinoxes.

The Chaco Anasazi built an elaborate road system of about fifteen hundred miles. The thirty-foot-wide roads were paved and curbed. Straight paths cut through or were built over gullies, hills, or cliffs. Roadside shrines were constructed in widened parts of the road. These roads may have served some ceremonial purpose.

By 1150, the Chacoan culture began to decline. The peace-loving people of Pueblo Bonito walled up the doors and windows facing the outside of the great houses. Stones closed the entrance to the pueblos, leaving access by ladder only. Slowly the people left the basin, never to return.

About 1100, the Mesa Verde Anasazi began to abandon many small settlements in the mesa. Large pueblos developed, which initially followed the traditional Mesa Verde pattern with the kiva in front of the main dwelling. Soon, the kivas were enclosed within the circle of houses and walls. Stone towers were built, perhaps as watchtowers. Walls were made of large rectangular sandstone blocks with little mortar. Mud plaster was applied inside and out. One hundred years later, the Mesa Verde Anasazi moved into the caves below the mesa, although they continued to farm the mesa. Some of the cliff dwellings became quite large. Cliff Palace numbered two hundred rooms with twenty-three kivas. The Mesa Verde Anasazi prospered for some time in their cliff dwellings, but decline fell upon these Anasazi, too. A savage, twenty-three-year drought occurred in the Southwest. The Mesa Verdeans left as the crisis intensified.

By 1300, few Anasazi remained in their once-large domain. As their legacy they left descendants who became the Hopi,

Zuñi, and other Pueblo peoples, as well as some of their religious and social traditions. Today the adobe pueblos of the Southwest serve as reminders of the great stone houses of their Anasazi forebears.

—*Mary Pat Balkus*

ADDITIONAL READING:

Brody, J. J. *The Anasazi*. New York: Rizzoli International Press, 1990. Presents a definitive view of the Anasazi, from prehistoric tribes to modern Pueblo people. Color photographs and illustrations.

Frazier, Kendrick. *People of Chaco*. New York: W. W. Norton, 1986. Concentrates on the Anasazi of Chaco Canyon, with details of each archaeological site. Photographs and illustrations.

Gabriel, Kathryn. *Roads to Center Place*. Boulder, Colo.: Johnson Books, 1991. Provides insight into the development of the Chaco roads. Photographs and illustrations.

Lister, Robert H., and Florence C. Lister. *Those Who Came Before*. Tucson: University of Arizona Press, 1983. Focuses on historical events that led to exploration, excavation, and interpretation of artifacts. Photographs and illustrations.

Pike, Donald. *Anasazi: Ancient People of the Rock*. Palo Alto, Calif.: American West, 1974. Illustrated with color photographs by David Muench.

SEE ALSO: 300 B.C., Hohokam Culture; A.D. 750, Mogollon Culture.

A.D. 700 ■ ZAPOTEC CIVILIZATION: *their early urban culture thrived and flourished at Monte Albán, influencing later generations of central Mexico*

DATE: A.D. 700-900
LOCALE: Oaxaca highlands and valleys of central Mexico
CATEGORIES: Latino American history; Native American history; Prehistory and ancient cultures
SUMMARY OF EVENT. Five hundred years before the Christian era, the Zapotec peoples of the mountains and valleys of central Mexico—the modern state of Oaxaca—laid foundations for a brilliant culture that reached its height between A.D. 700 and 900. Because the Zapotec had no written language (although they devised hieroglyphs), knowledge of their civilization depends entirely upon the discoveries and analyses of archaeologists and cultural anthropologists. The work of these experts ranges from studies of historic Mesoamerican farming, religion, political organization, and ecology to science, mining, metalworking, trade, and systematic archaeological reconstructions of the great urban site at Monte Albán, as well as lesser sites at Mitla, Etla, Tlacolula, and in the Zimatlán valleys.

Such evidence suggests that by the time Zapotec culture appears in the historical record, about 500 B.C., it was already characterized by increasing social and political complexity marked by communities of villages and temple centers. Between the opening of the Christian era and A.D. 500, the Zapotecs had developed a regional political state that reached its

cultural apogee at the great urban center at Monte Albán between two hundred and four hundred years later, even as Aztec expansion, military unrest, and large-scale migrations had begun to affect it adversely. Between the years 900 and 1520, the heart of Zapotec civilization shifted from Monte Albán to Mitla, as Aztec military expansion and attempts to incorporate the Zapotecs into an Aztec confederation marked a decline that was completed by the Spanish conquest of Mexico.

Zapotec origins are unknown, although the Zapotecs probably lived side by side with other central Mexican cultures during what archaeologists designate as the region's archaic, or Middle Formative and Late Formative, eras. The Zapotecs themselves ascribed their origins to their ancestors' birth directly from rocks, trees, and jaguars in a mythic past. From the earliest available records, they appear to have been a sedentary farming people, predisposed to living in communities and urban centers and committed to substantial trading activities involving products of their mines, as well as sophisticated, high-quality copper and gold work. Although much of Oaxaca consists of eroded mountains that were unsuitable for agriculture, the valleys of its central section were fertile, subtropical, and frost-free, and thus helped develop the Zapotecs' penchant for urban living.

Like other peoples of Mexico's central plateau, the Zapotecs broke the soil with digging sticks, planted corn, beans, tomatoes, and chili peppers, and supplemented their diets with fish and game. During the Formative era, they irrigated their fields with pots and canals. Having learned metalworking from cultures to their south, they not only were among the first Mesoamericans to work in metals but also soon exceeded all others except the Maya in their *repoussé* work, the quality of their bas-relief stonework (learned from the Olmecs to the south), and their gold, silver, and turquoise jewelry. Trade in these manufactures was facilitated by the Zapotecs' locational advantage in the paths of people moving north and south through Mesoamerica, as well as people traveling from the Pacific coast to the Gulf of Mexico.

The lives of the Zapotecs were dominated by religion. They worshiped a number of gods, the most important of which was Cosijo, the god of lightning and rain. Their affairs were partially ruled over by a hierarchy of priests; therefore, their political establishment functioned as a centralized theocracy, although it seems that power never was concentrated in the hands of a single individual. Power was divided between a monarch, who probably represented the army along with other worldly interests, and a high priest whose authority may have been greater than that of the king. Zapotecs also had developed an elaborate cult of the dead; accordingly, they were devoted to the worship of their ancestors, whom they believed inhabited an idyllic underworld. Their scientific achievements, which experts have ranked as equal to those of the Maya, related closely to their religious beliefs. Their ritual calendar, or *tonalpohuali*, consisted of 260 days, but they also were familiar with the solar calendar—evidence indicates that this had been true since before the Christian era.

At its height, between A.D. 700 and 900, Zapotec culture was epitomized by its capital, Monte Albán, the origins of which preceded the Christian era. The Zapotecs' first capital had been located at Teotitlán del Valle in the Tlacolula Valley. By the time a shift was made to Monte Albán—reasons for which are unclear—the Zapotecs had evolved an advanced culture comparable to others in the central highlands. Scholars estimate that between 600 and 200 B.C., the transformation of Monte Albán was under way and its superb plaza four hundred meters above the valley had begun taking shape. Toward the end of this Middle Formative period, Monte Albán had become the site of religious structures notable among archaeologists for their beautiful carved and inscribed columns and decorated bases that showed Olmec influences. After a transitional period, during which some of the earlier structures on Monte Albán were covered by newer buildings, the Zapotec culture that was centered there became one of the most influential—both politically and culturally—in Mesoamerica. Several scholars have described Monte Albán's Great Plaza as one of the most splendid civic spaces created by humankind, as well as the most beautiful in Mesoamerica. In conformity with the religious values that informed their construction, the score of impressive structures running along the mountaintop on a rough north-south axis close off views of the valleys below, heightening the feeling of completion and enclosure. When occupied, these structures—one of them an astronomical observatory—were painted but, unlike elsewhere in Mesoamerican cultures, they featured little decoration, although what little there was, was elegant. Their builders relied on the contrasting effects of sunlight and shadow to emphasize their meaning. It was from this mountaintop that Zapotec merchants and metal workers extended their commercial route, including the turquoise trade, across thousands of miles, from central Mexico as far northward as the Colorado Basin.

After A.D. 900, Monte Albán began to decline, and the focus of Zapotec civilization shifted to Mitla, now a well-researched ruin. Monte Albán remained occupied until the Spanish conquest that was carried into Oaxaca in 1521 by Francisco de Orozco. Mitla became a significant religious center as well as a necropolis, serving as the burial place of kings and the Zapotecs' chief priests during the years when the Zapotecs struggled to remain independent of the expanding Aztec confederation and then confronted the Spaniards. Neither Monte Albán nor Mitla was fortified, relying instead on the reputation of their great religious authority to dissuade potential enemies. Archaeological investigation of both Monte Albán and Mitla continues, as Monte Albán alone covered more than forty square kilometers and embraced a substantial population spread beyond its immediate precincts throughout nearby valleys.

—*Clifton K. Yearley*

ADDITIONAL READING:

Chinas, Beverly. *The Isthmus Zapotecs*. 2d ed. Fort Worth, Tex.: Harcourt Brace Jovanovich, 1992. Chinas, a specialist on Zapotec women, focuses on their traditional matrilineal roles, which cast light on lingering Monte Albán influences.

Flannery, Kent V., and Joyce Marcus, eds. *The Cloud People: Divergent Evolution of the Zapotec and Mixtec Civilizations*. New York: Academic Press, 1983. A comparison of the development of two major Mesoamerican cultures.

Hardoy, Jorge E. *Pre-Columbian Cities*. Translated by Judith Thorne. New York: Walker, 1973. Excellent synthesis of extant knowledge from archaeologists and cultural historians about Zapotec cities during their formation.

Kearney, Michael. *The Winds of Ixtepeji*. New York: Holt, Rinehart and Winston, 1972. Deals with modern Zapotec society in one town; also reveals myths and folkways that trace back to the Zapotecs' earliest origins.

Wiley, Gordon, and Jeremy A. Sabloff. *A History of American Archaeology*. London: Thames and Hudson, 1974. Includes numerous comments about archaeologists who studied the Zapotecs, what they discovered, and how they proceeded to design and classify chronologies that fit evidence about the ancient Zapotecs.

Wolf, Eric. *Sons of the Shaking Earth*. Chicago: University of Chicago Press, 1966. A historical-archaeological study of the peoples of Mexico and Guatemala and their cultures, which places the evolution of the Zapotecs in context.

SEE ALSO: 1500 B.C., Olmec Civilization; A.D. 200, Mayan Civilization.

A.D. 750 ■ MOGOLLON CULTURE: *with the Anasazi and Hohokam cultures, the Mogollon peoples created pueblo dwellings and a complex social order*

DATE: A.D. 750-1250
LOCALE: Central-southern New Mexico, eastern central-southern Arizona, and parts of northern Mexico
CATEGORIES: Native American history; Prehistory and ancient cultures

SUMMARY OF EVENT. The pre-Columbian Mogollon cultural tradition of the Southwest (distributed throughout central New Mexico and extending into eastern central Arizona and northern Mexico) is a subcultural variant of the "Pueblo Complex," which includes two other great traditions: Anasazi (of the Colorado Plateau) and Hohokam (central and southern Arizona, extending into the Sonoran Desert of northern Mexico). The Mogollon cultural complex and its Southwestern counterparts are among the most notable cultural developments in North American prehistory. Classic Mogollon culture reached its pinnacle at approximately 1200. By 1250, however, Mogollon culture as a cohesive tradition began to fall apart.

Diagnostic Mogollon culture traits first appear during a transitional phase from the older and more generalized Cochise period (7000 B.C. to A.D. 1000). Distinctively Mogollon culture came to dominate the core area of what is now central New Mexico by A.D. 750. This transition is characterized by a gradual shift away from an exclusively hunter-gatherer and foraging way of life to one dominated by domestication of plants, primarily maize, squash, and beans. Other traits include the presence of circular and semicircular house pits, brown and red pottery, tightly stitched basket weaves, cotton textiles, and distinctive burials. Through time, there was also a tendency toward increased sedentary settlement; but, unlike their highly sedentary neighbors—for example, the Anasazi and Hohokam—the Mogollon maintained numerous seasonal village sites and periodically shifted residence according to the availability of water and wild food resources.

The florescence of "classic" Mogollon culture (roughly A.D. 900 to 1200) is identified by the presence of multiple-room, pueblo-style dwellings, large and extensive settlements, polychrome pottery, advanced textile weave patterns, intensive agricultural systems, and indications of a complex social and political order.

Excavations carried out in the Mogollon area suggest that long-distance trade was an important component of the Mogollon economy. Materials that originated in regions as far away as the Mississippi Valley and Mesoamerica (particularly southern and central Mexico) have been found at Mogollon sites. For example, pipe stone sourced to the Mississippi and Wisconsin areas has been found at numerous Mogollon sites, while copper bells, shell beads, and a wide variety of effigy designs are most likely of Mexican origin.

Anthropologists and archaeologists who have worked on interpreting Mogollon artifacts have speculated that Mogollon society showed some signs of class or status differences. For example, some burial sites contained numerous and sumptuous grave goods, while others were sparse or contained only skeletal material with no grave goods present at all. These scholars have also speculated that these class differences indicate a general cultural evolutionary pattern favoring increases in intensive economic productivity. To maintain such economic systems, more centralized political authority must have become increasingly important so that various subsistence, trade, and construction projects could be effectively organized and conducted. Despite such archaeological evidence, an exact reconstruction of Mogollon society can never be made; it is sufficient, however, to acknowledge that Mogollon society must have been relatively complex, bordering on large-scale.

To understand what the Mogollon political system must have been like, anthropologists have looked at modern horticultural populations to provide a working analogy. The concept of a chiefdom has been used to describe sociopolitical structuring at this level. A chiefdom, as defined by anthropologists, refers to a sociopolitical system that depends on the redistribution of goods through a local chief or set of sub-chiefs. Chiefs found in contemporary horticultural societies enjoy higher status than other members of society but have little explicitly recognized political power. Their real power typically rests on their ability to redistribute goods effectively, often during festivals or ceremonies, and their ability to persuade or influence decision making through speeches. It is possible that Mogollon leaders operated in much the same way as their twentieth century counterparts.

Equally problematic have been attempts to reconstruct a tenable picture of Mogollon religion. Numerous artifacts suggesting religious themes have been found, but without specific ethnographic or historical data to indicate their actual cultural functions, interpretations have been highly speculative. Although few specific aspects of Mogollon religion can be described, there are some continuities between historical Southwestern Native American populations and religious traits that occur in earlier Mogollon contexts. Perhaps the most conspicuous is the kiva. Kivas are cylindrical, subterranean structures used primarily for purposes of carrying out religious ceremonies. Kivas are present at all significant late-period Mogollon sites and are still in use throughout much of the Native American Southwest. In addition, various general characteristics of contemporary Southwest practices suggest some general features of Mogollon religion. For example, among contemporary Zuñi and Acoma peoples, religion is integrated closely with other aspects of life; planting corn is considered a religious activity. Calling for rain by appealing to kachinas or nature spirits is also highly religious. Kachina symbols appear as art motifs in the Mogollon area, possibly as early as A.D. 1100. Moreover, the ritual cycles of the contemporary Acoma and Zuñi are closely tied to the annual growing cycle. It is likely that the Mogollon ritual cycle followed the same basic annual pattern, although contemporary researchers cannot describe in detail how these rituals were conducted.

From about 1200, and continuing into the fourteenth century, the Mogollon area, along with the neighboring Hohokam and Anasazi areas, experienced a period of rapid decline. Many of the large pueblo sites were abandoned, and much of the artistic splendor of the classic period disappeared. Archaeologists analyzing various types of artifactual remains (material culture, paleoclimatological, and human osteological data) have generated four basic theories to explain the decline. Some archaeologists have suggested that Mogollon decline resulted from severe changes in climate. These researchers have pointed out that tree ring and pollen data show that after 1200, the Southwest became much more arid than it had been previously. Researchers speculate that the Mogollon subsistence economy could not withstand this shift in climate and eventually collapsed. Other scholars have suggested that Mogollon society fell apart as a result of internal cultural disintegration. Some artifactual material suggests that Mogollon cultural institutions were highly inflexible and fragile, and may have become too disconnected from practical economic concerns. Still others have indicated that warfare may have delivered the final blow. The presence of Athapaskan-speaking groups (Navajo and Apachean), who were latecomers in the Southwest, offers evidence of cultural conflicts that, these researchers posit, might have permanently disrupted the Mogollon way of life.

Most scholars, however, take a synthetic or systemic view of Mogollon decline, believing that the combined forces outlined in all of these theories caused the decline. Some of this latter group of scholars have downplayed the idea of decline

and inferred that the Mogollon tradition did not disappear, but became fragmented and subsequently evolved into the various contemporary Native American traditions now found in central New Mexico and eastern Arizona.

Whatever may have stimulated their decline, it is accurate to say that the Mogollon have had a significant impact on modern views of precontact Native American societies of the Southwest and in North America in general. These were not simple societies, but complex, long-held traditions that rival any found in other parts of the world. Although it is difficult to measure precisely the impact Mogollon culture has had on contemporary Southwest native traditions, or the impact it has had on contemporary Euro-Americans, its influence is felt. Many Native American groups in central and southern New Mexico still make pottery, jewelry, and textiles that resemble Mogollon forms. Euro-Americans also have felt this influence when they visit ancient Mogollon sites, buy artwork, or observe native ceremonies as they continue to be practiced.

—*Michael Shaw Findlay*

ADDITIONAL READING:

Binford, Sally R., and Lewis R. Binford, eds. *New Perspectives in Archaeology*. Chicago: Aldine, 1968. A comprehensive overview of scientific approaches to archaeology. Includes many references to Southwest prehistory.

Cordell, Linda S., and George J. Gumerman, eds. *Dynamics of Southwest Prehistory*. Washington, D.C.: Smithsonian Institution Press, 1989. Contains a variety of high-quality articles on Southwestern prehistory.

Gladwin, Winifred, and Harold S. Gladwin. *Some Southwestern Pottery Types*. Series III. Glove, Ariz.: Gila Pueblo, 1933. An overview of ceramic types for most Southwestern cultural traditions.

Martin, Paul. "Prehistory: Mogollon." In *The Southwest*. Vol. 9 in *Handbook of North American Indians*, edited by Alfonso Ortiz. Washington, D.C.: Smithsonian Institution Press, 1979. A detailed article on the archaeology of the Mogollon culture area.

Snow, Dean R. *The Archaeology of North America*. New York: Chelsea House, 1989. A detailed, in-depth overview of North American archaeology. Includes a notable section on Southwestern archaeology.

SEE ALSO: 300 B.C., Hohokam Culture; A.D. 200, Anasazi Civilization.

A.D. 750 ■ MISSISSIPPIAN CULTURE: *a maize-based economy that dominated the Eastern Woodlands and built its largest city, Cahokia*

DATE: A.D. 750-1500
LOCALE: River valleys of the Eastern Woodlands
CATEGORIES: Native American history; Prehistory and ancient cultures

SUMMARY OF EVENT. "Mississippian" describes hundreds of Native American societies that populated the river valleys and the drainage system of the Mississippi River from about A.D. 750 to about 1500, a period of some forty generations. This period is the last prehistoric period in the Eastern Woodlands culture pattern. The Mississippian Culture Complex included six major areas: Oneota, around the Great Lakes; Fort Ancient in present-day Ohio; the Caddoan Mississippian, with a ceremonial center at Spiro, now in Oklahoma; Plaquemine Mississippian, with a center in Nunih Waya in present-day Mississippi; the Middle Mississippian area, with centers in Cahokia (Illinois) and in Moundville, now Alabama; and the South Appalachian Mississippian culture centered around Etowah in present-day Georgia.

The immediate source of this cultural pattern is not clear; however, between 800 and 1100, there were dramatic developments taking place in the area. Not just a time of change in the style of artifacts, the Mississippian period saw a new way of life with new kinds of technology and a new relationship to the surroundings. It has been said that the period was the closest to being a time of cultural revolution that the prehistoric Central Valley had experienced up to that time.

Chief among the developments of the period was a turning away from the traditional cultivation of native plant crops. A single species of corn, the nonindigenous maize, came to dominate both the fields and the lives of the Mississippian peoples. The Northern Flint variety of maize, an eight-rowed maize that matured more quickly and was more frost-resistant than earlier ten- to twelve-row varieties, thrived in some of the country's richest farmland. This development led to radical changes in the social and political fabric of the people. Maize would become the staple of the Oneota people on the Great Lakes, the Iroquoian Confederacy to the northeast, the people along the middle Ohio River Valley, and those in the river valleys to the southeast and in the Midwest.

Later, maize would be just as important in the lives of the Creek and Choctaw to the south, and the Mandan and Pawnee people in the Great Plains area. The Mississippians also cultivated two other crops, beans and squash, that along with maize formed what the Iroquois called the Three Sisters, crops available in quantities sufficient to provide the main food supply. These crops were supplemented by game and fish.

As these proliferating societies were connected by the common denominator of maize, there developed a need for more centralized authority and more concentrated social controls. Agricultural surpluses were needed for redistribution of food. One change led to others, and the people responded to the challenge by reorganizing their settlements into hierarchical arrangements. That is, the arrangement of housing gave greater distance between nobles and commoners.

The hub of much of this reorganization was under way by about 950, when the city of Cahokia in present-day Illinois emerged as a center of urban expansion. Cahokia was located north of the Central Valley, within what is called the American Bottom region just opposite what would become St. Louis, Missouri. Within a century, thousands of families poured into the area, making Cahokia the largest city north of Mexico. It is the largest archaeological site in the eastern United States. Its dispersed community covered an area of almost five square miles, and the population has been estimated at approximately thirty thousand.

The walled city of Cahokia was characterized by the presence of more than one hundred mounds of various sizes, shapes, and functions, and distributed in a pattern that indicates an organized community, perhaps arranged around plazas. The majority of the mounds were platform mounds, on which various kinds of structures were built. The greatest of the mounds, now called Monk's Mound, was originally taller because there was a conical mound atop it; it now is approximately 100 feet high and extends 1,037 feet north to south and 790 feet east to west. On some of the flat-topped mounds, palaces for the living ruler and housing for the new nobility, perhaps as much as 5 percent of the population, had been constructed. Thus, the elite literally towered over everyone and everything in the Cahokia area.

Not all the mounds were used as sites for palaces of royalty; some were burial mounds, and the burial offerings in the mounds reveal much about the extensive communication that the Mississippians had with other people on the Atlantic coast. The best-known of the burial mounds at Cahokia is the one now labeled Mound 72. This mound provides extensive information about the major trade contacts of the Mississippians. In it was found copper from Lake Superior and mica from the southern Appalachians. Examination of the style and content of arrow points has indicated sources in Wisconsin, Tennessee, east Texas, and eastern Oklahoma. In other locations in Cahokia, conch shells indicated contacts with people living along the Atlantic Ocean.

The Cahokian aristocrats presided over complex ceremonies and rituals that were at the center of the Mississippian's life. The sense of community was closely related to long-term political cycles. As long as chiefs were particularly effective, the people gladly accepted their rule and united as a regional community. When a chief died, the huge community became fragmented into several townships. The more social and political ranking increased, the more important ceremony and sacrament became to the people. These ceremonies expressed obligations to ancestors, celebrated successful harvests, hunts, and warfare, and involved elaborate death rituals in homage to social leaders.

The religious system that evolved is called the Southern Cult, the Southern Death Cult, or the Southeastern Ceremonial Complex. It included a network of artifacts and motifs. Ceramics modeled on animal and human forms could be found throughout much of the East during Mississippian times. Some of the important motifs included crosses, human hands with eyes or crosses on the palms, winged or weeping eyes, human skulls, long bones, dancing men in elaborate costumes, arrows, and symbols of the sun. Also important were animal

MOUND-BUILDING CULTURES AND MOUND SITES

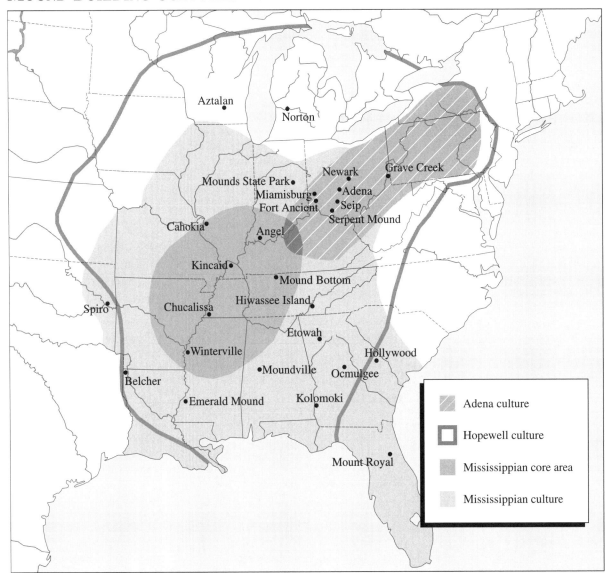

The earliest of the Ohio River Mound Builders, the Adena Indians, are thought to have lived between 700 B.C. and A.D. 200. The Adena gave rise to the Hopewell Indian culture, also centered in the valleys of the Ohio River and its tributaries, which is recognized from around 100 B.C. until about A.D. 400 or 500. The Hopewell developed vast, nearly continentwide, trading networks. Some researchers posit that Hopewellians were ancestral to the Iroquois. The last North American mound-building culture, the Mississippian, was centered along the Mississippi River, at Cahokia, where East St. Louis, Illinois, now stands. It developed around A.D. 700 and flourished until after 1500. Many scholars believe that the Mississippians were direct ancestors to the Cherokee, Sioux, and other American Indian tribes.

symbols such as the feathered serpent, woodpecker, falcon, raccoon, and eagle. These symbols are found on pottery and on shell and copper ornaments. The objects are associated with the burial of high-status personages, mostly at major centers such as Cahokia, and the distribution of particular styles is outside regional boundaries.

Although Cahokia and other great Mississippian centers were already in decline prior to Hernando de Soto's arrival in North America, their ultimate collapse is associated with the appearance of Europeans in their territory. Disease in epidemic proportions overtook people in the surviving towns, and by 1500, the complex political and social mores that defined the Mississippians were greatly diminished. Constructed public works such as the mounds and palisades were no longer built. Burial rituals for ancestors and support for royalty ended.

Nevertheless, many of the Mississippian beliefs lived on among southeastern tribes of later generations, such as the Cherokee, Creek, Choctaw, and Chickasaw. For example, the *puskita*, or Green Corn ceremony, shows the influence of the fertility rituals associated with the maize crop. Another ceremony of the Southern Cult, the Black Drink, also survived. The drink, made from roasted leaves of the sassina shrub, was taken with great ceremony and in the belief that the drink conferred spiritual purification upon all participants. Rich in caffeine, the drink was believed to clear the minds for debate and to cleanse and strengthen the bodies of warriors for battle.

—*Victoria Price*

ADDITIONAL READING:

Ballantine, Betty, and Ian Ballantine, eds. *The Native Americans: An Illustrated History*. Atlanta: Turner, 1993. Chapter 6 of this comprehensive treatment of Native American history discusses the emergence and demise of the Mississippian Culture Complex, in which the Indian confederacies of the southland were rooted.

Kehoe, Alice B. *North American Indians: A Comprehensive Account*. 2d ed. Englewood Cliffs, N.J.: Prentice-Hall, 1992. Systematically traces the Americas' earliest humans and discusses the people of each of seven geographical areas. Maps, charts, and recommended lists.

Morse, Dan F., and Phyllis A. Morse. *Archaeology of the Central Mississippi Valley*. New York: Academic Press, 1983. Places the complex origins of the Cahokia site in the context of the entire Mississippian complex. Focuses on environmental adaptation and ceramics and other important artifacts.

Silverberg, Robert. *Mound Builders of Ancient America: The Archaeology of a Myth*. Greenwich, Conn.: New York Graphic Society, 1968. A comprehensive study of various mound-building prehistoric societies. Discusses the emergence, triumph, and deflation of the myth that the Mound Builders were a lost race.

Smith, Bruce D., ed. *Mississippian Settlement Patterns*. New York: Academic Press, 1978. Discusses a number of Mississippian settlement patterns, including those of Cahokia and the American Bottom.

SEE ALSO: 700 B.C., Ohio Mound Builders.

A.D. 986 ■ NORSE EXPEDITIONS: *the first European attempts to establish settlements in North America*

DATE: A.D. 986-1008
LOCALE: South Baffin Island, Labrador, and Newfoundland, Canada
CATEGORIES: Canadian history; Exploration and discovery
KEY FIGURES:
Freydis Eiriksdottir (c. 965-1020), Greenlander woman who

led the fourth and last Norse expedition to attempt to colonize Vinland
Leif Eiriksson (c. 970-1035), prominent Greenlander who explored and first attempted to settle Vinland
Thorvald Eiriksson (c. 982-1002), Greenlander who led the second Norse expedition to Vinland and explored northern Labrador
Bjarni Herjolfsson (c. 965-1015), Norwegian-Icelandic navigator who first sighted North America in 986
Thorfinn Karlsefni (c. 983-1035), Greenlander who led the third and largest Norse expedition to Vinland

SUMMARY OF EVENT. Norse contact with North America dates to the Viking Age (c. 780-1070), when significant numbers of Scandinavians participated in Viking activities, which included piracy, trade, and settlement in Europe and the North Atlantic. By the 870's, Norwegian Vikings had settled Iceland, and by the 980's they had moved into Greenland. Although the Icelandic colony would be permanent, the Greenland colony was overly dependent on Europe and began to decline after 1400, as climatic changes resulted in colder winters. At its height, in the twelfth and thirteenth centuries, however, the Greenland colony sustained fourteen hundred farms and five thousand settlers.

During the last decades of the Viking Age (after 1000), the Greenlanders converted to Christianity with their brethren in Scandinavia and Iceland. However, they still possessed the maritime skills (including a knowledge of latitude and currents) and the daring that had carried their pagan forebears across an ever-widening world in the ninth and tenth centuries. Their seventy-six-foot-long oceangoing vessels held thirty-five crew members and provisions, and had a shallow draught enabling the ship to pull up close to the land. The ships usually were powered by wind and sail but carried sixteen pair of oars for rowers to maneuver in narrow straits or fjords.

According to Norse tradition, Greenland had been discovered accidentally by a navigator going to Iceland. *The Greenlanders' Saga* (c. 1200) reports that the earliest Norse contact with North America was accidental, when in the summer of 986, Bjarni Herjolfsson set sail from Iceland, intending to go to Greenland. Having only a rough course and descriptions of the Greenland coast by which to navigate, Bjarni was blown off course and sighted two unfamiliar coasts south of Greenland, which possessed dense forests and a topography of both flat land and small hills, which resembles eastern sub-Arctic Canada. Desiring to get to his destination in Greenland before winter, Bjarni did not disembark to explore. When he finally reached Greenland, however, he told his fellow mariners of the existence of the land of forests that lay to the south.

The exigencies of the colonization process in Greenland prevented any further exploration of the new land during the 980's and 990's. Sometime around the year 1000, Leif Eiriksson (son of Greenland pioneer Eirik "the Red" Thorvaldsson) purchased Bjarni's ship and set out to explore the new land with a crew of thirty-five. He explored and named three areas: Helluland ("flat stone land"), which most scholars identify as southern Baffin Island; Markland ("wood land"), which scholars identify as northern Labrador; and Vinland ("vine land"), at a distance of two days and two nights from Markland, identified as northern Newfoundland (with extant Viking-era Scandinavian archaeological remains).

Leif and his crew stayed in Vinland for a year, constructing huts and gathering grapes, wild wheat, salmon, and timber. Leif returned to a position of authority in Greenland and loaned the huts he had built to the leaders of the later expeditions. He did not wish to relinquish his control over the source of economically profitable ventures in the future by selling his property. The area of Leif's seasonal settlement in Vinland was called Leifsbudir ("Leif's booths") and became the focal point for later attempts at colonization. According to *The Saga of Eirik the Red* (c. 1263), the Greenlanders eventually distinguished between two areas in Vinland: Straumfjord ("stream ford") and Hop ("landlocked bay").

Leif's brother Thorvald undertook the second expedition to Vinland, in 1001-1002. He and his crew of thirty explored farther to the west in Labrador and encountered Native Americans whom they called Skraelings ("ugly men"). The Norsemen did not distinguish between the various native groups with whom they came into contact, but archaeological evidence (trade goods of Scandinavian provenance) suggests that the Skraelings were Dorset (Paleo) Eskimos, Thule Eskimos, and Algonquian-speaking American Indians. Thorvald was killed in a violent encounter with Skraelings in Markland, probably near Lake Melville, Labrador, and his men returned to Greenland without his body. In about 1002, Leif's other brother, Thorstein, set sail with a crew in order to recover Thorvald's body, but became lost and returned to Greenland without sighting the coast.

The first full-scale attempt to colonize Vinland occurred in 1003-1006, when Thorfinn Karlsefni led an expedition consisting of three ships, more than a hundred men and women, and cattle. The first European birth in the Americas occurred during this time—Snorri Karlsefnisson. The settlers traded Scandinavian red cloth and milk with the Skraelings in return for a variety of skins and furs, commodities of particular interest to Vikings everywhere. The Skraelings were unfamiliar with metal, and the sagas relate that they were interested in trading for the Norse settlers' metal-tipped weapons. Karlsefni's refusal to trade away the only military advantage his colonists possessed over their neighbors apparently led to tensions between the Vinland settlement and the Skraelings; not long after his refusal to trade in weapons came a large Skraeling attack on the colony, which induced Karlsefni and his band to abandon the venture.

The final recorded Norse attempt to colonize Vinland was undertaken by Leif's sister, Freydis Eiriksdottir. In about 1007-1008, she persuaded two Icelandic brothers, Helgi and Finnbogi, to pool their resources with her and make the journey with three ships and more than a hundred men and women. The sagas relate that Freydis' wrangling over scarce resources with the two brothers resulted in the murder of Helgi and Finnbogi and their followers, and in the theft of the commodities they had procured. A large Skraeling attack further demoralized the settlers, and this last Norse expedition returned to Greenland after only a year.

There may have been another Norse encounter with Vinland in 1121, when Bishop Eirik of Greenland set sail in search of the area. There is no reference to his motive (some have suggested missionary work) or to the result of the voyage. A Greenland ship briefly visited Markland in 1347, possibly to gather timber. The early documentary references to Vinland are Adam of Bremen (1075), who mentioned the area's wild grapes; Ari Thorgilsson (1125), who referred to Vinland as a land inhabited by Skraelings who used stone implements; twelfth and fourteenth century Icelandic annals; an anonymous "Geographical Treatise" (1387) that referred to the location of the colony; and the two previously mentioned thirteenth century sagas.

Helge Ingstad led seven archaeological expeditions to Newfoundland (1961-1968) and located the site of Vinland at L'Anse aux Meadows. Ingstad has made much of the fact that the Old Norse word *vin* actually means "meadow," but most sources corroborate the long-held belief that the colony's name comes from the abundance of wine grapes growing on vines. Ingstad's team uncovered remains of eight turf houses designed like typical Viking longhouses, four boat sheds, a smithy with a stone anvil, pig bones, a spindle whorl, and a bronze pin (evidence of wool-weaving technology, which was unknown to the American Indians and the Eskimos).

The Kensington Rune Stone discovered in 1898 in Minnesota has been identified as a fraud, but evidence of Norse trade with the natives has been uncovered in excavations of Native American sites in Arctic Canada (Ellesmere Island) and Maine. Ultimately, the Norse presence in North America ended for the same reasons as the later failure of the Greenland colony around 1500—inadequate lines of supply and communication with the home territory.   —*William E. Watson*

ADDITIONAL READING:

Guralnick, Eleanor, ed. *Vikings in the West*. Chicago: Archaeological Institute of America, 1982. An excellent short conference volume that contains six essays by experts on the Viking presence in Greenland, Newfoundland, and Arctic Canada.

Ingstad, Helge. *Westward to Vinland*. New York: Harper & Row, 1969. The definitive English-language book on the L'Anse aux Meadows archaeological expeditions of the Ingstad team.

Jones, Gwyn. *A History of the Vikings*. New York: Oxford University Press, 1984. One of the best English-language texts on the Viking Age. Chapter 5 contains a concise summary of the sources for the Vinland colony.

Wahlgren, Erik. *The Vikings and America*. London: Thames and Hudson, 1986. An interesting recent examination of the Vinland expeditions that suggests an alternative site for the colony.

1428 ■ AZTEC EMPIRE: *the greatest flowering of Mesoamerican culture, a militaristic civilization that stretched from Pacific to Atlantic*

DATE: 1428-1521
LOCALE: Central Mexico
CATEGORIES: Latino American history; Native American history; Prehistory and ancient cultures
KEY FIGURES:
Acamapichtli (died 1391), first supreme ruler of the Aztecs
Hernán Cortés (1485-1547), leader of the Spanish conquest of the Aztecs
Itzcóatl (c. 1382-1440), founder of the Aztec Empire
Montezuma II, also known as *Moctezuma Xocoytzin* (1467-1520), ruler when the Spaniards arrived

SUMMARY OF EVENT. Legend records that the Nahuatl-speaking Aztecs (or, more accurately, the Culhua Mexica) founded the city of Tenochtitlán in 1325 on a small island in Lake Texcoco (the site of modern Mexico City) and a century later emerged as the last great imperial power of indigenous Mesoamerica. Aztec civilization evolved from the legacy of earlier Mesoamerican groups, especially the Teotihuacán and Tula cultures. A widespread commercial network linked Tenochtitlán with the Maya to the south and extended as far north as the southwestern United States. Through strategic alliances, intimidation, and conquest, the Aztecs dominated central Mexico until the Aztec Empire fell victim to Hernán Cortés and his band of Spanish conquistadores and indigenous allies in 1519-1521.

According to their religious myths, the Mexica wandered southward into the valley of central Mexico, guided by their tribal god, Huitzilopochtli. Along the way, Huitzilopochtli's priests began the rite of tearing palpitating hearts from the chests of sacrificial victims. They eventually reached Lake Texcoco and encountered peoples whose culture was more advanced. In fact, these sedentary peoples despised the Mexica as primitive barbarians, but found them useful as mercenaries. Clashes with the city of Culhuacán forced the Mexica to take refuge in a marshy area of the lake, where they founded Tenochtitlán.

Early Aztec society in Tenochtitlán seems to have been egalitarian, based on clans (*calpulli*) that controlled access to agricultural land. As the city grew, however, the *calpulli* lost importance. The Mexica chose their first supreme ruler (*tlatoani*), Acamapichtli, who ruled from 1372 to 1391. Class divisions emerged, and nobles (*pipiltin*) dominated military leadership and monopolized access to the *calmecac* (a school where priests and pictorial writers were trained). Mexica rulers married into the royal families of Culhuacán and Azcapotzalco. Until the early fifteenth century, the Aztecs were subject to Azcapotzalco, which had a small empire around Lake Texcoco. Meanwhile, they expanded Tenochti-

tlán, providing it with drinking water and constructing *chinampas* ("floating gardens") to help feed the city. Around 1428, under the leadership of Itzcóatl, they joined with the cities of Texcoco and Tlacopan and defeated Azcapotzalco. After this victory, the Aztecs embarked on their own imperial quest, subordinating their two allies. On Itzcóatl's orders, Aztecs burned the recorded myths and history of the conquered peoples and imposed an official Aztec version of the past.

As lands around the lake fell to Aztec power, the state distributed them to the *pipiltin* and the most distinguished warriors. Expansion thus created a gulf between the elite and the commoners. Earlier, most Mexica were peasants (*macehualtin*), who shared the clan's communal lands. As the Aztec population grew, however, clans no longer possessed enough land to meet their needs. Dependent agricultural laborers (*mayeques*) and slaves became more prevalent, as noble estates proliferated and conquered peoples were incorporated into Aztec society.

The Aztec Empire stretched from the northern deserts to the strait of Tehuantepec and from the Gulf of Mexico to the Pacific Ocean. Some cities and villages succumbed to Aztec intimidation; others sought to become subordinate allies; some had to be conquered through military force. Only the Tarascans of Michoacán and the Tlaxcalans of Puebla escaped domination. The Aztec Empire was a hegemonic one. The Aztecs allowed the conquered to retain their lands and political leaders, as long as they obeyed imperial decrees and paid tribute. Imperial armies did not occupy conquered territories but exacted harsh vengeance on rebellious cities.

All men in Tenochtitlán were expected to be warriors. From infancy, boys received the physical markings and the training essential to warriors. Each *calpulli* had its young men's house (*telpochcalli*), where warriors taught the military arts. Society accorded great honors and rewards to those who distinguished themselves on the battlefield by capturing valiant enemy warriors. Public humiliation awaited those who showed cowardice on the battlefield.

Other social groups supported these military endeavors. Merchants (*pochteca*) carried out a far-flung trade but also served as spies and intelligence gatherers. At times, they may have purposely provoked hostilities with nonsubject peoples. Priests marched at the head of the army. Girls were raised to be mothers, to bear the next generation of warriors. A woman who died in childbirth had an afterlife status similar to the warrior who perished in battle or on the sacrificial slab. Even the lowliest members of society, the *tamemes* (carriers), served the military cause, transporting food and other supplies to the field of battle.

Environmental explanations have been given for Aztec militarism and human sacrifice (for example, population pressure demanded expansion; cannibalism derived from a protein-deficient diet), but religious ideology played a critical role. Human sacrifice was widespread in Mesoamerica, although not to the extreme practiced by the Mexica. The Az-

The supreme deity and god of war among the Aztecs and other tribes of the Nahua language group, Huitzilopochtli was said to have led his people to their home in central Mexico. His idol, a carved basalt block adorned with feathers and housed in a special temple dedicated in 1487, three decades before the arrival of the Spaniards, is believed to have witnessed ritual human sacrifice, with estimates ranging in the thousands. Montezuma II's claim to be Huitzilopochtli incarnate helped solidify his rule over the Aztecs. (Library of Congress)

tecs' cosmogony was also Mesoamerican. It held that the earth passed through cycles of creation and destruction. Humanity thus lived in a world doomed to disaster that could be forestalled only by nourishing the gods with human blood. Without human blood, the sun might not rise and preserve humanity. Not only priests but also all people provided blood through ritual self-laceration. Fatalism pervaded Aztec life: One's destiny was determined at birth. It mattered little whether one nourished the gods through self-sacrifice or as the captive victim.

Aztec militarism and religion became increasingly intertwined. The Mexica continued to worship other Mesoamerican deities, such as Quetzalcóatl, Tlaloc, and Tezcatlilpoca, in bloody rituals, but they raised the cult of Huitzilopochtli to an imperial obsession. Wars brought captives to sacrifice. By the

mid-1400's, the Mexica staged mock battles ("flowery wars") with rival cities so that both sides could take captives to sacrifice. In 1487, the Aztecs killed at least twenty thousand captives to appease Huitzilopochtli at the dedication of the enlarged Great Temple.

When Montezuma II became *tlatoani* in 1502, Aztec power was at its peak. Tenochtitlán had grown to 150,000 inhabitants, with perhaps 1.5 million living around Lake Texcoco. Social tensions were increasing, because commoners gained little material benefit from the conquests. To enhance his power, Montezuma II claimed to be the incarnation of Huitzilopochtli, creating the ultimate marriage of Aztec militarism and religion.

Montezuma II proved surprisingly ill-suited to deal with the crisis provoked by the Spaniards' arrival in 1519. More the meditative priest than the frenzied warrior, he vacillated, wondering if the strangers were Quetzalcóatl returning, as had long been prophesied. Spanish weapons and horses were superior to Aztec missiles and obsidian-edged swords. Hernán Cortés acquired important indigenous allies by playing upon their hatred of the Aztecs. Montezuma II allowed the Spaniards to enter Tenochtitlán, whereupon they took him hostage. He died while in their hands in 1520. The warlike Cuitlahuac replaced him as *tlatoani* but perished from smallpox a few months later. Driven from Tenochtitlán in a bloody rout in June, 1520, the Spaniards and their allies returned in 1521. Their siege destroyed most of the city, and the invaders captured the last *tlatoani*, Cuauhtémoc, as he tried to escape.

The Aztec legacy has provoked controversy. Rival indigenous peoples hated the Mexicas' bloody imperialism, and their human sacrifices and cannibalism horrified the Spaniards. Yet the Spanish invasion brought a demographic holocaust caused by Old World diseases (the empire's population probably declined by 90 percent) and a new oppressive colonialism. Aztec civilization produced a vibrant commerce, an elaborate belief system, and exquisite poetry. The Spaniards compared the splendors of Tenochtitlán to those of Venice, and conquistador Bernal Díaz del Castillo reported that it "seemed like an enchanted vision from the tale of Amadis." Rarely has a culture provoked such contradictory images. —*Kendall W. Brown*

ADDITIONAL READING:

Berdan, Frances E. *The Aztecs of Central Mexico: An Imperial Society*. New York: Holt, Rinehart and Winston, 1982. A brief overview of Aztec society, religion, and politics.

Broda, Johanna, David Carrasco, and Eduardo Matos Moctezuma. *The Great Temple of Tenochtitlan: Center and Periphery in the Aztec World*. Berkeley: University of California Press, 1987. Interprets the meaning of the Great Temple in Aztec life, emphasizing religion's role as a catalyst for Aztec militarism and human sacrifice.

Clendinnen, Inga. *Aztecs: An Interpretation*. New York: Cambridge University Press, 1991. A sensitive interpretation of Aztec religion and society as a context for understanding the Aztec's reaction to the Spanish invasion.

Díaz del Castillo, Bernal. *The Conquest of New Spain*. Translated by J. M. Cohen. London: Penguin Books, 1963. The famous narrative by one of Cortés' men.

Hassig, Ross. *Aztec Warfare: Imperial Expansion and Political Control*. Norman: University of Oklahoma Press, 1988. Excessively downplays religious ideology's role in Aztec warfare, but provides useful insights regarding the logistics of expansion.

Sahagún, Bernardino de. *General History of the Things of New Spain: The Florentine Codex*. Translated by Arthur J. O. Anderson and Charles E. Dibble. 13 vols. Santa Fe: School of American Research, 1950-1982. Ethnographic compilation about the religion, politics, society, flora, and fauna of pre-Hispanic Mexico, as reported by indigenous sixteenth century informants.

SEE ALSO: A.D. 200, Mayan Civilization; 1519, Cortés Enters Tenochtitlán.

1492 ■ COLUMBUS' VOYAGES: *the beginnings of major European colonization of the Western Hemisphere, accompanied by the decline of indigenous peoples*

DATE: October 12, 1492-1504
LOCALE: San Salvador (Watling), Bahama Islands
CATEGORIES: Exploration and discovery; Latino American history
KEY FIGURES:
Christopher Columbus (1451-1506), commander of the first Spanish voyages to the New World
Guacanagarí (died c. 1495), Arawak chief who befriended Columbus
Isabella I (1451-1504), queen of Castile

SUMMARY OF EVENT. Although not the first European to set foot in the New World, Christopher Columbus is credited with opening it to European settlement. His first voyage brought the area to the attention of Europe, and his second began the colonization by Spain.

Details of the birth and early life of Columbus are not definitely known. He was probably born in Genoa, Italy, in 1451. He had little schooling and went to sea as a young man. About 1476, he went to Portugal and settled in Lisbon, the center of Portuguese maritime activities. There Columbus received an education, sailed on several voyages, married a Portuguese lady of the lower nobility, and became a prosperous ship captain.

Columbus became convinced that the East Indies could be reached by sailing west. The idea was not new, but most experts agreed that the voyage was too long and difficult. When Columbus offered the plan to King John II of Portugal in 1484, the king rejected it in favor of the route around the tip of South Africa. Three years later, Bartolomeu Dias rounded the Cape of Good Hope and seemed to justify the king's decision.

In 1485, Columbus moved to Spain, and the Duke of Medina Celi introduced him to King Ferdinand and Queen Isabella. Isabella showed interest in Columbus' ideas but would not consider the project at the time because she was fighting an expensive war to expel the Moors. Columbus returned to Portugal to try a second time to persuade King John II. While Columbus was in Lisbon, Dias returned from his trip around the Cape of Good Hope, the voyage that gave Portugal her route to the spice wealth of India. King John had no interest in another route. Columbus then returned to Spain and sent his brother Ferdinand to King Henry VII of England and King Charles VIII of France to seek support. Both kings rejected the project.

In January, 1492, Granada, the last Moorish stronghold, fell. Isabella signed an agreement with Columbus on April 17, 1492, authorizing him to sail west, avoiding Portuguese territories. Under the terms of the agreement, Columbus and his heirs were granted the titles of don and admiral of the ocean,

VOYAGES OF COLUMBUS, 1492-1502

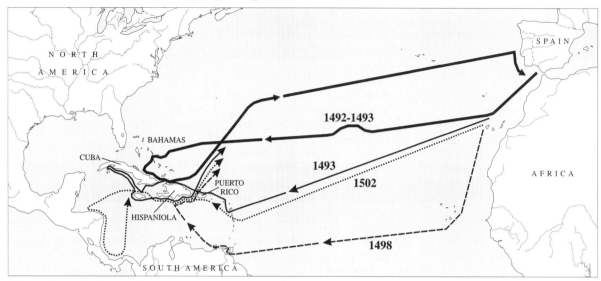

Christopher Columbus made the first European voyages to the New World following the aborted Norse expeditions five hundred years before. His four voyages—in 1492, 1493, 1498, and 1502—established a Spanish base in the Western Hemisphere.

the political positions of viceroy and governor, and one-tenth of all royal revenues from any new lands discovered.

The port of Palos owed Isabella a fine, and she required it to provide two ships free of cost for the expedition. Three ships were readied, the *Niña*, the *Pinta*, and the slightly larger *Santa Maria*. Ninety men and boys were enlisted. The expedition sailed on August 3, 1492. After a stop in the Canary Islands, the voyage west began. Thirty-three days later, on October 12, Columbus discovered an island that he named San Salvador. Because he believed he had reached Asia and had found the outer islands of the East Indies, Columbus gave the natives there the name Indians. He described them as without clothes, friendly and loyal, guileless and unwarlike, and ready for conversion to the true faith.

Martín Alonso Pinzón left in the *Pinta* on a private gold-hunting expedition. The remaining two ships sailed to the north coast of Haiti. Columbus named the island La Isla Española, later called Hispaniola. On Christmas morning, the *Santa Maria* was caught on a reef and wrecked. With help from the native Arawaks, led by their chief, Guacanagarí, the crew and most of the supplies were saved. Guacanagarí was a paramount chief, who had achieved status and power as one of the heads of a vast, interisland trading network. He trusted Columbus and exchanged gifts with him, thinking they were trading as equals. Columbus, however, interpreted Guacanagarí's gifts as a gesture of submission to the Spaniards.

Because of the gold ornaments worn by the Arawaks, Columbus determined that the island was suitable for settlement and decided to return to Spain. Before sailing, Columbus had a fort built at a site he called La Navidad (Christmas), and the forty-four men of the wrecked *Santa Maria* were left with orders to seek more gold. In mid-January, 1493, Pinzón in the

Pinta rejoined Columbus, and the two ships began the return voyage, reaching Palos on March 15, 1493. Columbus was greeted joyously by the people and with honors by Isabella and Ferdinand. No one questioned the tales he told.

To assure Spanish control of the new lands, Columbus was sent on a second voyage to get gold, keep out intruders, win souls, and find the kingdoms of China and Japan. Columbus began the second voyage on September 25, 1493, with seventeen ships and twelve hundred to fifteen hundred men, including soldiers, artisans, nobles, and five priests. They took with them horses, cattle, sheep, seeds, fruits, tools, and shoots of sugar cane, which would later become the chief crop of the Caribbean Islands. Women would come later.

Columbus sailed on a more southerly route, sighted Dominica in the Lesser Antilles, and turned north to Hispaniola, where he learned that the men he had left had disappeared and Fort Navidad had been destroyed. Greed for gold and women had led the Spaniards to mistreat the Arawaks, who finally killed the Spaniards and destroyed the fort. To replace La Navidad, Columbus founded a second settlement, La Isabela, farther east on the same coast.

In order to maintain support in Spain, Columbus had to deliver gold. He sent an expedition into the interior under the leadership of Alonzo de Ojeda, who forced the Arawaks to mine gold under penalty of death. The Arawaks turned against the Spaniards, running off or killing themselves. To satisfy the demand for wealth, Columbus sent five hundred Arawaks as slaves to Spain. More than half of them died on the voyage; Isabella, who opposed enslavement of the natives, freed the rest.

In further explorations, Columbus discovered Jamaica and Cuba, which he thought were the mainland. Upon returning to

La Isabela, he found the colonists in rebellion. To defend himself, Columbus sailed to Spain in June, 1496, leaving his brother Bartolomé as governor.

After some delay, Ferdinand and Isabella received Columbus but refused to provide any further support. Most Spaniards, disappointed with the financial returns from the Spanish colony, also denied him support, but after two years, Columbus was able to finance a third voyage (1498-1500). This time he sailed to Trinidad and continued along the Venezuelan coast. He became convinced that this area was Paradise and that the Oronoco River was one of the four rivers of Paradise.

Columbus decided to go to the new capital of Hispaniola, Santo Domingo, which Bartolomé had founded in 1496. When he arrived, he found the colony in civil war. Columbus appealed to the crown for reinforcements. In 1500, Isabella sent Francisco Bobadilla to Santo Domingo as governor, in violation of her 1492 agreement with Columbus. After an investigation, Bobadilla arrested Columbus and shipped him to Spain in chains. Six weeks after he arrived in Spain, Columbus was received by the monarchs, who treated him affectionately and assured him of his rights. Nevertheless, a new governor, Nicolás de Ovando, was sent to Hispaniola without Columbus' being consulted.

Isabella decided to give Columbus one last chance. She provided him four ships for his fourth and last voyage (1502-1504). He made his fastest crossing, twenty-two days. Passing through the Lesser Antilles, he headed for Santo Domingo, but Governor Ovando refused him permission to land.

Columbus sailed to Central America and for eight months explored the coast, convinced that it was the Malay Peninsula. Storm damage, diseases, and fights with hostile natives forced Columbus to sail back to Santo Domingo. His unseaworthy ships had to be beached in Jamaica, where he was stranded for one year and five days before rescuers arrived. Columbus returned to Spain in 1504 a broken man. He died on May 20, 1506, in Valladolid.

Columbus succeeded in reaching the New World because of his navigational skill, tenacity, courage, and faith. He began the expansion of Spain into new territory, an example the other European nations followed a century later. At first, he was genuinely concerned with the welfare of the natives but was unable to prevent his countrymen from abusing and exploiting them. He lacked political and managerial skills, causing him to be intensely disliked by the settlers. Columbus died believing he had actually found the route to the east by sailing west. In spite of his limitations, the greatness of Columbus and his influence on world history cannot be denied.

—*Robert D. Talbott*

ADDITIONAL READING:

Colon, Fernando. *The Life of Christopher Columbus by His Son Ferdinand*. Translated and annotated by Benjamin Keen. New Brunswick, N.J.: Rutgers University Press, 1959. Important source despite a son's bias. Illustrations and maps.

Fernandez-Armesto, Felipe. *Columbus*. New York: Oxford University Press, 1991. Written for readers who want un-

adorned facts from verified or reasonably inferred sources. Maps, illustrations, and notes.

Granzotto, Gianni. *Christopher Columbus*. Garden City, N.Y.: Doubleday, 1985. Translated by Stephen Cartarelli. Written by an Italian historian who retraced the first voyage. Nine maps.

Morison, Samuel Eliot. *Admiral of the Ocean Sea: A Life of Christopher Columbus*. Boston: Little, Brown, 1942. Condensation of author's two-volume biography, without much of the navigational data and notes. Maps and illustrations.

_____, ed. and trans. *Journals and Other Documents on the Life and Voyages of Christopher Columbus*. New York: Heritage Press, 1963. Accurate translations of the most interesting, significant, and informative documents on the life and voyages of Columbus. Chronology, maps, and illustrations.

SEE ALSO: 1495, West Indian Uprisings.

1495 ■ WEST INDIAN UPRISINGS: *Spanish policy of co-opting native West Indians ultimately resulted in rebellion*

DATE: 1495-c. 1510
LOCALE: Hispaniola, Greater Antilles
CATEGORIES: Native American history; Wars, uprisings, and civil unrest
KEY FIGURES:
Agüeybana, chief in the Higüey region
Anacaona, chieftainess in the western provinces
Caonabo, 1495 rebel leader
Christopher Columbus (1451-1506), explorer who made first European contact American indigenous peoples
Guarionex, 1495 rebel leader
Guarocuya (died 1509), nephew of Anacaona
Bartolomé de Las Casas (1460-1518), governor of Hispaniola, 1502-1509
Nicolás de Ovando (1460?-1518?), governor of Hispaniola
Diego Velázquez (1465?-1522?), Ovando's deputy commander
SUMMARY OF EVENT. The island of Hispaniola (today, the two independent states of Haiti and the Dominican Republic) was the key site of the first New World landing by Christopher Columbus in 1492. Historians have not only Columbus' own account of contacts with the native inhabitants of the Caribbean islands but also a number of descriptions by other explorers and missionaries who soon came to the first outposts in the Western Hemisphere. These accounts tended from the outset to distinguish two West Indian subgroups: Caribs and Arawaks. This conventional dualistic view gradually was reworked as ethnohistorians came to reserve the ethnolinguistic term "Arawak" for mainland populations, using the term "Taino" to refer to island groupings, including the native population of Hispaniola. The westernmost Tainos on Cuba and Jamaica appear to have been the most peaceful, both in their relations with other Taino groupings and in their reaction to the first

Spaniards. Ciguayan and Borinquen Tainos of Hispaniola and Puerto Rico had a pre-Columbian tradition of warring, mainly against aggressive raids from groupings now known archaeologically as Island Caribs (from the Lesser Antilles, mainly Guadeloupe). They were, however, relatively receptive in the first ten years after 1492 to trying to adapt to Spanish colonial presence.

It was among the eastern Tainos on the Virgin Islands that the Spaniards encountered the first signs of open hostility to their presence. After clashes with otherwise unidentifiable natives on St. Croix, whom Columbus called Caribs, a number of negative observations began to enter Spanish accounts, including presumed acts of cannibalism and enslavement of women captives (later identified as a ceremonial bride-capture tradition).

These early violent encounters with eastern Tainos stemmed more from the natives' fear of strangers than from a considered reaction against Spanish plans for colonization. However, by the time Columbus became Hispaniola's first governor, a policy had been defined that called for direct methods of colonial control, including the *encomienda* system. The latter involved forced attachment of native laborers to Spanish colonial economic ventures, both in agriculture and in mining. By 1495, when the first West Indian revolt against the Spaniards broke out, the long-term movement of all of Hispaniola's Tainos toward extinction had entered its first stage.

Historians have noted that the native population of Hispaniola declined most dramatically by the first decade of the sixteenth century, mainly because of a lack of immunological resistance to diseases brought by the Spaniards. Scores of thousands died from infectious diseases, others from the overwork and undernourishment associated with the notorious *encomienda* system. A surprising number, however, fell victim to violent repression of resistance movements led by their tribal chiefs.

Between 1495 and 1500, there were at least two armed uprisings against Spanish control. Each of these (that of Caonabo, in 1495, and that of Guarionex, in 1498) was headed by a native tribal head, or *cacique*, who had been able to retain his leadership (in Caonabo's case, as head of a chiefdom west and south of the island's central mountains; in Guarionex's case, local leadership in Magua, near the gold fields north of the mountains) by at first agreeing to cooperate with the main lines of Spanish colonial policy, including the *encomienda*. Especially after the appointment of Governor Nicolás de Ovando in 1502, however, the situation became worse, and Spanish excesses were bound to cause an escalation of violence.

A final royal note to Ovando, dated in September, 1501, authorized Spaniards to take natives into labor service "in order to get gold and do . . . other labors that we order to have done," probably presuming that reasonable wages would be paid for work carried out. In fact, this was the beginning of forced labor that reduced many natives to the status of slaves.

The excessive actions of Ovando against any sign of the *caciques'* discontent with Spanish control set a pattern of violent conflict that took a high toll, especially among the native leadership. Much of the discontent after 1502 came from the sudden dramatic increase in the numbers of Spaniards on Hispaniola. Ovando had arrived with a contingent of about twenty-five hundred persons, including not only soldiers, missionaries (among them the later famous author of the *History of the Indies*, Father Bartolomé de Las Casas), and administrators, but also private settlers, more than tripling the Spanish population of the previous decade. This increased settler population was certain to demand more native forced labor under the *encomienda* system.

The village chiefdom of Higüey, on the eastern tip of Hispaniola, was the first site of what became major clashes between Spanish troops and what seemed to be rebelling elements of the local population. Governor Ovando's decision in 1502 to kill seven hundred Higüey Indians who had reacted violently to the killing of one of their chiefs by a Spanish dog was followed a year later by a wholesale massacre, in the western province of Xaragua (the former territory of Caonabo, the 1495 rebel leader), of some eighty district chiefs. In the 1503 massacre, Caonabo's widow, Anacaona, assembled the chiefs to meet Ovando's party. While the Spanish murdered the subchieftains brutally in a mass slaughter, Ovando's "respect" for Anacaona compelled him to end her life by hanging. The future conquistador of Cuba, Diego Velázquez, at that time Ovando's deputy commander, followed up the massacre by systematic conquest of the entire western half of Hispaniola.

From 1503 forward, it became obvious that no previously offered Spanish promises to recognize the local ruling authority of *caciques* in any part of Hispaniola would hold. In 1504, some local chieftains, such as Agüeybana in the Higüey region, began trying to organize serious resistance forces before the Spanish dared to carry out added systematic removals or massacres of the remaining *caciques*. Despite the fact that Agüeybana's revolt was joined by diverse tribal elements, including groups the Spanish called Caribs, from the Lesser Antilles (more likely Eastern Tainos, not the traditional island Carib enemies of Hispaniola's shores), it was brutally repressed. Agüeybana's execution impelled any remaining potential leaders to leave Hispaniola, or at least to take refuge in the more remote eastern Taino region.

Five years after the bloody events in the western region of Xaragua, and shortly after the failure of Agüeybana's abortive efforts in the east, Chief Guarocuya, Anacaona's nephew, tried in 1509 to go into hiding in the island's mountain region of Baonuco. When local troops condemned this act as rebellion, the commanding authorities hunted him down and killed him. More out of fear than in active resistance, the neighboring provinces of Guahaba and Hanyguayaba rebelled, and immediately suffered violent repression by the hand of Diego Velázquez.

With such harsh actions, the short and uneasy period of cooperation between the Spanish and the native West Indians was over. As the native population died off under the overwhelming odds of disease, the process of importing African slave laborers began. They became the ancestors of most of today's West Indian population—the inevitable consequence of this breakdown of the *encomienda* system.

—*Byron D. Cannon*

ADDITIONAL READING:

Hulme, Peter. *Colonial Encounters: Europe and the Native Caribbean, 1492-1797*. New York: Methuen, 1986. Covers a longer time period than other listings here. Focuses on literary and anthropological approaches to understanding the psychological distances separating the colonial and colonized populations of the Caribbean.

Keegan, William F., ed. *Earliest Hispanic/Native American Interactions in the Caribbean*. New York: Garland, 1991. A series of specialized studies of both Spanish and native Indian institutions, including methods of agriculture and local administration, before and during the Ovando governorate.

Las Casas, Bartolomé de. *History of the Indies*. Edited and translated by Andrée Collard. New York: Harper & Row, 1971. A partial translation of the massive work (three volumes in the Spanish edition) of the Spanish missionary who, after coming to Hispaniola with Governor Ovando, turned critical of Ovando's repressive policies.

Rouse, Irving. *The Tainos: Rise and Decline of the People Who Greeted Columbus*. New Haven, Conn.: Yale University Press, 1992. Contains the most extensive coverage of the distant past of the native West Indian population, with a concluding chapter on their short history of contacts with Europeans before dying out.

Tyler, S. Lyman. *Two Worlds: The Indian Encounter with the European, 1492-1509*. Salt Lake City: University of Utah Press, 1988. Provides the most concise history of the circumstances of West Indian revolts and repression in this period.

SEE ALSO: 1492, Columbus' Voyages.

1497 ■ CABOT'S VOYAGES: *England begins to sponsor exploration and land claims in North America*

DATE: June 24, 1497-May, 1498
LOCALE: Newfoundland coast
CATEGORIES: Canadian history; Exploration and discovery
KEY FIGURES:

John Cabot (Giovanni Cabata, c. 1450-c. 1498), Italian explorer in the service in England
Sebastian Cabot (1476?-1557), one of Cabot's three sons, who carried out his own maritime exploration for England in 1508
John Day (1522-1584), English merchant who wrote a valuable surviving letter describing the voyages
Henry VII (1457-1509), king of England, who granted letters patent used first by John Cabot and then by Sebastian

SUMMARY OF EVENT. The late fifteenth century was an age of intense, increasingly national rivalry in Europe. When it be-

came known that Christopher Columbus, by sailing west, had landed on a hitherto unknown coast, all the nations fronting the Atlantic became interested in exploring the New World and laying claim to some of the lands that Spain and Portugal planned to reserve for themselves. England, at peace after the Wars of the Roses, with a strong government headed by the canny monarch Henry VII, had no intention of being left out. Like other monarchs of the era, Henry was willing to use the services of good seamen whenever they were available. He turned to an Italian, John Cabot, to begin his outreach for a piece of the New World.

Very little is known about John Cabot. No portrait, no personal description of him, no letter, not even a signature has been found. The assiduous researches of several scholars have, however, turned up a few facts. It is reasonable to conclude that Cabot was born in Genoa, nursery of seamen, possibly in 1450, a year before Columbus. In 1484, he was married and living in Venice, where he had resided the fifteen years required to gain Venetian citizenship. Between 1490 and 1493, a John Cabot, possibly the navigator, resided in Valencia, Spain. In 1495, Cabot was in England trying to interest Henry VII in trans-Atlantic explorations.

It is significant that Cabot, with his wife and three sons, was then living in Bristol. Bristol, with its good harbor on the Avon River, was the second largest port in England. It faced the Atlantic Ocean, carried on a large trade in spices, and was the headquarters of a large fishing fleet. It is little wonder that many of its inhabitants were deeply interested in western exploration.

Cabot was successful in his attempt to engage the king's interest. On March 5, 1496, Henry granted him letters patent to sail east, west, and north with five ships. Royal support was not just the product of enthusiasm for new discoveries. Henry no doubt hoped that Cabot could succeed in the famous venture originally undertaken in 1492 by his Genoese compatriot Columbus: gaining access to the valuable eastern silk and spice trade of Asia by sailing westward across the Atlantic. In fact, contemporaneous documents show that Columbus had earlier tried, unsuccessfully, to obtain the English crown's support for the trip he eventually carried out under the banner of Spain's Ferdinand and Isabella. Henry's 1496 letters patent only recognized Cabot's right to undertake oceanic explorations in the Crown's name; actual financial support had to come from elsewhere. Funds for this first trip, like those obtained for Cabot's second fateful voyage in 1498, came from wealthy Bristol merchants eager to profit from English entry, on their own terms, into what was still an Italian-dominated Eastern spice and silk trade. As the king's lieutenant, Cabot was to govern all lands he might find, but the king was to have one-fifth of all profits. Cabot was not to venture south, for Henry wanted no trouble with Spain or Portugal.

On or about May 20, 1497, Cabot set sail from Bristol. Instead of five ships, he had only one, the *Mathew*, a vessel of fifty tons' burden, with a crew of eighteen men. It was the equivalent of a fair-sized modern yacht. Going around the

MAJOR VOYAGES TO THE NEW WORLD AFTER COLUMBUS

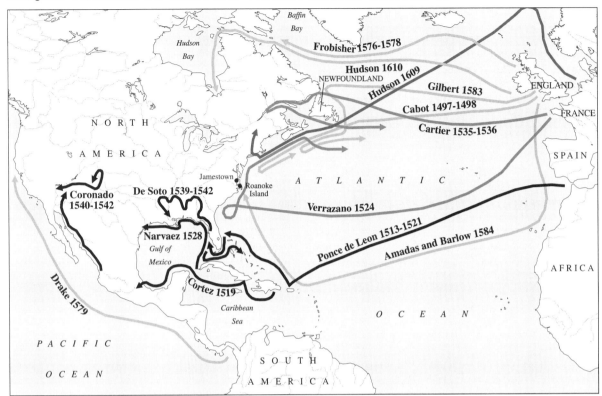

During the 1500's, the Spanish, English, and French made many voyages to the Western Hemisphere, especially North America, in search of natural resources and a Northwest Passage to the rich Asian trade.

south end of Ireland, he last sighted land at Dursey Head. His plan, a favorite with westbound mariners in that age, was to follow a parallel of latitude straight west. Dursey Head is in latitude 51°33'.

At 5:00 A.M. on June 24, Cabot came in sight of land again. He had made the Atlantic crossing in thirty-one days. The exact spot where he first saw the coast of North America has been much disputed, and the dispute has been made foggy by local patriotism, various places claiming to be the site. The famous historian Samuel Eliot Morison, whose account is one of the best, concluded that what Cabot saw was Cape Dégrat on the northeast tip of Newfoundland (latitude 51°37', only 4' off the Dursey Head latitude). If that is true, he had performed a real feat of navigation, having come almost straight west from the Irish coast. Furthermore, he was only five miles from where it is believed Leif Eirikson had landed nearly five hundred years before. Turning south, Cabot entered Griquet Harbor, where he made his only landing. There he formally took possession of the country in the name of Henry VII. Following this formality, Cabot is said to have performed a symbolic act, planting the flag of Saint Mark, the patron saint of Venice, his earlier adopted city-state and nationality, on North American shores. At the time of this first landing, Cabot's party found evidence of human inhabitants but no real contact—certainly

nothing comparable to Columbus' active interchange with the West Indian Tainos—took place. Although a few artifacts were found near abandoned campsites, Cabot decided, probably for security reasons, not to seek out their owners.

Continuing his southward course, Cabot skirted the whole east side of the island and rounded its southern tip into Placentia Bay. From Placentia he turned about, retraced his course to Cape Dégrat, and on July 20, left for home. After a fast passage of fifteen days, he made landfall at Ushant on the coast of Brittany, headed north, and on August 6 was in Bristol. Cabot had not found the way to Japan or China, and he had brought back neither gold nor spices, but he had found a coast teeming with codfish—a most important fact.

Cabot hurried to London to make his report to Henry. The king gave him ten pounds and on the thirteenth of the following December settled on the explorer a pension of twenty pounds per year. That, for Henry VII, was liberality.

On February 3, 1498, Henry issued new letters patent giving Cabot authority to impress six ships for a second voyage to the New World. Cabot was now to explore more thoroughly the coast he had touched, and when he had reached the source of the spice trade, to set up a trading factory with the intent of funneling that desired commodity to English ports. Cabot succeeded in obtaining five ships, with which he sailed from

Bristol at the beginning of May, 1498. In contrast to the *Mathew*, these ships were well stocked, not only with provisions to allow the crews to survive longer on their own if necessary, but also with goods to offer in trade for the Asian products they hoped to find. Bad weather caused damage to one ship soon after Cabot set sail. The damaged ship returned to port on the Irish coast while the others sailed on. After this event, Cabot and the other four ships disappear from the pages of history.

The Cabot story does not end with John's disappearance. Much more is known about his son Sebastian. At fifteen years of age, Sebastian may have accompanied his father on the first voyage. He said that he did, but his statement is not particularly good evidence. He also claimed to have made, in 1508, a voyage to discover the fabled Northwest Passage, but as he was a "genial and cheerful liar," this may not be true. He certainly knew how to promote himself. He set himself up as an expert adviser to would-be explorers and was paid by the kings of both England and Spain for his advice. He died in England about 1557. Eventually, John's name was practically forgotten, and historians took Sebastian to be the discoverer of North America.

The one voyage of John Cabot, for all the gaps in the story, may seem a small thing in the history of American exploration. However, it had great results, for on Cabot's voyage was laid the British claim to North America. After a long interval, English holdings in North America became one of the foundation stones of the British Empire.

—*Don R. Gerlach, updated by Byron D. Cannon*

ADDITIONAL READING:

Beazley, Charles R. *John and Sebastian Cabot: The Discovery of North America*. London: T. F. Unwin, 1898. A competent, documented study by an Oxford specialist in historical geography; easier reading than Williamson (below). Concludes, unlike other modern scholars, that John Cabot returned from his second voyage.

Biddle, Richard. *A Memoir of Sebastian Cabot, with a Review of the History of Maritime Discovery*. Philadelphia: Carey and Lea, 1831. Reprint. Freeport, N.Y.: Books for Libraries Press, 1970. Originally published anonymously, this book was the first attempt to apply serious scholarship to the Cabot story.

Harrisse, Henry. *John Cabot: The Discoverer of North America and Sebastian, His Son, a Chapter of the Maritime History of England Under the Tudors, 1496-1557*. London: B. F. Stevens, 1896. Written by the then foremost French expert in the history of American discovery. Attacks the fictions and inflated reputation of Sebastian Cabot.

Lawrence, A. W., and Jean Young, eds. *Narratives of the Discovery of America*. New York: Jonathan Cape and Harrison Smith, 1931. This valuable collection of original documents includes two letters by Italian observers of Cabot's organization for the 1497 voyage to America. One is an official account by the Milanese minister to England, reporting to the duke of Milan.

Quinn, David S. *Sebastian Cabot and the Bristol Exploration*. Bristol: Historical Association (Bristol Branch), 1968. Documents Sebastian Cabot's career, first under his father's guidance, then Sebastian's attempts to pursue English aims cut short by John Cabot's disappearance, and finally, his switching allegiance to the king of Spain.

Williamson, James A. *The Cabot Voyages and Bristol Discovery Under Henry VII, with the Cartography of the Voyages by R. A. Skelton*. Cambridge: Cambridge University Press, 1962. Generally recognized as the best book to date on the Cabots. Thorough research has produced some admittedly tentative conclusions that counter widely accepted views of Cabot's voyages, including the possibility that, as early as 1494, two other Bristol captains had discovered a "New Found Land" in North America.

SEE ALSO: A.D. 986, Norse Expeditions; 1492, Columbus' Voyages.

1500 ■ IROQUOIS CONFEDERACY: *the Haudenosaunee, or People of the Longhouse, controlled northeastern North America for three centuries*

DATE: c. 1500-1777
LOCALE: Hudson River west to Lake Michigan and St. Lawrence River south to the Cumberland Gap and the Ohio River
CATEGORY: Native American history
KEY FIGURES:
Atotarho, Onondaga chief
Deganawida, also known as *Peacemaker* (c. 1550-c. 1600), Huron or Mohawk prophet or holy man
Handsome Lake, also known as *Ganeodiyo* (c. 1735-1815), early eighteenth century prophet
Hiawatha (c. 1525-c. 1575), Mohawk chief

SUMMARY OF EVENT. The Iroquois are the prime example of the level of cultural evolution that American Indian tribes attained when they stayed in one place for a long time. Archaeologic evidence places the predecessors of the Iroquois in New York State for a thousand to fifteen hundred years prior to the emergence of the Iroquois Confederacy. A subsistence culture called Owasco preceded the Iroquois, which in turn was preceded by the Hopewell culture. Both cultures left traceable influences in Iroquois culture. By 1400, contemporary-style Iroquoian villages existed; by 1600, all the units of the confederacy were calling the larger group Haudenosaunee, the People of the Longhouse.

The Haudenosaunee lived in fortified, stockade villages, were agrarian and matrilineal (that is, passed property from mother to daughters), and banded together through a strong political and religious system, in which ultimate power was vested in the hands of the oldest "sensible" woman of each clan. The foundation of the culture was called the fireplace, or hearth. Each hearth—a mother and her children—was part of a larger extended family, or *owachira*. Two or more owachiras made a clan; eight clans made a tribe.

The purposes of the Iroquois Confederacy, League of the Iroquois, or League of Five Nations, which was established as early as 1500, were to unite and pacify the infighting Iroquois and to gain strength in numbers in order to resist the implacable opposition of Huron-and Algonquian-speaking neighbors. (The word *iroquois*, as spelled by the French, is probably from the Algonquian enemy name *iriokiu* or "spitting snake.") The confederacy, if later dates of its inception are accepted, may have formed as a response to the fur trade. Before the consolidation of the confederacy, warfare—primarily revenge feuds—was a constant among the Iroquois, who had no mechanism to bring the strife to an end. The consolidation of the confederacy was primarily a result of the efforts of the Mohawk chief Hiawatha and the Onondaga chief Atotarho, historical figures who based the religious and political principles of the confederacy on the teachings of Deganawida (the Peacemaker), whose historical authenticity is contested. The political rules and regulations, the cultural model, and the spiritual teachings and religious model all attributed to Deganawida were later qualified and codified by Handsome Lake, a Seneca visionary prophet responding to the pressures of Christianity after the Revolutionary War.

The League of the Iroquois included the Mohawk, Oneida, Onondaga, Cayuga, Seneca (the Five Nations), and, after 1722, the Tuscarora (the Six Nations). The league was based on a carefully crafted constitution. The "faithkeeper," or central religious leader, called a yearly council to recite the constitution and its laws and resolve differences. The council retained the roles of the leaders, which were defined from ancient times by clan system relationships. Fifty chiefs made up the council and served for life, but could be removed from office by the clan mothers if they violated moral or ethical codes.

Religious life was organized according to the teaching of the Peacemaker. Three men and three women supervised the keeping of the ceremonies. The cosmology was well defined, and the origin stories are detailed and sophisticated. Curing illnesses was a central part of daily religious life. The Iroquois had a profound sense of the psychology of the soul and understood dreams and divinations to be communications between one's personality and one's soul.

At the time of the arrival of the Europeans, the coastal regions of the Northeast were occupied by Algonquian-speaking peoples and the inland waterways were occupied by Iroquoian-speaking people. The entire area was crisscrossed by the trails of a vast trading network that reached to the sub-Arctic. Storable foods were traded for furs, nuts, obsidian, shells, flints, and other items. Wampum belts of shells and, later, beads described symbolically and mnemonically almost all dealings politically among and within tribes.

The fur trade and European economics changed the lives of the Iroquois drastically. Acquisition, exploitation, and competition became normal for Northeastern tribes. The confederacy created a combined military force of more than a thousand men that, in the mid-seventeenth century, effectively destroyed the Huron, Erie, Petun, and Illinois tribes as players in the fur trade.

The ever-increasing encroachment of the French and the British presented the Iroquois with three options: compromise; adoption of the ways of the Europeans, including their economics and religion; or use of violence to reject the wave of invaders. The Iroquois drew from all three options: They compromised whenever necessary to keep their neutrality and the peace; adopted the religions and much of the trade economy (thus becoming dependent upon metal items), but not the political and societal structures, of the Europeans; and chose to fight violently against the French and the tribal allies of the French.

The nations of the confederacy had a crucial role in U.S. history. After 1609, when a war party of Mohawks met a group of French and Huron soldiers under Samuel de Champlain and lost six Mohawk warriors to the muskets of the French, the Mohawks carried a dogged hatred of the French forward into alliances—first with the Dutch, from whom they obtained their firearms, and then with the British, from whom they obtained all forms of trade items and by whom they were converted to the Anglican version of Christianity. Thus the Hudson and Mohawk River Valleys were opened to the British, and the French were locked out. The subsequent British dominance of the New World was made much easier by Iroquois control of the waterways from the east coast into the interior of the continent.

In 1677, the Five Nations of the Confederacy met in Albany and wrote into history their memorized, mnemonically cued Great Law, best described as a constitution. At the end of the seventeenth century, the Iroquois had mastered the artful politics of their pivotal position. They played the various European traders one against the other, kept their neutrality with level-headed diplomacy, and maintained their control of the riverine system and the Great Lakes with intimidating success. Their hegemony included the territory from Maine to the Mississippi River, and from the Ottawa River in Canada to Kentucky and the Chesapeake Bay region.

In the eighteenth century, the Iroquois had more power than any other native nation in North America. Colonial delegates from all the states of the Americas traveled to Albany to learn about governing from the Iroquois. The longhouse sachems urged the colonists to form assemblies and to meet and discuss common interests. In 1754, the first intercolonial conference was held at Albany, and Iroquois delegates were in attendance.

The Iroquois maintained their power in spite of the assault of European culture and religion during the eighteenth century. Until about the end of the French and Indian War, the Iroquois were united in their resolve to stay neutral and not be drawn into the imperial wars between the French and the English. By the time of the American Revolution, however, the league's ability to stay neutral and to influence its members had less-

NATIVE PEOPLES OF EASTERN NORTH AMERICA C. 1600

Cree

Chippewa

Montagnais

Passamaquoddy

Algonquin

Ottawa

Penobscot

IROQUOIS
CONFEDERACY

Menominee

Mohawk
Oneida
Onondaga
Cayuga
Seneca

Abnaki

Sauk

Massachusett

Fox

Narragansett

Winnebago

Huron

Mohican
Pequot

Wampanoag

Pottawatomi

Kickapoo

Erie

Montauk

Illinois

Miami

Susquehannock

Honiason

Delaware

Monacan

Moneton

Pamunkey

Powhatan

Shawnee

Tutelo

Tuscarora

Pamlico

Yuchi

Cherokee

Chickasaw

Catawba

Santee

CREEK
CONFEDERACY

Choctaw

Alabama

Yamasee

Biloxi

Natchez

Apalachee

Timucua

Seminole

ened. During the Revolutionary War, the Seneca, Cayuga, and Mohawk fought with the British; the Onondaga tried to remain aloof; the Oneida and Tuscarora sided with the Americans.

The American Revolution ended the power of the Iroquois. By 1800, only two thousand survived on tiny reservations in western New York. Another six thousand had fled to Canada. Despite the conflicts and contacts with European cultures, the Iroquois have retained their society and many of their cultural practices, including kinship and ceremonial ties.

—*Glenn Schiffman*

ADDITIONAL READING:

Graymont, Barbara. *The Iroquois*. New York: Chelsea House Press, 1988. Graymont is an expert on the Haudenosaunee or Iroquois; this precise, concise text is essential for scholars of the Longhouse culture.

Henry, Thomas R. *Wilderness Messiah: The Story of Hiawatha and the Iroquois*. New York: W. Sloane, 1955. Defines the line between legend and history in the founding of the Iroquois league, and in the stories of Hiawatha, Deganawida, and Atotarho.

Jennings, Francis. *The Founders of America*. New York: W. W. Norton, 1993. An accurate history of special value to high school teachers.

Lyons, Oren, et al. *Exiled in the Land of the Free*. Santa Fe, N.Mex.: Clear Light Publishers, 1992. Lyons, faithkeeper of the Six Nations Confederacy, is distinctive in his understanding of the role of the American Indian in U.S. history.

Taylor, Colin F., ed. *The Native Americans: The Indigenous People of North America*. New York: Smithmark, 1991. Companion book to a 1990's televised series on Native Americans.

SEE ALSO: 700 B.C., Ohio Mound Builders; 1754, French and Indian War; 1776, Indian Delegation Meets with Congress.

1513 ■ PONCE DE LEÓN'S VOYAGES: *the Calusa people resisted Spanish attempts to explore the Gulf coast of Florida*

DATE: March 3, 1513-February, 1521
LOCALE: Florida's Gulf coast
CATEGORIES: Exploration and discovery; Native American history
KEY FIGURES:
Escambaba, or *Escambaha*, also known as *Chief Carlos* (died 1567), *cacique* of the Calusa until executed by the Spanish
Pedro Menéndez de Avilés (1519-1574), founder of St. Augustine, *adelanto*, and governor of Florida, 1565-1574
Juan Ponce de León (1460-1521), explorer and first *adelanto* and governor of Florida

SUMMARY OF EVENT. In 1492, when Christopher Columbus claimed the New World for Spain, the inhabitants of Florida numbered at least 100,000, perhaps as many as 925,000, and belonged to six major tribal groups with numerous subgroups. The major tribal groups were the Apalachee in the panhandle of Florida, the Tocobago near Tampa Bay, the Timucuan on the Atlantic coast, the Ais and the Jeaga in the coastal and Indian River region from Cape Canaveral to the St. Lucie River, the Tequesta from the area of Pompano Beach to Cape Sable, and the Calusa south of Tampa Bay to Cape Sable and inland to the area south of what is now Lake Okeechobee. By 1800, all of these tribes were virtually extinct, having fallen prey to European diseases, conquest, and incursions from the northern Creeks.

Although sometime around A.D. 1001 the Norse had made contact with indigenous peoples in what is today southeastern Canada, the Calusas were the first tribe officially to encounter the Europeans on the mainland of North America. However, it is probable that other Europeans had made landfall in Florida before Juan Ponce de León arrived at the peninsula in 1513. Scholars have asserted that it is nearly certain that Spanish slave hunters came to Florida from Cuba or Mexico prior to Ponce de León's voyages, thus accounting for his hostile reception and reports that he met at least one native who spoke some Spanish.

In 1493, Ponce de León had accompanied Columbus on his second voyage to Hispaniola, sent to plant a permanent settlement in the Caribbean. He found a place in the colonial establishment by commanding a force that put down a native insurrection. After conquering the native population of Borinquen (later Puerto Rico), he was named governor in 1508. Although he built a town, established Spanish authority, and enslaved rebellious natives there, he had to cede the governorship of that island to the prior claim of Diego Columbus, Christopher's son.

King Ferdinand granted Ponce de León a patent on February 2, 1512, to discover and govern the island of Bimini, about which the natives had told many tales, including that of the legendary fountain of youth. However, scholars generally agree that the explorer was more interested in claiming land and mineral wealth than in the elusive fountain as he set sail from Puerto Rico on March 3, 1513. On March 27, the expedition sighted land, and on April 2, 1513, the ships reached the Florida coast somewhere between St. Augustine and the St. Johns River. Ponce de León went ashore, claimed possession of all the contiguous land (in effect, all of North America) in the name of the Spanish crown, and called the land Florida after *Pascua florida*, the Easter feast of flowers. He continued his voyage northward to the mouth of the St. Johns River and then turned southward; he rounded the Florida Keys (which he named *Los Martires*, "the Martyrs") and the Dry Tortugas; he then sailed north up the Gulf coast at least to Charlotte Harbor, perhaps to Pensacola Bay. On returning to Puerto Rico in September, 1513, he had discovered the peninsula of Florida, found the Bahama Channel that would serve as a seaway for the Spanish fleet to travel from the Caribbean to the Atlantic, and made the first official contact with the inhabitants of the North American continent.

When Ponce de León sailed into Charlotte Harbor on June 4, 1513, he entered waters controlled by the Calusa, a highly organized tribe of skilled fishermen and warriors headed by a strong, centralized chiefdom. On the pretense of trading with the Spaniards, the Calusa attacked the Spanish ships with twenty canoes filled with warriors. The Spaniards managed to thwart this attack and sent a messenger with two battle prisoners to the Calusa chief to make peace. The *cacique* promised to come to Ponce de León's ship on the following day; he did—with eighty war canoes whose warriors fought the Spanish from morning until night. The Spaniards retreated and continued on their voyage.

On his return to Puerto Rico, the king made Ponce de León governor of all he had discovered, commissioning him to colonize the land and to convert the natives. However, he was unable to return to Florida until 1521, because he was first sent on a mission to subdue rebellious Caribs in the Lower Antilles. With two ships, two hundred colonists, fifty horses, livestock, and tools, Ponce de León set off from Puerto Rico to plant a

Setting sail from Puerto Rico in the spring of 1513, Juan Ponce de León landed on the west coast of Florida and laid claim to all contiguous land (North America) for the Spanish crown. Upon his return to Puerto Rico in September, he had discovered the peninsula of Florida, found the Bahama Channel that would serve as a seaway for the Spanish fleet to travel from the Caribbean to the Atlantic, and made the first official contact with the inhabitants of the North American continent. (Library of Congress)

colony on the Gulf coast of Florida, in February, 1521. The party landed on the coast of Charlotte Harbor and began to build shelter. Once again, the Spaniards had to retreat in the face of a fierce attack from the Calusas; several Spanish were killed in the battle, and Ponce de León received an arrow wound in his leg. The expedition sailed back to Cuba, where Ponce de León died. His body lies buried in Puerto Rico.

Numerous ill-fated attempts, including the expeditions of Pánfilo de Narváez in 1528, Hernando de Soto in 1539, and Tristán de Luna y Arellano in 1559, all proved unable to plant a permanent settlement in Florida. It was not until French Huguenots challenged the Spanish dominion of Florida by founding Fort Caroline on the East Coast that the Spanish finally managed to create a settlement that would set their imprint permanently on Florida soil.

Countering the French challenge, King Philip II appointed Pedro Menéndez de Avilés to drive out the French and to colonize and hold the coast. Subsequent to conquering the French at Fort Caroline and establishing a settlement at St. Augustine in 1565, Menéndez turned his attention to securing the Florida coastlines from pirates and establishing further settlements on the peninsula. When it came to his attention that the Calusa held Spanish captives from shipwrecked vessels and occasionally sacrificed them in religious rituals, he was determined to gain control over the natives.

He personally met with Chief Carlos twice in 1566 and 1567, and established a fort and mission at Calos, the principal village of the Calusas on what is now Key Marcos. Carlos nodded to Menéndez's superior power by an attempt to cement his alliance with the Spanish governor by giving him his sister, later baptized as Antonia, as a wife. Carlos' disappointment in the refusal of the Spanish to help him to defeat his Tocobago enemy and the Calusas' disinterest in Christianity quickly led to renewed strife and tension in their relations with the Spanish. In his frustration with the Calusa, Menéndez sanctioned the execution of Carlos and later his successor, Felipe. After Felipe's death, the Calusa burnt the village, and the Spanish left in defeat. This and later missions to the Calusa in the seventeenth century resulted in a number of documents about Calusa culture that have been significantly augmented only by archaeological research undertaken since the 1890's.

—*Jane Anderson Jones*

ADDITIONAL READING:

Devereux, Anthony Q. *Juan Ponce de León, King Ferdinand, and the Fountain of Youth.* Spartanburg, S.C.: Waccamaw Press, 1993. A biography of the Spanish explorer.

Dobyns, Henry F. "The Invasion of Florida: Disease and the Indians of Florida." In *Spanish Pathways in Florida*, edited by Ann L. Henderson and Gary R. Mormino. Sarasota, Fla.: Pineapple Press, 1991. Traces the devastation wrought by European diseases on the indigenous populations of Florida, who were virtually extinct by the first decades of the eighteenth century.

Hann, John H., ed. and trans. *Missions to the Calusa.* Introduction by William H. Marquardt. Gainesville: University of

Florida Press and Florida Museum of Natural History, 1991. Historical documents from the sixteenth through the eighteenth centuries, concerning political relations with and missions to the Calusa.

Jackson, W. R. *Early Florida Through Spanish Eyes*. Coral Gables, Fla.: University of Miami Press, 1954. An interpretive analysis of the Spanish reaction to the "discovery" of Florida and encounters with the native inhabitants.

Jones, Jane Anderson, and Maurice O'Sullivan, eds. *Florida in Poetry: A History of the Imagination*. Sarasota, Fla.: Pineapple Press, 1995. Contains bilingual excerpts of poems written by Spanish poets extolling the conquistadores and chronicling their encounters with Florida's inhabitants.

Tebeau, Charlton W. *A History of Florida*. 1970. Rev. ed. Coral Gables, Fla.: University of Miami Press, 1980. The first four chapters of this classic Florida history cover the indigenous inhabitants of Florida and their initial encounters with the Europeans.

Widmer, Randolph J. *The Evolution of the Calusa: A Nonagricultural Chiefdom of the Southwest Florida Coast*. Tuscaloosa: University of Alabama Press, 1988. An archaeological study of the development of the Calusa, positing that this highly developed hierarchical chiefdom evolved as a result of demographic elements.

SEE ALSO: 1528, Narváez's and Cabeza de Vaca's Expeditions; 1539, De Soto's Expeditions; 1565, St. Augustine Is Founded.

1519 ■ CORTÉS ENTERS TENOCHTITLÁN:

Spanish horses and guns put an end to Mesoamerica's greatest civilization and mark a new era of European domination of the Western Hemisphere

DATE: November 8, 1519
LOCALE: Central Mexico
CATEGORIES: Exploration and discovery; Latino American history; Native American history
KEY FIGURES:
Hernán Cortés (1485-1547), Spanish conqueror of Mexico
Montezuma II, also known as *Moctezuma Xocoytzin* (1467-1520), ruler when the Spaniards arrived
Diego Velázquez (c. 1465-1524), conqueror and governor of Cuba

SUMMARY OF EVENT. By 1515, Cuba had become the center of Spanish power in the Americas. The Spaniards, led by governor Diego Velázquez, continued to seek additional sources of wealth. The most tantalizing was the reputed gold and splendor of Mexico. Velázquez was served ably by several aides, one of whom was Hernán Cortés.

Cortés was born in 1485 in the arid, poor Spanish province of Extramadura, from which many of the conquistadores originated. He was born to an old, distinguished family with little wealth. In 1504, at nineteen years of age, he set sail for the Spanish Indies (Caribbean); in 1511, he accompanied Diego Velázquez in conquering Cuba. He gained influential positions and eventually became the *alcalde* (mayor) of Santiago.

Between 1517 and 1518, Velázquez, now governor of Cuba, sent two expeditions to Mexico in search of Indians to replace the native Cuban workforce, decimated by maltreatment and disease. Both parties sent back stories of distant cities and tales of a wealthy kingdom in the interior ruled by the king of the Aztec Empire, Montezuma II. These tales created excitement across the island, and Velázquez chose Hernán Cortés, because of his cunning and resourcefulness, to command an additional expedition to Mexico. When Velázquez heard about the zeal and increasing self-importance of his commander, he wondered if he could control this headstrong and unruly individual and sent an emissary to recall him. Anticipating this, Cortés hurriedly put together a large force consisting of eleven ships, 550 mercenaries and sailors, sixteen horses, and assorted cannons. He was able to convince his men to side with him over Velázquez and began his expedition on February 10, 1519.

Cortés first probed along the coast of the Yucatán peninsula of Mexico, where he acquired an interpreter, Jerónimo de Aguilar. Aguilar was luckily fluent in both Mayan (a major native language) and Spanish. Later, a violent skirmish with coastal Indians confirmed that people would not be easy to subdue. The Indians became convinced that the Spaniards were unbeatable, however, after losing two hundred men. Cortés accepted a gift of twenty young women as a peace settlement and proceeded north to San Juan de Ulúa.

Upon reaching this settlement, the Spaniards met a group of Indians who spoke a language unfamiliar to Aguilar. Again, Cortés was lucky to find a woman in his group, Doña Marina, who knew the language. Marina was a member of the Aztec nobility who had been sold to the Maya by her mother. Marina's knowledge of Nahuatl (the Aztec language) and Maya, and Aguilar's command of Maya and Spanish, made it possible for Cortés to communicate with these people. Marina became Cortés' interpreter, cunning adviser, mistress, and later, the mother of his son.

Cortés established a Spanish municipality, La Villa Rica de Vera Cruz (literally, "the rich town of the true cross," now Veracruz) and began moving into the interior. Soon, rich gifts of gold and jewels and encouragement to leave Mexico arrived from the Aztec capital, Tenochtitlán (modern Mexico City). The magnificent gifts only strengthened the Spaniards' resolve to move inland. Cortés also was aware of the legend of the Aztec wind god, Quezalcoatl, who was both fair-skinned and bearded like Cortés. Myths held that Quetzalcoatl's forced exile across the eastern sea would end upon his return in the year One Reed of the Aztec calendar (A.D. 1519). This prophecy was making Montezuma indecisive.

The Spaniards under Cortés' leadership were mercenaries, thus prone to mutiny in times of duress. Anticipating some of the dangers that lay ahead of them in that new land, some of the mercenaries tried to send a ship to inform Governor Velázquez of Cortés' intentions. Cortés responded by hanging two mutineers, having the feet of one cut off, and ordering two hundred lashes for the others. He then claimed his ships were unseaworthy and had them stripped and burned, leaving one intact. He encouraged anyone wanting to return to Cuba to identify themselves so they could board the ship. Once they were identified, Cortés had the ship burned.

Despite his ruthlessness, Cortés possessed many skills evident throughout his approach to Tenochtitlán and his conquest of Mexico. During his ventures, he had to cajole and threaten his tough troops. He led his men from the front ranks, experiencing hunger, fever, dysentery, and other hardships as they approached the Aztec capital. He also showed great skill in dealing with the different Indian chieftains on his marches. Some he flattered; others he defeated. He quit destroying local idols and convinced the natives that he was a great liberator seeking to end the hated rule of the Aztecs. He used the local myths to convince many that he was the god Quetzalcoatl.

As Cortés and his men moved inland, they encountered a fearsome group of Indians, the Tlaxcalans, who had thwarted repeated Aztec advances in their territory and were the Aztecs' chief rivals. Their initial response to Cortés was to attack him because of his repeated friendly communications with Montezuma, but after a terrible battle and subsequent Spanish victory, the Tlaxcalans became the Spaniards' chief allies against the Aztecs.

While Cortés was negotiating with the Tlaxcalans, envoys from Montezuma arrived, offering a yearly tribute to the king of Spain if the penetration of the interior were halted. Assuming the Spaniards to be gods, the envoys sacrificed captives so the Spaniards could drink their blood, an act that revolted the Spaniards. This further reinforced the belief that Cortés was Quetzalcoatl, because that god disliked human sacrifice.

Finally, the Spaniards arrived at the great basin where Tenochtitlán lay. They were amazed by the size and splendor of the capital city. On November 8, 1519, they were escorted into Tenochtitlán, where Montezuma waited. After initial greetings, the Spaniards were escorted to a grand palace, where they were housed.

Realizing his delicate strategic position in the heart of the Aztec capital, Cortés soon devised a plan, captured Montezuma, and used him as a puppet ruler. During the next several months, Montezuma revealed how the government operated, disclosed the location of royal treasure, gave Cortés tours, and introduced him to the Aztec idols. Among these was the dreaded temple where the Aztecs carried out human sacrifices.

The relative calm was broken in May, 1520, when news arrived that a large force from Cuba had landed to arrest Cortés. This came at a time when unrest was beginning to grow among the Aztecs. Cortés was forced to take his best troops to deal with the threat and leave the capital in the hands of Pedro de Alvarado, a ruthless soldier.

After defeating the Cuban force and assimilating its men, Cortés returned to Tenochtitlán, where he found his men surrounded and starving. Alvarado had slaughtered two hundred Aztec nobles during a celebration, mistaking it for an uprising. The Aztecs responded by refusing to provide them with food, deposing Montezuma, and choosing his half brother Cuitlahuac to rule. Cortés chose a night retreat with his men to Tlaxcala, during which he lost most of his treasure and most of his men. This retreat is remembered as *noche triste* (sorrowful night). Cortés spent the remainder of 1520 outfitting a new force. Smallpox ravaged many of the residents in Tenochtitlán and throughout the Aztec Empire, killing tens of thousands, including Cuitlahuac, who was replaced by Cuauhtémoc.

Cortés and his men attacked the capital and soon gained control of the surrounding lake and destroyed the causeways to the capital. Once the city could not acquire any food, the Spaniards proceeded to destroy the city block by block. A decisive battle was fought on August 13, 1521, breaking future Aztec resistance. Cuauhtémoc was captured and tortured for information about the Aztecs. He later died from this treatment, leaving the Spanish in control of Mexico and giving them a future center of power in North America.

—*Vincent Michael Thur*

ADDITIONAL READING:

Bannon, John Francis, ed. *The Spanish Conquistadores: Men or Devils*. Source Problems in World Civilization. New York: Holt, Rinehart and Winston, 1960. Primary sources and historiographic commentary.

Fagg, John Edwin. *Latin America: A General History*. New York: Macmillan, 1963. A thorough overview of Latin American history. Index and annotated bibliography.

Herring, Hubert. *A History of Latin America: From Beginnings to the Present*. 3d ed. New York: Alfred A. Knopf, 1968. One of the definitive Latin American sources. Extensive footnotes, bibliography, and index.

Keen, Benjamin, ed. *Latin American Civilization: History and Society, 1492 to the Present*. 4th rev. ed. Boulder, Colo.: Westview Press, 1986. Primary accounts with clear, concise commentary.

Meyer, Michael C., and William L. Sherman. *The Course of Mexican History*. 3d ed. Oxford, England: Oxford University Press, 1987. Revisionist overview, containing interesting information about Cortés' early life. Bibliography.

SEE ALSO: 1428, Aztec Empire.

1528 ■ NARVÁEZ'S AND CABEZA DE VACA'S EXPEDITIONS: *four survivors of the expeditions are the first Europeans to see the Gulf coast and the Southwest*

DATE: April 12, 1528-April, 1536
LOCALE: Florida, the Gulf coast, the Southwest, and northern Mexico
CATEGORIES: Exploration and discovery; Latino American history; Native American history

KEY FIGURES:

Álvar Núñez Cabeza de Vaca (c. 1490-1556), second-in-command of the Narváez expedition to Florida and one of its four survivors

Andrés Dorantes de Carranza, Spanish conqueror and survivor of the Narváez expedition

Francisco Vásquez de Coronado (1510-1554), governor of New Galicia and leader of a Spanish expedition into New Mexico, Texas, Oklahoma, and Kansas

Estevanico or *Estevén*, Moorish slave and survivor of the Narváez expedition

Alonso del Castillo Maldonado, Spanish conqueror, survivor of the Narváez expedition

Antonio de Mendoza (1490-1552), first viceroy of New Spain, later viceroy of Peru

Pánfilo de Narváez (1490?-1528), commander of the expedition to Florida

SUMMARY OF EVENT. After the conquest of the Aztecs in 1521, Spain had expanded its empire from a few islands to include Mexico, or New Spain (Mexico). Operating from bases in the Caribbean, Juan Ponce de León and other Spanish explorers had also explored and established a short-lived colony in Florida. These expeditions fueled the imagination of other Spaniards, and after the conquest of Mexico, Florida acquired important strategic value. In 1527, the Crown approved another expedition to Florida, to be commanded by Pánfilo de Narváez, a veteran of the conquests of Cuba and Mexico. The treasurer and second-in-command of the expedition was Álvar Núñez Cabeza de Vaca.

Although he had not been to America, Cabeza de Vaca had an impressive military background and pedigree. His mother's surname, which means "head of the cow," was an honorary title her family had received when an ancestor marked a mountain pass with a cow's skull that enabled the Christians to surprise the Muslims in a crucial battle. His paternal grandfather, Pedro de Vera, was the conqueror of the Gran Canary, and Cabeza de Vaca grew up with native Guanche slaves from the Canary Islands and his grandfather's stories of conquest and adventure. Born around 1490, Cabeza de Vaca reached manhood during Spain's imperial expansion and chose a military career. Before his assignment to the Narváez expedition, he had already served the Crown in Italy, Navarre, and Spain.

The commander of the expedition already had an ill-starred career. During the conquest of Cuba, Narváez oversaw the slaughter of thousands of natives. When he was sent to arrest Hernán Cortés, Narváez lost his men to the conqueror of Mexico and lost an eye in the process. The Florida expedition also started off badly when 140 men deserted shortly after arriving in Santo Domingo. On their way to Florida, the fleet was scattered by a hurricane off Cuba, several ships ran aground, and sixty men and twenty horses were lost.

The expedition finally reached Florida on April 12, 1528. After claiming the land in the name of the king of Spain and trading with the natives for food, the expedition moved inland in search of Apalachen, a province purportedly rich in gold.

Despite the objections of Cabeza de Vaca to separating the ships from the land force, Narváez ordered the ships to sail on to a port, leaving three hundred people on shore. It was the last time they would see their ships.

The Spaniards encountered a fierce resistance from native archers whose arrows could penetrate trees and Spanish armor. When they reached Apalachen, it was a disappointing village of forty thatched huts inhabited by women and children, and they were constantly under attack. Suffering from wounds, hunger, and disease, they tried to locate a harbor where they might find the ships. Failing that, they decided to build barges to escape to Pánuco, Mexico, by sailing along the Gulf coast. After consuming their horses, the 242 survivors embarked in five leaky and overcrowded barges. Narváez and his men, separating from the slower barges, disappeared, never to be seen again.

After almost two months at sea, Cabeza de Vaca and his troops crashed on Galveston Island, off what is now Texas. Although they were befriended by local tribes, they had little food. All but sixteen of the ninety Spaniards died from disease and hunger, while their hosts were dying from a disease they blamed on the Spaniards. Gradually, all but four of the Spaniards perished, some resorting to cannibalism before dying or being killed by shocked natives.

The four survivors, Cabeza de Vaca, Captains Andrés Dorantes and Alonso del Castillo Maldonado, and Estevanico (sometimes called Estevén), a Moorish slave, spent the next seven years wandering among the native tribes of the Southwest. Although initially worshiped for their medical powers, they were reduced to slaves and forced to work under harsh masters. After he escaped from his group, Cabeza de Vaca took up trade and became a successful merchant who could travel freely between hostile tribes. Despite his new status, he was naked and barely survived on the roots or plants he could scavenge.

When the four survivors were reunited, they became medicine men, praying over their patients, who experienced miraculous recoveries. Considered to have magical powers, they became famous, and their fame as healers spread. They were followed by hordes of believers and were welcomed and showered with presents in every village they visited. Although they developed an appreciation for their hosts and the native cultures, they never abandoned their Christian faith and viewed their own survival and medical cures as divinely inspired.

When they arrived in Mexico in the spring of 1536, eight years after landing in Florida, their reports of their experiences stimulated interest in further exploration. Seeking to preempt any competitors, the Spanish viceroy of New Spain, Antonio de Mendoza, dispatched Fray Marcos and Estevanico on a reconnaissance mission to northern Mexico. When Estevanico disappeared, apparently killed by resentful natives, Fray Marcos returned with reports of seven fabulous cities, rumored to be the Seven Cities of Cíbola founded by seven legendary bishops who had fled Portugal centuries earlier.

SHIPWRECKS AND WANDERINGS:
THE EXPEDITIONS OF NARVÁEZ AND CABEZA DE VACA, 1528-1536

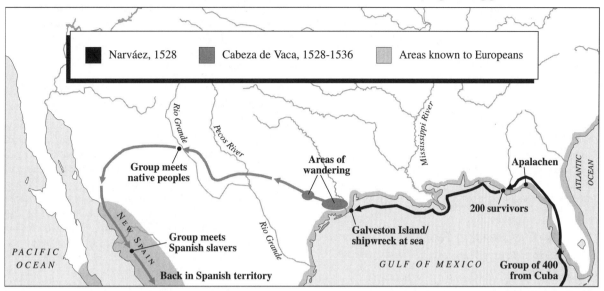

After beginning their journey with approximately four hundred men and several ships, Pánfilo de Narváez and his second-in-command, Álvar Núñez Cabeza de Vaca, split in Florida, where the seagoing expedition sailed on, leaving three hundred to search for the "riches" of Apalachen, which proved to be only a small village of hungry natives. Leaving in five leaky barges, Narváez and about two hundred survivors finally disappeared at sea; Cabeza de Vaca and about ninety survivors crashed off Galveston Island, went ashore, suffered disease and starvation, and became enslaved by Indians. Four survivors finally reached New Spain on the west coast of Mexico in the spring of 1536.

Acting on this news, Mendoza authorized Francisco Vásquez de Coronado to explore northern Mexico. With three hundred soldiers, seven Franciscans, and a thousand native allies, Coronado searched as far as Kansas without locating any fabulous riches, and returned to Mexico a broken man. Nevertheless, his expedition had initiated the Spanish conquest of Texas and New Mexico and the introduction of horses and cattle into these territories.

In 1537, Cabeza de Vaca returned to Spain and presented his official report to Charles I, king of Spain and Holy Roman Emperor. This document, along with a joint report prepared by Cabeza de Vaca, Castillo, and Dorantes, described the disastrous Florida expedition and is an important source of information on the explorers' experiences and the Native American cultures they encountered from Florida to Mexico, many of which were soon extinct. The report is also a dramatic story of survival and is the first European document to describe a hurricane, the buffalo and the opossum, numerous rivers and mountains, and the interaction of Europeans and natives in North America.

Although Cabeza de Vaca considered Florida to have great potential as a colony and believed in other fabulous civilizations in North America, he refused to offer his services as second-in-command of Hernando de Soto's ill-fated expedition to Florida. In 1540, Cabeza de Vaca sailed to South America in command of an expedition to relieve a struggling Spanish settlement in Paraguay and marched a thousand miles overland to Asunción. He was overthrown because of his efforts to protect the natives from enslavement and was sent back to Spain in chains. Although he was deprived of his titles and banished from the Indies, he was pardoned and given a pension by the king just before his death in 1556.

—*D. Anthony White*

ADDITIONAL READING:

Bishop, Morris. *The Odyssey of Cabeza de Vaca.* Westport, Conn.: Greenwood Press, 1991. The best biography of Cabeza de Vaca. Describes the conqueror's early life but has been challenged for the accuracy of Cabeza de Vaca's itinerary.

Cabeza de Vaca, Álvar Núñez. *Adventures in the Unknown Interior of America.* Translated and edited by Cyclone Covey. Albuquerque: University of New Mexico Press, 1990. The most readable and annotated translation of Cabeza de Vaca's official report.

Chipman, Donald. "In Search of Cabeza de Vaca's Route Across Texas: An Historiographical Survey." *Southwestern Historical Quarterly* 91 (October, 1987): 127-148. A survey of the literature on Cabeza de Vaca's route through Texas and New Mexico.

Hallenbeck, Cleve. *Álvar Núñez Cabeza de Vaca: The Journey and Route of the First European to Cross the Continent of North America, 1534-36.* Glendale, Calif.: Arthur H. Clark, 1940. A reconstruction of the itinerary of Cabeza de Vaca through Texas across the Rio Grande into Northern Mexico.

Hedrick, Basil C., and Carroll L. Riley, eds. and trans. *The Journey of the Vaca Party: The Account of the Narváez Expedition, 1928-1536, as Related by Gonzalo Fernández de Oviedo y Valdés.* Carbondale: University Museum, Southern Illinois University, 1964. Translation from the sixteenth century Spanish chronicler's general history of the Indies. Includes the joint report of Cabeza de Vaca, Castillo, and Dorantes, written in Mexico in 1536.

Sauer, Carl O. *Sixteenth Century North America: The Land and the Peoples as Seen by the Europeans.* Berkeley: University of California Press, 1971. An analysis of sixteenth century European descriptions of North America.

See also: 1513, Ponce de León's Voyages; 1519, Cortés Enters Tenochtitlán; 1539, De Soto's Expeditions; 1540, Coronado's Expedition; 1565, St. Augustine Is Founded.

1534 ■ Cartier and Roberval Search for a Northwest Passage: *one of the earliest attempts to find the elusive shortcut to the lucrative Asian trade*

Date: April 20, 1534-July, 1543
Locale: Gulf of St. Lawrence and the St. Lawrence River
Categories: Canadian history; Exploration and discovery
Key figures:
Jacques Cartier (c. 1491-1557), master mariner
Philippe de Chabot, sieur de Brion (1480-1543), French admiral who granted Cartier's commission for a second voyage
Donnacona (died c. 1539), chief of the principal Huron tribe near Quebec
François I (1494-1547), king of France, 1515-1547
Jean-François de La Roque, sieur de Roberval (1501?-1560?), soldier, courtier, and colonizer

Summary of event. From 1492 to about 1534, the exploration of the New World was almost the exclusive domain of Italian sailors. When England and France contested the Spanish and Portuguese monopolies, they employed John Cabot and Giovanni da Verrazano, both Italians. During the 1530's, however, Italian explorers were replaced by other nationals. As soon as Cabot's report of the marvelous shoals of fish he had observed off the coast of Newfoundland reached the mainland of Europe, fishing boats from Brittany, Normandy, and Portugal began to brave the hazardous crossings of the North Atlantic to reap the harvest of these new and teeming waters. From these fisheries sprang the beginnings of New France.

Jacques Cartier was born probably in 1491 in Saint-Malo, one of the most notable of French fishing ports. He went to sea early and became an experienced navigator, being awarded the coveted title of master pilot. He evidently visited the Newfoundland fisheries and voyaged to Brazil. In 1534, when he was forty years of age, Cartier was commissioned by the king of France to head an expedition across the Atlantic in search of a Northwest Passage to Asia. By the time of Cartier's first commissioned trip, he had gained a title that surpassed his earlier recognized but general function as master pilot—François I had named him Captain and Pilot for the king. Cartier's elevated title, as well as his assignment to seek a Northwest Passage, indicate that the French crown was placing itself in a position to take global actions of major significance.

Politically, French exploratory thrusts into the Atlantic invited hostile reactions from the colonizers of the Spanish New World and Portuguese Brazil, who, under the earlier terms of the 1494 Treaty of Tordesillas, claimed exclusive rights to all undiscovered areas of the Western Hemisphere. In the economic sphere, Cartier's Northwest Passage assignment is part of a broader context of international rivalries that were carried over from before 1492. Just as Cabot's first and second voyages to Newfoundland (1497 and 1498) reflected a strong English desire to gain access to the East Indian spice and Chinese silk trades without passing through foreign intermediaries (traditionally the Italian city-states), Cartier's goal was more than the discovery of new lands. François I viewed a possible Northwest Passage as a potential path to East Asian wealth. What Cartier accomplished during three voyages between 1534 and 1543, although extremely important for the future development of French settlements in the Saint Lawrence Valley, fell considerably short of this goal.

Setting out on April 20, 1534, from Saint-Malo with two ships of about sixty tons' burden each, Cartier made his landfall on May 10, at Cape Bonavista on the eastern coast of Newfoundland. After exploring the island, he crossed the Gulf of St. Lawrence to Cape Breton and Prince Edward Island, landing on the Gaspé Peninsula. There, upon the pledge that he would return them, he was given two sons of a Huron chief to take to France. From Gaspé, Cartier sailed north to Anticosti Island. Returning to Newfoundland on August 15, he set sail for home and arrived at Saint-Malo on September 5. Although he had not found the Northwest Passage, Cartier had explored extensively the Gulf of St. Lawrence and its islands, and he was enthusiastic about the new country.

His own manuscript accounts of the three voyages he made to the Saint Lawrence region provide an extensive narrative of the way of life of the Hurons living in the region, as well as detailed description of all manner of flora and fauna. While the latter information tended to be objective, French views of the American Indians show the biases of this early period of contact between what Cartier called the "civilized" and "savage" societies. Cartier's account of dealings with Hurons during his first expedition left at least two particularly revealing signs of future difficulties the French and other European settlers would face. One was his assumption that the natives were so simple that they could be "moulded in the way one would wish" (or, as a sixteenth century English translation "interpreted" Cartier's words, brought "to some familiaritie and civilitie"). A second came on July 24, 1534, when his party raised a wooden cross with an added coat of arms marked with the words "Long Live the King of France!" Huron dismay at the French expectation of immediate respect for the symbols of the French state and religion turned into a protest, led by the chief Donnacona. Donnacona met Cartier again under different terms at the end of Cartier's second voyage, when the French forced him and several other American Indians to accompany them as "specimens" on their return to François I's court.

As a result of Cartier's favorable reports, French leaders began to think of planting outposts of the kingdom in these new lands. By royal command, the admiral of France commissioned Cartier commander in chief of a second expedition of three ships, which was to sail beyond Newfoundland and discover and occupy lands for France. The little flotilla left Saint-Malo on May 19, 1535. This time, the crossing was imperiled by severe storms, but Cartier reached Blanc Sablon, Newfoundland, on July 15; not until July 26, however, did all three ships assemble there. He had with him the two American Indian boys he had taken from Gaspé the previous year. They had learned to speak French, and they told him of the great river that poured into the Gulf of St. Lawrence. Steering west and north of Anticosti Island, Cartier entered the great river, the first white man to travel that highway into the North American interior.

As Cartier progressed up the St. Lawrence River, piloted by his two Huron guides, he was welcomed by natives from the shore. Passing the Island of Orleans, in mid-September, he came to the tribal village of Stadacona, the magnificent site of the future city of Quebec. There he was greeted by Chief Donnacona, who welcomed the return of his two sons but tried to dissuade Cartier from further ascending the river. Donnaconna feared the loss of his French ally to the chief of Hochelaga, but ambition and curiosity drove the Frenchman on. He set out on September 19 with the smallest of his vessels, a pinnace, and on October 2 came to Hochelaga (now Montreal), the metropolis of the American Indians on the St. Lawrence. Here the Hurons feasted Cartier and tempted him with hints of a rich kingdom to the west called Saguenay. From the top of Mont Royal, however, Cartier saw that the rapids beyond blocked further travel inland, and he returned to Stadacona, above which his men had built a fort. There they wintered rather than risk an unseasonable Atlantic passage. Autumnal brilliance gave way to months of ice and deep snow. Scurvy became rampant but was conquered with an Indian bark remedy. Musing upon the fabled riches of Saguenay, Cartier and his men resorted to treachery. In May of 1536, they kidnapped Donnacona and four other Hurons as evidence to persuade King François that further exploration would be profitable. With five other American Indians, who apparently went without force, they set sail for France on May 6. As they came to Newfoundland and passed a group of islands they had named St. Peter's Islands, Cartier's crew realized they were not alone: Boats from France's northwestern seacoast (Brittany) had arrived and begun exploiting the rich North Ameri-

can fishing grounds. The Atlantic crossing was speedy, and on July 15, Cartier was back at Saint-Malo. On this voyage, he had opened the way for penetrating North America and had mapped out the principal sites of the future New France. After this date, concern for French settlements, combined with hopes that riches could be gained from finding and conquering Saguenay, tended to replace François I's original aim of sending explorers to find a Northwest Passage.

The king, impressed by Cartier's Huron captives, his samples of ores that promised diamonds and gold, and the reports of a land of spices and other abundant resources, determined to develop a colony in the New World—a New France. War between France and Spain interfered with his plans until 1538. Then followed three years of elaborate preparations and diplomatic difficulties. In 1540, Cartier received a royal commission to help lead the undertaking with a grant from the treasury. However, in January, 1541, Jean-François de La Roque, sieur de Roberval, was given command of the venture, and Cartier's authority could be exerted only in Roberval's absence.

While plans were being drawn up, France's main rival, Charles V, had been informed by the Cardinal of Toledo (speaking for the Spanish Councils of State and of the Indies) that François I was preparing a new fleet for New World exploration and that actions should be taken to thwart its movements. One action suggested was to organize a spy network, including close observation of the port of Saint-Malo. Eventually, two Spanish ships did try, unsuccessfully, to track the French ships sent on the third Cartier mission.

By the spring of 1541, Cartier had procured and equipped five vessels, and on May 23, he sailed from Saint-Malo on his third voyage. Roberval was to follow later. Settlement was now the main aim, although Christian missionary efforts and the search for Saguenay were also important objectives. After a rough Atlantic crossing, the expedition entered the Gulf of St. Lawrence and then proceeded up the river, arriving at Stadacona on August 23. Welcomed by the Hurons despite his earlier kidnapping exploits, Cartier proceeded to settle his colonists beyond Quebec at Cape Rouge for an easier approach to Saguenay. Two of his vessels were sent home with news and samples of spurious minerals. They reached Saint-Malo on October 3. Leaving the Vicomte de Beaupré in command, Cartier proceeded to Hochelaga and explored the rapids above it. The events of the winter of 1541-1542 are unknown, except for sailors' gossip later of American Indian attacks, scurvy, and misery.

On April 16, 1542, Roberval, with three ships and perhaps two hundred colonists, sailed from La Rochelle for New France. His delay in leaving to join Cartier had been much longer than he had expected. Part of the problem was the difficulties encountered in acquiring adequate armaments for what had become as much a military mission as a voyage for exploration. In fact, spies for Portugal and Spain had reported that Roberval was prepared to enter Atlantic waters as a pirate, and urged the closure of all ports he might try to enter. The ambassador of the English king Henry VIII reported that the French king was uncertain as to Roberval's intentions.

Whatever the circumstances of the splitting of command between Cartier and Roberval, on June 7, 1542, the follow-up expedition entered the harbor of what is now St. John's, Newfoundland. However, the winter in Canada had been too much for Cartier, and he had abandoned the settlement at Cape Rouge in June and struck out for Newfoundland. At St. John's, he found Roberval's reinforcements. In spite of Roberval's order, he slipped out into the Atlantic and returned to Saint-Malo.

The end of Cartier's third voyage marked the effective conclusion of his career as a sea captain and explorer. As for Roberval, he pushed on, ascended the St. Lawrence, and rebuilt Cartier's abandoned settlement. He sent two ships home for reinforcements in September. A difficult winter followed, in which Roberval was forced to resort to drastic disciplinary measures to maintain order. In June, 1543, Roberval began his search for the riches of Saguenay, but stopped when his boat was wrecked.

By mid-September, 1543, Roberval was back in France, so he probably had given up the settlement in New France by late July. His return marked the end of the first attempt of the French to settle Canada. François I died in 1547, and his son, Henry II, was uninterested in American exploration. The outbreak of religious wars in France prevented any further colonizing efforts for half a century. Cartier bought a manor near Saint-Malo where he lived until his death in 1557. He had revolutionized cartographical knowledge by his well-recorded findings, but for the moment neither his nor Roberval's exploits were promising enough to overcome France's European preoccupations.

—*Don R. Gerlach, updated by Byron D. Cannon*

ADDITIONAL READING:

Biggar, H. P. *Collection of Documents Relating to Jacques Cartier and the Sieur de Roberval.* Publications of the Public Archives of Canada 14. Ottawa: Canadian Public Archives, 1930. Combined with the Cartier volume, provides all the information available on the voyage.

Cartier, Jacques. *The Voyages of Jacques Cartier.* Translated, with notes and appendices, by H. P. Biggar. Publications of the Public Archives of Canada 11. Ottawa: F. A. Acland, 1924. A sourcebook that gives the principal documents in French, with an English translation and notes.

_____. *The Voyages of Jacques Cartier.* Introduction by Ramsay Cook. Toronto: University of Toronto Press, 1993. A new edition of Cartier's book that attempts to correct misinformation stemming from the earlier translation by H. P. Biggar.

Ganong, W. F. *Crucial Maps in the Early Cartography and Place-Nomenclature of the Atlantic Coast of Canada.* Toronto: University of Toronto Press, 1964. A standard reference source for tracing Cartier's route of exploration and the earliest names given to sites he discovered.

Hoffman, Bernard G. *Cabot to Cartier: Sources for a Historical Ethnography of Northeastern North America, 1497-1550.* Toronto: University of Toronto Press, 1961. Four chapters focus on Cartier's explorations. One chapter is a step-by-step historical account; the others delve into the problems of analysis faced by historians piecing together manuscripts purported to be authentic versions of Cartier's experiences.

Lehane, Brendan. *The Northwest Passage.* Alexandria, Va.: Time-Life Books, 1981. A readable, well-illustrated general history of the long search for the Northwest Passage, placing the significance of Cartier's attempts in broad perspective.

Morison, Samuel Eliot. *The European Discovery of America.* 2 vols. New York: Oxford University Press, 1971-1974. Summarizes the exploits of Cartier and Roberval in considerable detail. Fine scholarship, detailed bibliographical commentary, and attractive narration.

Pendergast, James F., and Bruce G. Trigger. *Cartier's Hochelaga and the Dawson Site.* Montreal: McGill-Queen's University Press, 1972. Analysis of archaeological data and ethnohistory concerning the size and location of the American Indian town visited by Cartier in 1535.

SEE ALSO: 1497, Cabot's Voyages.

1539 ■ DE SOTO'S EXPEDITIONS: *the first European penetration into the interior of North America, with severe consequences for Native Americans*

DATE: May 28, 1539-September 10, 1543
LOCALE: Southeast
CATEGORIES: Exploration and discovery; Native American history
KEY FIGURES:
Luis de Moscoso de Alvarado, governor of Florida and leader of the expedition from de Soto's death until the survivors reached Mexico
Juan Ortiz, Spanish interpreter for de Soto
Hernando de Soto (c. 1496-1542), Spanish governor who organized the expedition
Tascalusa, Choctaw chief who ambushed de Soto at Mabila
Vitachuco, Timucuan leader who fought de Soto at Napituca

SUMMARY OF EVENT. Hernando de Soto was a veteran of early Spanish campaigns in the New World, having served in Nicaragua, Panama, and Peru. As Francisco Pizarro's lieutenant, de Soto helped to topple the Incas' empire, acquiring a share of their treasure, which made him a wealthy man. He returned to Spain in 1537, where his drive for more riches led to his appointment as governor of Cuba and *adelantado* of Florida. This gave him Spanish permission to conquer coastal territories from the Gulf of Mexico all the way to Canada.

On May 28, 1539, de Soto landed near Tampa Bay with 622 soldiers, more than two hundred horses, and many slaves. They encountered the native town of Ucita, a well-organized compound with the chief's house on an earthen mound at one end and a temple guarded by a gilded-eyed bird at the other. They destroyed these and made camp.

On June 8, a Spanish patrol found Juan Ortiz, a shipwrecked survivor of the ill-fated Pánfilo de Narváez expedition. Ortiz had escaped death at the hands of Chief Hirrihugua of Ucita when the chief's daughter Ulele interceded on his behalf. Many believe that Captain John Smith was inspired to invent his own salvation from Powhatan by Pocahontas (which he did not report until some twenty years after the event) after reading Ortiz's story in the 1600's. Ortiz's abilities as translator proved invaluable to de Soto.

On July 15, the main army left Ucita in pursuit of gold. Living off native maize, they traversed northern Timucuan territories in late summer. They were continually harassed by ambushes, and a major uprising occurred at Napituca under the leadership of Vitachuco. On September 15, the deaths of hundreds of natives made apparent the advantages of Spanish horses, muskets, and war hounds.

Turning west, the entourage arrived at the principal Apalachee town of Anhaica on October 6. Near modern Tallahassee, this horticultural center of 250 houses and more than one thousand people had rich stores of food, and de Soto decided to winter there. It was there that de Soto's party heard rumors of a golden kingdom to the northeast ruled by a *cacica* (female chief) and on March 3, 1540, they crossed over into what is now Georgia to find it. Although delayed by pitched battles, the Spaniards extracted directions to the chiefdom of Cofitachequi from reluctant informants after burning some natives alive. De Soto used both negotiating and cruelty as political tools, resorting to kidnapping, murder, torture, and mutilation as a policy of intimidation.

Reaching Cofitachequi, de Soto received a gift of pearls from the chieftainess, and her temples produced hundreds of pounds more. She directed the party to nearby Talomeco, where her ancestors were interred. The five hundred houses of Talomeco had been abandoned as a result of pestilence, possibly caused by the 1526 slave-raiding foray of Lucas Vásquez de Ayllón along the Carolina coast. Talomeco's sumptuous mound temple was still intact, a one-hundred-by-forty-foot structure housing bodies of the elite, fine clothes, artworks, weapons, and chests of pearls. Many of de Soto's men wanted to stay in the abundance of Cofitachequi, but when demands for gold and silver produced only copper and sheet mica, de Soto left on May 3, 1540, to continue his treasure quest. Although she later escaped, he kidnapped the *cacica* to serve as guide.

During the summer of 1540, de Soto marched through the Carolinas and Tennessee, into the southern Appalachians and the Blue Ridge Mountains. He contacted the Cherokees at Xuala and Guasili, and then proceeded to the Creek frontier at Chiaha in northern Georgia. When the usual demands for treasure, food, bearers, and women were made, the Chiaha chief told de Soto that riches were to be found farther south, so the expedition continued.

The group passed through western Georgia in mid-July, briefly imprisoning the Coosa chief. It then passed through Itaba and Talisi, reaching Choctaw country in Alabama in early October. Here, the great Tascalusa chief by the same name was taken prisoner. Pressed for four hundred bearers and one hundred women, the chief provided bearers and promised that the women would be available at his town of Mabila. On October 18, 1540, Tascalusa led de Soto into an ambush.

Between four and five thousand warriors attacked the Spaniards, of whom twenty were killed and 150 wounded, including de Soto. Most of their goods—including the Cofitachequi pearls—were lost in the ensuing fire, but Mabila was destroyed and native losses may have been more than three thousand. This loss impacted native communities perhaps all the way to Coosa.

De Soto was within reach of his ships in the Gulf of Mexico, but he refused to quit. He turned the battered expedition northwest to invade Chickasaw territory at Apafalaya and Chicaca. They spent a cold winter in 1540-1541 near the Yazoo River in Mississippi. On March 3, 1541, two Chickasaw attacks killed twelve soldiers, sixty horses, and many pigs, and destroyed most of the supplies that had survived at Mabila.

Despite this setback, de Soto continued his spring march to the northwest, reaching the Mississippi River about ten miles south of modern Memphis, Tennessee. Crossing in dugout canoes on May 8, 1541, the expedition reached the chiefdom of Casqui in Arkansas. De Soto allied with the Casqui chief to jointly attack the rival chiefdom of Pacaha. They stripped the storehouses clean and scattered the bones of the Pacaha elite resting in the sacred mound temples.

De Soto then pressed up the Arkansas River to the very edge of the Great Plains, where he heard of great buffalo herds but little corn and, more important, no gold. Circling back to Casqui, de Soto and his group sought a place to spend their winter, settling at Autiamque, near Little Rock, on November 2, 1541. It was there that Juan Ortiz died, depriving de Soto of invaluable assistance, and the *adelantado* began to show signs of illness and despair.

The spring campaign of 1542 yielded more resistance and few successes, and at Guachoya, on the Mississippi River, de Soto became feverish. He gave his men a repentant speech about his shortcomings and died of what was probably a European illness on May 21, 1542. Luis de Moscoso de Alvarado took command and buried de Soto in the swirling waters of the great river Europeans would credit him for discovering.

Moscoso, after trying an unsuccessful overland trek through Texas, returned to the Mississippi River to attempt a watery route home. His small flotilla set out for the Gulf of Mexico on July 2, 1543. Before he reached the gulf, seven hundred miles and two weeks later, constant attacks by the natives claimed many more lives on both sides. The 311 bedraggled survivors made landfall at Panuco on Mexico's Gulf coast on September 10, 1543.

De Soto's precise route is not as important as the impact his expedition had on native cultures. He was the first European to see these vital and sophisticated societies, and—as a result of his legacy—among the last. Murder and casualties in battle took the lives of thousands. Virulent epidemics of European diseases were far worse. From this time, archaeologists have uncovered mass burials and skeletons bearing cuts from European weapons. Razing the mound temples, extinguishing sacred fires, scattering royal ancestral remains, and disrupting the leadership of elite rulers claiming direct descent from the Sun all may have undermined the religious and political fabric of these large and prosperous chiefdoms, sending them into chaos. Tristán de Luna y Arellano in the 1560's, and Robert Cavalier, sieur de La Salle in 1682, found only scattered villages where de Soto had described large populations.

The void was so complete that by the 1800's, no one remembered who had built the thousands of earth mounds dotting the waterways of eastern America. A popular myth attributed them to a "lost race" of Mound Builders, thereby denying Native Americans their authorship. The Smithsonian scientist Cyrus Thomas disproved this in 1894, citing de Soto's observations and archaeological findings to prove the contrary.

—*Gary A. Olson*

ADDITIONAL READING:

Ewen, C. R. "Apalachee Winter." *Archaeology* 42, no. 3 (1989): 37-41. Researches the 1539-1540 winter camp at Anhaica.

Garcilaso de La Vega. *The Florida of the Inca.* Translated by John Grier Varner and Jeannette Johnson Varner. Austin: University of Texas Press, 1951. Early secondhand account based on accounts of three expedition members. Originally published in 1605.

Milanich, J. T., and Susan Milbrath, eds. *First Encounters.* Gainesville: University of Florida Presses, 1989. Discusses specific traces of de Soto's expedition.

Silverberg, Robert. *Mound Builders of Ancient America: The Archaeology of a Myth.* Greenwich, Conn.: New York Graphic Society, 1968. Scrutinizes the myth of a lost race of Mound Builders.

Swanton, John R. *Final Report of the United States De Soto Expedition Commission.* Washington, D.C.: Smithsonian Institution Press, 1985. Classic analysis of de Soto's route and the ethnohistorical sources, originally published in 1939. New foreword and introduction.

SEE ALSO: A.D. 750, Mississippian Culture; 1513, Ponce de León's Voyages; 1528, Narváez's and Cabeza de Vaca's Expeditions; 1540, Coronado's Expedition; 1542, Settlement of Alta California.

1540 ■ CORONADO'S EXPEDITION: *the first extensive exploration of the Southwest, prompting later expeditions*

DATE: February 23, 1540-c. October 13, 1542
LOCALE: Southwest, primarily New Mexico
CATEGORIES: Exploration and discovery; Latino American history; Native American history

KEY FIGURES:

Álvar Núñez Cabeza de Vaca (c. 1490-1557), Spanish explorer who led three others out of Indian captivity in Texas to Spanish settlements in Old Mexico

Francisco Vásquez de Coronado (1510-1554), leader of the expedition

Estevanico or *Estevǎn* (died 1539), black Moorish slave who guided the first expedition into the American Southwest

Juan de Oñate (1550-1630), governor and captain general of New Mexico in 1595

Pedro de Peralta (c. 1584-1666), Oñate's successor, who moved the provincial capital of New Mexico to Santa Fe

SUMMARY OF EVENT. The Moors, a nomadic North African tribe, occupied the Iberian peninsula for several hundred years before finally being driven out in the late fifteenth century. They contributed much to Spanish culture. They also contributed to a myth that would have enduring consequences for North America. Legend had it that oppressed Christians led by seven bishops had fled the Moorish invasion and gone west by sea. These refugees were supposed to have landed on an island called Antilia and established seven cities of fabulous wealth. These cities then formed a utopian commonwealth, later called the Seven Cities of Cíbola.

Spanish explorers, motivated by the New World's promise of wealth, moved quickly to capitalize on its Mexican conquest of the early 1520's. Nuño Beltrán de Guzmán had been appointed governor of the central Mexican province of Panuco in 1527. Guzmán's young American Indian slave, Tejo, told the cruel governor that he had heard stories of seven rich cities to the north and west. In 1529, Guzmán and a force of four hundred soldiers set out to found the province of Nueva Galicia in what is today Northwest Mexico just below the Arizona border. He found treacherous terrain and, in bad temper, killed some natives along the way, but by 1531 he had abandoned his search for the cities of gold.

Then, in 1536, Alvar Núñez Cabeza de Vaca escaped Native American captivity in Texas and completed an eight-year odyssey from Florida, across south Texas, and across the Rio Grande into Mexico. He and his three companions—two other Spaniards and the black Moorish slave Estevanico—endured much hardship and had many tales to tell. They had not seen the fabulous seven cities, but had heard about advanced civilizations to the north. The islanders of Antilia just might have fled to a mainland sanctuary. Thus the rumor was revived.

In August, 1538, twenty-eight-year-old Francisco Vásquez de Coronado was appointed governor of Nueva Galicia. Meanwhile, the Viceroy of Mexico, Antonio de Mendoza, was seeking someone to lead an expedition to seek the seven cities. Estevanico was ready and willing, but a slave could not be expected to command Spanish soldiers. Conveniently, two padres arrived who were eager for the adventure. Fray Marcos de Niza and Fray Onarato sought grace in establishing church authority. Estevanico was ordered along.

The expedition went sour from the beginning. After leaving Nueva Galicia in the spring of 1539, Fray Onarato became ill

CORONADO'S EXPEDITION, 1540-1542

Fray Marcos reported that the legendary Seven Cities of Cíbola actually existed, prompting Francisco Vásquez de Coronado, governor of New Galicia in western Mexico, to assemble an expedition of 340 soldiers, several hundred natives, and a few African servants. Events in their travels included (1) exploration of the lower Colorado River by a splinter party led by Melchor Díaz; (2) a conflict in which two hundred Tiguex natives were killed; (3) discovery of the Grand Canyon by García López de Cárdenas; (4) Hernando de Alvarado's reconnaissance of the mighty Acoma pueblo, the Rio Grande Valley, and the environs of modern Albuquerque, Santa Fe, and Taos, New Mexico; and (5) Coronado's visit to the fabled city of Quivira in eastern Kansas. The great cities that Coronado sought proved to be thatched huts housing poor natives; he returned to Mexico in 1542, an exhausted and disappointed man.

In this drawing by the nineteenth century western illustrator Frederic Remington, Coronado leads an expedition of soldiers, natives, and clergy through the arid Southwest. The expedition reached eastern Kansas in search of the riches of Quivira. After two years, the exhausted group would return to Mexico, defeated but having left paths that would be followed by others in decades to come. (Library of Congress)

and had to return. Estevanico ignored Fray Marcos and went on ahead north into present-day Arizona and east across the Gila River into New Mexico. Fray Marcos likely never got as far as the Arizona country. Estevanico came to the city of Cíbola (the first use of this term) on Zuñi land in eastern New Mexico. The Zuñis were one of the many settled tribes in the American Southwest that the Spaniards labeled *pueblo* after their sophisticated architectural skills. The Zuñis killed Estevanico and dismembered his body in order to prove that he was not a god. Fray Marcos reported back to the viceroy that the trek to the land of the Zuñis was gentle, and that all indications were good that the Seven Cities of Cíbola actually existed. These lies spurred further exploration.

In mid-November of 1539, a scouting party led by Melchor Díaz took forty-five soldiers to Cíbola, mounted on the first horses to enter the western part of the continent. Díaz returned with a discouraging report. The terrain was rugged, and no evidence of gold, silver, or jewels was found. Coronado remained undaunted. He was a knight-errant in an exotic land, and his ethos was to serve God and country while serving himself. The Spanish relied on the *adelanto* (military chieftain) to secure new lands for the Crown. This warrior might

have to bankroll his own expeditions and the risks were great, but so too were the possible rewards.

Coronado set out on February 23, 1540, from Compostella on Mexico's west coast with 340 soldiers, several hundred natives, and a few African servants. He subjugated the Zuñi after a brief fight and sent emissaries ahead to scout the countryside. Captain García López de Cárdenas and his small band went north and became the first Europeans to gaze into the Grand Canyon. Captain Hernando de Alvarado moved east past the mighty fortress of the Acoma pueblos into the Rio Grande Valley and then north through the area that is now Albuquerque, Santa Fe, and Taos, New Mexico. All along, these conquistadores found sophisticated Pueblo settlements with good supplies of maize, turkeys, and beans. They found no gold or silver.

Alvarado then turned east toward what is now the New Mexico-Texas border. There he learned about the slave trade that existed between the Pueblo and Plains tribes. He met a captured Kansas Indian whom the Spaniards called the "Turk" because they thought he looked like one. The Turk knew what the Spanish craved. To get back to his own country, he concocted a story about precious minerals aplenty if the Spaniards would head north and east to the Kansas plain and the fabulous city of Quivira. The Turk was taken back to Coronado, who believed him because he wanted to believe.

Scattered fighting had broken out between the Spanish conquistadores and the native inhabitants of New Mexico during the harsh winter of 1540-1541. The Spaniards wanted food supplies and clothing, and so they took them. Coronado was nevertheless determined to march to Quivira. He pushed on all the way to eastern Kansas, in the area that is now Wichita, and found mostly grasslands. Coronado had the Turk executed, then returned to winter in the Rio Grande Valley before retreating to Old Mexico in the spring of 1542. The exhausted and tattered expedition reached Mexico City sometime before October 13. Coronado was a defeated and disappointed man.

For forty years, the frontier that Coronado had helped to establish lay neglected by the Spanish authorities. A combination of internal political squabbling and tribal uprisings preoccupied the viceroy in Mexico City. Gradually, Franciscan missionaries and Spanish miners pushed north and revived interest in Tierra Nueva, as Coronado's men had called the land. The authorities took note, and in 1595 granted the title of governor and captain general to Juan de Oñate. His job was "to carry out the discovery, pacification, and reconquest of the provinces of New Mexico."

The ruthless and ambitious Oñate went north from El Paso in 1598 and quickly subjugated the Pueblo tribes. He attracted soldier followers by the promise of their becoming *hidalgos*, which literally meant "son of someone" and was the lowest rank of Spanish nobility. He became *adelanto* and established a systematic repression of the Pueblo Indians through forced labor, murder, rape, torture, and extortion. The Franciscans competed with the civil authorities for plunder, until the only difference between the mission *encomiendas* (forced labor arrangements) and those of the governors was into whose pocket the profits went.

Oñate established the first settlement, called San Juan, north of Santa Fe. Because the site of Santa Fe had more room, a better defensive position, and a reliable source of water, colonists began settling the area as early as 1608. In 1609, Pedro de Peralta replaced the cruel Oñate; in 1610, he officially moved the provincial capital south to Santa Fe. He, too, used forced Indian labor to build the town. Eventually, in 1680, the Pueblo Indians organized a complete revolt throughout the Rio Grande Valley and drove the Spaniards out of New Mexico. The Spaniards were not able to recapture the area until 1693.

—*Brian G. Tobin*

ADDITIONAL READING:

Day, A. Grove. *Coronado's Quest*. Berkeley: University of California Press, 1964. A careful chronology derived from original sources.

Forbes, Jack D. *Apache, Navaho, and Spaniard*. Norman: University of Oklahoma Press, 1971. Focuses on Spanish incursions into Arizona, New Mexico, and Texas between 1540 and 1700.

Terrell, John Upton. *Pueblos, Gods, and Spaniards*. New York: Dial Press, 1973. A tribute to Pueblo culture and its resiliency.

Webber, David J. *The Spanish Frontier in North America*. New Haven, Conn.: Yale University Press, 1992. Smoothly written synthesis of an important cultural clash.

SEE ALSO: 1528, Narváez's and Cabeza de Vaca's Expeditions; 1539, De Soto's Expeditions; 1598, Oñate's New Mexico Expedition.

1542 ■ SETTLEMENT OF ALTA CALIFORNIA: *Spanish soldiers and explorers move into the present-day state of California*

DATE: June 27, 1542-April 21, 1782
LOCALE: California north of the Gulf of California
CATEGORIES: Exploration and discovery; Latino American history; Native American history
KEY FIGURES:
Juan Bautista de Anza (1735-1788), leader of land expeditions to Alta California, 1774-1776
Juan Rodríguez Cabrillo (1498?-1543), leader of a sea expedition to Alta California, 1542-1543
Gaspar de Portolá (1723?-1784?), leader of a land expedition to Alta California, 1769-1770
Junípero Serra (1713-1784), father-president of the Alta California missions, 1769-1784
Sebastián Vizcaíno (1550-1628), leader of a sea expedition to Alta California, 1602-1603
SUMMARY OF EVENT. After conquering the Aztec Empire in 1521 and establishing New Spain (Mexico) in its place, the Spanish were eager to expand northward in the hope of finding wealthy civilizations and a strait running through North America that would allow ships to sail directly from Europe to Asia. They also wanted to protect their empire from rival nations and to convert the Native Americans to Christianity.

In 1533, a ship sailing from New Spain under the command of Fortún Jiménez landed in a bay, later known as La Paz. The land Jiménez found was thought to be an island and was named California after an imaginary island in a novel. In 1539, Francisco de Ulloa sailed along the west coast of New Spain until it met the coast of California, proving that it was not an island but a peninsula. This peninsula became known as Baja California and the mainland above it as Alta California.

On June 27, 1542, three ships commanded by Juan Rodríguez Cabrillo left the port of Navidad in New Spain. They arrived in a bay, later known as San Diego, on September 28, marking the first time Europeans had landed in Alta California. Cabrillo continued to sail north along the coast, landing several times on the mainland and on nearby islands. He died on January 3, 1543, and the voyage continued under the chief pilot, Bartolomé Ferrelo, who sailed about as far north as the modern California-Oregon border, then returned to Navidad on April 14.

After Cabrillo's voyage, the Spanish gained new reasons to be interested in settling Alta California. In 1565, Spanish ships began carrying valuable cargo from Manila in the Philippines to Acapulco in New Spain. These ships, known as the Manila galleons, made enormous profits, but the voyage was long and dangerous. A port in Alta California would allow the galleons to take on supplies before continuing down the coast. An additional incentive to secure Alta California came in 1578, when the English privateer Francis Drake entered the Pacific Ocean and began raiding Spanish ships and settlements. In 1584, a Manila galleon commanded by Francisco de Gali observed the coast of Alta California but did not land. In 1587, English privateer Thomas Cavendish captured a Manila galleon, increasing the pressure on the Spanish to protect their territories. In 1595, a Manila galleon commanded by Sebastián Rodríguez Cermenho made landings in Alta California but was destroyed in a storm. Cermenho and his crew made their way to New Spain in an open boat, continuing to make landings and observations.

On May 5, 1602, three ships commanded by Sebastián Vizcaíno left Acapulco and began sailing up the coast of Alta California. Vizcaíno gave new names to places that had been visited previously by Cabrillo and Cermenho. Many of these names, such as San Diego and Santa Barbara, still exist today. On December 16, Vizcaíno sailed into a bay he named Monterey, which he described with some exaggeration as an excellent harbor.

Despite all the reasons Spain had for settling Alta California, little was accomplished for more than 150 years after Vizcaíno's voyage, because of the difficulty of the journey. In 1769, however, two ships and two land parties left Baja California to begin the first permanent Spanish settlements in Alta California. On January 9, the *San Carlos* left the settlement at La Paz, followed by the *San Antonio* on February 15. On March 22, the first land party left Baja California, followed by a second on May 15. This second party included Gaspar de Portolá, commander of the expedition, and Junípero Serra, a Franciscan friar who would serve as father-president of the missions in Alta California. The *San Antonio* arrived at San Diego on April 11, followed by the *San Carlos* on April 30. The first land party arrived on May 14, followed by the second on July 1.

Portolá arrived to find that so many sailors had died of scurvy on the voyage that the ships could not continue to Monterey as planned. On July 9, the *San Antonio* left San Diego to return to New Spain for supplies. On July 14, Portolá continued northward. Those who remained behind began building a mission and a presidio (a military settlement) on July 16. Portolá's party passed Monterey but failed to recognize it. They continued until November 1, when they reached an enormous bay they named San Francisco. Portolá turned back south, again missing Monterey, and arrived at San Diego on January 24, 1770.

The colony at San Diego was barely surviving and Portolá was about to abandon it when the *San Antonio*, returning with supplies, was sighted on March 19. On April 17, Portolá set out once again for Monterey, arriving on May 24. A mission and presidio were founded there on June 3. Portolá left Monterey on the *San Antonio* on July 9, arriving in New Spain on August 1. Serra remained in Alta California to found seven more missions. A total of twenty-one missions were founded by Serra and his successors between 1769 and 1823.

At the time of Spanish settlement, Alta California was more densely populated by a greater variety of Native Americans than any other region in North America. Although violent encounters were less common than elsewhere in the Spanish Empire, exposure to European diseases reduced the Native American population drastically.

The sea route to Alta California was long and dangerous because of contrary winds. The settlements in the barren land of Baja California were too poor to supply land parties. A new route had to be found. On January 8, 1774, Juan Bautista de Anza led a party overland from New Spain. The party obtained help in crossing the Colorado River from the Yumas, a Native American people inhabiting the region. They reached the mission of San Gabriel on March 22. Anza returned to New Spain on May 26. On October 23, 1775, Anza led a second party, arriving at San Gabriel on January 4, 1776. He continued on to San Francisco, where a presidio was founded on September 17 and a mission on October 9. Anza's route continued to be the main route into Alta California for later colonists. The first pueblo (town) in Alta California was founded at El Pueblo de San José de Guadalupe (later San Jose) in November of 1777, followed by El Pueblo de Nuestra Señora la Reina de los Angeles del Río de Porciúncula (later Los Angeles) in September of 1781.

On July 17, 1781, the Yumas, angered by demands made by Spanish colonists and by the damage done to their crops by Spanish cattle, attacked the two missions in their area, killing most of the men and capturing the women and children. The next day, they attacked a party of Spanish soldiers, killing all of them. After the Yuma Massacre, Alta California was effectively cut off from New Spain. A party of settlers who had left the area just in time to avoid the attack founded a presidio at Santa Barbara on April 21, 1782. This was the last important new settlement in the history of Spanish Alta California.

—*Rose Secrest*

ADDITIONAL READING:

Bean, Walton. "Discovery, Exploration, and Founding" and "Outposts of a Dying Empire." In *California: An Interpretive History*. 3d ed. New York: McGraw-Hill, 1978. These two chapters provide a clear, concise account of important events in the history of the Spanish settlement of Alta California, with an extensive bibliography.

Chapman, Charles Edward. *The Founding of Spanish California*. New York: Macmillan, 1916. Reprint. New York: Octagon Books, 1973. Despite its age, this is the classic scholarly work on the subject, based on the author's study of thousands of original documents from the period.

Daniels, George G., ed. "The Cruel Road to Empire." In

The Spanish West. New York: Time-Life Books, 1976. Includes a lively, anecdotal account of the settling of Alta California. Intended for general readers.

Kleber, Louis Charles. "California's Spanish Missions." *History Today* 42, no. 9 (September, 1992): 42-47. Discusses the impact of the missions on the Native Americans in Alta California, including the devastating drop in population as a result of disease.

Lyon, Eugene. "Track of the Manila Galleons." *National Geographic* 178, no. 3 (September, 1990): 5-37. A detailed account of the ships that helped promote the settling of Alta California. Colorful maps and photographs.

Weber, David J. *The Spanish Frontier in North America.* New Haven, Conn.: Yale University Press, 1992. An exhaustive, wide-ranging history of the northern borderlands of the Spanish Empire in the New World. Includes detailed accounts of the settling of Alta California.

SEE ALSO: 1519, Cortés Enters Tenochtitlán; 1540, Coronado's Expedition; 1579, Drake Lands in Northern California; 1769, Rise of the California Missions.

1565 ■ ST. AUGUSTINE IS FOUNDED: *the first permanent European settlement in North America begins with a failed crusade to convert native peoples*

DATE: September 8, 1565
LOCALE: Native village of Seloy in Florida
CATEGORIES: Exploration and discovery; Native American history; Settlements
KEY FIGURES:
Doña Antonia, Calusa Indian who "married" Menéndez
Carlos, also known as *Escambaba* or *Escambaha* (died 1567), the *cacique* of the Calusa
René de Laudonnière (died 1566), French Huguenot who settled Fort Caroline
Pedro Menéndez de Avilés (1519-1574), explorer who founded St. Augustine, Florida

SUMMARY OF EVENT. In September, 1565, the Saturiba occupants of the village of Seloy welcomed the Spaniards who had sailed into the inlet's shallow harbor by kissing them on their hands. Pedro Menéndez de Avilés stepped onto shore to the blare of trumpets and the echo of gunpowder. As banners were raised, Menéndez named the village San Agustín (St. Augustine) and claimed it for Spain and its king, Philip II.

Many countries saw the merit in gaining a foothold along the prized eastern coastline of North America. Spain believed that the vast empire belonged to her, because Spanish explorer Juan Ponce de León had taken possession of La Florida for the Crown. In addition, Philip II wished to protect the many unexplored waterways of Florida, thinking that one of them might be a passage to the East. In 1564, however, French Huguenot René de Laudonnière established the settlement of Fort

Caroline on the St. Johns River. When the news reached Philip, he contracted the services of Menéndez for a period of three years. Philip named Menéndez *adelantado* (contractual conqueror) of Florida and commissioned him to conquer and settle the land.

Menéndez, a native of Asturia, was an experienced seaman and leader. Although at one time he had been convicted and jailed for smuggling, Menéndez could boast of skills as a privateer, businessman, and captain-general of the Spanish fleet in 1555-1556, which had won him favor with the king. For Menéndez, the assignment took on many meanings. His only son, Don Juan Menéndez, had been shipwrecked along the coast, and he hoped to find him. He also wished to rid the land of heretic French Protestants, to convert the Native Americans to Catholicism, and to gain position and wealth.

After his successful landing at St. Augustine, Menéndez quickly launched an attack on the Huguenots (French followers of John Calvin) who had settled at Fort Caroline. Menéndez marched forty miles north through the rain to the fort with a force of five hundred harquebusiers. Eager to be rid of the French, the Saturibas aided the Spanish by leading the way. The soldiers met with little resistance, because most men of fighting age had struck out in pursuit of two ships from Menéndez's fleet. The women and children were spared and sent to Puerto Rico, but a reported 130 men were killed. In a letter to the king, Menéndez justified the killing by saying that the men were from the "evil Lutheran sect."

Menéndez renamed the fort San Mateo and, leaving a small garrison of soldiers to guard it, returned to St. Augustine. There, he learned that the French who had left Fort Caroline had been shipwrecked. Menéndez intercepted the survivors at a broad inlet eighteen miles south of St. Augustine. The French offered to surrender, providing their lives would be spared. Menéndez agreed to the surrender, only to kill all but a few Catholics, adolescents, and some musicians and tradesmen. The site of the massacre retained the name Matanzas ("slaughters"). Again, Menéndez explained his action by claiming that it was a necessary strike against heresy.

Although Menéndez contended that both the Native American and Protestant beliefs came from the same Satanic roots, he believed that he could convert the Native Americans in the area if he eliminated the French and kept the two cultures from becoming enmeshed. Conversion was one of his intentions when he visited the Calusa settlement in southwestern Florida in 1566. Menéndez also wished to find his son and establish a Spanish settlement in the same area to protect the coastal shipping lanes from the French, the English, and the Calusas, who were noted for their plundering of Spanish shipwrecks.

The cacique (chief), Carlos, eagerly formed a friendship with Menéndez, hoping to arrange a political alliance with Spain. Carlos' power was precarious, and he needed an ally to thwart his cousin and rival, Don Felipe. In order to cement his relationship, Carlos demanded that Menéndez take his middle-aged sister, called Doña Antonia by the Spaniards, to be his wife. Menéndez did not wish to offend the Calusas, and although he already had a wife, he acquiesced and consummated the marriage. The Calusas were not an agricultural people, but rather survived through fishing and trading. The Calusa had a highly sophisticated culture, with art that included carved wooden figures and painted wooden masks. Scavengers of wrecked Spanish ships, they recovered gold, silver, and copper, then developed hammering and embossing techniques.

Menéndez did not meet with success in either converting the natives or settling Calusa lands. He did make peace between Carlos and the Tequestas, who were blood relations. In a series of plots and counterplots, Menéndez's captain, Francisco de Reinoso, murdered Carlos, placing Don Felipe in power. The Calusas nevertheless retaliated, and the Spanish abandoned their fort. The Calusas retained their power in southwestern Florida, and although they decreased in numbers over the centuries, it is believed that they still occupied the area in the mid-nineteenth century as part of the Seminole and Miccosukee tribes.

Menéndez's initial goal was to establish two or three fortified and populated settlements within three years. The first winter was harsh. Few supply ships came into port to provide the residents with food, and the palm thatch huts of St. Augustine barely kept out the elements. Those who took the advice of Native Americans to drink boiled sassafras tea survived. Despite all the hardships, within a year and a half Menéndez had established five forts along the east coast and two garrisons on the west coast. Before long, however, the French rallied against the Spanish, allying again with the Native Americans. The Saturiba had changed their allegiance after being assaulted by the Spanish soldiers and condemned by missionaries for their religious beliefs and practices. In 1568, they joined the French privateer Dominique de Gourgues in destroying Fort San Mateo. In retaliation for the earlier massacre of his fellow countrymen, de Gourgues hanged the remaining Spaniards from the same trees, it is said, that the Spaniards had used for hanging the French. The French destroyed all the Spanish garrisons except Santa Elena and St. Augustine.

Although Florida was a key element in protecting Caribbean interests, its lack of precious gems was a detriment. Unable to get funding from the Crown to reclaim lost settlements, and given the added office of the governorship of Cuba, Menéndez's leadership began to wane. Menéndez could not comprehend the Native Americans' turnaround, and he condemned them as warlike and having bad dispositions. He recommended that the entire population of Florida Indians be sold into slavery in the Caribbean. The Spanish government opposed the move, however. Menéndez's legacy, nevertheless, was to secure Spanish domination of Florida that would last for more than two centuries.

Menéndez died in 1574, at Santander, Spain. In 1576, Orista Indians forced Santa Elena to be abandoned, and in 1587, it was dismantled. St. Augustine remained a Spanish colony, except for a twenty-one-year British occupation, for more than

two and one-half centuries, until Spain ratified the Adams-Onís Treaty (1819), ceding Florida to the United States.

—Marilyn Elizabeth Perry

ADDITIONAL READING:

Bushnell, Amy. *The King's Coffer: Proprietors of the Spanish Florida Treasury, 1565-1702*. Gainesville: University Presses of Florida, 1981. Uses correspondence to piece together economic, social, and cultural history of the early days of St. Augustine, Florida.

Deagan, Kathleen A., ed. *America's Ancient City, Spanish St. Augustine: 1565-1763*. New York: Garland, 1991. Selected writings by noted Florida historians on different aspects of the first period of Spanish occupation in Florida, through investigation of documents, archaeological findings, and cartography.

Milanich, Jerald, and Samuel Proctor, eds. *Tacachale: Essays on the Indians of Florida and Southeastern Georgia During the Historic Period*. Gainesville: University Presses of Florida, 1978. A thoroughly researched series of essays depicting the interaction of native and European cultures at the time of conquest.

Reilly, Stephen Edward. "A Marriage of Expedience: The Calusa Indians and Their Relations with Pedro Menéndez de Avilés in Southwest Florida, 1566-1569." *The Florida History Quarterly* 59, no. 4 (April, 1981): 395-421. A detailed account of the relationship between Menéndez and the Calusas.

Waterbury, Jean Parker, ed. *The Oldest City: St. Augustine, Saga of Survival*. St. Augustine, Fla.: St. Augustine Historical Society, 1983. A detailed chronology of St. Augustine, with each chapter written by a Florida historian knowledgeable in a particular period.

Weber, David J. *The Spanish Frontier in North America*. New Haven, Conn.: Yale University Press, 1992. A well-researched narration of the Spanish colonization of America and its impact on the peoples, institutions, and lives of the explorers, the colonists, and those with whom they came in contact.

SEE ALSO: 1513, Ponce de León's Voyages; 1528, Narváez's and Cabeza de Vaca's Expeditions; 1819, Adams-Onís Treaty.

1570's ■ POWHATAN CONFEDERACY:
Wahunsonacock makes political alliance with native tribes in the Virginia region against encroaching European settlers

DATE: Mid-1570's-1644
LOCALE: Eastern Virginia
CATEGORY: Native American history
KEY FIGURES:
Robert Beverly (1673?-1722), Virginia member of the House of Burgesses who handled Indian affairs
Japasus or *Iopassus*, king of the Potomacs
Kekataugh, the ruler of the village of Pamunkey

Opechancanough (c. 1544-1644), chief of the Pamunkey
　Indians and a Powhatan successor
Opitchapam, Powhatan's successor
Pocahontas or *Matoaka* (c. 1596-1617), daughter of
　Powhatan, wife of John Rolfe
Powhatan, also known as *Wahunsonacock* (c. 1550-1618),
　leader of the Powhatan Confederacy
John Smith (1580-1631), second president of the council of
　Jamestown
William Strachey (1572-1621), English writer who described
　the Virginia Indians during his 1610-1611 stay

SUMMARY OF EVENT. The term "Powhatan" is used in several
ways. It was the name given to a group of tribes of Virginia
Indians; the name of an Indian village; the "throne name" of a
chief; and the name of the man who created the Powhatan
Confederacy in eastern Virginia. Geographically, the Powhatan Confederacy extended north to Alexandria along the
Potomac River, south to the Neuse River in North Carolina,
west along Virginia's fall line, and east to the Atlantic Ocean.
Although historians have consistently referred to the chief of
the Powhatan Indians and the ruler of the Powhatan Confederacy as Powhatan, his birth name was Wahunsonacock. This
discrepancy was caused by the English, who either did not
know his birth name or found it more convenient to call him
Powhatan because he had so many names.

It has been suggested that Powhatan or his father came from
the south. This contention is supported by the fact that Powhatan succeeded his father as chieftain, a practice in opposition
to the matriarchal system of succession practiced by the Algonquians of eastern Virginia. Upon his father's death, Powhatan
inherited control over six tribes in eastern Virginia: the Arro-
hattoc (Arrohateck), Appomattoc (Appomattox), Mattapanient
(Mattaponi), Pamunkey, Youghtanund, and Powhatan. By the
time of Jamestown's founding in 1607, Chief Powhatan's control extended to more than twenty additional tribes: the Acco-
hannock, Accomac, Chesapeake, Chickahominy, Chiskiack,
Cuttatawomen, Kecoughtan, Moraughtacund (Morattico),
Nandtaughtacund, Nansemond, Onawmanient, Opiscopank
(Piscataway), Paspahegh, Piankatank, Pissaseck, Patawomeck
(Potomac), Quiyoughcohannock, Rappahannock (Tappahan-
nock), Sekakawon (Secacawoni), Warraskoyack, Weanoc
(Weyanock), Werowocomoco, and Wiccocomico (Wiccomico).

Most historians agree that the Powhatan Confederacy was
forged by Powhatan's treachery, fear, and force. Powhatan
allegedly attacked the Piankatank tribe at night and then
slaughtered all the captives. When Powhatan invaded the Kecoughtan, he slaughtered all resisters and distributed the captives throughout his domain. He was reputed to have slaughtered the entire Chesapeake tribe because an oracle had
divined that Powhatan would be overthrown by a force from
the east. He then transplanted his own people to the area
formerly occupied by the Chesapeake.

Powhatan consolidated his power by conferring chiefdoms
on his relatives, by his own multiple marriages with the daughters of chieftains, and by the intermarriage of his family with
the sons and daughters of locally powerful chiefs. The four
known brothers of Powhatan all became chiefs: Opitchapam,
Powhatan's successor; Opechancanough, the chief of the Pamunkey Indians and a Powhatan successor; Kekataugh, the
ruler of the village of Pamunkey; and Japasus (Iopassus), the
king of the Potomacs. William Strachey, an English writer who
lived in Virginia in the early 1600's, suggested that Powhatan's
twelve marriages increased his authority among Virginia's native tribes. A thirteenth wife has been attributed to Powhatan—
Oholasc, the regent of the Tappahannocks.

There is no accurate listing of the number of children fathered by Powhatan. At the time of the English arrival in 1607,
it was estimated that Powhatan had twenty living sons and
twelve living daughters. The better-known Powhatan offspring
included Taux-Powhatan, the eldest son and ruler of the Powhatans; Na-mon-tack, who was presented to James I; Pocahontas; Cleopatre; Tohahcoope, chief of the Tappahannocks; Nan-
taquaus, described by John Smith as the manliest, comeliest,
and boldest spirit in a "savage"; Matachanna; and Pochins,
chief of the Kecoughtan.

Powhatan's original capital, Werowocomoco, was about ten
miles from Jamestown. In 1608, Werowocomoco was abandoned for Orapax on the Chickahominy River to keep Powhatan geographically distant from the English. Powhatan used
his retreat to the interior and the threat of the English presence
to increase his control over the tribes of the confederacy.

The domain over which Powhatan ruled was a collection of
villages. There is dispute about the exact number. William
Strachey counted thirty-four villages; historians have estimated from thirty to more than one hundred villages. Often a
tribe would people more than one village. Regardless of the
number, Powhatan ruled about thirty tribes in eastern Virginia
with an estimated population of at least 14,300, although this
figure is also in dispute. Each village was expected to pay
eight-tenths of its rude wealth in tribute to Powhatan. The
village was the administrative unit of the Powhatan Confederacy, with power invested in a cockarouse, the weroance or
war-leader, the tribal council, and the priest.

The cockarouse was the first person in dignity in the village,
a member of the tribal council, and the highest elected civil
magistrate, chosen for experience and wisdom. The cockarouse exercised authority only during times of peace, received
the first fruits of the harvest, and was in charge of all public
and private concerns of the village. The cockarouse presided at
tribal councils, was a delegate to Powhatan's council, and held
the office for life on condition of good behavior. Although
elective, the position of cockarouse might be hereditary in the
female line. Women could be cockarouses.

Powhatan appointed the weroance. The weroance was a
member of Powhatan's council, the leader in hunting and
fishing expeditions, and in charge of all military affairs. The
weroance exercised the power of life and death over the members of his tribe, collected the tribute due Powhatan, declared
war, maintained a crude ceremonial state, and presided over
the village council in the absence of the cockarouse.

A somewhat idealized German rendering of Powhatan, or Wahunsonacock, the head of a sophisticated political structure of some thirty tribes in eastern Virginia at the time of first contact with the British. Here he is depicted at the head of a council of tribal chiefs and others, as he might have appeared upon receiving Captain John Smith. (Library of Congress)

The tribal council regulated matters of concern to the whole confederacy. It governed by a sense of right and wrong, by custom, by fashion, by public opinion, and by a sense of honor. It is difficult to determine whether the tribe or the village was the basic political unit of the Powhatan Confederacy, because they were frequently one and the same. Historians generally agree that a king or queen ruled over a tribe. Usually, the king was a weroance. Strachey mentions one queen, Opossunoquonuske of the Mussasran, who was also a weroance. This is probably an exception, because Oholasc was a queen but her son was the weroance.

The highest political authority resided with Powhatan and his council (Matchacomoco). The council was composed of cockarouses, weroances, and the priests of all the subject and allied tribes. The council shared the supreme authority over the Powhatan Confederacy with Powhatan, was convened by the people, and held open meetings. Powhatan presided over this advisory body to declare war or peace, conduct foreign relations, and manage domestic affairs. A unanimous vote of the council was required to implement council decisions, but the personal authority of Powhatan greatly affected council policy.

Powhatan's increasing association with the English may have led to his coronation ceremony, which elevated him both in his own eyes and among his subjects. The Ashmolean Museum at Oxford has an object called "Powhatan's Mantle." It measures approximately 233 by 150 centimeters and is made of four pieces of tanned buckskin bearing a design in shell depicting a standing human figure flanked by two quadrupeds and a series of large rosettes. It is unlikely that this particular mantle was Powhatan's coronation cloak, but it is judged to be authentically seventeenth century Virginia Indian.

During Powhatan's lifetime and because of the religious conversion of Pocahontas, his daughter, and her subsequent marriage to John Rolfe, relations between the Powhatan Confederacy and the Jamestown settlement steadily improved. After the deaths of Pocahontas (1617) and Powhatan (1618), Powhatan's successors, particularly his brother Opechancanough, viewed the English as intruders and sought to remove the English from the ancestral native lands. From 1622 until 1676, Native American rebellions occurred intermittently until the eastern Virginia tribes were either defeated or fled westward, leaving the English in firm control of the lands of the Powhatan Confederacy. —*William A. Paquette*

ADDITIONAL READING:

Barbour, Philip L. *Pocahontas and Her World*. Boston: Houghton Mifflin, 1970. A good synthesis of seventeenth century accounts of Jamestown's founding, including much information on Powhatan.

Beverly, Robert. *The History and Present State of Virginia*. Indianapolis: Bobbs-Merrill, 1971. A study of Indian life and customs in the seventeenth century, first published in 1705.

McCary, Ben C. *Indians in Seventeenth Century Virginia*. Williamsburg: Virginia 350th Anniversary Celebration Corporation, 1957. Reviews the history of seventeenth century Native Americans in Virginia.

Rountree, Helen C. *Pocahontas's People: The Powhatan Indians of Virginia Through Four Centuries*. Norman: University of Oklahoma Press, 1990. Written by an ethnohistorian and anthropologist, this is one of the best studies of Jamestown and the settlement's relationship to the Powhatan Confederacy.

_____. *The Powhatan Indians of Virginia: Their Traditional Culture*. Norman: University of Oklahoma, 1989. A comprehensive study of all aspects of life among the Powhatan Confederacy tribes.

Smith, John. *The General History of Virginia, New England, and the Summer Isles*. Philadelphia: Kimber and Conrad, 1812. An account of life in Virginia by the first Englishman to meet Chief Powhatan.

Strachey, William. *The Historie of Travell into Virginia Britania (1612)*. Edited by Louis Wright and Virginia Freund. 1953. Reprint. Nendeln, Liechtenstein: Kraus Reprint, 1967. A contemporary account of Virginia's Native Americans.

SEE ALSO: 1607, Jamestown Is Founded; 1622, Powhatan Wars.

1576 ■ FROBISHER'S VOYAGES: *Britain's first attempt to discover an Arctic passage to China leads to a gold rush*

DATE: June 7, 1576-July, 1578
LOCALE: Southeast Baffin Island, Canada
CATEGORIES: Canadian history; Exploration and discovery
KEY FIGURES:

Arnaq (died 1577), Inuit woman captured during the second Frobisher voyage

George Best (died 1584), official chronicler of the three expeditions, who published one of the earliest written accounts of the Inuit

Martin Frobisher (c. 1535-1594), British privateer, Arctic explorer, and naval hero

Charles Francis Hall (1821-1871), U.S. explorer who rediscovered the Frobisher sites and collected Inuit oral histories

Kalicho (died 1577) Inuit man kidnapped by Frobisher, along with Arnaq and her child, and exhibited with them as curiosities to the English public

Michael Lok (1532?-1615?), merchant, financier, and governor of the Cathay Company

John White (fl. 1575-1595), Elizabethan artist known for his watercolor paintings of the Indians in the Virginia Colony

SUMMARY OF EVENT. On June 7, 1576, Martin Frobisher set off from Deptford, England, in search of a Northwest Passage to India and the Far East. This former privateer headed a flotilla consisting of a pinnace and two small ships, the *Gabriel* and the *Michael*. The pinnace sank off the coast of Greenland, and the *Michael* turned back toward England after losing sight of the *Gabriel* in stormy seas. Although the captain of the *Michael* incorrectly reported that Frobisher was lost at sea, on

August 11, 1576, the *Gabriel*, with its party of nineteen, sailed into a large bay along southeastern Baffin Island. They sailed 150 miles along the coast, finding neither an outlet nor a dead end. Thinking that he had found a northern sea route to the Indies, Frobisher named the waterway Frobisher Straits. This body of water is now known as Frobisher Bay.

The group had its first encounter with Inuit natives eight days later when Frobisher, his sailing master Christopher Hall, and several others landed on a small island near the mouth of the bay. While scanning the area from a small hill, a party of Inuit in kayaks landed on the beach and attempted to prevent the intruders from returning to their boat. The sailors reached the *Gabriel* only by rushing to the boat landing just ahead of

the Inuit. This and several other incidents suggest that the Inuit had had prior experience with European sailors, probably Portuguese fishermen.

The next day, Hall led a small party ashore and engaged in some friendly trade. This was followed by a visit to the ship by a group of Inuit. A day later, on August 21, 1576, five sailors took the ship's boat ashore to continue the contacts. It remains uncertain what transpired, but the sailors were apparently taken captive. Frobisher attempted various strategies to recover his men, but without the ship's boat, the crew of the *Gabriel* was unable to go ashore to rescue them. The crew attempted to sink one of the Inuit's *umiaks* (large skin boats) and take hostages to exchange for the sailors, but the Inuit

FROBISHER'S VOYAGES, 1576-1578

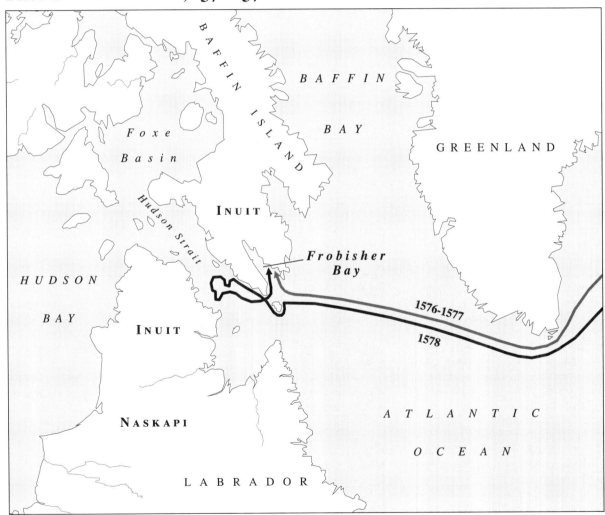

During his first voyage, in 1576, Frobisher captured an Inuit native and samples of a mineral that seemed to be gold, returning to England with both. The Inuit man died; the rock, when tested, proved to contain no gold. Nevertheless, Frobisher formed the Cathay Company and returned in 1577 to mine the ore, bringing 180 tons of it back to England. A third trip, in 1578, occurred before Frobisher had received confirmation from the assayers that his ore was worthless. He mined more worthless ore and transported it back to England, only to have the Cathay Company declared insolvent.

remained wary and out of range of the ship's ordnance. Frobisher then lured a lone kayaker to the ship by holding out a bell. When the Inuit came alongside the *Gabriel*, he was, according to George Best, official chronicler of the expedition, "plucked . . . boat and al . . . out of the sea." The unfortunate man was reported to be so upset by his capture that "he bit his tong[ue] in twayne [in half] within his mouth."

Unable to rescue the missing sailors, Frobisher set sail for England with his Inuit captive and an unusual black rock as tokens. The captive died soon after his arrival in London, but the black rock set in motion a series of events which, in retrospect, can only be considered a comic disaster.

The rock, which seemed unusually heavy and appeared to sparkle, was presented to Michael Lok, the merchant who had financed the voyage. Lok came to believe it contained gold. At least two assayers assured Lok that the rock was ordinary, but he refused to be dissuaded. He continued to consult assayers until one finally assured him that the rock contained considerable quantities of gold. The Cathay Company, quickly formed by Lok and Frobisher in order to mine the gold, succeeded in attracting numerous investors, including Queen Elizabeth I.

Frobisher sailed from Blackwell on May 25, 1577, with three ships, the *Michael*, the *Gabriel*, and his flagship, the *Ayde*, which had been loaned by the queen. They entered Frobisher Bay on July 19, 1577, and remained there for five weeks. There were two goals of this second expedition: to mine as much "gold" as possible and to recover the five men lost the previous year.

The thirty miners included among the 120 passengers and crew succeeded in loading approximately 180 tons of ore in the allotted time. The second goal proved more troublesome. After a fruitless search of the southern margin of the bay, Frobisher and his sailing master went ashore and attempted to capture two natives. The Inuit escaped and managed to wound Frobisher with an arrow to his buttocks. A small skirmish, in which three Inuit were captured, ensued. This event is the subject of a highly detailed painting by Elizabethan artist John White, who may have witnessed the incident. The trio, a man named Kalicho and a woman, Arnaq, with her infant son, Nutaaq, were transported back to England, where they caused quite a stir. The three, who died within months of their capture, are the subjects of several drawings by White. Their Asiatic features reinforced the notion that Frobisher had found a northern water route to the Far East.

Numerous delays in obtaining assays of the ore meant that Frobisher sailed a third time before any results were known or profits could be realized. In fact, the subscribers were forced to increase their investments in order to outfit the fifteen ships that sailed from in England on May 31, 1578. Frobisher planned to leave one hundred men to mine gold throughout the winter, but the sinking of the ship that carried most of the building materials caused him to abandon that idea. Thick ice and bad weather forced Frobisher into what is now known as the Hudson Strait, and he concluded that this, and not Fro-

bisher Bay (or "Strait," as he still believed it to be), was the true Northwest Passage. It was not until the end of July that the party reached its mining site at the mouth of Frobisher Bay. Although the group had no further encounters with natives, they built a small house that they left stocked with small trade items and freshly baked bread. The latter was intended as a means to educate the Inuit in the ways of civilization. They returned to England with 1,225 tons of worthless ore.

The Cathay Company was declared insolvent, and Lok spent part of 1581 in debtors' prison. Frobisher went on to distinguish himself in naval battle and was knighted in 1588 for heroism against the Spanish Armada. The search for an Arctic route to Asia continued for another few years, but then was largely abandoned until the early years of the nineteenth century. The Inuit were spared further attempts at colonization until those later years.

In 1861, U.S. journalist and explorer Charles Francis Hall visited southeastern Baffin Island and made the first systematic ethnographic observations of the Inuit living there. He collected detailed oral histories and was astonished to discover that these included extremely accurate references to the Frobisher expeditions nearly three hundred years earlier. According to his informants, many years earlier two ships had come to the area. The following year, three ships arrived; the next year, there were many ships. The five men that Frobisher lost on the first voyage were said to have built a ship with a mast and attempted to sail away. They were blown back to shore and later, all died. With the aid of his Inuit informants, Hall visited the site of Frobisher's mines and collected a number of artifacts.

—*Pamela R. Stern*

ADDITIONAL READING:

Fitzhugh, William W., and Jacqueline S. Olin, eds. *Archeology of the Frobisher Voyages*. Washington, D.C.: Smithsonian Institution Press, 1993. Combines historical documents, oral histories, and archeological evidence to provide a full account of the Frobisher expeditions. Numerous black-and-white photographs and maps.

Francis, Daniel. *Discovery of the North: The Exploration of Canada's Arctic*. Edmonton, Canada: Hurtig, 1985. Chapter 1 contains a thorough description of the Frobisher voyages.

Hall, Charles Francis. *Life with the Esquimaux*. 2 vols. London: Sampson Low, Son, and Marston, 1864. Hall's observations and oral histories of the Baffin Island Inuit.

Halton, P. H. "John White's Drawings of Eskimos." *The Beaver* 41 (Summer, 1961): 16-20. Reproduction and discussion of several of White's lesser-known works.

Oswalt, Wendell H. *Eskimos and Explorers*. Novato, Calif.: Chandler and Sharp, 1979. Chapter 2 presents a thoughtful discussion of contacts between Inuit and the Elizabethan-era British.

Payne, Edward John. *Voyages of the Elizabethan Seamen: Selected Narratives from the "Principal Navagations" of Hakluyt*. Oxford, England: Clarendon Press, 1907. Contains George Best's sixteenth century accounts of the three Frobisher voyages, with the spellings modernized.

See also: 1497, Cabot's Voyages; 1534, Cartier and Roberval Search for a Northwest Passage; 1603, Champlain's Voyages; 1610, Hudson Explores Hudson Bay.

1579 ■ Drake Lands in Northern California: *the explorer announces the first British land claim in North America*

Date: June 17, 1579
Locale: New Albion
Category: Exploration and discovery
Key figures:

Francis Drake (c. 1540-1596), explorer who established the first British colonial claim in North America
Elizabeth I (1533-1603), British monarch, 1558-1603
Martin Frobisher (c. 1535-1594), Drake's rival in exploration, who attempted to discover the Northwest Passage in 1576
Philip II (1527-1598), Spanish monarch, 1556-1598, and British consort, 1554-1558

Summary of event. On November 15, 1577, Sir Francis Drake, commanding five ships, set sail from Plymouth, England, obeying Elizabeth I's order to "encompass the world." Before the voyage was completed, the sole surviving flagship, the *Pelican*, later renamed the *Golden Hind*, had circumnavigated the globe. Rounding the Strait of Magellan, Drake navigated up the western coast of South America to Peru, plundering Spanish ships and settlements along the way. Heavy with Spanish gold, silver, trade route maps, and occasionally human captives, his ship cruised up the North American coast past Mexico and California, going as far north as Oregon. Inclement weather forced him back south to what is today Marin County, California. There he anchored for repairs before setting sail across the Pacific Ocean. Drake, who eight years later was to play an important role in England's defeat of the Spanish Armada, reached as far as the Pelew Islands (Palau) before returning home to Plymouth, England, in 1580 by way of Ternate (in the Moluccas), Java, the Cape of Good Hope, and Sierra Leone.

The contemporaneous political situation in England must be examined for the significance of Drake's 1579 excursion to California to become clear. Thirty-five years earlier, Prince Philip of Spain had become king of England by marrying Mary Tudor, queen of England. When his reign ended upon Mary's death in 1588, he attempted to maintain his powerful position by marrying the new monarch, Mary's sister Elizabeth. After Elizabeth rejected his marriage proposal, Philip canceled all commerce, including trade treaties, between England and the Spanish colonies. Thus, finding new English trade routes in the South Pacific became paramount for England's economic survival. Finding a way through the Northwest Passage, formerly thought of as a possible route from the Atlantic to the Pacific, seemed the most expedient way to accomplish this goal.

The search for this Northwest Passage, attempted in 1576 by Martin Frobisher, brought Drake to "a faire and good baye" in California. It was popularly believed at that time that the west coast of North America ran in a northeasterly direction until the passage was reached. After reaching at least 40° north latitude (possibly as much as 48° north latitude), Drake concluded that the passage did not exist, or, if it did, that it would be unnavigable. Backtracking to 38° north latitude, the *Golden Hind* dropped anchor on June 17, 1579.

The exact location of Drake's anchorage remains controversial. It was not far from contemporary San Francisco, and it is likely that it was the unsheltered bay known as Drake's Bay, behind the hook on the end of the Point Reyes Peninsula. Although scholars continue to argue, placing Drake's landing at various points around San Francisco—Drake's Bay, San Francisco Bay, Bodega Bay, Drake's Estero, Bolinas Lagoon, and Tomales Bay—a geographical feature chronicled in the journal of Drake's chaplain, Francis Fletcher, provides evidence for historians to name Drake's Bay the original landfall site. Fletcher recorded that, because of its similarity to England's white banks and cliffs, Drake renamed the country New Albion (New England). A line of white diatomaceous shale cliffs stretches for miles across from Drake's Bay. Although not as striking as the English chalk cliffs, these are the only white cliffs in the area.

On shore, Drake erected a commemorative metal plaque, rediscovered in 1936 by a group of picnickers at Greenbrae Hill overlooking Point San Quentin, which reads:

> Be it known unto all men by these presents, June 17, 1579, by the Grace of God in the name of Her Majesty Queen Elizabeth of England and Her successors for ever, I take possession of this Kingdom, whose King and people freely resign their right and title in the whole land unto Her Majesty's keeping, now named by me and to be known unto all men as Nova Albion.
> —*Francis Drake*

The rediscovery of this commemorative brass plate at Greenbrae Hill fueled the controversy over Drake's actual landfall site and added credence to the claim that San Francisco Bay was the anchorage location. A comparison of modern charts to explorer Jodocus Hondius' 1589 commemorative Drake and Cavendish World Map supports this claim. In addition, the chaplin Fletcher's description of "Barbarie Conies" and "Deere" in the area better reflects the ecology of Greenbrae than that of Point Reyes. Significantly, if Drake anchored in San Francisco Bay, he would have been the first European at this geographical site, antedating Gaspar de Portolá's land expedition by 190 years. The inhospitable coastline, prevalent fog, and narrow entrance long prevented earlier explorers such as Juan Rodríguez Cabrillo, who had charted the entire coast of California by 1542, from finding the Golden Gate.

Anthropologists determined from fragments of speech recalled by one of Drake's crew that the people referred to by Drake were Coast Miwoks who lived in the area now occupied by Marin and Sonoma Counties, north of San Francisco. The

EXPLORATIONS OF DRAKE, OÑATE, AND VIZCAÍNO, 1579-1602

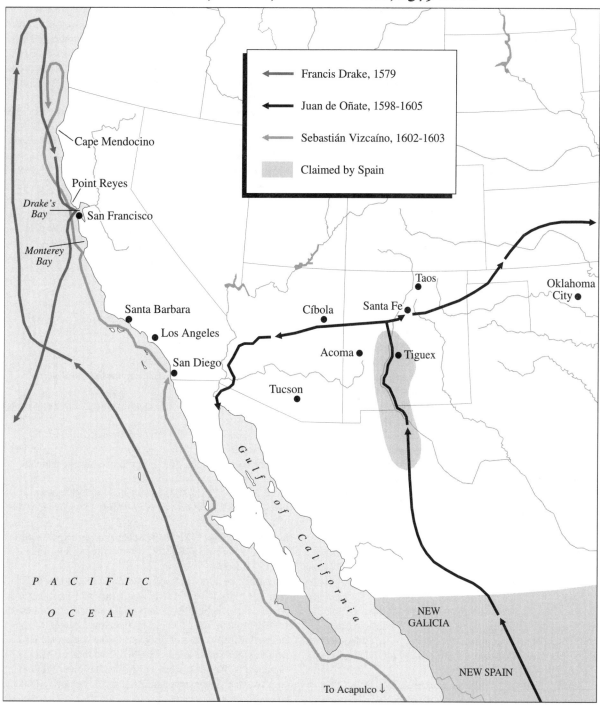

Francis Drake, 1579

Juan de Oñate, 1598-1605

Sebastián Vizcaíno, 1602-1603

Claimed by Spain

Cape Mendocino

Point Reyes

Drake's Bay

San Francisco

Monterey Bay

Taos

Oklahoma City

Santa Barbara

Cíbola

Santa Fe

Los Angeles

Acoma

Tiguex

San Diego

Tucson

Gulf of California

PACIFIC

OCEAN

NEW GALICIA

NEW SPAIN

To Acapulco ↓

Francis Drake was the first Englishman to visit the California coast, on a voyage around the world. After raiding Spanish ships and sailing as far north as the Oregon coast, he dropped anchor somewhere near San Francisco on June 17, 1579. In 1598, Juan de Oñate led a Southwestern land expedition that resulted in the decimation of the Acoma pueblo. Oñate went on to lead an expedition east in a failed attempt to reach Quivira, encountering Apaches and buffalo herds along the way. On May 5, 1602, Sebastián Vizcaíno left Acapulco with three ships to sail up the coast of Alta California. He gave new names to places that had been visited in 1542 by Juan Rodríguez Cabrillo, including San Diego, Santa Barbara, and Monterey Bay.

native people left no record of their first impressions of Drake and his crew, but according to Fletcher, they were happy upon the arrival of the British, referred to Drake as "Hich," or king, gave over their land voluntarily, and were saddened when the British left.

Aside from the fact that Drake and his crew were the first white people to set foot in the San Francisco area, Drake's arrival in California is even more significant for the impact it had on British and U.S. history. This event greatly impacted England's expansion policy. Because this landing predates England's earliest North American colonies—Sir Walter Raleigh's Roanoke Colony by six years (1584) and the permanent Virginia settlement by twenty-eight years (1607)—scholars maintain that it was the first consolidation of non-Europeans under a British sovereign. It was the original protectorate colony in what was to become the British Commonwealth of Nations. This milestone marks the beginning of Great Britain's worldwide system of empire that acknowledged local authority but maintained jurisdiction under the British crown.

Drake's crew spent six weeks coping with a cold, foggy summer in California repairing the leaking *Golden Hind* before setting sail on July 23. They stopped briefly at the Farallon Islands to replenish supplies before riding the northeast trade winds across the Pacific Ocean bound for the Moluccas (Spice Islands). It was not until the British navigator's return to England in 1580 that the significance of the California expedition started to solidify: The Spanish ambassador to Elizabeth's court, Don Bernardin de Mendoza, pronounced the goods that Drake brought home as Spanish property and demanded their return to the Spanish crown. In the document that was to become England's central expansion doctrine for the next three centuries, Elizabeth claimed that since the Spaniards had prohibited commerce with the British, England had been forced to take their own exploratory steps. Because protestant England was not under Rome's jurisdiction, she continued, it need not honor Spain's papal title to the New World. Until Drake claimed the Coast Miwok country, there was no British interest in North America. By 1609, the Virginia Charter extended to the Pacific Ocean and included Drake's Nova Albion.

—*M. Casey Diana*

Additional reading:

Drake, Sir Francis. *The World Encompassed by Sir Francis Drake.* Cleveland: World Publishing, 1966. Offset edition of the Huntington Library copy of the first edition (London, 1628). Recounts the complete circumnavigation, including the six weeks spent in Marin County. Based on the journal of Fletcher, the chaplain of the voyage.

Jenkins, Dorothy G. "Opening of the Golden Gate." Part 1 in *Geologic Guidebook of the San Francisco Bay Counties: History, Landscape, Geology, Fossils, Minerals, Industry, and Routes to Travel.* Bulletin 154. San Francisco: California Division of Mines, 1951. Detailed natural history of San Francisco Bay counties. Illustrations include Drake's brass plate.

Kelsey, Harry. "Did Francis Drake Really Visit California?" *Western Historical Quarterly* 21, no. 4 (1990): 444-462. A

scholarly article that discusses the uncertainties and contradictions inherent in nearly every aspect of Drake's voyage.

Power, Robert H. *Francis Drake and San Francisco Bay: A Beginning of the British Empire.* Keepsake Number 6. Davis: University of California, 1974. Posits San Francisco Bay as Drake's landfall site; emphasizes the interaction that the Coast Miwok people had on British expansion policies. Short, scholarly work.

Williams, Neville. *Francis Drake.* London: Weidenfeld & Nicolson, 1973. Readable account of Drake's life and the historical forces that shaped it. Many illustrations, no index.

See also: 1542, Settlement of Alta California; 1576, Frobisher's Voyages; 1584, Lost Colony of Roanoke; 1769, Rise of the California Missions.

1584 ■ Lost Colony of Roanoke: *the first British attempt to colonize North America ends in mystery*

Date: July 4, 1584-August 17, 1590
Locale: Roanoke Island, Virginia
Category: Settlements
Key figures:
Philip Amadas (born 1565?) and
Arthur Barlowe (1550?-1620?), captains of the 1584 expedition
Virginia Dare (born 1587), first child born of English parents in America
Richard Grenville (1542-1591), commander of the 1585 expedition
Thomas Harriot (1560-1621), astronomer, mathematician, and scientist
Ralph Lane (1530?-1603), governor of the 1585 colony
Pemisapan, also known as *Wingina* (died 1586), chief of the Roanoc tribe
Walter Raleigh (c. 1552-1618), sponsor of the expeditions
John D. White (fl. 1575-1595), artist and governor of the 1587 colony

Summary of event. During the reign of the Queen Elizabeth I, England experienced prosperity, and mariners were interested in establishing colonies in America. On March 25, 1584, Elizabeth I issued to one such mariner, Walter Raleigh, a charter for the purpose of discovering and occupying lands in America that were not held by Christians. In April, two ships, captained by Philip Amadas and Arthur Barlowe, left England on a reconnaissance expedition and on July 4 arrived off the coast of the Outer Banks.

On the third day after their arrival, the two English captains had their first encounter with a member of the Roanoc tribe. He was Granganimeo, brother of the chief, Wingina. After delivering a welcoming speech to the captains, he was taken aboard their ships for a tour and given presents.

For several days, Granganimeo and other members of his

tribe visited the English on their ships and received more gifts. These meetings led to a period of extended trade between the two groups. Granganimeo and his family dined with the English on their ships. After developing a trusting relationship, Captain Barlowe and seven sailors went to the Roanoc's village, where they received a cheerful and friendly welcome and partook of the hospitality of Granganimeo's wife. Barlowe described his hosts as kind and loving. After six weeks of exploration and trade, the English carried back favorable reports and two Roanocs, Manteo and Wanchese. Staying at Raleigh's estate, Manteo and Wanchese learned English from Thomas Harriot.

On January 6, 1585, when Raleigh was knighted by the queen, he called the land Virginia in her honor and made plans for a permanent settlement. The second expedition of approximately six hundred men left Plymouth, England, on April 9, with seven ships under the command of Sir Richard Grenville. With Manteo and Wanchese, they arrived at Ocracoke Inlet on June 26. Sir Ralph Lane served as governor. They reached Roanoke Island, constructed Fort Raleigh, and built small houses.

After two months of careful exploration, Grenville returned to England with detailed maps. Left with 107 men, Lane spent nearly a year organizing numerous exploratory expeditions that gathered information about the country, its resources, and the Native Americans. John White, a painter, drew many pictures of the surroundings and the inhabitants. Harriot, an astronomer, mathematician, and scientist, made a lengthy report on the area.

Having arrived too late to plant crops, Lane expected a shipment of supplies from Grenville to arrive before winter. Winter passed with no supplies having come, however. In addition, Lane's colony was plagued by internal rivalries, a preoccupation with gold, and a pathetic inability to find food in an abundant region. Efforts to grow sugarcane, wheat, oranges, and lemons failed. Therefore, Lane established a close relationship with Wingina and his people. Harriot learned about local products including grass silk, worm silk, flax, and hemp. The Roanocs constructed fish weirs for the English, taught them the medicinal properties of local herbs, and demonstrated how to extract flour from chestnuts.

In return, the colonists demonstrated such advanced goods as iron weapons of war, the compass, and spring clocks. Because the workings of such items exceeded the comprehension and technologies of the Native Americans, they thought they were the works of gods rather than of men.

Lane's men had little interest in learning the ways of the Roanocs. They were more interested in the hints of pearl fisheries farther to the north and of gold to the west. In March, 1586, Lane dispatched an expedition north to find the pearl fisheries, while he took another group to look for gold in the western mountains. Each evening, they stopped at a different Native American village. They stopped at Choanoke on the Chowan River, where Chief Menatonon of the Chawonoac Kingdom lived. Impressed with the chief's knowledge of the

surrounding area and wanting to learn more, Lane took the chief as prisoner on his expedition. To ensure Menatonon's cooperation, Lane took Skiko, the chief's son, prisoner and sent him to Roanoke Island. Menatonon was then released and Lane took a group of thirty men to sail up the Roanoke River looking for gold.

Lane assumed that members of the Moratuck and Mangoak tribes would provide him with the necessary supplies along the way. The Native Americans were forewarned that the English were conquerors; therefore, Lane found their villages abandoned and stripped clean. With little food, Lane and his men decided to return to Roanoke Island. On the way back, they were attacked by Native Americans who were dispersed by Lane's men.

When they reached Roanoke Island in April, Grenville had not arrived, and Wingina, who had changed his name to Pemisapan, had heard of Lane's activities. After his initial request for the release of Skiko was denied, Menatonon sent a large delegation to Lane seeking his son's release in exchange for his loyalty to the English crown.

This shattered Pemisapan's hopes for a unified action against Lane. With the support of Wanchese, he united the different tribes, including the Chanoacs, Moratucks, and Mangoaks, in a conspiracy to destroy the white men. Instead, Lane, Harriot, and some soldiers made a preventive attack on Pemisapan's village and killed him and other Native Americans.

On June 1, Sir Francis Drake stopped by to look in on the colonists. Turning down an offer of supplies, Lane convinced Drake to take his colony and Manteo back to England. They left in such a rush that Lane left behind an exploratory party.

Immediately afterward, Grenville arrived with the anticipated supplies. Finding the colony gone, he left fifteen men with supplies for two years, but they would not be heard from again. Had Lane waited a little longer, he would have succeeded in establishing England's first permanent American colony. Instead, he demonstrated that the land was hospitable for Englishmen.

Raleigh sent another expedition to Roanoke in May, 1587, under the command of John White. This group of 110 was to pick up the men left by Lane and Grenville and to establish the city of Raleigh on the Chesapeake Bay. However, the pilot, Simon Fernandez, refused to take them any farther than Roanoke Island. When White's party reached Fort Raleigh, they learned from the evidence at the site and from friendly Native Americans that the men left by Grenville had been murdered by unfriendly natives from the mainland. The houses left by Lane were repaired and new ones were built. Manteo, who had returned with White, was baptized and made Lord of Roanoke.

Like the Lane colony, the White colony discovered it had arrived too late to plant crops. Having inadequate supplies and receiving little help from the Native Americans, White was encouraged to return home for supplies. He left his daughter and newborn granddaughter, Virginia Dare, with the colonists and set sail. Because England was involved in a war with

Spain, White could not return to Roanoke Island immediately. After Spain was defeated, White set sail for Roanoke in 1590.

Upon arriving, he found no one, only a stake in the ground with the word "Croatoan" written or carved on it. White assumed his colony had migrated southward to Croatoan Island, south of Cape Hatteras and the birthplace of Manteo. The following day, White set sail for Croatoan Island. A storm developed that pushed his ship into the North Atlantic and did such severe damage that he had to return to England for repairs. By this time, Raleigh and England had lost interest in building colonies and were concentrating on raiding Spanish vessels directly from England. Because of the lack of interest in the colonies, White could not raise enough money for a return trip and, heartbroken, retired to his Irish plantation.

—Bill Manikas

ADDITIONAL READING:

Hunter, John L. *Backgrounds and Preparations for the Roanoke Voyages, 1584-1590*. Raleigh: North Carolina Department of Cultural Resources, 1986. Includes chapters on the personnel, ships, food and supplies, and financing of the expeditions.

Quinn, David B. *The Lost Colonists, Their Fortune and Probable Fate*. Raleigh: North Carolina Department of Cultural Resources, 1984. The first five chapters describe the setting, the relations with Native Americans, and the problems among the colonists.

Quinn, David B., and Alison Quinn. *The First Colonists: Documents on the Planting of the First English Settlements in North America, 1584-1590*. Raleigh: North Carolina Department of Cultural Resources, 1982. Contains narratives, reports, and letters from the principals on the expeditions.

Sinclair, Andrew. *Sir Walter Raleigh and the Age of Discovery*. New York: Penguin Books, 1984. The first three chapters explain the interest and attempts by the queen and Raleigh to establish colonies in the New World.

Stick, David. *Roanoke Island: The Beginnings of English America*. Chapel Hill: University of North Carolina Press, 1983. A detailed description of each expedition and the geography, Native Americans, and principals involved.

SEE ALSO: 1579, Drake Lands in Northern California; 1607, Jamestown Is Founded; 1620, Pilgrims Land at Plymouth.

1598 ■ OÑATE'S NEW MEXICO EXPEDITION: *native Puebloan peoples rise up against early Spanish efforts to colonize present-day New Mexico*

DATE: January, 1598-February, 1599
LOCALE: Acoma Pueblo, New Mexico
CATEGORIES: Latino American history; Native American history; Wars, uprisings, and civil unrest

KEY FIGURES:
Alonso Martínez, father commissary of the expedition's Franciscan contingent
Juan de Oñate (1549?-1624), leader of the expedition
Luis de Velasco (1534-1617), the Spanish official who granted the contract to colonize New Mexico
Vicente Zaldívar Mendoza (1565-1625?), nephew of Oñate and his principal lieutenant
Juan de Zaldívar (died 1599), Vicente's brother, who was killed at Acoma

SUMMARY OF EVENT. Spanish intrusion into New Mexico began in the sixteenth century, after early explorers had reported that there were cities of great wealth there. The legend of these golden Seven Cities of Cíbola grew until Francisco Vásquez de Coronado explored the territory in 1540. After two years, the disillusioned Coronado returned to Mexico, concluding that New Mexico was a barren land that would never yield much wealth and that any attempt to colonize would require constant financial support from the Spanish crown. Thus, New Mexico was protected for a time against any further large-scale Spanish invasion.

Eventually, however, rumors again arose of a fabulous mineral wealth in the territory. Economic opportunism, along with Franciscan desire to establish missions there, prompted Viceroy Luis de Velasco to award a contract for the colonization of New Mexico to Don Juan de Oñate, a wealthy mine owner from Zacatecas. Oñate's contract, issued on September 21, 1595, gave him the powers of a dictator, with the title of governor and captain general of New Mexico. He would be the highest judicial officer in the territory, with the right to award patronage to those who accompanied him.

From the beginning, it was obvious that Oñate's own intentions with regard to the colonization of New Mexico conflicted with the spirit of the Law of 1573. This law had been enacted by Philip II, who, concerned about some of the early conquistadores' cruel abuse of native populations, intended to set guidelines for future exploration of the New World. The Law of 1573 replaced the idea of conquest with that of pacification, stating that American Indians were to be given the opportunity to become Christians and vassals of the king, with the same rights to property, freedom, and dignity enjoyed by all subjects of the Crown. Oñate, however, had insisted upon the right to allot sections of the land and its native residents to himself and his people and to levy tribute upon those whom he did not claim in servitude.

By January, 1598, Oñate had assembled an expedition of more than four hundred people, including settlers, soldiers, and seven Franciscan friars and two lay brothers led by Fray Alonso Martínez, the father commissary. Eighty-three ox carts carried supplies, and a herd of animals provided meat. After crossing the Rio Grande at El Paso del Norte, Oñate took formal possession of New Mexico for the Crown and made his first demand for supplies from the Puebloans, loading eighty pack animals with grain from Teypana pueblo. The expedition then traveled across the Jornada del Muerto (the Journey of

Death), ninety miles of waterless desert, which they crossed with no casualties.

At one of the first pueblos he came to, Oñate discovered two Mexican Indians who had lived among the Puebloans for many years, and they became his interpreters. Proceeding up the Rio Grande Valley, Oñate visited the pueblos at Tiguex, San Felipe, and Santo Domingo. Although many Puebloans fled in terror before the invaders, those who remained received Oñate and his men hospitably. On July 7, 1598, Oñate met in council with Pueblo leaders at Santo Domingo pueblo. Declaring that he had come to protect the Puebloans and save their souls, Oñate demanded that they swear allegiance and vassalage to their new rulers, the Spanish king and the Catholic church. Oñate explained the advantages to be gained if the Puebloans voluntarily submitted to the two majesties, while also informing them that disobedience of the law would result in severe punishment.

At this point, serious misunderstanding undoubtedly occurred on both sides. One of Oñate's soldiers translated his Castilian into a Mexican Indian language understood by the two interpreters, who then translated the message into a Pueblo tongue. It is highly unlikely that this double translation communicated a complete understanding of the complex structure of vassalage to the Puebloans. Nevertheless, the Pueblo leaders, always courteous in council, indicated their acceptance. On the other hand, Oñate completely misunderstood the system of government in the pueblos. He thought he was dealing with Pueblo chiefs who had authority to speak for all the people, when no such system of chieftainship existed. In all probability, the representatives from each pueblo were either war captains, delegates chosen by a council of elders to attend this one meeting, or leaders of small factions promoting peaceful coexistence with the Spaniards. In any case, what occurred was the acceptance of something that was little un-

This modern pen-and-ink drawing depicts Don Juan de Oñate and members of his Spanish expedition meeting Apache natives in the Texas panhandle around 1601. Oñate had been drawn to the Southwest in search of the same riches of Cíbola that had drawn Francisco Vásquez de Coronado half a century before. The effect of Spain's Law of 1573, which replaced the idea of conquest with that of pacification and assimilation, can be seen in the presence of the Franciscan friar to Oñate's right; however, the actions of Oñate and his expedition belied the official Spanish policy against native abuse. (Jaxon)

derstood by a few people who had no authority to speak for anyone but themselves. Oñate, however, thought that he had achieved an agreement from all the Puebloans to render obedience and vassalage to crown and church.

Oñate next turned his attention to establishing permanent quarters for his colony. Requiring the natives to vacate the pueblo of Ohke, he changed its name to San Juan de los Caballeros and moved his people in. When they needed more space, the Spaniards occupied the larger pueblo of Yunque, which they renamed San Gabriel. The Spaniards, having arrived too late in the year to plant crops, demanded food, blankets, skins, and firewood from the Puebloans, as their own supplies dwindled.

That autumn, Oñate traveled north up the Rio Grande Valley, convening councils with Pueblo leaders and administering the oath of vassalage as he went. The Franciscans accompanied him, building churches and establishing missions. Oñate then explored westward, looking for wealth to satisfy the demands of his colonists and to recoup his own fortune. In October, he reached Acoma pueblo, where, after the usual ceremony of swearing allegiance to king and church, the inhabitants were asked to give generously of their food, robes, and blankets. Oñate continued on to the Zuñi and Hopi pueblos. In early December, Juan de Zaldívar and thirty soldiers, following Oñate, arrived at Acoma and demanded to be provisioned, ignoring the Indians' pleas that they had nothing left to spare. When the Spaniards insisted, the Puebloans attacked, killing Zaldívar and twelve of his men.

Oñate vowed to avenge this serious blow to Spanish authority. At San Juan, planning the punishment of Acoma, he consulted the Franciscans. They agreed this was a just war under Spanish law, because the Puebloans, having sworn obedience and vassalage to the Spanish crown, were now royal subjects who were guilty of treason. On January 21, 1599, Juan's brother, Vicente Zaldívar Mendoza, and his forces reached Acoma, where they found the Puebloans ready to defend themselves. Fighting with arrows and stones, the natives were no match for men armed with guns. After two days of bitter fighting, Acoma was defeated, with more than eight hundred dead. The pueblo was destroyed and some five hundred men, women, and children were captured. Those who did not immediately surrender were dragged from their hiding places and killed.

On February 12, Oñate himself decreed the punishment of the captives: All men more than twenty-five years of age had one foot cut off and served twenty years in slavery; all men between the ages of twelve and twenty-five years and all women over twelve years of age served twenty years in slavery; the old men and women were given to the Querechos (Plains Apaches) as slaves; the children less than twelve years of age were given to Fray Martínez and to Vicente Zaldívar Mendoza. Two Hopi men who were visiting Acoma when the battle began had their right hands cut off and were sent back to the Hopi as an object lesson to those pueblos. To discourage future rebellions, the Spaniards carried out the sentences of

mutilation in public at several different pueblos. Evidently, this was as effective as Oñate had planned; it would be eighty years before the Puebloans dared to organize another rebellion against Spanish rule. —*LouAnn Faris Culley*

ADDITIONAL READING:

Fergusson, Erna. *New Mexico: A Pageant of Three Peoples*. Albuquerque: University of New Mexico Press, 1973. Relies greatly on *Historia de la Nueva Mexico*, published in 1610 by Gaspar de Villagrá, a member of Oñate's expedition.

John, Elizabeth A. *Storms Brewed in Other Men's Worlds*. College Station: Texas A&M Press, 1975. The most complete and detailed account of the expedition. Explains Oñate's eventual fall from official favor.

Minge, Ward Alan. *Acoma: Pueblo in the Sky*. Albuquerque: University of New Mexico Press, 1976. A less detailed account of the expedition than John's, but includes the trial text of Oñate's sentence upon the Acoma survivors.

Sando, Joe S. *The Pueblo Indians*. San Francisco: Indian Historian Press, 1976. Summarizes the facts of the expedition, and explains the Spanish system of *encomienda*—a way of exacting taxes from the Puebloans.

Terrell, John Upton. *Pueblos, Gods, and Spaniards*. New York: Dial Press, 1973. Provides a brief summary of the expedition and a detailed account of the Battle of Acoma.

SEE ALSO: 1540, Coronado's Expedition; 1542, Settlement of Alta California; 1632, Zuñi Rebellion; 1680, Pueblo Revolt.

1603 ■ CHAMPLAIN'S VOYAGES: *the founding of Quebec, exploration of Canada and New England, and early records of a vast, uncharted land*

DATE: March 15, 1603-December 25, 1635
LOCALE: Eastern Canada and New England
CATEGORIES: Canadian history; Exploration and discovery; Settlements
KEY FIGURES:
Samuel de Champlain (c. 1567-1635), explorer, cartographer, and founder of Quebec
Pierre du Gua, sieur de Monts (c. 1560-1630), colonizer who helped establish the first French settlement in America
Henry IV (1553-1610), king of France and Champlain's personal and financial supporter
François Pont-Gravé (died 1629), commander of and investor in several voyages, and commander of Quebec
SUMMARY OF EVENT. At the end of the sixteenth century, distracted by civil war, France had not made any significant attempt to develop its claims in the New World for more than six decades. In March, 1603, with the help of funds from King Henry IV of France, Samuel de Champlain traveled as an observer to eastern Canada with François Pont-Gravé. Champlain previously had traveled to the West Indies and Mexico as

CHAMPLAIN AND FRENCH EXPLORATIONS, 1603-1616

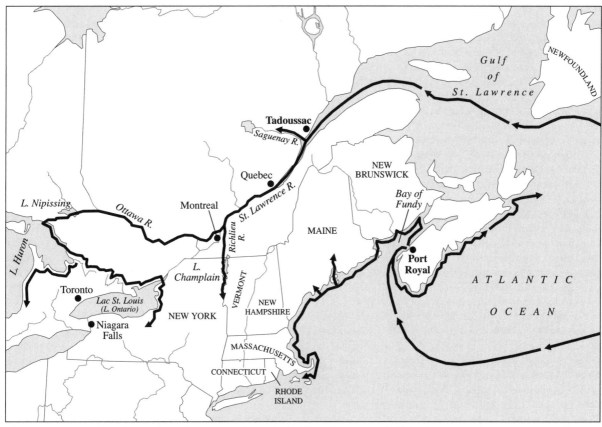

The greatest French explorer of North America, Samuel de Champlain, spent half his lifetime making numerous voyages to the regions surrounding the Gulf of St. Lawrence and the St. Lawrence River. He founded the city of Quebec, traversed the rapids near Montreal that had barred the way to the Great Lakes, and spent months with Algonquian and Huron Indians during his explorations of the lands near Lakes Huron and Ontario.

passenger on his uncle's ship. In May, 1603, Champlain and Pont-Gravé landed in Tadoussac, Canada, and sailed up the St. Lawrence River to explore the surrounding areas. In June, Champlain passed the future site of the city of Quebec. He was immediately impressed with the location because it was well suited for shipping and military defense; its close proximity to friendly Canadian Indians was another advantage. He later suggested the area as a site for the first permanent settlement in Canada. Champlain and Pont-Gravé also explored the Richelieu River area, where they were met by Anadabajin, leader of the Montagnais Indians. The French became friends and trading partners with the Montagnais, trading with them for furs and cured fish before starting home in August, 1603.

Champlain returned to France with fish, furs, and descriptions of the lands and wildlife he had seen. He wrote about the voyage in *Des Sauvages, ou, Voyage de Samuel Champlain, de Brouage* (1603). In it, he described the natives, lands, and rivers he had seen in Canada. His talents for drawing and cartography were demonstrated in intricate maps of the regions he had explored and pictures of indigenous people and

culture he had witnessed. Champlain's descriptions of the Montagnais were the first detailed information Europeans had received of Montagnais dress, tools, religious ceremonies, hunting practices, and dance.

Champlain returned to the New World as a geographer in April, 1604. This voyage was under the command of Pierre du Gua, sieur de Monts, who also financed the expedition. In May, the party landed in Nova Scotia. Champlain traveled up and down the Atlantic coastline, drawing maps and searching for possible sites for a permanent settlement. Champlain explored the Bay of Fundy to Sainte Croix Island and southward along the coast of New England to the Penobscot River, Cape Cod, and Boston Harbor.

In 1608, Champlain returned to Canada from France to establish a permanent settlement. On July 3, he planted the French flag in the soil of the site of Quebec, Canada, which became Canada's first successful permanent settlement. Champlain and his men set about felling trees, clearing ground, and building storehouses and cellars. He made friends and allies with the Huron and Algonquian Indians in the area. The Huron,

Algonquian, and Montagnais tribes all had a common enemy in the Five Tribes of the Iroquois Confederacy. The three tribes asked Champlain and his men to demonstrate their loyalty by accompanying them in a campaign against the Iroquois. Champlain agreed, and so it was with a war party of sixty Indians that he reached the lake named after him, Lake Champlain, in July of 1609. Champlain shot two Mohawk chiefs on this victorious campaign, thus making enemies of the large and powerful Iroquois Confederacy, who would later side with the British against the French. The Hurons, Algonquians, and Montagnais continued to assist the French in trade and friendship.

Champlain returned to the New World in the spring of 1611, under the leadership of Captain Pont-Gravé. Finding the Quebec settlement progressing well, he traveled up the St. Lambert River, past the La Chine rapids, and explored the surrounding area. Champlain made plans to establish another permanent settlement at Montreal; however, his plans were not carried out until 1642, seven years after his death. It was after this voyage that Champlain wrote *Les Voyages du Sieur de Champlain Xaintongeois* (1613), in which he shared his discoveries with the world in an attempt to encourage future investment, settlement, and exploration.

Champlain returned to Canada in March, 1613. He checked on the settlers at Quebec and traveled up the Ottawa River, through numerous rapids, to explore the Muskrat and Lower Allumette Lakes. Back in France in September of that year, Champlain wrote *La Quatrième Voyage du Sr. de Champlain* (1613), in which he described his trip up the Ottawa River. He used his writings to encourage new investors in the New World. Investors were given exclusive rights to the fur trade in the St. Lawrence River area for eleven years. In return, Champlain received a salary. Investors would arrange for six families to move to Canada to begin a permanent population there. Champlain also agreed to take four Franciscan priests with him to the New World in an attempt to convert the Native Americans to Catholicism.

In 1615, Champlain again moved up the Ottawa River to Lower Allumette Lake and the mouth of the Mattawa River to Lake Nipissing. He traveled up the French River into Lake Huron. He later landed near Penetanguishene, where he discovered numerous Huron Indian settlements. He went from village to village, meeting and gathering tribesmen for a war party against the Iroquois. With several hundred Hurons in his party, Champlain traveled west to Lake Ontario. They then moved southward to Lake Oneida, where the party came upon the Onondaga tribe at an Iroquois fortress. Champlain and the Huron chiefs immediately attacked the fortification and laid siege. However, they were unable to take the stronghold, and Champlain was wounded in the leg and knee in the battle. On their journey homeward to Quebec, the Huron Indians stopped for a month to hunt deer. Champlain later described the intricacies of their deer hunt and other experiences in *Voyages et descouvertures faites en la Nouvelle France* (1619). During the winter of 1615-1616, Champlain spent four months with the Huron tribe. By the time he returned to Quebec, Champlain had explored large undiscovered regions of interior lands surrounding the Great Lakes.

French friars were finding it impossible to convert the Native American populations to Catholicism. Champlain contended that a permanent French population of at least three hundred families was needed to demonstrate the believed benefits of French civilization to the Canadian Indians. He encouraged the building of more trading posts in Canada, the development of fisheries, and the exploitation of Canada's mineral wealth of iron, lead, and silver. Champlain warned that failure to develop these areas might mean losing French holdings in the New World to the English or Dutch.

On successive trips to the New World, Champlain monitored the progress of the habitation at Quebec and encouraged improvements. He brought cattle, oxen, seeds, building materials, and necessary annual provisions. He encouraged settlers to till their own fields instead of depending on unreliable annual shipments for their survival. Champlain also was called upon to settle disputes among the tribal allies, the French, and the Iroquois. In 1632, Champlain published *Les Voyages en la Nouvelle France Occidentale*, detailing his most recent travels and experiences.

Champlain returned to Canada for the last time in 1633. He brought permanent colonists and saw to the rebuilding of Quebec, which had been burned down during an English attack. He reestablished trade with the Montagnais and Algonquians, who had been trading with the English, and built trading posts on Richelieu Island and Sainte-Croix. Samuel de Champlain died in Canada on Christmas Day in 1635. His contributions remained in the settlement of the territories he explored and the many descriptions of Canadian lands and Native American culture that he left. —*Leslie Stricker*

ADDITIONAL READING:

Biggar, Henry P., ed. *The Works of Samuel de Champlain*. Toronto: The Champlain Society, 1922-1936. An eight-volume English translation of Champlain's works.

Grant, W. L., ed. *Voyages of Samuel de Champlain 1604-1618*. New York: Barnes & Noble Books, 1959. An English translation of Champlain's *Voyages*.

Lanctot, Gustave. *A History of Canada*. Cambridge, Mass.: Harvard University Press, 1963. Canadian history from a French historian. Focuses on the last ten years of Champlain's work.

Morison, Samuel Eliot. *Samuel de Champlain: Father of New France*. Boston: Little, Brown, 1972. Focuses on Champlain's voyages and personal life.

Parkman, Francis. *Pioneers of France in the New World*. Vol. 1 in *France and England in North America*. New York: Literary Classics of the United States, 1983. Canadian history by an English historian noted for his narrative style.

SEE ALSO: 1500, Iroquois Confederacy; 1534, Cartier and Roberval Search for a Northwest Passage; 1610, Hudson Explores Hudson Bay; 1627, Company of New France Is Chartered; 1670, Hudson's Bay Company Is Chartered; 1673, French Explore the Mississippi Valley.

1607 ■ Jamestown Is Founded: *the first commercially viable British settlement in North America and the beginning of the Virginia colony*

Date: May 14, 1607
Locale: Jamestown, Virginia
Category: Settlements
Key figures:

Christopher Newport (died 1617), commander of the first voyagers to Jamestown

Opechancanough (c. 1544-1644), chief of the Pamunkey Indians and Powhatan's half brother

Pocahontas or *Matoaka* (c. 1596-1617), daughter of Powhatan and wife of tobacco planter John Rolfe

Powhatan, also known as *Wahunsonacock* (c. 1550-1618), leader of the Powhatan Confederacy

John Smith (1580-1631), second president of the council in Jamestown

Thomas Smythe (1558?-1625), head of the Virginia Company from 1609

George Somers (1554-1610), commander of the ill-fated fleet of 1609 to Jamestown

Thomas West, Lord De La Warr (1577-1618), first governor of Virginia

Edward Maria Wingfield (1560?-1613?), first president of the council in Jamestown

Summary of event. In 1605, England and Spain had finally made peace, and in England capital was accumulating and commerce flourishing. Captain George Waymouth had returned from a voyage to Nantucket and Maine to explore a possible refuge for Catholics. Five Abenaki Indians whom Waymouth had brought with him and a glowing account of the expedition by Catholic scholar James Rosier had attracted much attention.

Their interest having been aroused, Sir John Popham, Lord Chief Justice of England, and Sir Ferdinando Gorges, both powerful members of the mercantile community, petitioned the Crown in the name of a group of adventurers for a charter incorporating two companies, one of London and one of Plymouth. The patent issued on April 10, 1606, granted them the territory known as Virginia, located between latitudes 34° and 41° north. The London Company was authorized to settle between latitudes 34° and 41° north, and the Plymouth Company, between latitudes 45° and 38° north, but neither was to settle within one hundred miles of the other. Because of Sir Walter Raleigh's explorations in the Chesapeake Bay area and Waymouth's investigations in Maine, the adventurers knew exactly what to request.

The absence, before 1618, of the official minutes of the Virginia Company, as the two companies were jointly called, has forced historians to turn to fragmentary and often biased sources, including the sometimes conflicting accounts of Captain John Smith in his memoirs and some settlers' incomplete journal entries. However, enough facts have been ascertained that a basic chronology can be reconstructed.

On December 20, 1606, the Virginia Company of London dispatched for America three ships, the *Godspeed*, the *Discovery*, and the *Susan Constant*, carrying 144 men and boys. Captain Christopher Newport was to be in charge until the expedition reached land. After making landfall on the southern shore of Chesapeake Bay on April 26, 1607, and following a brief skirmish with local members of the Powhatan Confederacy, the 105 survivors turned up the Powhatan (renamed the James) River to search for a favorable site to settle. On May 14, they disembarked on a peninsula extending from the north shore, where they would begin to build James Fort, later called "James Towne." Although the area was low and marshy, it was beautiful, seemed defensible, and provided anchorage for deepwater vessels. The great James River offered the possibility of penetration into the interior for exploring and trading with natives.

Only when the settlers had landed and opened the sealed box containing their instructions did they learn the names of their council, the governing body that had been appointed by the Virginia Company. This council would prove an inferior mode of governance: Its seven members quickly disagreed with one another (there had been contention, for example, over their settlement site), and a considerable number of the other settlers were headstrong adventurers. This lack of concentrated authority in Virginia resulted in bickering and the formation of factions. The strong if near-dictatorial leadership of Smith, the second president of the council, held the settlement together after fear and suspicion led to the ousting of the council's weaker first president, Edward Maria Wingfield.

More pressing than matters of government was the necessity of providing for the settlers' physical needs. Upon their arrival in America, they had divided themselves into three groups: the first was to concentrate on construction and fortifications; the second was to plant crops and keep watch downriver; and the third was to explore the surrounding area. Although the company hoped to find a water route through the continent to the South Sea and encouraged search for minerals, there was little time for such activity. Establishment of a settlement and development of trade were more urgent.

The accomplishment of both these aims depended on the amicable relations with native peoples, members of the great Powhatan Confederacy of about thirty tribes. The Powhatans occupied most of Tidewater Virginia south of the Potomac River. The naïve settlers, rather than meeting the simpleminded "lovable savages" touted by the London promoters, soon realized that these people were both sophisticated and highly wary of the English intrusion into their domain.

James Towne (not yet even a half-moon bunker) lay in the middle of Paspehege hunting grounds. On May 26 approximately two hundred Powhatans attacked the infant settlement, killing one or two and wounding more than a dozen—the first of many such skirmishes that would occur over the next several years. In mid-June, the confederacy's leader Wahunsona-cock (known as Powhatan) sent envoys from upriver to make peace and provide food for the now-starving travelers. In the fall, Smith undertook a reconnaissance trip and was detained by Powhatan's half brother Opechancanough, who delivered Smith to Powhatan. The famous story of Powhatan's mercy at the behest of his young daughter Pocahontas was Smith's fabrication some two decades after this episode; Powhatan more likely expected to bargain with the Europeans, knowing well that he had the upper hand in being able to supply them with food and hoping to strike a deal for weapons in return. Smith agreed but tricked the Indians who escorted him back to Jamestown into accepting trinkets in exchange for valuable corn. It was also during this time that the Indians had their first taste of aqua vitae, or 100-proof alcohol. Powhatan would continue to supply food (at times by force), punctuated by minor attacks on the settlers, during the settlement's early years until, in 1622, after repeated abuse at the hands of the English, he would mount a major uprising.

Returning to the settlement, Smith found disease, death, and dissension. The settlers had made little headway in building the storehouse and adequate shelter, and although the river was full of sturgeon and they knew that they must boil the water to make it potable, they were eating barley soaked in slimy, brackish water and dying of influenza, typhoid, and starvation. Although the strict discipline of John Smith's council presidency and the addition of more immigrants improved conditions at the settlement, the first two years must be judged as disappointing. Not only had the settlers failed in the basics of healthy survival; they had also failed to return commercially valuable resources to England.

The backers in London therefore embarked upon a more ambitious program to be financed on a joint-stock basis. Having negotiated a new charter, the Virginia Company, under the leadership of Sir Thomas Smythe, launched a campaign for financial support. Sixteen hundred persons were to emigrate to Virginia on two great expeditions in the summer of 1609. The joint-stock arrangement would allow a pooling of labor with common stock, since each person's migration to America was counted as equal to one share of stock. By this means a community of interest was developed between the adventurer in England and the colonist. The new charter of 1609 abolished the royal council and placed control in the hands of the council of the company. A governor with absolute authority was to replace the local council in the colony.

The first great contingent of settlers set out on May 15, 1609, with Sir George Somers in command. Ironically, the ship carrying the leaders was blown away from the others in a hurricane and foundered in Bermuda, its passengers not arriving in Jamestown until nearly a year after they had set out. When the other ships arrived in Virginia, Smith refused to give up his post as council president, though he yielded leadership after a famous accident (some have speculated conspiracy) in which he was injured when his gunpowder pouch ignited and exploded.

The departure of Smith for England and the arrival of almost four hundred new settlers in weakened condition placed considerable strain on the economy of the colony. When the leaders of the expedition arrived the following summer, they found only sixty settlers still living, with the settlement in ruins about them. Famine, disease, and attacks by Indians had left even the few survivors on the brink of death or reduced to a subhuman existence that sometimes involved cannibalism. Since the new arrivals were without sufficient provisions, the settlers abandoned hope of maintaining the colony and prepared to leave for England by way of Newfoundland.

As the disheartened colonists were sailing down the James River, miraculously they met Thomas West (Lord De La Warr), their new governor, coming upriver with a year's provisions. Lord De La Warr ordered the colonists to return and reestablish the settlement. The new leadership, with additional supplies and manpower, gave the colonists courage to continue.

In 1612, John Rolfe, who would eventually marry Pocahontas, discovered Virginia's "gold" when he planted the first West Indies tobacco in its soil. Used initially for medicinal purposes, the new American commodity was soon being smoked "for fun" by Europeans—an "aqua vitae" made of smoke. —*Warren M. Billings, updated by Christina J. Moose*

ADDITIONAL READING:

Bridenbaugh, Carl. *Jamestown: 1544-1699.* New York: Oxford University Press, 1980. This brief (200-page) history emphasizes the "people—red, white, and black—who lived on or near Jamestown Island." Four illustrations; index.

Hawke, David Freeman, ed. *Captain John Smith's History of Virginia: A Selection.* Indianapolis: Bobbs-Merrill, 1970. Reprints sections on Virginia from Smith's *Generall Historie of Virginia, New-England, and the Summer Isles.* A major primary source, if suspect given its discrepancies with Smith's more contemporaneous account in his *True Relation.*

Hume, Ivor Noël. *The Virginia Adventure: Roanoke to James Towne.* New York: Alfred A. Knopf, 1994. Historical archaeologist Hume provides an extremely detailed account of the settling of Virginia, comparing primary documents as well as physical evidence and deftly teasing out fact from legend. Black-and-white illustrations, index.

Josephy, Alvin M., Jr. *500 Nations: An Illustrated History of the North American Indians.* New York: Alfred A. Knopf, 1994. Powhatan and Smith are covered in chapter 4 of this lavishly illustrated history of North America from its original occupants' viewpoint.

Morgan, Edmund S. *American Slavery, American Freedom: The Ordeal of Colonial Virginia.* New York: W. W. Norton, 1975. Early chapters include an excellent description of the difficulties faced by Smith and the other settlers.

Rountree, Helen C. *Pocahontas's People: The Powhatan Indians of Virginia Through Four Centuries.* Norman: University of Oklahoma Press, 1990. Written by an ethnohistorian and anthropologist, this is one of the best studies of Jamestown and the settlement's relationship to the Powhatan Confederacy.

Vaughan, Alden T. *American Genesis: Captain John Smith and the Founding of Virginia.* Boston: Little, Brown, 1975. A short, balanced biography of Smith combined with a detailed history of Virginia from Smith's departure in 1609 until his death in 1631.

SEE ALSO: 1570's, Powhatan Confederacy; 1619, First General Assembly of Virginia; 1622, Powhatan Wars.

1610 ▪ HUDSON EXPLORES HUDSON BAY:
establishment of the main water route to northwestern Canada for trade and settlement

DATE: Beginning June, 1610
LOCALE: Hudson Bay, Canada
CATEGORIES: Canadian history; Exploration and discovery
KEY FIGURES:
Henry Hudson (1560's?-1611), English explorer and navigator
Martin Frobisher (1535?-1594), the explorer thought to be the first European to sail into Hudson Strait
Médard Chouart des Groseilliers (1625-1698), explorer and cofounder of the Hudson's Bay Company
Robert Juet, mate aboard the Discovery and leader of the mutiny against Hudson
Pierre Esprit Radisson (c. 1636-c. 1710), fur trader, explorer, and cofounder of the Hudson's Bay Company
Rupert (1619-1682), prince of Bavaria, cousin of Charles II of England, an early supporter of the Hudson's Bay Company

SUMMARY OF EVENT. On April 27, 1610, Henry Hudson and a crew of twenty-three men, including his son, sailed the ship *Discovery* from London to search for the Northwest Passage to Asia. Bold and determined, Hudson had made several earlier attempts to locate the Northwest Passage. Among these was a voyage in 1608 for the Dutch, which resulted in the exploration of the Hudson River when his crew lost confidence in his plans to sail through Hudson Strait. On this his final voyage to the New World, Hudson established the existence of Hudson Bay; the Hudson Strait, which is the main conduit to Hudson Bay; and James Bay, the southern appendix to Hudson Bay. Others, including Martin Frobisher, had made earlier, less conclusive attempts to explore the territory, but Hudson was the most successful.

Over the next three months, Hudson and his crew sailed north from London past Iceland and Greenland, arriving in Ungava Bay in June, 1610. They entered the strait and were in the bay proper at the end of June. By September, they had pushed south and begun to explore James Bay, still desperately persisting in the belief that they could find the Northwest Passage. Following the eastern coast of James Bay, the decision was made to winter on the southern shores, near the mouth of the Rupert River. Hudson and crew passed an un-

comfortable and fractious winter, troubled by too few provisions and unexpected cold. The arrival of spring found the crew uncertain of Hudson's leadership and unwilling to trust his promises of an immediate return to England. Mutiny occurred in June, 1611, when Hudson, his son, and seven sailors, including several sick crewmen, were placed in an open boat and set adrift. Presumed dead, Hudson and the others were never seen again. Only eight of Hudson's crew returned to England six months later, carrying with them Hudson's records, including a fragment of his logbook. Four of these men were tried and acquitted by the Admiralty for their part in the mutiny.

Several times between 1612 and 1616, the *Discovery* returned to Hudson Bay, with crews that included some of Hudson's men, to retrace Hudson's route, confirm his findings, and look for survivors. Other explorers—Bylot and Foxe (1631) and Thomas James (1631)—would follow Hudson's route, trying yet again to find the elusive passage to Asia. However, permanent European settlement of the area would not begin for more than fifty years. The bare and heavily forested regions of the Canadian Shield would prove somewhat inhospitable to Europeans, and their main settlements continued to be in the area of the St. Lawrence Valley and the coastal regions to the east. Native settlement in the area of Hudson Bay, however, was fairly extensive. Ringing Hudson Bay to the north and on the east and west sides were the Inuit; to the south, the Cree, an Algonquian people; to the west, the Chipewyan. The company undoubtedly encountered native peoples on this voyage, especially the Cree, who were in the region where the company camped for the winter. Hudson's hopes to rely on native peoples for food through the winter failed, which is why food was so scarce in the 1610-1611 winter. In addition, it seems that the crew was fatally attacked while retreating through the strait after the mutiny, with the loss of several crewmen.

Ultimately, the English, drawn by the fur trade, would settle Hudson Bay. While the fur trade had begun in the early part of the sixteenth century as a subsidiary to European coastal fishing, by century's end the seemingly insatiable European demand for furs guaranteed the independence of the trapping industry. Competition between the Dutch and the French in the St. Lawrence region proved the profitability of the industry but also left some areas nearly depleted of animals. The English, eager to stake their share in the fur trade, sought their opportunity in the northwest. In 1688, an English trading post was established at the opening of the Rupert River by Médard Chouart des Groseilliers, who, with Pierre Radisson, sought further funding to develop the venture. The venture was offered first to the French, who declined, as their settlement farther south along the St. Lawrence River was firmly established. A joint stock trading company then was formed in England in 1665. On May 2, 1670, the Hudson's Bay Company received its charter from the English crown. To assure the English presence against the French, the company received a monopoly to trade furs in all the territory drained by rivers that

HUDSON'S VOYAGE OF 1610-1611

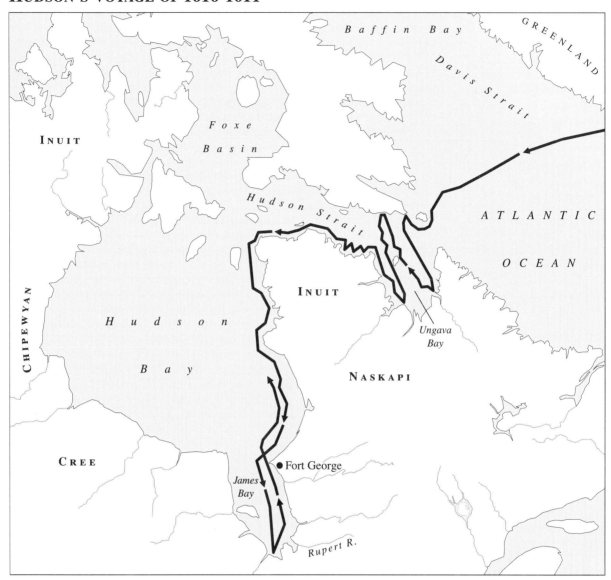

On April 27, 1610, Henry Hudson and a crew of twenty-three men sailed from London to search for the Northwest Passage to Asia, arriving in Ungava Bay in June, 1610. They entered Hudson Strait, the bay proper, and followed the eastern coast of James Bay, spending the cold winter on the southern shores near the mouth of the Rupert River. The crew, uncertain of Hudson's leadership, mutinied in June, 1611. Hudson, his son, and seven sailors were placed in an open boat and set adrift, never to be seen again.

flowed into Hudson Bay. The area covered by the monopoly was named Rupert's Land for Prince Rupert, an early supporter of the venture and the first governor of the company. The Hudson's Bay Company was the primary agent for both settlement and government in Rupert's Land for almost two centuries.

The Hudson's Bay Company was unique among contemporaneous trading companies in the degree of its organization and self-sufficiency, both traceable to its remoteness from London, where the company was chartered. Basic policy and procedures were set in London; an elected governor acted for the company in Rupert's Land. A series of posts was built at the mouths of important rivers—part military fortress, part trade town—led by a chief factor aided by a council of officers. The presence of the company and its success in securing pelts for the European market seem to have raised the ire of the French fur traders along the St. Lawrence River. For fifty years, the French traders moved westward and upward in their search for beaver and other animals, encroaching on lands claimed by the company. Several times, the French campaigned to capture the English posts as part of their attempt to claim all of North America.

In 1713, the French were forced to recognize English claims to the area as part of the Treaty of Utrecht. The French government completely withdrew from the competition in 1763, when it ceded its holdings in North America at the close of the French and Indian War. Taking its place in competition for furs came an English trading company based in Montreal, the North West Company. Established in the 1760's by Scottish immigrants to Canada, in 1790 the North West Company challenged the Hudson's Bay Company by attempting to end the latter's monopoly. By establishing inland posts and exploring the western regions, the North West Company gained the upper hand. The Hudson's Bay Company was forced to do the same, and a rivalry for land, loyalty, and furs ensued. The competition culminated in a merger of the two companies in 1821, engineered and approved by the British Parliament, which furthermore extended the territory covered by the original monopoly. Rupert's Land remained in private hands until 1869, when it was claimed by Canada.

—*Kelley Graham*

ADDITIONAL READING:

Davis, Richard C., ed. *Rupert's Land: A Cultural Tapestry.* Waterloo, Ont.: Wilfrid Laurier University Press for the Calgary Institute for the Humanities, 1988. Articles covering a variety of subjects relating to exploration and trade in Rupert's Land.

Edwards, Philip. *Last Voyages: Cavendish, Hudson, Ralegh.* Oxford, England: Oxford University Press, 1988. A narrative of Hudson's final voyage, using contemporary accounts.

Francis, Daniel, and Toby Morantz. *Partners in Fur: A History of the Eastern James Bay, 1600-1870.* Kingston, Ont.: McGill-Queens University Press, 1983. A study of the structure of the European fur empire and its impact on native peoples.

Krech, Shepard, III, ed. *The Subarctic Fur Trade: Native Social and Economic Adaptations.* Vancouver: University of British Columbia Press, 1984. Detailed articles on the effects of the fur trade from the seventeenth century onward.

Stewart, Gordon. *History of Canada Before 1867.* Washington, D.C.: Association for Canadian Studies in the United States, 1989. Presents a detailed picture of conflicts and issues in early Canadian history. Concise and historiographically current.

Woodcock, George. *A Social History of Canada.* Markham, Ont.: Viking, 1988. An introductory work on the history of the people of Canada, including the native peoples.

SEE ALSO: 1576, Frobisher's Voyages; 1603, Champlain's Voyages; 1626, Algonquians "Sell" Manhattan Island; 1627, Company of New France Is Chartered; 1664, British Conquest of New Netherland; 1670, Hudson's Bay Company Is Chartered.

1619 ■ FIRST GENERAL ASSEMBLY OF VIRGINIA: *the earliest manifestation of representative government in the British colonies*

DATE: July 30-August 4, 1619
LOCALE: Jamestown, Virginia
CATEGORY: Government and politics
KEY FIGURES:
Samuel Argall (c. 1572-c. 1620), deputy governor of Virginia, 1617-1619
John Pory (1570-1636), secretary of the Virginia colony and speaker of the General Assembly during its first session
Edwin Sandys (1561-1629), treasurer of the London Company, who instructed Yeardley to call the first General Assembly
George Yeardley (1587?-1627), governor of Virginia, who presided over the first session of the General Assembly

SUMMARY OF EVENT. The first permanent English colony in America was established at Jamestown, Virginia, in 1607. By 1618, the colony had neither prospered greatly nor realized the full expectations of the London Company, which had been responsible for its founding. Twice before 1618, the London Company had been reorganized in unsuccessful efforts to make the Virginia venture turn a profit, but it was again on the verge of bankruptcy. In 1617, as an inducement to settlement, the company had sanctioned the introduction of private land tenure and the creation of particular plantations, which had resulted in widely scattered settlements and confused land titles. This emergence of private landowners soon made possible and feasible the establishment of a representative assembly, but the colony's economic base was still insecure. The colonists grew more restive, especially after 1617, when Sir Samuel Argall became deputy governor and returned the colony to stricter discipline by rigorously enforcing the *Lawes, Divine, Morall, and Martiall*, which had been adopted by the Virginia Company in 1612 and provided for partial government by martial law.

Against this background, the London Company resolved anew in 1618 to revitalize its Virginia venture. Led by Sir Edwin Sandys, the company embarked on an ambitious course of action that aimed at a comprehensive reorganization of the entire colonial operation. The company embodied its plans in a series of instructions and commissions, the so-called Great Charter, which was designed to reform land tenure, improve local administration, and replace the *Lawes, Divine, Morall, and Martiall* with English common law and a more representative and resident government.

In 1619, Governor Argall was accused of self-interested dealings, including his being responsible for the importation of the first African slaves into Virginia, which had put the Virginia Company heavily in debt. Argall was relieved of his duties by the London Company; he escaped arrest only by fleeing Virginia, with most of his wealth, before the arrival of his replacement. The new governor, Sir George Yeardley, was instructed to call an assembly consisting of himself, a council of state appointed by the London Company, and burgesses elected by the freemen of the colony. The assembly would meet not more than once a year, except on "very extraordinary and important occasions." It would serve as a court of justice, and it was to have the power to enact such general laws and ordinances for the colony's welfare as should be deemed necessary. These laws were to be subject to a gubernatorial veto and to review by the London Company. The legal name for the new assembly was "The Treasurer and Company of Adventurers and Planters of the City of London, for the First Colony in Virginia."

Following his arrival in Jamestown, Yeardley issued a call for the assembly, and on July 30, 1619, the first meeting of a representative legislative body in the New World convened in the church in Jamestown. This church, measuring only fifty by twenty feet, had been built in 1617 by Argall to replace one that had collapsed. It was apparently situated along the James River, outside the protective walls of James Fort. The assembly was composed of the governor, six councilors, and twenty-two burgesses—two from each of eleven settlements (plantations, "hundreds," and towns). The burgesses had been elected by the votes of all freemen who were seventeen years of age or older. After selecting John Pory (secretary of the colony and one of the councilors) as Speaker and taking the necessary oaths of allegiance and supremacy, the General Assembly proceeded to its business.

After deliberating the qualifications of its members, a tradition followed by the later Congress of the United States, two members were rejected pending clarification of the patents from the London Company. Beginning their legislative work, the assembly adopted several revisions of the Great Charter which the company suggested. It then enacted a series of laws dealing with relations with the Indians, the dress and conduct of the settlers, church attendance, and measures to promote certain industries, including flax, hemp, silk, and wine. With the completion of the legislative work, the assembly switched to a court of justice and resolved several criminal cases.

This first session of the General Assembly was remarkably short, lasting only six days. General Yeardley—"by reason of extream heat, both paste and likely to ensue," which had apparently caused the illness of several burgesses and the governor himself—ordered a review of all they had done and then adjourned on August 4, 1619. The next session was scheduled for March 1, 1620.

Despite the brevity of the meeting, the General Assembly of Virginia had made an important beginning. It had ushered in a new era in colonial government and had transformed Virginia from a plantation colony, supported and governed by a trading company largely for profit, into a self-supporting and partially self-governing political community. Although the assembly would undergo modifications in its functions and its right to exist would be challenged after the London Company lost its

charter in 1625, that first meeting in July, 1619, established the precedent for the development of representative political institutions in British North America. However, this House of Burgesses, as the General Assembly is sometimes called, did not represent a radical departure from European political institutions. It was basically the transplanting to America of the traditional form of representative government.

Although its legality was questioned when the Virginia Company was dissolved in 1624 and Virginia became a royal colony controlled directly by the king, the General Assembly survived and nurtured the elusive goal of self-government until it bore fruit in 1776.

—Warren M. Billings, updated by Glenn L. Swygart

ADDITIONAL READING:

Andrews, Matthew Page. *Virginia: The Old Dominion.* Richmond, Va.: Dietz Press, 1949. Chapters 7 and 8 detail the beginning and the early history of the General Assembly.

Bridenbaugh, Carl. *Jamestown: 1544-1699.* New York: Oxford University Press, 1980. Chapter 7 explains the problem of self-interest in relation to the establishment of the General Assembly.

Hume, Ivor Noël. *The Virginia Adventure: Roanoke to James Towne.* New York: Alfred A. Knopf, 1994. Chapter 13 covers the background for the first assembly, including the problems that made it necessary.

Morton, Richard L. *The Tidewater Period, 1607-1710.* Vol. 1 in *Colonial Virginia.* Chapel Hill: University of North Carolina Press, 1960. Chapter 4 describes the land distribution in 1617 that made possible a representative assembly.

Randolph, Edmund. *History of Virginia.* Charlottesville: University of Virginia Press, 1970. Chapter 3 covers events relating to the assembly from 1619 until the end of the Virginia Company in 1624.

Tyler, Lyon Gardiner, ed. *Narratives of Early Virginia, 1606-1625.* New York: Charles Scribner's Sons, 1907. Includes the proceedings of the assembly in 1619, taken from primary accounts, plus editorial comments. Also lists the original burgesses.

Willison, George F. *Behold Virginia: The Fifth Crown.* New York: Harcourt, Brace, 1952. Chapter 15 details problems in Virginia preceding the first meeting of the General Assembly.

SEE ALSO: 1607, Jamestown Is Founded; 1619, Africans Arrive in Virginia; 1622, Powhatan Wars.

1619 ■ AFRICANS ARRIVE IN VIRGINIA:
the beginnings of slavery in the British colonies

DATE: August 20, 1619
LOCALE: Point Comfort, Virginia
CATEGORY: African American history
SUMMARY OF EVENT. In August of 1619, a Dutch warship carrying "20 and odd" Africans landed at Point Comfort, Vir-

ginia. These Africans, the first to arrive in the British colonies, were probably put to work not as slaves but as servants. Neither the laws of the mother country nor the charter of the colony established the institution of slavery, although the system was developing in the British West Indies at the same time and was almost one hundred years old in the Spanish and Portuguese colonies. To be sure, African servants were discriminated against early on—their terms of service were usually longer than those of white servants, and they were the object of certain prohibitions that were not imposed on white servants—but in the early seventeenth century, at least some black servants, like their white counterparts, gained their freedom and even acquired some property. Anthony Johnson, who labored on Richard Bennett's Virginia plantation for almost twenty years after he arrived in Virginia in 1621, imported five servants in his first decade of freedom, receiving 250 acres on their headrights. Another former servant, Richard Johnson, obtained one hundred acres for importing two white servants in 1654. These two men were part of the small class of free blacks that existed in Virginia throughout the colonial period.

Such cases as the two Johnsons were rare by midcentury. As early as the 1640's, some African Americans were in servitude for life, and their numbers increased throughout the decade. In 1640, for example, in a court decision involving three runaway servants, the two who were white were sentenced to an additional four years of service, while the other, an African named John Punch, was ordered to serve his master "for the time of his natural Life." In the 1650's, some African servants were being sold for life, and the bills of sale indicated that their offspring would inherit slave status. Thus, slavery developed according to custom before it was legally established in Virginia.

Not until 1661 was chattel slavery recognized by statute in Virginia, and then only indirectly. The House of Burgesses passed a law declaring that children followed the status of their mothers, thereby rendering the system of slavery self-perpetuating. In 1667, the Virginia Assembly strengthened the system by declaring that in the case of children that are slaves by birth "the conferring of baptisme doth not alter the condition of a person as to his bondage or freedome; that divers masters, freed from this doubt, may more carefully endeavor the propagation of christianity." Until this time, Americans had justified enslavement of Africans on the grounds that they were "heathen" and had recognized conversion as a way to freedom. This act closed the last avenue to freedom, apart from formal emancipation, available to African American slaves. In 1705, Virginia established a comprehensive slave code that completed the gradual process by which most African Americans were reduced to the status of chattel. Slaves could not bear arms or own property, nor could they leave the plantation without written permission from the master. Capital punishment was provided for murder and rape; lesser crimes were punished by maiming, whipping, or branding. Special courts were established for the trials of slaves, who were barred from serving as witnesses, except in the

cases in which slaves were being tried for capital offenses.

In the other British colonies, the pattern was similar to that of Virginia. African racial slavery existed early in both Maryland and the Carolinas. Georgia attempted to exclude slavery at the time of settlement, but yielding to the protests of the colonists and the pressure of South Carolinians, the trustees repealed the prohibition in 1750. The Dutch brought slavery to the Middle Colonies early in the seventeenth century. The advent of British rule in 1664 proved to be a stimulus to the system in New York and New Jersey; but in Pennsylvania and Delaware, the religious objections of the Quakers delayed its growth somewhat and postponed legal recognition of slavery until the early eighteenth century. In seventeenth century New England, the status of Africans was ambiguous, as it was in Virginia. There were slaves in Massachusetts as early as 1638, possibly before, although slavery was not recognized by statute until 1641, which was the first enactment legalizing slavery anywhere in the British colonies. New England became heavily involved in the African slave trade, particularly after the monopoly of the Royal African Company was revoked in 1698. Like Virginia, all the colonies enacted slave codes in the late seventeenth or early eighteenth century, although the New England codes were less harsh than those of the Middle or Southern colonies. In all the colonies, a small class of free blacks developed alongside the institution of slavery, despite the fact that formal emancipation was restricted.

Slavery grew slowly in the first half of the seventeenth century. In 1625, there were twenty-three Africans in Virginia, most of whom probably were servants, not slaves. By midcentury, a decade before the statutory recognition of slavery, the black population was only three hundred, or 2 percent of the overall population of fifteen thousand. In 1708, there were twelve thousand African Americans and sixty-eight thousand whites. In a little more than fifty years, the black population had jumped from 2 percent to 15 percent of the total Virginia population. In the Carolinas, blacks initially made up 30 percent of the population, but within one generation outnumbered whites, making South Carolina the only mainland colony characterized by a black majority. In New England, blacks numbered only about one thousand out of a total population of ninety thousand. The eighteenth century would see the rapid development of the system of African racial slavery, particularly in the Southern colonies, where it became an integral part of the emerging plantation economy.

—Anne C. Loveland, updated by Laura A. Croghan

ADDITIONAL READING:

Davis, David Brion. *The Problem of Slavery in Western Culture*. Ithaca, N.Y.: Cornell University Press, 1966. The first in a trilogy examining slavery. Analyzes the sources of the ideas in Western culture that justified slavery.

Greene, Lorenzo J. *The Negro in Colonial New England, 1620-1776*. New York: Columbia University Press, 1942. Studies the condition of free and enslaved blacks in colonial New England and the region's participation in and economic dependence on the slave trade.

Jordan, Winthrop D. *White over Black: American Attitudes Toward the Negro, 1550-1812*. New York: W. W. Norton, 1968. Examines the British colonists' attitudes toward Africans, especially concerning their religions and color. Characterizes the establishment of slavery as an unthinking decision.

Morgan, Edmund S. *American Slavery, American Freedom: The Ordeal of Colonial Virginia*. New York: W. W. Norton, 1975. Argues that the switch to black slavery was intended to curb the growth of a discontented lower class by decreasing the number of freemen coming out of indentures and looking for land.

Morgan, Philip D. "British Encounters with Africans and African-Americans, Circa 1600-1780," In *Strangers Within the Realm: Cultural Margins of the First British Empire*, edited by Bernard Bailyn and Philip D. Morgan. Chapel Hill: University of North Carolina Press, 1991. Posits a useful model to distinguish between a slave-owning society and a slave society. In Virginia, this transition culminated in 1710, once slaves represented 20 percent of the population.

Vaughan, Alden T. "The Origins Debate: Slavery and Racism in Seventeenth Century Virginia." *Virginia Magazine of History and Biography* 97 (July, 1989): 311-354. Comprehensive examination of the scholarly literature on the origins of slavery and racism.

Wood, Peter H. *Black Majority: Negroes in Colonial South Carolina from 1670 Through the Stono Rebellion*. New York: Alfred A. Knopf, 1974. Recounts the establishment of the South Carolina colony and Africans' integral role in shaping its society and economy.

SEE ALSO: 1641, Massachusetts Recognizes Slavery; 1661, Virginia Slave Codes; 1671, Indian Slave Trade; 1712, New York City Slave Revolt.

1620 ■ PILGRIMS LAND AT PLYMOUTH: *establishment of the second major center of English colonization, founded on a search for religious freedom*

DATE: December 16, 1620
LOCALE: Plymouth, Massachusetts
CATEGORIES: Religion; Settlements
KEY FIGURES:
William Bradford (1590-1657), Puritan political leader and
   historian of the Plymouth Colony
William Brewster (1567-1644), Puritan layman and religious
   leader at Plymouth
John Carver (1576?-1621), first elected governor of the
   Plymouth Colony
Christopher Jones (1570?-1622), captain of the *Mayflower*
Massasoit (c. 1580-1661), grand sachem of the Wampanoags
Samoset (c. 1590-c. 1653), member of the Pemaquid tribe
   from Maine who aided the colonists at Plymouth
Squanto, also known as *Tisquantum* (c. 1580-1622), member

of the Pawtuxet tribe who served as an interpreter for the colonists
Miles Standish (1584-1656), non-Puritan leader of the
   Plymouth Colony

SUMMARY OF EVENT. In 1534, King Henry VIII of England separated the Christian church in England from the Roman Catholic church. About 1560, Queen Elizabeth I began creating a national Church of England by including the beliefs and practices of both the Roman Catholic church and the Protestants who were emerging from the Protestant Reformation throughout Europe. However, many Protestants sought to "purify" the new church of all Roman Catholic ideas. These Puritans, as they soon became known, included nonseparatists who desired to remain in a purified Church of England and separatists who saw no hope in remaining and favored complete separation.

By the early seventeenth century, the Separatist Puritans were being persecuted by the Church of England and the English government. In 1607, many of them, including a group called the Scrooby Congregation, fled to Holland to escape the persecution. Within a few years, conditions in Holland became unsatisfactory, and the Scrooby Congregation decided to seek a better home in the new land of America, where Jamestown had been established in 1607.

The Scrooby Congregation returned to England in 1620 and soon received permission to settle in the northern part of Virginia, where the actual boundaries had been surveyed only vaguely. After arranging financial backing from London merchants, the group secured two vessels, the *Speedwell* and the *Mayflower*, to transport them to their new home. For financial reasons, Pastor John Robinson and part of the congregation remained in England with plans to make the trip later, but Robinson died before he could do so. The major leaders of the initial group were two laymen, William Bradford and William Brewster.

The original departure date for America was August 5, 1620. However, this journey was aborted six days later, when the *Speedwell* proved unseaworthy for an Atlantic crossing. The *Mayflower* then sailed alone from Plymouth, in southwestern England, on September 6, 1620. Aboard, besides officers and crew, were 102 passengers. Because one died and one was born en route, they arrived in America with the same number. The passengers were divided into two categories. The thirty-five Separatist Puritans, led by Bradford and Brewster, were called Saints. The remaining sixty-seven passengers were mostly young men sent by the London merchants to guarantee the economic success of the colony. Led by Miles Standish, these were called Strangers.

After a rough voyage of sixty-four days in a leaky ship, the weary occupants of the *Mayflower* rejoiced to sight land on November 9. They had intended to land near the mouth of the Hudson River, then within the northern boundary of the Virginia Company's territory, in what later became New York City. However, the violent Atlantic winds had blown the vessel much farther north. The land they saw on that day was Cape

Cod, in what was to become Massachusetts. After a brief attempt to sail south failed because of the dangerous coastline, the leaders of the expedition decided to seek a landing site near Cape Cod. After five weeks of scouting and several landing parties, they chose an area near the western end of Cape Cod, which a 1614 map by Captain John Smith of Jamestown already had called Plymouth. It was here that the *Mayflower* landed on December 16, 1620. (This was the date by the Julian calendar then in use; by the present-day Gregorian calendar, the date would be December 26.) A large rock near the landing was later called Plymouth Rock.

Before disembarking from the *Mayflower*, realizing their need for unity and order, the leaders of the expedition drew up the Mayflower Compact. This historic document was then signed by all of the adult men; in it, they agreed to obey all laws passed by elected leaders. Some historians classify the Mayflower Compact as the beginning of democracy in America. John Carver was elected as the first governor of the colony.

Soon after their landing, the Pilgrims, as they later became known, were ravaged by disease and starvation, similar to the fate of the Jamestown colonists in 1607 but complicated by more severe weather. They built crude shelters but had to spend most of the winter aboard the *Mayflower*. By early spring, only about fifty of the colonists had survived. However, warm weather brought new hope, and when the *Mayflower* sailed for England in April, not one of the survivors was on board.

In March of 1621, the colonists were shocked when a young native walked into their village and addressed them in English. He identified himself as Samoset, a sachem (chief) of the Pemaquid tribe in what became the state of Maine. Samoset apparently had learned English from English fishermen along the coast. Two weeks later, Samoset returned with Tisquantum, better known as Squanto, a member of the Pawtuxet tribe, which occupied much of present-day Massachusetts and Rhode Island. In 1605, Squanto and two others of his tribe had been taken to England by English adventurers. He was returned to his tribe by Captain John Smith in 1614 during Smith's mapmaking exploration of New England. Squanto's nine years in England explain his fluency in the English language and made him a valuable interpreter between English colonists and native tribes. Before this service could be utilized, however, Squanto was again captured, this time by Thomas Hunt, a ship's captain left behind by John Smith. Squanto and about thirty other natives were sold as slaves in Spain. After escaping to England, Squanto was again returned to his home in 1619, only to find his tribe decimated by disease, probably smallpox brought by Europeans. The area that had been occupied by Squanto's tribe soon became the Plymouth Colony.

Samoset and Squanto soon arranged a meeting between Governor John Carver of Plymouth and Massasoit, grand sachem of the Wampanoags, who controlled southeastern Massachusetts. At this historic meeting, Carver and Massasoit signed a treaty of friendship that lasted until Massasoit died in

1661. Carver's contribution to Plymouth was strong but short. His wisdom helped guide the colonists through the first winter, but he died soon after his meeting with Massasoit and only four months after the landing. William Bradford was then elected governor, serving every year except five until his death in 1657.

During the summer of 1621, with the aid of their native friends and Miles Standish, the colonists planted, hunted, and fished. By fall, their harvest was so bountiful that Governor Bradford proclaimed a thanksgiving celebration. Their native friends were invited and about ninety, led by Massasoit, arrived with five deer.

From 1621 to 1630, the Plymouth Colony experienced slow but steady growth. Periodically, ships from England brought more settlers, including the rest of the Scrooby Congregation. The debts to the London merchants, with their exorbitant interest rates, were paid. By 1643, the colony had ten towns and a population of twenty-five hundred. It continued growing until 1691, when the Plymouth Colony became a part of the larger Massachusetts Bay Colony. In the course of that merger, the Separatist Puritans of Plymouth were absorbed by the more numerous nonseparatists, who had established the Puritan Congregational church while still officially recognizing the Church of England.
—*Glenn L. Swygart*

ADDITIONAL READING:

Bradford, William. *Of Plymouth Plantation: 1620-1647*. Edited with notes and introduction by Samuel Eliot Morison. New ed. New York: Alfred A. Knopf, 1966. A primary source by one of the major participants of the Plymouth Colony. Valuable appendices.

Caffrey, Kate. *The Mayflower*. Briarcliff Manor, N.Y.: Stein & Day, 1974. Provides background for the *Mayflower* and its historic voyage. Many appendices, including passenger lists and the Mayflower Compact. Maps and illustrations.

Dillon, Francis. *The Pilgrims*. New York: Doubleday, 1975. Presents the economic, political, and religious background of the Puritan exodus from England. Explains the difficulties of a frontier settlement.

Fiore, Jordan D., ed. *Mourt's Relation: A Journal of the Pilgrims of Plymouth*. Plymouth, Mass.: Plymouth Rock Foundation, 1985. A primary account of the early years at Plymouth, from accounts by Bradford and others. Illustrations and maps, including the 1614 map by John Smith.

Goodwin, John. *The Pilgrim Republic*. Boston: Houghton Mifflin, 1899. A historical review of the Plymouth Colony. Compares Plymouth with other New England colonies and explains Puritan beliefs.

Marshall, Cyril. *The Mayflower Destiny*. Harrisburg, Pa.: Stackpole Books, 1975. General description of the Pilgrims and by other Europeans. Covers life and customs at Plymouth and presents a political history of the colony.

Willison, George. *Saints and Strangers*. New York: Reynal and Hitchcock, 1945. Discusses the lives of both groups of Pilgrims at Plymouth and the trials of establishing a new colony. Appendix lists major leaders.

SEE ALSO: 1584, Lost Colony of Roanoke; 1607, Jamestown Is Founded; 1630, Great Puritan Migration; 1641, Massachusetts Recognizes Slavery; 1643, Confederation of the United Colonies of New England; 1662, Half-Way Covenant; 1686, Dominion of New England Forms.

1622 ■ POWHATAN WARS: *early friction between Virginia natives and European settlers escalates into a multigenerational conflict*

DATE: March 22, 1622-October, 1646
LOCALE: Virginia
CATEGORIES: Native American history; Wars, uprisings, and civil unrest
KEY FIGURES:

Opechancanough (c. 1544-1644), Powhatan's half brother and first Southeast tribal leader to stage a major offensive against European settlers

Pocahontas or *Matoaka* (c. 1596-1617), daughter of Powhatan and wife of tobacco planter John Rolfe

Powhatan, also known as *Wahunsonacock* (c. 1550-1618), leader of the Powhatan Confederacy

John Rolfe (1585-1622), settler who introduced the regular cultivation of West Indies tobacco in 1612

John Smith (1580-1631), Jamestown founder who established trade relations with the Powhatans

Thomas Smythe (1558?-1625), head of the Virginia Company

SUMMARY OF EVENT. In 1607, the twenty-eight horticulturally based, egalitarian Powhatan tribes residing between the Potomac River and the James River of the Chesapeake Bay region of Virginia were the first American Indians to encounter the arrival and development of the first permanent English settlement, Jamestown. The Powhatan Confederacy was composed of approximately nine thousand individuals who resided in perhaps two hundred palisaded, sedentary villages along the Chesapeake Bay. A major figure and leader of the confederation was Powhatan, a high priest and paramount chief, described by Captain John Smith as a tall, well-proportioned man. Powhatan had inherited the office of chief upon his father's death in the mid-1570's and began to expand his own power and authority through intimidation and even force over nonaligned contiguous tribal groups. Some Europeans considered Powhatan to be a king, while others referred to him as an emperor. The English addressed his daughter Pocahontas as "empress."

Although the success of the Euro-American colony was dependent upon the accommodation and often-needed assistance of the Powhatans, conflict commenced almost immediately and continued in varying degrees, ultimately forming a pervading pattern of hostile intergroup relationships between the two different cultures. There is no indication of why the powerful Powhatan chief did not annihilate the small group of early colonists, but he chose rather to save the English from famine on several occasions with generous contributions of food. In fact, Powhatan had his people instruct the early settlers about the traditional horticultural techniques and necessary predation skills for hunting and fishing. Despite continual encroachment by the settlers and an increase in the number of immigrants, the Powhatans continued to refrain from exercising any concerted military power against the English. Even Powhatan's half brother, Opechancanough, who had captured Captain John Smith, chose not to kill the Englishman, indicating Powhatan's respect for the settlement leader. There has been speculation that Powhatan may have believed the British would later assist him in consolidating other indigenous nonconference groups of the area into the confederation. It soon became apparent to Powhatan, and certainly to others of his tribe, that the primary intent of the English was to possess and control their once-traditional Indian lands.

This uncertain relationship between the Powhatan tribes and the English settlers was exacerbated by several factors: intermittent armed conflict; the dire effects of newly introduced diseases and alcohol upon the natives; a general sense of deprivation resulting from white encroachment; and the increased immigration of Europeans to Virginia. Because of intermarriage, it also was apparent that many English were attempting to assimilate the Powhatans into the Anglo culture. In 1614, Pocahontas, who had converted to the Anglican religion and been baptized as Lady Rebecca, married the very literate entrepreneur John Rolfe, who first introduced West Indian tobacco to the colonies in 1612. This celebrated marriage probably helped to ameliorate overt hostility, as did the realization that the number of Powhatan warriors had been reduced through armed conflict. Consequently, for eight years prior to the Powhatan Wars, relative peace existed between the English and the Powhatan people, undoubtedly a reflection of Powhatan's policy of accommodation. As early as 1609, he realized the potential threat of the English to his people, particularly with their firearms and edged steel weapons. Relations with the settlers generally deteriorated, and warfare intensified from 1609 to 1614. Powhatan claimed he wanted to live in peace, which he did from 1614 until April, 1618, when he died and his half brother, Opechancanough, succeeded him.

As paramount chief, Opechancanough attempted to continue the policy of accommodation, despite the colonists' increasing refusal to respect the Powhatans' unqualified sovereignty. With the realization that the English settlers were expanding their claim to and use of lands, and their constant attempts to proselytize and assimilate his people, Opechancanough began to resent these incursions and planned to drive the English from Powhatan territory with a major uprising. His plan required that he negotiate with the thirty tribes of the Powhatan Confederacy to join with him in expelling the English. The plan was implemented on March 22, 1622, when the highly regarded prophet and warrior Nemattanow was murdered by the British, who suspected he had killed a white trader. Opechancanough took advantage of his people's feelings by having them simultaneously attack the colonists.

The surprise Indian attack annihilated 347 settlers, nearly a third of the English settlement in Virginia. It is believed that more would have died had not a Pamunkey servant forewarned his master, who then alerted some of the settlers of Jamestown and surrounding communities. Thus, many settlers were prepared for the attack. Even more devastating, however, was the successful coordinated counterattack by the English, who conducted military expeditions against many Powhatan villages, which they burned, destroying crops and great quantities of stored foodstuffs. The Virginia company took advantage of the massacre to dispossess of their land most Powhatans who lived in and near the various settlements, and even encouraged the enslavement of young girls and boys. In fact, the governor and council initiated a policy of extermination, and wrote: "Wee have anticipated your desire by settinge uponn the Indiyans in all places." After a decade of almost continual fighting, a treaty was negotiated in 1632, ending the Powhatan Wars, but even during the peace ceremony, poison was placed in the Indians' wine.

The truce was effective for approximately twelve years, until Opechancanough, now nearly one hundred years old and quite debilitated and feeble, was able to persuade the Powhatan Confederacy tribes again to wage war against the English. On April 18, 1644, the combined tribes staged a coordinated attack against the English, killing nearly five hundred. The natives' efforts to expel the English were futile, for the settlers in Virginia now numbered approximately eight thousand. The fighting continued for two years.

Warfare ceased in October, 1646, when the colonial assembly joined in a peace agreement with Necotowance, Opechancanough's successor. This treaty recognized the York River as separating the Powhatans and English, and only with the colonial governor's permission could one enter the other's territory. In essence, the Powhatan Wars effectively stopped any further Indian opposition to the expansion of the colonial settlers and their ultimately taking control of Powhatan lands and resources. Two decades of conflict, along with introduced diseases, had greatly reduced the Powhatan population, and the natives of Virginia began a difficult period of deculturation brought on by an increasing Euro-American population.

—*John Alan Ross*

ADDITIONAL READING:

Craven, Wesley Frank. *White, Red, and Black: The Seventeenth Century Virginian*. Charlottesville: University Press of Virginia, 1971. A comprehensive study of different resident groups in Virginia.

Josephy, Alvin M., Jr. *500 Nations: An Illustrated History of the North American Indians*. New York: Alfred A. Knopf, 1994. Chapter 4 covers the conflict, placed in the context of European colonization. Lavishly illustrated.

Lowe, William C. "Powhatan Confederacy" and "Powhatan Wars." In *Ready Reference: American Indians*. 3 vols. Pasadena, Calif.: Salem Press, 1995. Brief but informative accounts of the development of intertribal internal functions and tribal conflict with white settlers.

Paredes, J. Anthony, ed. *Indians of the Southeastern United States in the Late Twentieth Century*. Tuscaloosa: University of Alabama Press, 1992. An excellent ethnographic compendium of the effects of Euro-American socioeconomic and political policies upon Native Americans of this area.

Roundtree, Helen C. *Pocohontas's People: The Powhatan Indians of Virginia Through Four Centuries*. Norman: University of Oklahoma Press, 1990. A thorough, well-presented ethnographic history of the Powhatan Indians.

SEE ALSO: 1570's, Powhatan Confederacy; 1607, Jamestown Is Founded.

1626 ■ ALGONQUIANS "SELL" MANHATTAN ISLAND: *the Dutch gain a stronghold in North America that they will relinquish to the British four decades later*

DATE: May 6, 1626

LOCALE: Manhattan Island, New Netherland

CATEGORIES: Expansion and land acquisition; Native American history; Settlements

KEY FIGURES:

Henry Hudson (1560's?-1611), English navigator who explored the Hudson River for the Dutch East India Company

Willem Kieft (1597-1647), fifth governor of New Netherland

Cornelius Jacobsen May, first governor of New Netherland, who brought settlers to the area

Peter Minuit (1580-1638), third governor and first director-general of New Netherland

Peter Stuyvesant (c. 1610-1672), last Dutch governor of New Netherland

Willem Verhulst, second governor of New Netherland

SUMMARY OF EVENT. In the early seventeenth century, the Netherlands, like other nations of northern Europe, sent out explorers to search for a sea route around North America to the riches of eastern Asia. The principal explorer for the Dutch was Henry Hudson, an Englishman, who, in 1609, explored the river that bears his name. When Hudson and other navigators failed to find the Northwest Passage, the Dutch, like other Europeans, decided to claim the lands that they had found in the Americas and exploit their resources. While hoping to discover gold and silver, as the Spanish had done to the south, the Dutch soon found that furs were the most readily exploitable resource of the middle Atlantic coastal region that they claimed. The Dutch could obtain these furs by trading with the Native Americans, who would do most of the trapping in exchange for European goods. The demand for pelts was so great in Europe that one shipload could make its investors wealthy.

In the interests of further discovery and to stimulate trade, the Dutch legislative body, the States-General, granted to its traders and explorers the exclusive right to make four voyages

New Amsterdam, as it was illustrated in the first edition of a Dutch work, Beschrijvinghe Van Virginia, Nieuw Nederlandt, Nieuw Engelandt, En d'Eylanden Bermudes, Berbados, en S. Christoffel, *published in 1651 by Joost Hartgers, Amsterdam. As can been seen by the writing in the upper right-hand corner and the ships entering from the "west," the picture was incorrectly engraved and should be reversed. The moated fort can be seen in the middle ground.* (Library of Congress)

to any new lands that they might explore. Under this grant, in 1614, five ships visited the Hudson River, which the Dutch then called Mauritius. Later that same year, these traders combined as the United New Netherland Company and received a monopoly on the trade of the Hudson Valley from the States-General. Ignoring Manhattan Island, these early traders sailed up the Hudson River to the site of present-day Albany, where they erected Fort Nassau on Castle Island as a base of operations. There they exchanged their goods for furs with the Mohican tribal peoples. Following the expiration of the charter of the United New Netherland Company in 1618, a succession of different companies plied the Hudson River fur trade.

In 1621, a number of influential merchants obtained from the States-General a charter for the Dutch West India Company with the sole right to trade on the Atlantic coasts of Africa and North and South America for twenty-four years. Although the new company organized primarily to challenge Spanish control of Latin America, it also was interested in the Hudson River area. In 1624, the company dispatched Captain Cornelius May with a shipload of thirty families to settle in North America. Opposite Castle Island, the group founded a trading post they named Fort Orange; to the south, they formed a settlement on the Delaware River. They also may

have established a trading house on Governor's Island, in what would become New York City's harbor. Coastal Algonquian tribes probably were in the process of forming a coalition when the Dutch arrived and disrupted that maneuver.

The first two governors of New Netherland, Cornelius May and Willem Verhulst, lived at the Delaware River site and administered the colony from there. Peter Minuit, the third governor and first director-general of New Netherland, shifted his center of operations to Manhattan Island. A native of Wesel, then in the Duchy of Cleves, he was probably of French or Walloon descent. He impressed many as a shrewd and somewhat unscrupulous man.

One of his first acts after arriving on Manhattan Island early in 1626 was to buy the rights to the island from an Algonquian tribe, the Canarsee, for trinkets worth about sixty guilders, or about twenty-four dollars. There is some debate whether Minuit actually arranged the purchase himself or if his predecessor, Verhulst, did, but a May, 1626, letter revealed Minuit's intentions to buy it. Controversy also surrounds the morality of the purchase. Tradition commonly calls the sale an unconscionable steal or a tremendous bargain. However, some historians suggest that the conversion to twenty-four dollars is too low and that, refiguring the payment in 1986 dollars, the Dutch paid $31 billion. Moreover, the Canarsee certainly placed a different value on the beads, other trade goods, and land than did the Europeans; the concept of land "ownership" did not exist among most indigenous people or, at least, it had a meaning completely different from that of Europeans. Because the Manhattan tribe, whose name the island reflected, had a better claim to it than did the Canarsee, Minuit later apparently also bought the island from them. Through this, their first major land purchase from the Native Americans, the Dutch secured a semblance of a legal title to Manhattan. At the time of the purchase, it was a beautiful island, covered with a great forest and abounding with wildlife and wild fruits.

Minuit made New Amsterdam, at the southern tip of Manhattan, the nucleus of Dutch activity in the area. A large fort, pentagonal in shape, surrounded on three sides by a great moat and fronting on the bay, was one of the first structures built. When it was complete, Minuit brought several families from Fort Orange to settle in the town. He also ordered the evacuation of Fort Nassau on the South River, near present-day Gloucester, New Jersey, and transferred the garrison to New Amsterdam. Despite his vigorous administration of the colony, the parent country recalled him for examination in 1632 and dismissed him from the Dutch West India Company's service.

In the meantime, in 1629, the directorate of the company, with the approval of the States-General, had issued a charter of Freedoms and Exemptions that provided for the grant of large estates, called patroonships, to those members of the company who would recruit at least fifty settlers more than fifteen years of age to settle their lands within four years. These grants ostensibly were to promote farming in New Netherland, but their primary intention was to encourage settlers to go up the Hudson River to settle and make additional contacts with the Native Americans and thereby extend the fur trade. Traders presumably would ship the furs down the river to New Amsterdam, from where the Dutch West India Company had the sole right to export them. With one exception, Rensselaerwyck, these patroonships never measured up to Dutch expectations.

Relations with the Native Americans remained mostly harmonious and the fur trade continued to prosper until 1641, when hostilities broke out. The fighting, called Kieft's War after Governor Willem Kieft, resulted from his attempt to collect taxes from the Algonquian tribes for Dutch "protection." The conflict ended with a treaty on August 29, 1645, but it had already disrupted the fur trade and forced Kieft to relinquish some of his arbitrary power to advisory bodies to obtain popular support for the prosecution of the war. In 1647, Peter Stuyvesant succeeded Kieft and became the last Dutch governor or director-general of New Netherland. It was he who surrendered the colony to the British in 1664. The brightness of the early promise of New Netherland, lustrous with the purchase of Manhattan in 1626, faded within the half century. Although the Dutch would retain significant economic and cultural influence in the renamed New York, the English would benefit even more from one of the world's best harbors.

—*William L. Richter, updated by Thomas L. Altherr*

ADDITIONAL READING:

Brasser, Ted J. "The Coastal New York Indians in the Early Contact Period." In *Neighbors and Intruders: An Ethnohistorical Exploration of the Indians of Hudson's River*, edited by Laurence M. Hauptman and Jack Campisi. Ottawa: National Museums of Canada, 1978. Argues that the coastal Algonquians were probably in the process of forming a coalition when the Dutch purchased Manhattan.

Condon, Thomas J. *New York Beginnings: The Commercial Origins of New Netherland.* New York: New York University Press, 1968. Monograph examining the Dutch purchase decision as part of a wider commercial policy.

Francis, Peter, Jr. "The Beads That Did Not Buy Manhattan Island." *New York History* 67, no. 1 (January, 1986): 4-22. Asserts that the trinkets the Dutch paid for the island were much more valuable than common assumptions hold.

Gehring, Charles. "Peter Minuit's Purchase of Manhattan Island: New Evidence." *De Halve Maen* 54 (Spring, 1980): 6ff. Discusses a letter from Minuit suggesting his intention to buy Manhattan Island.

Rink, Oliver A. *Holland on the Hudson: An Economic and Social History of Dutch New York.* Ithaca, N.Y.: Cornell University Press, 1986. Argues strongly for Minuit's mastery in establishing New Amsterdam.

Trelease, Allen W. *Indian Affairs in Colonial New York: The Seventeenth Century.* Ithaca, N.Y.: Cornell University Press, 1960. Places the Dutch purchase in the context of other relations with Native Americans around New Netherland. Argues that the money paid was worth more to the Canarsee tribal people than usually is presumed.

Weslager, C. A. "Did Minuit Buy Manhattan Island from the Indians?" *De Halve Maen* 43 (October, 1968): 5-6. Questions whether Minuit actually purchased the island and suggests that Verhulst did instead.

SEE ALSO: 1610, Hudson Explores Hudson Bay; 1643, Confederation of the United Colonies of New England; 1664, British Conquest of New Netherland; 1670, Hudson's Bay Company Is Chartered.

1627 ∎ COMPANY OF NEW FRANCE IS CHARTERED: *creation of the most important French colonizing power in North America until 1663*

DATE: April 27, 1627
LOCALE: Canada
CATEGORIES: Canadian history; Economics; Organizations and institutions
KEY FIGURES:
Samuel de Champlain (c. 1567-1635), founder of Quebec in 1608
David Kirke (c. 1597-1654), Anglo-Scots privateer
Armand-Jean du Plessis, cardinal de Richelieu (1585-1642), King Louis XIII's first minister

SUMMARY OF EVENT. France's first permanent settlements in the Western Hemisphere were Acadia, which included parts of present-day Nova Scotia, New Brunswick, Prince Edward Island, and Maine, founded in 1605, and New France, founded in 1608 with its capital at Quebec. These colonization efforts were fledgling and precarious. Both were financed by merchant investors, who expected profits in fishing and the fur trade. Harsh winters, underfunding, and conflicts between colonial leaders and the private companies that had been granted monopolies for the fur trade resulted in weak development. New France, on the St. Lawrence River, fared better than Acadia, which suffered from its physical isolation, but even New France had a population of fewer than one hundred by 1627. Those consisted mostly of clerks, interpreters, and missionaries, with only one actual settler family present.

In that year, Cardinal Richelieu, King Louis XIII's chief policymaker and the de facto ruler of France, carried out widespread reforms in colonial policy with the goal of increasing the prestige, wealth, and power of his employer. He revoked all previous charters and concessions given for New France and initiated the chartering of a new and much more powerful group of investors, the Company of New France (la Compagnie de la Nouvelle-France) or, as it came to be known, the Company of One Hundred Associates (la Compagnie des Cent Associés). This company was so named because initially one hundred men and women, the latter being wealthy widows, invested 3,000 livres each (one livre was roughly equal to four U.S. dollars in 1990), creating a capital pool of 300,000 livres for the initial investment. Many of the shareholders were government officeholders, merchants, and clergy. Some of the latter were motivated by religion as much as or more than by the drive for profit. The charter granted the new organization full title to all lands from the Arctic Circle to Florida and from Newfoundland in the Atlantic Ocean to the Great Lakes.

The company was required to bring two hundred to three hundred settlers to New France in 1628 and at least four thousand more over the following fifteen years. The fur trade, New France's only important export trade, and the encouragement of settlement were to be the highest priority. The charter, issued by Richelieu in April, 1627, and receiving official approval the following month, discriminated against Huguenots (French Protestants) who had been instrumental in the establishment of Acadia. Only Roman Catholics were allowed to colonize New France, according to the new charter. Surprisingly, and probably unique in the history of European colonization of North America, Article XVII of the charter stated that native people in the colonized area who became Catholic "will be considered and reckoned natural born subjects of France, and as such will be allowed to settle in France whenever they please, acquire property therein, make wills, inherit, accept donations and legacies, in the same manner as those born in France." It is difficult to imagine a Native North American pursuing these privileges, and none is known to have done so, but that it was allowed in the charter demonstrates an openness on the part of French colonizers at that time.

This experiment in interracial harmony had a rocky start. War broke out between France and England in 1628, and the initial convoy sent to Quebec in the spring of that year was captured in the Gulf of St. Lawrence by an English privateering force led by David Kirke. Those waiting for the ships to arrive at Quebec waited in vain and barely survived the following winter subsisting on wild plants. Samuel de Champlain, who had been governing the colony for years, was forced by hunger and lack of supplies to surrender to Kirke's English forces in the summer of 1629. The Company of One Hundred Associates depleted its treasury in futile attempts to recapture the colony for France, and by 1630, the investment group Richelieu had initiated was nearly bankrupt.

In the Treaty of Saint-Germain-en-Laye, signed by the English and French in 1632, the colony of New France was returned to the French, and the company was allowed to continue its efforts to develop the colony. Champlain was named governor once again. The royal government was preoccupied with the Thirty Years' War in Europe for the next few decades and therefore neglected its fledgling colony in North America. In the absence of strong leadership on the part of the company and the French crown from the 1630's to 1663, the Roman Catholic church, and particularly religious orders such as the Jesuits, took a prominent role in governing New France. In the 1640's, Montreal was founded as a religious community of both nuns and male missionaries, and Jesuit missionary efforts influenced much of what transpired in northeastern North America in the mid-seventeenth century.

The company lacked the funds to satisfy its obligations as stated in the charter, so its directors farmed out land grants to wealthy French investors who agreed, in turn, to settle these lands with colonists who would farm on the banks of the St. Lawrence. The number of colonists who came for this purpose would be credited to the company's quota of four thousand. Hence, what became known as the seigneurial system in New France was inaugurated. By 1642, there were still only three hundred people in the colony, although the number climbed to two thousand by 1653.

One of the reasons for such slow population increase was that, although the fur trade was a much more lucrative way to make a living than settling down to farm, fur trading meant traveling into the interior to live with Native Canadians, and perhaps contributing to the growth of native population, but not to the enlargement of New France's population and number of families. Also, the French had allied with many native nations along or near the St. Lawrence—Algonquians, Montagnais, Hurons—and had, through these alliances, gained a formidable set of enemies, the Iroquois Confederacy of Five Nations—the Senecas, Cayugas, Onondagas, Oneidas, and Mohawks. These nations, particularly the Mohawks, were determined to undermine or even expel the French presence in the St. Lawrence Valley, and the mutual hostility that developed resulted in frequent surprise attacks on each other's communities. The French attacked Iroquois civilian populations at times, and the Iroquois reciprocated in like fashion from the 1630's through the 1650's. This situation made stable settlement by French colonists from the mother country a frightful proposition. It contributed to a lack of enthusiasm for crossing the Atlantic even by those in France who lived on the economic margins and might have benefited from farming on a seigneurial estate, which would have given them an improved standard of living and more autonomy than peasant farming back home.

Although the Iroquois ability to undermine the colony made the Company of One Hundred Associates look bad in France, the company struggled on until 1663, when the French crown took a much more activist role in its colonies. Colonization under commercial arrangements was considered a failure by 1663, and New France became a royal colony at that time, but the company chartered in 1627 had been more successful than previous attempts to promote French settlement in the St. Lawrence Valley.　　　　　　　　　—*Gretchen L. Green*

ADDITIONAL READING:

Adair, E. R. "France and the Beginning of New France." *Canadian Historical Review* 13 (September, 1944): 3-37. A detailed and highly respected account of the early years of New France.

Delâge, Denys. *Bitter Feast: Amerindians and Europeans in the American Northeast, 1600-64.* Vancouver: University of British Columbia Press, 1993. A native perspective on the history of French and Dutch colonization in northeastern North America.

Eccles, William J. *France in America.* Rev. ed. East Lansing: Michigan State University Press, 1990. Up-to-date account of French colonization in North America, including a brief mention of the 1627 company chartered for New France.

Lescarbot, Marc. *The History of New France.* Edited by W. L. Grant and H. P. Biggar. 3 vols. Toronto: Champlain Society, 1907-1914. An important primary source on the history of New France; the first volume deals with the Company of New France.

Thwaites, R. G., ed. *The Jesuit Relations and Allied Documents.* 73 vols. Cleveland: Burrows, 1896-1901. A collection of letters written by Jesuit missionaries in New France and Acadia, mostly dealing with the seventeenth century. An invaluable source of information on the native nations, both allied and enemy, with which the priests dealt. Provides an excellent window into early New France.

Zoltvany, Yves F., ed. *The French Tradition in America.* New York: Harper & Row, 1969. A collection of documents related to the French presence in North America. Includes an English translation of the text of the charter of the Company of One Hundred Associates.

SEE ALSO: 1534, Cartier and Roberval Search for a Northwest Passage; 1603, Champlain's Voyages; 1670, Hudson's Bay Company Is Chartered; 1673, French Explore the Mississippi Valley.

1630 ∎ GREAT PURITAN MIGRATION: *establishment of the Massachusetts colony and the birth of Puritan influence in New England*

DATE: May, 1630-1643
LOCALE: Massachusetts Bay
CATEGORIES: Religion; Settlements
KEY FIGURES:
John Cotton (1584-1652), teacher at the First Church in Boston and an eminent clergyman
Anne Hutchinson (1591-1643), an enthusiastic disciple of John Cotton
Roger Williams (1603?-1683), one of the founders of Rhode Island
John Winthrop (1588-1649), governor of Massachusetts and its leading citizen

SUMMARY OF EVENT. Credit for the successful establishment of a Puritan commonwealth in North America belongs as much to Charles I, king of England and Puritan antagonist, as to any other single individual. On March 2, 1629, he dissolved Parliament, thereby denying the Puritans a public forum from which to continue their agitation for reforming the Church of England; a few days later, on March 14, he granted a royal charter to the Puritan-controlled Massachusetts Bay Company, which provided the framework for establishing a colony in the New World. By thus harassing the Puritans in old England even as he allowed them to procure a beachhead in New England, Charles virtually guaranteed the success of their colonizing venture.

The charter granted to the Massachusetts Bay Company contained, contrary to established custom, no clause stipulating that the company should hold its meetings in England. This omission enabled several leading Puritan stockholders to carry the charter with them to the New World and so transfer control of both company and colony to North America. Massachusetts thus became an autonomous commonwealth, the government of which evolved out of a transplanted joint-stock company. The stockholders who emigrated to Massachusetts became the voting citizens of the state; the board of directors, known as assistants, developed into a legislative assembly; and the company president served as governor of the colony.

The first contingent of settlers came to America in 1630, the earliest ships arriving in May and June. In the Great Migration, which lasted until 1643, some twenty thousand people came to Massachusetts to make the greatest colonizing exodus that England has ever known. They came mainly in family groupings, sometimes from the same parish, and largely from the east of England, especially the region known as East Anglia. Most were middle-class farmers or tradesmen. Religious reasons played a major role in their coming, although economic hard times no less than political problems influenced them as well.

Those who moved through Boston and settled the land, as most of the early migrants did, generally favored the open-field system of land tenure. Under that plan, quite common in England, each household had a village lot, where they built their home and raised their garden, living in rather close proximity to their neighbors. Village life centered on the meeting house, where in town meetings the villagers discussed issues of common interest with the elected selectmen. The meeting house also was the church, and although the settlers of the Great Migration had different experiences that brought them to New England, they more or less shared the religious outlook that was called Puritanism.

John Winthrop, first governor of Massachusetts Bay, made it clear to those traveling with him in 1630 that they were on a mission for God. Their objective was not just to settle a new land; it was to establish a "City upon a Hill," a holy commonwealth that would serve as an example so that old England might learn from New England. Winthrop realized soon after his arrival in the colony that too few members of the company had emigrated to provide a secure basis for government. In 1631, therefore, Winthrop arranged for the admission of more than a hundred settlers to the status of freemen, as stockholders were then called in England, and this number was gradually increased as the colony grew. Although the original stockholders had hoped to contain the rights of these newly created citizens within definite limits, such restrictions proved to be increasingly difficult to enforce. By 1644, the freemen had broadened their participation in the legislative process through the establishment of a lower house in the legislature consisting of two deputies from each town who shared, along with the governor and assistants, in the enactment of laws for the affected territory.

Despite these changes in the structure of government and the remarkable growth of the colony, Massachusetts remained safely under the control of a Puritan oligarchy. A law in 1636 helped to maintain this alliance of the church and the state by providing that only members of an approved congregation could apply for the status of freemen. Moreover, Puritan political theory held that although the people had a right to elect their leaders, once magistrates were installed in office, they held a commission from God and were responsible to the deity rather than to the electorate. Therefore, as Boston's influential minister John Cotton repeatedly pointed out, the freemen had no right to deprive a man of elective office unless they found him guilty of some grave offense. The remarkable durability of Puritan magistrates attests to the effectiveness of this advice.

The difficulty of maintaining orthodoxy in a congregational system of church government presented the Puritan commonwealth with its greatest challenge during the early years of settlement. Despite John Winthrop's efforts to maintain unity within the colony, zealots, such as Roger Williams, one of the founders of Rhode Island, and Anne Hutchinson, an enthusiastic disciple of John Cotton, threatened to divide the province into warring factions by convincing their respective congregations that the church stood in need of further purification. Since each congregation was presumably independent of out-side authority, it was difficult to discipline any heretic who succeeded in winning support from his or her local church.

Williams arrived in Massachusetts in 1631 and almost immediately began to challenge the purity of the New England churches, as well as the basis on which the Puritans had erected their civil government. He contended that the Massachusetts congregations retained too many contacts with the Church of England, that the civil government had no right to enforce religious uniformity, and that the king had acted illegally in granting a charter to the colony. These arguments threatened established authority and yet, because Williams enjoyed the confidence of his congregation at Salem, both the magistrates and the ministers found it difficult to deal with him.

Hutchinson presented an even greater problem. She argued that personal revelation might supplant the teachings of the minister and that each person must obey the voice of God rather than the commands of either church or state (a philosophy that came to be known as Antinomianism). Although she held no official church position, she enjoyed the support of a majority in the Boston congregation and, like Williams, proved a thorny problem for the ministers and magistrates.

The ultimate expulsion of both Williams and Hutchinson demonstrated that orthodoxy would continue to protect itself in Massachusetts. Williams pioneered the colony of Rhode Island; Hutchinson joined him before going on to Long Island, then under Dutch jurisdiction. Her son-in-law, John Wheelwright, would head north, founding Exeter in what became New Hampshire. Others who had differences with the Puritan oligarchs left Massachusetts Bay of their own accord.

Thomas Hooker, a Puritan clergyman whose eminence almost equaled John Cotton's, may have led a portion of his Cambridge congregation to the Connecticut Valley in 1636 because of his rivalry with the preeminent Cotton, whose influence on John Winthrop clearly made Hooker increasingly uncomfortable with the blending of church and state in Winthrop's colony. Others followed the remarkable Hooker, who penned the most elaborate of early America's constitutions, the Fundamental Orders of Connecticut (1639). Unlike Hooker, the Reverend John Davenport and his rich patron, merchant Theophilus Eaton, believed that the relationship between church and state in Massachusetts was not close enough. In 1638, Davenport and Hooker founded New Haven, whose founders were inspired by a vision of a religious utopia based on the Mosaic.

The Puritans of Massachusetts Bay continued to insist upon the autonomy of each congregation, but they managed to maintain uniformity through their control of the government. In theory, the ministers of the colony exercised no authority over a particular congregation except through persuasion. They could, however, declare a person a heretic, and it then became the duty of the civil government to see that that person was punished. Through this partnership of the church and the state, formalized by the Cambridge Platform of 1649, the Puritans maintained a ritually unchallenged control of Massachusetts throughout the first half of the seventeenth century.

—*David L. Ammerman, updated by Ronald W. Howard*

ADDITIONAL READING:

Anderson, Virginia DeJohn. *New England's Generation: The Great Migration and the Formation of Society and Culture in the Seventeenth Century.* New York: Cambridge University Press, 1991. A searching analysis of who came, why they came, and what they hoped to do in Massachusetts Bay.

Battis, Emery. *Saints and Sectaries: Anne Hutchinson and the Antinomian Controversy in the Massachusetts Bay Colony.* Chapel Hill: University of North Carolina Press for the Institute of Early American History and Culture, 1962. A detailed study of the Antinomian controversy, with suggestions about the psychological, sociological, and physiological undercurrents of the event.

Cressy, David. *Coming Over: Migration and Communication Between England and New England in the Seventeenth Century.* New York: Cambridge University Press, 1987. Emphasizes the essential English nature of the Puritan enterprise in New England.

Fischer, David Hackett. *Albion's Seed: Four British Folkways in America.* New York: Oxford University Press, 1989. Argues that Puritan folkways were transferred largely from East Anglia and remained a potent force throughout U.S. history.

Miller, Perry. *Orthodoxy in Massachusetts, 1630-1650.* Cambridge, Mass.: Harvard University Press, 1933. Comprehensive account of Miller's theories of the establishment of congregationalism in Massachusetts Bay.

Morgan, E. S. *The Puritan Dilemma: The Story of John Winthrop.* Edited by Oscar Handlin. Boston: Little, Brown, 1958. Relates with eloquence and precision the "middle way" that Winthrop chose as he and other Puritans sought to build a society upon biblical principles.

SEE ALSO: 1620, Pilgrims Land at Plymouth; 1632, Settlement of Connecticut; 1636, Rhode Island Is Founded; 1641, Massachusetts Recognizes Slavery; 1643, Confederation of the United Colonies of New England; 1662, Half-Way Covenant; 1686, Dominion of New England Forms; 1692, Salem Witchcraft Trials.

1632 ■ ZUÑI REBELLION: *a century after the first Spanish inroads into New Mexico, Puebloan peoples resist*

DATE: February 22-27, 1632

LOCALE: Zuñi pueblos, New Mexico

CATEGORIES: Latino American history; Native American history; Wars, uprisings, and civil unrest

KEY FIGURES:

Martín de Arvide (died 1632), one of two priests killed in the rebellion

Francisco Vásquez de Coronado (1510-1554), Spanish explorer who conquered the Zuñi

Estevanico or *Estevén* (died 1539), black Moorish slave who

guided the first expedition into the American Southwest

Francisco Letrado (died 1632), first priest killed by the Zuñi

SUMMARY OF EVENT. Zuñi Indian contact with Spanish explorers began in violence. The Zuñi lived in six pueblos widely scattered across what is now western New Mexico. They occupied communities of apartment houses built on the sides or tops of mesas. They had no central government, and each pueblo spoke a distinct language.

Spaniards first entered this territory in 1539. They came north from Mexico, hunting for great cities of gold reported to be in the area. The legend of the Seven Cities of Gold, called Cíbola, had spread through Spanish possessions in the New World three years earlier, when Álvar Núñez Cabeza de Vaca—a sailor who had spent eight years wandering through Texas and the Southwest after a shipwreck on the Gulf coast—brought to Mexico City the story he had been told by native peoples. The governor of New Spain sent an expedition led by a Franciscan priest, Marcos de Niza, and a former slave named Estevanico into the region to verify the story. Estevanico reached a Zuñi pueblo a few days before the priest. By the time Fray Marcos arrived, the Zuñi had killed Estevanico reportedly for taking liberties with Zuñi women. The priest returned south and, contrary to all evidence, told the governor what the latter wanted to hear: that the Seven Cities of Cíbola did exist and were as magnificent as legend had held.

In the summer of 1540, the Spanish launched an expedition of more than a hundred men, including several priests, led by Francisco Vásquez de Coronado, the governor of Nueva Galicia, a state in western Mexico. After six months of travel, the explorers reached the Zuñi villages previously visited by Fray Marcos and were greatly disappointed by the poverty they discovered. The Zuñis, fearing that the invaders were looking for slaves, met the Spaniards in front of their village and warned that trying to enter their homes meant death. Coronado explained through an interpreter that he had come on a sacred mission to save souls for Christ. A priest then read the *requerimiento*, a statement read by a priest before all battles, warning the Zuñi that if they did not accept Spain's king, Philip IV, as their ruler, and if they did not embrace Christianity, they would be killed or enslaved.

The Zuñis responded with arrows, killing several Spaniards, but Spanish muskets and steel swords proved far superior to native weapons, and Coronado's forces quickly destroyed much of the village. The Zuñis fled, leaving behind a large quantity of corn, beans, turkeys, and salt, but no gold. Coronado, who had traveled much of the way in full armor, received several wounds during the battle but survived. He concluded that Cíbola must be somewhere else. Before continuing his search, however, he destroyed the village, called Hawikuh by the Zuñis. Despite the victory, no Spaniard returned to Zuñi territory until 1629.

By 1629, Franciscan missionaries had more than fifty churches in the area of New Mexico. Their headquarters in Santa Fe had been built by Pueblo Indian laborers in 1610.

Most of the mission churches had been constructed by native labor, with women building the walls and the men doing the carpentry. The priests decided to reestablish contact with peoples living farther to the west. In 1629, eight priests traveled to Acoma, a village built on top of a four-hundred-foot mesa, where a church was built. The next year, Fray Estevan de Pereá, sixty-four years of age, was sent to Hawikuh, about sixty miles west of Acoma. He found a village of eight hundred people, who greeted him peacefully. An interpreter told the Zuñis that the expedition had come to free them from slavery and the "darkness of idolatry." This was the same message brought to them a hundred years before by Coronado, and it had led to bloodshed. This time, however, the Zuñi allowed the Spanish to remain and build a church. Three years later it was completed.

Zuñi religious leaders, called sorcerers by the Christian fathers, fought the new religion from the very beginning. In their religion, there were many gods, not just one, who lived on the earth in trees, mountains, plants, and various animals. Zuñis worshiped water gods, according to Coronado, because water made the corn grow and sustained life in a very harsh climate. Water seemed almost as valuable to them as gold did to the Spaniards, something the Spaniards could not understand. Zuñi priests taught that people should live in harmony with the earth and learn to live with nature, not conquer it as Christians seemed to believe. Zuñis sought harmony in every aspect of their lives, which to them meant compromise and getting along with everything. They did fight wars, especially with Apache raiders, but violence and aggression were generally to be avoided. The Spaniards found little of value in these teachings and believed their god had chosen them to conquer the heathen, bring light to those living in darkness—which meant anyone who was not Christianized—and then grow rich, as God meant them to do. Compromise meant weakness to them; conquest, the highest good. These conflicting values would finally lead to rebellion and violence.

Another source of conflict between Zuñis and Spaniards was the system of labor that developed. Zuñis and other native peoples did most of the manual labor on construction projects; they also worked in mines and in the fields. Spanish nobles, government officials, and settlers simply did not work in these types of jobs; hard labor was beneath their dignity. Native Americans were forcibly recruited for this backbreaking labor. Wealthy Spanish landlords supposedly owned the right to the labor of all Indians living on their land under the *encomienda* system. They also received tribute from all families on their extensive properties, usually 1.6 bushels of maize (corn), and a cotton blanket or deer or buffalo hide each year. In times of drought, these payments were especially harsh and deeply resented.

Native peoples also hated the compulsory labor demanded of them by Spanish authorities. Thousands of Pueblo Indians, including Zuñis, had built Santa Fe under this system. They were supposed to be paid for their work, but many were not. In other places, the native peoples were used largely as pack animals to carry logs and heavy mining equipment across the desert. Many mines used slaves captured on frequent slaving expeditions into tribal territory. Slavery and economic exploitation added to Native American resentment of the Europeans.

On February 22, 1632, according to Spanish government records, Zuñi warriors killed Fray Francisco Letrado, the missionary at Hawikuh, during a mass he was celebrating to honor the completion of his church. The Zuñis then abandoned the pueblo and did not return for several years. Upon hearing of the killing, Governor Francisco de la Mora Ceballas sent a party of soldiers after the Zuñis. The soldiers found the Zuñi's hiding place and took revenge on the population, killing some and enslaving others.

Five days after the murder of Fray Letrado, Zuñis killed another priest, Fray Martín de Arvide, at a pueblo fifty miles west of Hawikuh. Two soldiers in Fray Martín's party were killed also. The governor sent another military expedition to avenge these deaths. Several Zuñis were killed in battle, and at least one was later executed for participating in the murders. The rebellion spread no further at this time, although Christian missionaries did not return to the Zuñi pueblos until 1660. The missionaries remained in the area until the rebellion of 1680, when violence between Spaniards and Zuñi again broke out and the Zuñi mission churches again were destroyed.

—*Leslie V. Tischauser*

ADDITIONAL READING:

Crampton, C. Gregory. *The Zuñis of Cíbola.* Provo: University of Utah Press, 1977. A general history of the Zuñi people. Black-and-white photographs illustrate how the Pueblos have changed over time.

Ganner, Van Hastings. "Seventeenth Century New Mexico." *Journal of Mexican American History* 4 (1974): 41-70. Provides a pro-Indian view of tribal relations with the Spanish. Includes a brief description of the events leading up to 1632.

Hodge, Frederick Webb. *History of Hawikah, New Mexico, One of the So-Called Cities of Cíbola.* Los Angeles: Southwest Museum, 1937. Contains translations of Spanish mission records and early histories of Spanish-Zuñi relations. The only detailed history of the revolt.

Scholes, France V. *Church and State in New Mexico, 1610-1650.* Historical Society of New Mexico Publications in History 7. Albuquerque: University of New Mexico Press, 1942. Takes a pro-Spanish point of view, treating Native Americans in a condescending manner. Based on translations of Spanish documents.

Weber, David J. *The Spanish Frontier in North America.* New Haven, Conn.: Yale University Press, 1992. A general overview and detailed history of the Spanish presence in North America, from the early 1500's to the 1830's. A balanced view of relations between Native Americans and the Spanish, with much useful information on religion, social structure, and culture.

SEE ALSO: 1540, Coronado's Expedition; 1598, Oñate's New Mexico Expedition; 1680, Pueblo Revolt.

1632 ■ SETTLEMENT OF CONNECTICUT:
expansion of Puritan influence in New England

DATE: Fall, 1632-January 5, 1665
LOCALE: Connecticut River Valley and the coast of Long Island Sound
CATEGORIES: Religion; Settlements
KEY FIGURES:
John Davenport (1597-1670), founder and coleader of the New Haven colony
Theophilus Eaton (1590-1658), English merchant and cofounder of the New Haven colony
Thomas Hooker (1586?-1647), pastor and leader of the Hartford settlement
Roger Ludlow (1590-1664?), leader of the settlement at Windsor
Robert Rich, second earl of Warwick (1587-1658), president of the Council for New England, who solicited a patent for Connecticut from the council in 1632
Edward Winslow (1595-1655), Plymouth colonist who explored the Connecticut River Valley in 1632
John Winthrop, Jr. (1638-1707), founder of the settlements at Saybrook and New London; governor of Connecticut
SUMMARY OF EVENT. As more and more settlers poured into Massachusetts Bay as part of the Great Puritan Migration, towns that at first had seemed partly settled began to seem congested. The first settlers obtained the best agricultural land; those who came later were left with second-best. New groups often brought their favorite pastor with them, but these Puritan pastors often found their ideas of the Puritan way of life somewhat at odds with that espoused by the earlier groups. Both these forces worked to motivate the groups coming later to seek new ground for their settlements.

In the fall of 1632, Edward Winslow of the Plymouth Colony explored westward and discovered the Connecticut River Valley, the site of some of New England's most productive farmland. Moreover, the most desirable land was cleared land, and the river valley contained extensive meadows that had few trees because of the frequent flooding. News of the rich meadows to the west rapidly reached the congested settlements in Massachusetts Bay, and a number of settlers attached to the minister Thomas Hooker resolved to move to the new area. Although the Dutch traders centered at Albany had earlier laid claim to the portion of the river valley near the present site of Windsor, the settlers chose to ignore this claim. Instead, they bought the claim Winslow's explorations had created from Plymouth, and in 1635, they moved to the site of the present city of Hartford. Other groups soon followed, settling at Windsor and Wethersfield on the Connecticut River.

Robert Rich, earl of Warwick and president of the Council for New England, had secured a patent for at least part of what is now Connecticut; the boundaries of the patent were ill-defined. In 1635, Warwick and his associates authorized

John Winthrop, Jr., son of the leader of the Massachusetts Bay Colony, to build a fort and create a settlement at the mouth of the Connecticut River, where it flows into Long Island Sound. He negotiated an agreement with the followers of Thomas Hooker, proposing to settle in the Connecticut River Valley, as a result of which Winthrop became governor of the colony.

Because Winthrop's authority did not include the right to establish a governing body, he secured the cooperation of the Massachusetts General Court, which authorized the establishment of basic government institutions similar to those existing in the Massachusetts Bay Colony. These institutions provided for the participation of all Christian freeholders in the election of individuals to office in the towns and in the General Court for Connecticut. This franchise—relatively broad compared to that in the older colony, which restricted participation to those who were recognized members of a church—has led many commentators to view Connecticut as fundamentally more democratic than the Massachusetts Bay Colony.

In 1637, the first General Court of Connecticut met at Hartford, comprising representatives of the towns of Hartford, Windsor, and Wethersfield. This general court prepared for war against the powerful Pequots, whose lands lay between these settlements and the coast. In a three-week campaign, the settlers vanquished the Pequots and eliminated them as a threat to the new colony. Shortly after the victory over the Pequots, a new group of settlers, under the leadership of John Davenport and Theophilus Eaton, founded a new colony at New Haven. The coastal settlement proved successful, and soon other groups settled in the vicinity.

The settlers in the Connecticut River Valley, flush with their victory over the Pequots, immediately turned their attention to creating a stable government for the colony. They drew up a constitution, called the Fundamental Orders, that provided for a General Court, or legislature, to meet twice a year, and a governor. Representatives of the towns sat in the General Court; every qualified householder could vote in the Town Meeting to choose the town's representatives, but only settlers who were freemen and held substantial property were eligible to serve in the General Court. The settlers around New Haven were not included, as they were a separate colony. Attempts were made to include representatives from the settlements on the eastern end of Long Island, but the difficulties of travel ensured that they would rarely participate in governmental decisions. The formal drafting of the Fundamental Orders relied heavily on the advice of Roger Ludlow, the only one of the earlier settlers with legal training.

All of these settlements flourished under the neglect of the British government, for during most of the first thirty years of Connecticut settlement, the British were wholly preoccupied with their own civil war and the Protectorate under Oliver Cromwell. With the restoration of the Stuart kings in 1660, the lack of a royal charter for any group in Connecticut (in contrast to Massachusetts Bay) became an urgent issue. In 1661,

SETTLEMENTS OF THE AMERICAN COLONIES, 1600-1760

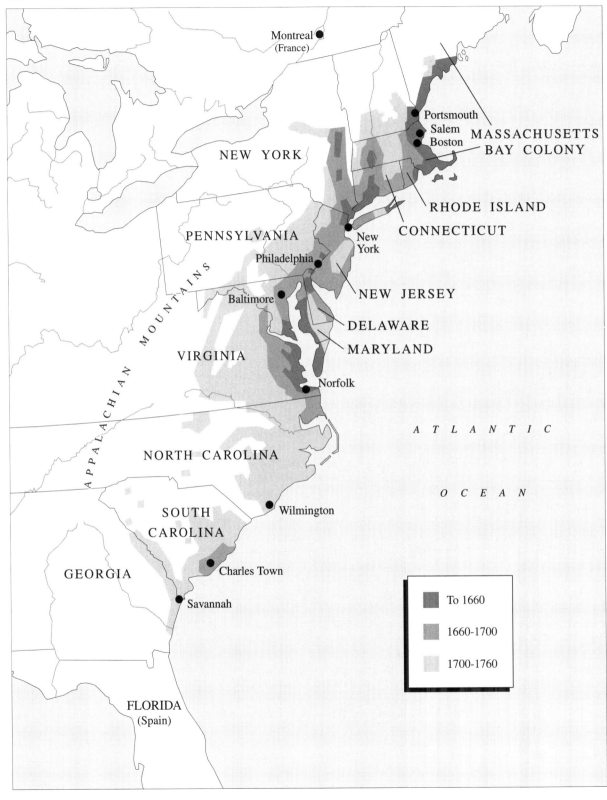

Montreal ●
(France)

NEW YORK

Portsmouth ●
Salem ●
Boston ●

MASSACHUSETTS
BAY COLONY

RHODE ISLAND

PENNSYLVANIA

CONNECTICUT

New
York

Philadelphia ●

NEW JERSEY

Baltimore ●

DELAWARE

MARYLAND

APPALACHIAN MOUNTAINS

VIRGINIA

Norfolk ●

ATLANTIC

NORTH CAROLINA

OCEAN

SOUTH
CAROLINA

Wilmington ●

GEORGIA

Charles Town ●

Savannah ●

■	To 1660
■	1660-1700
■	1700-1760

FLORIDA
(Spain)

John Winthrop, Jr., was commissioned to go to England and secure a royal charter. Winthrop proved to be a highly successful maneuverer, and in 1662, he won for Connecticut the desired charter, issued on May 3. On January 5, 1665, although somewhat reluctantly, the independent colony at New Haven agreed to be incorporated into Connecticut. The conquest of New Amsterdam by the English that same year eliminated any competitors for control of Connecticut.

The first thirty years of settlement in Connecticut brought many new émigrés from England, although new immigrants were few during the l640's. The supply of good land during these years ensured that this overwhelmingly agricultural society would remain relatively homogeneous socially. Although some who came subsequently left, those who stayed were soon able to acquire enough land for a "competency," that is, a standard of living that enabled them and their families to live with modest comfort. Few would have been able to achieve this level had they remained in England. For them, living in Connecticut was the realization of a dream.

—*Nancy M. Gordon*

ADDITIONAL READING:

Andrews, Charles M. *The Settlements.* Vol. 2 in *The Colonial Period of American History.* New Haven, Conn.: Yale University Press, 1964. Still a valuable account, chapters 3 through 5 present a straightforward narrative of the settlement of Connecticut and its political organization. Argues the importance of the availability of cleared land along the river as a major motivation for settlement.

Jones, Mary Jean Anderson. *Congregational Commonwealth: Connecticut, 1636-1662.* Middletown, Conn.: Wesleyan University Press, 1968. Argues that a search for religious freedom was the primary motive behind the settlement of Connecticut. The desire for new, uninhabited land drove some early settlers to move on to the Connecticut River Valley. Asserts that the rudimentary government created for Connecticut was less democratic than it is usually depicted. The chief book-length account.

Lucas, Paul R. *Valley of Discord: Church and Society Along the Connecticut River, 1636-1725.* Hanover, N.H.: University Press of New England, 1976. Describes the deep dissension within the churches of the first Connecticut settlements.

Main, Jackson Turner. *Society and Economy in Colonial Connecticut.* Princeton, N.J.: Princeton University Press, 1985. An innovative study presenting details of the economic and social conditions of the early settlers of Connecticut, based on an extensive collection of statistical materials. Concludes that the colonial society of Connecticut was substantially homogeneous.

Martin, John Frederick. *Profits in the Wilderness: Entrepreneurship and the Founding of New England Towns in the Seventeenth Century.* Chapel Hill: University of North Carolina Press, 1991. Argues that individuals of means played a larger role in the creation of new towns in New England than has previously been recognized, and that the founding of new towns was driven as much by profit as by religious motives.

SEE ALSO: 1620, Pilgrims Land at Plymouth; 1630, Great Puritan Migration; 1636, Rhode Island Is Founded; 1643, Confederation of the United Colonies of New England; 1650, Harvard College Is Established; 1662, Half-Way Covenant; 1686, Dominion of New England Forms.

1636 ■ RHODE ISLAND IS FOUNDED: *dissatisfied members of the Massachusetts Bay Colony seek freedom from the Puritan oligarchy and religious intolerance*

DATE: June, 1636
LOCALE: Narragansett Bay region of Rhode Island
CATEGORIES: Religion; Settlements
KEY FIGURES:
Canonicus (c. 1565-1647), elderly leader of the Narragansetts
John Clarke (1609-1676), physician and minister who was Rhode Island's agent in England
William Coddington (1601-1678), founder of the Aquidneck Island settlements of Portsmouth and Newport
Samuel Gorton (1592?-1677), controversial supporter of Anne Hutchinson, who established Warwick
Anne Hutchinson (1591-1643), who was banished from Massachusetts Bay Colony and helped found Portsmouth
Massasoit, also known as *Pokanokets* (c. 1580-1662), sachem among the Wampanoags Plantations, later called Rhode Island
Roger Williams (c. 1603-1683), founder of Providence

SUMMARY OF EVENT. The founding of Rhode Island was more complicated than the founding of most of the other American colonies, because it involved five separate settlements and unusual leaders bent on expressing their individualistic beliefs. The earliest settlers in Rhode Island represented those who were forced out of Massachusetts Bay Colony for their "dangerous" opinions or who left of their own accord because they were dissatisfied with certain aspects of the Puritan oligarchy.

The first of these, with the exception of the recluse William Blakston, was Roger Williams, who was ordered to leave the colony on October 9, 1635. Escaping deportation to England, he set out for the Narragansett region in January, 1636, and took refuge among the natives for several months. Aware of his impending arrest, Williams had set out three days earlier during a blinding blizzard. Walking eighty to ninety miles during the worst of a New England winter, he suffered immensely and likely would have died without the aid of Indians. Williams went to the lodge of Massasoit at Mount Hope. Williams had first met the Wampanoag sachem when the latter was about thirty years of age and considered him to be a great friend. Near the end of his trek, Williams lodged with Canonicus—an elderly leader of the Narragansetts, whom he also counted as a friend—and his family. The scars of that winter trek hindered Williams' health for the rest of his life.

Soon after purchasing land near the Seekonk River from Massasoit, Williams was joined by five other men. A warning from the governor of Plymouth that they were trespassing forced them to establish a new settlement in June, 1636, which they called Providence, on the Great Salt River. It is not known whether Williams had an actual plantation in mind or simply envisioned a trading post or mission, but other outcasts were soon welcomed, and each settler was given a home lot and a farm from the land that Williams had purchased from the natives.

Providence was strictly an agricultural community. The colony was built without capital or outside assistance, and its population and economy grew slowly. The heads of families participated in a town-meeting type of government and signed a compact agreeing to obey the laws passed by the will of all. The compact was intended to be operative "only in civil things," signifying a commitment to the separation of church and the state.

Williams' house at Providence Plantations quickly became a transcultural meeting place. He lodged as many as fifty Indians at a time—travelers, traders, sachems on their way to or from treaty conferences. If a Puritan needed to contact a native or vice versa, he more than likely did it with Williams' aid. Among the Indian nations at odds with each other, Williams became known as "a quencher of our fires." When citizens of Portsmouth needed an American Indian agent, they approached Williams. The Dutch did the same thing after 1636. Williams often traveled with Canonicus, Massasoit, and their warriors, lodging with them in the forest. The Narragansetts' council sometimes used Williams' house for its meetings.

In April, 1638, another band of exiles, led by William Coddington, left Boston in search of religious freedom. They had been preceded in March by Anne Hutchinson, whose Antinomian emphasis on "grace" over "works" minimized the clergy's role and elevated personal revelation. Arriving at Providence, they all arranged to purchase the island of Aquidneck from the natives, and by the following spring they had laid out the new settlement of Pocasset (Portsmouth). By seventeenth century standards, the settlement had a democratic form of government, with Coddington serving as judge.

Two such dominant personalities as Coddington and Anne Hutchinson could not exist in harmony for long. When their two factions split over Hutchinson's eccentric supporter Samuel Gorton, Coddington was ousted and, with his followers, began the new plantation of Newport. In March, 1640, he succeeded in uniting the two settlements on Aquidneck so that they could manage their own affairs apart from Providence. The union, the most orderly civil organization in the Narragansett region, was to endure for seven years. By today's standards, the democracy that they proclaimed in 1641 was limited, because it excluded half the adult males from participating in government. Probably because Coddington was unsuccessful in obtaining a patent for Aquidneck, the people of Portsmouth became disillusioned and broke away from Newport in 1648.

Meanwhile, the controversial Gorton, driven from both Portsmouth and Providence for defying the authority of the government, purchased Indian lands to establish Warwick. After enduring harassment and imprisonment by Massachusetts officials, he obtained an order compelling Massachusetts to cease molesting him and lived in peace as an honored citizen of Warwick.

Of all the Rhode Island leaders, Williams emerged as the dominant figure. His efforts to maintain peace among the tribes were of inestimable service to the whole of New England. Yet the ambitions of other political leaders in the British settlements in and around Rhode Island were to remain his chief problem. Convinced that the settlements of Rhode Island had to cooperate in order to remain intact, he worked selflessly for a federation of the four main towns. When the formation of the United Colonies of New England in 1643 threatened Rhode Island's integrity, Williams sailed for England to obtain a charter from the Long Parliament. The patent that he brought back in September, 1644, authorized the union of Providence, Portsmouth, and Newport as "The Incorporation of Providence Plantations." Warwick was included later.

The uncertainty of the civil war in England caused a delay in putting the newly authorized government into effect, but in May, 1647, an assembly of freemen met at Portsmouth to organize the government and to draft laws. A federal system, whereby the towns maintained their individual rights as parts of the larger community, was created. Their code of laws was one of the earliest made by a body of men in America and the first to embody in all its parts the precedents set by the laws and statutes of England. By 1650, a representative assembly composed of six delegates from each town was operating. The assembly also served as a judicial body, until a separate court for trials was established in 1655. Town courts preserved the local peace.

Coddington continued to deal underhandedly in an attempt to separate Aquidneck from the union. In 1651, he succeeded in obtaining a lifetime appointment as governor of Aquidneck and Conanicut Islands from the Council of State. The residents of the islands supported Williams' successful mission to England, which resulted in the annulment of Coddington's patent in 1652. Distrust of central government and antagonism between the mainland and islands persisted until 1654, when Williams, with the support of Oliver Cromwell, restored the atmosphere of cooperation.

The Restoration in England imperiled the validity of Rhode Island's charter of 1644. Dr. John Clarke, its agent in London, petitioned the Crown for confirmation. Confirmation of Connecticut's grant to include half of Rhode Island's territory necessitated submitting the matter to arbitration. The decision was in favor of Rhode Island, and the new charter of July 18, 1663, also confirmed the colony's policy of complete liberty of conscience, the only charter to do so.

Although they were couched mainly in a religious context, Williams' ideas also engaged debates regarding political liberty that would fire the American Revolution more than a century later. His ideas of "soul liberty," political freedom, and economic equality presaged the later revolution of continental scope. —*Warren M. Billings, updated by Bruce E. Johansen*

ADDITIONAL READING:

Andrews, Charles M. *Our Earliest Colonial Settlements: Their Diversities of Origin and Later Characteristics.* New York: New York University Press, 1933. Chapter 4 details the political turmoil of the early years and the lives of the colony's principal leaders.

_____. *The Settlements.* Vol. 2 in *The Colonial Period of American History.* New Haven, Conn.: Yale University Press, 1964. Chapters 1 and 2 present a detailed overall account of Rhode Island's founding.

Brockunier, Samuel H. *The Irrepressible Democrat: Roger Williams.* New York: Ronald Press, 1940. Presents Roger Williams as the first great American democrat, a fighter against the tyranny of the Puritan oligarchy.

Greene, Theodore P., ed. *Roger Williams and the Massachusetts Magistrates.* Boston: D. C. Heath, 1964. This collection of readings presents disparate views from the seventeenth century to the present on the question of Williams' banishment.

Grinde, Donald A., Jr., and Bruce E. Johansen. *Exemplar of Liberty: Native America and the Evolution of Democracy.* Los Angeles: UCLA Native American Studies Center, 1991. Includes a chapter on Williams' founding of Rhode Island and his use of Native American aid and ideas about political society.

Miller, Perry. *Roger Williams: His Contribution to the American Tradition.* New York: Atheneum, 1962. Liberally interspersed with selections from Williams' writings, Miller's study contends that Williams was concerned basically with theology, not democratic political reforms.

Morgan, Edmund S. *Roger Williams: The Church and the State.* New York: Harcourt Brace & World, 1967. Concentrating upon the thought of Roger Williams as presented in his writings, Morgan seeks "to expose the symmetry of the ideas that lay behind the polemics."

Rugg, Winnifred K. *Unafraid: A Life of Anne Hutchinson.* Boston: Houghton Mifflin, 1930. The Rhode Island experience is treated only in the final chapter of this book, which focuses on the Antinomian controversy in the Massachusetts Bay Colony.

Williams, Roger. *The Complete Writings of Roger Williams.* 7 vols. New York: Russell & Russell, 1963. The most complete collection of Williams' writings on the founding of Rhode Island.

_____. *A Key into the Language of America.* 5th ed. Reprint. Providence, R.I.: Tercentenary Committee, 1936. Williams' views on religion, politics, and society, in the context of a guide to Native American languages.

SEE ALSO: 1620, Pilgrims Land at Plymouth; 1630, Great Puritan Migration; 1632, Settlement of Connecticut; 1643, Confederation of the United Colonies of New England; 1649, Maryland Act of Toleration.

1636 ■ PEQUOT WAR: *the first major conflict between Native Americans and New England settlers*

DATE: July 20, 1636-July 28, 1637
LOCALE: Connecticut
CATEGORIES: Native American history; Wars, uprisings, and civil unrest
KEY FIGURES:
John Endecott (1588-1665), first governor of Massachusetts Bay Colony
John Mason (1600-1672), soldier who led the combined Massachusetts-Connecticut force
Miantonomo (c. 1600-1643), chief of the Narragansetts
Sassacus (c. 1560-1637), sachem of the Pequots
Uncas (c. 1606-c. 1682), relative of Sassacus who rebelled
John Underhill (1597?-1672), trained warrior and Massachusetts militia captain
Roger Williams (c. 1603-1683), founder of Rhode Island

SUMMARY OF EVENT. As suggested by their name (from *pek-awatawog*, "the destroyers"), the Pequots were once the most formidable tribe in New England. Part of the Eastern Algonquian language family, the Pequots, by the dawn of the seventeenth century, were well established in what is now Connecticut. Their powerful sachem (principal chief) was the venerable Sassacus, who was born near what is now Groton. In spite of many years of experience, Sassacus faced, in his seventies, the biggest crisis in his people's history. Although the Pequots had a virtual hegemony over their adjacent nations—as the leader of the Mohegans, Uncas was married to the daughter of the Pequot chief—the Pequots had trouble coping with the impact of the European powers in the Connecticut Valley. The Pequots found themselves caught between the Dutch moving eastward from New Netherlands and the English moving westward from the Massachusetts Bay Colony and Connecticut. European competition for control over trade on the Connecticut River proved to be a destabilizing factor in intertribal relationships.

The political climate was ripe for violence. It began when two English traders were killed in Connecticut—John Stone in 1633 and John Oldham on July 20, 1636. It has never been firmly established that the Pequots were responsible for their deaths. When John Gallup, an English merchant, found natives in control of Oldham's ship, anchored off Block Island, he fought with them in July, 1636, for control of it. Captain John Endecott, the first governor of the Massachusetts Bay Colony, with ninety soldiers, conducted a punitive raid on Block Island, killing every male native there. Although most of the casualties were Narragansetts, not Pequots, Endecott pushed eastward along the Connecticut coast, demanding reparations from the Pequots, who refused, resisted, and suffered at least one death, as well as the destruction of several villages.

Sassacus, outraged, invited the Narragansetts to join him in war on the English. Their chief, Miantonomo, was favorably disposed toward the colonists, probably due to the influence of Roger Williams, the founder of Rhode Island. Even without Narragansett support, Sassacus acted, laying siege to Fort Saybrook, situated on the Connecticut River, during the winter of 1636-1637 and concurrently attacking several outlying English settlements, including Wethersfield, where at least nine settlers were killed.

Puritan retaliation was not long in coming. Captains John Mason and John Underhill shared command. Born in England, Mason had served as an army officer in the Netherlands before his arrival in Massachusetts in 1632. From Hartford, he set forth with a band of eighty, supported by the Mohegans and Narragansetts. Like Mason, Underhill had been born in England and then was reared in the Netherlands, where his father had fought the Spanish. Since 1630, he had lived in Massachusetts. Mason and Underhill initially went eastward, by ship, along the Connecticut coast, making landfall at Narragansett Bay. Then, with their native allies, they moved westward by land. After crossing the Pawcatuck and Mystic Rivers, they were poised to attack the main Pequot village at sunrise on May 25, 1637. The Puritan forces divided, each half attacking one of the two main gates, located at opposite ends of the stockaded native settlement. The English did not profit as much as expected by their surprise attack; their opening forays were repulsed. Then the colonials set fire to the wigwams, and as the village burned, the Pequots faced horrible alternatives. Some, mostly women and children, remained inside the fort, perishing in the flames. Those who fled, mostly the warriors, were cut down by the English and their Narragansett, Mohegan, and Niantic allies. Between six hundred and one thousand Pequots perished in this massacre. Only two colonials were lost, a mere twenty wounded. Underhill rejoiced in the "mighty victory," comparing his annihilation of the Pequots to David's destruction of his foes in biblical times.

A large group of Pequot refugees sought sanctuary in a swamp near New Haven, only to be discovered and destroyed on July 28, 1637. In the subsequent confusion, Sassacus and a handful of followers fled, seeking asylum in Mohawk territory. Desiring to prove their loyalty to the English, the Mohawks beheaded Sassacus.

As a consequence of the Pequot War, Uncas, the son-in-law of Sassacus, seized control of the Mohegan tribe. With English support, Uncas began a career of conquest that made him the most powerful sachem in New England. Miantonomo, sachem of the Narragansetts, was killed by command of Uncas in 1643, perhaps as a political act asked by his English allies. Although Uncas initially prospered as a prominent warrior and ruler, he discovered his English allies to be unpredictable. When he attacked Massasoit in 1661, the Puritans forced him to give up prisoners and plunder; during Metacom's War (1675-1676), Uncas surrendered his sons as hostages to the colonists, who, defeating Metacom (or King Philip) of the Wampanoags, effectively ended Indian resistance to European settlement.

The Pequot War also marked the advent of almost constant conflict between the Puritan settlers and the natives, and its results were ultimately tragic for all the Native Americans. The Pequots, who (together with the Mohegans) had counted perhaps four thousand men when the English arrived at Plymouth Rock in 1620, steadily declined in numbers. An estimate made in 1643 suggested that there were twenty-five hundred men in their group. Following their defeat, many of the Pequots were massacred or enslaved; those enslaved were shared between the Europeans and other natives, some being deported as far from home as Boston or the island of Bermuda. Others were assimilated into other tribes, by being resettled among their former enemies. In 1655, the Pequots were moved to two reservations on the Mystic River. By 1674, there were only three hundred men in this once-proud nation. Pequot place names disappeared: The Pequot River, for example, became the Thomas. Their power had been forfeited, their identity nearly eradicated. In 1990, there were between nine hundred and sixteen hundred Pequots. —*C. George Fry*

ADDITIONAL READING:

De Forest, John W. *History of the Indians of Connecticut from the Earliest Known Period to 1850.* Hartford, Conn.: W. J. Hammersley, 1851. Reprint. Hamden, Conn.: Shoestring Press, 1988. A classic study of the native peoples of Connecticut.

Josephy, Alvin M., Jr. *500 Nations: An Illustrated History of the North American Indians.* New York: Alfred A. Knopf, 1994. This generously illustrated volume is sympathetic to the point of view of the Native Americans. References to the situation in New England are corrective to earlier writings.

Orr, Charles, ed. *History of the Pequot War: The Contemporary Accounts of Mason, Underhill, Vincent, and Gardener.* Cleveland, Ohio: Helman-Taylor, 1897. A valuable anthology of eyewitness reporting on the Pequot War from the Puritan perspective, drawing on the recollections of major English participants.

Peale, Arthur L. *Memorials and Pilgrimages in the Mohegan Country.* Norwich, Conn.: Bulletin Company, 1930. Peale, author of a groundbreaking study of Uncas, was celebrated for his knowledge of the Mohegans and the Pequots. Remarkably readable reflections.

Salisbury, Neal E. *Manitou and Providence: Indians, Europeans, and the Making of New England, 1500-1643.* New York: Oxford University Press, 1982. A thorough, objective study of the contrasting attitudes and values of the Native Americans and the Europeans during a century and a half of contact and conflict.

Stoutenburgh, John L., Jr. *Dictionary of the American Indian.* New York: Philosophical Library, 1960. A concise resource with excellent brief biographies and summary descriptions of key events in Native American history.

Vaughan, Alden T. *New England Frontier: Puritans and Indians, 1620-1675.* Boston: Little, Brown, 1965. This helpful study of a half-century of relationships between Native Americans and European settlers is a fine starting point for research.

SEE ALSO: 1620, Pilgrims Land at Plymouth; 1632, Settlement of Connecticut; 1675, Metacom's War.

1641 ■ MASSACHUSETTS RECOGNIZES SLAVERY: *the granting of formal status to slavery makes it an institution in the British colonies*

DATE: November, 1641
LOCALE: Massachusetts Bay Colony
CATEGORIES: African American history; Laws and acts
KEY FIGURES:
John Cotton (1584-1652), Puritan clergyman and church leader
Nathaniel Ward (1578-1652), Puritan clergyman and author and architect of Body of Liberties
John Winthrop (1588-1649), first governor of Massachusetts Bay

SUMMARY OF EVENT. From its outset, the Massachusetts Bay Colony endorsed the idea of unfree labor. One hundred eighty indentured servants arrived with the original colonists. Subsequent food shortages led to the surviving servants' being set free in 1830. Unfree labor, however, continued on a private basis, and some white criminals were made slaves to court-appointed masters. Captives from the Pequot War of 1636-1637 were given over into slavery. Some of these captives were subsequently transported to a Puritan enclave off the coast of Nicaragua, and black slaves were introduced from there to the Massachusetts colony. The colony, however, remained without a formal endorsement of slavery until the promulgation of the Body of Liberties in 1641.

The Body of Liberties was controversial in many respects. It evolved out of the gradually weakening authority of Governor John Winthrop and his first Board of Assistants, and the emergence of the General Court as a representative body of freemen. The document was crafted and adopted by Elizabethan men who had grown up in the age of Shakespeare and the King James Bible. They were not democrats, but they had a strong sense of destiny and a healthy fear of absolute authority. In a larger sense, the document came to reflect the classic and ancient struggle between church and state.

In 1635, the General Court had appointed a committee to draw up a body of laws for the rights and duties of the colonists. This committee stalled over the church-state conflict, and another committee was impaneled in 1636. John Cotton sat on this committee. Cotton was a devout churchman who saw a government based on the theocracy of Israel and drafted a document that derived much of its authority from scripture. Cotton did, however, believe in limitations on authority. He also resisted adopting biblical statutes wholesale. Winthrop, who was lukewarm to the entire idea, called Cotton's Code, "Moses his Judicialls."

Cotton's counterpart in drawing up the code was Nathaniel Ward. Ward was a Puritan with a sense of humor and a literary bent. He later penned a humorous pamphlet of observations entitled *The Simple Cobler of Aggawam*. Like most Puritans,

he was a friend to strict discipline, but he also was a foe to arbitrary authority. He could agree with Winthrop and Cotton that all law was the law of God, but with a view toward local conditions and universal morality. He insisted that the code be based on English common law rather than on the Bible. He became the chief architect and intellectual godfather of the "Massachusetts Magna Charta," the Body of Liberties. His contribution would be a government of laws and not men. The Pequot War slowed deliberations, but by 1638, the committee had a fresh start and by 1639 had ordered a document that combined Cotton's and Ward's work. The final document, which owed more to Ward than to Cotton, was adopted in November, 1641.

In many ways, the Body of Liberties was an enlightened document and certainly remarkable by seventeenth century standards. A compilation of one hundred laws, the Body of Liberties, while not democratic, allowed for wide judicial discretion and for each case to be judged on its merits. It also effectively barred the legal profession from defending anyone for pay, and it protected married women from assault. It also addressed the liberties of servants in humanitarian terms for those times. The number of lashes given to servants was limited to forty, and the capital laws were more lenient than those of England. The distinguished historian Samuel Eliot Morison wrote that the Body of Liberties was "an enlightened body of laws and of principles that would have done credit to any commonwealth in the 17th century. . . ." The one problem, however, was slavery. This bold document addressed the slavery issue thus:

> There shall never be any bond slaverie, villainage or captivitie amongst us unles it be lawfull captive, taken in just warres, and such strangers as willingly selle themselves or are sold to us. And these shall have all the liberties and Christian usages which the law of God established in Israell concerning such persons doeth morally require. This exempts none from servitude who shall be judged thereto by authoritie.

Although not a ringing endorsement of slavery, the Body of Liberties nevertheless admits of it. Thus it opened the way for the official sanction of slavery. Later and stricter codes would formalize the institution in New England on a colony-by-colony basis. The reasoning was a business decision. An early realization that the price of slaves was greater than their worth as laborers led the Yankee businessmen to market some of their slave cargoes to the plantation colonies. In the triangular trade of West Africa, the West Indies, and North America, the vast majority of slaves taken by New England traders ended up in the West Indies. Shrewd New England traders shipped rum, fish, and dairy products out; they imported slaves, molasses, and sugar. Those few slaves who were not dropped off in the West Indies or on Southern plantations were taxed rather heavily. In 1705, Massachusetts imposed a duty of four pounds sterling per slave imported into the colony.

By 1680, Governor Simon Bradstreet estimated the number of "blacks or slaves" in the Massachusetts colony at one hundred to two hundred. Some special laws were passed restricting the movement of African Americans in white society, but the Puritans encouraged Christian conversion and honored black marriages among themselves. Slavery was mild compared to the Southern kind. Slaves needed to read and write to do their jobs. Although there were occasional isolated rebellions, the slaves benefited from the New England love for learning and the strong Puritan emphasis on marriage and family.

Slavery gradually faded away in Massachusetts, perhaps because of its vague legal status. In the aftermath of the American Revolution, a national clamor for a Bill of Rights led individual colonies to adopt their own. While none expressly forbade slavery, the institution seemed at odds with the rhetoric. By 1776, the white population of Massachusetts was 343,845 and the black population was 5,249. The census of 1790 showed Massachusetts as the only state in which no slaves were listed.

As John Winthrop stated, "wee shall be as a Citty upon a Hill, the Eies of all people are uppon us; soe that if wee shall deale falsely with our god in this worke wee have undertaken and soe cause him to withdrawe his present help from us, wee shall be made a story and a by-word through the world. . . ." Despite the legalization of slavery in the Body of Liberties, slavery was never popular in Massachusetts except as incidental to trade—and the slave trade was an accepted practice by seventeenth century European standards. The Puritans themselves were products of a rigorous, harsh, isolated experience. They were humanists and intellectuals with contradictions. They prized sincerity and truthfulness, yet practiced repression and inhibition to steel themselves against life's ills. They had a strong element of individualism in their creed, believing that each person must face his maker alone. Puritan humanism thus never squared with the institution of slavery.

—*Brian G. Tobin*

ADDITIONAL READING:

Franklin, John Hope. *From Slavery to Freedom: A History of Negro Americans*. 3d ed. New York: Alfred A. Knopf, 1967. Classic text on the evolution of American slavery contains a chapter on "Puritan Masters."

Miller, Perry, ed. *The American Puritans: Their Prose and Poetry*. New York: Columbia University Press, 1982. Includes selected writings from John Cotton, Nathaniel Ward, and John Winthrop.

_____. *Errand into the Wilderness*. Cambridge, Mass.: The Belknap Press of Harvard University Press, 1984. A timeless source that delves into the theological underpinnings of Puritanism.

Morgan, Edmund S. *The Puritan Dilemma: The Story of John Winthrop*. Edited by Oscar Handlin. Boston: Little, Brown, 1958. A simplified view of Puritan politics, with Massachusetts Bay's first governor as the focal point.

Morison, Samuel Eliot. *Builders of the Bay Colony*. Boston: Northeastern University Press, 1981. Contains individual chapters on the Elizabethan architects of Massachusetts, including John Cotton, Nathaniel Ward, and John Winthrop.

Phillips, Ulrich B. *American Negro Slavery*. Baton Rouge: Louisiana State University Press, 1966. Rich in original source material about the development of slavery.

SEE ALSO: 1619, Africans Arrive in Virginia; 1636, Pequot War; 1661, Virginia Slave Codes; 1671, Indian Slave Trade.

1642 ■ BEAVER WARS: *the Iroquois Five Nations challenge the French-Huron trade monopoly, leading to large-scale intertribal warfare*

DATE: 1642-1685

LOCALE: Northeastern woodlands, from the Hudson River west to the Great Lakes and from the Ohio River north to Ontario

CATEGORIES: Economics; Native American history; Wars, uprisings, and civil unrest

KEY FIGURES:

Edmond Andros (1637-1714), English governor of New York, partner in the Covenant Chain

Samuel de Champlain (c. 1567-1635), French explorer, fur trader, and founder of Quebec

Henry Hudson (1560's-1611), English explorer, employed by the Dutch at Albany

Iroquet, Algonquian chief

Isaac Jogues (1607-1646), Jesuit priest and intermediary between the Hurons and the Iroquois

Kiotsaeton, Mohawk orator who presented wampum belts at peace council

Paul Le Junne, Jesuit priest who wrote extensively about the Hurons

Peter Stuyvesant (c.1640-1672), Dutch director general of New Netherlands

Tandihetsi, Huron chief married to an Algonquian woman

SUMMARY OF EVENT. During the seventeenth century, the principal mode of subsistence for the Iroquois changed from farming to trapping. After the Iroquois had traded successfully with the Dutch for several decades, a seemingly insatiable demand for furs to make fashionable top hats for European gentlemen had depleted the Iroquois' source of beaver pelts. Meanwhile, the French had become allies with the Algonquians and Hurons to the north, establishing a lucrative monopoly on the fur trade in the upper Great Lakes. Acting as middlemen, the Hurons bought huge quantities of furs from the Ottawa, then sold them to the French. Seeking an expedient solution to the problem of a diminishing supply of furs, the Iroquois began attacking Huron villages and intercepting and confiscating fur shipments along trade routes, provoking a series of conflicts known as the Beaver Wars.

The name "Iroquois" refers both to the members of the Iroquois Confederacy, or League of Five Nations (Senecas, Cayugas, Onondagas, Oneidas, and Mohawks), and to their language. Consolidation of the league in 1570 (although it had existed informally for several decades before that) helped end centuries of warring among these neighboring tribes and protected them from attacks by surrounding tribes. Although known throughout the woodlands as fierce warriors, the Iroquois had met European advances into their territory peacefully and created profitable alliances, such as their trade agreement with the Dutch at Albany.

In 1608, French explorer Samuel de Champlain established Quebec at a deserted Iroquois site on the St. Lawrence River. In the area, the Huron Confederacy of four tribes and their Algonquian allies began a trade agreement with the French that was coveted by the Iroquois. This rivalry increased long-existing hostility between Hurons and Iroquois.

In July, 1609, Champlain, two soldiers, and sixty Algonquians and Hurons followed a war party of two hundred Mohawks along what is now called Lake Champlain. In the traditional manner, both sides agreed to engage in battle in the morning. Iroquois warriors preferred close-in fighting with wooden clubs and leather shields, and were accustomed to using bows and arrows only for ambushes. As the battle began, both sides advanced, but the French remained hidden among the Hurons. Advancing closely, the French fired their guns, killing two Mohawk chiefs instantly and mortally wounding the third. Many Mohawks died and a dozen captives were taken, one of whom was tortured during the victory celebration. This dramatic battle was the Iroquois' first encounter with Europeans and their dreadful weapons. Their humiliation left the Iroquois with a fierce hatred of the French. A few weeks later, Henry Hudson arrived at Albany to initiate the Dutch fur trade, which eventually brought guns to the Iroquois.

In the next three decades, the Hurons and Iroquois lost many warriors in battle. The Jesuit priests who brought Christianity to Quebec also brought European diseases. By 1640, through warfare and epidemics, only ten thousand Hurons remained, less than half of their previous number. However, they retained their alliance with the French. Iroquois offers of peace with the Hurons were dissuaded by the French. In 1640, five hundred Iroquois approached a French village to negotiate for peace and trade a French captive for guns. When French offers were not acceptable, the council disbanded and the Iroquois began planning for war.

Early Iroquois warfare was guerrilla-style fighting by small bands, so the beginning date of the Beaver Wars is difficult to determine, but an attack by a Seneca war party on the Huron village of Arendaronon in 1642 is marked as the first event. Iroquois also raided the Algonquian village of Chief Iroquet on the Ottawa River, capturing and later releasing Father Isaac Jogues.

In 1645, the French bargained for peace, using Iroquois captives. The Iroquois wanted to share the middleman role with the Hurons and continue trading with the Dutch. At the council, the great Mohawk orator Kiotsaeton appealed to the French, Hurons, and Algonquians, presenting fifteen wampum belts. He translated the symbolic messages coded in the shell beads. After the council, Father Jogues and Father Paul Le Junne continued to support the peace effort.

Months later, some Mohawks reported to Huron chief Tandihetsi about secrecy and intrigue involving the possible exclusion of the Algonquians. The chief had a wife and many relatives among the Algonquians. Finally, a trade-related treaty was made, honored for a time, then broken when a huge shipment of furs passed down the Ottawa River and the Iroquois were given no share. In retaliation, the popular Father Jogues was killed when he returned to visit a Mohawk village.

European presence in North America affected Iroquois social and cultural systems that had provided earlier stability. Ecological balance was upset by the high demand for beaver pelts; economic balance, by the shift from farming to trapping; and political balance, by rivalries among tribes. The Iroquois

A Mohawk Indian chief c. 1709. The Mohawks were among the most powerful of the Five Nations of the Iroquois Confederacy, early becoming British allies against the French and playing a key role from the early seventeenth century through the French and Indian War. (Neg. No. 19312. Courtesy Department Library Services, American Museum of Natural History)

had become dependent upon the Dutch for food, metal tools, weapons, and ammunition. Since the primary commodity was beaver pelts and the agreement had been broken, the Iroquois began attacking Huron villages and intercepting travel along their trade routes, confiscating whole shipments of pelts. In times of warfare, one gun was well worth the price of twenty beaver pelts.

By March of 1649, the Iroquois had declared open warfare, and a thousand Iroquois set out for the Huron homeland. The starving Hurons, fearing annihilation, burned their villages and escaped into the woods, some to a Jesuit encampment, others divided into clan groups. Eventually, several thousand Hurons were adopted into the five Iroquois tribes. By late 1649, the Iroquois had defeated the Tobaccos; from 1650 to 1656, they warred against the Neutrals on the Niagara peninsula and the Eries on southern Lake Erie, devastating them and taking over their hunting territories. They successfully maintained trade with the Dutch under Governor Peter Stuyvesant.

By 1654, the Ottawas had taken over the Hurons' position as middlemen for the French. When the Iroquois attempted to displace them, the Ottawas moved westward to the Straits of Mackinac. For the next thirty years, they supplied two-thirds of the furs sent to France. By 1670, the Iroquois controlled the woodland territory surrounding the eastern Great Lakes, while the French claimed Lakes Huron and Superior.

In 1680, several hundred Iroquois invaded the territory of the Illinois and Miami tribes. In 1684, an unsuccessful attempt to take Fort St. Louis from Illinois marked the end of the nearly century-long Iroquois campaign to overturn the French-Huron trade monopoly.

During the Beaver Wars, the Iroquois had established a political agreement with the English through Governor Edmond Andros. This Covenant Chain was forged for two purposes: safe access to Albany for Iroquois traders and easy entry into the natives' affairs for the English. By 1685, the League of Five Nations had been consolidated to deal with external affairs.

Leagues, alliances, treaties, covenants, and confederacies all worked against the Europeans' establishing a niche in the New World. The powers of France and England had been balanced almost equally for many years, but long-held Iroquois hostility turned the scale against the French, and their magnificent schemes of colonization in the northern part of America were lost. Had it not been for the determination of the Iroquois, the official language throughout North America might have been French. 　　　　　—Gale M. Thompson

ADDITIONAL READING:

Cleland, Charles E. *Rites of Conquest: The History and Culture of Michigan's Native Americans.* Ann Arbor: University of Michigan Press, 1992. A multiethnic, regional approach to the history of the Ojibwa, Ottawa, and Potawatomi, from precontact to the late twentieth century. Maps, photographs, biographical sketches, chapter notes, bibliography, index.

Grinde, Donald A., Jr. *The Iroquois and the Founding of the American Nation.* San Francisco: Indian Historian Press,

1977. Provides cultural and historical background; discusses Iroquois relationships with colonists before and after the American Revolution. Photographs, maps, illustrations, references, sources. Constitution of the Five Nations and Albany Plan of Union are included as appendices.

Harvey, Karen D., and Lisa D. Harjo. *Indian Country: A History of Native People in America.* Golden, Colo.: North American Press, 1994. Written and illustrated by American Indians. Presents ten culture areas, historical perspectives, contemporary issues, major ceremonies, and time lines from 50,000 B.C. to the twentieth century. Summaries, lesson plans, resources, and index; appendices include "Threats to Religious Freedom," the text of the Fort Laramie Treaty of 1868, and a list of Indian activist organizations and events.

Magill, Frank N., and Harvey Markowitz, eds. *Ready Reference: American Indians.* Pasadena, Calif.: Salem Press, 1995. Comprehensive survey of Indians of the Americas, prehistory to late twentieth century. Discusses archeology, architecture, arts, crafts, culture, history, language, religion, and social organization of tribes in ten culture areas. Contains features on well-known persons, events, acts, and treaties. Tables, maps, illustrations, photographs, listing of organizations.

Steele, Ian K. *Warpaths: Invasions of North America.* New York: Oxford University Press, 1994. Discusses American Indian-European warfare in eastern North America, from the defeat of Juan Ponce de León (1513) to negotiated peace with the British (1765); combines social and military history for a balanced perspective. Maps, illustrations, extensive chapter notes, index.

SEE ALSO: 1500, Iroquois Confederacy; 1603, Champlain's Voyages; 1610, Hudson Explores Hudson Bay; 1627, Company of New France Is Chartered.

1643 ■ CONFEDERATION OF THE UNITED COLONIES OF NEW ENGLAND: *early cooperation among the colonies sets a precedent for later union*

DATE: September 8, 1643
LOCALE: Massachusetts Bay, Plymouth, Connecticut, and New Haven colonies
CATEGORY: Government and politics
KEY FIGURES:
William Collier (c.1612-1670), commissioner from Plymouth of the United Colonies of New England
Thomas Dudley (1576-1653), deputy governor of Massachusetts Bay Colony and commissioner of the United Colonies of New England
Theophilus Eaton (1590-1658), governor of the New Haven Colony and commissioner of the United Colonies of New England
George Fenwick (1603-1657), commissioner from Connecticut of the United Colonies of New England

John Haynes (1594-1654), governor of Connecticut and commissioner of the United Colonies of New England

Thomas Hooker (1586?-1647), Puritan divine and a leader in Connecticut

Edward Hopkins (1600-1657), governor and deputy governor of Connecticut and commissioner of the United Colonies of New England

Edward Winslow (1595-1655), commissioner from Plymouth of the United Colonies of New England

SUMMARY OF EVENT. In 1607, a shipload of settlers arrived in the New World and established Jamestown, in what is now Virginia. The next colonial settlement was founded in 1620 at Plymouth, in New England, by the Pilgrims, religious separatists who had been persecuted in Britain. When their ship, the *Mayflower* was blown off course and arrived farther north than expected, the colonists decided to create a new community there.

As New England settlement expanded north, south, and west during the 1630's, territorial conflicts became inevitable. Not only did the Puritan colonies attempt to encroach upon one another's territory, but they also came into hostile contact with the American Indians, the Dutch, and the French. Although the British had nearly destroyed the natives in the brief Pequot War of 1636-1637, the lack of coordinated effort had convinced the British that some form of intercolonial cooperation was necessary for determining military policies, ensuring participation, arbitrating territorial disputes, and regulating trade. Religious and political turmoil in Great Britain prevented the mother country from supervising colonial affairs directly, and the colonies preferred it that way. In the absence of formal control from above, however, the Puritan colonies saw the need for defending their expanding boundaries against foreign aggression.

The joint action in the Pequot War apparently had fostered a feeling of unity among the Puritan colonies. Furthermore, if the smaller, weaker colonies of Plymouth, Connecticut, and New Haven could enter into an agreement with the Massachusetts Bay Colony as political equals, they should be free from that powerful colony's attempts to encroach upon their territory. The Massachusetts Bay Colony, in turn, would profit from a union by gaining legal approval from the other members in its efforts to annex territory in Maine.

In the late summer of 1637, a synod of New England church leaders meeting in Cambridge seriously broached the subject of union for the first time, but disagreements marred that and several other attempts to achieve union during the next few years. Fear of an American Indian uprising in 1642, however, spurred Plymouth to send representatives to negotiate with the Massachusetts Bay Colony about their mutual defense. About the same time, Connecticut also sent a proposal for mutual defense efforts to Massachusetts. The Massachusetts General Court, therefore, ordered the magistrates to meet with the deputies of Connecticut, Plymouth, and New Haven on the matters of unification and defense.

Meeting in Boston on May 29, 1643, the American colonies of Massachusetts Bay, Connecticut, New Haven, and Plymouth formed a military alliance. Members of the alliance agreed to coordinate their military operations while retaining their independence in internal affairs. The representatives "readily yielded each to the other, in such things as tended to the common good," and drew up articles of confederation. When the last of the four General Courts ratified them on September 8, 1643, these articles of confederation became binding. The United Colonies of New England thereby established encompassed all the settlements along the coast and rivers from Long Island to New Hampshire. Rhode Island, which the Puritans disdainfully considered anarchical, and Maine were not included.

As stated in the preamble to the articles of confederation, the purposes of the confederation were to preserve the purity of the Puritans' religion and their ability to worship free of interference, to promote cooperation, and to provide for defense. The articles themselves specified the duties and powers of the confederation's commissioners, the structure of the confederation, and the rules of procedure. Because there was no judicial authority over all the members, each colony could interpret the articles of confederation to its own liking—a situation that was to cause problems later.

The governing body of the confederation was to consist of two commissioners chosen annually from each colony. The only qualifications demanded were that they be church members and that they bring full power from their general courts. The commissioners were to convene each September and meet in each colony successively. Anyone who had advice to offer was welcome to speak before them. Three magistrates from any colony could call a special meeting if necessary. Approval of a matter required the votes of six commissioners, although war could be declared by only four in a state of emergency. Thus, the Massachusetts Bay Colony could not veto the wishes of the other three colonies.

How much actual power did the commissioners possess? The answer to this question is essential to understanding the accomplishments and defects of the confederation. The United Colonies of New England did not consider themselves a nation, but rather individual governments allied by a treaty. Each commissioner actually served as one of his colony's ambassadors. In matters of military preparation, declaration of war, and arbitration, the four colonies did surrender to the commissioners their individual power to act. Although the confederation, in theory, possessed vague executive and judicial powers, in actuality it had only advisory powers in most areas.

The articles of confederation specified that each colony's military obligation should be in proportion to its means and population. Each colony was expected to send aid if one of the other three colonies should be invaded and was to participate in all just wars. The commissioners were empowered to decide if the confederation should wage an offensive war, and no colony could do so without its approval.

Apart from military affairs, actual power rested with the general courts of the member colonies. The commissioners could not pass legislation binding on the general courts, nor were they directly responsible to the people. They could neither levy taxes nor requisition supplies. Because the commissioners had no powers of enforcement, a colony that disagreed with a particular decision could nullify it simply by refusing to comply. To avoid conflict, the remaining colonies usually compromised.

Although lacking in power, the Board of Commissioners did perform numerous important services for the four participating colonies. It established various civil agreements of interest to all four colonies and arbitrated intercolonial disputes. Policies concerning American Indians, and regulations governing runaway slaves and the extradition of criminals were also within its domain. In the judicial realm, the commissioners established uniform standards for probating wills and served as an admiralty court. Other duties included fund-raising for Harvard College, settling tariff disputes, and promoting religious orthodoxy.

The successful achievement of the aims of the alliance was hampered by the development of bitter rivalries among the signatories. Massachusetts Bay Colony, for example, attempted to win a predominant position within the confederation on the grounds that it had the largest population; failing in this attempt, it refused, in 1653, to participate in the projected war against the Dutch colonies in America.

The major specific achievement of the military alliance of the confederation was the successful cooperation of its members in King Philip's (Metacom's) War of 1675, in which the colonies crushed an uprising of American Indian tribes in New England. On a less tangible but more significant level, the confederation of the United Colonies of New England was essential to the colonies' survival in the colonies' early years and, despite its flaws, offered a means of coordinating intercolonial resources and resolving disputes. In 1684, shortly after the charter of the Massachusetts Bay Colony had been revoked by the British government, the confederation was dissolved.

Unquestionably, serious flaws were inherent in the confederation of the United Colonies of New England. The illusion of power survived only for the first decade of its existence. Yet, it was to be the longest-lived interstate confederation in American history. The leadership that the confederation provided was essential to the existence of the colonies in their early years. It concentrated the colonies' resources in military emergencies and protected the three weaker colonies from encroachment by the Massachusetts Bay Colony. Most important of all, it preserved the peace in New England.

—*Warren M. Billings, updated by Susan M. Taylor*

ADDITIONAL READING:

Andrews, Charles M. *The Settlements.* Vols. 1 and 2 in *The Colonial Period of American History.* New Haven, Conn.: Yale University Press, 1964. The chapters on the New England colonies contain frequent references to the affairs and problems of the Confederation of the United Colonies of New England.

Francis, Mark. *Governors and Settlers: Images of Authority in the British Colonies.* London: Macmillan, 1992. Discusses administration and cooperation in the early New England colonies and provides historical background.

Fraser, Gary. *Ambivalent Anti-Colonialism: The United States and the Genesis of West Indian Independence.* Westport, Conn.: Greenwood Press, 1994. Provides a detailed discussion of the early history of the colonies and British relations with the United States.

Greene, Jack P. *Pursuits of Happiness: Social Development of Early Modern British Colonies and the Formation of American Culture.* Chapel Hill: University of North Carolina Press, 1988. Explains the models of English colonization from 1600 to 1660.

Osgood, Herbert L. *The American Colonies in the Seventeenth Century.* Gloucester, Mass.: Peter Smith, 1957. Provides an institutional history of England's mainland colonies, focusing on the commercial relationship between Great Britain and America.

Ward, Harry M. *The United Colonies of New England, 1643-1690.* New York: Vantage Press, 1961. Examines the ideas that influenced the Founding Fathers and explains what prompted attempts at unification.

SEE ALSO: 1620, Pilgrims Land at Plymouth; 1630, Great Puritan Migration; 1632, Settlement of Connecticut; 1636, Rhode Island Is Founded; 1636, Pequot War; 1650, Harvard College Is Established; 1671, Indian Slave Trade; 1686, Dominion of New England Forms.

1649 ■ MARYLAND ACT OF TOLERATION: *the first codification of the policy of religious toleration*

DATE: April 21, 1649

LOCALE: St. Mary's, Maryland

CATEGORIES: Laws and acts; Religion

KEY FIGURES:

Cecilius Calvert, second Lord Baltimore (1605-1675), son of George Calvert and the first proprietor of Maryland

George Calvert, first Lord Baltimore (1580?-1632), who petitioned Charles I for a charter to found a colony north of the Potomac River

Leonard Calvert (1606-1647), brother of the first proprietor and the first governor of Maryland

SUMMARY OF EVENT. In his instructions to his brother Leonard Calvert and the commissioners leading the first settlers to Maryland in 1633, the colony's first proprietor, Cecilius Calvert, second Lord Baltimore, cautioned that "they be very carefull to preserve unity and peace amongst all the passengers on Shipp-board, and that they suffer no scandall nor offence to be given to any of the Protestants. . . ." George Calvert, the first Lord Baltimore and father of Cecilius and Leonard, had died the previous year before his goal of founding a colony free from religious animosity could be realized. While the sincerity of Lord Baltimore's position is unquestionable, it was nonetheless necessary to the recruitment of Protestant settlers for the venture. It would have been impossible to find enough British Catholics willing to emigrate; so advantages had to be offered men of humbler rank, usually loyal practicing members of the Church of England, to persuade them to participate in an undertaking led by Catholic gentlemen.

Some Catholics took advantage of the freedom of religion to proselytize among colonists as well as among the native populations of the colony. To seek to convert colonists was illegal and it was punished because religious toleration was practiced from the first. Maryland was indeed unique. Nowhere else had anyone experimented with the concept that Protestants and Catholics could live together amicably and enjoy political and religious equality. Anyone who dared attempt to force his beliefs upon another could expect to meet the fate of one William Lewis, a Catholic who was fined heavily in 1638 for proselytizing among the Protestants. Cecilius Calvert, loyal to his father's purpose, encouraged missionary work by all Christians among the Indians, and Catholics and Protestants used the same chapel for their services of worship. That there should be no established church in Maryland Cecilius Calvert had determined; likewise, the government should not interfere in spiritual matters. Because of this policy Maryland was able to attract non-Catholics from England and even Puritans and Anglicans from New England.

In ensuring the first of these tenets, the first proprietor became involved in a long dispute with the Jesuit missionaries in the colony. Claiming that they were exempt from the civil authority, the Jesuits wanted to obtain land directly from the Indians rather than through the proprietary, as the charter specified. They also demanded special privileges, such as exemption from paying quitrents, and preferred treatment for their retainers and servants. Lord Baltimore finally prevailed when the Jesuits' father provincial ordered them to renounce their claims.

The decade between 1640 and 1650 was an inauspicious time for trying to stabilize a colony founded on the principle of religious toleration. Leonard Calvert barely managed to recover the province after having been forced to flee to Virginia in 1644 when William Claiborne, a troublemaker of long standing, captured Kent Island, and Richard Ingle took St. Mary's and plundered the colony. The combination of American discord and England's civil war was almost fatal for Lord Baltimore's proprietorship. Only through his shrewdness was he able to ward off revocation of his charter by the triumphant Puritans, and as it was, Catholics and loyalists were threatened with imprisonment and confiscation of their property.

Amid this turmoil Lord Baltimore drafted the famous document "An Act Concerning Religion," which has come to be known as the Toleration Act. The General Assembly passed the measure on April 21, 1649. Since toleration had been practiced from the colony's founding, the act represented no change in Lord Baltimore's policy. It apparently was passed in order to refute the charge by those who had tried to annul the charter that the colony was a hotbed of popery. The act had two parts, each with its own preamble, but the second part, positive in its sentiment, was apparently framed by Cecilius Calvert. This section proclaimed that no person "professing to believe in Jesus Christ shall from henceforth be any waies troubled, molested or discountenanced, for or in respect of his or her Religion, nor in the free Exercise thereof within this Province. . . ." It further provided for the punishment of anyone failing to respect these rights. The first clause of the act was added later by the General Assembly, then controlled by a Protestant-Puritan majority, to accord with an act passed by Britain's Long Parliament in 1648 to punish heresies and blasphemies. As punishment for blasphemy, or for denying the Holy Trinity, or that Jesus Christ was the Son of God, it prescribed the penalty of death and confiscation of property. Paradoxically, the next section again emphasized toleration, prohibiting disparagement "in a reproachful manner" of any religious group and stipulating penalties for offenders. Finally, the act forbade swearing, drunkenness, recreation, and labor on the Sabbath.

"An Act Concerning Religion," therefore, did not guarantee complete religious liberty, freedom of thought, or separation of church and state. The first part, added by the General Assembly, actually represented a regression, since it formally limited toleration to Trinitarian Christians. What the act did accomplish was the official, formal expression of the toleration of Catholics and Protestants for each other's beliefs which had been practiced since 1634.

Following an investigation into the colony by parliamentary commissioners, the Puritan-dominated Assembly which was called on October 30, 1654, repudiated Lord Baltimore's authority, repealed the Toleration Act, and replaced it with an act denying Catholics protection. When the Calverts regained control in 1657, however, Lord Baltimore promised to stand firm for "An Act Concerning Religion."

—*Warren M. Billings, updated by Daniel A. Brown*

ADDITIONAL READING:

Andrews, Charles M. *The Settlements*. Vol. 2 in *The Colonial Period of American History*. New Haven, Conn.: Yale University Press, 1964. Writing from the English point of view, the author places the Calverts into their British context, demonstrating the practical nature of the proprietors in promoting religious toleration.

Andrews, Matthew P. *The Founding of Maryland*. Baltimore: Williams and Wilkins, 1933. The Catholic founders of the colony, from the start, promoted religious toleration and punished only those who bothered their colonial neighbors by proselytizing.

Craven, Wesley F. *The Southern Colonies in the Seventeenth Century, 1607-1689*. Baton Rouge: Louisiana State University Press, 1949. Chapters 6 and 7 provide an introduction to Maryland's beginnings, especially in religious matters.

Hall, Clayton C., ed. *Narratives of Early Maryland, 1633-1684*. New York: Barnes and Noble, 1946. This collection of original documents includes Lord Baltimore's instructions to the colonists, the text of the Act of Toleration, and various firsthand accounts of the early years of the Maryland colony.

Hanley, Thomas. *Their Rights and Liberties: The Beginnings of Religious and Political Freedom in Maryland*. Westminster, Md.: Newman Press, 1959. The principles of religious freedom were in evidence long before the Act of Toleration, and those principles were much more extensive than the Puritan Assembly eventually permitted.

Hennessey, James. "Catholics in an American Environment: The Early Years." *Theological Studies* 50 (1989): 657-675. Lord Baltimore considered conscience, not political expedience or civil authority as paramount when it came to colonists—even if not to the natives of the colony who were "idolaters."

Jordan, David. "The Miracle of This Age: Maryland's Experiment in Religious Toleration, 1649-1689." *Historian* 47 (1985): 338-359. A careful account of the Act of Toleration and its subsequent rocky history.

Lasson, Kenneth. "Free Exercise in the Free State: Maryland's Role in Religious Liberty and the First Amendment." *Journal of Church and State* 31 (1989), 419-449. The author argues that Maryland colonial experience helped shape the eventual policy of the new nation.

Steiner, Bernard C. *Beginnings of Maryland*. Baltimore: The Johns Hopkins University Press, 1903. Relations between Protestants and Catholics are covered well in this general history.

Terrar, Edward. "Was There a Separation Between Church and State in Mid-Seventeenth Century England and Colonial Maryland?" *Journal of Church and State* 35 (1993): 61-82. Not only was there religious toleration in the colony, but there was also an inchoate separation of church and state, largely through the leadership of the Calverts.

SEE ALSO: 1630, Great Puritan Migration; 1636, Rhode Island Is Founded.

1650 ■ HARVARD COLLEGE IS ESTABLISHED: *the birth of higher education and the foundation for public education*

DATE: May 30-31, 1650
LOCALE: Massachusetts Bay Colony
CATEGORIES: Education; Organizations and institutions
KEY FIGURES:
Richard Bellingham (1592?-1672), treasurer of Massachusetts Bay Colony and member of the Board of Overseers
Thomas Dudley (1576-1653), deputy governor of Massachusetts Bay Colony and member of the Board of Overseers

Henry Dunster (1609-1659), first president of Harvard College
Nathaniel Eaton (1609?-1674), first professor to be appointed by the Board of Overseers
John Harvard (1607-1638), first benefactor of Harvard College
Anne Hutchinson (1591-1643), central figure in the Antinomian crisis that delayed the founding of Harvard
Henry Vane (1613-1662), governor of Massachusetts Bay Colony in 1636
John Winthrop (1588-1649), governor of Massachusetts Bay Colony after 1637 and charter member of the Board of Overseers

SUMMARY OF EVENT. In *New England's First Fruits*, the famous tract extolling the virtues of New England to possible supporters in the old country, the Puritans proclaimed that one of their first concerns had been "to advance *Learning* and perpetuate it to Posterity; dreading to leave an illiterate Ministry to the Churches, when our present Ministers shall be in the Dust." Because the Puritan church's tenets emphasized interpretation and discussion of the Scriptures rather than mere ritual or emotion, it required a learned clergy. Therefore, on October 28, 1636, the Massachusetts General Court passed a legislative act to found "a schoale or colledge" and voted four hundred pounds sterling for its support. The Antinomian crisis revolving around Anne Hutchinson delayed action on the matter until November 15, 1637, when, after debating whether the college should be built in Salem, the Massachusetts General Court passed an order that the college be built at Newetowne. A few days later, the building of the college was committed to the first Board of Overseers, consisting of six magistrates and six church elders. The location for the school was chosen partly because of its resemblance to Oxford and Cambridge in England; hence, Newetowne was renamed Cambridge on May 2, 1638.

By June, 1638, Nathaniel Eaton, the professor engaged by the overseers, had moved into the house acquired for him in the midst of a cow pasture, and the Massachusetts General Court had granted three lots to him for the college. Within a few months, the first classes were being taught, the building was being constructed, and a library was being assembled.

The college already was operating when, on September 14, 1638, a young clergyman named John Harvard died and left his library and half of his estate, amounting to about eight hundred pounds sterling, to the new institution. Although Harvard was not responsible for the founding of the college, nor did his legacy make its establishment possible, his gift was a remarkable one for the times, and the Massachusetts General Court voted on March 13, 1639, to name the college after him.

Unfortunately, Professor Eaton's most praiseworthy accomplishment was the planting and fencing of the yard to keep the cows out and the students in. His tyrannical tenure was marred by beatings and dismal living conditions for the students who boarded at his home. Mistress Eaton's "loathsome catering," featuring such items as "goat's dung in their hasty pudding,"

Harvard College, c. 1725. Some three-quarters of a century after its founding, the college was already a venerable institution. (Library of Congress)

provided an inauspicious beginning for that much-maligned institution, the college dining hall. When Eaton's cruelty finally came to the attention of the Massachusetts General Court, he was fined and dismissed, and the college closed its doors at the beginning of its second year. Lacking an instructor, the school remained closed for nearly a full year, although construction work continued.

On August 27, 1640, Henry Dunster, a graduate of Magdalene College, Cambridge, was invited to become the school's first president. He accepted and began teaching classes that fall, infusing life into the college and providing a firm foundation for its growth. The class of 1642 returned, a new freshman class entered, and a three-year course in the arts was established. A thorough knowledge of Greek and Latin was required for admission. Dunster personally instructed the three classes in the arts, philosophies, and Oriental languages, and he also moderated the students' disputations. Although the Puritans believed that knowledge without Christ was vain, Harvard College was less ecclesiastical than the universities at

Oxford and Cambridge, for it strove to provide a course in philosophy and the liberal arts that would be suitable either for a general education or as a basis for entering one of the professions.

Determined to establish in America the collegiate system as it was practiced in England, under which the students lived, studied, ate, and disputed together with their tutors, Dunster and the overseers were anxious to complete the first building despite the economic depression. Donations made possible the occupation of the "Old College" in September, 1642, in time for the commencement of the first nine graduates. Within this building, the students attended classes, studied, ate, and slept.

During its early years, Harvard College had serious financial problems. Lacking any sort of endowment or income-producing lands, it struggled along on tuition fees, and the ferry rents and town levies that it was granted. A fund-raising mission to England met with moderate success, and in 1644, representatives at the meeting of the United Colonies of New England agreed that all the Puritan colonies should share in supporting the college. Each family was obligated to give a peck of wheat or one shilling annually. Governor Thomas Dudley signed Harvard College's first official charter on May 30-31, 1650.

The establishment and support of a college was an ambitious undertaking for such a new, economically insecure community. Only the strong religious faith of the Puritans in the purpose of their endeavor carried it through. Contrary to the claims of various educational historians, the Puritans took a greater interest in intellectual pursuits than other Englishmen of their day. Their concentrated system of settlement in towns rendered the accomplishment of popular education easier than in Virginia, where the population was dispersed. Even before the law required it, a number of towns established schools: Boston hired a master in 1635, as did Charlestown in 1636. The first New England school legislation, the Massachusetts Act of 1642, required the heads of families to teach their children and servants "to read and understand the principles of religion and the capital laws of the country" and to see that they were employed in useful occupations. Thus the Puritans envisioned education serving social and economic needs: It provided training for citizenship and service in the community.

The laissez-faire system apparently proved to be unsatisfactory: In 1647, the Massachusetts General Court passed a law requiring every town of fifty families to appoint a schoolmaster "to teach all such children as shall resort to him to write and read." His wages were to be paid by the parents or the town, as the town should choose. Towns of one hundred families were to establish grammar schools to instruct youth "so far as they may be fitted for the Universitie." The cost of supporting the schools was a hardship on some of the smaller communities, and the uneducated complained of the ruling class trying to force its high standards upon the poor. Thus, interest in public education did not work its way up from the bottom but down from the top.

—Warren M. Billings, updated by Geralyn Strecker

ADDITIONAL READING:

Bailyn, Bernard, et al., eds. *Glimpses of the Harvard Past.* Cambridge, Mass.: Harvard University Press, 1986. Contains essays on each major phase of the school's development. Bailyn's essay, "Foundations," deals with Harvard's early years.

Lipset, Seymour Martin, and David Riesman. *Education and Politics at Harvard.* New York: McGraw-Hill, 1975. Critical discussion of political controversies at Harvard. The chapter on "The Colonial Period" deals with discipline and academic freedom, among other issues.

Maddocks, Melvin. "Harvard Was Once, Unimaginably, Small and Humble." *Smithsonian* 17, no. 6 (June, 1986): 140-160. This accessible article describes the hardships faced by Harvard students from the school's beginnings through the nineteenth century.

Morison, Samuel Eliot. *The Founding of Harvard College.* Cambridge, Mass.: Harvard University Press, 1935. This first

volume of Harvard's official tercentennial history sets the school's founding and early development up to 1650 in context with the rise of liberal arts and European universities during the Renaissance.

_____. *Harvard College in the Seventeenth Century.* 2 vols. Cambridge, Mass.: Harvard University Press, 1936. These books continue Morison's tercentennial history of the college, from the granting of its first charter in 1650 through 1708.

_____. "The Puritan Age, 1636-1707." *Three Centuries of Harvard: 1636-1936.* Cambridge, Mass.: Harvard University Press, 1936. A condensed history of Harvard's founding.

Quincy, Josiah. *The History of Harvard University.* 2 vols. Cambridge, Mass.: John Owen, 1840. Reprint. New York: Arno Press, 1977. The official history of the college, written in celebration of its bicentennial.

SEE ALSO: 1630, Great Puritan Migration; 1632, Settlement of Connecticut; 1643, Confederation of the United Colonies of New England; 1820's, Free Public School Movement.

1654 ■ FIRST JEWISH SETTLERS: *their right to live and work in New Netherland, despite intense opposition, lays the groundwork for greater religious toleration*

DATE: August-September, 1654
LOCALE: Manhattan Island
CATEGORIES: Jewish American history; Religion
KEY FIGURES:
Asser Levy (1628?-1682), first Jew to own land and obtain burgher right in New Amsterdam
Dominie Johannes Megapolensis (1603-1670), preacher in New Amsterdam
Peter Stuyvesant (c. 1610-1672), director general of New Netherland, 1647-1664

SUMMARY OF EVENT. The first Jewish settlers of record in New Amsterdam were Jacob Barsimon and Solomon Pieterson, both of whom came from Holland in the summer of 1654. The next month, twenty-three other Jews arrived, both old and young, refugees from the Portuguese conquest of Dutch Brazil (New Holland), which had been the richest property of the Dutch West India Company in America. After leaving Recife, Brazil, their ship had been captured by Spanish pirates, from whom they were saved by a French privateer, the *St. Charles,* captained by Jacques de La Motthe. Having little more than the clothes on their backs, the Jewish migrants convinced La Motthe to carry them to New Amsterdam for twenty-five hundred guilders, which they hoped to borrow in that Dutch port. They shortly discovered, however, what Jacob Barsimon and Solomon Pieterson were already learning: There was much opposition to Jews settling in New Netherland.

Their poverty made the Dutch Jews from Brazil especially vulnerable. Unable to borrow the money, they asked La Motthe for extra time to contact friends and receive money from Amsterdam. Rather than waiting, La Motthe brought suit in the City Court of New Amsterdam, which ordered that their meager belongings should be sold at public auction. Even after all that was worth selling had been sold, the unfortunate exiles still owed almost five hundred guilders. The City Court then ordered that two of the Jews—David Israel and Moses Ambroisius—should be held under civil arrest until the total debt was paid. In October, the matter finally was resolved after the crew of the *St. Charles*, holding title to the remainder of the Jewish debt, agreed to wait until additional funds could be sent from Amsterdam.

Yet the ordeal of the Jewish refugees was far from over. They wanted to remain in New Amsterdam, Director General Peter Stuyvesant complained to the Amsterdam Chamber of the Dutch West India Company. Stuyvesant was against their staying, as were the city magistrates, who resented "their customary usury and deceitful trading with the Christians," and the deacons of the Reformed Church, who feared that in "their present indigence they might become a charge in the coming winter." Indicating that the colonists generally shared his anti-Semitic views, Stuyvesant informed the Amsterdam directors that "we have for the benefit of this weak and newly developing place and the land in general, deemed it useful to require them in a friendly way to depart." As for the future, he urged "that the deceitful race—such hateful enemies and blasphemers of the name of Christ—be not allowed further to infect and trouble this new colony, to the detraction of your Worships and the dissatisfaction of your Worships' most affectionate subjects."

Despite his vehemence against the Jews, Stuyvesant delayed his expulsion order, waiting instead for guidance from the Amsterdam Chamber of the Dutch West India Company, to whom the unwanted refugees were also appealing. The Jewish community in Amsterdam took up their cause. During the early sixteenth century, the embattled United Provinces—and especially the city of Amsterdam—had become a haven for persecuted European Jews, whose many contributions to Dutch economic and cultural life had brought them considerable religious freedom, political and legal rights, and economic privileges. Not only did Jewish investors own approximately 4 percent of the Dutch West India Company's stock, but also, more than six hundred Dutch Jews had participated in colonizing Dutch Brazil. Virtually all of them left Pernambuco in 1654 with other Dutch nationals, losing practically everything, although the conquering Portuguese had urged them to remain and promised to protect their property. Their loyalty to the Dutch republic could hardly be questioned. Moreover, thinly populated New Netherland desperately needed settlers.

On the other hand, Dominie Johannes Megapolensis, one of the leading Dutch Reformed preachers in New Netherland, was especially disturbed because a few additional Jewish families recently had migrated from Amsterdam. He called upon the Amsterdam Classis of the Reformed Church to use its

influence to have the Jews expelled from the American colony. "These people have no other God than the Mammon of unrighteousness," warned Dominie Megapolensis, "and no other aim than to get possession of Christian property, and to overcome all other merchants by drawing all trade toward themselves." Surely, Megapolensis pleaded, these "godless rascals" should be expelled.

Expressing some sympathy for Stuyvesant's anti-Jewish prejudice, the Amsterdam Chamber nevertheless announced in early 1655 that Jews could travel, trade, and live in New Netherland, provided they cared for their own poor. Over the next few years, while not directly defying the company's directive, Stuyvesant and other civil officials delayed, obstructed, and otherwise made life more difficult for the Jews of New Amsterdam. In March, 1655, for example, Abraham de Lucena was arrested for selling goods on Sunday. In July, de Lucena and others petitioned to purchase land for a Jewish cemetery, but were denied. Indeed, Jews were not allowed to purchase land in New Amsterdam. They also were exempted from the city militia, on grounds that other colonists would not serve with them, but were required to pay a heavy tax each month in lieu of service.

The Jews of New Amsterdam resented and resisted such treatment. In November, when Asser Levy and Jacob Barsimon, two young Jews with little money, protested the tax and asked to do service with the militia instead, the town council dismissed their protest and noted that the petitioners could choose to go elsewhere. The same message was conveyed by the heavy rates imposed upon Jews in the general levy to raise funds for rebuilding the city's defense wall. Most discouraging were the restrictions placed on Jews who wished to trade to Albany and Delaware Bay.

In 1656, the Amsterdam Chamber chastised Stuyvesant and insisted that Jews in New Netherland were to have the same rights and privileges as Jews in old Amsterdam. They could trade wholesale, rent and buy property, and enjoy the protection of the law as other Dutch citizens did. However, their religious freedom did not extend to public worship, and they were not allowed to sell retail, work as mechanics, or live and work outside a designated area of town. Despite the opposition of the Burgomasters and Schepens, Stuyvesant, ever the faithful servant of the Dutch West India Company, insisted that Asser Levy be admitted to the burgher right, which allowed him to run a business, vote in town elections, and even hold office. New Amsterdam Jews were not ghettoized, and they could work as mechanics and tradesmen as well as shopkeepers and merchants. Asser Levy became the first Jewish landowner and was one of two Jews licensed as butchers in 1660.

Prejudice remained, but social and economic acceptance came to the Jewish community in New Amsterdam. They were allowed their separate burial ground, and their right to observe the Sabbath on Saturday was respected. They never established a synagogue and may not have had enough people to maintain a congregation, but regular religious services apparently were held. Asser Levy owned a Torah, and others had prayer books and shawls. Most of the Jews in New Amsterdam were Sephardim, descended from Portuguese Jews, although a few were Ashkenazim Jews from Germany, France, and Eastern Europe. Their numbers remained quite small, never more than a handful of families, and there seems to have been a good deal of migration in and out. However, the Jews of New Amsterdam were pioneers who prepared the way for the more extensive Jewish community that would emerge in early New York.

—*Ronald W. Howard*

ADDITIONAL READING:

Hershkowitz, Leo. "Judaism." In *The Encyclopedia of the North American Colonies*, edited by Jacob Ernest Cook. Vol. 3. New York: Charles Scribner's Sons, 1993. Brief but incisive summary of colonial Judaism.

Kessler, Henry H., and Eugene Rachlis. *Peter Stuyvesant and His New York*. New York: Random House, 1959. Gives insight into the anti-Semitism of Dutch Calvinism and the cooperative efforts of Stuyvesant and the Dutch Reformed preachers against the Jews.

Marcus, Jacob R. *The Colonial American Jew, 1492-1776*. 3 vols. Detroit, Mich.: Wayne State University Press, 1970. Presents a detailed survey of the Jewish experience in early America, relating connections between the various Jewish communities.

Oppenheim, Samuel. *The Early History of the Jews in New York, 1654-1664*. New York: American Jewish Historical Society, 1909. Basic source for details on early Jewish settlers and their trials, tribulations, and successes.

Rink, Oliver A. *Holland on the Hudson: An Economic and Social History of Dutch New York*. Ithaca, N.Y.: Cornell University Press, 1986. An account that relates the Jewish migration to larger economic and social developments in New Netherland.

Smith, George L. *Religion and Trade in New Netherland: Dutch Origins and American Development*. Ithaca, N.Y.: Cornell University Press, 1973. An analysis of religious toleration that emerged in the northern Netherlands and its transference to New Netherland.

1660 ■ BRITISH NAVIGATION ACTS:
attempts to force the American colonies to trade only with England

DATE: September 13, 1660-July 27, 1663
LOCALE: British Empire, including the American colonies
CATEGORIES: Economics; Laws and acts
KEY FIGURES:
Charles II (1630-1685), king of England
George Downing (1623-1684), member of Parliament and commissioner of customs
Edward Hyde, earl of Clarendon (1609-1674), lord chancellor appointed by Charles

George Monck, earl of Torrington (1608-1670), privy councilor
Thomas Povey, influential English merchant
John Shaw, English financier who brought the Navigation Act of 1660 before Parliament
Thomas Wriothesley, fourth earl of Southampton (1607-1667), lord high treasurer of England

SUMMARY OF EVENT. During the Elizabethan era, England, hitherto an agricultural country, began to emerge as a great nation ready to compete with the other European nations for wealth and power. The doctrine of mercantilism that the Crown adopted decreed that a nation must attain a favorable balance of trade—that is, to export more than it imported—in order to accumulate bullion for financing war efforts and maintaining national security. Because the navy was thought to be essential to the strength of the nation and because commercial maritime activity enhanced naval power, attention in the seventeenth century centered upon the promotion of English shipping. Success demanded the overthrow of the Dutch monopoly in the carrying trade.

All the great commercial rivals of the seventeenth century accepted the tenets that colonies existed for the benefit of the mother country and that the colonies' trade should be restricted to the mother country. As England's knowledge of its colonies and of the new products to be reaped from them increased, so did its expectation of the colonies' potential contribution to its grand scheme. England lacked definite laws relating to commercial policy until 1650, when a combination of private corporate interests and the national interest motivated Parliament to enact legislation designed to attain the national goals. In an attempt to break Dutch control of commerce, Parliament in 1650 forbade foreign ships to trade with the colonies without a license. The following year, Parliament enacted a law stating, in part, that only British-owned ships of which the master and majority of the crew were British could import goods from Asia, Africa, and America into Great Britain, Ireland, or the colonies; only British ships or ships of the country of origin could import European goods into Great Britain, Ireland, or the colonies; and foreign goods could be imported into England only from the place of production. The act also prohibited British merchant ships from sailing from country to country to take on produce for import; more seriously, it provoked a two-year war with the Dutch. The entire period from 1651 to 1660 was marked by a great commercial struggle among the powers of western and northern Europe. Furthermore, the last years before the Restoration in Great Britain were fraught with uncertainty and financial difficulties.

When Charles II came to the throne in 1660, he acted upon the urging of the merchants to promote British commerce. He established two councils, one for trade and one for plantations, consisting of lords, merchants, planters, and sea captains. Through the Crown's instructions to these councils, commercial policies gradually were defined. At the same time, Parliament gave the policies statutory authority. The first of such measures was the Navigation Act of 1660, sponsored by John

Shaw, a prominent financier, and Sir George Downing, later commissioner of customs. Enacted by the Convention Parliament on September 13, 1660, and confirmed by the first regular Restoration Parliament on July 27, 1661, the act was similar to that of 1651 in many respects. Certain defects and ambiguities in the earlier act had hindered enforcement, and certain revisions were necessary. The act of 1660 provided that only British-built or British-owned ships of which the masters and three-quarters of the crew were British could import or export goods or commodities, regardless of origin, to and from the British colonies. It further restricted shipment of certain enumerated articles produced in the colonies (sugar, tobacco, cotton, indigo, ginger, speckle wood, and dye-woods) to Great Britain or its colonies, and required ships sailing from the colonies to give bond that they would unload their cargoes in the realm. The enumeration clause was intended to increase England's customs revenues, to ensure its access to raw materials, and to advance domestic industries by creating employment in the trades that employed the enumerated products.

In practice, the 1660 regulations created many problems, and shippers took advantage of loopholes and ambiguities to evade the law. Probably to facilitate enforcement, Parliament passed the Act of Frauds in 1662. It restricted the privileges of the act of 1660 to ships built in England, except for ships bought before 1662.

Great Britain still had to clarify the dependent relationship of its colonies to the mother country. If the government were to recover from virtual bankruptcy incurred by the Puritans and royal debts, it could not allow the colonies to buy European products at cheaper prices, and it had to gain customs revenues from the colonial merchants. To make Great Britain the sole exporting center for colonial imports and thus constitute it a "staple," Parliament, on July 27, 1663, passed the "Act for the Encouragement of Trade." Henceforth, European goods could be imported to the colonies only from England and in English-built ships. The only exceptions to the rule were salt for the New England and Newfoundland fisheries, wine from Madeira and the Azores, and provisions, servants, and horses from Ireland and Scotland.

Because of the complexity of the Navigation Acts, administrative discretion was important in determining how they should be interpreted and enforced. In the colonies, enforcement lay with the governors, who were required to send to England reports of all vessels trading within their jurisdiction and copies of the bonds required of all ships' masters. Both colonial and English sea captains, however, found ways of continuing direct trade with Europe, and smuggling was common. In the period immediately following passage of the Navigation Acts, the colonists protested about the restriction on their markets. As English markets became glutted with colonial goods, the returns that the colonists could expect decreased. The Puritans of the Massachusetts Bay Colony objected to the acts on the basis that, since they were not represented in Parliament, they were not subject to the laws passed by Parliament. Gradually, however, most colonists ad-

justed to compliance, and the insurrections that occurred in the years following cannot be attributed in any large sense to the Navigation Acts.

As far as England was concerned, the legislation did achieve its purpose. Colonial trade with England and British overseas shipping increased more rapidly than before. There were sufficient causes for the American Revolution apart from the Navigation Acts, and the habits of trade that the acts established lasted beyond the eighteenth century. Great Britain had become the world's greatest commercial and maritime power.
                                                    —*Warren M. Billings*

ADDITIONAL READING:

Andrews, Charles, M. *England's Commercial and Colonial Policy*. Vol. 4 in *The Colonial Period of American History*. New Haven, Conn.: Yale University Press, 1964. Argues that the Navigation Acts were expressions of Great Britain's goal to develop a great commercial and colonial empire.

Brenner, Robert. *Merchants and Revolution: Commercial Change, Political Conflict and London's Overseas Traders, 1550-1653*. Princeton, N.J.: Princeton University Press, 1993. Provocative revisionism on mercantilism, colonialism, the English merchant class, the role of politics, and the place of London in the commercial and maritime structure of the British Empire.

Clark, Sir George. *The Later Stuarts, 1660-1714*. Vol. 10 in *The Oxford History of England*. Oxford, England: Clarendon Press, 1955. A standard history of the late seventeenth century England. Depicts the Restoration period, 1660-1685, as characterized by an elaborate and rigid system of trade regulation and protectionism, policies that originated under the Commonwealth.

Davies, Godfrey. *The Early Stuarts, 1603-1660*. Vol. 9 in *The Oxford History of England*. Oxford, England: Clarendon Press, 1959. Stresses the link between the powerful Dutch commercial empire and the aspiring English determined to compete with and surpass the Dutch.

Dickerson, Oliver M. *The Navigation Acts and the American Revolution*. Philadelphia: University of Pennsylvania Press, 1951. Analyzes the impact of the Navigation Acts in the seventeenth and eighteenth centuries, the role of mercantilism, and the origins of the American Revolution.

Farnell, J. C. "The Navigation Act of 1651, the First Dutch War, and the London Merchant Community." *Economic History Review*, 2d ser., 16 (1963-1964): 439-454. Credits Adam Smith with enunciating the rationale for the Navigation Acts; traces the origins of the acts to Maurice Thompson, who was engaged in colonial trade in the late 1620's.

Harper, Lawrence A. *The English Navigation Laws*. New York: Octagon Books, 1964. The definitive work on the series of Navigation Acts of the 1650's and 1660's. Argues that the English acts were an experiment in social engineering and an early manifestation of the economic system of mercantilism.

SEE ALSO: 1643, Confederation of the United Colonies of New England; 1664, British Conquest of New Netherland; 1686, Dominion of New England Forms.

1661 ■ Virginia Slave Codes: *first laws recognizing and institutionalizing slavery in Virginia*

Date: March, 1661-1705
Locale: Virginia
Categories: African American history; Laws and acts

Summary of event. In March, 1661, the Virginia General Assembly declared that "all children borne in this country shalbe held bond or free only according to the condition of the mother." Enacted to alleviate confusion about the status of children with English fathers and African mothers, this law was the first in a series of laws recognizing perpetual slavery in Virginia and equating "freedom" with "white" and "enslaved" with "black." This law is especially indicative of the hardening of race relations in mid-seventeenth century Virginia society, as status in the patriarchal society of England traditionally was inherited from the father. By reversing this legal concept, perpetuation of enslavement for blacks was ensured for their children, whether of black or white ancestry.

Despite the extent to which the 1661 law narrowed the options for defining Africans' status, this act did not in itself establish slavery. Africans had two available windows through which they could obtain freedom—conversion to Christianity and manumission (formal emancipation). In 1655, mulatto Elizabeth Key brought a successful suit for her freedom, using as her main argument the fact that she had been baptized. In 1667, a slave named Fernando contended that he ought to be freed because he was a Christian and had lived in England for several years. Not only did the court deny Fernando's appeal, but also that same year the General Assembly took another step toward more clearly defining blacks' status, by declaring "that the conferring of baptisme doth not alter the condition of the person as to his bondage or freedome." Planters felt that if baptism led to freedom, they would be without any assurance that they could retain their slave property. The 1667 law thereby built on the earlier one to define who would be a slave, and was clarified in 1670 and again in 1682, when the Assembly declared that any non-Christian brought into the colony, either by land or by sea, would be a slave for life, even if he or she later converted.

In 1691, colonial leaders provided a negative incentive to masters wishing to free their slaves by declaring that anyone who set free any "negro or mulatto" would be required to pay the costs of transporting the freedmen out of the colony within six months. Although manumissions still occurred and some free blacks managed to remain in the colony, the primary status for African Americans in Virginia was that of chattel.

Although who was to be a slave in Virginia had now been defined, it had yet to be determined precisely what being a slave meant on a daily basis for Africans and their descendants. Between 1661 and 1705, nearly twenty separate laws were passed limiting, defining, and prescribing the rights, status, and treatment of blacks. In general, these laws were designed to protect planters' slave property and to protect the order and stability of white society from an "alien and savage race."

The greater the proportion of black slaves in the overall Virginia population, the more restrictive and oppressive the laws became. Whereas Africans were only 2 percent of the total population of Virginia in 1648, they were 15 percent in 1708. In certain coastal counties, such as York, the demographic picture was even more threatening. In 1663, blacks already made up 14 percent of the total county population; by 1701, they counted for 31 percent of the county's inhabitants. In large part, the slave codes were motivated by the growth of the black population and whites' fears of slave uprisings.

The piecemeal establishment of slavery in these separate laws culminated in 1705 in a comprehensive slave code in Virginia. This code reenacted and strengthened a number of earlier slave laws, added further restrictions and harsher punishments, and permanently drew the color line that placed blacks at the bottom of Virginia society. Whites were prohibited from trading with, having sexual relations with, and marrying blacks. Blacks were forbidden to own Christian servants "except of their own complexion," leave their home plantation without a pass, own a gun or other weapon, or resist whites in any way.

In this society in which private property was a basic legal tenet, a slave's property was not protected: "be it enacted . . . that all horses, cattle or hoggs marked of any negro . . . shall be forfeited to the use of the poore of the parish . . . seizable by the church warden thereof." Neither was slave life or limb protected by the codes. It was legal both to kill a slave accidentally while correcting him or her, and to dismember a slave guilty of running away as a means of dissuading other slaves from trying to escape. Slaves were not allowed to assemble for prayer, for entertainment, or to bury their dead. They could not testify against white people in court and were not given the right of trial by jury. The only protection mandated in the slave code was that masters must provide adequate food, clothing, and shelter for their slaves, and that they "not give immoderate correction."

Many of these enactments lacked any means of enforcement, including the sole protection, and remained as almost dead letters in the statutes. Many of the harsher penalties for slave crimes, for example, the death penalty and maiming, were not carried out nearly as frequently as the laws suggest, because doing so would harm or destroy the master's property. Laws prohibiting slaves from trading or hiring themselves out were disregarded almost routinely. The disadvantage for slaves of this lack of enforcement was that laws prohibiting cruel treatment or defining acceptable levels of correction often were ignored as well. Where abuse was noticeably blatant, action against white offenders was taken only reluctantly, and punishments were insignificant and rare. Generally, laws in the economic and political interest of the white planter elite were enforced and respected; laws that restrained planters' pursuits were not.

To a large extent, these laws grew out of the early- to mid-seventeenth century laws regulating indentured servitude. Servants also were prohibited from having sexual relations with or marrying their masters; indentured women who became pregnant through such liaisons were fined, made to serve extra time, and had their children bound out to labor. Like slaves, servants were punished for attempting to run away or for resisting their masters. Servants also were treated harshly and exploited by ruthless masters eager to get every penny's worth of effort from their laborers. Unlike African slaves, white indentured servants had legal rights and were protected by the laws and courts of the colony. Furthermore, white servants ultimately served out their time, became freemen and full citizens, acquired land and servants of their own, and became respected members of the community, regardless of their earlier status. Indentured servants had rights and opportunities, but African and African American slaves, by the turn of the eighteenth century, virtually had neither.

—*Laura A. Croghan*

ADDITIONAL READING:

Boskin, Joseph. *Into Slavery: Racial Decisions in the Virginia Colony*. Philadelphia: J. B. Lippincott, 1976. Provides a brief account of the evolution of perpetual slavery and a representative selection of relevant primary documents. Good bibliographical essays.

Catterall, Helen T., ed. *Judicial Cases Concerning American Slavery and the Negro*. 5 vols. New York: Octagon Books, 1968. Comprehensive examination of court records related to American slavery and the experiences of African Americans in slavery. Abstracts, index.

Hening, William Waller, ed. *Statutes at Large: A Collection of All the Laws of Virginia*. 13 vols. New York: R & G & W Bartow, 1823. Reprint. Charlottesville: University Press of Virginia, 1969. Chronological listing of all the laws of the Virginia colony, with index.

Higginbotham, A. Leon, Jr. *In the Matter of Color: Race and the American Legal Process, the Colonial Period*. New York: Oxford University Press, 1978. Recounts the events culminating in the legal recognition of slavery in all the British mainland colonies.

Jordan, Winthrop D. *White over Black: American Attitudes Toward the Negro, 1550-1812*. New York: W. W. Norton, 1968. Examines the attitudes of British colonists toward Africans, especially concerning their religions and color. Characterizes the establishment of slavery as an "unthinking decision."

Schwartz, Philip J. *Twice Condemned: Slaves and the Criminal Laws of Virginia, 1705-1865*. Baton Rouge: Louisiana State University Press, 1988. Uses criminal trial records to examine slave resistance and whites' efforts to control threatening slave behavior. Interprets the seventeenth century as a time of adjustment or negotiation.

Shaw, Robert B. *A Legal History of Slavery in the United States*. Potsdam, N.Y.: Northern Press, 1991. Illustrates the history of slavery in terms of its legislative and judicial back-

ground, from settlement through emancipation. Early chapters discuss the evolution of early slave codes.

SEE ALSO: 1619, Africans Arrive in Virginia; 1641, Massachusetts Recognizes Slavery; 1671, Indian Slave Trade.

1662 ■ HALF-WAY COVENANT: *expansion of eligibility for Puritan baptism encourages increased membership in the church*

DATE: 1662
LOCALE: Boston, Massachusetts
CATEGORY: Religion
KEY FIGURES:

Charles Chauncy (1592-1672), president of Harvard College and leading opponent of the movement to revise membership requirements

Increase Mather (1639-1723), son of Richard, who initially opposed the Half-Way Covenant

Richard Mather (1596-1669), minister and principal leader in devising the Half-Way Covenant

John Woodbridge, Jr., minister who led his congregation beyond the Half-Way Covenant and opened membership to all

SUMMARY OF EVENT. One of the most compelling questions about the Puritan Commonwealth established in Massachusetts during the seventeenth century concerns the reasons for its decline. Historians have found it difficult to determine not only why the rule of the "Saints" came to an end but also the time when the deterioration began. Some have contended that the system of the church and the state established under the leadership of such men as John Winthrop and John Cotton was so well constructed that it remained almost unchanged for many years. Others believe that Puritan ideals began to falter from the beginning, and that too much stress has been placed on the pervasiveness of a group of attitudes defined as the "Puritan mind." Some historians argue that church membership declined because rigid Puritan beliefs could not survive when confronted with harsh life on the frontier. Others, however, credit the decline to natural causes: The years between generations were not always sufficient time for parents to become full church members before their children were born.

Among the controversial issues that have enlivened the debate over Puritan decline is the so-called Half-Way Covenant of 1662. The most important provision of this document, endorsed by a Massachusetts General Court-sponsored synod of more than eighty ministers and laity meeting in Boston, was that children whose parents had not been admitted to full membership in a Puritan church might nevertheless be eligible for baptism. This created a new class of church membership, because those who had been baptized but had not yet testified were only partial members—they could pass church privileges on to their children but could not participate in Holy Communion or vote on church issues.

The Half-Way Covenant provided the Puritan Commonwealth with one of its most prolonged controversies. Along with his father Richard and his brother Eleazar, Increase Mather (seen in this engraving from Cases of Conscience Concerning Evil Spirits, *1693), charged that, despite claims to the contrary, the covenant would open up the church to persons who were not among God's elect.* (Library of Congress)

The question of membership was one that long had plagued the churches of New England. On the one hand, Puritans believed that no one should be admitted to full communion in the church who had not demonstrated sufficiently a personal experience by which he or she had become convinced that God had elected him or her to salvation. Yet if one believed that prospective church members must await a message from God, what part was the church itself to play in recruiting new adherents? This problem became increasingly acute as the proportion of Puritans in New England declined in relation to the growing population of the area. It began to seem, as Jonathon Mitchel wrote, that the churches had been set up "onely that a *few old Christians* may keep one another warm while they live, and then carry away the Church into the cold grave with them when they dye."

The Half-Way Covenant did not concern the admission of new members from outside the church but attempted rather to deal with the problems raised by the children and grandchildren of the "elect." Because the Puritans believed in infant baptism, they always had permitted church members to have their children brought under the care of the congregation, although each had to await the conversion experience before being admitted to full membership. It was expected that a significant umber of these young people ultimately would experience conversion, but until that time, they were not permitted to participate in communion or vote on church business. This arrangement did not provide for the third generation, however.

During the early days of the Puritan Commonwealth, the churches did not have to concern themselves about the grandchildren of the "elect," because there were none. When they did begin to appear, there was no difficulty about those whose parents had been received into full communion with a church. The problem arose with those members of the third generation whose parents had not yet achieved full membership: Were such infants to be baptized or not? No one could say for certain that the parents of these children would not experience a conversion at some later time, because the Puritans did not believe that God necessarily informed the "saints" of their election at any certain age. Moreover, if these infants were to be denied baptism, would it not then become necessary to expel their parents from the privileged position they had held in a church since childhood?

The answer that the Half-Way Covenant provided to this question may have confirmed a practice that already was developing in New England. It stated that, in cases where children were born to parents who had not yet attained full church membership, the congregation should baptize the new infants. Such persons could not, however, become full members of a church unless they subsequently experienced conversion. Both they and their parents enjoyed a kind of "half-way" membership that enabled the Puritans to maintain their rigid standards for full communion in a church and yet to provide for the possible conversion of new members. Infants baptized into a church obviously were more likely to achieve full membership than those who were excluded from the fold.

The Half-Way Covenant provided the Puritan Commonwealth with one of its most prolonged controversies. Although the Synod of 1662 had strongly endorsed the covenant, it was opposed by a small and determined group of ministers and temporarily rejected by a significant number of congregations. Most of its opponents charged that, despite claims to the contrary, the covenant would open up a church to persons who were not among God's elect. Richard Mather, one of those most responsible for the decision of the synod, found his congregation at Dorchester skeptical about the covenant, and his sons, Increase and Eleazar, were among its most vocal opponents. Another influential leader of the opposition was Charles Chauncy, who, as president of Harvard College, was among the most respected scholars in the province. Nevertheless, despite such pockets of resistance as that evidenced by the refusal of Boston's Second Church to accept the covenant until 1693, the Puritan churches in New England gradually came to accept the idea of "half-way" membership. John

Woodbridge, Jr., a minister in Killingworth, Connecticut, took the new covenant a step further and opened membership in his church to anyone. Not until the great religious revivals of the 1730's swept through the colonies did the covenant again come under serious attack, and by then, the Puritan Commonwealth, as such, had ceased to exist.

—David L. Ammerman, updated by Geralyn Strecker

ADDITIONAL READING:

Bremer, Francis J. *Shaping New Englands: Puritan Clergymen in Seventeenth-Century England and New England*. New York: Twayne, 1994. This survey of Puritan history discusses the strong connection between church and state and the role the Half-Way Covenant had in trying to maintain that bond.

Burg, Barry R. *Richard Mather*. Boston: Twayne, 1982. This biography of the leading proponent of the Half-Way Covenant explains the major religious and political factors leading to membership reform.

Middlekauff, Robert. *The Mathers: Three Generations of Puritan Intellectuals, 1596-1728*. New York: Oxford University Press, 1971. Traces the Mather family's central role in the Half-Way Covenant controversy through Richard's support of the new doctrine and Increase's initial objection, then later support.

Miller, Perry. *From Colony to Province*. Vol. 2 in *The New England Mind*. New York: Macmillan, 1939. Cambridge, Mass.: Harvard University Press, 1953. Argues that New England Puritanism retained its pristine quality for only one generation and that the Half-Way Covenant clearly reveals the decline of Puritan self-assurance.

Morgan, Edmund S. *Visible Saints: The History of the Puritan Idea*. New York: New York University Press, 1963. Because children were inevitably born to members not yet in full communion, some provision had to be made for them. Argues that the Half-Way Covenant was not a symptom of decline but rather evidence of the Puritans' determination to maintain rigid standards of membership.

Pope, Robert G. *The Half-Way Covenant: Church Membership in Puritan New England*. Princeton, N.J.: Princeton University Press, 1969. Detailed discussion of the Half-Way Covenant by a scholar who accepts, in general, that the covenant was a sign of decline within the church.

SEE ALSO: 1620, Pilgrims Land at Plymouth; 1630, Great Puritan Migration; 1636, Rhode Island Is Founded; 1643, Confederation of the United Colonies of New England; 1730's, First Great Awakening.

1663 ■ SETTLEMENT OF THE CAROLINAS: *the seat of the South in British North America*

DATE: March 24, 1663-July 25, 1729
LOCALE: Eastern Carolinas
CATEGORIES: Expansion and land acquisition; Settlements

KEY FIGURES:

William Berkeley (1606-1677), governor of Virginia and an original Carolina proprietor

John Colleton, wealthy Barbadian planter who took the initiative in acquiring the proprietary charter for the Carolinas

John Culpeper, leader of a rebellion against Albemarle's proprietary government

William Drummond, first governor of Albemarle County, which became North Carolina

Edward Hyde, earl of Clarendon (c. 1650-1712), first governor of North Carolina independent of South Carolina

John Locke (1632-1704), English political philosopher, who helped to prepare the Fundamental Constitutions

Philip Ludwell, first governor of both Carolinas

Francis Nicholson (1655-1728), first royal governor of South Carolina

Anthony Ashley Cooper, earl of Shaftesbury (1621-1683), proprietor and architect of the Carolina proprietary system

John Yeamans (1610?-1674), leader of South Carolina's Goose Creek faction

SUMMARY OF EVENT. Settlement of the Carolinas had its origin in 1629, when Charles I of England granted all land between 31° and 36° north latitude to Sir Robert Heath, who called the area "New Carolana." Heath planned to open the territory to French Protestants, who were under siege in the latest of French religious conflicts. Agents of the Carolina settlers attempted to obtain supplies in Virginia to the north but were largely unsuccessful, and no settlements were established. Heath shortly thereafter gave up on the enterprise, and nothing further was attempted during Charles's reign.

The introduction of large-scale sugar production during the early 1660's to Barbados in the West Indies, among the wealthiest of the British colonies, had forced many small British planters to consider emigration from the island. When Sir John Colleton, a wealthy Barbadian, returned to England and gained a seat on the Council for Foreign Plantations, he conceived the idea of establishing a proprietary colony and recruiting Barbadians to settle it. For fellow proprietors, Colleton turned to powerful Englishmen who had been associated with colonial expansion: the earl of Shaftesbury (Anthony Ashley Cooper), Sir William Berkeley, John Lord Berkeley, the duke of Albemarle (George Monck), the earl of Clarendon (Edward Hyde), the earl of Craven, and Sir George Carteret. On March 24, 1663, Charles II granted to the proprietors a charter similar to that of his predecessor, redefined as all land between 29° and 36°30′ north latitude and extending west to the "South Seas"; they called the area Carolina after King Charles. Required only to pay a nominal annual sum to the king, the proprietors possessed vast powers—to fill offices, erect a government, establish courts, collect customs and taxes, grant land, confer titles, and determine military matters. They were obliged to guarantee the rights of Englishmen to their settlers, however, and could enact laws only with the consent of the freemen. The proprietors in England also constituted a Palatine Court, which, in addition to appointing the governor of the colonies, was empowered to disallow laws and hear appeals from the colony.

Having devised plans for the creation of three counties and having begun negotiations with two groups of prospective settlers in Barbados and New England, the proprietors drafted the "Declaration and Proposals to All That Will Plant in Carolina," which outlined a headright system of land distribution and a framework for participatory government. Sir William Berkeley received authorization to appoint a governor and council for Albemarle County (later North Carolina), and in October, 1664, he named William Drummond of Virginia as its governor. A few months later, Sir John Yeamans was commissioned governor of Clarendon County. As a further inducement to settlement, in January, 1665, the proprietors drew up the Concessions and Agreements, which provided for a unicameral legislature that included representatives of the freemen and ensured religious toleration. However, friction between new arrivals and original settlers, combined with hostility from Native American tribes and the news of better land to the south, led to abandonment of Clarendon County in 1667.

Settlement of Carolina during this period was focused primarily on the estuaries of the southern regions rather than the large bays and dangerous banks of the north. Settlers in the region were a varied lot, consisting of a mixture of English Dissenters, French Huguenots, and Presbyterian Scots. The largest contingent, however, consisted of emigrants from Barbados; by 1671, they constituted half the population in the region. As a system of laws, the Concessions and Agreements had proven unsatisfactory, so in 1669, the earl of Shaftesbury collaborated with his protégé, John Locke, to write the Fundamental Constitutions of Carolina. Essentially, the program called for development of a landed aristocracy for the region, in the form of 12,000-acre baronies. Two-thirds of the land would be held by a colonial nobility. Although a "parliament" consisting of the nobility and popular representatives would sit in the colony, the proprietors in England, functioning as a Palatine Court, could veto the legislature's decisions. Certain provisions were implemented, but the proprietors never succeeded in winning approval of the system as a whole. Few baronies were ever surveyed, and no manorial system was ever established. Reflecting the exigencies of a governing body in England removed from the day-to-day running of a colony, the actual government consisted of a governor and council appointed by the proprietors, and representatives elected by the freemen. Until a supreme court was established in 1700, the governor and council would constitute the colony's highest court.

Despite the abandonment of the Clarendon region, Carolina proprietors continued to develop plans for settlement of the region. Shaftesbury was able to convince the proprietors that a larger investment was essential for success. Drawing upon earlier experience and the expertise and resources of investors from Barbados, it was decided to attempt to establish a settlement at Port Royal. More than one hundred settlers, led by

Joseph West, left England in August, 1669. However, after landing at Port Royal, already an important anchorage, they were persuaded by the local tribes to travel to another estuary some sixty miles up the coast. There in April, 1670, they established Charles Town (today, Charleston).

Because the settlers were predominantly tradesmen ignorant of farming methods, many went into debt and deserted the colony. Recruitment efforts proved successful, however, and a rapid influx of settlers from Barbados and elsewhere continued to populate the colony. Many of these men moved inland, searching out the best land along the estuaries. They quickly learned the ways of agriculture. Disparate ethnic enclaves began to form, such as French Huguenots settled along the Santee and Scottish settlement at the anchorage of Port Royal. Despite religious contention, prosperity within the colony increased. In 1674, Dr. Henry Woodward was commissioned Indian agent to establish trade with local Native American tribes; the colonists developed a thriving trade in furs and naval stores with England, and in meat, lumber, and Indian slaves—a practice frowned upon by the proprietors—with the West Indies.

A large proportion of the colonists having emigrated from Barbados, this particularly significant group soon gained control of the government. Known as the "Goose Creek men," from the site of their settlement just outside of Charles Town, this faction was to determine the colony's politics for the next fifty years. Despite success in the areas of trade and farming, conflict between the proprietors and settlers over debts, land distribution, and the slave trade nearly brought an end to the colony in the 1670's. Attracted by the proprietors' promise of toleration, many Dissenters also came, only to encounter the resentment of the conservative Anglican Barbadians, who resisted the proprietors' efforts at reform; both pro- and anti-proprietary factions were formed.

During the 1670's, dissension culminated in what became known as Culpeper's Rebellion. In 1677, Thomas Miller, governor and leader of the proprietary faction, attempted to combine his position with that of the duties of custom collector. In December, an anti-proprietary faction established a revolutionary government and imprisoned Miller. Miller escaped to England and pleaded his case before the Privy Council; John Culpeper, a leader of the dissident group, represented the rebels. The council decided that Miller had indeed exceeded his authority. Culpeper was tried for treason but through the influence of Shaftesbury was acquitted.

When Governor James Colleton declared martial law in February, 1690, in an attempt to halt the abuses of the Native American trade and collect the quitrents, the Goose Creek men ousted him and replaced him with Seth Sothel. In 1691, Sothel was suspended by the Palatine Court and charged with treason, though Sothel's death in 1694 settled the controversy. Meanwhile, Philip Ludwell was appointed governor by the proprietors (1691), and the popular freemen's branch of the legislature was allowed to meet separately and to exercise parliamentary privileges.

Unlike the turmoil of earlier decades, the 1690's would be one of relative peace and prosperity. Ludwell and his successors were to reside in Charles Town, while Albemarle (northern Carolina), governed by Ludwell's deputy, was to retain a separate legislature. Trade with Native American tribes prospered. Perhaps even more important, during this period it became apparent that a new crop, rice, was perfectly suited for the swampy lowlands of Carolina. Rice quickly became a staple export. Critical to development of rice farming was the large influx of African slaves into the region, bringing with them knowledge of rice cultivation. By the beginning of the eighteenth century, the black population equaled that of the white: approximately four thousand of each.

The region of Albemarle, known as North Carolina after 1691, was repeatedly torn by religious strife in the first decade of the new century. Huguenots from Virginia had settled the area south of Albemarle Sound; German Palatines and Swiss had settled in the region of what would be founded as New Bern (1710). Although toleration had prevailed in the earlier years and many Dissenters held positions of power, Anglicans were determined to establish the Church of England in the colony. With the passage of the Vestry Act of 1704, Assembly members were required to take an oath of loyalty to the Church of England. The act aroused such intense opposition that deputy governor Thomas Cary was removed for attempting to enforce the law. In 1712, North Carolina was established as a separate colony; the proprietors appointed Edward Hyde deputy governor, the first governor of North Carolina to be independent of the royal governor of Carolina. The new legislature nullified the laws of the previous administrations.

The crisis in North Carolina was exacerbated by the war with the Tuscaroras, the worst Indian war in the colony's history. In September, 1711, the Tuscaroras, seeking revenge for encroachment by the settlers on their land, enslavement of their people, and unfair trading practices, attacked New Bern and other settlements from the Neuse to the Pamlico Rivers. Before the raids were over, hundreds of settlers had been massacred and their farms destroyed. Two expeditions, led by Colonel Jack Barnwell and Colonel James More in 1712 and 1713, and aided by men from South Carolina, finally defeated the Tuscaroras. Although the war had placed the colony in dire financial straits, it drew the people together, and they entered a new period of peace.

The choice of rice as a staple crop had its greatest impact in the south. Unlike the tobacco crop, grown in the region of the Chesapeake to the north, rice growing required special water facilities to maintain an annual flooding of the fields. However, once the facilities were established, the rice crop could be grown in the same fields year after year. It was unnecessary to plant new fields or to continue shifting the settlements themselves. Thus the settlements, once established, could maintain a semblance of stability, except for the frequent internal rivalries. Consequently, settlement followed the river systems as extensions from the city of Charles Town. By 1708, the population of the district (and in essence the entire colony) consisted of four thousand whites, forty-one hundred African Americans, and fourteen hundred Native Americans; most of the African Americans and Native Americans in the settlements were slaves.

Factional rivalries were revived at the beginning of the eighteenth century. The selection of an Anglican governor for Carolina in 1700 aroused the opposition of the Dissenters to the establishment of the Church of England in the colony; indeed, in 1704, the parish vestries had become the seats of power. The popular division over religion was superseded by a division over the issue of paper currency in 1712. As early as 1703, the colony had emitted its first bills of credit to pay for an expedition against the Spanish in Florida. Other emissions followed. The planters and tradesmen who did business solely within the colony favored the use of paper money, but the Charles Town merchants who had to pay their English creditors in specie bitterly opposed its use.

The proprietors had never moved decisively to control the long-standing abuses of trade with Native American tribes. As a result, in 1715, the Yamasee War, the longest and costliest war with Native Americans in South Carolina's history, erupted. During the conflict, the people were driven from their homes to seek refuge in Charles Town. To end the abuses of trade, the Commons House of Assembly created a monopoly of the Native American trade under its own direction.

In 1718, the proprietors launched a strong attack upon some of the colony's most popular laws, disallowing measures providing for bills of credit and import duties, removing the monopoly on trade, and weakening the power of the legislature; consequently, antiproprietary sentiment crystallized in favor of royal government. All that lacked for rebellion was a catalyst.

The catalyst came in November, 1719, in the form of the rumor of an imminent invasion of the colony by the Spanish. When the Assembly convened in December, it declared itself a convention and petitioned the Board of Trade to be made a royal colony. Because the region represented a major line of defense against both the French and Spanish, King George I accepted the removal of the proprietary government, and South Carolina became a royal colony in 1719.

The "royalizing" process also had its counterpart in North Carolina. The Crown bought out the proprietors on July 25, 1729, and North Carolina also became a royal colony.

—Richard Adler

ADDITIONAL READING:

Andrews, Charles M. *The Colonial Period of American History.* 4 vols. New Haven, Conn.: Yale University Press, 1934-1937. Includes a detailed discussion on the government of the Carolinas.

Craven, Wesley F. *The Southern Colonies in the Seventeenth Century, 1607-1689.* Baton Rouge: Louisiana University Press, 1949. Places the settlement of the Carolinas in the context of British expansion in America. Written by noted author on colonial America.

McCusker, John, and Russell Menard. *The Economy of British America, 1607-1789.* Chapel Hill: University of North

Carolina Press, 1985. A detailed description of economic factors behind the development of North and South Carolina.

Meinig, D. W. *Atlantic America, 1492-1800*. Vol 1 in *The Shaping of America: A Geographical Perspective on Five Hundred Years of History*. A detailed discussion on the merging of diverse societies into what became the Southern colonies.

Meriwether, Robert L. *The Expansion of South Carolina, 1729-1765*. 1940. Reprint. Philadelphia: Porcupine Press, 1974. A concise history of the later years of Carolina's development.

Salley, Alexander S., Jr., ed. *Narratives of Early Carolina, 1650-1708*. New York: Barnes & Noble Books, 1946. Presents original accounts, including descriptions of the early explorations and life in the settlements.

SEE ALSO: 1670, Charles Town Is Founded; 1671, Indian Slave Trade; 1711, Tuscarora War.

1664 ■ BRITISH CONQUEST OF NEW NETHERLAND: *mercantile and territorial ambitions lead to the dominance of the British in colonial North America*

DATE: March 22, 1664-July 21, 1667
LOCALE: Dutch colony in the New World
CATEGORIES: Economics; Wars, uprisings, and civil unrest
KEY FIGURES:
James, duke of York and Albany (1633-1701), proprietor of New York after March, 1664; later, king of England
Richard Nicolls (1624-1672), James's deputy and first governor of New York
Peter Stuyvesant (c. 1610-1672), Dutch director general of New Netherland, 1647-1664

SUMMARY OF EVENT. The restoration of the Stuart monarchy to the British throne in 1660 ushered in an era of colonial expansion in America. This expansion was driven by a rigorous mercantilism that called forth efforts to make colonial administration more unified. New Netherland's existence as an alien wedge between Great Britain's New England and Chesapeake colonies threatened not only English territorial and mercantile ambitions but also plans for strengthening imperial government. Playing an important role in all of this, James, King Charles II's brother and heir to the throne, was at the center of a group of merchants and noblemen who were deeply concerned by the Dutch in North America and exercised considerable influence over the king.

Charles II, James, and their supporters viewed land grants in America as a device for recouping their lost fortunes, and the region occupied by the Dutch enticed such land-grabbers. Furthermore, the Crown's attempt to unify colonial administration was frustrated by the situation of New Netherland, for its strategic geographic location impeded communications between the Chesapeake and New England colonies and made more difficult the task of defending those colonies from the French. The stubborn independence demonstrated by Puritan

New England particularly disturbed the Restoration government. Following upon the earlier policy of Oliver Cromwell and the Commonwealth government, King Charles and Parliament continued to enact trade regulations against their commercial rivals, the Dutch. However, New Netherland's existence rendered enforcement of the Acts of Trade and Navigation ineffective.

England's mainland colonies used New Netherland as a means of circumventing the British navigation system, and the Dutch colony became a breeding ground for smugglers. Despite laws to the contrary, Dutch merchants did a thriving business in tobacco from Virginia and Maryland, and Boston regularly had Dutch ships carrying goods to and from her harbor. In fact, officials in the British colonies would not enforce the trade acts against the Dutch, and it was argued that if New Netherland were in England's hands, it might well generate ten thousand pounds annually in uncollected customs revenues. The prospect of acquiring an American colony that could make him money appealed mightily to debt-ridden James.

The Crown eventually concluded that the only effective remedy for these difficulties lay in wresting control of New Netherland from the Dutch. As early as 1663, the Council for Foreign Plantations—an advisory board of merchants and privy councillors, several of whom were close advisers to James—investigated the matter of Dutch power and examined the possibility of a military operation against New Netherland. Information from English residents on the eastern end of Long Island suggested that such a military undertaking would meet with little resistance from the Dutch garrison at New Amsterdam. Plans were even made to enlist the New England militia against the Dutch.

Based upon the council's recommendations, Charles moved swiftly. March 22, 1664, he gave brother James a proprietary grant of all the land between Delaware Bay and the Connecticut River, which included the Dutch colony. Parliament approved the grant, and in April, the king nominated Colonel Richard Nicolls as lieutenant governor of the proprietary, put him in charge of a small military force, and sent him to America. Nicolls was charged with more than seizing New Netherland: He headed a special commission whose members were instructed not only to take over lands claimed by the Dutch but also to settle boundary disputes among the New England colonies and make sure that the New England governments understood they were expected to enforce the navigation acts. With the Duke of York in firm control of the colony next door, it was generally thought by the Council for Foreign Plantations that New Englanders would be more likely to fall into line behind imperial policy.

Nicolls and his squadron of four ships carrying three hundred soldiers arrived off New Amsterdam in August, 1664. The lieutenant governor immediately demanded the surrender of the colony, offering liberal terms as bait. Among the terms were guarantees to the inhabitants of all the rights of Englishmen, trading privileges, freedom of conscience, the continuance of Dutch customs and inheritance laws, and up to eighteen months for the settlers to decide whether or not to leave. At first, Director General Peter Stuyvesant, who had led New Netherland for the Dutch West India Company since 1647, refused to surrender and began to make preparations for the defense of his colony. However, the peg-legged Stuyvesant, having angered his people with his high-handed rule, received little support from the residents, who felt they would be no worse off under the British. Moreover, the English villages on Long Island were in full-scale revolt, and the British had spread rumors that if Stuyvesant did not surrender, New Amsterdam would be brought under siege, burned, and sacked. Bowing to the inevitable, Stuyvesant surrendered the town and its garrison of 150 soldiers on August 26, 1664. New Amsterdam was immediately renamed New York, in honor of James, duke of York.

Nicolls sent British forces both north and south to secure the surrender of the rest of New Netherland. Sir George Cartwright went up the Hudson River and obtained the surrender of Fort Orange without a fight. Cartwright renamed the town Albany, after James's other dukedom. The inhabitants there were pleased that the British were willing for them to have a monopoly on the fur trade. Nicolls also instructed Cartwright to negotiate a treaty with the Iroquois, whose friendship the English needed if the French and their American Indian allies were to be bested. This first British-Iroquois treaty was signed on September 26, 1664. Contrary to his expressed orders, Sir Robert Carr, who had been sent with British soldiers to the South River (Delaware Bay), provoked a fight and stormed the small fort there, killing and wounding several and plundering the settlement of New Amstel. Outraged by Carr's violence on the Delaware, Governor Nicolls wanted erstwhile New Netherlanders to remain in New York, understanding full well that the province's most valuable resource was its settlers. In fact, most of New Netherland's estimated population of nine thousand did remain, including Stuyvesant. Against the advice of Nicolls, however, James gave away choice lands and settlements in what became New Jersey, thereby inhibiting the demographic and economic progress of his own colony.

On July 21, 1667, the Treaty of Breda, which ended the Second Anglo-Dutch War, confirmed the British conquest. Except for a brief loss of control during the Third Dutch War (1673-1674), the British retained a firm grip upon the former Dutch colony that they called New York. The acquisition of New York was part of a more extensive effort to centralize government that led, in the 1680's, to the creation of the Dominion of New England, which included New York, New Jersey, and the New England colonies.

Great Britain's conquest of New Netherland plugged the breach between the British colonies, thus forming a continuous English presence from Canada to Florida. It eliminated the Dutch as commercial rivals on the continent, gained an alliance with the Iroquois, and ultimately brought the British and the French into confrontation for continental supremacy.

—*Warren M. Billings, updated by Ronald W. Howard*

ADDITIONAL READING:

Andrews, Charles M. *England's Commercial and Colonial Policy*. Vol. 4 in *The Colonial Period of American History*. New Haven, Conn.: Yale University Press, 1964. Discusses Anglo-Dutch rivalry; relates the conquest of New Netherland to overall British efforts to create a self-contained colonial empire.

Kammen, Michael. *Colonial New York: A History*. New York: Charles Scribner's Sons, 1975. Chapters 3 and 4 deal with the reasons for the British conquest, the Articles of Capitulation, and adjustments under Governor Nicolls.

Kessler, Henry H., and Eugene Rachlis. *Peter Stuyvesant and His New York*. New York: Random House, 1959. Chapters 14 and 15 consider the British conquest from the perspective of Stuyvesant and the Dutch in New Netherland.

Merwick, Donna. *Possessing Albany, 1630-1710: The Dutch and English Experiences*. Cambridge, England: Cambridge University Press, 1990. A provocative work, less concerned with the British conquest than with the cultural differences that emerged between the Dutch and English in New York, particularly Albany.

Rink, Oliver A. *Holland on the Hudson: An Economic and Social History of Dutch New York*. Ithaca, N.Y.: Cornell University Press, 1986. Chapter 8 relates the stresses and strains that weakened the hold of the Dutch West India Company on New Netherland.

Ritchie, Robert C. *The Duke's Province: A Study of New York Politics and Society, 1664-1691*. Chapel Hill: University of North Carolina Press, 1977. Chapter 1 deals extensively with the reasons for the British conquest.

SEE ALSO: 1626, Algonquians "Sell" Manhattan Island; 1660, British Navigation Acts; 1686, Dominion of New England Forms.

1670 ■ CHARLES TOWN IS FOUNDED: *first permanent European settlement in South Carolina, eventually displacing Spanish claims*

DATE: April, 1670
LOCALE: Charles Town, South Carolina
CATEGORY: Settlements
KEY FIGURES:
Charles II (1630-1685), king of England, 1660-1685
Henry Woodward (c. 1646-c. 1686), liaison between
  Europeans and Kiawah Indians

SUMMARY OF EVENT. In 1562, Huguenots (French Protestants) escaping from the Catholic-Protestant wars in France settled in Port Royal, South Carolina, under the leadership of Jean Ribaut, but this settlement quickly failed. In 1629, King Charles I of England gave a grant to Sir Robert Heath to resettle Huguenot refugees from England to South Carolina, but this plan also failed. In 1669, the Spanish were still the major European power trading and visiting in the Carolina area.

"An Exact Prospect of Charles Town, the Metropolis of the Province of South Carolina," as rendered for the London Magazine *before 1739.* (Library of Congress)

Although the Spanish claimed Carolina, their closest settlement was two hundred miles away in St. Augustine, Florida.

England also claimed Carolina and challenged Spain's claim. Charles II became king of England in 1660, and in 1662-1663 gave Carolina as a grant to the eight Lord's Proprietors, who had helped him regain the throne his father had held. In 1669, one of the proprietors, the earl of Shaftesbury (Anthony Ashley-Cooper), took charge of the project and began to develop the area for economic reasons. Three ships, the *Carolina*, the *Port Royal*, and the *Albemarle*, left England for the seven-month voyage to America. The *Albemarle* wrecked and was replaced in Barbados by the *Three Brothers*, and the *Port Royal* wrecked and was not replaced, but in April, 1670, the *Carolina* entered what is now called Charleston harbor, followed by the *Three Brothers* on May 23. The two ships brought approximately 148 people.

The immigrants had planned to settle at Port Royal (about sixty miles from present-day Charleston), but landed by mistake a little north of Charleston. They still planned to go to Port Royal, but the chief (cacique) of the local tribe, the Kiawahs, persuaded them to settle in the Charleston area, partly to help protect the Kiawahs from the Spanish and Spanish-allied Native Americans, such as the Westoes. Contrary to the "wild savage" image, the natives lived in semipermanent homes in villages, practiced some diversified agriculture, and had a fairly developed political system. Dr. Henry Woodward, an Englishman, had lived with the Kiawahs for several years and had good relations with them, which in turn helped develop good relations between the Kiawahs and the settlers.

The English went five miles northwest up the Ashley River, and then west a short distance up Old Towne Creek, to the first high land that afforded a view of the river so Spanish ships could be seen before they reached the settlement. Marshlands and a short palisade also helped the defense. Because of the threat of attack by Spanish or Spanish-allied natives, Charles Town (briefly called Albemarle Point) was developed as a fort, with people sleeping inside and working outside during the day. In 1670, Spaniards from St. Augustine attempted to attack, but were defeated because Native Americans friendly to the English warned them of the planned attack. In the 1670's, there were battles with the Westoe and Stono tribes. In 1686, another attempted attack by the Spanish and their native allies was stopped by a hurricane.

The settlers traded with the natives, largely for animal furs and skins, and obtained lumber, tar, and pitch from the forests. About fifteen different crops were experimented with, but corn was the main food raised. Cattle were raised, and fish and wild animals were plentiful. There were problems (for example, malaria), but fewer than in most other settlements.

Charles Town was very popular among Barbadians, who needed a place to move to escape from overcrowding and a lack of land on Barbados. In 1671, more than a hundred Barbadians (mostly of English heritage) had joined the settlement. Industrious and business-oriented, the Barbadians soon exercised a powerful economic and political influence. By 1672, there were thirty houses and about two hundred people at Charles Town. By 1680, the settlers had moved the settlement back down the Ashley River to where it joined the Cooper River to form the bay or harbor area, a few miles west of the Atlantic Ocean.

One of the unique features of Charles Town at its new location was that it was a planned city, following the checkerboard plan proposed for London after the great fire of 1666. At the time, only in Philadelphia and Charles Town were the streets laid out before the city was built. By 1680, approximately a thousand people lived in Charles Town. By 1690, with a thousand to twelve hundred residents, Charles Town was the fifth largest city in the North American colonies that would become the United States—after Boston, Philadelphia, New York, and Newport. By 1700, Charles Town still was an eighty-acre fortified city-state, four squares long by three squares wide, surrounded by a wall. Six bastions helped protect the city. Many farms and plantations existed outside the city, and the city had become a trading center for the farms, plantations, and native villages, with rivers and original Indian trails becoming the avenues of commerce into the city. Deerskins and beaver skins remained important, but rice had become the major economic harvest by the early 1700's.

By 1717, the Spanish threat had waned, unfriendly local natives had been defeated in the Yamasee War, and friendly local tribes had settled primarily as farmers and hunters along local river areas in South Carolina. In 1717, the wall was removed from around the city to allow growth. Pirates remained a problem until 1718.

Charles Town was unique in its early ethnic mixture. Some scholars think that one African slave was on the *Carolina* in 1670, but even if this were not the case, African slaves were brought in soon afterward. Some of the Africans were free, and many, whether slave or free, were skilled craftsmen. There was a relatively small white middle class, because the large white wealthy class stymied middle-class growth, and an even smaller white craftsman class because of the predominance of free Africans and African slaves as expert craftsmen. Against strong opposition from the Lord's Proprietors, some local natives were enslaved. Huguenot refugees from England, France, and other places began moving to the city in the mid-1680's. The Barbadians and Huguenots soon formed the largest part of the cultural and political elite of the area.

Close contact was maintained with Barbados, and these ties also helped the Barbadians and the city to prosper. Barbadian architecture, Huguenot wrought iron, and formal gardens became hallmarks of Charles Town. The Proprietors encouraged Dissenters (Protestants who were not members of the Church of England) to move to Charles Town in order to limit the power of the Barbadians. Immigrants, mostly Calvinist Presbyterians, came from Scotland and Ireland, and they engaged in political conflict with the Barbadians and Huguenots. Quakers, and by 1695 Spanish and Portuguese Jews, also settled in Charles Town. Charles Town remained unique in its tolerance of religious and ethnic diversity. It was the only major city in the colonial era that did not exclude undesirable strangers and probably was the least religious of the early major cities. In fact, Charles Town developed a well-deserved reputation as a cultured, wealthy, and pleasure-oriented city—a place of theaters, gambling, horse racing, dancing, and drinking. Much of this was possible only through exploitation of African slaves to provide most of the manual labor.

In 1970, Charles Town Landing was developed as a state park and major tourist attraction on the site of the original Charles Town settlement, celebrating the tricentennial of the 1670 settlement, which is also considered the tricentennial of South Carolina. A reconstruction of a village of the 1600's, a forest with animals found in Charles Town in 1670—such as black bears, bison, bobcats, alligators, snakes, and puma—a crop garden with tobacco, rice, indigo, cotton, sugar cane, and other crops grown in season, a reproduction of a seventeenth century trading vessel docked at the original landing area, a museum, a theater, and other activities showed many facets of the 1670 settlement.   —*Abraham D. Lavender*

ADDITIONAL READING:

Fraser, Walter J. *Charleston! Charleston! The History of a Southern City*. Columbia: University of South Carolina Press, 1989. A detailed account of Charleston's settlement and history.

Jones, Lewis P. *South Carolina: A Synoptic History for Laymen*. Rev. ed. Orangeburg, S.C.: Sandlapper Publishing, 1978. Includes several chapters on the early history of the Charleston area.

Lavender, Abraham D. *French Huguenots: From Mediterranean Catholics to White Anglo-Saxon Protestants*. New York: Peter Lang, 1990. A general history of Huguenots that includes analysis of naming patterns in Charleston, illustrating early cultural assimilation among Huguenots, English, and others.

Osborne, Anne Riggs. *The South Carolina Story*. Orangeburg, S.C.: Sandlapper Publishing, 1988. Includes a detailed discussion of Charles Town's settlement and a chapter on the pirates in the Charles Town area.

Rosen, Robert. *A Short History of Charleston*. 2d ed. Charleston, S.C.: Peninsula Press, 1992. Separate chapters are devoted chronologically to Charleston's history, including two chapters on its early history.

Wallace, David Duncan. *South Carolina: A Short History, 1520-1948*. Columbia: University of South Carolina Press, 1961. Considered to be a classic history of South Carolina. Gives detailed information on Charleston's settlement and history.

SEE ALSO: 1663, Settlement of the Carolinas; 1671, Indian Slave Trade; 1711, Tuscarora War.

1670 ■ HUDSON'S BAY COMPANY IS CHARTERED: *the company's political as well as economic power ensures British dominance in Canada*

DATE: May 2, 1670
LOCALE: Hudson Bay (Rupert's Land)
CATEGORIES: Canadian history; Economics; Expansion and land acquisition; Organizations and institutions
KEY FIGURES:
Charles II (1630-1685), king of England
Zachariah Gillam (died 1682), captain of the *Nonsuch*
Médard Chouart des Groseilliers (1625-1698) and
Pierre Esprit Radisson (c. 1636-c. 1710), French-Canadian explorers who were influential in forming Hudson's Bay Company
Pierre Le Moyne, sieur d'Iberville (1661-1706), Hudson Bay raider who almost drove the English out
Rupert (1619-1682), prince of Bavaria, first governor of Rupert's Land

SUMMARY OF EVENT. In 1670, England and France were deeply entrenched in the struggle for North America. Although outwardly friendly, King Louis XIV of France and King Charles II of England secretly struggled for dominance. Two French Canadian *coureurs de bois* (woodrunners) and explorers, Pierre Esprit Radisson and Médard Chouart des Groseilliers, became pawns in the battle for North America.

Radisson was alleged to be the first white explorer to enter Minnesota; Groseilliers, his brother-in-law and partner, prob-

ably journeyed as far as Lake Michigan, the Straits of Mackinac, and Green Bay. In 1659-1660, the two men traded for furs
in the northern fur areas with the Illinois, Sioux, and Cree
tribes. Upon their return to New France (now Quebec), leading
a flotilla of sixty fur-laden canoes, they were prosecuted by the
French authorities for illegal trading and their furs were confiscated. Although they appealed to the French court in 1661,
their petitions were ignored. Acting through Colonel George
Cartwright, a commissioner sent to Boston by the newly restored British monarchy to help settle British colonial boundaries, the brothers-in-law entreated Charles II and his cousin,
Prince Rupert, duke of Bavaria, to fund an expedition to Hudson Bay. This area had been located sixty years earlier by
Henry Hudson during his fourth voyage, in which he attempted to discover the Northwest Passage to Cathay.

Radisson and Groseilliers arrived in England during 1665,
the year of the bubonic plague. The British referred to them as
Mr. Radishes and Mr. Gooseberry (*groseilliers* means gooseberry bushes in French). Fascinated by the adventurers' idea
that the Bay of the North could be approached by sea rather
than the normal St. Lawrence River route by canoe (information given to the explorers by the Cree natives), King Charles
and Prince Rupert envisioned rich fur harvests. In 1667, Sir
George Carteret invested the first twenty pounds in the new
venture. It took until June 5, 1668, to equip two decrepit but
serviceable ships—the *Eaglet*, captained by William Stannard,
with Radisson on board, and the *Nonsuch*, commanded by
Captain Zachariah Gillam, with Groseilliers on board—with
the necessities for an exploratory journey to Hudson Bay. The
Eaglet was forced to return to England on August 5; the
Nonsuch continued to Hudson Bay where, on the east coast of
James Bay, on a stream he called the Rupert River, Groseilliers
established Fort Charles, a trading station. The party wintered
with the help of friendly Cree natives, with whom Captain
Gillam signed a treaty of amity and traded muskets, hatchets,
steel knives, needles, and trinkets for pelts.

Groseilliers left Hudson Bay in June, 1669, and returned to
the court of Charles in October with a shipload of luxurious
furs: ermine, lynx, and beaver. For the British monarchy, this
shipment represented an alternative source to the Baltic fur
market. At that time, Baltic furs were used by Great Britain in
trade with Russia in exchange for commodities vital to the
shipbuilding industry, including hemp and tar. Charles now
realized that fur, rather than gold, was the real treasure of the
New World.

On May 2, 1670, Charles granted a royal charter, composed
on five sheepskin parchment sheets, under the Great Seal of
England to his privy councillor, Prince Rupert. The charter
granted the newly established "Governor and Company of
Adventurers of England tradeing into Hudson's Bay" title to
all land, and a trade monopoly within the drainage basin of
Hudson Bay: "all those Seas Streightes Bayes Rivers Lakes
Creekes and Soundes in whatsoever Latitude they shall be that
lye within the entrance of the Streightes commonly called
Hudsons Streightes together with all the Landes and Territo-

ryes." The area was to be called Rupert's Land, with the
company maintaining the mineral and fishing rights and the
right of exclusive trade. Traders encroaching on this expanse
of land would be imprisoned and forfeit their ships and merchandise, with one-half the value going to the company, the
other half to the British crown. The charter also included in its
right of exclusive trade all lands accessed by the waterways of
Rupert's Land.

Other founding adventurers, whose investment shares were
priced at three hundred pounds, included Anthony Ashley
Cooper, the first earl of Shaftesbury; Sir Robert Boyle, chem-
ist and founding member of the Royal Society; Robert Vyner,
the king's banker; Francis Millington, customs commissioner;
John Fenn, paymaster of the Admiralty; Sir George Carteret,
financier; John Portman, banker and goldsmith; Sir John Griffith, city magnate; James Hayes, private secretary to Prince
Rupert; John Kirke, merchant; Kirke's brother-in-law, Sir
Edgar Hungerford; Henry, earl of Arlington; Sir John Robinson, lieutenant of the Tower of London; and William Prety-
man, merchant to India. Lady Margaret Drax, a colonial
widow advised by Hayes, became the first female stockholder.

The charter granted the company complete judicial power,
including the right to sue and be sued, to hold land and dispose
of it, and, if necessary, to wage war. The company was to be
controlled by a governor and an elected committee of seven.
Charles named Prince Rupert the first governor of Rupert's
Land, a position he maintained until his death in 1682. The
only provision mandated upon the company was the payment
of two elk and two black beavers should the British monarch,
or his successors, ever decide to set foot on Rupert's Land.

Charles had no idea of the expanse of Rupert's Land, which
spread over nearly 40 percent of modern Canada: Ontario,
Quebec, Manitoba, most of Saskatchewan, southern Alberta,
the northern area of the Laurentian Mountains, south past
the forty-ninth parallel, and west through the Red River Valley to the Rocky Mountain divide. The area covered by all
streams draining into Hudson Bay encompasses 1.5 million
square miles.

The desire for ermine, lynx, and beaver, used for the immensely fashionable beaver felt hats and as insignias of rank
and wealth, grew. Soon, trading posts, or bay posts as they
were called, lined Hudson Bay, James Bay, the Arctic Ocean,
and the interior. As trade escalated, the beaver skin became
the monetary unit, the "coin of the realm," with a single skin
worth five pounds of sugar and ten skins worth a gun. Hudson's Bay Company outfitted the indigenous people and used
them to trap.

Intermittent problems with France continued. In 1697,
Pierre Le Moyne, sieur d'Iberville, raided Hudson Bay and
almost drove the English out. In 1713, the Peace of Utrecht
sanctioned the British possession of Hudson Bay, but this new
land became the site of a ruthless fur trade, which became
most vicious from 1789 to 1821, after the rival North West
Company arrived. During this era, John Jacob Astor made his
fortune by forming the American Fur Company. The Hudson's

Bay Company maintained domination over Rupert's Land until the Deed of Surrender in 1869, at which time it sold its land to the new Dominion of Canada in exchange for 300,000 British pounds and western farmland. Ultimately, the company sold all its land, preserving some mineral rights; after World War I, it cultivated interests in retail department stores, real-estate investment, and petroleum and natural gas production. — *M. Casey Diana*

ADDITIONAL READING:

Newman, Peter C. *Company of Adventurers*. New York: Viking, 1985. A concise study of Hudson Bay; includes a comprehensive bibliography and maps.

_____. *Empire of the Bay*. Toronto: Madison Press, 1989. Oversized book filled with colorful illustrations, including photographs, depicting the history, past and present, of Hudson's Bay Company. Includes a comprehensive chronology.

Nute, Grace Lee. *Caesars of the Wilderness: Médard Chouart, Sieur des Groseilliers, and Pierre Esprit Radisson, 1618-1710*. 1943. Reprint. St. Paul: Minnesota Historical Society Press, 1978. A comprehensive biography of both Groseilliers and Radisson, covering the discovery and exploration of New France and the development of the fur trade. Extensive bibliography.

Ray, Arthur J. *The Canadian Fur Trade in the Industrial Age*. Toronto: University of Toronto Press, 1990. Covers the history and economic conditions of Hudson's Bay Company, the fur trade, and the natives of North America. Plates, illustrations, many bibliographical references.

Rich, Edwin Ernest. *Hudson's Bay Company, 1670-1870*. 2 vols. New York: Macmillan, 1961. Extensive and approachable, with illustrations of key players, a map, and a foreword by Sir Winston Churchill.

SEE ALSO: 1603, Champlain's Voyages; 1610, Hudson Explores Hudson Bay; 1627, Company of New France Is Chartered; 1673, French Explore the Mississippi Valley.

1671 ■ INDIAN SLAVE TRADE: *British colonists use intertribal rivalries and natives' desire for European goods to gain slaves and establish dominance over Spanish claims*

DATE: 1671-1730

LOCALE: South Carolina

CATEGORIES: Economics; Native American history

KEY FIGURES:

Francis Le Jau (1665-1717), French Huguenot minister who opposed Indian slavery

James Moore (died 1706), Carolina governor who led an attack on Florida Indians in 1704

SUMMARY OF EVENT. The earliest known record of Carolina natives being captured and enslaved was in 1520, when Span-

ish explorers took them to provide slaves for sugar plantations in Santo Domingo. In 1663, William Hilton, an Englishman, also captured natives from the Carolina coast for Caribbean slave owners. In 1670, Charleston was settled by the English. In 1671, after the defeat of Kusso warriors and the taking of numerous captives, English colonists initiated the Indian slave trade when Henry Woodward was commissioned to open trade in Indian slaves with Indians of rival tribes.

Carolina included what is now South Carolina and North Carolina until 1713, but between the 1670's and 1730, almost all of Carolina's American Indian trading was out of Charles Town, or Charleston, which was the hub of the area that became South Carolina. Agriculture and forest industries also were part of Carolina's economy, but trading with the natives became the most lucrative aspect of the Carolina economy. Deerskins, leathers, and furs were the most important exports from this trading, but slavery also early became an important part of the trade. Although American Indian slaves existed in other areas (Virginia, for example), only South Carolina developed Indian slavery as a major part of its commerce. As a result, South Carolina enslaved more natives than any other English colony.

The Carolina traders had an advantage in developing a thriving trade with natives all the way to the Mississippi River for several reasons: The Carolina colony got an early start in the trade; there were no mountains blocking the westward expansion of Carolina trading; and Carolina traders could trade directly with American Indians rather than going through other natives as middlemen (in the northeastern United States, the Iroquois acted as middlemen between other American Indians and the Europeans).

The enslavement of natives by Carolina traders did have some opposition. From 1680 until 1730, South Carolina was under the active or nominal leadership of eight Lord Proprietors (headquartered in London) who recognized the crucial financial importance of developing trade with the natives. The Lord Proprietors knew that the enslavement of natives ultimately would hurt their general trade with Indians by leading to uprisings. A few proprietors also owned stock in the Royal African Company (begun in 1672), which was bringing slaves from Africa, and did not want competition from American Indians. Some prominent local leaders also spoke against American Indian slavery. For example, Francis Le Jau, a French Huguenot minister, publicly criticized the slave trade. In 1720, sixteen prominent businessmen issued a statement against the enslavement of American Indians. As a group, Charleston's Huguenot merchants were more opposed to native slavery, although a few did own Indian slaves. The proprietors were not opposed to slavery in principle, however, and they wavered in their opposition.

Despite some opposition, major factors encouraged slavery. The selling of captives into slavery in order to pay volunteer soldiers was an old custom in Europe, with military commanders and pirates routinely enslaving people on ships they captured. For example, some Jews escaping the Spanish Inquisition in the 1490's were captured by pirates and sold into slavery. The idea that slavery was better than death, and that the natives would murder their captives if they did not have the option of selling them, was used as a moral justification for slavery. Although this rationale was accurate in some cases, it did not take into account the great increase in natives capturing other natives because a market existed for slaves—a market made by the Europeans. Prior to European contact, slavery had been practiced by some American Indians, who frequently sold captives as slaves, but not on a large scale and generally without the harsh treatment common to European slavery. In addition, the enslavement of both American Indians and Africans got strong support in Charleston because a large number of Charleston's political and economic establishment were from the Caribbean and brought a strong tradition of slavery with them to South Carolina.

The trade in American Indian slaves became an important part of the national conflicts involving Great Britain, Spain, and France for control of the Americas. Indians were drawn into these conflicts, often allying with a European power against other natives allied with another European power. In 1680, for example, Indians allied with the British in Carolina began raids against Indians allied with the Spanish Catholic missions in Georgia and northern Florida. The British and Spanish had attempted attacks on each other, and the English feared that the natives in Georgia and Florida would ally with the Spanish to attack Carolina. At the same time, the availability of a large number of Indians who were easy to capture because of their sedentary village life was tempting to slave traders for nondefense reasons. In 1704 under James Moore, for example, fifty British soldiers and a thousand Indians from Carolina took large numbers of Indian slaves from the Spanish areas. The French settled on the Gulf coast in 1699, putting them in proximity with natives in the lower Mississippi River area who were being threatened by attack and enslavement from Carolinian slave traders or (more likely) their Indian allies. This opposition from the French increased the risk and cost of capturing lower Mississippi River natives and, by 1720, largely ended the English slave trading.

Although the Europeans actually kidnapped or captured American Indians in the early years of the slave trade, mostly from coastal areas, they soon began to rely on other Indians to do the capturing as the slave trade increased and moved farther away from the coast. Encouraging native allies to capture other natives for slavery became a major part of the strategy of the slave dealers. In 1712, for example, the Tuscaroras of North Carolina killed some English and German settlers who had taken their land. The governor of North Carolina announced the availability of Indian slaves to induce South Carolina officials to send him military help. South Carolina expeditions—comprising mostly American Indians—killed more than a thousand Tuscaroras, mostly men, and more than seven hundred, mostly women and children, were sold into slavery. Peaceful natives along the route back to South Carolina also were captured and enslaved.

In 1715, the Yamasees in South Carolina revolted against the Carolina traders because of the traders' dishonest practices such as cheating when weighing deerskins and furs. The Yamasees were defeated only because the Cherokees allied with the Carolina traders to capture Yamasees to sell as slaves, the proceeds from which they used to buy ammunition and clothing from the Carolinians. After that time, Carolina deliberately played one tribe off against another. The exposure of natives to European clothing, ammunition, rum, and other goods led to a rising desire for more European products, which further encouraged Indians to capture other Indians for exchange.

Indians comprised one-fourth of the slaves in Carolina in 1708, numbering fourteen hundred out of fifty-five hundred slaves, but the percentage generally decreased after that, for several reasons. Natives were more likely than Africans to try to escape. Although Indians had to beware of other hostile Indians, they frequently were successful in their attempts because they were in the same country as their original homes. For this reason, and because of the heavy demand for slave labor on the Caribbean sugar plantations, native slaves usually were sold to Caribbean traders. Some were also sold to New England. In addition, native slaves were more susceptible to European diseases and hence had a greater death rate than African slaves. Early writers also described American Indian slaves as being more docile than African slaves, ascribing this alleged trait to the Indians' sense of independence. For these reasons, native slaves usually were less desirable than, and cost much less than, African slaves. Because large numbers of native men were killed, a high percentage of American Indian slaves were women, partly explaining a significant mixture of African and Indian genealogies.

Although some American Indian slavery continued for several more decades, the practice basically had ended by 1730 in Carolina, with the Carolina traders turning to other trades and the English turning their American Indian slavery concerns to central America. —*Abraham D. Lavender*

ADDITIONAL READING:

Crane, Verner. *The Southern Frontier, 1670-1732*. Ann Arbor: University of Michigan Press, 1929. A classic work on relations between European settlers and American Indians in the South.

Rozema, Vicki. *Footsteps of the Cherokees: A Guide to the Eastern Homelands of the Cherokee Nations*. Winston-Salem, N.C.: John F. Blair, 1995. Devotes several pages to American Indian slavery, helping to correct the previously small amount of attention given to this topic.

Waddell, Gene. *Indians of the South Carolina Lowcountry, 1562-1751*. Spartanburg, S.C.: Reprint Company, 1980. Describes how enslavement was one of several major factors in the extinction of South Carolina's lowcountry tribes.

Weatherford, Jack. *Native Roots: How the Indians Enriched America*. New York: Fawcett Columbine, 1991. One chapter is devoted to American Indian slaves, with a section describing the important part played by Charleston merchants in Indian slavery.

Wright, J. Leitch, Jr. "Brands and Slave Cords." In *The Only Land They Knew: The Tragic Story of the American Indians in the Old South*. New York: Free Press, 1981. Gives details on the Carolina slave trade in American Indians, with emphasis on historical details.

SEE ALSO: 1663, Settlement of the Carolinas; 1670, Charles Town Is Founded.

1673 ■ FRENCH EXPLORE THE MISSISSIPPI VALLEY: *French exploration and occupation of the trans-Mississippi West, laying the foundation for conflict with the British a century later*

DATE: 1673-1740's
LOCALE: Mississippi River Valley
CATEGORIES: Expansion and land acquisition; Exploration and discovery
KEY FIGURES:

Louis de Buade, comte de Frontenac (1622-1698), the Iron Governor, who sponsored La Salle's expeditions

Étienne de Bourgmound, explorer of the Missouri River

Louis Jolliet (1645-1700), explorer and trapper to whom Talon entrusted the task of finding the Mississippi River

René Robert Cavelier, sieur de La Salle (1643-1687), French nobleman who first followed the Mississippi River to the Gulf of Mexico

Pierre Gaultier de Varennes, sieur de La Vérendrye (1685-1749), explorer of Manitoba and the Dakotas sixty years before the Lewis and Clark expedition

Pierre Le Moyne, sieur d'Iberville (1661-1706), Frenchman who established the first French settlement on the Gulf of Mexico

Peter Mallet and

Paul Mallet, brothers who pioneered the Santa Fe Trail in 1739

Jacques Marquette (1637-1675), Jesuit priest whose journal is the only record of Jolliet's journey

Jean-Baptiste Talon (c. 1625-1694), colonial intendent who licensed the first expeditions to the Great Lakes

Charles Claude du Tisné, first Frenchman to explore the Kansas and Republican Rivers

SUMMARY OF EVENT. Expanding upon Samuel de Champlain's explorations in the early 1600's, Jean Nicolet opened the Ottawa River route to Lake Huron, Lake Michigan, and Green Bay in 1634. Nicolet then traveled up the Fox River, probably crossed the portage at what is now Portage, Wisconsin, to enter the Mississippi Valley, and may have proceeded south into what is now northern Illinois. During this trip, natives of the Mascouten tribe told him of a "great water" three days' travel to the west. Although this probably was the Mississippi River, Nicolet thought it was the Pacific Ocean.

In 1671, Nicholas Perrot guided Simon François Daumont, sieur de St. Lusson, to Sault Sainte Marie. St. Lusson formally took possession of the area for France and signed trade treaties with sixteen western tribes in 1672. Perrot was the first man licensed to explore the Great Lakes by Jean-Baptiste Talon, intendent in charge of the colonial judiciary and finances. Earlier, however, Médard Chouart des Groseilliers and Pierre Esprit Radisson had led an illegal exploratory trade mission to Chequamegon Bay on Lake Superior, from 1654 to 1660. It appears that Radisson also traveled west to Mille Lacs (Minnesota) and perhaps to the Mississippi River.

Talon also engaged Louis Jolliet to explore the Mississippi River. In 1673, Jolliet, accompanied by Jacques Marquette, a Jesuit priest, left Michilimackinac and traveled across Lake Michigan to Green Bay and up the Fox River. They then portaged the Wisconsin River, thus entering the Mississippi Valley, and descended the Wisconsin River to its mouth. They then canoed down the Mississippi River to the mouth of the Arkansas River. Convinced that the Mississippi River flowed into the Gulf of Mexico, not the Gulf of California, they returned up the Mississippi River. Discovering the mouth of the Illinois River, they ascended it. From the Illinois River, they portaged to the Chicago River, leaving the Mississippi Valley and entering Lake Michigan.

In 1672, Talon had left for France, turning over the colonial government to Louis de Buade, comte de Frontenac. Frontenac envisioned a series of forts west of the Appalachian Mountains to exclude the British from the Mississippi Valley. He then hoped to tap the rich fur supply and ship it to France from either Quebec or a new city near the mouth of the Mississippi River. Frontenac made René-Robert Cavelier, sieur de La Salle, who was fluent in eight American Indian languages and very effective in dealing with the tribes, his chief agent. La Salle already had explored the Ohio River to the falls at present-day Louisville in 1669-1670.

On May 12, 1678, King Louis XIV and Jean Baptiste Colbert, the king's minister, signed letters patent giving La Salle a five-year trade monopoly in the West. In the spring of 1679, La Salle sent a party westward toward the land of the Illinois and began building his own sailing ship, the *Griffon*, which became the first to sail the lakes. On August 27, he arrived aboard his ship at Michilimackinac. Sending the *Griffon* back from Green Bay, La Salle then proceeded south to the mouth of the Miami River (now St. Joseph). During the next two years, he made three trips into the Illinois River Valley, penetrating to the Mississippi in futile attempts to continue on down the Mississippi River to the Gulf. Forts were built and destroyed, the *Griffon* was lost, and trading parties failed. On April 9, 1682, La Salle found the mouth of the Mississippi River, claimed the whole area for France, and named it Louisiana after Louis XIV.

In 1683, La Salle again returned to France and obtained royal support to establish a fortified colony about 180 miles above the mouth of the Mississippi River. In 1684, La Salle left France with four ships, one hundred soldiers, and three hundred settlers. Failing to find the river's mouth and plagued by Spanish raiders, shipwreck, and desertion, La Salle and 180

MISSISSIPPI VALLEY:
THE MARQUETTE/JOLLIET AND LA SALLE EXPEDITIONS, 1573-1682

Among the many French explorations of the Mississippi River Valley, that of Jacques Marquette and Louis Jolliet is famous as the first major expedition into the region. That of René Robert Cavelier, sieur de La Salle, was the first to reach the mouth of the Mississippi River, confirming that the great midcontinental waterway emptied into the Gulf of Mexico.

survivors finally landed at Matagorda Bay, Texas, where he constructed a fort. After an exploratory trip to what is now West Texas, he returned to Fort St. Louis. A few days later, the expedition's only remaining ship was lost and La Salle decided that the expedition's only hope was to seek relief overland from Illinois. Starting on January 27, 1687, La Salle took seventeen men, leaving twenty-three behind to guard the fort. La Salle was murdered during a mutiny near the Brazos River,

but six men struggled onward to Post aux Arkansas near the junction of the Arkansas and Mississippi Rivers. La Salle's lieutenant, Henri de Tonti, had established the post while searching for La Salle.

Meanwhile, Daniel Greysolon, sieur du Lhut, explored the western Lake Superior region, discovering the Falls of St. Anthony at present-day Minneapolis. Pierre Le Moyne, sieur d'Iberville, rediscovered the mouth of the Mississippi River and was instrumental in founding Fort Maurepas (Biloxi) in 1699. His brother, Jean Baptiste Le Moyne, sieur de Bienville, established Mobile in 1702 and New Orleans in 1718.

Étienne de Bourgmound made the first extensive journey up the Missouri River in 1715. He was followed by Charles du Tisné, who advanced westward on the Kansas River to the Pawnee country, where he was blocked from contacting the Comanche farther west.

The upper Missouri River was explored by the La Vérendrye family and others going west from Lake Superior. Pierre Gaultier de Varennes, sieur de La Vérendrye, and his three sons received a government fur trade monopoly for the regions in 1730. Basing their operations at Fort La Reine on the Assiniboine River (in what is now Manitoba) in 1737, they traveled over much of the present-day Dakotas, searching for a water route to the Pacific Ocean and trading with the natives.

At the same time that the La Vérendryes were exploring the upper Missouri River, two brothers, Peter and Paul Mallet, were journeying to New Mexico, the farthest west any Frenchman had ventured. Passing through the Osage, Pawnee, and Comanche lands along what became the Santa Fe Trail, the Mallets arrived in Santa Fe, only to be jailed by the Spanish. Released in 1740, they returned to Louisiana.

French exploration and occupation of the interior valley led directly to the clash with Great Britain in the French and Indian War (1754-1763). This cost France its American empire and ultimately contributed to the American Revolution. Nevertheless, the French left a substantial legacy: The *coureurs de bois* had gathered basic information about the trans-Mississippi West that was used by American mountain men and the British Hudson's Bay Company nearly a century later. The French also made a lasting contribution to the culture of the north woods and Louisiana.

—*William L. Richter, updated by Ralph L. Langenheim, Jr.*

ADDITIONAL READING:

Balesi, Charles J. *The Time of the French in the Heart of North America: 1673-1818.* Chicago: Alliance Francaise Chicago, 1992. Focuses on the history of the Illinois country.

Crouse, Nellis M. *Lemoyne d'Iberville: Soldier of New France.* Ithaca, N.Y.: Cornell University Press, 1954. Biography of the founder the first French Gulf coast settlements.

Kellogg, Louise P. *The French Regime in Wisconsin and the Northwest.* Madison: State Historical Society of Wisconsin, 1925. Discusses early exploration, mining, and the fur trade in the Great Lakes and Wisconsin.

Nasatir, Abraham P. *Before Lewis and Clark: Documents Illustrating the History of the Missouri, 1785-1804.* 2 vols. St. Louis: St. Louis Historical Documents Foundation, 1952. The author's introduction to the first volume is a fine narrative of French Missouri River exploration between 1673 and 1804.

Parkman, Francis. *The Discovery of the Great West: La Salle.* 1889. Reprint. Westport, Conn.: Greenwood Press, 1986. The first comprehensive account of La Salle's explorations; based on copies of most of the original documents in French and other archives.

Speck, Francis B. *The Jolliet-Marquette Expedition, 1673.* Glendale, Calif.: Arthur H. Clark, 1928. A definitive study of the Jolliet-Marquette expedition.

Weddle, Robert S., Mary Christine Morkovsky, and Patricia Galloway, eds. *La Salle, the Mississippi, and the Gulf.* Translated by A. L. Bell and Robert S. Weddle. College Station: Texas A & M University Press, 1987. Documents pertaining to La Salle's exploration of the Mississippi Valley and Texas.

SEE ALSO: 1603, Champlain's Voyages; 1610, Hudson Explores Hudson Bay; 1627, Company of New France Is Chartered; 1670, Hudson's Bay Company Is Chartered; 1754, French and Indian War.

1675 ■ METACOM'S WAR: *the first large-scale conflict between New England colonists and Native Americans*

DATE: June 20, 1675
LOCALE: New England colonies
CATEGORIES: Native American history; Wars, uprisings, and civil unrest
KEY FIGURES:
Benjamin Church (1639-1718), prominent soldier
Massasoit, also known as *Ousamequin* (c. 1580-1661),
Metacom, also known as *King Philip* (c. 1640-1676), and
Wamsutta, also known as *Alexander* (died 1661), paramount Wampanoag sachems
Mary White Rowlandson (c. 1635-c. 1678), war captive and writer

SUMMARY OF EVENT. Metacom's War, also known as King Philip's War, began on June 20, 1675, when Wampanoag, or Pokanoket, warriors began looting English houses in southern Plymouth Colony (now Massachusetts) on the edge of Wampanoag country. Serious fighting began at Swansea on June 24.

The causes of the conflict were both economic and cultural. Through a series of treaties, much native land had passed into the hands of English settlers, and the remaining Wampanoag homeland, Mount Hope Peninsula on Narragansett Bay, was in danger of being completely surrounded by English settlements. This expansion of English-controlled territory had brought many Indians under English political control, with the imposition of alien social mores. English courts, for example, sometimes sentenced tribesmen to fines or whippings for violating the Sabbath by such activities as firing a gun on Sunday. There also was growing pressure on Native Americans to convert to Christianity. Tribal chiefs (called sachems in New England) and religious leaders (powwows) strongly opposed conversion, because it tended to weaken their traditional influence.

Massasoit (renamed Ousamequin late in life), the paramount sachem of the Wampanoags and an ally and friend of the English since 1621, had died about 1661, and after his death, tensions rapidly mounted. Massasoit's eldest son, Wamsutta, called Alexander by the English, became sachem on his father's death. Wamsutta died in 1661, shortly after being required by English authorities to explain rumors that he was considering an uprising. Then another son, Metacom or Meta-comet, known to the English as King Philip, became sachem, and the next few years witnessed a series of disputes. By 1671, friendly Native Americans were warning Puritan authorities that Philip was organizing an alliance of tribes to join with the Wampanoags in a war of extermination against the English.

While the evidence for such a conspiracy is strong, war, sparked by the trial and execution at Plymouth of three Wam-panoags for murder, seems to have broken out before Meta-com's alliance was perfected. In January, 1675, a Christian Wampanoag named John Sassamon, who had just warned Plymouth of Metacom's plans, was found murdered. On the testimony of an Indian who claimed to have witnessed the deed, three Wampanoags, including an important counselor of Metacom, were convicted and hanged on June 8. Metacom apparently was unable to restrain the rage of his warriors, and violence broke out before he was ready.

The war quickly spread to Connecticut and Massachusetts Bay colonies, and later to Rhode Island, as other tribal groups, drawn in by Metacom's diplomacy or angered by threats from colonial authorities, went on the attack. The Wampanoags were joined by the related Sakonnet and Pocasset bands to the east of Narragansett Bay, by Nipmucks from the interior of Massachusetts, by the Narragansetts of present-day Rhode Island, and by smaller groups such as the river tribes of the Connecticut Valley.

The English colonists were supported by American Indians who often were the traditional enemies of tribes in Metacom's alliance, so Indian New England was not united in Metacom's War. The Mohegans and Pequots of southern Connecticut served with the English, as did hundreds of Christian Indians from the "praying towns" of Massachusetts Bay Colony. The Niantics of southern Rhode Island remained neutral. Metacom sought the assistance of the Mohawks of New York Colony to the west, but the Mohawks aided the English by attacking their old Wampanoag enemies.

In the early months, the Wampanoags and their allies, well armed with trade muskets, were too skillful and aggressive for the English. They repeatedly ambushed parties of colonial militiamen and assaulted and burned outlying English towns. Unskilled in forest warfare and distrustful of friendly tribes-men, the colonists were unable to pin down the enemy. The English usually had no inkling of the town chosen for attack, so hostile chiefs concentrated their forces and often greatly outnumbered the defending garrison. By using Indian allies as scouts, English militia officers learned to avoid ambush and to operate more effectively in the forest. Eventually, special colo-nial units that could remain in the field for weeks were used to pursue American Indian bands; disease, cold, and starvation aided the colonists in wearing the tribes down. The most effective such unit was a small, mixed force of English militia and Indian allies commanded by Captain Benjamin Church of

Plymouth Colony. It was Church's company that eventually ran down Metacom and the handful of Wampanoags still with him, directed by a surrendered Wampanoag to a swamp where they had taken refuge. Metacom was killed, shot by an Indian while trying to slip away once more, on August 12, 1676. By this time, as starving groups of Indians straggled in to surren-der, the war was dragging to a close. The much larger popula-tion and economic resources of the English had won out. In spite of the warriors' initial successes, it had become clear that there was no real prospect of driving the English into the sea. To the northeast in New Hampshire and Maine, where the Abenaki peoples had risen against the English, the war contin-ued into 1678.

Both sides used ruthless methods, often killing women, children, and the elderly. Indian attackers regularly attempted to burn colonists' houses with the inhabitants inside them, and sometimes tortured prisoners. Perhaps the most strikingly ruthless act committed by the English took place in the Great Swamp Fight, December 19, 1676. A force of a thousand militiamen marched into a frozen swamp deep in the Rhode Island forest, led there by a Narragansett turncoat, and at-tacked perhaps a thousand Narragansetts sheltered in a log-walled fort. Forcing their way inside, the English set the fort afire. As many as six hundred Narragansetts, many of them women and children, perished in the blaze. Some eighty En-glishmen were killed or died of wounds.

Metacom's War has been called the bloodiest war, propor-tionally, in the nation's history, with some nine thousand of the eighty thousand people in New England killed. Of these, one-third were English and two-thirds Indians. Of New England's ninety towns, fifty-two were attacked and seventeen com-pletely burned. The frontier of settlement was pushed back many miles. The military power and the independence of the tribal people of southern New England had been crushed for-ever. Hundreds of Native American captives, including Meta-com's wife and small son, were sold into slavery by the colo-nial governments to help defray the war's cost. Other captives, considered to be important war chiefs or those responsible for particular atrocities, were tried and publicly executed.

—*Bert M. Mutersbaugh*

ADDITIONAL READING:

Bourne, Russell. *The Red King's Rebellion: Racial Politics in New England, 1675-1678.* New York: Oxford University Press, 1990. A detailed treatment of the war that is especially critical of the motives and acts of the colonists. Maps, illustra-tions, and index.

Leach, Douglas Edward. *Flintlock and Tomahawk: New England in King Philip's War.* New York: Norton Library Edition, 1966. This elegantly written study, long considered the standard modern account of the war, indicts English land hunger as a cause of the war. Maps, illustrations, and index.

Lincoln, Charles A., ed. *Narratives of the Indian Wars, 1675-1699.* New York: Scribner's, 1913. Reprint. New York: Barnes & Noble Books, 1941. Contains a number of contem-poraneous accounts of the war, including *The Sovereignty &*

Goodness of God . . . the Captivity and Restoration of Mrs Mary Rowlandson, Rowlandson's account of her capture in the attack on Lancaster, Massachusetts, in 1676. Her often reprinted classic is the earliest American captivity narrative. Rowlandson reports firsthand exchanges with Metacom, who at times traveled with the mixed band that held her prisoner.

Malone, Patrick M. *The Skulking Way of War: Technology and Tactics Among the New England Indians.* Baltimore: The Johns Hopkins University Press, 1991. Study of Native American military tactics and their evolution under the influence of European weapons and methods. Argues that New England's natives adopted the more ruthless methods of total war through English influence and example. Map, illustrations, and index.

Slotkin, Richard, and James K. Folsom, eds. *So Dreadful a Judgment: Puritan Responses to King Philip's War, 1676-1677.* Middletown, Conn.: Wesleyan University Press, 1978. Six contemporaneous accounts, including Rowlandson's narrative and the liveliest, best contemporary description of the fighting, Thomas Church's *Entertaining Passages Relating to Philip's War* (1716), based on the recollections of his father, Captain Benjamin Church.

SEE ALSO: 1620, Pilgrims Land at Plymouth; 1630, Great Puritan Migration; 1636, Pequot War.

1676 ■ BACON'S REBELLION: *planters rise up against both Virginia's governor and Native Americans, causing destruction and death*

DATE: May 10-October 18, 1676
LOCALE: Eastern Virginia
CATEGORIES: Government and politics; Native American history; Wars, uprisings, and civil unrest
KEY FIGURES:
Nathaniel Bacon (1647-1676), English planter
William Berkeley (1606-1677), governor of Virginia
John Berry (died 1715) and
Francis Moryson (died 1678?), two of the royal commissioners sent to investigate causes of the rebellion
Robert Beverly, clerk of the General Assembly and Berkeley's chief lieutenant in the suppression of the rebellion
Henry Chicheley (1615-1683), lieutenant governor of Virginia
Joseph Ingram, commander of the rebel forces after Bacon's death
Herbert Jeffreys (died 1678), third royal commissioner, who succeeded Berkeley as governor
Philip Ludwell (1638?-1723?), member of the Council of State and close adviser to Governor Berkeley
SUMMARY OF EVENT. Instability was inherent in the rapid growth of the English population in Virginia after 1640. Competition for political power and social position increased after 1660, as the earlier settlers entrenched themselves in local

political offices. Land hunger was also a problem: Since the end of the second Powhatan War in 1646, the Powhatans had held the land north of the York River, which had the effect of hemming in English expansion. Landownership was a requirement for the vote as well as the key to personal fortune. Later settlers, many of whom had come to Virginia as indentured servants, found high land prices and limited opportunities, and they began to view the land held by the Powhatans as the answer to their problem. At the same time, the return of the Susquehannocks to the northern Chesapeake meant the extension of their war with the Iroquois into the area. That European settlers should be caught in the crossfire of this war was inevitable, and also helped fuel frustrations.

A prosperous economy might have counteracted unstable political and social conditions, but Virginia's economy stagnated after 1660. Chronic overproduction of an inferior quality of tobacco, aggravated by restrictive features of the Navigation Acts, drove the price of tobacco down. Expensive experimentation with methods of diversifying the economy and the need for defense measures against the Dutch and the natives resulted in high taxes. In 1674, the colonists were further taxed to send agents to London to lobby against proprietary land grants. Circumstances conspired to exacerbate the planters' miseries, and Governor Sir William Berkeley's ineffectual leadership led to a general disaffection toward the government. Berkeley's own comfortable circumstances, derived in part from a profitable monopoly in the fur trade with local tribes, seemed to prove his indifference to the planters' troubles.

The events immediately leading to the rebellion grew out of a dispute between a planter and members of the Doeg tribe in June, 1675. After forces of Virginians pursuing the Doegs murdered numbers of friendly Susquehannocks on two separate occasions, the natives increased the intensity of their raids throughout the fall and winter. Governor Berkeley angered the planters in the frontier settlements when he countermanded the order for a force to proceed against the marauding warriors. In keeping with Berkeley's overall American Indian policy, the Assembly committed the colony to a defensive war, and the governor ordered the erection of a chain of forts on the frontier. Berkeley's solution was no solution in the planters' view, as the forts would add to the burden of taxation and hemmed in further settlement. The settlers' worst fears about Berkeley had been confirmed.

In April, an impatient group of upcountry planters persuaded one of their number, Nathaniel Bacon, Jr., to lead a band of volunteers against the natives. What followed on May 10 was a war of extermination, in which Native Americans of all tribes, friendly or hostile, were killed. Bacon, the son of an English gentleman and related to Berkeley through marriage, had not arrived in Virginia until 1674, but he had already been appointed to the Council of State. Governor Berkeley refused Bacon's request for a commission to raise volunteers and sent several letters warning him against becoming a mutineer. Unable to head off Bacon with his force of three hundred men, Berkeley, on May 26, 1676, declared him a rebel. On the same day, the governor dissolved the Long Assembly and called for the first general elections in fifteen years, promising that the new Assembly would deal with the American Indian threat and any other grievances.

Bacon's success in killing some natives prompted the residents of Henrico County to send him to Jamestown as one of their new burgesses, but the governor ordered his capture before he could take his seat. Bacon confessed his error and received a pardon from the governor. Several days later, he slipped off to Henrico.

The June Assembly met for twenty days and passed a series of acts dealing with the prosecution of the war with the natives and with various local problems, especially concerning the misuse of political power. Although Bacon has often been credited with pushing through reform legislation, he did not return to Jamestown until June 23, when the session was nearly over. Arriving with five hundred armed men, he terrorized the governor and the burgesses into granting him a commission to fight the natives.

As soon as Bacon marched toward the falls of the James River, Berkeley again proclaimed him a rebel and tried to raise a force against him. Failing in his attempt, Berkeley fled to the eastern shore, leaving Bacon in control of the western shore. Upon arriving in Middle Plantation, Bacon issued a manifesto, the Declaration of the People, that accused the governor of numerous offenses against the colonists and called for his surrender. While Bacon then proceeded to seek out and fall upon the friendly Pamunkey Indians, Berkeley returned to Jamestown and, having reached agreement with Bacon's garrison, took possession of the capital. Several days later, Bacon arrived with six hundred troops and besieged the town. The faintheartedness of Berkeley's men forced the governor to concede the town. Bacon burned it on September 19. A little more than a month later, the rebellion fell apart at the news of Bacon's sudden death of the "bloody flux" and "lousey disease," possibly dysentery.

On January 29, the royal commissioners John Berry, Francis Moryson, and Herbert Jeffreys arrived from England, along with a thousand British soldiers, to investigate the uprising and restore order. Berkeley nullified the royal pardons that they brought for the rebels and ordered the execution of twenty-three men. His extreme cruelty was criticized by the commissioners, and Sir Herbert Jeffreys formally took over the government in April upon Berkeley's recall by the Crown. Although Bacon was dead, the disorder and protest would not end until 1683, with the reconfiguring of imperial government in Virginia. —*Warren M. Billings, updated by Kelley Graham*

ADDITIONAL READING:

Fausz, J. Frederick. "Merging and Emerging Worlds: Anglo-Indian Interest Groups and the Development of the Seventeenth-Century Chesapeake." In *Colonial Chesapeake Society*, edited by Lois Green Carr et al. Chapel Hill: University of North Carolina Press, 1988. Details the changing English view of the Native Americans in the Chesapeake from "noble savages" to important trading partners.

Horn, James. *Adapting to a New World: English Society in the Seventeenth-Century Chesapeake*. Chapel Hill: University of North Carolina Press, 1994. A scholarly but lively study of the extent to which English colonists in the Chesapeake were influenced by their homeland in their attitudes about race, authority, and other matters.

Middlekauff, Robert. *Bacon's Rebellion*. Chicago: Rand McNally, 1964. A good collection of the primary documents associated with the uprising, beginning with Berkeley's American Indian policy and concluding with the official report submitted to London.

Tate, Thad W., and David L. Ammerman. *The Chesapeake in the Seventeenth Century: Essays on the Anglo-American Society*. Chapel Hill: University of North Carolina Press, 1979. An essential collection of articles addressing race relations, class structure, and the demographics of the seventeenth century Chesapeake. Includes an historiographic discussion of Bacon's Rebellion.

Washburn, Wilcomb E. *The Governor and the Rebel*. Chapel Hill: University of North Carolina Press, 1957. A classic study of the small details of the uprising; generous in its forgiveness of Governor Berkeley.

Webb, Stephen Saunders. *1676: The End of American Independence*. Cambridge, Mass.: Harvard University Press, 1985. Places the rebellion in a larger context, as a prerevolutionary condition, while providing a detailed study of the events of 1676-1677.

SEE ALSO: 1570's, Powhatan Confederacy; 1622, Powhatan Wars; 1660, British Navigation Acts.

1680 ■ PUEBLO REVOLT: *the most successful uprising against European colonial authority, ensuring the survival of Puebloans as a distinct people*

DATE: August 10, 1680
LOCALE: Rio Grande River Valley
CATEGORIES: Native American history; Wars, uprisings, and civil unrest
KEY FIGURES:
Alonso Garcia, Otermín's lieutenant governor in 1680
Antonio Malacate, Keresan leader of the revolt
Juan de Oñate (1549?-1624), founder and first Spanish governor of New Mexico
Antonio de Otermín, governor of New Mexico in 1680
Popé (died 1688), major instigator of the revolt
Luis Tupatú, successor to Popé and a principal aid during the revolt
Diego José de Vargas (1643-1704), New Mexico governor in 1692
SUMMARY OF EVENT. The first permanent European colony in Pueblo territory was established by Juan de Oñate in 1598. The jewels and gold of the fabled Seven Cities of Cíbola had

Taos Pueblo, c. 1927. Ceremonial kivas, or circular rooms below ground for ritual ceremonies, were built next to the dwelling places of the Pueblo peoples of the Southwest. A century of Spanish influence, from Juan de Oñate's arrival in New Mexico (1598) to the time of Popé's rebellion, took its toll on the traditions of the Puebloans, reducing their numbers by more than half. (Library of Congress)

proven to be a myth, but the Spanish still intended to settle the land. Franciscan friars came to seek converts to Catholicism, the civilian authorities and settlers to seek their fortunes in mining, trading, and ranching. The entire Spanish system was based on the need for American Indian labor. In order to get it, the Spanish imposed the *encomienda* system, which gave large land grants to holders, known as *encomanderos*. The part of this program known as *repartimiento* bestowed upon the encomanderos the right to the labor of any nearby natives. Annual taxes also were collected from the natives in the form of produce, textiles, or other resources.

The Spanish were able to impose these measures by access to guns and horses and frequent displays of force. Harsh physical punishments were meted out for even slight infractions. The Franciscans—who recognized no belief system except their own and thus felt justified in exterminating Pueblo religion—saved the most extreme measures for natives practicing their traditional beliefs. Father Salvador de Guerra, in 1655, had an "idolator" at Oraibi whipped, doused with turpentine, and burned to death. Even missing the daily Mass could bring a public flogging.

This unrelenting assault on native beliefs and practices was the single greatest cause of the Pueblo Revolt. The people believed that harmony within the community and with the environment was maintained through their relationships with a host of spirit figures called kachinas. They communicated with the kachinas at public dances and in ceremonies conducted in their circular churches, called kivas. It seemed no coincidence to the natives that when priests stopped these practices, things began to go wrong.

Severe droughts, famine, Apache raids, and epidemics of European diseases reduced a population of fifty thousand in Oñate's time to seventeen thousand by the 1670's. Three thousand were lost to measles in 1640 alone. At times between 1667 and 1672, people were reduced to boiling hides and leather cart straps for food. The abuse of women and sale of slaves south to work the silver mines of Mexico made it seem that the moral as well as the physical universe was collapsing. Calls were made to return to the old ways.

In 1675, forty-seven Puebloans were arrested for practicing their religion. All were whipped, three were hanged, and one committed suicide. One deeply resentful survivor was a Tewa medicine man for San Juan Pueblo named Popé. Incensed by this oppression, he began planning retribution, but his task was formidable.

The Spanish label "Pueblo" obscured the fact that these people were not of one tribe, but members of a collection of autonomous villages that cherished their independence and rarely acted in unison. Although they shared many cultural features, three major language families were represented in the Rio Grande area alone: Zuñi, Keresan, and Tanoan. The latter had three distinct dialects of its own: Tiwa, Tewa, and Towa. Hopi villages of Uto-Aztecan speech lay farther west. Previous revolts had been localized affairs and were suppressed quickly.

In hiding at Taos Pueblo, fifty miles north of the Spanish capital at Santa Fe, Popé began building a multilingual coalition. He enlisted the great Picuris leader Luis Tupatú, a Tiwa speaker who was influential in the northern Rio Grande pueblos; Antonio Malacate, a Keresan spokesman from pueblos to the south; the Tewa war leader Francisco El Ollita of San Ildefonso; and many others. His role becoming more messianic, Popé claimed inspiration from spirit contacts. Gradually, a plan emerged to expel the Spanish from Pueblo territory entirely.

The time came in August of 1680. Runners were sent out bearing knotted maguey cords, each knot representing one day. The uprising was to begin the day the last knot was untied. Governor Antonio de Otermín was told by informants that that day was August 13, but Popé had advanced it to August 10 and the Spanish were caught completely by surprise. Just nine miles north of Santa Fe, the citizens of Tesuque killed Padre Juan Pio early that morning as he came to gather them up for Mass, and upheaval soon swept the countryside as eighty years of frustration came to a boil.

Lieutenant Governor Don Alonso Garcia led soldiers on a sweep to the south of the capital and encountered such destruction that he organized the survivors for evacuation south. They left for El Paso del Norte (now Juarez) on August 14. The next day, Governor Otermín found himself besieged in Santa Fe by five hundred Puebloans who demanded that he free any slaves and leave the territory. He responded by attacking, but when the opposition increased to more than two thousand warriors and Otermín's water supply had been cut, he abandoned the capital. On August 21, Otermín led more than a thousand settlers south, meeting Garcia's group on September 13, and the whole bedraggled column reached El Paso on September 29.

Four hundred civilians and twenty-one of thirty-three priests had been killed. To undo their conversions, baptized Puebloans had their heads washed in yucca suds. A new kachina entered the pantheon of Pueblo spirit figures known among the Hopi as Yo-we, or "Priest-killer." In the years following the revolt, the coalition began to unravel, as drought, disease, and Apache raids continued to plague the tribes. Popé, who had become something of a tyrant himself, died in 1688. In 1692, Spain reconquered the area, and the new governor, Don Diego José de Vargas, entered Santa Fe on September 13.

The Pueblo Revolt did much more than dispel the stereotype that Puebloans were unassertive and peaceful farmers who could not unify. It also was much more than a twelve-year respite from colonial oppression. It catalyzed transformations in Native American cultures in many directions. Large numbers of Spanish sheep came into the hands of the Navajo, forming the core of a new herding lifestyle. Weaving skills, possibly passed along by Puebloans fleeing Spanish reprisals, soon turned the wool into some of the world's finest textiles. Previously forbidden horses, now freed by the hundreds, became widely traded. Within a century, tribes such as the Nez Perce, Cayuse, and Palouse to the northwest, Plains Cree to the north, and Sioux, Cheyenne, and others to the east became mounted. With the mobility to access the great bison herds of the Plains, the economic complex that became the popular image of the Native American evolved.

The continued importance of the Pueblo Revolt to all Native Americans was demonstrated during the tricentennial of 1980. Cultural events celebrating the "First American Revolution" were held all across the United States. The revolt was seen as a symbol of independence and religious freedom. It was also recognized that some Puebloans who chose to settle with Otermín at El Paso in 1680 subsequently had lost most of their language, arts, and customs. After three centuries, the Puebloans see their ancestors' revolt as a key reason for their survival as a distinct people.   —*Gary A. Olson*

ADDITIONAL READING:

Hackett, Charles W. *Revolt of the Pueblo Indians of New Mexico and Otermín's Attempted Reconquest, 1680-1682.* Translated by Charmion Shelby. 2 vols. Albuquerque: University of New Mexico Press, 1942. The definitive report on the subject to date.

Hait, Pam. "The Hopi Tricentennial: The Great Pueblo Revolt Revisited." *Arizona Highways* 56, no. 9 (September, 1980): 2-6. The entire issue is a beautifully illustrated exploration of Hopi culture, and persistence of which is a tribute to the Pueblo Revolt.

Hill, Joseph. "The Pueblo Revolt." *New Mexico Magazine* 58 (June, 1980): 38. An overview of the subject, with nine illustrations.

Josephy, Alvin M., Jr. *The Patriot Chiefs: A Chronicle of American Indian Resistance.* Rev. ed. New York: Penguin Books, 1993. Gives an account of the precursors to the revolt, but presents no consideration of the aftermath.

Page, James K., Jr. "Rebellious Pueblos Outwitted Spain Three Centuries Ago." *Smithsonian* 11 (October, 1980): 221. Tells the story through Padre Pio's last day. Good observations on the revolt's modern significance.

Sando, Joe S. "The Pueblo Revolt." In *Handbook of North American Indians.* Vol. 9, edited by Alfonso Ortiz. Washington, D.C.: Government Printing Office, 1979. A brief article that gives details on the planning of the revolt.

Silverberg, Robert. *The Pueblo Revolt.* Introduction by

Marc Simmons. Lincoln: University of Nebraska Press, 1994. An account based mainly on Hackett's earlier work. Introduction considers the revolt's legacy three centuries later.

SEE ALSO: 1598, Oñate's New Mexico Expedition; 1632, Zuñi Rebellion.

1681 ■ PENNSYLVANIA IS FOUNDED:
William Penn establishes a haven for the Society of Friends, or Quakers, and their "holy experiment"

DATE: March 4, 1681
LOCALE: Pennsylvania
CATEGORIES: Religion; Settlements
KEY FIGURES:
Charles II (1630-1685), king of Great Britain, 1660-1685
David Lloyd (1656?-1731), leader of the Popular Party
Thomas Lloyd (1640-1694?), president of the council, 1684-1686, 1690-1691, and deputy governor, 1691-1692
James Logan (1674-1751), leader of the Proprietary Party
William Markham (1635?-1704), Penn's cousin and personal agent in the colony
William Penn (1644-1718), proprietor of the Pennsylvania Colony
Israel Pemberton (1715-1779), leader of the strict Quakers in the 1740's and 1750's

SUMMARY OF EVENT. On March 4, 1681, King Charles II of Great Britain granted to William Penn a charter creating the colony of Pennsylvania. Named after his father, Sir William Penn, an admiral who had aided Charles's accession, Penn received the charter in payment of a debt of sixteen thousand pounds sterling that the king owed to him.

The charter made Penn proprietor of the colony. It was similar to other proprietary charters, in that it made Penn the owner of all lands in the province, with authority to structure and run the colony. Under the charter, Penn was empowered to grant property, establish the form of government, appoint the governor, and initiate and promulgate laws with the advice and consent of the freemen in the assembly. This particular charter was unique, however, in its restriction of proprietary prerogatives. Three provisions assured the enforcement of the Navigation Acts passed by Parliament prior to the establishment of the colony: Laws passed in the colony were to be submitted to the king for his confirmation or disallowance, with the king retaining the right to hear and decide appeals from the courts of the province; the Church of England was assured a place in the colony; and the charter contained a promise that the king would not impose taxes "unless the same be with the consent of the proprietary, or chiefe governour, or assembly, or by act of Parliament." These provisions implemented Great Britain's new colonial policy of limiting provincial self-government and centralizing the empire as a means of securing the commercial and defensive interests of Great Britain.

Penn's avowed purpose in establishing a colony in America was to found a "holy experiment" based on Quaker principles. Pennsylvania was to be a holy commonwealth, similar to other religion-based colonies like Massachusetts Bay, characterized by peace, brotherly love, and religious toleration, which would serve as "an example . . . to the nations." At the same time, the colony would offer a haven to Quakers who were being persecuted in England for their nonconformist beliefs.

One month after receiving his charter from the king, Penn began advertising the new province to prospective settlers in England, Ireland, and Wales. *Some Account of the Province of Pennsylvania* was published in April, 1682, the first of eleven such publications designed to attract colonists. Settlers began to arrive in Pennsylvania in the summer of 1682. The promise of community drew many of them: Immigrants coming to Pennsylvania would be settling among those of the same country, or even of the same region.

Penn dispatched his cousin William Markham to the colony to serve as his deputy governor until the proprietor's arrival. Not until August 30, 1682, did Penn himself set sail for the colony in the ship *Welcome*, along with about one hundred colonists. Shortly before leaving England, he had obtained the Lower Counties (Delaware) from the Duke of York, an intimate friend, thereby gaining ocean access for his new colony. In fact, the Duke of York did not possess clear title to these lands, and Penn found himself defending his claim to the territory against Lord Baltimore. Pennsylvania's right to rule the region persisted until a charter in 1701 granted the Lower Counties the right to self-government.

Negotiations for the land that was to become Philadelphia and its surrounding area were concluded with the Lenni Lenape, whom the settlers called the Delaware, in the summer of 1682. Blankets, bolts of cloth, and other goods were exchanged for the signatures of twelve Lenni Lenape sachems, or chieftains. Later purchases would be made from the native peoples of the Susquehanna River region, the Susquehannocks, and the Iroquois, as the Pennsylvania colony expanded. Despite other Europeans' poor record of promises made and quickly broken in the New World, Penn seems to have been genuinely concerned with being fair to the Native Americans with whom he dealt.

Like other proprietors in the New World, Penn hoped to profit from the sale or rent of land in his colony, but his primary aim was a religious one. He was a member of the Society of Friends, or Quakers, founded by George Fox in the late 1640's. One of the many radical religious sects that emerged from the turbulence of the English Civil War, the Quakers embraced the Puritan social ethic but went beyond Puritanism to reject formal creeds and worship. The faith was founded on the belief that the Holy Spirit, which Quakers called the "inner light," dwelled within each person. Belief that one's inner light placed one in communication with God meant that Quakers, like Puritans, rejected the idea of clergy as intermediaries. Their ecclesiastical organization shows the influence of the Puritan theory of congregationalism: Each congregation, or "meeting," was completely autonomous, although a hierarchy of meetings ultimately developed, similar in structure and purpose to that of the Presbyterians. Quakers differed from Puritans in their rejection of a national church. Like other sectarians, Quakers insisted on separation of church and state and viewed the meeting as a voluntary association composed only of believers. Two important consequences of Quaker religious beliefs were equalitarianism and humanitarianism.

Before sailing to America, Penn had drawn up the "first frame of government" to serve as a constitution for the new colony. It provided for a governor appointed by the proprietor; a council of seventy-two members, which was to be the source of all legislation; and an assembly of two hundred, which had the power to accept or reject bills initiated by the council. Both the council and the assembly were elective bodies. More than 150 laws were passed by the legislature implementing the "holy experiment." In 1696, Governor William Markham issued a third frame, which further modified suffrage requirements, reduced the council to twelve members and the assembly to twenty-four, and granted the latter body the right to initiate legislation. A fourth frame, known as the Charter of Privileges, was drawn up by Penn in 1701. It created a one-house legislature by vesting legislative power in the assembly, subject to the governor's veto, and limiting the council to executive and judicial powers. The council was appointed by the governor instead of being elected by the freemen. This marked the end of proprietary rule in Pennsylvania, save in the appointment of a governor. The unicameral legislature that was created endured until the American Revolution.

Penn issued the Charter of Privileges in order to end almost twenty years of quarreling between council and assembly, the former asserting its superior status against the latter's demands for a greater share in the government of the colony. The assembly had considerably enlarged its power from 1692 to 1694, when the colony was under royal rule. Markham's third frame, issued after the Crown returned Pennsylvania to Penn, had extended the prerogatives of the assembly, and the Charter of Privileges' establishment of a unicameral legislature represented a further triumph for that body.

Although he had inherited wealth, one reason Penn embarked on the troublesome business of a new colony was to make his personal fortune. It is, however, difficult to say whether Pennsylvania was a success from the viewpoint of the Penn family. Penn spent much of the first twenty years of his colony's life in England, entrusting his interests to a series of governors and agents. The result was less than satisfactory, as Penn was imprisoned for debt and was forced to mortgage Pennsylvania in 1708.

With the council eliminated as both a legislative and an elective body, the assembly transformed its opposition to the governor. In the early eighteenth century, two parties dominated Pennsylvania politics: the Proprietary Party, led by James Logan, which sought to centralize authority in the hands of the governor and the council; and the Popular Party, led by David Lloyd, which sought to expand the powers of the assembly. The main political issue was the Quaker principle of pacifism, which underwent a critical test in 1756 when warfare between the Iroquois tribes and European settlers erupted on the frontier. A declaration of war against the Lenni Lenape and Shawnee Indians by the governor and the council resulted in the Quakers' decision to withdraw from the assembly rather than compromise their stand against the war. This withdrawal ended almost seventy-five years of Quaker rule over the colony of Pennsylvania.

—Anne C. Loveland, updated by Kelley Graham

ADDITIONAL READING:

Doerflinger, Thomas. *A Vigorous Spirit of Enterprise: Merchants and Economic Development in Revolutionary Philadelphia*. Chapel Hill: University of North Carolina Press, 1986. An interesting study that challenges the older concept of a Quaker merchant aristocracy in prerevolutionary Philadelphia.

Dunn, Richard, and Mary Maples Dunn, eds. *The World of William Penn*. Philadelphia: University of Pennsylvania Press, 1986. An outstanding collection of articles reevaluating the politics and religious issues of early Pennsylvania history.

Nash, Gary B. *Quakers and Politics: Pennsylvania, 1681-1726*. Princeton, N.J.: Princeton University Press, 1968. Unlike earlier historians of colonial Pennsylvania, Nash approaches his subject not from a religious angle but from the viewpoint of the sociology of politics.

Penn, William. *The Papers of William Penn*, edited by Mary Maples Dunn et al. 5 vols. Philadelphia: University of Pennsylvania Press, 1981-1987. An essential collection of primary materials, with informative introductions and bibliography.

Schwartz, Sally. *"A Mixed Multitude": The Struggle for Toleration in Colonial Pennsylvania*. New York: New York University Press, 1987. Explores the development and consequences of Quaker toleration in an increasingly diverse colony.

Soderlund, Jean R., et al. *William Penn and the Founding of Pennsylvania, 1680-1684: A Documentary History*. Philadelphia: University of Pennsylvania Press, 1983. A documentary study of the political, economic, and social origins of Pennsylvania on both sides of the Atlantic.

SEE ALSO: 1660, British Navigation Acts; 1737, Walking Purchase; 1754, French and Indian War.

1686 ■ DOMINION OF NEW ENGLAND FORMS: *the British crown's first major effort to centralize control over the American colonies*

DATE: June, 1686-April, 1689
LOCALE: New England colonies, New York, and the Jerseys
CATEGORY: Government and politics
KEY FIGURES:
Edmond Andros (1637-1714), governor of the Dominion of New England

James II (1633-1701), king of England from 1685 until his overthrow in 1688

Jacob Leisler (1640-1692), merchant and militia captain who assumed control of the New York government in 1689

Edward Randolph (1632-1703), royal collector of customs and secretary of the Dominion of New England

William III (1650-1702), who acceded with Mary to the throne of England in 1689

SUMMARY OF EVENT. Only after the restoration of the Stuart monarchy in 1660, when Great Britain recognized the advantages of bringing the American colonies into its expanding commercial system, did the lack of an adequate colonial policy become apparent; but by then, it was too late. Great Britain had permitted its colonies a large measure of local self-government and had demanded little of them. The governments in the American colonies (which had never experienced direct royal control) had become accustomed to independence and wanted no interference, even from a relatively liberal mother country. Massachusetts, the most independent and rebellious of the colonies, not only violated the Navigation Acts and refused to cooperate with Edward Randolph (whom the Crown had appointed collector and surveyor of customs in 1678) but also usurped powers not granted by its corporate charter and denied that the laws of Parliament applied in the Massachusetts Bay Colony. The Crown had no choice but to declare the colony's charter null and void, and did so in 1684.

By this time, it had become evident that revocation of the colonial charters was necessary for the development of Great Britain's commercial plans. The Lords of Trade issued writs of *quo warranto* ("by what authority?") to Connecticut, Rhode Island, the Jerseys, Pennsylvania, Maryland, the Carolinas, Bermuda, and the Bahamas in preparation for nullifying their charters. Because the establishment of royal governmental machinery in each colony would have been too expensive, a plan for three unions was devised: one for New England, one for the Middle Colonies, and one for the South.

Only the New England union materialized. It began in the fall of 1685 as a provisional government for Massachusetts, Maine, New Hampshire, and the Narragansett Bay region, and it was to last until a royal governor could be commissioned and sent to America. On December 20, 1686, Sir Edmond Andros arrived to assume the governorship and to organize the Dominion of New England. Rhode Island was incorporated into the union almost immediately, and Connecticut was brought in within a year. New York and the Jerseys entered in 1688. The commission and instructions drafted for Andros by the Lords of Trade provided for a governor and council appointed by the king and a representative assembly chosen by the people, but James II had eliminated the provision for an assembly. The governor was empowered to appoint all officials; with the council, the governor was to legislate, levy taxes, establish courts, and sit as a supreme court. All laws were to be sent to England for approval.

Until a committee for codification could develop a uniform body of laws consistent with those of England, each colony was to operate in accordance with its old laws. In the absence of any revenue acts in effect in Massachusetts, the governor and council enacted increased customs, import and tonnage duties, excises, and land and poll taxes. The Puritans habitually had ignored or nullified laws that they disliked, and although the new taxes represented only a small increase, the selectmen of Ipswich led a revolt against them, claiming taxation without representation.

The matter of taxation was one of several areas of conflict between the Dominion government and the Puritans. In an effort to achieve conformity in the method of granting land and to make the new government self-supporting, the king had ordered that quitrents be collected on all new land granted, and that fees be charged for the compulsory confirmation of all old titles. The New Hampshire and Maine colonists welcomed the opportunity to ensure their titles, but the Puritans could not understand why the land was not theirs by right. Because Andros enforced the hated Navigation Acts, New England trade dropped off drastically. The continuing need for English manufactured goods created a drain on the colonies' hard money.

When the Dominion government attempted to make the administration of justice conform to English law, the Puritans resented the change. Jurors no longer had to be chosen from among the landowners, eliminating some of the power of the leaders of the theocracy. Even more alarming to the Puritans was the Declaration of Indulgence of April 4, 1687, granting liberty of conscience to all the king's subjects. No longer were the Puritan ministers and schools supported by the taxes of the entire population. When Andros appropriated one of Boston's Congregational churches for Anglican worship, the Puritans began to fear that the Church of England would become established in the colonies.

The Puritans regarded themselves as God's chosen people and interpreted the interference of Great Britain as a divine punishment for the younger generation's having slipped from the straight and narrow path. Thus, they anticipated their eventual deliverance from the oppressors. In the spring of 1688, Increase Mather, the influential Puritan clergyman, traveled to England to petition for an assembly and other reforms. When James II was forced to publish a proclamation restoring rights to corporations, Mather and his fellow agents interpreted this concession to include colonial corporations. Mather gained the favor of the attorney general, and the Lords of Trade agreed to promote a new charter granting more powers to the colonists.

The Glorious Revolution of 1688 and the accession of William and Mary in 1689 embodied the sign of deliverance that the Puritans had been expecting. The Lords of Trade recommended, however, that the Dominion be continued, with two commissioners replacing Andros. In an effort to create the impression that the Puritans were allied with William and Mary against the Dominion and James, Mather suggested to the Massachusetts Puritans that they overthrow Andros in the name of the new sovereigns.

DOMINION OF NEW ENGLAND, 1686-1689

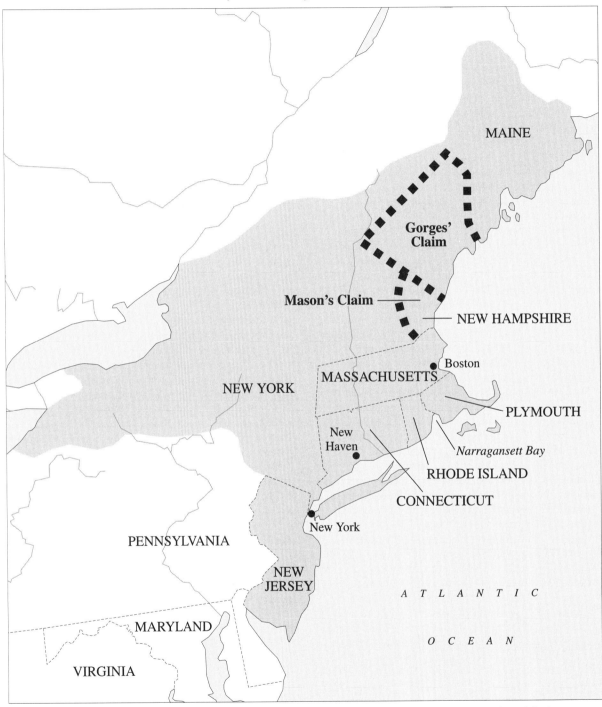

The Dominion of New England, established in 1686 shortly after the arrival of a new governor, Sir Edmond Andros, was an attempt by the British king and the Lords of Trade to break Massachusetts' resistance to the British Navigation Acts and to combine the New England colonies—initially Massachusetts, Maine, New Hampshire, and the Narragansett Bay region, and eventually Connecticut, Rhode Island, New Jersey, and New York—into a single political unit that could be easily governed by royal authority. As the British government placed pressure on the colonists to adhere to increasing regulations, they resisted. Finally, in April, 1689, armed overthrow of Andros in Boston effectively ended the Dominion.

On April 18, 1689, when troops who had mutinied on the Maine frontier marched into Boston, insurrection broke out and Andros was imprisoned. Within a month, all the colonies had overthrown the Dominion government. In New York, where Francis Nicholson served as Andros' deputy, the Long Island militia rose in revolt and was joined by the New York City militia, while Nicholson abandoned the province and returned to England. Jacob Leisler, a New York City merchant and militia captain, proclaimed William and Mary the sovereigns of England and assumed the position of commander in chief of the province for the next two years. Leisler's Rebellion was driven by a number of complex motives, including Dutch resentment toward English rule and the dominant elite of Anglo-Dutch merchants and landowners, anti-Catholicism, and genuine fear of a French invasion.

On May 9, a convention of delegates from the New England colonies voted to restore the governments and laws of 1686. Once back in power, the Puritan officials of Massachusetts Bay returned to their authoritarian policies, evoking many complaints from non-Puritans. Both pro- and anti-Dominion forces pleaded their cases before William and Mary on the question of New England's future government. William was more concerned about gaining the Puritans' support for his war with the French than with colonial policy.

Thus, the new charter for Massachusetts was sealed on October 7, 1691. It allowed for a governor appointed by the Crown, but it also provided for an elected assembly and a council chosen by that assembly. New Hampshire became a separate royal colony, Maine and Plymouth were annexed to Massachusetts, and Connecticut and Rhode Island operated under their old charters. Massachusetts had gained a charter, but new policies ensuring religious freedom and broadening the franchise had destroyed the Puritan oligarchy. In New York, Leisler and his son-in-law, Jacob Melburne, had resisted turning the government over to Governor Slaughter, sent by William and Mary. They were hanged for treason at the behest of their political enemies, the Anglo-Dutch elite that Leisler had so resented and harassed while in authority. William and Mary did call for elections to a legislative assembly for New York, its first permanent one, but politics in the province remained bitterly divided over Leisler's Rebellion for the next twenty years.

—*Warren M. Billings, updated by Ronald W. Howard*

ADDITIONAL READING:

Andrews, Charles M., ed. *Narratives of the Insurrections, 1675 to 1690*. New York: Barnes and Noble, 1959. Includes descriptions of the revolt against Andros in Boston and materials related to Leisler's Rebellion in New York.

Barnes, Viola. *The Dominion of New England: A Study in British Colonial Policy*. New York: Frederick Ungar, 1960. Dated but comprehensive monograph that emphasizes the reasons that the Dominion was established and why it failed.

Hall, Michael G. *Edward Randolph and the American Colonies, 1676-1703*. Chapel Hill: University of North Carolina Press, 1960. Focuses on the role played in the formation

and government of the Dominion by the dedicated public servant who was England's foremost expert on the colonies.

_____. *The Last American Puritan: The Life of Increase Mather*. Middletown, Conn.: Wesleyan University Press, 1988. Demonstrates the important role this remarkable Puritan leader played in both the overthrow of Andros and the acquisition of the royal charter for Massachusetts Bay.

Harper, Lawrence A. "Enforcement in the Colonies." In *The English Navigation Laws*. New York: Octagon Books, 1964. Explains the changes in English policy that brought about colonial resistance, thus necessitating the imposition of royal government.

Miller, Perry. *From Colony to Province*. Vol. 2 in *The New England Mind*. Cambridge, Mass.: Harvard University Press, 1953. Discusses the decline of Puritan power in the years following the Restoration.

Sosin, J. M. *English America and the Revolution of 1688: Royal Administration and the Structure of Provincial Government*. Lincoln: University of Nebraska Press, 1982. Takes a comprehensive view of the American colonies during the Restoration era; emphasizes the social and economic tensions behind the political upheavals inspired by the Glorious Revolution in England.

Voorhees, David Williams. "The 'Fervent Zeale' of Jacob Leisler." *William and Mary Quarterly* 51 (July, 1994): 447-472. A provocative interpretation that stresses the religious motivation of Leisler amid the ethnic and economic antagonism in New York.

SEE ALSO: 1620, Pilgrims Land at Plymouth; 1630, Great Puritan Migration; 1632, Settlement of Connecticut; 1636, Rhode Island Is Founded; 1643, Confederation of the United Colonies of New England; 1660, British Navigation Acts; 1662, Half-Way Covenant; 1664, British Conquest of New Netherland.

1692 ■ SALEM WITCHCRAFT TRIALS:
religious, emotionally hysterical, and perhaps politically motivated fervor leads to tragic persecution

DATE: June 2, 1692-May, 1693
LOCALE: Salem, Massachusetts
CATEGORIES: Religion; Women's issues
KEY FIGURES:
Simon Bradstreet (1603-1697), provisional governor of Massachusetts after the fall of the Dominion of New England
Jonathan Corwin and
John Hathorne, assistants of the Massachusetts General Court who conducted the examinations of the accused witches
Cotton Mather (1663-1728), son of Increase, a Puritan minister interested in psychic research and author of *Wonders of the Invisible World*

Increase Mather (1639-1723), pastor of the Boston Puritan church and president of Harvard College

Nicholas Noyes (1647-1717), Puritan pastor of Salem Town

Samuel Parris (1653-1720), Puritan pastor of Salem Village

William Phips (1651-1695), royal governor of Massachusetts, 1692-1694

Samuel Sewall (1652-1730), Massachusetts magistrate and a judge at the witch trials

William Stoughton (1631-1701), deputy governor and presiding justice at the witch trials

Tituba (1648?-1692), West Indian slave in the Parris household

SUMMARY OF EVENT. Early in 1692, a circle of young girls began to meet in the home of Samuel Parris, the Puritan pastor of Salem Village. The minister's nine-year-old daughter, Betty, and Betty's eleven-year-old cousin, Abigail Williams, were fascinated by the voodoo-like tales and tricks of the family's Barbados slave, Tituba, and soon they began to invite their friends to share in the entertainment. Before long, some of the girls in the circle began to behave strangely, complaining of physical maladies, reporting visions, lapsing into trances, and trembling and babbling without restraint.

Among the Puritans, inexplicable afflictions were customarily attributed to the work of the devil, so most of the inhabitants of Salem Village believed the young girls when they charged that Tituba and two village women of doubtful respectability were practicing witchcraft upon them. Two assistants of the Massachusetts General Court, John Hathorne and Jonathan Corwin, were called upon to conduct a legal examination of the accused women. Placing no store in lawyers, the Puritans were governed essentially by Old Testament law. When they found a statement in the Scriptures that witches must not be allowed to live, their duty became clear. The two magistrates conducted their examination more like prosecuting attorneys than impartial investigators. They accepted the dreams and fancies of the young girls as positive evidence and concluded that a "strange tit or wart" on the body of one of the women was a "witches' tit," at which the devil and his familiars, or messengers, sucked the blood of the witch.

As in any system of law, the identity of the accused was essential to the Salem proceedings. One method of identification was a search of the accused's body for physical signs left behind by the devil. These bodily searches were performed on the woman accused by matrons and midwives, by order of the sheriff. The first six women to be identified as witches through this method were executed. Ironically, women who had knowledge of medicine and who used astrology (an acceptable form of prediction in certain cultures) to forecast illness were historically the victims of accusation themselves. As early as 1441, the Duchess of Gloucester had been accused of witchcraft for her "uncanny knowledge of medicine and astrology."

Parris had planned to implicate Tituba as a witch and force her into naming others. When Tituba confessed her own connection with the devil, she implicated the other accused witches, and on March 7, all three were sent to prison. Tituba

later said that Parris beat her into a confession, claiming that her accusations of Sarah Good and Sarah Osborne, as well as two other women, were the result of his abuse.

Although many of the villagers were skeptical of the claims of the girls, the examiners, supported by Parris and Nicholas Noyes, his colleague in Salem Town, called upon other ministers of the area to consult with them. More accusations—this time against respectable, pious women of the community— came almost immediately, and it seemed that the devil was carrying out his deception by possessing seemingly innocent persons. The panic soon enveloped not only the residents of Salem but also those of neighboring towns. The trials would begin in Salem Village, but most of the accused resided in

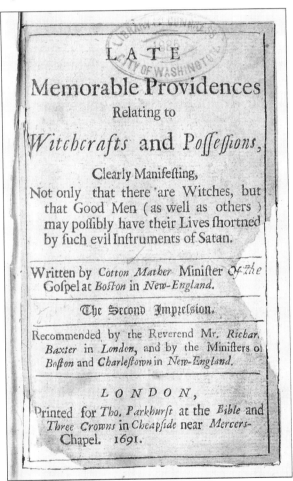

The title page from a major work by the Congregational minister Cotton Mather, first published in 1689, only a few years prior to the witchcraft trials in Salem. Mather, from a venerable Puritan family, was considered not only a preeminent divine but also a scholar, an expert on the presence of the supernatural in daily life whose writings were taken quite seriously. Although he is often identified as the instigator of the witchcraft trials, in fact he criticized the court's methods. (Library of Congress)

Andover. Warrants for three Salem Village women were issued on February 29, 1692. The devil's timing was faultless, for the Massachusetts Bay Colony was still agitated over the loss of its charter in 1684 and the overthrow of the Dominion of New England in 1689. The weak provisional government, headed by the ailing governor Simon Bradstreet, was merely awaiting the arrival of the new governor and did nothing to avert the crisis. When Sir William Phips, royal governor of Massachusetts, arrived in May, 1692, with the new Massachusetts charter, he decided immediately that proper courts must be established for the trying of witches. On the last Wednesday in May, the Governor's Council set up a general court, which promptly appointed seven judges to constitute a special Court of Oyer and Terminer to convene on June 2. The witchcraft fever continued to spread, but the accused were confident that the distinguished judges Bartholomew Gedney, Samuel Sewall, John Richards, William Sergeant, Wait Winthrop, Nathaniel Saltonstall (later replaced by Jonathan Corwin), and Presiding Justice William Stoughton represented some of the best minds in the colony and would deal justly with the witchcraft problem. The court, however, accepted the testimony gathered at the examination as proven fact. At the trials, the judges simply heard new evidence, and a jury decided the prisoners' fate. On June 8, the General Court revived an old law making witchcraft a capital offense. Two days later, Bridget Bishop, the first condemned witch, went to the gallows.

A schism among the judges over the validity of spectral evidence necessitated a delay in the proceedings while they sought the advice of clergy of the Boston area. Although the ministers urged caution in the handling of spectral evidence, they praised the judges and encouraged further prosecution of the witches. As the summer brought more hangings, the remaining prisoners began to fear for their lives, and several managed to escape. The judges, as good Puritans, accepted confession as evidence of possible regeneration and were merciful to those who would confess their dealings with the devil and repent, but few of the staunch Puritans were willing to belie themselves, even to save their lives.

On July 15, Martha Carrier, a resident of Andover, was arrested after being accused by several of the afflicted girls from Salem. Carrier's courage and defiance during her legal examination may have been considered malicious and imprudent by the seventeenth century audience. Testimony by her neighbors may suggest why she first came under suspicion: ". . . and there happening some difference betwixt us she gave forth several threatening words, as she often used to do," testified one male neighbor. According to religious faith during this time, such threats were considered a curse. The Court of Oyer and Terminer condemned Carrier on August 5, 1692. Five days later, her children—Thomas Jr., ten years of age, and Sarah, age seven—were imprisoned and tricked by magistrate Hathorne into naming their mother. The court further abused all four of her children in hopes that she would confess, but she never did. On August 19, 1692, Martha Carrier was hanged at Salem.

By the time the last of the twenty convicted witches had been executed on September 22, public support of the trials was waning. There were numerous reasons for this change: Several of those who were executed in August died calmly, forgiving their accusers and judges and protesting their innocence to the end; the court's procedures seemed to be aggravating the witchcraft problem rather than alleviating it; and as the witch hunt spread, persons were being accused who no one could believe were guilty. The panic had been confined almost exclusively to Essex County, and ministers from outside the immediate area began taking a stand against continuing the trials. Increase Mather, the great Boston divine, warned against reliance on spectral evidence and traveled to Salem to investigate the method of obtaining confessions. A petition from Andover was the first of many to call for release of the remaining prisoners and to denounce the accusing girls. On October 29, Governor Phips dismissed the Court of Oyer and Terminer. Its end marked the end of the witch hunt.

The tragedy of Salem extends beyond the number executed. Added to the list of victims should be Sarah Good's nursing infant, who died while Good was incarcerated; Roger Toothaker, who was murdered in prison; Lydia Dustin, who was found innocent but never released, and died in prison in 1693; and others, including slaves who suffered not only from bondage but also from witchcraft accusations. By acts of the General Court of November 23 and December 16, special sessions of the Superior Court of Judicature were ordered to complete the trials. The new circuit court was composed largely of the same judges as the recently dissolved court, but it now held spectral evidence to be inadmissible. Fifty-two accused witches came to trial early in January, 1693, and forty-nine were released immediately for lack of evidence. The governor soon reprieved the others, and by May, all the remaining prisoners had been discharged.

While some people were disappointed to see the trials end, most were relieved to return to their long-neglected work. Blaming Parris for allowing the death of innocent relatives and friends, the congregation of the Salem church voted to void his salary. In the ensuing years, many of the accusers of the condemned repented, and in 1709 and 1711, the Massachusetts General Court restored to many of those who had been accused of being witches, as well as the children of the executed victims, their good names and awarded them compensation for financial losses. The names of some, however, were never cleared.

During the Salem witchcraft trials, both Increase and Cotton Mather expressed their doubts about the proceedings, especially concerning the use of spectral evidence. Increase Mather insisted that the special Court of Oyer and Terminer be terminated because it might be guilty of shedding innocent blood. Cotton Mather, one of the most cogent critics of the court's methods while it was sitting, afterward offered a strongly partisan defense of the judges. Because of this defense, historians have incorrectly presented Cotton Mather as the instigator of the witchcraft trials. He was, in fact, guilty of not opposing the trials vigorously enough. Although the Salem trials were not the last, because of the Massachusetts authorities' actions in discovering, acknowledging, and disowning their errors, the Salem experience helped to end witchcraft trials in Western civilization.

A number of reasons have been offered to explain this tragic period in colonial history: Generational, racial, and sexual hostility, opposition to law, social stresses, and food poisoning all have been advanced as the causes of anxiety and hysteria in Salem during this time. However, the causes were complex and no single explanation is sufficient in itself. The Salem witchcraft trials marked the first of a series of political and criminal witch hunts that have plagued American society ever since. —*Warren M. Billings, updated by Kimberly Manning*

ADDITIONAL READING:

Fox, Sanford J. *Science and Justice: The Massachusetts Witchcraft Trials*. Baltimore: The Johns Hopkins University Press, 1968. Describes the role of science in prosecuting the accused witches. Examines the scientific awareness, attitudes, and ethos at the time of the trials.

Goodbeer, Richard. *The Devils Domain: Magic and Religion in Early New England*. New York: Cambridge University Press, 1992. Examines the inconsistencies of folk magic as practiced by ordinary men and women in early New England. Focuses on the similarities between Puritanism and magic that enabled even church members to switch from one to the other without questioning their actions. Chapter 5 is devoted to the witch hunt of 1692.

Levack, Brian P., ed. *Articles on Witchcraft, Magic, and Demonology: A Twelve-Volume Anthology of Scholarly Articles*. New York: Garland, 1992. Articles from a variety of disciplines—history, sociology, anthropology, literature, and art history—range from being informative to advancing arguments. Volume 8 deals exclusively with witchcraft in colonial America; volume 10 focuses on the societal implications of witchcraft for women.

Robinson, Enders A. *The Devil Discovered: Salem Witchcraft 1692*. New York: Hippocrene Books, 1991. Begins with a chronological sequence of events and concludes by analyzing the lives of the first seventy-five accused witches. Tables, illustrations, and maps clarify the intricate relationships of the accusers and accused.

Rosenthal, Bernard. *Salem Story: Reading the Witch Trials of 1692*. New York: Cambridge University Press, 1993. Investigates the assumptions surrounding the trials, the mythologizing of the event, and the stereotyping of witches regarding gender and age. Uses surviving documentation to illustrate that many of the accusers used logic and reason, rather than hysteria, to charge their victims.

Weisman, Richard. *Witchcraft, Magic, and Religion in Seventeenth Century Massachusetts*. Amherst: University of Massachusetts Press, 1984. Contends that the cultural response to the witch hunts of 1692 was aided, in part, by a lack of consensus over how to define and deal with witchcraft. Political and legislative issues are addressed. Appendices and bibliography.

SEE ALSO: 1620, Pilgrims Land at Plymouth; 1630, Great Puritan Migration; 1643, Confederation of the United Colonies of New England; 1686, Dominion of New England Forms.

1702 ■ QUEEN ANNE'S WAR: *conflict resulting in British acquisition of French territory and commercial concessions from Spain*

DATE: May 15, 1702-April 11, 1713
LOCALE: Hudson Bay, Newfoundland, Acadia, New England, Carolinas, Florida, and the Caribbean
CATEGORIES: Canadian history; Expansion and land acquisition; Wars, uprisings, and civil unrest
KEY FIGURES:
Anne (1665-1714), queen of England
John Churchill, duke of Marlborough (1650-1722), commander of English troops on the European continent
Joseph Dudley (1647-1720), governor of Massachusetts
John Hill (died 1735), commander of troops in the Walker expedition
James Moore (died 1706), governor of Carolina
Francis Nicholson (1655-1728), military leader and governor of several English colonies
Henry St. John, first Viscount Bolingbroke (1678-1751), English secretary of state who planned the Walker expedition
Samuel Vetch (1668-1732), merchant, military commander, colonial governor
Hovenden Walker (died 1728), commander of the Walker expedition

SUMMARY OF EVENT. By the seventeenth century, colonial rivalries had involved European powers in global conflicts. The first, the Nine Years' War (1689-1697), primarily an Anglo-French conflict, was known as King William's War in North America, where all captured territory was restored by the Treaty of Ryswick in 1697. Warfare was renewed in the War of the Spanish Succession (1702-1713), whose North American phase was known as Queen Anne's War.

This conflict's origins involved the question of who would succeed the sickly, childless Charles II as ruler of the vast Spanish Empire. Attempts to partition the empire between Louis XIV's son and Emperor Leopold I's son came to naught when Louis XIV accepted Charles II's will, which left the Spanish Empire to Philip of Anjou, Louis XIV's grandson. Provocative actions by Louis XIV and the new Spanish king, Philip V, coupled with the fear that one person might eventually rule France and Spain, led William III, ruler of England and the Netherlands, to organize the Grand Alliance of England, the Netherlands, and the emperor. The object of the alliance was to prevent the union of France and Spain and to gain commercial and territorial benefits. On May 15, 1702, the Grand Alliance formally declared war against France and

Spain. English and allied troops under the command of John Churchill, duke of Marlborough, won significant victories on the Continent, while the English navy captured Gibraltar in 1704 and established a presence in the Mediterranean.

In North America, fighting between English colonists and their Native American allies on one side, and the French, the Spanish, and their Native American allies on the other, occurred in Canada, New England, the southern border of Carolina, Florida, and the Caribbean, where privateers operated. New York escaped attack by the French because the latter feared disturbing the neutrality of the Iroquois.

The English fleet seized the French West Indian island of St. Christopher (St. Kitts) in July, 1702, but an attack on Guadeloupe was unsuccessful in 1703. James Moore, governor of Carolina, led a raid of five hundred militia and three hundred Yamasees on St. Augustine, Florida, in October, 1702. Although they sacked the town, they were unsuccessful in capturing the fort. The following year, Moore led fifty militia and one thousand Native Americans in an attack on Spanish missions west of St. Augustine, destroying thirteen missions and carrying off thirteen hundred Native Americans to be used as slaves. Actions such as these led to a joint French-Spanish retaliatory attack on Charleston in August, 1706. This assault failed, and the following year, the Carolinians raided Pensacola, Florida. Repeated requests by the Carolinians to the English government for military assistance and the construction of forts went unanswered.

In New England, members of the Abenaki tribe, urged on and sometimes held by the French, attacked isolated settlements. The worst of these episodes was the February, 1704, attack on Deerfield, Massachusetts, which resulted in the death of fifty and the capture of more than one hundred residents. Some of the captured residents were later killed, others were ransomed, and the remainder settled in Canada. Massachusetts' governor, Joseph Dudley, made a secret peace overture to the French governor of Quebec, Philippe de Rigaud, marquis de Vaudreuil. This attempt failed, as the French insisted that New York and the other northern colonies be brought into the plan and that the English relinquish their right to fish off the coast of Newfoundland, an area that the French and English regarded as valuable for training sailors.

One colonial objective was to eject the French from North America, and colonists expected English assistance to accomplish that end. One target of colonial aggression was Port Royal in Acadia (Nova Scotia). Several raids against the town had failed. After 1709, the English increased their military involvement in North America. Samuel Vetch, a merchant and soldier, had devised a plan to attack Quebec. Supported by the governors of New York and Massachusetts, Vetch journeyed to England and received cabinet support for a joint Anglo-colonial attack on Canada in 1709. New York, Massachusetts, Connecticut, Rhode Island, and New Hampshire provided fifteen hundred men, who were to march on Montreal from Albany. One thousand others were to join English forces for an assault on Quebec and Port Royal by sea.

Preparations were made in England and North America, but favorable developments in European peace negotiations led the English to assign their forces to occupy Spain in anticipation of a peace treaty. When Louis XIV did not consent to the peace terms, the English determined that additional pressure on France in Europe was required and canceled their plans for Canada. Upon learning of the change in English plans, the colonial governors decided to postpone the assault until the following year.

Vetch and Colonel Francis Nicholson, a former colonial governor, commanded a successful raid on Port Royal (renamed Annapolis Royal) in September and October, 1710, which involved colonial forces and five hundred English troops. Buoyed by success, Nicholson and four Mohawks met with the new Tory ministry in London to plan an attack on Canada. The ministers saw French Canada as a threat to English colonies and trade, and were anxious to offset Marlborough's popularity with an American victory. First Viscount Bolingbroke Henry St. John, one of the secretaries of state, was the strongest proponent of action. He took the lead in planning the Walker expedition, the first significant action against Canada launched from England.

An army commanded by Nicholson was to march from Albany to Montreal, and Admiral Sir Hovenden Walker's sixty ships were to land General John Hill's five thousand troops to attack Quebec. Because of navigational errors, the fleet foundered on rocks in the St. Lawrence River, losing about nine hundred men. The remnant of the fleet returned to England. News of the expedition's failure reached London in October, 1711, after secret preliminary peace articles had been signed by England and France. Nicholson was ordered to halt his overland march.

Although this expedition had been launched, the English ministry had initiated secret peace negotiations with France in late 1710 and by October, 1711, had established a general framework for peace. In December, 1711, Marlborough was dismissed, and the Congress of Utrecht (1712, 1713) convened to force England's allies to accept the Anglo-French terms and put them into the formal treaty. In May and June, 1712, the English and French agreed to a suspension of arms in Europe, which was extended to North America in September, 1712.

The war was ended by the Peace of Utrecht, signed on April 11, 1713. Among its major provisions were the recognition of Philip V as Spanish king, who renounced any claim to the French throne. England won significant advantages through the grant of the *asiento* contract to supply Spanish colonies with slaves and by its acquisition of Gibraltar from Spain. However, England's greatest acquisitions came in North America, where France relinquished Hudson Bay, Acadia, and Newfoundland. France retained Cape Breton Island and the right to catch and dry fish on Newfoundland's coast. St. Christopher in the Caribbean was acquired by the English. These advantages secured for England commercial and territorial benefits that weakened the American colonial empires of France and Spain.

Casualties among the American colonists were about four

hundred. The English lost approximately nine hundred in the Walker expedition and hundreds more in the failed raid on Guadeloupe. Native American losses were high, and the peace settlement recognized the Iroquois as English subjects and allowed English merchants to trade with western Native Americans. Intercolonial cooperation had improved, but cooperation between the colonists and England was not good. Anglo-French and Anglo-Spanish rivalries resumed in subsequent conflicts for control of North America. —*Mark C. Herman*

ADDITIONAL READING:

Arnade, Charles W. *The Siege of St. Augustine in 1702.* Gainesville: University of Florida Press, 1959. This short monograph provides background information and an account of the colonial attack.

Crane, Werner W. *The Southern Frontier: 1670-1732.* 1929. Reprint. Ann Arbor: University of Michigan Press, 1956. Provides a detailed narrative of action along the southern border of the English colonies in the era of the war.

Eccles, William J. *France in America.* New York: Harper & Row, 1972. Discusses the war from the French colonial perspective.

Graham, Gerald S., ed. *The Walker Expedition to Quebec, 1711.* Toronto: Champlain Society, 1953. Reprint. New York: Greenwood Press, 1969. The introduction examines the expedition and analyzes the relevant primary sources.

Hattendorf, John B. *England in the War of the Spanish Succession: A Study of the English View and Conduct of Grand Strategy, 1702-1712.* New York: Garland, 1987. The only major work to date to examine the formation and implementation of English strategy in the war. Analyzes the place of the Walker expedition in the conduct of the war.

Parkman, Francis. *A Half-Century of Conflict.* 1892. Reprint. New York: Collier Books, 1962. This classic account needs to be read in conjunction with other sources to correct a strong colonial bias.

Peckham, Howard H. *The Colonial Wars, 1689-1762.* Chicago: University of Chicago Press, 1964. Sets the war in the context of other Anglo-French conflicts of the eighteenth century.

1711 ■ Tuscarora War: *decimation of the Tuscaroras dispersed their society and opened the way for westward expansion by European settlers*

DATE: September 22, 1711-March 23, 1713

LOCALE: Fort Neoheroka on Contentnea Creek in North Carolina

CATEGORIES: Expansion and land acquisition; Native American history; Wars, uprisings, and civil unrest

KEY FIGURES:

John Barnwell (1671-1724), leader of the first attacks on the Tuscaroras

King Tom Blunt (died 1739?) and

King Tom Hancock (died 1712), leaders of hostile Tuscarora towns

James Moore (1667-1723), leader of the attacking forces at Fort Neoheroka

Thomas Pollock (1654-1723), governor of North Carolina during Moore's attack

SUMMARY OF EVENT. When European settlers began arriving in North America, the Tuscarora tribe controlled nearly all the North Carolina coastal plains. The tribe's territory stretched from today's Virginia state line, south to the Cape Fear River, and inland to the Appalachians. Tribal land cut a wedge between the Algonquian tribes of the coast and the Siouan tribes of the piedmont. The Tuscaroras held a trade monopoly throughout the area.

Information about the Tuscaroras and their western holdings was limited, because the tribe denied passage through the area. Contact with settlers was infrequent as a result of the natural protection provided by swamps, sand reefs, and shallow harbors. Conflict between the tribe and the settlers began, however, when the two groups started occupying the same areas and the Indians began raids on settlers' livestock and crops. The Indians saw no problem with their actions, because there was no Tuscarora law or custom that discouraged stealing from an enemy. Settlers were helpless to prevent these attacks, because the tribe had a vicious policy of revenge. In 1705, the Tuscaroras became such a problem for the settlers that Virginia passed a law forbidding natives from hunting on patented land.

Trade agreements were established between the tribe and the settlers, but things did not go smoothly. The Tuscaroras felt the settlers were taking advantage of them and complained about being cheated. Tuscarora tribal leaders approached the Pennsylvania government in 1710. They presented eight wampum belts, signifying various grievances concerning the safety of American Indian families. No agreement was reached. Unscrupulous traders accelerated the Tuscarora discontent by describing the settlers as easy targets with no government backing or protection. Then the Tuscaroras declared war.

On September 22, 1711, approximately five hundred Tuscaroras and their allies attacked at widely scattered points along the Neuse, Trent, and Pamlico Rivers. Men, women, and children were butchered and their homes destroyed by fire. The Indians' frenzy was slowed only by fatigue and drunkenness. At the end of the two-day rampage more than 130 whites were dead and nearly 30 women and children had been captured. The frightened survivors scrambled to reach fortified garrisons.

The situation in North Carolina was desperate. Planters west of the river could not help protect those under attack without weakening their own defenses. Quaker settlers refused to fight. Governor Edward Hyde appealed to Virginia and South Carolina for help. Virginia worked to secure the loyalty and assistance of the neutral Tuscaroras who had not participated in the raids, but met with little success. South Carolina responded by sending Colonel John Barnwell and a force of five hundred native allies and thirty white men.

Barnwell's departure was delayed, and his winter march was difficult. He crossed the Neuse River in late January and marched an entire day and night to attack the Tuscarora town of Narhontes. Although the natives knew of his approach, Barnwell's raid was successful. For the next four months, Barnwell led several victorious attacks in Tuscarora territory, but he was displeased by the weak North Carolina support. In April, against orders from North Carolina, he signed a treaty with the Tuscaroras. During Barnwell's return to South Carolina, he broke the treaty by capturing native women and children to sell as slaves, thereby provoking new raids.

The summer of 1712 brought no relief. Settlers and natives were starving; no one could plant crops or hunt in safety. Residents along the Neuse and Pamlico Rivers had their homes burned, their stock stolen, and their plantations destroyed. The North Carolina Assembly held a special session in July and passed a law requiring all men between sixteen and sixty years of age to fight the natives or pay a fine. The law was widely disliked and few men obeyed it. Then a yellow fever epidemic hit the area. North Carolina's governor was one of those who died.

Thomas Pollock was chosen as the new governor until the colony could receive instructions from the Lord Proprietors. Pollock appealed to South Carolina for aid but suggested that Colonel Barnwell would not be suitable. Barnwell went before the South Carolina assembly and advised that it was necessary to prosecute the Tuscarora War to a successful conclusion. South Carolina agreed to help. A force of nine hundred Indians and approximately thirty-three soldiers was placed under the leadership of Colonel James Moore, who was experienced in fighting the American Indians.

Governor Pollock reopened negotiations with King Tom Blunt, the chief ruler of the neutral Tuscaroras in the upper towns. In September, Blunt requested peace with North Carolina. Pollock insisted Blunt's people fight on the side of the settlers and would not accept neutrality. Pollock demanded the capture of King Tom Hancock, the chief who had authorized the massacre in September, 1711. In mid-November, 1712, Hancock was delivered and executed. King Blunt then signed a treaty with North Carolina on behalf of nine Tuscarora towns.

Colonel James Moore and his forces arrived in the Neuse River region in late December. Although the people were thankful for the protection, they were angered when the troops consumed all the provisions in the area. It was nearly a month before Moore's forces left for Fort Barnwell to prepare an attack on Fort Neoheroka.

Fort Neoheroka lay within a wide curve of Contentnea Creek and was protected on three sides by deep water and steep river banks. The fourth side was enclosed by an angled palisade, a fence created by pointed stakes. There were bastions, or projections, on the four main corners, and an angled passageway led from the fort to the water. The natives also had access to a network of tunnels and caves within the fort.

Moore instructed his men to create zigzag trenches to within gun range of the fort's east wall. He then built a triangular blockhouse to allow his troops to provide crossfire while men raised a battery against the fort wall. Moore also ordered a mine tunneled under the wall near the blockhouse and lined it with explosives.

Once preparations were completed, Moore placed his forces around the fort. Two captains, a battery of artillery, and more than three hundred Cherokees were assigned to the northwest area of the fort and stream to block off the most likely escape route. East of the fort and in the trenches, Moore's brother, two other captains, ten whites, and fifty Yamasees took their positions. Colonel Moore placed himself, four other commanders, eighty whites, and four hundred members of Siouan nations in the southeast. Mulberry Battery took its place within the southern curve of the creek.

The attack began on March 20, 1713, with the blast of a trumpet. The powder in the mine failed, but the attack on the northeast quickly succeeded. Captain Maule went against the southern side of the fort instead of the southeast, as he had been ordered. This caused Maule's troops to be caught in the crossfire, and only twenty of his men escaped unhurt. Colonel Moore erected a low wall and managed to set two of the fort's blockhouses on fire. By the next morning, the fire had destroyed the structures as well as several houses within the fort. Some of the Tuscaroras hid in the caves and created problems for the attackers, but by Sunday, March 23, Moore's forces controlled the fort. Destruction of Fort Neoheroka was complete. Moore had lost fewer than sixty men and had fewer than one hundred wounded. Nearly one thousand Tuscaroras were killed or captured.

As word of the defeat spread, other members of the Tuscarora tribe fled. Many of the refugees headed to Virginia, where they endured great hardships and found little food. Several raiding bands continued guerrilla warfare in North Carolina, but Moore's help was no longer needed. He returned to South Carolina in September, 1713. —*Suzanne Riffle Boyce*

ADDITIONAL READING:

Graymont, Barbara, ed. *Fighting Tuscarora: The Autobiography of Chief Clinton Rickard.* Syracuse, N.Y.: Syracuse University Press, 1973. Introduction includes information about Tuscarora history. Main text chronicles the life of Chief Clinton Rickard (1882-1971) and his work for American Indian rights.

Johnson, F. Roy. *The Tuscaroras.* Vols. 1 and 2. Murfreesboro: Johnson, 1967. Discusses history, traditions, culture, mythology, and medicine. Maps, illustrations, index, and many footnotes. Provides listings of numerous original resources.

Snow, Dean R. *The Iroquois.* The Peoples of America series. Cambridge: Blackwell, 1994. Follows the development of the Iroquois Confederacy. Extensive bibliography, index.

Waldman, Carl. *Encyclopedia of Native American Tribes.* New York: Facts On File, 1988. One page summarizes events leading to Fort Neoheroka and gives some details about tribal life.

Wilson, Edmund. *Apologies to the Iroquois.* New York: Farrar, Straus & Cudahy, 1959. Contains a chapter on Tuscarora history. Also discusses land disputes at Niagara Falls in the 1960's.

See also: 1663, Settlement of the Carolinas; 1671, Indian Slave Trade.

1712 ■ New York City Slave Revolt:
an abortive uprising that shaped the institution of slavery in New York

Date: April 6, 1712

Locale: Manhattan Island

Categories: African American history; Wars, uprisings, and civil unrest

Key figures:

May Bickley (died 1723), attorney general who led the prosecution of those indicted in the conspiracy and revolt

Cuffee and

Dick, two slaves who presumably were promised immunity to testify against others implicated in the rebellion

Robert Hunter (1666-1734), royal governor of New York, 1709-1719

Elias Neau (1662-1722), Huguenot merchant who ministered to New York City slaves

John Sharpe, Anglican chaplain to the British garrison at Fort Anne

Summary of event. The New York City Slave Revolt of 1712 calls attention to the fact that slavery had become more firmly established in colonial New York than in any other British province north of Chesapeake Bay. Slaves were already an integral part of the labor force when England conquered Dutch New Netherland in 1664. As European immigration lagged, slave labor became increasingly important. Between 1703 and 1723, New York's total population almost doubled, increasing from 20,540 to 40,564; but its black population (slaves and free blacks were always lumped together and listed in the census as Negroes) almost tripled, jumping from 2,253 to 6,171.

As the number of bondsmen increased, so did the anxiety level of white New Yorkers. In 1708, following the grizzly murder of a Long Island planter and his family, four slaves were tried, convicted, and executed "with all the torment possible for a terror to others." Shortly thereafter, the provincial assembly passed An Act for Preventing the Conspiracy of Slaves, which defined the judicial proceedings and made death the penalty for any slave found guilty of murder or attempted murder. Fear of slave conspiracy led whites to look with ambivalence upon Anglican catechist Elias Neau's teaching among New York City blacks and Native Americans.

Small-scale slave owning prevailed in New York. Few white families owned more than a slave or two, so slave husbands, wives, and children might be scattered among several households. Regulations restricting their freedom of movement were bitterly resented by slaves, because they inter-

fered with their domestic life. Such restrictions often were more apparent than real, because slavery in New York City and surrounding villages, where slaves were most heavily concentrated, was tied to a developing urban economy that demanded a flexible, if not free, labor supply. Slaves in New York City and Albany often hired themselves out, splitting the pay with their respective owners, but otherwise lived separately from their masters. The hustle and bustle of the urban economic scene afforded slaves considerable opportunity to meet, socialize, and discuss common grievances, despite the best efforts of whites to keep them under surveillance.

The slave uprising of 1712 apparently began as a conspiracy on March 25, then celebrated as New Year's Day. The ringleaders reportedly were of the Cormantine and Pawpaw peoples, Africans who had not been long in New York; a few Spanish Indian slaves; and at least one free black, a practitioner of African medicine and magic who reportedly supplied special powder to protect the rebels from the white man's weapons. Their motivation, according to both Governor Robert Hunter and Chaplain John Sharpe, was revenge for ill treatment at the hands of their respective masters. Their goal was freedom, which, claimed Hunter and Sharpe, was to be achieved by burning New York City and killing the white people on Manhattan.

During the early morning hours of Sunday, April 6, 1712, about two dozen conspirators, armed with guns, swords, knives, and clubs, gathered in an orchard in the East Ward on the northeast edge of New York City. They set fire to several outbuildings and waited in ambush for the whites who came to put out the blaze, killing nine and wounding seven. Soldiers were dispatched from the fort, but when they arrived, the rebels had dispersed, taking refuge in the woods surrounding the town. The next day, local militiamen systematically searched Manhattan Island for the rebellious blacks. Rather than surrender, six slaves killed themselves, several cutting their own throats.

White New Yorkers were in full panic. "We have about 70 Negro's in Custody," read a dispatch from New York, dated April 14 but published in the *Boston News-Letter* on April 21, but it was "fear'd that most of the Negro's here (who are very numerous) knew of the Late Conspiracy to murder the Christians." Fear of another uprising drove the judicial proceedings. On April 9, a coroner's jury implicated thirty-eight slaves, identifying fourteen of them as murderers. In accordance with the 1708 Conspiracy Act, the coroner's findings were turned over to the Court of Quarter Sessions of the Peace, which convened on April 11. Attorney General May Bickley handled the prosecution, moving the trials on from the Quarter Sessions to the State Supreme Court on June 3.

Forty-two slaves and one free black were indicted and tried. Crucial to both the indictments and trials was the testimony of two slaves, Cuffee, who belonged to baker Peter Vantilborough, and Dick, a boy slave owned by Harmanus Burger, a blacksmith. The coroner's jury had found Cuffee and Dick guilty of at least two murders, but Attorney General Bickley apparently promised them immunity, and they became the Crown's prime witnesses. Some whites, including such substantial citizens as former mayor David Provost, coroner Henry Wileman, and lawyers Jacob Regnier and David Jamison, testified for a few of the defendants. However, the general adequacy of defense counsel may well be doubted. Many of the convictions hinged upon the dubious testimony of Cuffee and young Dick, both of whom were manipulated by Attorney General Bickley, described by Governor Hunter as "a busy waspish man." Bickley also demonstrated considerable bias against certain slave defendants, depending upon who owned them. For example, Mars, belonging to Jacob Regnier, a rival attorney with whom Brickley had a private quarrel, was tried twice and acquitted before being found guilty in the third trial and sentenced to be hanged.

Most of the trials were over by early June. Twenty-three slaves were convicted of murder; fifteen slaves were acquitted, along with one free black. Two slaves were found guilty of assault with intent to kill, and two were acquitted of that charge. The twenty-five who were convicted were sentenced to death. Twenty were to be hanged; three were burned alive, one in a slow fire for eight to ten hours until consumed to ashes. Another was broken upon the wheel and left to die, and one was hung in chains and "so to continue without sustenance until death." Eleven were "executed at once," including those burned, broken at the wheel, and chained without food or water. These barbaric executions were defended by Governor Hunter as "the most exemplary that could be possibly thought of."

Yet even Hunter doubted the justice of it all. He postponed the execution of six slaves, including two Spanish American Indians taken during Queen Anne's War (1702-1713) and sold as slaves despite their claim of being free men, a pregnant slave woman, and the much tried and finally convicted Mars. At Hunter's request, the queen pardoned several of them, and perhaps all of those he had reprieved (the record is rather vague), despite the efforts of Bickley in New York and Lord Cornbury, a former governor of New York, in London to obstruct the pardons.

There were other ramifications of the slave uprising. The provincial government passed laws making it impossible to free slaves without putting up a two-hundred-pound bond and paying the freed slave twenty pounds per year for life. Africans, American Indians, and mulattoes were prohibited from inheriting or otherwise owning property. Finally, due process rights were weakened for slaves accused of murder or conspiracy. In the wake of the revolt, Elias Neau, the preacher and catechist of Trinity Church, found it difficult to continue his school for blacks and Indians. Only two of his many pupils were implicated in the conspiracy, and Chaplain John Sharpe doubted that either was involved in the violence.

After the rebellion, New Yorkers were reluctant to import slaves directly from Africa or to purchase Spanish Indians as slaves. Black slaves from the West Indies were preferred over the other two groups. Yet slavery remained a primary source of labor for both the province and city of New York, slaves constituting about 15 percent of the population. In 1730, other regulations were added to the slave code because "many Mischiefs had been Occasioned by the two great Liberty allowed to Negro and other Slaves." In 1741, white paranoia and slave discontent provoked a so-called slave conspiracy in which 150 slaves and twenty-five whites were jailed. Of that number, eighteen slaves and four whites were hanged, thirteen blacks burned alive, and seventy were sold and sent to the West Indies.

—*Ronald W. Howard*

ADDITIONAL READING:

Goodfriend, Joyce D. *Before the Melting Pot: Society and Culture in Colonial New York City, 1664-1730*. Princeton, N.J.: Princeton University Press, 1992. Chapter 6 provides considerable insight into the life and labors of New York City slaves, both before and after the 1712 revolt.

Kammen, Michael. *Colonial New York: A History*. New York: Charles Scribner's Sons, 1975. Chapter 11 relates the slave revolts of 1712 and 1741 to larger social and economic problems in colonial New York society.

Lustig, Mary Lou. *Robert Hunter, 1666-1734*. Syracuse, N.Y.: Syracuse University Press, 1983. Gives a brief but pertinent summary of the slave revolts and the persons most associated with the trials.

McManus, Edgar J. *A History of Negro Slavery in New York*. Syracuse, N.Y.: Syracuse University Press, 1966. Goes into considerable detail regarding the conditions that contributed to the 1712 uprising.

Scott, Kenneth. "The Slave Insurrrection in New York in 1712." *The New-York Historical Society Quarterly* 45 (January, 1961): 147-165. Describes the revolt and the trials that followed. Notes the pertinent source collections.

Wood, Peter. "Slave Resistance." In *Encyclopedia of the North American Colonies*. Vol. 2. New York: Charles Scribner's Sons, 1993. Relates the 1741 New York revolt to other examples of slave resistance in North America.

SEE ALSO: 1619, Africans Arrive in Virginia; 1641, Massachusetts Recognizes Slavery; 1661, Virginia Slave Codes; 1671, Indian Slave Trade; 1739, Stono Rebellion; 1777, Northeast States Abolish Slavery.

1714 ■ FOX WARS: *generations of intertribal warfare and French attempts to obtain peace*

DATE: Summer, 1714-1741
LOCALE: West and southwest of Lake Michigan
CATEGORIES: Canadian history; Native American history; Wars, uprisings, and civil unrest
KEY FIGURES:
Charles de Beauharnais (1670-1749), governor general of New France, 1726-1747, responsible for critical decisions that ended the Fox Wars

Kiala, war chief during the most brutal period of repression of Fox tribes fleeing French and other tribes' assaults

Mekaga, minor chief who negotiated the 1738 "pardon" of the remaining tribal groups in the Rock River Valley

Philippe de Rigaud, marquis de Vaudreuil (1643-1725), governor general of New France, 1703-1725

SUMMARY OF EVENT. Although the Fox people trace their own origins to the northeastern seaboard, they clearly emerged in Native American history in the late seventeenth century in the western Great Lakes region. First known under their Algonquian name, Mesquakis (People of the Red Earth), early French explorers' journals called them *renards*, or Foxes, a name that persists in the literature. Most of what is known about the Fox tribe and their often hostile relations with a number of their neighboring tribes comes from the eighteenth century Québécois (New France colonial) archives. Hardly a year passed between 1699 and 1742 without some reference to relations between the Foxes and representatives of Onontia, the natives' name for the French governor general of New France.

In 1699, Governor General Louis-Hector de Callières tried to obtain a peace treaty, not only between France and the tribes of the western Great Lakes region but also among the tribes themselves. His goal was to increase profitable trade in a vast region that remained unpredictable because of recurring intertribal strife. The natives invited to Montreal were well-known tribes associated with the Iroquois Five Nations (including the Senecas) and lesser-known tribes along the western shore of Lake Michigan, including the Sacs, Winnebagos, Kickapoos, Menominees, and Foxes. In September, 1700, peace was signed by several important tribes, but many, including the Foxes, held back. Although the Foxes and Chippewas agreed to cease fighting each other in the Wisconsin area, Fox hostilities with neighboring Sioux still raged, disrupting fur trading as far as Sioux territory in Minnesota. In their attempt to stop these conflicts, the French invited Fox chieftains Noro and Miskousouath to Montreal. There the chiefs were assured that, if they remained peaceful in their newly fortified villages at the portage point between the Fox and Wisconsin Rivers, they would have their share of French fur trade in Sioux territory.

The shortcomings of these agreements were particularly evident to Antoine de La Mothe, sieur de Cadillac, commander of the strategic post at Michilimackinac on the straits between Lakes Michigan and Huron. Cadillac's goal was to develop another, eventually much better-known, post at Detroit into a major trading center for various tribes. In 1710, he invited a number of Algonquian tribes located in the area from the Green Bay to the Wisconsin River, including Sacs, Foxes, Mascoutens, and Kickapoos, to move to eastern Michigan.

Some Foxes, together with other Wisconsin tribes, did go to the Detroit area, but the venture soon was reversed by Montreal's governor general, the marquis de Vaudreuil. Not only did the Foxes expect that their cooperation with the resettlement scheme should be rewarded, but they also became entangled in skirmishes with other tribes, especially Hurons and members of the Illinois Confederacy. They even raided French colonial farms, stealing food and livestock. Instead of heeding French orders in 1711 to return to Wisconsin, the Foxes became even more belligerent, proceeding to build a fort near Fort Pontchartrain on the Detroit River. It took more than a year for the French, taking advantage of alliances with Huron and Illinois Confederacy tribes, to expel the Foxes by force. Most of the besieged Foxes were massacred brutally by French-allied American Indians, despite the French commander's assurance of safe passage upon surrender. Those who escaped sought refuge among the Seneca Iroquois. These violent events on the Detroit River were bound to have repercussions among the Fox tribes that had stayed behind in Wisconsin alongside their allies, the Sacs and Winnebagos. When the defeated Foxes returned to Wisconsin, new alliances were built; by the summer of 1714, they had begun attacks on French traders passing from Detroit to Michilimackinac.

In this first stage of the Fox Wars, some Wisconsin natives hoped that the French would seek an accommodation with the Foxes. As the situation deteriorated and trade became paralyzed, many American Indians began to call for a strong French military campaign against the Foxes. Before long, it appeared that the Foxes had long-distance ties with other allies in British territory, especially the Senecas. This complicated French strategy considerably, forcing the French to try diplomatic intervention far to the east of Wisconsin. Vaudreuil was unable to report any progress for at least three years.

Although Fox chieftains Okimaoussen and Ouchala agreed to de-escalate the conflict, warfare against the Foxes by their inveterate enemies, the Chippewas and Potawatomis, caused strife to spread into Illinois tribal areas in 1719. By 1721, the Foxes had even sealed peace with their former enemies, the Sioux, to have an ally against the Illinois. In 1725, the French reported that their own hopes to tap the Sioux fur market were seriously hampered by the Sioux-Fox alliance.

By the time of Vaudreuil's death in October, 1725, King Louis XV himself sent orders to replace the French commander at Green Bay, François Amariton, suspected of encouraging Fox raids into Illinois territory, and to step up activities against the Foxes. This task, which would lead to disastrous consequences for the Fox tribe, fell to Charles de Beauharnais, governor general of New France from 1726 to 1747.

A major campaign was set for 1728. French forces of four hundred soldiers were joined by *coureurs de bois* (freelance French fur trappers and traders) and hundreds of western natives. The French claimed success, but in reality the Foxes had withdrawn into Iowa rather than risk a battle.

The next stage of conflict came when Fox chief Kansekoe tried to force his Kickapoo allies to hand over a dozen French traders who were being held as hostages. Kickapoo refusals incited younger Fox warriors to break away from Kansekoe and attack both Kickapoo and Mascouten hunters. Both tribes soon asked for French alliance status. Then, some Winnebagos and Menominees also joined attacks against the Foxes. Declining chances for a victory again divided the Foxes. Some factions favored a peace, while more hostile tribesmen decided to leave Wisconsin and seek asylum, preferably among the Senecas. The attempted migration left them open to reprisal attacks, especially by members of the Illinois Confederacy, supported by the Foxes' former neighbors, the Potawatomis, Kickapoos, and Mascoutens. A major siege of Fox fortifications on the Illinois prairie in 1730 involved French relief forces, who joined in a general massacre of more than five hundred Foxes, including women and children.

Governor General Beauharnais reported that the remaining Foxes no longer could consider resistance. Continuing reprisals caused Foxes under Chief Kiala to try to resettle peacefully on the north bank of the Wisconsin River and to send emissaries to Montreal. Kiala's apparent failure to meet French terms tempted Beauharnais to allow Huron the Iroquois "volunteers" to pursue the refugee Foxes spread out in areas of Iowa and Illinois. Intertribal fighting continued until 1735, when two refugee groups separated, one to the Rock River in Illinois and the other to the mouth of the Wisconsin. In 1736, White Cat, a friendly Sac chief, asked Beauharnais to grant a pardon. Beauharnais tried unsuccessfully to persuade the Sacs to gain peace by allowing the French to disperse the Foxes among other American Indian nations.

Finally, unable to hold out in the Rock River Valley against other Indians' attacks, and fearful of massive French reprisals for Fox assistance to Sioux warriors near Lake Peoria who had killed French travelers in the area, Fox chief Mekaga agreed to accept French terms of forced relocation. By the fall of 1741, the Foxes and Sacs were trekking to new settlements: ten lodges to the Chicago River, three to Milwaukee, and the rest to their old homeland village on the Fox River in Wisconsin. Although the formal Fox War was over in 1741, these settlements still suffered from attacks by their Chippewa, Menominee, and Ottawa neighbors. In 1743, Beauharnais himself had to intercede to gain another joint pledge of peace.

—*Byron D. Cannon*

ADDITIONAL READING:

Edmunds, R. David, and Joseph L. Peyser. *The Fox Wars: The Mesquaki Challenge to New France*. Norman: University of Oklahoma Press, 1993. The most complete study to date of the specific events of the Fox Wars.

Hagen, William T. *The Sac and Fox Indians*. 2d ed. Norman: University of Oklahoma Press, 1980. A general history, including cultural and religious topics.

Parkman, Francis. *Count Frontenac and New France Under Louis XIV*. 1877. Reprint. New York: Library of America, 1983. A pioneering work providing background on French interests in the Great Lakes area just before dealings with the Foxes became focal.

White, Richard. *The Middle Ground: Indians, Empires and Republics in the Great Lakes Region, 1650-1815*. Cambridge, England: Cambridge University Press, 1991. Places the Fox Wars in a wider chronological and geographical context of French, British, and American Indian relations.

SEE ALSO: 1642, Beaver Wars; 1754, French and Indian War.

1728 ■ RUSSIAN VOYAGES TO ALASKA: *Russian scientific excursions and occupation of the northern Pacific region, heralding later settlement*

DATE: July, 1728-1769
LOCALE: North Pacific
CATEGORIES: Expansion and land acquisition; Exploration and discovery
KEY FIGURES:

Vitus Jonassen Bering (1681-1741), Danish navigator employed by Peter the Great

Aleksei Ilyich Chirikov (1703-1748), Russian explorer who captained the *St. Paul* on Bering's second expedition

Mikhail Spiridonovich Gvozdev (born 1699?), land surveyor who sighted Alaska, but did not realize what he had found

Pyotr Kuzmich Krenitsyn (died 1770) and

Mikhail Dmitrievich Levashov (1739-1775), cartographers who sailed for the Aleutians

Grigorii Ivanovich Shelikov (1747-1795), Russian merchant and fur trader

Georg Wilhelm Steller (1709-1746), German naturalist who accompanied Bering

SUMMARY OF EVENT. After a cossack discovered the Chukotskiy peninsula—the easternmost "nose" of Siberia—in 1648, reports about Alaskan fur traders led people to believe that water divided America from Asia. The German philosopher Gottfried Leibniz convinced Czar Peter I in 1716 to send an expedition eastward to confirm its existence. Peter undoubtedly was interested for scientific and imperial reasons, but also because Siberian furs were bringing less state revenue than earlier and he wished to rejuvenate this trade. In 1719, he dispatched two men to explore the Kamchatka region. Although the expedition of Ivan Evreinov and Fedor Luzhin failed to show that America lay near the Kuriles, both were praised for locating them in relation to Japan and Kamchatka. Peter gave the next expedition more precise instructions.

The most important person associated with the early voyages to the North Pacific was Vitus Bering. Although Danish, Bering became a captain commander of the Russian fleet, first under Peter I and later under Empress Anna. From his native seaport of Horsens, Denmark, Bering had traveled to the East Indies in 1703. Recruited as a sublieutenant for the young navy of Czar Peter, Bering engaged in Russia's wars in the Baltic, Black, and Azov Seas. By 1720, he had beem promoted to captain second class. Desirous of greater rewards, he retired from service in 1724 to live on his Vyborg estate, only to be recalled by Peter later that year. Peter elevated him to captain first class and, heeding the advice of Admiral Peter Sievers, another Dane, entrusted Bering with the difficult mission to determine whether America was connected with Siberia. Days before his death on January 28, 1725, Czar Peter gave his personal instructions for this mission, which called for Bering

VOYAGES TO ALASKA, 1728-1769

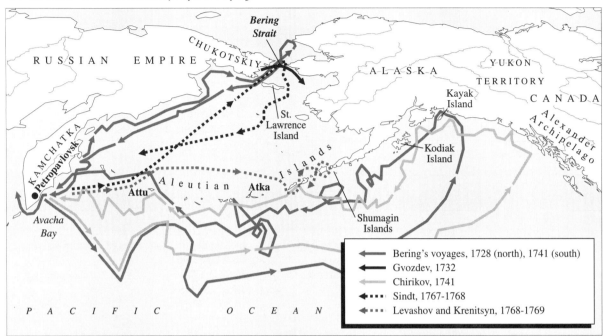

Between 1728 and 1769, the Russian goverment sponsored several important expeditions to explore the waters and lands across what came to be known as the Bering Strait, named after the most important of these explorers, Vitus Bering.

to sail east to America's coast and then south to the nearest European settlement.

Bering's party made the arduous Siberian journey, then built a ship, the *Saint Gabriel*, in Kamchatka. Aleksei Chirikov and Martin Spanberg, another Dane, were officers with Bering when the ship was launched in July, 1728. In August, they discovered Saint Lawrence Island, and, after discussing the option of returning to Kamchatka, they proceeded northward. The ship passed through the strait that would bear Bering's name at 67°18′ north latitude. On their return, they discovered Big Diomede Island, but the fog was so heavy that Bering could not see the Alaskan shores twenty-five miles away. In September, Bering arrived at Kamchatka to spend the winter, only to put up sails again in June in search of land to the south and southeast. Failing that endeavor, he returned to Saint Petersburg.

When Bering arrived in the capital on March 30, 1730, his reception was warm, but he soon fell prey to petty politics at the Admiralty. He was certain that he had discovered the strait—as he had—but failed to appreciate the need for proof. As a result of indefatigable labor by the Senate secretary, Ivan Kirillov, Anna was persuaded to send Bering on another, more ambitious, mission to the East. Bering was instructed by the Senate to map the Siberian rivers, including the Amur, and the Pacific coast of Siberia before proceeding to America. This Great Northern Expedition was to include six hundred sailors, five hundred guards, and up to two thousand laborers to haul supplies. Beginning his journey across Siberia in 1733, he

found the assignments overwhelming. Forty men died before setting sail, and expenses mounted far in excess of expectations. At Okhotsk, workers constructed two ships, the *Saint Peter* and *Saint Paul*, which sailed to Kamchatka in November, 1740.

A Kolyma cossack, Afanasy Shestakov, had organized another expedition to the East in 1726, and left for the North Pacific in 1732. Led by Ivan Fedorov and Mikhail Gvozdev, a land surveyor and former student at the Moscow Navigation School and Naval Academy, they sailed to the later Bering Strait. Parts of the Asiatic and American coastlines were charted by Gvozdev as his ship circumnavigated Big Diomede and, on August 21, sighted Alaska, thinking it another large island. Inclement weather prevented the crew from disembarking. Gvozdev's report of this discovery was ignored and not dispatched to the Admiralty until 1743. On June 4, 1741, Bering, on the *Saint Peter*, and Chirikov, commanding the *Saint Paul*, set sail to the south, with specific orders to find and claim the American coastline. Within days, fog became so heavy that the ships separated, although both had changed course to the northeast. When on July 15, Chirikov sighted land in the Alexander archipelago, fifteen of his crew went ashore, never to return. More would later die of scurvy. Before Chirikov returned to Kamchatka on October 10, he had discovered several islands, including Kayak Island.

A German naturalist, Georg Wilhelm Steller, kept a journal of the voyage of the *Saint Peter*. Catching sight of Alaskan mountains, Bering laid anchor near the Copper River, where

Steller and some crewmates spent a few hours looking for ore and flora. Bering discovered Kodiak and other islands, but severe storms and a shortage of fresh water forced him to return. En route, he discovered what he called the Shumagin Islands before a storm wrecked his vessel as they anchored on November 6 at an uninhabited island. Bering died December 8 on the island that bears his name. Although thirty of his seventy-seven men died of scurvy, the survivors built another ship from the remains of the *Saint Peter*, reaching Avacha Bay on August 26, 1742.

Chirikov had gone back to sea in May in search of Bering. After reaching Attu Island, he returned to Kamchatka in July, later taking part in the charting of Russian discoveries in the Pacific Ocean, including the capes in Kyusha Island, the Anadyr Gulf, and Taui, Guba, and Atka Islands. An underwater peak in the Pacific Ocean was named after him.

After 1743, the government tired of expensive voyages and allowed merchants to organize their own expeditions. For two decades, private voyagers exploited the Aleutians rather than sailing eastward to the American mainland. Traders pooled their resources into small venture companies and, with permits from the state, exploited all the Aleutian Islands, sending 10 percent of their furs to the state treasury. One merchant from Irkutsk, Nikifor Trapeznikov, promoted eighteen such voyages from 1743 to 1764.

Authorities could not allow persistent reports of abuse, even slaughter, of natives to go unheeded. Some traders seized all local women and children as hostages, and the natives supplied them with food. This concern, and the desire to map all discoveries of the merchant adventurers, led Catherine the Great to send expeditions to Alaska after 1764. One was led by a Baltic German, Ivan Sindt, who was with Bering's second expedition, but his work proved unsatisfactory, even fraudulent. Catherine then dispatched Mikhail Levashov and Pyotr Krenitsyn eastward. Viewing their roles as cartographers, in 1764, they sailed for the Aleutians from Kamchatka and continued east to Alaska. Forced to winter on separate islands and defend against hostile natives, they returned to Kamchatka in 1769. There, Krenitsyn drowned in a river. Levashov compiled a useful ethnographic description of the natives of Unalaska and Unimak. His charts of the Aleutians proved accurate in relation to each other, but the islands were placed too close to Kamchatka.

Although the expeditions never achieved all that officials had desired, the northern Pacific waters became Russian. Okhotsk became a base for the Russian navy, and Bering's settlement at Avacha Bay became the port of Petropavlovsk. The Great Northern Expedition (officially ended in 1749) amassed a prodigious amount of scientific data, including Steller's treatises on plants, fruits, insects, sea otters, fish, and the languages of the native peoples. More expeditions would be undertaken, but Russia's interest in Alaska was transformed in 1784 when Grigorii Shelikov established the first Russian settlement in the Americas on Kodiak Island.

—*John D. Windhausen*

ADDITIONAL READING:

Barratt, Glynn. *Russia in Pacific Waters, 1715-1825*. Vancouver: University of British Columbia Press, 1981. A closely written narrative with special insights into the politics, grand and minor, of the expeditions and their participants.

Dmytryshyn, Basil, E. A. P. Crownhart-Vaughn, and Thomas Vaughn, eds. and trans. *Russian Penetration of the North Pacific Ocean, 1700-1799*. Vol 2. Portland: Oregon Historical Society, 1988. Contains a valuable introduction to many translated documents about the explorations of Siberia and America.

Golder, Frank A. *Bering's Voyages*. 2 vols. New York: American Geographical Society, 1922-1925. Reprint. New York: Octagon Books, 1968. The definitive study, with documents, of the earliest expeditions to North America, viewing these voyages in the perspective of Russia's traditional eastward expansion.

Starr, S. Frederick, ed. *Russia's American Colony*. Durham, N.C.: Duke University Press, 1987. Especially valuable essays by B. P. Polevoi and James R. Gibson on differing Russian and American views of the early explorations.

Steller, Georg Wilhelm. *Journal of a Voyage with Bering, 1741-1742*. Edited and with an introduction by O. W. Frost; translated by Margritt A. Engel and Frost. Stanford, Calif.: Stanford University Press, 1988. A beautifully written account of science, politics, and personalities, by the naturalist who accompanied Bering on his second voyage.

SEE ALSO: 1959, Alaska and Hawaii Gain Statehood.

1730's ■ FIRST GREAT AWAKENING: *a colonywide spiritual revival gives birth to religious tolerance and inclusiveness in American society*

DATE: 1730's-1760
LOCALE: American colonies
CATEGORIES: Religion; Social reform
KEY FIGURES:
Charles Chauncy (1705-1787), minister of Boston's First Church and chief critic of the Great Awakening
Samuel Davies (1723-1761), organizer and propagator of Presbyterianism in Virginia and founder of the Hanover Presbytery in 1755
Jonathan Edwards (1703-1758), minister and principal theological architect of the Great Awakening; author of *A Treatise Concerning Religious Affections*
Theodore J. Frelinghuysen (1691-1748), Dutch Reformed minister who sparked the first stirrings of revival in the Middle Colonies
Gilbert Tennent (1703-1764), William's son and pastor of the church from which revival spread among Presbyterian congregations
William Tennent (1673-1745), key figure in the outbreak of a

spiritual awakening among the Presbyterians in the
Middle Colonies

George Whitefield (1714-1770), Anglican preacher whose
1739 visit to America sparked the Great Awakening

SUMMARY OF EVENT. Between 1739 and 1742, the American
colonies experienced a general, colonywide quickening of religious faith that became known as the Great Awakening. The
young Anglican preacher George Whitefield, whose reputation as a great pulpit and open-air orator had preceded his visit,
traveled through the colonies in 1739 and 1740. Everywhere,
he attracted large and emotional crowds, eliciting countless
conversions as well as considerable controversy. Critics condemned his enthusiasm, his censoriousness, and his extemporaneous and itinerant preaching; yet his extemporaneous
preaching, his use in sermons of plain language, and his appeal
to the emotions were to contribute to the emergence of the
democratic and popular style of American Christianity. This
manner of preaching also won for him numerous imitators,
who spread the Great Awakening from New England to Georgia, among rich and poor, educated and illiterate, and in the
backcountry as well as in seaboard towns and cities.

In the Middle Colonies, Gilbert Tennent was the leader of
the revival among the Presbyterians. Led by Jonathan Dickinson, Presbyterians of New England background also joined in

*George Whitefield, an Anglican preacher whose open-air services attracted huge crowds, traveled through the colonies in
1739 and 1740. His enthusiastic, plain-speech sermons and his appeal to the emotions are generally credited with instigating
the democratic and popular style of American Christianity manifested in the First Great Awakening. (Library of Congress)*

the revival. In New England, the most notorious evangelist was James Davenport, whose extravagances were even denounced by Tennent and other revivalists. Jonathan Edwards, Samuel Buell, and Eleazar Wheelock, less controversial than Davenport, were likewise instruments of the Awakening in New England. In the Southern colonies, the Great Awakening made its greatest headway on the frontier. Samuel Davies preached revivalism among the Presbyterians of Virginia and North Carolina; Shubal Sterns and Daniel Marshall drew converts to the Separate Baptist fold; and Devereux Jarratt inaugurated the Methodist phase of the Great Awakening.

The colonists were not unprepared for the Great Awakening. Prior to 1739, there had been indications of a religious quickening among several denominations. In the 1720's, the Dutch Reformed Church in New Jersey experienced a series of revivals led by Theodore Frelinghuysen, a native of Germany who had been influenced by the pietistic movement within the Lutheran church. In the mid-1730's, a "refreshing" occurred among the Presbyterians of New Jersey and Pennsylvania as a result of the preaching of a group of Scotch-Irish ministers led by Gilbert Tennent's father, William, and trained in William's Log College. The revivals continued throughout the 1730's, coinciding with the "subscription controversy" within American Presbyterianism. New England was also the scene of religious excitement before 1739. The "harvest" of Solomon Stoddard, known as the "pope" of the Connecticut Valley, and the Northampton revival of 1734-1735, led by his grandson Jonathan Edwards, foreshadowed the later, more general, awakening. Thus Whitefield's tour provided the catalyst, not the cause, of the Great Awakening, which represented the culmination of impulses that were already beginning to transform colonial Protestantism.

At first, the Great Awakening was celebrated as a supernatural work, the "pouring out of the grace of God upon the land." However, controversy over the origins and effects of the revival soon displaced the earlier consensus. Prorevivalists continued to defend the Great Awakening as the work of God, but opponents of the revival reacted negatively both to what they regarded as unlearned preaching and to the religious enthusiasm that it fomented. The assault by the revivalists on the orthodox clergy as "without spiritual taste and relish," an assault classically expressed in Gilbert Tennent's "The Danger of an Unconverted Ministry," could only have amplified the hostility.

The root of the disagreement between the pro- and antirevivalist parties reached to the source of religious faith. The orthodox clergy, the most famous of whom was Charles Chauncy of Boston, tended toward a "rational" theology. It was from this group that the Unitarians later emerged. By contrast, the revivalists held that religion was a matter of the heart or the "affections," as Jonathan Edwards called them. Yet Edwards and his disciples, in what was known as the New England Theology, held that both reason and the emotions were rightfully a part of religious experience. In keeping with their Puritan heritage, these Edwardseans also reaffirmed the Calvinist convictions about the depravity of human beings, the sovereignty of God,

and the necessity of unmerited grace for salvation. For them, regeneration was not a matter of good conduct but the result of a "new birth" or a "change of heart" wrought by God.

In many cases, the controversy over the Great Awakening split denominations into opposing factions. The revival produced a temporary schism among the Presbyterians—between Old Sides who opposed the Great Awakening and New Sides who approved it. Congregationalism was split between Old Lights and New Lights. Some prorevivalist New Lights became Separatists, withdrawing from the established Congregational churches and forming new churches of the regenerate; most of these Separate churches ultimately became Baptist, with the result that the majority of New England Baptists shifted from an Arminian to a Calvinist theology. No denomination entirely escaped the divisive effects of the Great Awakening.

Divisiveness was not the decisive consequence of the Great Awakening, however. Revival contributed to the unity of the diverse colonies and ultimately to the emergence of a "national consciousness" by communicating to the colonists a common experience and a transcending conviction about America's special destiny. As for separations among the churches, these were far outweighed by a new denominational understanding of the church that the revivalists fostered. Of great significance for American religion, diverse Christian churches were coming to be regarded as but different expressions of one reality. As Gilbert Tennent remarked, all Christian societies professing the foundational principles are but diverse denominations of the "one Church of Christ."

The establishment of colleges was another institutional consequence of the revivalist impulse. As early as 1727, William Tennent established his Log College for the education of a clergy imbued with a vital inward faith. Other colleges dedicated to the education of ministerial recruits and a Christian laity were to follow. The Presbyterian Synod of New York secured a charter for the College of New Jersey (now Princeton); the Hanover Presbytery established Hampden-Sidney College; the Baptists founded the College of Rhode Island (Brown); and the Dutch Reformed opened Queens College (Rutgers). Charitable schools also were established to provide educational opportunities for the children of indentured servants, and Dartmouth College originated as a charitable school for the education of Native Americans.

Charitable schools were but one expression of the spirit of inclusiveness encouraged by the Awakening. Revivalism gave rise also to missionaries such as David Brainerd, who worked among the Delaware of eastern New Jersey, and Samuel Davies, who took his ministry to African American slaves. The first generation of revivalists paid slight attention to the institution of slavery, yet the followers of Jonathan Edwards, armed with the revivalists' conviction about the essential dignity of all created beings, spoke out against the practice of slavery. Some itinerants of the Baptist and Methodist churches worked among black slaves, welcomed them with a surprising degree of equality into their churches, and utilized African Americans with special talents as exhorters and preachers in evangelistic endeavors. This revivalist impulse toward inclusiveness and tolerance held promise for a future pluralism that was to become a distinctive feature of religion in the United States.   —Anne C. Loveland, updated by Thomas E. Helm

ADDITIONAL READING:

Gaustad, Edwin S. *The Great Awakening in New England.* New York: Harper & Row, 1957. A compact study of the New England awakening. Gives descriptions of the events, personages, and long-range effects of the revival.

Goen, Clarence C. *Revivalism and Separatism in New England, 1740-1800: Strict Congregationalists and Separate Baptists in the Great Awakening.* Hamden, Conn.: Archon Books, 1969. A study of the separatist movement in New England during the Great Awakening, with attention to the Congregationalists and Baptists.

Hudson, Winthrop S. "The American Context as an Area for Research in Black Church Studies." *Church History* 52, no. 2 (1983): 157-171. An account of the emerging African American church experience through the efforts of itinerant Protestant preachers during the Great Awakening.

Maxson, Charles H. *The Great Awakening in the Middle Colonies.* Chicago: University of Chicago Press, 1920. A study locating the awakening among the Dutch Reformed and Presbyterian churches in the Middle Colonies in the context of an international evangelical revival.

Stout, Harry S. *The Divine Dramatist: George Whitefield and the Rise of Modern Evangelicalism.* Grand Rapids, Mich.: Wm. B. Eerdmans, 1991. Posits Whitefield as a hinge figure in American religious history, who transformed revivals from local to regional and national experiences.

Trinterud, Leonard J. *The Forming of an American Tradition: A Re-examination of Colonial Presbyterianism.* Philadelphia: Westminster Press, 1949. Examines the process by which an American understanding of Presbyterianism emerged out of the theological controversy and spiritual quickening of the Great Awakening.

SEE ALSO: 1630, Great Puritan Migration; 1649, Maryland Act of Toleration; 1662, Half-Way Covenant; 1768, Methodist Church Is Established; 1786, Virginia Statute of Religious Liberty; 1789, Episcopal Church Is Established; 1790's, Second Great Awakening.

1732 ■ SETTLEMENT OF GEORGIA: *the last and southernmost of the original thirteen British colonies was an experiment in social engineering*

DATE: June 20, 1732
LOCALE: Southeast coast
CATEGORY: Settlements
KEY FIGURES:

John Martin Bolzius (1703-1765), leader of the German Salzburger settlers

Mary Musgrove (1700-1763), Native American interpreter and trader who, with her husband John, assisted the Georgia settlers

James Edward Oglethorpe (1696-1785), British Parliament member who proposed the founding of Georgia and was its first civil and military leader

John Perceval (1683-1748), promoter and recorder of the Georgia venture

Tomochichi (1650-1739), chief of the Yamacraw Indians who resided in the Savannah area

James Wright (1716-1785), the most successful of the royal governors

SUMMARY OF EVENT. The founding of Georgia attracted more attention in England than that of any other colony. Because the project suited both philanthropic and imperial interests, it drew support from all segments of society. Philanthropists, such as James Edward Oglethorpe, a member of Parliament, and Thomas Bray, founder of the Society of the Gospel in Foreign Parts, hoped the new colony would relieve the plight of thousands of destitute debtors and provide a haven for persecuted Protestants from other European countries. The Crown, on the other hand, was concerned with the Spaniards who had gradually expanded northward from their Florida settlement, establishing presidios and missions, first on the Sea Islands and then on the mainland of Georgia. In addition to protecting their frontier against the Spanish, the British government had to contend with the Yamasee Indians, who were resentful of the encroaching European settlers. The Crown also perceived economic advantages from a new colony that could contribute raw materials for English manufacturers, provide a market for their goods, and ease the mother country's unemployment problem. Therefore, when John Perceval (later earl of Egmont), an associate of the late Dr. Bray, acted upon the suggestion of Oglethorpe and petitioned the Crown for a tract of land south and west of Carolina between the Savannah and Altamaha Rivers, the request was approved.

On June 20, 1732, the Crown conferred upon the twenty-one members of the Board of Trustees for Georgia a charter empowering them to found and to manage for twenty-one years the land between the Savannah and Altamaha Rivers, stretching as far westward as the "South Sea" (the Gulf of Mexico). Although the government took a calculated view of their enterprise, the trustees considered it the greatest philanthropic and social experiment of their age. Numerous churches, organizations, and individuals responded to their promotional campaign with contributions.

Because the settlers were to participate in a social experiment, they were individually selected from among applicants who included imprisoned debtors, the poor, and the downtrodden. Each received free passage to Georgia, tools, seeds, provisions until their first harvest, and fifty acres of land. Slaves, hard liquor, Catholics, and lawyers were prohibited in early Georgia.

In November, 1732, 114 settlers set sail on the boat *Anne*, with Oglethorpe leading the expedition to America. Disembarking in the Carolinas at Charleston in January, 1733, Oglethorpe soon chose a settlement site. With Mary Musgrove, a Native American, serving as interpreter, Oglethorpe reached an agreement with Tomochichi, chief of the Yamacraws, a Creek group who lived in the area. On February 12, 1733 (Georgia's founder's day), the colonists arrived. With the aid of Colonel William Bull, a Carolinian, Oglethorpe laid out the city of Savannah, where settlement began. The communal arrangement provided that each family own a town lot with a garden and a piece of farmland nearby. Settlers held their land through "tail male," meaning that tenure was for life and only eldest sons could inherit land. The prohibition against the sale or rental of property eliminated the possibility of unselected immigrants becoming part of the community. Hoping once again to make silk production a profitable colonial enterprise, the Crown required each settler to clear ten acres and plant one hundred mulberry trees within ten years. Moreover, Georgia's colonial settlers were to produce wine, grow tropical plants, and provide other raw materials that would benefit the British mercantile system.

In addition to the "charity settlers," the trustees admitted approved adventurers, persons who paid their own passage to the colony. Persecuted Protestants, such as the Lutheran Salzburgers from Germany, also came. The Salzburgers, under the dynamic leadership of John Martin Bolzius, settled outside Savannah in the town of Ebenezer and quickly became the most prosperous group in early Georgia. Their church, New Jerusalem, is the oldest brick structure in the state.

Authority over Georgia's affairs was officially shared by the Board of Trustees and the British government, although in practice a smaller body known as the Common Council did most of the work. Among the most active trustees were Oglethorpe, Perceval, James Vernon, the earl of Shaftesbury (Anthony Ashley-Cooper), and Benjamin Martyn, the secretary. Although all laws passed by the trustees had to be reviewed by the king, the trustees neglected the political side of the Georgia colony. While the trustees held the philanthropic and social goals to be of primary importance, the government was concerned chiefly with the economic and defensive advantages that Georgia might contribute to the British Empire. The trustees came to distrust Sir Robert Walpole, the chancellor of the exchequer, and in order to evade the authority of the government, tried, as far as possible, to govern by regulations rather than laws. In the absence of local governmental institutions, Oglethorpe acted as Georgia's unofficial leader.

Georgia's most serious problems in the early years were caused by the conflicting purposes it was expected to fulfill. Times were hard, rewards few. Inevitably, Georgia assumed a military character, and the colonists were distracted from the business of building a stable society. Oglethorpe focused much of his time on negotiating with the Native Americans and leading his regiment into a series of skirmishes against the Spanish, for which he was rewarded military rank. When the fighting ended in 1743, General James Edward Oglethorpe left Georgia, never to return. In the absence of a leader, hard times increased for

the Georgia settlers; they ignored the liquor and slave prohibitions; and many resettled in other colonies. Furthermore, the trustees abandoned the colony a year before their charter ended. Consequently, Georgia became a royal colony under the auspices of King George II, for whom the colony was named. The royal colony was under the leadership of three governors from 1754 to 1776: Captain John Reynolds, an unpopular leader who was forced back to England after serving two years; Henry Ellis, who was in poor health and did not last; and finally Sir James Wright, who was appointed in 1760. Under Governor Wright, colonial Georgia began to stabilize as its population grew. Among the new colonists were more than fifteen thousand African slaves who contributed much to colonial development. Wright remained governor of Georgia until the changes wrought by the American Revolution forced him from power. In 1777, under a new constitution, John Truetlen, a Salzburger, was elected the state's first governor as colonial Georgia theoretically ended.

—Warren M. Billings, updated by Linda Rochell Lane

ADDITIONAL READING:

Ettinger, Amos A. *James Edward Oglethorpe, Imperial Idealist.* Hamden, Conn.: Archon Books, 1968. A definitive biography of Georgia's founder that carefully analyzes his strengths, his weaknesses, and his life.

Jackson, Edwin L., Mary E. Stakes, Lawrence R. Hepburn, and Mary A. Hepburn. *The Georgia Studies Book.* Athens: University of Georgia Press, 1992. A standard textbook in many Georgia public schools, this is a comprehensive, illustrated work on the history of Georgia.

Jones, George Fenwick, ed. *The Salzburger Saga: Religious Exiles and Other Germans Along the Savannah.* Athens: University of Georgia Press, 1984. Commemorating the 250th anniversary of the Salzburgers' arrival in Georgia, this work overviews the Salzburgers' religious persecution in Germany, their trek to America, and their hardships and triumphs in colonial Georgia.

Lane, Mills, ed. *General Oglethorpe's Georgia.* 2 vols. Savannah: Beehive Press, 1975. Contains colonial letters written by James Oglethorpe, colonial settlers, and others involved with Georgia's early settlement from 1733 to 1741.

McPherson, Robert G., ed. *The Journal of the Earl of Egmont: Abstract of the Trustees Proceedings for Establishing the Colony of Georgia, 1732-1738.* Athens: University of Georgia Press, 1962. An indispensable primary source. A private record of the meeting of the Georgia trustees kept by Perceval in addition to the official minutes.

Robinson, W. Stitt. *The Southern Colonial Frontier, 1607-1763.* Albuquerque: University of New Mexico Press, 1979. Places colonial Georgia in perspective against other Southern colonies and provides background information.

Spalding, Phinizy, and Harvey H. Jackson, eds. *Oglethorpe in Perspective: Georgia's Founder After Two Hundred Years.* Tuscaloosa: University of Alabama Press, 1989. Collection of essays that analyze facets of James Oglethorpe, his work in Parliament, and his time in Georgia as a soldier and administrator.

SEE ALSO: 1739, King George's War.

1734 ■ TRIAL OF JOHN PETER ZENGER:
early precedent for freedom of the press and freedom of speech, including the freedom to criticize government

DATE: August 4, 1734
LOCALE: New York
CATEGORIES: Civil rights; Court cases; Government and politics
KEY FIGURES:
James Alexander (1691-1756), lawyer and leader of the anti-Cosby faction
Richard Bradley, attorney general of the Province of New York
William Cosby (c. 1690-1736), governor of New York
James De Lancey (1703-1760), chief justice appointed by Cosby to the Supreme Court of the Province of New York
Andrew Hamilton (died 1741), Zenger's defense counsel
Lewis Morris (1671-1746), chief justice removed by Cosby from the Supreme Court of the Province of New York
John Peter Zenger (1697-1746), printer and publisher of the *New York Weekly Journal*

SUMMARY OF EVENT. John Peter Zenger's fame rests upon his role in what is perhaps the best-known free speech case in American history. Born in Germany in 1697, Zenger emigrated to New York in 1710 and took up an apprenticeship with William Bradford, publisher of the *New York Gazette*. Bradford was then the only printer in New York and the printer for the colonial government. Zenger became a master printer whose graphic skills exceeded those of his master. He never had any formal schooling and never made any pretense of being a writer, just a printer. At age twenty-one Zenger traveled through the colonies and then settled in Maryland from 1720 to 1722. He married and served for a time as the printer for the colonial administration. When his wife died, he returned to New York and entered into a partnership with Bradford.

In 1726 Zenger dissolved his partnership with Bradford to establish his own printing shop, which was patronized by a small group of New Yorkers who were leading members of the bar: Supreme Court Chief Justice Lewis Morris, Lewis Morris, Jr., James Alexander, and William Smith. He published their political broadsides and pamphlets. When Chief Justice Morris lost his office after issuing an opinion against Governor William Cosby in a dispute over the salary still owed to Cosby's immediate predecessor in office, Morris engaged Zenger to publish a pamphlet giving his side of the controversy.

Encouraged by the success of the pamphlet, Zenger's patrons persuaded him to publish an opposition newspaper for which they would anonymously write articles. Zenger was happy to oblige since a newspaper gave a printer steady work and profits. On November 5, 1733, the first issue of Zenger's *New York Weekly Journal* appeared. The *Journal* printed essays on liberty and attacks on Governor Cosby detailing his corruption and incompetence. The newspaper became an immediate success, partly because of the unpopularity of the governor and partly because of the wit and style of the articles.

Governor Cosby was not willing to tolerate the attacks and, after two months' restraint, ordered Chief Justice James De Lancey to convene a grand jury to bring Zenger to trial for libel. The first attempt in January, 1734, failed, and a second unsuccessful attempt was made in November. On October 17, 1734, a resolution was introduced into the General Assembly to have copies of Zenger's newspaper brought into the council and burned by the hands of the common hangman, to authorize the governor to offer a reward to discover the authors of the seditious libel, and to demand the prosecution of the printer. The resolution was passed in amended form to authorize the public burning of the newspaper.

Zenger was jailed on a warrant signed by the clerk of the governor's council while another grand jury met and again refused to indict him. In January, 1735, Attorney General Richard Bradley in a bill of indictment charged Zenger with "printing and publishing several Seditious Libels" in two issues of his newspaper. One of these two issues, dated January 28, 1734, had asserted that the people of New York "think, as matters now stand, that their liberties and properties are precarious, and that slavery is likely to be entailed on them and their posterity." The second issue, dated April 8, 1734, contained a statement by a New York resident which declared: "We see men's deeds destroyed, judges arbitrarily displaced, new courts erected without consent of the legislature by which . . . trial by jury is taken away when a governor pleases." Because reasonable bail was denied, Zenger remained in jail nine months awaiting trial. Zenger's wife continued publication of the newspaper while he was in jail.

James Alexander, a former attorney general and author of several of the newspaper articles, and William Smith, a future attorney general and New York Supreme Court justice, defended Zenger. They argued for the removal of Chief Justice De Lancey and Justice Frederick Philipse from the case, arguing that their commissions were defective. Both were disbarred, and the court appointed John Chambers, an inexperienced lawyer and an advocate of Governor Cosby, to represent Zenger at the trial set for August 4.

After an unsuccessful attempt to pack the jury with a preselected list of the governor's supporters, the prosecution tried to equate the criticism of the governor with action against the king. Andrew Hamilton from Philadelphia had been secretly brought to New York to defend Zenger. He dramatically arose in the court to assume the defense of Zenger. He admitted the fact of publication but added that it was supported with truth. Attorney General Bradley countered that the jury must find a verdict for the king. He added that even if the charges were true, the law said that they are libel and that truth is an aggravation of the crime. Hamilton replied that to ignore truth in matters of libel was a return to the wickedness of the Star

Chamber and offered to prove the truth of the articles in the newspaper. This defense was not permitted by the court. Hamilton then argued that to determine the proper punishment for libel, the truth must be determined, since truth aggravated the libel. Again the court disallowed his argument. In summing up, Hamilton reminded the jury that an essential part of liberty was the right to oppose arbitrary power by speaking and writing the truth. The argument had an effect upon the jury. After a brief deliberation, the jury returned a verdict of not guilty. The victory was celebrated with cheers, salutes from guns aboard ships, and a dinner in honor of Hamilton. The case became widely known in the colonies and in England.

Although the Zenger case did not establish a binding precedent in libel cases, it was an important step toward truth as a defense against libel. Up to that time, the role of the jury had been limited to ascertaining whether or not the accused had in fact published the material in question. Two important new rules were derived from Zenger's case: that juries in libel cases are competent to decide on questions of the "law" as well as those of "fact"; and that truth is a defense in a libel prosecution. These principles were not adopted into U.S. law, however, until the enactment of the Sedition Act of 1798. Zenger's trial occurred during a period of increasing demand for liberty. It proved that citizens could speak their minds, take on the authorities, and win. The trial is therefore a symbol of the fundamental freedom to criticize government and the right to publish such criticism, which is necessary to make that freedom meaningful.

—*James J. Bolner, updated by Robert D. Talbott*

ADDITIONAL READING:

Alexander, James. *A Brief Narrative of the Case and Trial of John Peter Zenger, Printer of the New York Weekly Journal.* Edited by Sidney N. Katz. Cambridge: Harvard University Press, 1963. Katz states that the indirect effect of the Zenger trial was most important and that Hamilton's argument reflected the prevailing feeling on the proper relationship between government and citizens.

Burancelli, Vincent. *The Trial of Peter Zenger.* New York: New York University Press, 1957. A leading commentary on the Zenger trial emphasizing its importance in libel defense.

Emord, Jonathan W. *Freedom, Technology, and the First Amendment.* San Francisco: Pacific Research Institute for Public Policy, 1991. Author says that no legal precedent was set but gave colonial juries a means to thwart libel prosecutions.

Peck, Robert S. *The Bill of Rights and the Politics of Interpretation.* St. Paul, Minn.: West, 1992. Peck states that no precedent was established but the trial reflects a growing public sentiment for liberty.

Rutherford, Livingston. *John Peter Zenger: His Trial, and a Bibliography of Zenger Imprints.* New York: Dodd, Mead, 1904. A reprint of the account of the trial written by Zenger and published in his *New York Weekly Journal.*

SEE ALSO: 1791, U.S. Bill of Rights Is Ratified; 1798, Alien and Sedition Acts.

1737 ■ WALKING PURCHASE: *Pennsylvania's acquisition of Native American land enhances Iroquois dominance over eastern Pennsylvania tribes*

DATE: September 19, 1737

LOCALE: Bucks County, Pennsylvania

CATEGORIES: Expansion and land acquisition; Native American history

KEY FIGURES:

James Logan (1674-1751), prominent Penn family adviser, provincial official, and entrepreneur

Nutimus (c. 1660-c. 1742), chief of the Lenni Lenape

Thomas Penn (1702-1775), son of William Penn and governor of Pennsylvania

SUMMARY OF EVENT. The first half of the eighteenth century was a time of profound population growth in Pennsylvania. Europeans, especially Scotch-Irish and German settlers, came into the colony in unprecedented numbers. The steadily expanding population put considerable pressure on the provincial government to make additional acreage available for settlement. The demand for land also created potentially lucrative opportunities for aggressive speculators, particularly speculators who also served as provincial officials. Such was the case with those who initiated the 1737 Walking Purchase.

The Lenni Lenape, or Delaware as they were also known, were among the first Native American tribes to negotiate with William Penn. At the time that Pennsylvania was founded, the Lenni Lenape occupied much of the land between the Delaware and Susquehanna Rivers. Penn's policies toward the Lenni Lenape were more benevolent than were the tribal policies of most colonial administrators. Penn generally recognized native land rights and usually was tolerant of the native lifestyle.

By the 1730's, Pennsylvania settlers along the Delaware River had moved well north of Philadelphia. This was Lenni Lenape territory, and the natives refused to share possession. Some provincial officials, including William Penn's son Thomas, disputed the Native American claim. The younger Penn maintained that the Lenni Lenape had promised his father that they would surrender a portion of the land. The younger Penn no doubt also had ulterior motives for contesting the Lenni Lenape land. While serving as the colony's governor, he was beset with ever-growing family debts. In an effort to solve his financial woes, he chose to sell some of his family's real estate. Among the most desirable and salable parts of his acreage was the Lenni Lenape land along the Delaware.

When confronted by Thomas Penn's claim to their land, the Lenni Lenape acknowledged that the Penn family had title to a portion of the land along the Delaware. They agreed that Mechkilikishi, one of their chiefs, had granted to William Penn some acreage north of Philadelphia. According to Nutimus, a

Lenni Lenape chief who was present when land was given, the Penn claim ended at the Tohickon Creek, which is about thirty miles north of Philadelphia. James Logan, an influential member of Thomas Penn's council, led several Pennsylvania officials in challenging Nutimus' assessment. He contended that Penn's land extended beyond the Forks of the Delaware, which was more than fifty miles to the north.

To resolve the dispute, Thomas Penn called Nutimus and two other Lenni Lenape chiefs to his home at Pennsbury Manor. Assisted by Logan, Penn showed the Native Americans a copy of a deed dated 1686. The agreement transferred to the Penn family a large tract of land west of the Delaware and extending "back into the woods as far as a man can walk in one day and a half."

Nutimus argued that the walk had been made and ended at the Tohickon. The creek, therefore, was the formal border between Penn land and Lenni Lenape territory. Additionally, since Nutimus' village had for several centuries occupied the Forks area, Mechkilikishi, who was chief of another Lenni Lenape village, had no authority to turn over land at the Forks to William Penn.

Nutimus' arguments were greeted with disdain by several influential Pennsylvania officials who, like Penn, had interests in the Forks area beyond providing more land for settlers. One of the most concerned Pennsylvanians was James Logan. A few years earlier, he had begun operating an iron furnace in the region and hoped to expand his facility. Two other interested parties were Andrew Hamilton and his son-in-law, William Allen. Hamilton was mayor of Philadelphia, and Allen was on his way to becoming one of the colony's most successful entrepreneurs and the chief justice of the provincial court. Allen already had begun negotiating quietly for a large tract in what is today Allentown. Once he acquired the land, he hoped to divide it into lots and sell the lots to settlers.

Although the Pennsylvanians passionately argued their claim, the 1686 deed upon which they based their arguments was suspicious in several ways. Among other shortcomings, it lacked signatures and seals. There were also blank spaces in several crucial places, including the spot where the final dimensions of the tract should have appeared. In most cases, such a document would have been voided by the British courts. When questioned about the flaws, Penn and Logan claimed that it was a copy of an original that had been lost. Nevertheless, they continued to uphold the document as valid.

In the months that followed the Pennsbury meeting, Logan quietly expanded his plan of attack. To undermine Nutimus' authority, he appealed to Iroquois representatives for support. The powerful Iroquois nation dominated most tribes throughout Pennsylvania; without their support, the Lenni Lenape had little hope of retaining the disputed land along the Delaware. Assisted by Conrad Weiser, Logan was able to get the Iroquois to confirm the Penn claims. With Iroquois approval secured, it was just a matter of time before the Lenni Lenape conceded to Penn's claims. On August 25, 1737, Nutimus and three other Lenni Lenape chiefs grudgingly endorsed Governor Penn's

furtive 1686 treaty. A walk that would determine the extent of Penn's holdings along the Delaware was soon scheduled.

The walk began at the Wrightstown Quaker Meeting House at daybreak on September 19. Three local men known for their athletic prowess were hired by provincial authorities to make the hike. Two Native American representatives accompanied the Pennsylvanians. The Lenni Lenape expected that the walk would conform to native customs. The walkers would walk for a while then rest, smoke a peace pipe, and share a meal before resuming their trek. The Lenni Lenape expected that the journey would cover about twenty miles. Pennsylvania officials, however, had much different plans.

It became clear immediately that the walk would not be a leisurely stroll along the Delaware. Instead it proceeded northwest toward the Kittatiny Mountains and followed a path that had been cut through the backcountry to aid the walkers. Additionally, much of the time the walkers did not walk. They ran. The Pennsylvanians also were accompanied by supply horses carrying provisions, and boats that were used to ferry the hikers across streams.

By early afternoon, the unsuspecting Lenni Lenape escorts fell far behind the Pennsylvanians. A few hours later, already well beyond the Tohickon, one Pennsylvanian dropped from exhaustion. A second walker gave up the following morning. The final Pennsylvanian persevered until noon on the second day. In all, he covered sixty-four miles, more than three times what the Lenni Lenape had expected.

Even after the walk had ended, the Penn land grab continued. Rather than draw a straight line from start to finish and then a right angle to the river, surveyors were instructed by Logan to set the borders of the walk in a zigzag course that followed the flow of the Delaware. As a result, another 750,000 acres were acquired from the Lenni Lenape.

During the months that followed, Nutimus and his tribe complained bitterly about the devious tactics employed by provincial officials. However, the Lenni Lenape had few alternatives to accepting the results. With Walking Purchase completed, the new land was soon opened to Pennsylvania settlers and the Lenni Lenape relegated to diminished status among Native American tribes living in the colony.

—*Paul E. Doutrich*

ADDITIONAL READING:

Jennings, Francis. *The Ambiguous Iroquois Empire*. New York: W. W. Norton, 1984. Offers a detailed explanation of the duplicitous tactics used by Pennsylvania officials to acquire the Walking Purchase acreage.

Kelley, Joseph J., Jr. *Pennsylvania: The Colonial Years, 1681-1776*. Garden City, N.Y.: Doubleday, 1980. Describes the Walking Purchase and many other episodes in Pennsylvania's colonial history.

Thomas, David Hurst, et al. *The Native Americans: An Illustrated History*. Atlanta, Ga.: Turner Publishing, 1993. A colorful history that includes a concise accounting of the purchase.

Tolles, Frederick B. *James Logan and the Culture of Provincial America*. Boston: Little, Brown, 1957. Details the life and career of James Logan, including his role in the Walking Purchase.

Wallace, Paul A. W. *Indians in Pennsylvania*. Harrisburg: Pennsylvania Historical and Museum Commission, 1981. Survey of Native Americans, including a general description of the Walking Purchase.

SEE ALSO: 1681, Pennsylvania Is Founded.

1739 ▪ STONO REBELLION: *open violence triggers other slave insurrections and forces white settlers to cooperate to prevent additional uprisings*

DATE: September 9, 1739
LOCALE: St. Paul's Parish near the Stono River, twenty miles from Charles Town, South Carolina
CATEGORIES: African American history; Wars, uprisings, and civil unrest
KEY FIGURES:
William Bull (1683-1755), lieutenant governor who discovered the band of rebels
Jemmy, slave leader of the rebellion

SUMMARY OF EVENT. Conditions in South Carolina in the 1730's led to white fear of slave uprisings. The high numbers of Africans imported through Charles Town port led to legislation against Africans congregating, holding meetings, and appearing in public after night hours. Charles Town had a watch committee to guard the port city, and the rest of the colony had a white patrol system to police Africans in militia districts. South Carolina used public punishment as a deterrent.

Contrary to their intent, these white controls increasingly led to greater resistance from newly imported Africans. Cases of verbal insolence joined arson as a recurring feature of colonial life. Whites blamed illnesses and deaths on African knowledge of plants and their poisonous powers. In the 1730's, massive importations from the Congo-Angola region meant that more than half of the colony's slaves had been there fewer than ten years. Slave unrest was blamed on outside agitators— Native Americans with assistance from both the Spanish and French. Rumors of a Spanish invasion increased after the Spanish king granted liberty to African fugitive slaves in 1733.

Tension thus was high in 1739. Then, a smallpox epidemic, coupled with the escape of slaves to Spanish Florida, led to massive loss of investments. A yellow fever epidemic hit during the summer months. In the fall, deaths decreased with the return of cool weather, but the situation was ripe for insurrection. Since Sundays afforded slaves their best opportunity for meeting in communal activities, the legislature passed the Security Act in August, 1739, requiring all white men to carry firearms to churches beginning September 29 or pay a stiff fine. News of conflict between England and Spain reached Charles Town the weekend before the uprising began, explaining why the Stono Rebellion began immediately without be-

trayal, caught white masters in church unarmed, and had slaves marching toward Spanish St. Augustine.

The insurrection included elements typical of early rebellions in South Carolina: total surprise, brutal killings, extensive property damage, armed fighting, and extended consequences. On the morning of September 9, 1739, twenty slaves, mostly Angolans, gathered in St. Paul's Parish near Stono River, twenty miles from Charles Town. Led by a slave named Jemmy, the group broke into Hutchenson's store near the Stono Bridge to gather guns and ammunition. Storekeepers Robert Bathurst and Mr. Gibbs were beheaded. The slave band moved on to the Godfrey house, killing the family, gathering supplies, and burning the building. The slaves took the main road to Georgia, stopping at Wallace's Tavern but sparing the innkeeper, who was known to be a kind master. His white neighbor, however, lost his life, along with his wife and child. The band continued, sacking and burning houses on Pons Pons Road and killing all the white occupants. Slave owner Thomas Rose was successfully hidden by his slaves as the band moved through. The group's numbers grew as reluctant slaves were forced to join. Increased numbers led to diminished discipline. The group took up a banner, beat on two drums, and shouted, "Liberty!" They pursued and killed any whites they encountered.

Lieutenant Governor William Bull and four other white men were traveling to Charles Town for legislative session when they encountered the rebel slaves. They escaped to warn others. By late Sunday afternoon, the band of nearly one hundred rebel slaves stopped in an open field, showing their confidence and hoping to be joined by other slaves by morning.

Nearby, white colonists had been alerted by Sunday afternoon and had organized an armed and mounted resistance of somewhere between twenty and one hundred men. Moving to the field, the white forces caught the slaves off guard, killing or wounding at least fourteen rebels. They surrounded other rebels, who were briefly questioned before being shot to death. They released the slaves who had been forced to participate. Almost one-third of the rebeling slaves escaped the fighting. Some returned to their plantations, hoping not to be missed. Upon their return, planters cut off their heads and placed them on posts to serve as a reminder for other slaves seeking freedom.

The white colony engaged in an intensive manhunt to recapture those participants who remained at large. Whites armed themselves, and guards were posted at ferry posts. By some accounts, twenty to forty rebels were captured, hanged, disemboweled, or beaten within the two following days. Another account, a month later, reported the rebels had been stopped from doing further mischief by having been "put to the most cruel Death." The Georgia general James Oglethorpe called out rangers and American Indians, garrisoned soldiers at Palachicolas—a fort guarding the only point on the Savannah River where fugitives could cross—and issued a proclamation for whites to keep a watchful eye on any Africans.

Despite these acts of retribution and retaliation against both free blacks and slaves, white fears did not subside. Most whites thought persons of African descent were dangerous and possessed of a rebellious nature. By the fall of 1739, many planters near Stono had moved their wives and children in with other families for greater security. The Assembly placed a special patrol along the Stono River. Outlying fugitives were still being brought in for execution by early 1740. Finally, two fugitive slaves seeking a large reward captured the last remaining leader, who had been at large for three years following the insurrection.

The white minority responded to the Stono Rebellion in several ways. First, the colony tightened restrictions on all blacks, giving South Carolina the harshest penalties of any mainland colony. The colony also sought to improve conditions that provoked rebellion. Finally, the colony sought to lessen the influence of the Spanish settlement in St. Augustine as a constant source of incitement. The war against the Spanish curbed that stimulant. The white minority also tried to correct the numerical racial imbalance. A prohibitive duty on new slave imports cut the rate of importation from one thousand per year in 1730 to one hundred per year by 1740. Collected duties went to recruit white immigrants. The legislature required one white man present for every ten Africans on a plantation. Fines from this infraction went to fund additional patrols.

The government intensified efforts to control the behavior of slaves. Through the Negro Act of 1740, the legislators shaped the core of the South Carolina slave codes for more than a century. Masters who failed to retain control of slaves received fines. The right to manumit slaves was taken out of the hands of owners and turned over to the legislature. No longer could slaves have such personal liberties as freedom of movement, of education, of assembly, to raise food, and to earn money. Surveillance of African American activity increased. Slaves received rewards for informing on the actions of other slaves. The legislature discouraged the presence of free blacks in the colony.

The white minority developed several strategies of calculated benevolence. The government assessed penalties on masters known for excessive labor requirements or brutality of punishments for their slaves. A school was founded in Charles Town to train slaves to teach other slaves about selective Christian principles requiring submission and obedience.

These efforts did not lessen white dependency on African labor. Machines did not supplant their labor until after the American Revolution. White immigration did not increase substantially, despite offers of free land on the frontier. High duties reduced the importation of slaves, but the racial proportions varied slightly from those prior to insurrection.

The suppression of the Stono Rebellion was a significant turning point for the white minority. White factions had to cooperate to maintain the English colony. Techniques used to maintain white control shaped the race relations and history of South Carolina. The heightened degree of white repression and the reduction in African autonomy created a new social equilibrium in the generation before the American Revolution.

—*Dorothy C. Salem*

ADDITIONAL READING:

Aptheker, Herbert. *American Negro Slave Revolts.* Rev. ed. New York: Columbia University Press, 1969. The pioneering work on slave revolts.

Jordan, Winthrop. *White Over Black: American Attitudes Toward the Negro, 1550-1812.* Chapel Hill: University of North Carolina Press, 1968. Discusses how slave revolts influenced the status of both slaves and free blacks in the United States.

Kilson, Martin. "Toward Freedom: An Analysis of Slave Revolts in the United States." *Phylon* 25 (1964): 175-189. Analyzes the distribution of slave revolts and the environments that contributed to their occurrence.

Wood, Peter H. *Black Majority: Negroes in Colonial South Carolina from 1670 Through the Stono Rebellion.* New York: W. W. Norton, 1974. Examines the patterns of white control and African resistance within the socioeconomic context of colonial South Carolina. Both a narrative and an analysis of the event and its effects on the colony.

SEE ALSO: 1663, Settlement of the Carolinas; 1670, Charles Town Is Founded; 1671, Indian Slave Trade; 1712, New York City Slave Revolt.

1739 ■ KING GEORGE'S WAR: *colonial skirmishes merge into a war among European powers and prove the significance of America in world affairs*

DATE: October 19, 1739-October 18, 1748
LOCALE: Eastern North America
CATEGORIES: Canadian history; Economics; Wars, uprisings, and civil unrest
KEY FIGURES:
Louis du Chambon, governor of Louisbourg and leader of an unsuccessful defense in 1745
Manuel de Montiano, governor and defender of St. Augustine who led the invasion of Georgia
James Oglethorpe (1696-1785), governor of Georgia and leader of the struggle against the Spanish in the early 1740's
William Pepperrell (1669-1759), commander of the expedition against Louisbourg in 1745
William Shirley (1694-1771), governor of Massachusetts who promoted and helped plan capture of Louisbourg
SUMMARY OF EVENT. Although the declaration of colonial war was made by the mother country, technicalities had little to do with actual fighting. The conclusion in 1713 of Queen Anne's War (the War of Spanish Succession in Europe) was followed by a period of peace. For British colonies in America, however, skirmishes with natives along the frontiers, and occasional confrontations with the French in Canada and the Spanish in Florida, continued. The establishment of Georgia in 1733 as a buffer against Florida shows that London was aware

of the military situation. A conflict that the colonists would call King George's War and Europeans called the War of Austrian Succession began in October of 1739.

The fighting began over trade in the Caribbean. England held the *asiento*, a privilege that gave control of the slave trade plus an annual shipload of merchandise. English merchants cheated blatantly. This early struggle is called the War of Jenkins' Ear, after an English smuggler who lost an ear, which he preserved in a bottle of brandy, in a scuffle with a Spanish *guardacosta*. Although he had commonly used his grisly souvenir to cadge drinks, in the late 1730's Jenkins became a *cause célèbre* as the political opposition led by William Pitt the Elder and others began to press for war to protect the freedom of the seas against Spanish claims of a right to search. For Pitt, this began a career focused on shifting English policy to empire, but he was unusually farsighted. Many leaders were more concerned with continental matters than with imperial ones. The latter seemed more pressing the next year, when Prussia seized the province of Silesia from Austria, initiating a war that would draw all the powers into confrontation. Ultimately, England supported Austria and, because Spain and her ally France were on the other side, the colonial war merged into the European struggle. The Anglo-French declaration of war did not come until 1744, so the initial campaigns of King George's War involved the Southern colonies and Spain.

The 1739 fighting was started by Admiral Edward Vernon in the Caribbean, and the Georgia-Florida border was soon embroiled. For the Georgians, led by General James Oglethorpe, St. Augustine was tempting. It was an important Spanish center, from which American Indians were courted; in English hands, it would be a base from which to attack Spanish fleets. After gaining an accommodation with the Creek Indians, Oglethorpe mounted a raid on Florida but lacked strength to occupy territory. Returning to Georgia, he secured the promise of a regiment from South Carolina, which was to meet the Georgians at the St. John's River in the spring.

In April, the Royal Navy began patrolling the Florida coast and the eager Oglethorpe invaded. After attacks on forts along the St. John's River, he planned a combined sea and land assault on St. Augustine. The Spanish blocked amphibious operations, and the assault degenerated into a siege. The navy failed to prevent resupply of the city, and in late June, Oglethorpe went home, blaming others for his own failure to adapt to changing circumstances.

Colonial involvement in the war expanded later in 1740, when numerous ships and thirty-six companies of troops became part of an attack against Cartagena. This expedition proved disastrous. No preparation had been made for the colonials' arrival, and they had to wait several disease-ridden months for the English contingent to appear. The force did not reach Cartagena until March, 1741, and after a month, marked by illness and futile fighting, gave up. Only a few of the colonial troops survived. For the first time, there was open colonial disdain for English arms—a harbinger of feelings that later contributed to revolution.

Their morale buoyed by the English failures, the Spanish launched an invasion of Georgia in the fall of 1741. The prospects looked good. The Royal Navy was committed to the Caribbean; the small Georgian population was scattered and divided; help from South Carolina was unlikely, due to lingering hard feelings from the failure at St. Augustine and fears of slave revolt; and once the attack was launched, the Spanish would be in place to block any seaborne relief. A combination of bad luck, poor generalship, and effective defense doomed the invasion, however. The defenders were concentrated on St. Simon's Island, and a storm scattered the Spanish shallow-draft vessels needed for maneuver, providing time to organize the defense. A landing was achieved, but in the Battle of Bloody Marsh, the Spanish were battered and fell back on their beachhead. False rumors that a Royal Navy squadron had arrived convinced them to go home. After this, both sides in the South fell onto the defensive.

With the declaration of war between England and France in 1744, the focus of King George's War shifted northward. Skirmishing began in Nova Scotia, with an attack by the French and natives. The cooperation of Governor William Shirley of Massachusetts, an imperialist who looked beyond the narrow interests of his own colony, resulted in the French returning to their main base of Louisbourg, on Cape Breton Island.

Louisbourg provided domination of the Gulf of St. Lawrence, a commercial center, and control of access to the St. Lawrence River, a highway into the interior of the continent. Shirley, initially to distract the French, began to talk about taking Louisbourg. Two Englishmen who had been prisoners there reported weakened defenses, and the talk became serious. Shirley began organizing an expedition of three thousand troops, seeking support from all the Northern colonies. Connecticut was the most enthusiastic, but Rhode Island and New Hampshire sent some troops, New York provided artillery, and New Jersey and Pennsylvania contributed provisions. Commodore Peter Warren in the West Indies approved of the effort and promised naval support if orders were received from London.

Shirley wisely picked William Pepperrell of Maine to head the force. Although inexperienced, he was bright and popular enough to draw volunteers, which combined with the hope of plunder to fill the ranks. By April, the colonial force, with considerably more than the hoped-for three thousand, was in Nova Scotia training. Commodore Warren arrived with four warships to tighten the blockade of Cape Breton Island. The French defenders, led by Acting Governor Louis du Chambon, were no more than adequate but believed Louisbourg's guns would destroy any hostile ship entering the harbor. Showing his ability, Pepperrell landed away from the city and attacked from landward.

The colonials' effort was risky. They had not been able to bring enough cannons for a siege and had no experience in such operations. Luck and determined effort paid off, however. A major French artillery position was taken, and the guns, although spiked, were easily repaired. Another position,

Chambon's last significant defense outside the city, fell in early June. There were numerous casualties, and resupply efforts were frustrated by Warren's blockade. In mid-June, more Royal Navy ships arrived, assuring English control of the sea. June 15, Chambon asked for terms, and surrender was negotiated.

Reactions to the victory were mixed. The people of the Northern colonies and England were overjoyed, but the English government wanted peace and was forced by public sentiment into more war. The soldiers at Louisbourg were unhappy that the negotiated surrender denied them the chance to plunder. Their annoyance worsened as the navy, by leaving up the French flag, trapped a series of valuable prizes. However, nothing could deny the surge of pride among the colonists—they had won a major victory against European foes and proven for the first time that American events had a notable impact on world affairs.

The war continued. A colonial invasion of Canada was dropped due to European politics. The French in Canada struck by using their Native American allies, while the Six Nations of the Iroquois, the most important American Indian friends of the English, moved toward neutrality. In late 1745, Saratoga, New York, was burned; for the next two years, isolated settlements in English colonies were at risk. The French, even with their American Indian allies, were not able to mount a major American campaign. On other fronts, however, they scored major gains in the Low Countries and took Madras in India.

In April, 1748, the Anglo-French negotiations opened at Aix-la-Chapelle, and on October 18, peace was concluded. The terms suggest that continental considerations remained primary to English politicians. The French made concessions in the Low Countries and returned Madras in return for regaining Louisbourg and Cape Breton Island. In North America, the result was *status quo ante bellum*, with no resolution of border disputes, north or south. Although some merchants were pleased to have French commerce reestablished at Louisbourg, most colonists were disgusted and began to suspect that the English talked a better war than they fought. The English, in their turn, were less than impressed with colonial military practice, which seemed to allow the rank and file to influence decisions—Pepperrell had delayed an attack because his men had objected. The resulting miscalculations contributed to the willingness to fight in 1775. *—Fred R. van Hartesveldt*

ADDITIONAL READING:

Dorn, Walter L. *Competition for Empire, 1740-1763*. New York: Harper & Brothers, 1940. Remains the best account of the European aspects of King George's War.

Garrison, Webb. *Oglethorpe's Folly: The Birth of Georgia*. Lakemont, Ga.: Copple House, 1982. Provides a useful focus on the role of Oglethorpe, the key leader of the war in the South.

Ivers, Larry E. *British Drums on the Southern Frontier: The Military Colonization of Georgia*. Chapel Hill: University of North Carolina Press, 1974. Discusses the war's early

phases, when the English and Spanish struggled for control of Georgia-Florida border areas.

Leach, Douglas Edward. *Arms for Empire: A Military History of the British Colonies in North America, 1607-1763*. New York: Macmillan, 1973. A detailed and well-written account of military activities in both the Southern and Northern theaters.

Peckham, Howard, *The Colonial Wars*. Chicago: University of Chicago Press, 1964. A lively account of the late seventeenth and first half of the eighteenth centuries.

SEE ALSO: 1732, Settlement of Georgia.

1754 ■ FRENCH AND INDIAN WAR: *defeat of French and Native American forces establishes British dominance in North America but increases the mother country's dependence on colonial resources*

DATE: May 28, 1754-February 10, 1763
LOCALE: North America
CATEGORIES: Canadian history; Expansion and land acquisition; Native American history; Wars, uprisings, and civil unrest
KEY FIGURES:
William Pitt the Elder (1708-1778), British prime minister who led the war effort
Pontiac (c. 1720-1769), Ottawa (Algonquian) leader who led a coalition of Indian nations against the British to defend Indian lands in the Ohio Valley in 1763
George Washington (1732-1799), young officer in charge of the military mission that set off the war
James Wolfe (1727-1759), British general who won the crucial battle of Quebec

SUMMARY OF EVENT. The French and Indian War was the North American part of a larger conflict called the Seven Years' War, fought between France and Great Britain for control of colonies in North America and India and for hegemony in Europe. Both Great Britain and France claimed large territories in North America. In addition to the thirteen colonies spread out along the Atlantic coast, the British claimed what is now northern Canada. The French claimed a huge section of the inner continent, stretching from New Orleans in the south to what is now Montana in the northwest and Quebec in the northeast. The French built a series of forts along the Mississippi River and its tributaries to defend their claims. One of these tributaries, the Ohio River, flows southwest along the western frontier of Pennsylvania and Virginia. Both French and British claimed this land. British colonists worried about a French invasion and resented the French presence, which limited western expansion.

In 1754, 150 soldiers from Virginia, led by the twenty-two-year-old officer George Washington, headed west to secure

MAJOR BATTLES IN THE FRENCH AND INDIAN WAR, 1754-1763

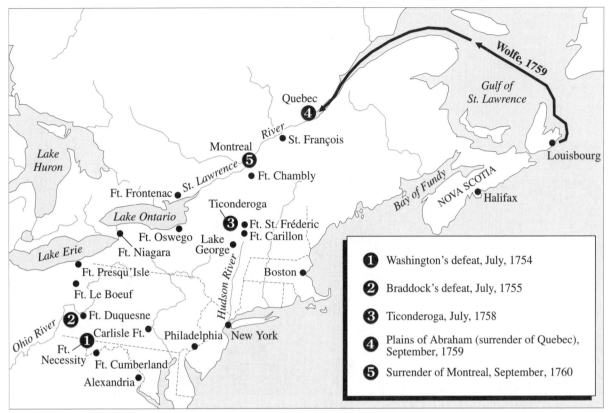

Both Great Britain and France claimed large territories in North America, overlapping on the soutwestern frontier of Pennsylvania and Virginia. Algonquians and Hurons allied themselves with the French; Mohawks allied with the British. In the end, the French lost much of their stronghold in North America.

British claims by building a fort at the fork where the Monongahela and Alleghany Rivers meet to form the Ohio River. When they arrived, they discovered that the French had built a fort there already, Fort Duquesne. Washington's troops lost the ensuing battle (May 28), which marked the beginning of the war.

As they struggled to expand their North American empires, the British and French did not consider the rights or needs of the people who had been living on the land for thousands of years before Europeans arrived. The only time Europeans took serious notice of the First Americans was when they needed allies in wartime. Both the French and the British sought and received support from some native peoples. For their part, Native Americans, by siding with one party or the other, could get access to European weapons and perhaps succeed in driving at least one group of invading Europeans from the land. Algonquians and Hurons allied themselves with the French, whom they had known mainly as fur traders over the past century and a half. The French seemed less intrusive and permanent than the British, who cleared the land for farming. The Algonquians were, moreover, traditional rivals of those tribes allied with the Iroquois Confederacy. By selling goods

at low prices and exploiting traditional enmities, the British also were able to find native allies, including the Mohawks, one of the most powerful Iroquois nations, who agreed to help the British against the French and Algonquians.

The war went poorly for the British at first. With thirteen separate colonial governments involved, decisions were difficult to make. Nor were British soldiers accustomed to the American landscape. In 1755, the British general Edward Braddock was badly defeated when he attacked the French at Fort Duquesne. The French and their Native American allies easily scouted out and ambushed Braddock's troops, shooting from behind trees at the British soldiers, whose red coats made good targets. The French won a series of battles until 1757, when the tide changed.

The British had had some advantages from the beginning. There were twenty times as many British in North America as French, and the British had the most powerful navy in the world. Then, in 1757, a dynamic new leader, William Pitt, took over the British government. Pitt sent Britain's best generals to lead the war against the French and motivated British colonists to support the war effort by offering high prices for supplies purchased in America.

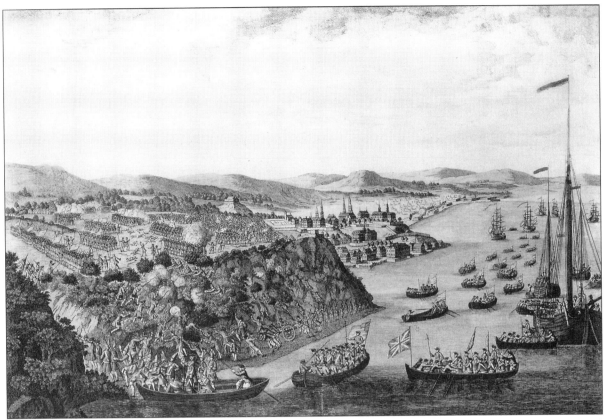

The taking of Quebec, September 13, 1759. The decisive battle came when Pitt sent General James Wolfe to attack the French capital, Quebec. Located at the top of a high cliff that rose steeply from the banks of the St. Lawrence River, this city was easier to defend than to attack. British general Wolfe moved four thousand troops across the St. Lawrence River in small boats, surprising the French general Montcalm by attacking in the early hours of the morning. This Battle of the Plains of Abraham effectively ended the French stronghold in North America. (Library of Congress)

A year later, the Lenni Lenape (Delawares), an Algonquian people living in Pennsylvania, withdrew their support from the French, leaving Fort Duquesne vulnerable to attack. The British attacked successfully and renamed the fort to honor their new leader. The city that grew on the site of the fort, Pittsburgh, still contains William Pitt's name.

The decisive battle came in 1759, when Pitt sent General James Wolfe to attack the city of Quebec, the French capital. If the British could take this city, they would win the war. Quebec, located at the top of a high cliff that rose steeply from the banks of the St. Lawrence River, was easier to defend than to attack. The French general in charge, the Marquis de Montcalm, was an experienced leader, but even he was taken by surprise when Wolfe moved four thousand troops across the St. Lawrence River in small boats, found ways to scale the cliffs, and attacked in the early hours of the morning. Both generals were killed in the battle, but news of the British victory reached Wolfe before he died. This Battle of the Plains of Abraham was the turning point for the French, effectively ending their stronghold in North America.

When the British took Montreal in 1760, fighting ended in North America. There was no formal peace treaty until the war between France and Prussia, Great Britain's ally in central Europe, finally ground to a halt three years later.

Then, in the Treaty of Paris (February 10, 1763), the French ceded Canada and all French lands east of the Mississippi to Great Britain. France retained the land it claimed west of the Mississippi, including the key port of New Orleans. Spain, which had allied itself with France against Great Britain, was forced to give up Florida. The rights of the indigenous nations that had prior claim to all of this land were not considered.

The French and Indian War had important consequences for the early development of American history. It increased Great Britain's needs for its North American colonies, but had the opposite effect on the colonists' needs for Great Britain. With the French gone, the need for the protection of the British military began to disappear as well. To some colonists, it seemed that the redcoats were starting to get in the way. The British Proclamation of 1763 forbade colonists from settling land west of a line drawn along the Appalachian Mountains. Welcomed by the followers of the Ottawa chief Pontiac, who earlier that year had brought many American Indian nations together to defend their lands against European invasion, the proclamation disappointed those colonists who had expected to benefit from land opened up by the French defeat. In effect, the Proclamation of 1763 had little effect in preserving western lands for their Indian inhabitants as colonists began to push west anyway.

The war brought the colonies closer together. There had been a first effort, called the Albany Plan of Union, to unite the colonies under one government. Although the Albany Plan, discussed by representatives of several colonies in Albany, New York, in 1754, was unsuccessful—the individual colonial governments being hesitant to give up any power—the fact that some sort of union was even discussed reflected a growing tendency to see the colonies as a unified entity distinct from the mother country, England.

Seven years of fighting on three continents and all the world's oceans had exhausted British resources as well. War debts forced the British government to increase tax rates drastically. These rates, however, only applied to British citizens in Great Britain. British citizens in North America continued to pay relatively low taxes. To many British, it seemed only fair that the British in the colonies pay their share for the war that had made their homes safe from invasion.

The self-confidence of the colonists had grown as they helped fight a successful war. They believed they had the same rights to representative government as British citizens in Great Britain. One of these was the right to send representatives to the body of government that levies taxes. Colonists accepted taxes levied by colonial governments, where they were represented, but rejected taxes levied by the British Parliament, to which they were not allowed to send representatives. British efforts to tax the colonies, despite colonial protest, thus became one of the causes for the outbreak of the American Revolution.   —*T. W. Dreier*

ADDITIONAL READING:

Anderson, Fred. *A People's Army: Massachusetts Soldiers and Society in the Seven Years' War*. Chapel Hill: University of North Carolina Press, 1984. This illustrated regional study reveals how average colonists experienced and affected the war.

Auth, Stephen F. *The Ten Years War: Indian-White Relations in Pennsylvania, 1755-1765*. New York: Garland, 1989. Includes Native American perspectives missing in many studies. Final chapter shows the war's implications for later treatment of Native Americans.

Hamilton, Edward P. *The French and Indian Wars: The Story of Battles and Forts in the Wilderness*. Garden City, N.Y.: Doubleday, 1962. The first chapters of this narrative history discuss the role played by George Washington.

Jennings, Francis. *Empire of Fortune: Crowns, Colonies, and Tribes in the Seven Years War in America*. New York: W. W. Norton, 1988. A comprehensive study by a major scholar; offers easily accessible information on all aspects of the war. Illustrations, maps, and indices.

Schwartz, Seymoor. *The French and Indian War, 1754-*

1763: The Imperial Struggle for North America. New York: Simon & Schuster, 1994. A concise, well-illustrated study that provides a thoughtful, readable overview.

SEE ALSO: 1739, King George's War; 1754, Albany Congress; 1759, Cherokee War; 1763, Pontiac's Resistance; 1763, Proclamation of 1763; 1763, Paxton Boys' Massacres.

1754 ■ ALBANY CONGRESS: *to resolve Iroquois land and trade complaints, colonial delegates draft the Plan of Union*

DATE: June 19-July 10, 1754
LOCALE: Albany, New York
CATEGORIES: Government and politics; Laws and acts; Native American history
KEY FIGURES:
James De Lancey (1703-1760), New York's lieutenant governor
Benjamin Franklin (1706-1790), proponent of confederation
Hendrick (c. 1680-1755), Mohawk leader
Thomas Hutchinson (1711-1780), Massachusetts legislator who some scholars believe wrote the Plan of Union

SUMMARY OF EVENT. In June of 1753, the Mohawk leader Hendrick declared the Covenant Chain—a term used to symbolize the Iroquois Confederacy's alliance with New York and the other colonies—to be broken. Hendrick's action shocked colonial and imperial officials. From their perspective, Hendrick's timing could not have been worse. Tensions between the French and English were increasing, and British officials had based their military strategy for North America on an Anglo-Iroquois alliance. Just when the Iroquois alliance was most needed, the Mohawks had voided the centerpiece of Britain's military strategy for North America. Something had to be done, and that something was the Albany Congress of 1754.

Hendrick's declaration represented a culmination of events dating back a decade. In 1744, the Onondaga, believing they were ceding the Shenandoah Valley to Virginia, agreed to the Treaty of Lancaster. Virginians, however, used this treaty to claim the entire Ohio region. Over the next decade, Virginian officials opened nearly three hundred thousand acres of land to settlement through land companies such as the Ohio Company of Virginia. King George's War (1739-1748) temporarily delayed settlement. Once the war ended, however, the Ohio Company renewed its efforts at settling the region. French officials responded by sending Captain de Céleron into the Ohio Valley in 1750. French soldiers also began building forts in the region. One such outpost, Presque Isle, was in the heart of Iroquoia. When the Iroquois asked for assistance in removing the French from Presque Isle, Virginian officials refused to help. By the early 1750's, the Mohawks and other Indian groups felt themselves trapped between the English and French.

Hendrick, chief of the Mohawks, who in 1753 declared the Covenant Chain—the Iroquois Confederacy's alliance with New York and the other British colonies—to be broken as a result of Iroquois attacks against westward-expanding settlers. The Albany Congress was designed to allow the British to make peace with their long-standing Iroquois allies in the face of mounting French-British tensions. Mohawk leaders such as Hendrick hoped that the congress' proposed Plan of Union would allow all British colonists to speak with a single voice, thus alleviating Iroquois-settler tensions, but the plan was rejected. (Library of Congress)

Following Virginia's response to the Iroquois, members of the Board of Trade recommended that King George II call a congress to address Indian complaints about colonial behavior. In September, 1753, the Board of Trade notified colonial governors that King George II wanted all colonies having a relationship with the Iroquois to attend a conference that was to resolve existing Iroquois complaints about land and trade with the colonists. The resulting Albany Congress was unlike any other Anglo-Iroquois conference. It was the first intercolonial-Indian conference called by London officials.

The proposed conference met with the approval of Massachusetts governor William Shirley and the Pennsylvanian Benjamin Franklin. However, the lieutenant governors of New York and Virginia were less enthralled with the board's directive. New York lieutenant governor James De Lancey could not escape the conference. Robert Dinwiddie of Virginia, however, failed to send a representative to Albany. Still, when the conference began in June of 1754, representatives from nine colonies attended.

The delegates met at Albany for specific reasons. It was the historic meeting place for Iroquois-European conferences. Albany was the site of one of the two council fires the English and Iroquois maintained. As one of the anchors of the Covenant Chain, official business could be conducted and ratified there. It was also the closest city to the frontier that delegates could reach by boat.

When representatives met at Albany, they needed not only to address Iroquois complaints but also to prepare for war. Delegates saw the two issues as interrelated. On June 19, 1754, they created a seven-person committee to prepare James De Lancey's opening speech to the American Indians. Five days later, the representatives created a second committee to consider "some Method of affecting the Union between the Colonies." This latter delegation produced the Plan of Union associated with the Albany Congress. It did so, however, "as a Branch of Indian Affairs." Mohawk leaders such as Hendrick hoped confederation would allow the colonists to speak with a single voice. Some delegates agreed. They though colonial confederation would alleviate the problems of which the Iroquois complained. Therefore, the Albany Plan of Union was designed primarily as a mechanism for conducting Indian affairs.

Besides improving colonial policy toward the natives, representatives thought colonial confederation would improve their military preparedness and help them defeat New France. There were mutual security reasons for confederation. Politicians did not prepare their plan to tamper with each colony's internal autonomy.

Common wisdom maintains that Benjamin Franklin is the father of the colonial confederation. There is, however, some evidence to suggest that Thomas Hutchinson of Massachusetts wrote the plan. If Hutchinson was the author, then American Indian affairs were probably an important influence on the Plan of Union, because Hutchinson was a member of the original subcommittee appointed to study American Indian affairs. Franklin was not.

Whoever the author was, the Plan of Union contained specific proposals. It created a unicameral legislature, to be called the Grand Council. This council would consist of forty-eight representatives chosen from the lower houses of the colonies. Representation in the Grand Council was limited to members of the lower houses of assembly in the colonies, because it was assumed that only directly elected representatives had the right to tax the colonists. Initially, representation in the Grand Council would be based on the population of each colony. After three years, representation would be based on the revenue a colony generated for the confederation, so as to reward participation. In both its name and the number of delegates, the Plan of Union paid homage to the Iroquois League.

The new government also would have a president general. This executive would receive his salary directly from England, so the president general would be independent of the colonial legislatures. This proposal recognized the problems confronting the relationship between governor and lower house in colonial America.

The proposed confederation government had eight functions. One of the most important was the right to direct all Indian treaties for the colonies. The government also would make declarations of war and peace toward the natives, make all land purchases from the natives in the name of the king, and regulate trade with the natives. Purchased land would reside outside the existing boundaries of established colonies. The government would direct the creation of settlements in the territory, would rule them in the name of the king, and would be responsible for the defense of the frontier.

The Plan of Union also gave the proposed government the ability to tax. The Grand Council could enforce an excise tax on luxury goods. The government would secure additional money by regulating the Indian trade. Traders would be required to carry licenses and post bonds of good behavior before being allowed to trade with the natives. Traders were to purchase these licenses and bonds from the confederation government. Trade would be restricted to specific forts, built just for that purpose. It was hoped that by regulating trade with the Indians, many of the problems associated with the traders would be curtailed. Finally, the government would receive quitrent from colonists as they settled lands newly purchased from the Indians. Politicians thus pursued colonial confederation as a method of addressing Indian affairs.

The Albany delegates approved the Plan of Union on July 10 and adjourned to take the proposals back to their respective colonies. Not one colonial legislature accepted the plan. Legislators in seven colonies voted the Plan of Union down. The other six legislatures let the issue die away during the Seven Years' (French and Indian) War. Each colonial legislature had specific reasons for rejecting the Albany Plan. Some politicians feared that the plan gave too much power to the governor. Others feared the creation of a president general. Still others believed that the confederation government threatened the western lands included in their original charters.

Colonial legislators were not the only ones to repudiate the

Plan of Union. The Board of Trade rejected it too, believing the idea of a Grand Council to be cumbersome. They wanted a smaller council, with delegates chosen by the royal governors. They also thought that the Albany Plan gave too much power to colonial assemblies. From the Board of Trade's perspective, the Albany Congress was a failure.

If the Albany Congress was a failure, it was an important one. The congress showed how different England and America had grown since the Glorious Revolution in the 1680's. The Seven Years' War would strain the imperial-colonial relationship even more. The failure of delegates to the Albany Congress to address Iroquois complaints directly forced the home government to become an active participant in colonial-Indian relations. The result was the creation of an Indian superintendent system. This new system, begun in 1755, made imperial policies, not colonial desires, the primary focus of Anglo-Iroquois dialogue in the years to come.

—*Michael J. Mullin*

ADDITIONAL READING:

Alden, John R. "The Albany Congress and the Creation of the Indian Superintendencies." *Mississippi Valley Historical Review* 27, no. 2 (September, 1940): 193-210. Describes how the Albany Congress led British officials to create the Indian superintendent system.

Gipson, Lawrence Henry. "The Drafting of the Albany Plan of Union: The Problem of Semantics." *Pennsylvania History* 26, no. 4 (October, 1959): 291-316. Argues that Thomas Hutchinson was responsible for writing the Albany Plan of Union.

Hopkins, Stephen. *A True Representation of the Plan Formed at Albany.* Providence, R.I.: Sidney S. Rider, 1880. Hopkins, who represented Rhode Island at the Albany Congress, details the issues that delegates discussed concerning Indian affairs.

Mullin, Michael J. "The Albany Congress and Colonial Confederation." *Mid-America* 72, no. 2 (April-July, 1990): 93-105. Discusses the role of Indian affairs at the Congress.

Newbold, Robert C. *The Albany Congress and Plan of Union of 1754.* New York: Vantage Press, 1955. A summation of the scholarship on Albany at the time.

SEE ALSO: 1500, Iroquois Confederacy; 1754, French and Indian War.

1759 ■ CHEROKEE WAR: *total destruction of several Cherokee communities presages the Cherokee alliance with the British in the Revolutionary War*

DATE: October 5, 1759-November 19, 1761

LOCALE: Charles Town, South Carolina, and several Cherokee territories

CATEGORIES: Native American history; Wars, uprisings, and civil unrest

KEY FIGURES:

Attakullakulla (1714?-1781?), Cherokee diplomat

William Bull (1710-1791), Lyttleton's successor

James Grant (1720-1806), commander of the third campaign against the Cherokees

William Henry Lyttelton (1724-1808), governor of South Carolina and commander of the first campaign against the Cherokees

Archibald Montgomery (1719-1796), commander of the second campaign against the Cherokees

Oconostota (c. 1710-1783), Cherokee military leader

SUMMARY OF EVENT. The Cherokees, a Native American people inhabiting the southern Appalachian highlands, first encountered visitors from the Old World on May 30, 1540, during the wanderings of the Spanish explorer Hernando de Soto. For more than a century after this first meeting, the Cherokees had little direct contact with European colonists. During the late seventeenth century and early eighteenth century, trade began to develop between the Cherokees and the English colonies of Virginia, North Carolina, and South Carolina. This relationship was strengthened during the Yamasee War (1715-1716), when the Cherokees were allied with the colonists against other Native American peoples. The relationship was enhanced in 1730, when Scottish aristocrat Alexander Cuming visited the Cherokees and took seven of them to England, where they met King George II and signed a trade agreement. One of the seven was the young Attakullakulla, who would turn out to be the strongest advocate for peace with the English colonists.

The 1750's saw increasing rivalry between France and England, which evolved into the Seven Years' War (1756-1763), a conflict that had already begun to manifest itself in North America as the French and Indian War (1754-1763). Because of the threat of the French and their Native American allies, the South Carolinians built Fort Prince George near the Cherokee town of Keowee in 1753 and Fort Loudoun near the town of Chota in 1756. These forts were designed to offer protection to the Cherokees in exchange for their aid to the English in the war with the French.

From 1756 to 1759, even as the forts were being built, several violent incidents between Cherokees and colonists led the way to war. The most critical of these occurred when a group of Cherokees making their way home from an abortive battle with the French-allied Shawnee through the backcountry of Virginia were attacked by settlers, who killed twenty-four of them. The settlers defended their action by accusing the Cherokees of stealing their horses and food. The governor of Virginia, Robert Dinwiddie, offered gifts and apologies to the relatives of the victims, but many Cherokees demanded retribution. Cherokee warriors killed twenty-four settlers in South Carolina in revenge.

The Cherokee War can be thought of as officially beginning on October 5, 1759, when William Henry Lyttelton, governor of South Carolina, announced his intention to lead an army into Cherokee territory. On October 20, a peace delegation led by Oconostota, the head warrior of the Cherokees, arrived in Charles Town in an attempt to prevent further hostilities. They were placed under arrest and forced to march with the troops. When Lyttelton arrived at Fort Prince George on December 10, the prisoners were held captive inside the fort. Attakullakulla, the most important negotiator for the Cherokees, arrived on December 17 and managed to secure the release of Oconostota and several other prisoners, but twenty-two remained hostages. Lyttelton refused to release them until twenty-four Cherokees were executed for the killing of the settlers. He was forced to retreat on December 28, when symptoms of smallpox, which had been raging in the town of Keowee, began to appear among his troops.

Cherokee warriors led by Oconostota surrounded the fort as soon as Lyttelton left. On February 16, 1760, the commander of the fort was lured out with the promise of negotiation and shot by concealed warriors. In retaliation, the soldiers at the fort killed the hostages. This ended any possibility of preventing a full-scale war and led to attacks on settlers.

William Bull, lieutenant governor and Lyttleton's successor, appealed to General Jeffrey Amherst, supreme commander of British forces in North America, for help. On April 1, twelve hundred soldiers commanded by Colonel Archibald Montgomery arrived in Charles Town. On June 1, they reached Keowee, which they burned to the ground. Other towns in the area, known to the colonists as the Lower Towns, were also destroyed, along with all the crops being grown there.

During these attacks, Montgomery's troops killed sixty Cherokees and took forty prisoners, while facing little opposition. Montgomery relieved the garrison at Fort Prince George and marched toward the area known as the Middle Towns. On June 27, near the town of Echoe, Cherokee warriors launched a surprise attack on the British troops, killing twenty of them and wounding seventy. Although the Cherokees withdrew, the British were forced to retreat. A month later, they left South Carolina to rejoin the war against the French in Canada.

Meanwhile, Oconostota's warriors had surrounded Fort Loudoun. Deprived of the relief given to Fort Prince George, Captain Paul Demere, commander of the fort, surrendered on August 8 rather than face starvation. The surrendering garrison was to turn over all its munitions and be escorted safely out of Cherokee territory. Because Demere attempted to conceal some of the fort's munitions, he and thirty-two of his soldiers were killed and the rest taken prisoner.

Amherst sent two thousand troops under the command of Colonel James Grant to avenge the loss of the fort. On March 20, 1761, Grant left Charles Town, arriving at Fort Prince George on May 27. There he met with Attakullakulla, but Grant refused the Cherokee's offer to intercede with the warriors. On June 7, Grant left the fort and headed for the Middle Towns. On June 10, within two miles of the place where Montgomery's troops were attacked, Grant fought a battle with the Cherokees, leaving ten British soldiers killed and fifty wounded. The Cherokees withdrew because of a lack of ammunition. Grant spent the next month destroying fifteen

Middle Towns and fifteen hundred acres of crops. Approximately five thousand Cherokees were forced to flee into the forest to survive on whatever food they could find in the wild.

After this devastating attack, Attakullakulla and several other Cherokee leaders met with Grant at Fort Prince George to ask for peace. A treaty was prepared demanding the execution of four Cherokee leaders, the elimination of all relations between the Cherokees and the French, the sovereignty of the British courts over all offenders within Cherokee territory, and the establishment of a line twenty-six miles east of Keowee as the border of South Carolina. The Cherokees could not accept the demand for executions. Attakullakulla asked to speak to Bull directly. He was allowed to travel to Charles Town and was welcomed by the governor as a loyal friend of the English. The demand for executions was dropped, and the treaty was signed on September 23. A separate treaty was signed with Virginia on November 19, officially ending the Cherokee War.

Conflicts between the Cherokees and the colonists continued until well after the end of the American Revolution (1783), during which the Cherokees were allied with the British. A series of land cessions to the newly independent United States during the late eighteenth and early nineteenth centuries left the Cherokees with only a small portion of their land. In a final attempt to survive as an independent people, the Cherokees adopted the ways of the Americans, even going so far as to set up a government modeled after that of the United States. Despite this effort, the Cherokees were finally forced to leave their native land for Oklahoma during the infamous Trail of Tears removals in the 1830's.   —*Rose Secrest*

ADDITIONAL READING:

Corkran, David H. *The Cherokee Frontier: Conflict and Survival 1740-1762*. Norman: University of Oklahoma Press, 1962. A detailed account of the complex relations between the Cherokees and English colonists during the mid-1700's.

Hatley, Tom. *The Dividing Paths: Cherokees and South Carolinians Through the Era of Revolution*. New York: Oxford University Press, 1993. Focuses on the multicultural aspects of the Cherokee War, including a discussion of the roles of women and African slaves.

Mails, Thomas E. "Transformation of a Culture." In *The Cherokee People: The Story of the Cherokees from Earliest Origins to Contemporary Times*. Tulsa, Okla.: Council Oak Books, 1992. Describes the history of relations between Cherokees and Europeans up to the Trail of Tears.

Milling, Chapman J. "The Cherokee War." In *Red Carolinians*. Chapel Hill: University of North Carolina Press, 1940. A detailed, carefully documented account of the war. An important reference despite its age.

Woodward, Grace Steele. "'The King, Our Father.'" In *The Cherokees*. Norman: University of Oklahoma Press, 1963. A history of the Cherokee people from the start of the Yamassee War until the end of the Cherokee War.

SEE ALSO: 1539, De Soto's Expeditions; 1754, French and Indian War; 1777, Battle of Oriskany Creek.

1763 ■ PONTIAC'S RESISTANCE: *a pan-Indian uprising presents the greatest threat to British expansion before the American Revolution*

DATE: May 8, 1763-July 24, 1766
LOCALE: Great Lakes region
CATEGORIES: Native American history; Wars, uprisings, and civil unrest
KEY FIGURES:
Jeffrey Amherst (1717-1797), commander of British forces in America during the French and Indian War
Henry Gladwin (1729-1791), British major who resisted Pontiac's siege of Detroit
William Johnson (1715-1774), British commander who imposed a lenient peace on Pontiac's forces
Pontiac, also known as *Obwandiag* (c. 1720-1769), Ottawa war chief who organized pan-Indian resistance to the British
William Petty Shelburne (1737-1805), British statesman who recommended separating western lands from the colonies
Tenskwatawa, also known as *the Prophet* (1768-1837), religious leader who reportedly inspired Pontiac

SUMMARY OF EVENT. Having signed the Treaty of Paris on February 10, 1763, Great Britain and France concluded the French and Indian War, nearly a decade of battle for empire in North America. Victorious, Great Britain then had to decide how to organize its vast new territories, embracing Canada and the area lying between the Appalachians and the Mississippi River. At issue in these trans-Appalachian lands were the rights, vital interests, profits, and responsibilities of the remaining Frenchmen, fur traders and trappers, British governors and colonials with claims to these territories, land speculators, the British Army, and, not least, Native Americans. A plan to separate trans-Appalachia from eastern British colonies and keep out settlers had been recommended by William Shelburne, then president of Britain's Board of Trade. Shelburne had hoped that his plan would be implemented by 1767, but despite amounting political pressure for Parliament to act on imperial reorganization, nothing was done until Shelburne had left office. What determined his successor's action and his issuance of the Proclamation of 1763 was an native uprising and the siege of the British fort at Detroit by a little-known Ottawa war chief, Pontiac.

A large, imposing figure, Pontiac was born in present-day northern Ohio, the son of an Ottawa father and an Chippewa (Ojibwa) mother. Although he married several times (as was customary), only one of his wives and two sons have been identified. Esteemed for his strategic skills and his intelligence, he had become a war chief by 1755, when he was in his mid-thirties. The Ottawa, like most of their neighbors, were traders who had profited from close relationships with the French and who, therefore, fought with French forces in America during the French and Indian War. Pontiac had fought with the French when they defeated British troops commanded by General Braddock at Fort Pitt in western Pennsylvania.

France's defeat, sealed by the Treaty of Paris, proved disastrous to frontier natives, who were constrained thereafter to deal with the British. Contrary to the intent of the Proclamation of 1763, colonial settlers poured across the Appalachians into American Indian territories. In addition, Lord Jeffrey Amherst, commander in chief of British forces, discontinued bestowing on the tribes gifts and supplies, the most import of which was gunpowder. During the war, Amherst had also provided alcohol to the natives, but he refused to dispense it at war's end. Thus, genuine hardship from a lack of gunpowder, which curtailed their hunting and disrupted their fur trade, an unslaked addiction to drink, discomfort due the diminution of other supplies, and increasing white encroachments on their lands furnished many Great Lakes tribes with serious grievances against the British.

On April 27, 1763, Pontiac convened a general war council in order to finalize war plans that envisaged a wholesale assault on British forts along the frontier. His call to arms solicited support from Chippewas, Lenni Lenapes (Delawares), Hurons, Illinois, Kickapoos, Miamis, Mingos, Potawatomis, Senecas, and Shawnees. On May 8, 1763, he and three hundred warriors—mostly his own tribesmen, along with Chippewas and Potawatomis—entered Fort Detroit, weapons concealed and ready to strike. Previously alerted to Pontiac's intentions, however, Major Henry Gladwin foiled Pontiac's attack from within and the natives put Gladwin's fort under what became a six-month siege. Within weeks, every British fort west of Niagara was destroyed: Forts Sandusky, St. Joseph, Miami, Quiatenon, Venango, Le Boeuf, Michilimackinac, Edward Augustus, and Presque Isle. Forts in the Monongahela Valley, such as Fort Ligonier, were attacked. Only Fort Pitt and Detroit survived. Before the winter of 1763, the British had suffered costly ambushes such as one outside Detroit at Blood Ridge and counted two thousand casualties overall.

Fearful that their entire frontier would collapse, the British counterattacked. By late fall, tribal resistance weakened, as the natives were unused to protracted warfare and lacked the measure of aid they had expected from the French. At Fort Pitt, blankets distributed by the fort commander, Captain Simon Ecuyer, infected besieging natives and produced a devastating smallpox epidemic, while another of Amherst's commanders tracked them with English hunting dogs. In late autumn, Pontiac lifted the siege of Detroit, although elsewhere some Indian forces continued fighting throughout 1764. Other tribes, however, had concluded peace treaties with Colonel John Bradstreet at Presque Isle as early as August, 1763. By July, 1765, Pontiac had entered peace negotiations that resulted in a treaty signed with the British at Oswego on July 24, 1766, a treaty under which he was pardoned.

Following his pardon, Pontiac was received with hostility by neighbors in his Maumee River village and he, his family, and a handful of supporters were driven out by tribe members who wanted resistance to continue. While at a trading post in Cahokia (Illinois), Pontiac was murdered in April, 1769, by Black Dog, a Peoria Indian whom the British may have paid in hopes of forestalling future rebellions.

In the aftermath of Pontiac's resistance, the British, apprehensive about a renewal of Native American resistance, altered their Indian policy. They abandoned their Indian posts everywhere in the West, except at Detroit, Michilimackinac, and Niagara, and cross-mountain trade was placed again in colonial hands. British authorities, seeking to remove yet another cause of native grievances, renewed the practice of favoring tribes with sumptuous gifts. Unable to stem the tide of European settlers into trans-Appalachian tribal lands, as the Proclamation Line of 1763 was intended to do, British representative William Johnson negotiated a new boundary with Iroquois leaders at Fort Stanwix in September, 1768. This line was drawn farther west, in hopes of lessening chances of friction between the natives and the settlers. Britain's concerns over Native American affairs soon gave way to coping with rising resistance among its own colonials.

In retrospect, Pontiac's pan-Indian alliance represented the greatest threat mounted by Native Americans against Great Britain's New World expansion prior to the outbreak of the American Revolution. It dramatically launched Native American resistance to white civilization, resistance that subsequently included uprisings by Little Turtle (1790-1794) and by Tecumseh (1809-1811) and, during the last three decades of the nineteenth century, drew the U.S. military into the lengthiest and most numerous succession of campaigns in its history, ending with the Battle of Wounded Knee in 1890. —*Mary E. Virginia*

ADDITIONAL READING:

Hawke, David. *The Colonial Experience.* Indianapolis: Bobbs-Merrill, 1966. Chapter 13 brilliantly places Pontiac's resistance in the context of Great Britain's halting steps toward imperial reorganization.

Leach, Douglas E. *Arms for Empire: A Military History of the British Colonies in North America, 1607-1763.* New York: Macmillan, 1973. A formidable study that details the increasingly impossible task Great Britain faced in trying to devise an effective military defense for a vast colonial empire against France and Spain, British colonists, and Native Americans. The latter chapters provide excellent background on Pontiac's resistance.

_____. "Colonial Indian Wars." In *History of Indian-White Relations,* edited by Wilcomb B. Washburn. Vol. 4 in *Handbook of North American Indians.* Washington, D.C.: Smithsonian Institution Press, 1988. More specific in its focus than the Leach study, this article combines British and American Indian politics and perspectives in the context of colonial wars.

Parkman, Francis. *The Conspiracy of Pontiac and the Indian War After the Conquest of Canada.* 7th ed. Boston: Little, Brown, 1874. Despite minor inaccuracies, this remains the classic study of the subject. Based on original documents and written by one of the greatest of American historians.

Peckham, Howard. *Pontiac and the Indian Uprising.* Princeton, N.J.: Princeton University Press, 1947. Corrects Parkman's inaccuracies, updates the subject, and provides fresh insights into American Indian attitudes.

Sosin, Jack M. *Whitehall and the Wilderness: The Middle West in British Colonial Policy, 1760-1775.* Lincoln: University of Nebraska Press, 1961. Concentrates on the evolution of British policy in trans-Appalachia between 1760 and 1765, including British adjustments to Pontiac's resistance.

SEE ALSO: 1754, French and Indian War; 1763, Proclamation of 1763.

1763 ■ PROCLAMATION OF 1763: *the British draw a frontier line between Native Americans and colonists, hoping to avoid more costly conflicts*

DATE: October 7, 1763
LOCALE: London, England
CATEGORIES: Canadian history; Expansion and land acquisition; Laws and acts; Native American history
KEY FIGURES:
Jeffrey Amherst (1717-1797), British commander in chief in North America from 1759, and governor general of British North America, 1760-1763
George Montagu Dunk, earl of Halifax (1716-1771), president of the Board of Trade, 1748-1761
Thomas Gage (1721-1787), British general in North America, 1763-1776
Wills Hill, earl of Hillsborough, marquis of Downshire (1718-1793), president of the Board of Trade, 1763-1765
William Johnson (1715-1774), superintendent of Native American affairs, 1755-1774
William Petty, second earl of Shelburne, marquis of Lansdowne (1737-1805), president of the Board of Trade, 1763, and secretary of state for the Southern Department, 1766-1768
Charles Wyndham, second earl of Egremont (1710-1763), secretary of state for the Southern Department, 1761-1763

SUMMARY OF EVENT. How would Great Britain, victorious in the French and Indian War against France and its allies, control the vast domain between the Appalachian Mountains and the Mississippi River after 1763? The answer to that question interested not only Native Americans, French Canadians, and British colonial administrators but also American fur traders, merchants, and land speculators. The trans-Appalachian West had increasingly occupied the attention of British and colonial officials since the Albany Congress of 1754. During the ensuing war, the Crown appointed superintendents to coordinate Native American affairs—Sir William Johnson for the Northern Department and Edmund Atkin (replaced by John Stuart in 1762) for the Southern Department—but exigencies of the moment made the new arrangement inadequate. In the eyes of

PROCLAMATION LINE OF 1763

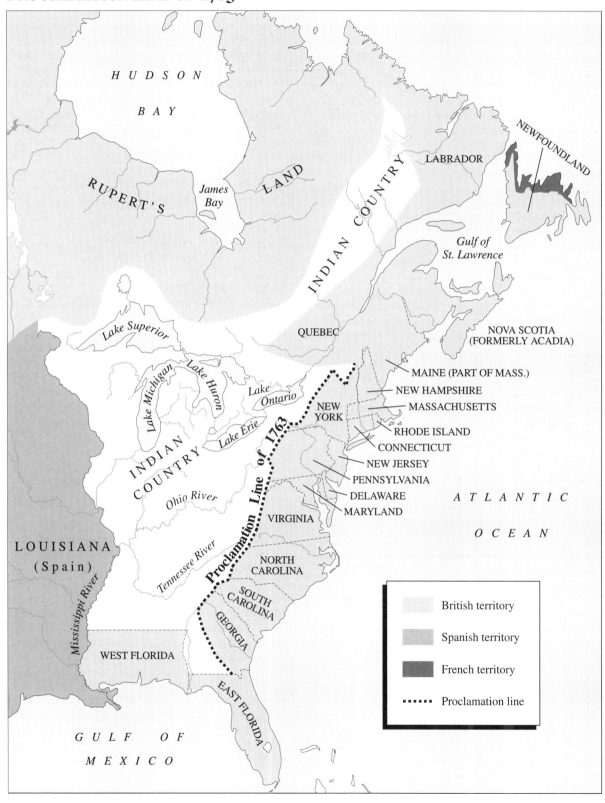

HUDSON

BAY

RUPERT'S

James
Bay

LAND

INDIAN COUNTRY

LABRADOR

NEWFOUNDLAND

Gulf of
St. Lawrence

Lake Superior

QUEBEC

NOVA SCOTIA
(FORMERLY ACADIA)

Lake Michigan

Lake Huron

Lake
Ontario

MAINE (PART OF MASS.)

NEW HAMPSHIRE

MASSACHUSETTS

NEW
YORK

RHODE ISLAND

Lake Erie

CONNECTICUT

INDIAN
COUNTRY

NEW JERSEY

PENNSYLVANIA

Ohio River

DELAWARE

MARYLAND

ATLANTIC

VIRGINIA

OCEAN

Tennessee River

LOUISIANA
(Spain)

NORTH
CAROLINA

Mississippi River

SOUTH
CAROLINA

GEORGIA

WEST FLORIDA

Proclamation Line of 1763

EAST FLORIDA

GULF   OF

MEXICO

British territory

Spanish territory

French territory

Proclamation line

Whitehall officials, the old policy of leaving control of the frontier to the individual colonies had been chaotic and ruinous. The line of Euro-American agricultural settlement had steadily edged westward, with scant regard for Native American land claims or indigenous culture. Royal governors, superintendents for Native American affairs, and British military men repeatedly had complained that the colonists disregarded Native American treaties and made fraudulent land purchases, and that Euro-American traders mistreated the tribal peoples.

The necessity of reaching an accord with the Native Americans seemed even more urgent with Pontiac's Resistance, which had begun in the spring of 1763. The indigenous population, already uneasy over the defeat of their French allies, encountered repeated insults from the British commander in chief, General Jeffrey Amherst, who refused to present them with guns, ammunition, and other gifts, as had been the French custom. Striking first in the remoter sections of the West, such as at Fort Michilimackinac, and later on the Pennsylvania frontier, roving parties of Ottawas, Chippewas, Lenni Lenapes (Delawares), and Senecas overran one British-occupied post after another; by the end of June, only Forts Detroit, Pitt, and Niagara still held out against the warriors. Amherst, near recall from the home government, dispatched relief expeditions to his remaining garrisons, and several colonies raised troops to repel the indigenous combatants. The prospect of fire and sword, the diplomatic skills of William Johnson, Pontiac's calling off the sieges, and the breakup of the coalition of tribes—which never was united on ultimate objectives—explain the demise of the rebellion and restoration of peace in 1764. Anxious to bring an end to hostilities and avoid another outbreak, the British exacted little retribution from the western tribes.

During the uprising, the government announced its new policy for the West, one that had evolved from British experience in the French and Indian War. It was the work of no single minister or subminister, although Charles Wyndham (the earl of Egremont and secretary of state for the Southern Department, 1761-1763), William Petty (the earl of Shelburne, president of the Board of Trade in 1763 and later secretary of state for the Southern Department), and Wills Hill (the earl of Hillsborough, president of the Board of Trade from 1763 to 1765 and later secretary of state for the colonies) were keenly interested in the matter.

On October 7, 1763, King George III signed the edict now known as the Proclamation of 1763. By its terms, the recently acquired territories of Canada and East and West Florida became Crown colonies, and their inhabitants became entitled to the same rights as the English at home. The proclamation nullified all colonial claims to territories west of the crest of the Appalachians and set those lands aside for Native Americans "for the present, and until our further Pleasure be known." Wishing to monopolize the substantial and lucrative fur trade of the area, Whitehall hardly wanted colonial farmers crowding out the furbearers' habitat and local traders competing for the business. The trade with the tribal peoples would be "free and open," although traders would have to obtain a license and obey any pertinent regulations. As the Proclamation of 1763 contained no provision for law enforcement in the area beyond provincial boundaries, an ad hoc system of confining trade to a few forts under superintendent and military supervision developed. The Crown expected that the colonials would obey the edict out of allegiance to England. Moreover, the royal government hoped that restless colonists would move northward into the thinly settled districts of Maine, Nova Scotia, and New Brunswick to offset the Catholic French Canadian population there and in Quebec, or relocate southward into Georgia to bolster that buffer province against the Spaniards.

Native Americans in the region heard about the Proclamation Line and watched some of the actual surveying with distrust and bemusement. The document promised that

> the several Nations or Tribes of Indians with whom We are connected, and who live under Our Protection should not be molested or disturbed in the Possession of such Parts of our Dominions and Territories as, not having been ceded to, or purchased by Us, are reserved to them, or any of them, as their Hunting Grounds.

British general Thomas Gage rushed copies westward, because he imagined that "these Arrangements must be very satisfactory to the Indians." The tribes, however, had witnessed earlier attempts at boundary treaties, such as at Easton and Lancaster, Pennsylvania, in 1758 and 1760 respectively, and in South Carolina in 1761, crumble as squatters leapfrogged the line.

In the long run, Great Britain's "western policy" failed. Land-hungry settlers spilled over into the trans-Appalachia area in defiance of the Proclamation of 1763. British troops could not guard every mountain gap, nor could they and royal superintendents force traders to patronize specific posts. Several ambitious Virginia speculators, some of whom later joined the patriot cause in the revolution, had claims across the divide. Faced with the prospect of worthless holdings, they pressed for repeal of the order. The maintenance of western garrisons was expensive, especially when American revenues for the army's upkeep failed to materialize, and when the troops did not accomplish their mission. In 1768, the British government, beset with these problems and colonial rebelliousness in the eastern regions, adopted a policy of retrenchment in the West. Control of the trade with Native Americans reverted to the individual colonies, and British troops received orders to abandon all the interior posts except Niagara, Detroit, and Michilimackinac. Almost simultaneously, the government bowed to pressure to push the Native American boundary westward. The Treaty of Fort Stanwix (1768) with the Iroquois Confederacy and the Treaties of Hard Labor (1768) and Lochaber (1770) with the Cherokee signified this change. No longer did the trans-Appalachian West loom uppermost in British imperial policy.

—*R. Don Higginbotham, updated by Thomas L. Altherr*

ADDITIONAL READING:

Jennings, Francis. *Empires of Fortune: Crowns, Colonies, and Tribes in the Seven Years War in America*. New York: W. W. Norton, 1988. Contains a short discussion of the Proclamation of 1763 and the Native American response.

Martin, James Kirby. *In the Course of Human Events: An Interpretive Exploration of the American Revolution*. Arlington Heights, Ill.: Harlan Davidson, 1979. Links the Proclamation of 1763 with other British decisions to control the colonies, such as stationing ships in American waters.

"Proclamation of 1763: Governor Henry Ellis' Plan May 5, 1763." In *The American Revolution, 1763-1783: A Bicentennial Collection*, edited by Richard B. Morris. Columbia: University of South Carolina Press, 1970. Demonstrates the thinking by one colonial official that prompted the Proclamation of 1763.

Sosin, Jack M. *Whitehall and the Wilderness: The Middle West in British Colonial Policy, 1760-1775*. Lincoln: University of Nebraska Press, 1961. Detailed examination of royal decisions leading to the Proclamation of 1763.

Stagg, Jack. *Anglo-Indian Relations in North America to 1763 and an Analysis of the Royal Proclamation of 7 October 1763*. Ottawa: Research Branch, Indian and Northern Affairs Canada, 1981. Provides a detailed interpretation of the text of the Proclamation of 1763 and the Crown's motives.

Steele, Ian K. *Warpaths: Invasions of North America*. New York: Oxford University Press, 1994. Places the decisions for the Proclamation of 1763 within the context of the military actions of the recent war and earlier treaties.

SEE ALSO: 1754, French and Indian War; 1763, Pontiac's Resistance; 1784, Fort Stanwix Treaty.

1763 ■ PAXTON BOYS' MASSACRES:
growing tensions between Pennsylvania backcountry settlers and Native Americans reflect western resentment of inequitable representation

DATE: December 14-27, 1763
LOCALE: A Conestoga village near Lancaster, Pennsylvania
CATEGORIES: Expansion and land acquisition; Native American history; Wars, uprisings, and civil unrest
KEY FIGURES:
John Elder (1706-1792), Presbyterian minister who became a spokesman for the Paxton Boys
Benjamin Franklin (1706-1790), prominent Philadelphia politician who negotiated with the Paxton Boys
John Penn (1729-1795), governor of Pennsylvania
SUMMARY OF EVENT. The French and Indian War was a particularly difficult time for settlers in the Pennsylvania backcountry. By the early 1750's, the harmony that had characterized the relationship between Native Americans and the colony since the time of William Penn had ended. Led by the

Six Nations of the Iroquois Confederacy, various Pennsylvania tribes, encompassing numerous Native American villages throughout the region, fought to limit future European expansion onto ancestral lands. The struggle engendered much bloodshed and carnage on both sides.

During the war, the Pennsylvania Assembly, influenced by pacific Quakers, pursued a policy of negotiations rather than resorting to armed confrontation. Despite pleas from embattled backcountry residents for military assistance, provincial leaders steadfastly refused to organize or outfit an official militia. As a result, western residents were left to fend for themselves. By the 1760's, the Quaker policy had produced some minimal results. Pennsylvania authorities were able to reestablish peaceful relations with a few villages. Cooperative tribes were promised land rights, commercial opportunities, and protection from their enemies. However, many villages questioned the sincerity of the offers and remained at war. This put backcountry residents in a particularly difficult situation. It was virtually impossible for them to differentiate between peaceful and hostile natives, a distinction that could become a matter of life or death. Therefore, many homesteaders chose simply to label all of the indigenous population as hostile until all had agreed to a peace.

On the morning of December 14, 1763, the tensions generated the first of two massacres. A band of approximately four dozen angry Pennsylvania backwoodsmen attacked an unsuspecting Conestoga village situated approximately fifty miles northwest of Lancaster. The village was inhabited by fewer than two dozen Susquehannocks. A month earlier, in a petition to Governor John Penn, these same Susquehannocks had promised to maintain the peace that they claimed they had always honored. Nevertheless, the Pennsylvanians, who called themselves the Paxton Boys, complained that villagers were assisting and sheltering Native American warriors. Several of the warriors were believed to have murdered nearby settlers. In the assault, the Paxton Boys struck quickly, burning the village's huts and killing three Susquehannock men, two women, and a child.

Panicked by the raid, fourteen Susquehannock survivors fled to the safety of provincial authorities in Lancaster. Upon their arrival, the refugees were placed under protective custody and held in the town jail. It was there that the Paxton Boys found them on December 27, and it was there that the backwoodsmen committed a second massacre. Enraged that local officials would shelter the natives, a force of about one hundred well-armed Paxton Boys rode up to the jailhouse. They burst into the building, seized the keeper, and then shot and tomahawked the defenseless Susquehannocks. A few minutes later, with their task accomplished, the backwoods raiders rode off to their homes, satisfied that they had taken an important step toward easing the Native American threat within the region.

News of the two attacks created a flurry of activity in Philadelphia. Governor Penn immediately issued a proclamation instructing western magistrates to apprehend those involved in the massacres. Colonial officials, fearing additional assaults, rounded up 125 friendly Native Americans, many of whom had converted to Moravianism, and brought them to Philadelphia. Meanwhile, the colonial Assembly asked New York authorities to provide a sanctuary for the refugees. However, the New York governor denied the request. Instead, a regiment of British regulars was assigned to escort the "Moravian Indians" to a military barracks on a Delaware River island and to defend them against all potential assailants. The Assembly's precautions were not popular in the backcountry. John Elder, a Presbyterian minister and militia colonel who was alleged to be the Paxton Boys' organizer, warned that "the minds of the inhabitants are so exasperated against the Quakers" that western residents were ready to confront the Assembly and take matters into their own hands.

By late January, 1764, reports about an impending attack by the Paxton Boys swirled through Philadelphia. One letter to Governor Penn claimed that fifteen hundred well-armed backwoodsmen, a force three times larger than the British regiment guarding the Native Americans, were planning to march on the city and go door to door until they had found all the Native Americans in Philadelphia. The westerners intended to burn down the houses of those who resisted. The letter ended with a prediction that the backwoodsmen would fight to the death, if necessary.

The rumored march became a reality in early February. Although considerably smaller than most reports had forecast, a force of two hundred backwoods residents, comprising primarily Scotch-Irish Presbyterians from the lower Susquehanna River region, began a hike toward the provincial capital. Armed with muskets, tomahawks, and pistols, they announced that they were coming to Philadelphia to rectify the various abuses directed at them by the Assembly.

Intercepting the westerners at Germantown, five miles northwest of the city, Benjamin Franklin led a delegation appointed by the governor. Matthew Smith and James Gibson, two militia officers, presented Franklin with a petition that identified nine specific grievances. Surprisingly, the primary complaint had nothing to do with the colony's Native American policy. Instead, the Paxton Boys protested that the four western counties had significantly less representation in the Assembly than did the three eastern counties. If this inequity were rectified, the backwoodsmen claimed that the other eight complaints, all of which dealt with policies concerning Native Americans, would be remedied.

While Franklin conferred, other Philadelphians prepared for an attack. Some local residents insisted that the force in Germantown was simply an advance unit of Paxton Boys and that hundreds more would soon arrive. To defend the city against the "Lawless Party of Rioters," the Assembly swiftly enacted emergency legislation. Six companies, each with one hundred volunteers, were hastily organized. Cannons were pulled into defensive positions around the courthouse. Shops were closed. The roads and ferries leading into the city were blockaded. The British regiment guarding the Native American refugees was placed on alert.

Aided by the city's impressive mobilization, Franklin's deliberations proved fruitful. The westerners agreed that if their petition were promptly delivered to the governor and Assembly, they would return home. In a gesture aimed at compromise, the Philadelphia delegation announced that the Paxton Boys had been misunderstood and were, in fact, "a set of worthy men who laboured under great distress." The delegation then accompanied about thirty backwoodsmen into the city. The following day, one of the visitors was permitted to inspect several Native Americans to determine whether they had been involved in recent attacks upon settlers. They had not. Several days later, the westerners' petition was presented to the legislature.

In July, the Assembly responded legislatively to the Paxton Boys' demands. Pennsylvania formally declared war against the Lenni Lenape and Shawnee tribes. A bounty for Native American scalps, another of the westerners' demands, was enacted. Money also was appropriated for the creation of an official provincial militia, something the Quaker government had steadfastly refused to do, even during the French and Indian War. The colony's search for the Paxton Boys involved in the two massacres had ended months earlier, with no arrests made.

Pennsylvania felt the impact of the Paxton Boys' activities for years to come. Most important, the crisis initiated an ongoing dispute about fair and equitable representation for western counties. It was a contest in which political power eventually shifted away from Philadelphia Quakers and toward a diverse and democratic coalition of political leadership. Ultimately, the crisis surrounding the Paxton Boys' massacres served as an initial step toward the political divisions that generated an independence movement within the colony.

—Paul E. Doutrich

ADDITIONAL READING:

Franz, George W. *Paxton: A Study of Community Structure and Mobility in the Colonial Pennsylvania Backcountry*. New York: Garland, 1989. Focuses on political and socioeconomic development of the Paxton community.

Hindle, Brooke. "The March of the Paxton Boys." *William and Mary Quarterly*, 3d ser., 3 (October, 1946): 461-486. Still one of the best narrative accounts of the massacres.

Jacobs, Wilbur R. *The Paxton Riots and the Frontier Theory*. Chicago: Rand McNally, 1967. A brief booklet that includes many primary documents produced during the episode.

Kelley, Joseph J., Jr. *Pennsylvania: The Colonial Years*. Garden City, N.Y.: Doubleday, 1980. Includes a general description of the Paxton Boys episode.

Schwartz, Sally. *"A Mixed Multitude": The Struggle for Toleration in Colonial Pennsylvania*. New York: New York University Press. 1987. A general history that describes the various tensions within colonial Pennsylvania and how the colony dealt with them.

SEE ALSO: 1681, Pennsylvania Is Founded; 1737, Walking Purchase; 1754, French and Indian War; 1763, Proclamation of 1763.

1765 ■ STAMP ACT CRISIS: *the first direct tax on the colonies leads to the first in a series of events culminating in the Revolutionary War*

DATE: March 22, 1765-1766
LOCALE: America and Great Britain
CATEGORIES: Economics; Laws and acts; Wars, uprisings, and civil unrest
KEY FIGURES:
Daniel Dulany (1722-1797), Maryland lawyer who wrote the most significant pamphlet attacking the Stamp Act
Benjamin Franklin (1706-1790), colonial agent in London
George Grenville (1712-1770), head of the British ministry, 1763-1765, chiefly responsible for the program of American taxation
Patrick Henry (1736-1799), colonist who led the Virginia House of Burgesses in adopting resolutions against taxation
Charles Watson Wentworth, second marquis of Rockingham (1730-1782), Grenville's successor as first minister, who secured the Stamp Act's repeal
Thomas Whatley, treasury official who prepared the Stamp Act
SUMMARY OF EVENT. In 1763, the British national debt had soared to a level double that prior to the French and Indian War. Besides finding revenues to meet the interest on this war debt, George Grenville, the first minister, needed additional funds to administer a greatly enlarged empire. Although Parliament had never before placed direct taxes on the colonies, Grenville persuaded that body to approve the Sugar Act of 1764 and the Stamp Act of 1765. The decision to tax America was momentous in its consequences. The intensity of the colonists' opposition shocked most people in England, and on both sides of the Atlantic the crisis produced an atmosphere of tension and mistrust that influenced all subsequent Anglo-American relations before the American Revolution.

Grenville, a narrow-minded financial expert, amassed impressive statistics to show that the prosperous colonists were lightly taxed compared to the English at home. The Sugar Act grew out of Grenville's discovery that the American customs service was costing the government more to maintain than it was collecting in revenues. The colonists were evading payment of the import duties—sixpence a gallon—on foreign molasses, which was required under the Molasses Act of 1733. Grenville revamped the customs service and ordered the Royal Navy to guard against smuggling. The Sugar Act itself cut the molasses duty to threepence a gallon, a sum Grenville believed would be enforceable without ruining the New England rum industry. It was clear that colonial rum distillers needed more molasses than the British West Indian sugar islands could provide. The new statute placed additional duties on colonial imports, increased restrictions on colonial exports, and added to the difficulties of smugglers by strengthening the

system of vice-admiralty courts. The preamble to the Sugar Act, unlike the Molasses Act, made it clear that the law of 1764 was not designed primarily to regulate trade; it stated "that a revenue be raised" in His Majesty's dominions. Subsequently, Grenville introduced his Stamp Act, passed by Parliament and signed by the king on March 22, 1765, to become effective on November 1. Taxes fell on every kind of legal document and on playing cards, dice, and almanacs. Each item was to carry a stamp indicating payment of the tax. Offenders were to be tried in vice-admiralty courts (without trial by jury), which formerly had jurisdiction only over affairs relating to

As a result of the tension surrounding the hated Stamp Act—the first direct tax levied on the American colonists—secret societies such as the Sons of Liberty rose during the summer of 1765 and organized demonstrations against the tax. Violence was one means of making their voices heard, and in a famous instance in Boston on August 26, 1765 (not 1764, as this German depiction of two decades later indicates), Stamp Act papers were burned and the homes of British officials were ransacked and looted. (Library of Congress)

the sea and commerce. New taxes meant payments in cash, but money—always scarce in the agriculturally oriented colonies—became tighter than ever because Grenville, in 1764, had persuaded Parliament to adopt the Currency Act, which forbade the provincials from continuing to make their own paper money as legal tender.

The colonists found much to displease them in Grenville's program. Merchants thought the rum industry would not be able to stand the threepence duty on molasses, and they found the new customs procedures complicated and difficult. The currency restrictions promised to make silver in shorter supply than ever. Colonists also thought it was unfair to try Stamp Act offenders in courts, devoid of juries, possessing authority beyond that permitted the courts in England. Even more important to Americans, Parliament's direct taxes seemed to deprive them of their rights as British subjects to be taxed only by their elected representatives. The colonists were represented in their own assemblies but not in the House of Commons. They vigorously approved the pamphlet written by Maryland lawyer Daniel Dulany, who denied the contention of Englishman Thomas Whatley that all residents of the empire were, in effect, represented in Parliament, which allegedly looked after the interests of all, regardless of whether one had the opportunity (as many local Englishmen did not) to vote for members of the House of Commons. American writers quoted John Locke, political philosopher of the England's Glorious Revolution of 1688, who said that the most esteemed right of people was the right of property, without which both life and liberty were endangered.

The Virginia House of Burgesses, prodded by young Patrick Henry, took the lead in drafting remonstrances against Parliamentary taxation. Soon afterward, the Massachusetts legislature issued a call for a congress from all the colonies to meet to consider ways of securing relief. The Stamp Act Congress, Meeting October 7 to 27, 1765, in New York and attended by delegates from nine colonies, acknowledged Parliament's authority to regulate trade (to legislate) for the welfare of the whole empire, while rejecting its right to tax America. By November 1, the date the stamps were to go on sale, none were available. The Sons of Liberty had "persuaded" almost every designated stamp distributor to resign. Colonial merchants also aided the cause by curtailing imports from Britain until the oppressive Stamp Act was repealed.

In 1766, Grenville was out of office (for reasons unrelated to America), and the ministry was under Charles Watson Wentworth, marquis of Rockingham. The marquis, who had opposed the Stamp Act, now listened to the outcries of British merchants suffering from the colonial economic boycott. By stressing the disruption of trade and ignoring American rioting, and by employing Benjamin Franklin's erroneous testimony that the colonists opposed only internal taxes (the Stamp Act), Rockingham secured repeal of the Stamp Act—after Parliament passed the vaguely worded Declaratory Act, a bill that affirmed Parliament's right "make laws and statutes . . . to bind the colonies . . . in all cases whatsoever." Americans rejoiced at the outcome without knowing the Declaratory Act's precise meaning.

In the latter half of the twentieth century, many historians have posited that the American Revolution was not predestined, not in the third quarter of the eighteenth century at least, especially if the mother country had displayed more enlightened leadership. Some historians place the blame for the first imperial controversy squarely upon George Grenville. Grenville, although pretending otherwise, had made no real effort to allow the colonies to raise revenues on their own to aid in the upkeep of the empire; in fact, the first minister discouraged Massachusetts and the agents of various colonies and London from devising means to acquire needed revenue in America. From this viewpoint, Americans appear less irresponsible in facing up to their imperial obligations than they have been depicted to be by more traditional historians. In this more modern view, the actual stamp tax would have been a small expense to almost all the colonists and the crux of the American opposition was, therefore, a matter of the constitutional principle of no taxation without representation. These later historians also part company from previous historians by demonstrating that Americans objected not only to internal taxes (the Stamp Act) but also to external taxes (the Sugar Act) in 1765-1766. During the following decade, the colonists consistently adhered to this constitutional principle, while they continued to recognize the need for Parliament to legislate in the interest of harmonizing trade and commerce for the welfare of all the empire's parts—but not for revenue.

—R. Don Higginbotham, updated by Liesel Ashley Miller

ADDITIONAL READING:

Bridenbaugh, Carl. *Mitre and Sceptre: Transatlantic Faiths, Ideas, Personalities, and Politics, 1689-1775.* New York: Oxford University Press, 1962. Asserts that American fears of an Anglican establishment throughout the colonies were a factor in the growth of American nationalism and a hitherto neglected cause of the American Revolution.

Gipson, Lawrence H. *The Coming of the Revolution, 1763-1775.* New York: Harper & Row, 1954. Representative of the traditional imperial school of American historiography, Gipson sees the American Revolution as an inevitable development, with growing American nationalism as the prime cause.

Knollenberg, Bernhard. *Origin of the American Revolution: 1759-1766.* New York: Macmillan, 1960. Complements and amplifies the Morgans' account of the first imperial crisis. Knollenberg discovers little evidence of colonial unhappiness with the British Empire as it existed before the Seven Years' War.

Morgan, Edmund S., and Helen M. Morgan. *The Stamp Act Crisis.* Chapel Hill: University of North Carolina Press, 1995. Provides a revisionist look at the events surrounding the Stamp Act crisis and blames Grenville for the crisis. Focuses on constitutional principles and the ideas of the Revolutionists.

Thomas, P. D. G. *British Politics and the Stamp Act Crisis.* Oxford, England: Clarendon Press, 1975. A study of the policies and attitudes of Great Britain toward the American colonies in the years leading up to the American Revolution.

Weslager, C. A. *The Stamp Act Congress*. Newark: University of Delaware Press, 1976. A thorough documentation of the Stamp Act Congress, wherein the principles of opposition to the Stamp Act were first formulated. Contains the first available journal of the Stamp Act Congress in its entirety.

SEE ALSO: 1754, French and Indian War; 1767, Townshend Crisis.

1767 ■ TOWNSHEND CRISIS: *British laws, designed to tighten economic and political controls on the colonies, prompt American resistance*

DATE: June 29, 1767-April 12, 1770
LOCALE: America and Britain
CATEGORIES: Economics; Laws and acts; Wars, uprisings, and civil unrest
KEY FIGURES:
John Dickinson (1732-1808), Philadelphia lawyer who disputed the constitutionality of the Townshend duties
Thomas Gage (1721-1787), British commander in chief in North America
Frederick North, second earl of Guilford (1732-1792), former chancellor of the Exchequer who became prime minister of Great Britain in 1770
William Pitt the Elder (1708-1778), prime minister of Great Britain
Charles Townshend (1725-1767), chancellor of the Exchequer

SUMMARY OF EVENT. In 1766, after repealing the Stamp Act and imposing new domestic taxes in England, Lord Rockingham and his ministry were recalled by King George III and replaced by a coalition of diverse politicians under the ailing William Pitt. Because of his poor health, Pitt often was absent from Parliament for long periods, which enabled his ministers to pursue their own individual agendas. Pitt's most powerful minister was the chancellor of the Exchequer, Charles Townshend, who inherited Great Britain's financial crisis. The problems became considerably worse after Parliament, in an attempt to appease its constituents, slashed the land tax. As a result, the British government was deprived of more than four hundred thousand pounds in annual revenue. In searching for solutions to his dilemma, Townshend seized upon colonial American arguments made during the Stamp Act protest. Colonial leaders had claimed that they opposed in principle only internal taxes, not external taxes. Never a friend of the colonial protest, Townshend declared that if the colonists adhered to such a distinction, then they should be saddled with extensive external duties.

Despite warnings from several influential members of Parliament, Townshend steered three laws through the British government during June and July, 1767. Collectively, the three acts became known as the Townshend Acts. Two of the three,

the American Board of Customs Act and the New York Suspending Act, were designed to strengthen British authority within the colonies. The third, the Revenue Act of 1767, was intended to raise forty thousand pounds by taxing glass, paint, lead, paper, and tea imported into the colonies. Because the act taxed only imported goods and therefore was an external tax, supporters of the legislation expected Americans to submit to it. Townshend planned to use the new revenues to pay for the administrative changes embodied by the first two pieces of legislation.

The colonists had grave reservations about each of the three acts. The danger in the Revenue Act of 1767 was not in the quantity of cash extracted from colonial pockets but in its potential to extend Parliament's authority over colonial American affairs. Unlike legislation prior to the Stamp Act, the new act was created to collect money, or revenue, for the British treasury exclusively from colonial America. Since the mid-seventeenth century, British trade laws had been designed to regulate commerce throughout the empire. Colonial leaders contended that, constitutionally, before Parliament could create a tax solely on the colonies, Parliament would have to include colonial representation. Colonists also feared that if they accepted the Revenue Act, a precedent would be established and additional revenue-raising acts directed only at the colonies would soon follow. Additionally, a portion of the act's revenues was to be used to administer the colonies. This deeply troubled many Americans. During the eighteenth century, colonial legislatures had acquired significant powers to control the salaries and general remuneration of British administrators in America. By the 1760's, these powers provided a way for colonists to keep the Crown's appointed officials responsive to the will of the colonial population they served. The Revenue Act threatened to do away with those powers and, therefore, further threatened the constitutional rights of the colonists.

Adding to Parliament's perceived assault upon American rights were the American Board of Customs Act and the New York Suspending Act. The Customs Act created an American Board of Customs, with headquarters in Boston, that reported directly to the British Treasury. The new agency, which included vice-admiralty courts in three colonial cities, had the power to administer virtually all American activities with little regard for colonial assemblies. The Board of Customs was expected to be zealous in the handling of its assignment, for a third of all fines received in the vice admiralty courts went to the customs agents. Parliament also made British regulars stationed in the colonies available to the new Board of Customs, should the need arise.

The New York Suspending Act was an attempt to force New York to comply fully with the Quartering Act, passed in 1765, which required provincial assemblies, at their own expense, to lodge British regulars in taverns and other public houses when military barracks were not available. Firewood, candles, bedding, and other essential items also were to be provided by the province. New York, a colony frequently asked to provide such assistance, refused to comply with the law completely. In retaliation, Parliament, through the Suspending Act, sought to shut down the New York Assembly until the colony thoroughly obeyed the Quartering Act. From the colonial American perspective, this act was clearly punitive and, therefore, an abuse of constitutional authority. Colonists also considered the act an indirect tax, because it required assemblies to levy money for the upkeep of royal regiments.

The American reaction to the Townshend Acts came slowly, in part because Parliament was able to implement the acts before the colonists had time to plan their resistance. Likewise, Parliament took steps to nullify the strong-arm tactics that had been so effective during the Stamp Act protest. Nevertheless, by early 1768, colonial leaders had begun to rally their fellow Americans. Among the more influential critics was Pennsylvania lawyer John Dickinson, whose *Letters from a Farmer in Pennsylvania* became popular reading throughout America. What Dickinson lacked in originality he made up for by vigorously and clearly expressing the colonists' constitutional opposition to all forms of taxation in which the colonies were not represented. Other writers, including Massachusetts firebrands James Otis and Samuel Adams, joined the battle, as did several colonial assemblies, with remonstrance and petitions against the unpopular actions. The Massachusetts legislature, through what it called a "circular letter," led the way with a bitter denunciation of parliamentary taxation and the scheme to pay judges and royal governors from funds other than those appropriated by the colonial assemblies. In Boston, merchants again resorted to a nonimportation agreement, as they had during the Stamp Act protest. Aided by the reappearance of various Sons of Liberty organizations, the Boston boycott slowly spread southward during 1768 and 1769. Eventually, the tactic cut British imports to the colonies by 40 percent.

While the Townshend Acts prompted a less violent reaction in the colonies than had the Stamp Act, the new legislation collectively represented an even greater threat to American rights. The point was made obvious when, in response to the customs collectors' appeal for protection, the secretary of state for the colonies, Wills Hill, the earl of Hillsborough, attempted to dissolve the Massachusetts Assembly and ordered General Thomas Gage, British commander in chief in North America, to station British troops in Boston. Hillsborough's moves confirmed to many colonists that a conspiracy against American rights existed in Parliament.

In 1770, after the sudden death of Charles Townshend and William Pitt's retirement, Lord North came to power in Parliament. With the colonial boycott still in place and American resistance growing, North was able to persuade Parliament to repeal all the Townshend duties except the one on tea; the king gave his consent on April 12. The tea duty would remain as a symbol of Parliament's authority to tax. North was a practical man whose way out of the crisis seemed to offer a return to more cooperative Anglo-American relations.

—Paul E. Doutrich

ADDITIONAL READING:

Brooke, John. *The Chatham Administration, 1766-1768.* Vol. 1 in *England in the Age of the Revolution,* edited by Louis Namier. New York: St. Martin's Press, 1956. Mirrors the approach and conclusions of the author's mentor.

Butterfield, Herbert. *George III and the Historians.* New York: Macmillan, 1957. This historiographical monograph finds serious fault with some of the conclusions of Namier and Brooke concerning parties and principles.

Jacobson, David L. *John Dickinson and the Revolution in Pennsylvania, 1764-1774.* Berkeley: University of California Press, 1965. A useful narrative of Dickinson's political ideas and activities.

Knollenberg, Bernard. *Growth of the American Revolution, 1765-1775.* New York: Free Press, 1975. Places the British policy toward colonial America in context and describes the American reaction.

Namier, Lewis B., and John Brooke. *Charles Townshend.* New York: St. Martin's Press, 1964. In this biography, completed after his death by Brooke, Namier depicts the charming and eloquent Townshend as also erratic, amoral, and a determined imperialist in favor of strong royal authority in the colonies. Namier maintains that the "Townshend duties" of 1767 were pushed through Parliament despite opposition from Pitt and others—they were not in fact the result of Parliament's need to prime the American pump. The Revenue Act had been worked out before the defeat of the land tax and, far from being the result of that defeat, was the realization of Townshend's long-planned design to bolster British authority.

Pares, Richard. *King George III and the Politicians.* Oxford, England: Oxford University Press, 1953. A brilliantly written account of the monarch's place in the political and constitutional picture, reflecting Namier's point of view.

Thomas, Peter D. G. *The Townshend Duties Crisis: The Second Phase of the Revolution, 1767-1773.* Oxford, England: Clarendon Press, 1987. A thorough assessment of how the Townshend Acts affected both England and colonial America.

Ubbelohde, Carl. *The Vice-Admiralty Courts and the American Revolution.* Chapel Hill: University of North Carolina Press, 1960. This carefully researched work asserts that "the Vice-Admiralty Courts were a mirror, but persistent, cause of the American Revolution."

SEE ALSO: 1765, Stamp Act Crisis.

1768 ■ CAROLINA REGULATOR MOVEMENTS: *protesting lack of representation in the western backcountry, the Regulators inspire vigilante insurrections*

DATE: 1768-May 16, 1771
LOCALE: Carolinas' backcountry
CATEGORIES: Government and politics; Native American history; Wars, uprisings, and civil unrest

KEY FIGURES:

William Bull (1710-1791), governor of South Carolina, who was friendly to the backcountry

Edmund Fanning (1739-1818), justice of the peace and recorder of deeds of Orange County, who was hated by the North Carolina Regulators

Charles Garth, South Carolina agent in London who sought legislation to cope with the colony's interior region

Herman Husband (1724-1795), pamphleteer who stated the case for the North Carolina backcountry

Samuel Johnston (1733-1816), conservative leader in the North Carolina assembly

Moses Kirkland, aggressive planter and businessman who emerged as leader of the South Carolina Regulators

William Tryon (1729-1788), British governor of North Carolina

Charles Woodmason (1720?-1776?), Church of England clergyman who wrote a petition of grievances for the South Carolina frontiersmen

SUMMARY OF EVENT. Conflicts between the East and the West, between old established societies and new primitive settlements of the frontier, recurred throughout the history of North America. The breadth and depth of these sectional antagonisms have varied sharply according to time and place. The Regulator movements of the late 1760's and 1770's in the Carolinas illustrate the complexity of the phenomenon.

In Maryland and Virginia, the frontier folk harbored no deep-seated grievances against the East. The legislatures, although dominated by tidewater aristocrats, had established counties—with courts, justices of the peace, sheriffs, and representation in the assemblies—and had enacted statutes to build roads and bridges for facilitating trade. In North Carolina, despite the fact that the same political institutions had made their appearance in the piedmont, there was serious regional discord because of the malpractices of local officials, and, to a lesser extent, because of high quitrents, inadequate arteries of transportation, and underrepresentation in the legislature. Sheriffs, by failing to publish the tax rate, collected far more than the law permitted and lined their own pockets in the process. If a taxable person could not pay—and cash was ever in short supply—his property was seized and sold, with the auctions rigged in favor of insiders. There was little opportunity for redress, because corrupt sheriffs acted in collusion with other county officials. These "courthouse rings" charged exorbitant fees for performing routine legal services. The symbol of the people's unhappiness was New York-born, Yale-educated Edmund Fanning, justice of the peace and recorder of deeds of Orange County.

Although violence erupted as early as 1759 in the Granville District, the initial pattern of the Regulators (a name that the aroused victims of these discriminatory practices borrowed from a simultaneous but separate reform movement in South Carolina) was to lodge formal protests with the governor and the Assembly. Humble in tone and legalistic in concept, these petitions were largely ignored or condemned on the seaboard.

Only after many rebuffs did the Regulators broaden their goals to include dividing western counties and instituting secret voting so as to increase their representation in the colonial legislature. New elections in 1769 brought Herman Husband, one of their principal spokesmen, into the Assembly, along with several other Regulators and their sympathizers. James Iredell, a conservative, declared that a majority of the lower house was "of regulating principles." With their new strength, they won approval for the creation of four new counties in the backcountry.

This measure and other modest reforms concerning officers' fees and court costs in litigation lacked enforcement at the county level. Violence increased, and in September, 1770, Regulators invaded the Orange County court at Hillsborough, drove out the justices, and tried cases themselves. Fear of rebellion led the assembly to abandon its "regulating principles" by enacting the repressive Johnston Act against unlawful gatherings and by backing Governor William Tryon in sending a militia army against the Regulators. On May 16, 1771, near the banks of the Alamance Creek, twenty miles from Hillsborough, a motley throng of two thousand farmers gathered to oppose Tryon's force of fourteen hundred well-armed militias. After desultory firing and ludicrous field movements on both sides, the Regulators fled, each side sustaining nine dead. Many Regulators left the province with their families, moving across the mountains into northeastern Tennessee. The majority accepted the governor's offer of clemency.

The Regulation ended at Alamance, but in the 1770's, justices and sheriffs in the piedmont appear to have paid stricter attention to the law in performing their duties, for patriot leaders saw the need to placate the West to achieve unity in the face of the challenge from Great Britain. There is little evidence to indicate that erstwhile Regulators supported the British cause in the American Revolution.

The backcountry of South Carolina was settled somewhat later than that of the Tarheel colony, and its chief grievance was the absence of government rather than the abuses of government that plagued frontier North Carolina. In the 1760's, newcomers flooded into the backcountry, a region suffering from the aftermath of the Cherokee War of 1759-1761. Life in the "up country" (a South Carolina expression), precarious at best, threatened a total breakdown in the face of rising lawlessness and social and economic maladjustment. The parishes of South Carolina, the local units of political and ecclesiastical authority, only theoretically extended to the backcountry. There were, it is true, justices of the peace, but their authority was limited to minor civil cases. The absence of courts meant a visit to Charleston if one desired to transact any important legal business, and the journey entailed a week on horseback or two weeks by wagon from distant stations, such as Ninety-six. In 1767, as roving bands of outlaws terrorized the region while Charleston authorities looked the other way, leading citizens, with the support of other respectable persons, formed an association for "regulating" the backcountry. Dedicated to law and order and the protection of property, the

Regulators, by 1768, had dealt harshly and effectively with the criminal part of the population. Many honest men, however, felt the Regulators had gone too far by punishing immorality as well as lawlessness. An anti-Regulator group, the Moderate movement, brought the excesses of the extremist Regulators to an end and restored control of the area to respectable property owners. A direct confrontation between the Regulators and constituted authority in Charleston never took place, partly because Lieutenant Governor William Bull and others in authority recognized the need to bring tranquillity to the interior. In addition, the Commons House of Assembly finally endeavored to solve backcountry problems, providing more legislative representation and establishing schools. These well-intentioned undertakings ran afoul of British policy and the emerging Anglo-American conflict, but passage of the Circuit Court Act of 1769 ended a major grievance by creating four backcountry courts, with full jurisdiction in civil and criminal matters, and provisions for jury trials and the strict regulation of legal fees.

Although there were obvious differences, the broad objectives of the two Regulator movements in the Carolinas were the same. Eschewing theoretical political innovations or radical social leveling, the Regulators asked principally for a redress of specific grievances, for government that was just and responsible, for the political and legal rights to which freeborn Englishmen were everywhere entitled. Despite initial setbacks, the Regulator movements helped bring about better government in the backcountry of the Carolinas. They also gave witness to the growth of a powerful tradition of popular or vigilante justice that has come to characterize the reaction of Americans to real or perceived failures of courts and police to deal with crime.

—*R. Don Higginbotham, updated by Charles H. O'Brien*

ADDITIONAL READING:

Brown, Richard M. *The South Carolina Regulators.* Cambridge, Mass.: Harvard University Press, 1963. A significant monograph contending that the Regulators were upstanding citizens concerned with protecting property rights and restoring order.

Cooper, William J. *The American South: A History.* 2 vols. New York: McGraw-Hill, 1990. Volume 1 offers a useful survey of conditions on the Southern frontier in the eighteenth century.

Dill, Alonzo T. *Governor Tryon and His Palace.* Chapel Hill: University of North Carolina Press, 1955. Readable, informative study of the governor who put down the North Carolina Regulators and his times.

Gipson, Lawrence H. *The Rumbling of the Coming Storm, 1766-1770: The Triumphant Empire.* Vol. 9 in *The British Empire Before the American Revolution.* New York: Alfred A. Knopf, 1965. Devotes two chapters to what the author calls "the struggle for political equality" in the Carolinas.

Meriwether, Robert L. *The Expansion of South Carolina, 1729-1765.* Kingsport, Tenn.: Southern Publishers, 1940. Meticulous scholarship by a leading authority on South Carolina history.

Powell, William. *North Carolina Through Four Centuries.* Chapel Hill: University of North Carolina Press, 1989. A readable yet scholarly narrative, a third of which is devoted to the colonial period.

Woodmason, Charles. *The Carolina Backcountry on the Eve of the Revolution: The Journal and Other Writings of Charles Woodmason, Anglican Itinerant.* Edited by Richard J. Hooker. Chapel Hill: University of North Carolina Press, 1953. Woodmason, an itinerant Church of England clergyman who sympathized with the Regulators, paints a vivid and sometimes amusing picture of life in their region.

SEE ALSO: 1663, Settlement of the Carolinas; 1759, Cherokee War; 1763, Paxton Boys' Massacres.

1768 ■ METHODIST CHURCH IS ESTABLISHED: *the Methodist movement becomes institutionalized in America*

DATE: October 30, 1768
LOCALE: New York City
CATEGORIES: Organizations and institutions; Religion
KEY FIGURES:

Francis Asbury (1745-1816), leader of the Methodist church in America in the late eighteenth century
Philip Embury (1728-1773), director of the Methodist Society in New York City
Barbara Ruckle Heck (1734-1804), Embury's cousin, who encouraged members of the Methodist Society at New York City
Thomas Webb (c. 1724-1796), military captain who joined Embury in leading the Methodist Society in New York City
John Wesley (1703-1791), leader of the Methodist movement in England
George Whitefield (1714-1770), Anglican preacher whose visit to North America sparked the First Great Awakening

SUMMARY OF EVENT. The founding of the first Methodist church in America is rooted in the Methodist revival movement that spread across England after 1740. The movement was centered in the Anglican church and focused on the notion of assurance of salvation through faith in Jesus Christ. In 1738, an Anglican priest, John Wesley, had a transforming religious experience, which he believed brought such an assurance to him personally. Soon thereafter, an old friend from Oxford University who shared a similar belief, George Whitefield, asked Wesley to come to Bristol, England. Whitefield wanted Wesley to organize and lead those who believed they also had found this assurance during a revival that had occurred during Whitefield's preaching there. Wesley's work at Bristol initiated the Methodist movement. He organized the new believers into societies, approximately corresponding to church congregations, for teaching, spiritual growth, and religious discipline. Whitefield subsequently traveled to North America, where for several decades he experienced similar results from his preaching in the English colonies.

The Methodist movement spread rapidly from Bristol, taking John Wesley to Ireland on a preaching tour during the early 1740's. By 1744, more than fifty thousand persons in Ireland had come under the influence of the Methodist movement. Among these were a group of German refugees from the Palatinate, who had settled in Limerick. One of their number was a carpenter, Philip Embury, who became a Methodist lay preacher (that is, a person authorized by Wesley to preach, but not ordained to offer any church sacraments). Unhappy with their life in Ireland, eight or ten of these refugee families departed for the English colonies in America in 1760. Among the emigrants were Embury, his cousin Barbara Ruckle Heck, and her new husband, Paul Heck.

Settling in New York City, the immigrants found life difficult and fell into quiet inactivity in their religious life. According to tradition, one evening in October, 1766, Barbara Heck found her brother, her cousin Philip, and some others playing cards and gambling. This was a common amusement of the time, but to some, it was a morally questionable activity. The scene kindled Barbara's religious ardor. Collecting the cards from the table into her apron, she disposed of them in the fire and warned the players to repent. She then turned her comments specifically to Philip Embury, urging him to preach "or we shall all go to hell, and God will require our blood at your hands!" At first, he objected that he had neither a place to preach nor a congregation. Soon Heck had gathered a congregation of five persons into Embury's house. These included Barbara and Paul Heck, John Lawrence, a hired man, and a black slave, Betty. Together, these individuals constituted the first Methodist Society in New York City, and apparently the second in the English colonies in America, since perhaps half a year earlier, a group had been formed in Maryland (with neither Wesley's knowledge nor his authorization).

Under Embury's preaching, the small house soon overflowed. The Methodist Society began meeting in a rented storeroom on Barrack Street, near the British military headquarters. Some musicians from the regimental bands began attending the meetings, drawn there by the different style of music they overheard during the Methodists' services. A British military captain, Thomas Webb, was drawn there too. In 1766, there had been tension in New York City over the quartering of British soldiers, resulting in clashes and violence not far from where the Methodists were meeting. When Webb entered the meeting for the first time, he stirred fears of repression similar to that which Methodists had known in England, where soldiers had tried to break up several Methodist Societies. However, Webb had fallen under Wesley's influence when he had heard Wesley preach in Bristol in the late 1750's.

Webb began preaching as well, and soon he received a local preacher's license from Wesley. Having returned to America in 1766, Webb announced to the New York City Methodist Society that he was not only a soldier of the Crown but also "a soldier of the cross and a spiritual son of John Wesley." Within a week, Webb was participating in the preaching activity and the leadership of the Society. Webb's persuasiveness, and the sheer spectacle of a uniformed military officer preaching with his sword laid across the pulpit, reinforced Embury's preaching ability. Soon the storeroom became too small for the congregation.

In early 1767, the Methodist Society moved to a rigging loft on Williams Street (then called Cart and Horse Street). The new facility provided twenty-four hundred square feet of space, was lit by a large candelabra, and was heated by a corner fireplace. In this location, the congregation continued to grow. After a year, even the loft was becoming cramped, and the group prepared to build a "preaching house." A site on John Street was located, and a fund-raising effort began. Captain Webb gave thirty pounds for the building—a third more than any other gift—and loaned an additional three hundred pounds to the effort. He also lobbied support from all parts of the city. Subscriptions to the building fund were made by Anglican clergymen, the mayor, African slaves, and some leading aristocratic families of New York City, including the Livingstons, the Stuyvesants, and the Lispenards.

A carpenter by profession, Embury designed and built the new preaching house, which was called Wesley Chapel. The new building, believed by many Methodist historians to be the first Methodist church building in America, was dedicated for religious services on Sunday, October 30, 1768. Because there was also a Methodist Society in Maryland, some Methodist historians have suggested that a log meeting house there may actually have predated the building in New York City. Nevertheless, in terms of growth and development of the Methodist movement in America, if not also in physical structures, Wesley Chapel in New York City takes priority.

On April 11, 1768, one of the members of the Methodist Society in New York City, Thomas Taylor, wrote John Wesley about the congregation's progress. Until this communication, Wesley was apparently unaware of Methodist activities in America, which were being concluded without his authorization. Taylor's goal in writing was primarily to urge Wesley to send authorized assistants to the colony to help further and direct the work there. He believed that while Embury and Webb were doing good work, they lacked the qualifications to develop the church further. Similar requests for assistants were dispatched by Captain Webb to Wesley as well. At the 1769 Methodist Conference in Leeds, Wesley responded to these requests by accepting two volunteers, Richard Boardman and Joseph Pilmoor, who were quickly sent to America. While Pilmoor worked in Philadelphia, Boardman traveled to New York City to work with the congregation meeting in Wesley Chapel.

Still not satisfied, Webb continued to urge Wesley to provide more assistants. At the 1771 Methodist Conference in Bristol, one of the volunteers chosen to work in America was Francis Asbury. When Asbury arrived in America in late 1771, he made his way to New York City. Within a decade, Asbury had become the unquestioned leader of Methodism in America. Webb later worked in Philadelphia; Heck and her family moved to Canada, as did many other colonists during the American Revolution. Embury died in 1773. From his base in the Northeast, Asbury's untiring work spread the movement southward and to the frontier. New congregations multiplied yearly, until Methodist churches were to be found in virtually every city and town in the growing United States.

—*Richard A. Bennett*

ADDITIONAL READING:

Bucke, Emory Stephens, gen. ed. *The History of American Methodism.* 3 vols. New York: Abingdon Press, 1964. A voluminous scholarly work that covers virtually every aspect of the subject through the 1950's.

Luccock, Halford, and Paul Hutchinson. *The Story of Methodism.* New York: Abingdon-Cokesbury Press, 1949. A popular general survey of the growth of Methodism in both England and America, from Wesley to the twentieth century.

McEllhenney, John G., gen. ed. *United Methodism in America: A Compact History.* Nashville, Tenn.: Abingdon Press, 1992. A history of the development of the Methodist church in the United States. Includes a survey of the expansion and division of U.S. Methodism.

Norwood, Frederick A. *The Story of American Methodism.* Nashville, Tenn.: Abingdon Press, 1974. Focuses on Methodism in the United States, with only limited information of other parts of the world. Well-researched; useful footnotes.

Richey, Russell E. *Early American Methodism.* Bloomington: Indiana University Press, 1991. A brief history surveying the development of Methodism in the United States, primarily in the eighteenth and nineteenth centuries. Bibliography.

SEE ALSO: 1730's, First Great Awakening; 1773, African American Baptist Church Is Founded; 1789, Episcopal Church Is Established; 1790's, Second Great Awakening; 1816, AME Church Is Founded; 1819, Unitarian Church Is Founded.

1769 ■ RISE OF THE CALIFORNIA MISSIONS: *twenty-one Catholic missions, four military installations, and several towns establish Spain's claim to Alta California and alter the lives of thousands of Native Americans*

DATE: July 17, 1769-1824

LOCALE: Coastal regions of California, from San Diego to Sonoma

CATEGORIES: Expansion and land acquisition; Native American history; Religion

KEY FIGURES:

José de Gálvez (1729-1787), *visitador general* to New Spain, responsible for the expansion of the Spanish frontier into Alta California

Fermín de Lausen (1736-1803), Serra's successor as head of the California missions

Gaspar de Portolá (1723-1785?), first governor of California

Junípero Serra (1713-1784), Franciscan friar who established the first California missions

SUMMARY OF EVENT. The worldwide Spanish Empire had gradually developed a mission system that suited imperial policy in places as distant as the Philippines, Paraguay, and Baja California. With a relatively modest investment, the Crown could extend its frontiers and establish opportunities for further expansion later. Two or three missionaries per location could attract indigenous peoples to a different way of life. The native peoples would learn manual trades, farming, cattle-raising, smithing, tanning, weaving, and other rudimentary skills, so that they could manage the institution on their own. A few soldiers at each mission—never more than ten—enforced discipline. On occasions of serious trouble, appeal could be made to strategically placed presidios that housed sizable, highly mobile military forces capable of putting down any rebellions. When the missions developed enough, a pueblo might be established nearby, able to make use of the growing mission economy without having to follow the often austere mission routine.

The Spanish missionaries, usually members of religious orders (the regular clergy), expected to complete their work in ten years, after which the establishments were to be secularized: The administration of church affairs would be in the hands of the secular clergy, and all the mission's properties and possessions would be dispersed. Church authorities would receive the church buildings and some surrounding land. Indigenous peoples would receive at least half of all the possessions and land.

For 160 years, missionaries in New Spain sought to evangelize the peoples of the Upper California territories, claimed for Spain by Juan Rodríguez Cabrillo in 1524 and Sebastián Vizcaíno in 1611. Without royal approval, however, ecclesiastical initiatives were not implemented in the Spanish Empire. Even many popes, as well as lowly missionaries, discovered this policy.

In 1741, Captain Vitus Bering had reached Alaska and claimed much of North America's west coast. Carlos Francisco de Croix became the Viceroy of New Spain in 1766. Along with Don José de Gálvez, *visitador general* of King Charles III, Croix laid plans for a series of missions in Alta California to blunt Russian expansionist plans. Galvez's plans called for a mission and fort at Monterey Bay in the north. They chose San Diego in the south as the site of the first mission, because it was about half the distance from the base in Loreto, Baja California. Gálvez selected Don Gaspar de Portolá to be governor of California and Fray Junípero Serra as president of the missions.

Four foundation parties, two by land and two by sea, set out from Baja for the arduous journey. Most of the sailors died, as did many of those taking part in the overland trek. On July 17, 1769, Serra dedicated the mission of San Diego de Alcalá on a site five miles west of the present mission. Portola pushed on to Monterey with a small party, but left no permanent settlement. That came about the following year, under Serra. Between Serra and his immediate successor, Fray Fermín de Lausen, eighteen of the twenty-one missions were built by 1798.

Economics determined the sequence of building the missions. Largely dependent on shipping for supplies in the earliest years, the missions were first clustered in three areas: south (San Diego), central (Santa Barbara Channel) and north (Monterey). Gradually, the gaps between the missions were closed to lessen their reliance on the vagaries of eighteenth century shipping. In 1776, Juan Bautista de Anza led an arduous overland expedition to San Francisco through the southern deserts, demonstrating that New Spain no longer need rely on the sea to supply California. In all, Spain founded twenty of the missions. After independence, Mexican authorities founded the last of the missions at Sonoma, San Francisco Solano, dedicated in 1824.

In late eighteenth century California, there were about 130,000 Native Americans living in many small bands. The land supported them well in a life that was not much different from the one they had lived five thousand years before. Abundant potable water, fish, and game were within easy reach. Of all the indigenous peoples of what would become the United States, they made the swiftest, most seaworthy boats, without knowing metal trades. Their loosely structured societies lacked a central organization. They had no writing system for their six languages and several dialects. There were no orga-

nized wars, although occasional raids to steal goods were not unknown. Shelter was modest, at most.

It quickly became clear to the missionaries that they needed more workers if the missions were to become self-sufficient. They stepped up recruitment of the indigenous people as laborers, often luring them with trinkets. The Franciscan missionary plan initially included teaching the native populations in their own languages, but the diversity was so extensive that that plan was abandoned, and Spanish was chosen instead to be the *lingua franca* of California.

The missions attracted people from surrounding areas with the promise of better living conditions and some amenities unavailable to those on the outside. If the natives converted to Christianity—a condition for remaining within the economic ambit of the mission—they were no longer at liberty to return to their previous way of life, although many did, in fact, escape. Native Americans living in the mission were permitted, even encouraged, to visit their families for weeks at a time. This policy proved to be the best recruiting tool the missionaries possessed.

The workers did learn trades and some even learned to read and write. Daily work usually finished by mid-morning, and numerous feast days provided diversion from the normal regimen. By the time of secularization in 1834, approximately thirty thousand natives resided at the missions, with only sixty friars and three hundred soldiers along the 650 miles from San Diego to Sonoma. The missions held 230,000 cattle, 34,000 horses, and 268,000 hogs, sheep, and goats.

Mission San Juan Capistrano, May 9, 1865, south of present-day Los Angeles. This Vischer drawing was made less than a century after the founding of the mission. (Security Pacific Collection/Los Angeles Public Library)

The life was far removed from that visited upon the natives' ancestors by the savage conquistadores of the sixteenth century. The process of colonization was relatively peaceful, and on balance the native population fared better under the Spanish friars than people in other colonies and received better treatment than they received subsequently in Mexico or in the United States. However, because the mission system destroyed their previous tranquil existence and failed to prepare them for the promised secularization, it cannot escape historical criticism. The Indians were introduced into an alien culture as little more than slaves; they suffered tragically from European diseases and, in the end, were ill-equipped for any other existence, either that of their own rapidly declining culture or that of the new California.

When Mexico gained independence from Spain, the new government resolved to secularize the missions. When secularization began, Native Americans were either tricked into giving up their rights or their rights simply were ignored in the land grab of what had been the missions. Stranded after secularization, many of the natives at the missions had nowhere else to go, so they stayed on, continuing menial work under new masters. Only in the twentieth century were there some modest advances in their status. The U.S. government gave most of the mission buildings back to the Catholic church after California entered the Union. Many of the missions have been restored to a romantic, tranquil, even charming condition that belies their troubled history. —*Daniel A. Brown*

ADDITIONAL READING:

Cook, Sherburne Friend. *The Conflict Between the California Indian and White Civilization.* 4 vols. Berkeley: University of California Press, 1943. A scholarly collection that chronicles the troubled history of Native Americans during and after the mission period. Rich bibliographies.

Costo, Rupert, and Jeannette Henry Costo, eds. *The Missions of California: A Legacy of Genocide.* San Francisco: Indian Historian Press, 1987. A collection that vigorously indicts the evils of the mission system.

Englehardt, Zephyrin. *The Missions and Missionaries of California.* 4 vols. Santa Barbara, Calif.: Mission Santa Barbara, 1929. The monumental standard reference work on the missions, giving an overall positive evaluation of the system.

Font Obrador, Bartolome. *Fr. Junipero Serra: Mallorca, Mexico, Sierra Gorda, Californias.* Palma, Mallorca, Spain: Comissio de Cultura, 1992. A biography of Serra that depends on, but summarizes well, the work of many earlier authors.

Geiger, Maynard J. *The Life and Times of Fray Junipero Serra, OFM.* 2 vols. Washington, D.C.: Academy of American Franciscan History, 1959. A large, sympathetic biography that relies heavily on original sources.

Johnson, Paul C., et al., eds. *The California Missions: A Pictorial History.* Menlo Park, Calif.: Lane, 1985. A colorful, popular, accessible, and reliable work.

Kroeber, Alfred Louis. *Handbook of the Indians of California.* New York: Dover, 1976. A large anthropological tome.

SEE ALSO: 1542, Settlement of Alta California.

1770 ■ BOSTON MASSACRE: *American fears of British standing armies result in a bloody confrontation and epitomize colonial unrest*

DATE: March 5, 1770
LOCALE: Boston, Massachusetts
CATEGORY: Wars, uprisings, and civil unrest
KEY FIGURES:
John Adams (1735-1826), Boston lawyer
Crispus Attucks (c. 1725-1770),
James Caldwell,
Patrick Carr,
Samuel Gray, and
Samuel Maverick (c. 1753-1770), casualties of the Boston Massacre
Thomas Gage (1721-1787), British commander in chief in North America
John Hancock (1737-1793), wealthy Boston merchant in conflict with customs collectors
Wills Hill, earl of Hillsborough, marquis of Downshire (1718-1793), secretary of state for the colonies
Thomas Preston, officer of the main guard at Boston

SUMMARY OF EVENT. On the night of March 5, 1770, a small crowd gathered around a soldier at the guard post in front of the Customs House at Boston, accusing him of striking a boy who had made disparaging remarks about a British officer. John Adams depicted the hecklers as "a motley rabble of saucy boys, negroes and mulattoes, Irish teagues and outlandish Jack tars." The sentinel's call for aid brought eight men from the Twenty-ninth Regiment and Captain Thomas Preston, officer of the day. The crowd increased, especially after someone rang the bell in the old Brick Meeting House; men and boys hurled snowballs and pieces of ice at the crimson-coated regulars and, with cries of "lobster," "bloody-back," and "coward," taunted them to retaliate.

The crowd's hostility stemmed from more than this particular incident; it rested on a series of occurrences between the Bostonians and the military during the seventeen months that the troops had been garrisoned in the city. If possible, the townspeople had expressed even more antipathy for the Customs Commissioners, who that very evening gazed uneasily from the windows of the Customs House on the scene before them in King Street. They were the real source of the trouble; their cries for protection had brought troops to Boston in the first place.

The Americans were right about the role of the commissioners, but their version of what transpired shortly after nine o'clock on the night of March 5 is highly questionable. Captain Preston probably did not order his nervous troops to fire into the angry throng, but fire they did after one of their number was clubbed on the head. Three Americans died instantly, two a short time later, and six more received wounds.

British troops shoot Crispus Attucks and others during the Boston Massacre. (The Associated Publishers, Inc.)

The "Boston Massacre" may have been a misnomer, the result of extreme harassment of the redcoats, and triggered, according to John Adams, by an unprincipled mulatto, Crispus Attucks, "to whose mad behavior, in all probability, the dreadful carnage of that night is chiefly to be ascribed."

Attucks, son of an African American father and a Massachuset Indian mother, was the first casualty of the Boston Massacre of March 5, 1770, the first death in the cause of the American Revolution. Attucks' father was a black slave in a Framington, Massachusetts, household until about 1750, when he escaped and became a sailor. Crispus' mother lived in an Indian mission at Natick. Attucks was known around Boston as one of the Sons of Liberty's most aggressive agitators. When the British claimed that he had provoked their soldiers, they may have been right. Attucks and Paul Revere were among the earliest Sons of Liberty, a clandestine society that agitated against the British by engaging in acts of propaganda and creative political mischief. The Sons of Liberty tormented Tories and their supporters, often stripping, tarring, and feathering tax collectors, then walking free at the hands of sympathetic colonial juries. They later would form the nucleus of a revolutionary armed force, but in the early years, their main business was what a later generation would call "guerrilla theater."

Americans elsewhere wondered whether their respective colonies would be the next to have a standing army in their midst, an army seemingly intent on destroying their liberties, not only by its presence but also by the use of fire and sword. At the time, however, Massachusetts had been singled out ostensibly because of the Customs Commissioners' appeal for protection. Undoubtedly, another consideration made the decision to comply an easy one for London politicians: the Massachusetts Bay Colony, with its spirited opposition to the Stamp Act (1765) and the Townshend Revenue Act (1767), had long been viewed as a hotbed of sedition.

The conduct of His Majesty's revenue collectors had incited colonial opposition. They were considered by many to be "customs racketeers," a lecherous band who played fast and loose with the complicated provisions of the Sugar Act (1764) in order to win, in Vice-Admiralty Courts, judgments that lined their own pockets. This was substantially the opinion of New Hampshire's Governor Benning Wentworth, and the British commander in chief in North America, General Thomas Gage, admitted almost as much to the secretary of state for the colonies, Wills Hill, earl of Hillsborough and marquis of Downshire. Nevertheless, the secretary of state ordered the general to dispatch regulars to the Massachusetts capital.

Gage's troops met no resistance when they landed on October 1, 1768. Despite the obvious displeasure of the populace, reflected in the town fathers' reluctance to aid in securing quarters for the soldiers (soon increased by two additional regiments), there followed months of relative calm with no mob activity against either the redcoats or the customs collectors. Lord Hillsborough, however, was determined to deal harshly with Massachusetts, and had he been able to impose his will, Parliament would have wrought changes to equal or surpass in severity the Coercive Acts of 1774.

Because of troubles in Ireland, threats from France and Spain, and the colonial boycott of British goods in protest against the Townshend duties, the government rejected Hillsborough's schemes and eventually repealed all the Townshend taxes except the one on tea. The employment of troops against civilians was ticklish business to George III and Englishmen in general, calling forth memories of Stuart days. The logical step was to remove all the troops, but two regiments remained in Boston.

Serious tension began to build in the late summer and fall of 1769, when Bostonians believed that the redcoats were becoming permanent residents. The soldiers were subjected to every form of legal harassment by local magistrates, to say nothing of mounting acts of violence against the men in uniform. The redcoats in the ranks, like all European soldiers of their day, were hardly of the highest character, often recruited from the slums and the gin mills, and stories of theft, assault, and rape by the regulars were not without considerable foundation. The culmination, foreseen by the army and townspeople alike, was the Boston Massacre. Only then were the last regiments pulled out of the city, leaving behind a legacy of fear and suspicion that was revived every succeeding March 5. "Massacre Day," as it was called, was commemorated by the tolling of bells and a patriot address that stressed the danger of standing armies.

Tension in Boston rose again in 1773, due to another act of political mischief by the Sons of Liberty, who remembered the victims of the Boston Massacre at the Boston Tea Party. In 1888, a monument to Attucks was erected at the Boston Common. —*R. Don Higginbotham, updated by Bruce E. Johansen*

ADDITIONAL READING:

Alden, John R. *General Gage in America*. Baton Rouge: Louisiana State University Press, 1948. The redcoats in Boston are treated with sympathy and fairness by Alden in his two chapters relevant to the subject.

Beer, George L. *British Colonial Policy, 1754-1765*. New York: Macmillan, 1907. Contains information about military affairs, including the once-traditional interpretation of why redcoats remained in the colonies after 1763.

Boston (Mass.) City Council. *A Memorial of Crispus Attucks, [et al.] from the City of Boston*. Miami, Fla: Mnemosyne, 1969. A remembrance of the Boston Massacre lauding the sacrifices of its victims.

Hansen, Harry. *The Boston Massacre: An Episode of Dissent and Violence*. New York: Hastings House, 1970. A comprehensive account of the event and its context. One of several works on the massacre published for its bicentennial.

Miller, John C. *Sam Adams: Pioneer in Propaganda*. Boston: Little, Brown, 1936. Stresses the role of Adams as a manipulator and agitator, whose talents helped, indirectly at least, lead to the bloodshed in King Street.

Zobel, Hiller B. *The Boston Massacre*. New York: W. W. Norton, 1970. A comprehensive treatment of the event and its political and economic context.

SEE ALSO: 1765, Stamp Act Crisis; 1767, Townshend Crisis; 1773, Boston Tea Party.

1773 ■ AFRICAN AMERICAN BAPTIST CHURCH IS FOUNDED: *an amalgamation of African and European forms of religious worship finds expression*

DATE: 1773-1788
LOCALE: Savannah River Valley
CATEGORIES: African American history; Religion
KEY FIGURES:
Andrew Bryan (1737-1812), slave who was converted, purchased his freedom, and founded the Savannah Church
David George (born 1742?) and
George Liele (1750?-1825?), slaves who became preachers and founded churches for African Americans

SUMMARY OF EVENT. The religious revivals collectively known as the (first) Great Awakening transformed the spiritual climate of British North America in the mid-eighteenth century. Church membership grew and evangelical religious ideas, which emphasized a person's own relationship with God, began to acquire hegemony over the religious values propagated by the established churches. Among those people who embraced evangelical ideals were African American slaves, who found attractive the notion of a personal God, the hope for salvation, and the less formal style of evangelical worship. This was especially true in the South, where African Americans benefited from a practice among some white evangelicals of allowing blacks to preach to other blacks and where African Americans were the targets of white missionary activity.

African Americans were particularly drawn to the Baptist faith, especially in the latter part of the eighteenth century. White Baptists, themselves often among the poorest in southern society, actively recruited African Americans. Furthermore, Baptists did not require formal education as part of ministerial training, and what learning they did encourage centered on mastering the contents of the Bible. Even African Americans held in bondage and denied opportunities for formal education could fulfill these expectations, and more than a few became ministers. African American slaves not only joined biracial Baptist churches but also fashioned their own fellowships, where they blended the traditional folk religions they brought from Africa with the evangelical nostrums of the Europeans, thus creating a hybrid African American religion. The cosmologies and churches fashioned by African Ameri-

1773 ■ African American Baptist Church Is Founded

cans helped them survive and transcend the harsh realities of Southern slavery.

One area where African American Baptists flourished was the Savannah River Valley, which connected the hinterlands around Augusta, Georgia, with the port city of Savannah. Here, evangelical revivals among whites and blacks bore organizational fruit among African Americans. Indeed, African Americans formed their own Baptist church at Silver Bluff, near Augusta, in 1773, following one such revival.

About that time, a slave named George Liele heard a sermon preached by Reverend Matthew Moore, a white minister, and became convinced that he needed to respond to the gospel. "I was sure I should be found in hell, as sure as God was in heaven," Liele recalled. Baptized by Moore, Liele became a preacher and began to exhort other slaves in the vicinity of Augusta to become Christians. Liele's master, who was loyal to the British during the American Revolution, temporarily had to flee Georgia for his life and freed Liele. For the next several years, Liele and a colleague, David George, preached regularly at Silver Bluff, South Carolina, at the first black Baptist church in the Savannah River Valley region. George had been born a slave in Virginia and had run away from a cruel master before coming to the Deep South as the slave of George Galphin. Becoming convinced of his own iniquity and borrowing from whites an evangelical vocabulary and worldview, he was converted after hearing sermons in the mid-1770's by several African American preachers, including Liele.

Both George and Liele initially had become Baptists because of their own desire to go to heaven, but quickly they took it upon themselves to preach to their fellow slaves. Having found a sense of inner peace because of his religion, Liele wanted others to experience in themselves "the work which God had done for my soul." Liele and George organized other churches, including the congregation at Yama Craw, outside Savannah, in 1777.

Among those who heard Liele preach at Yama Craw was Andrew Bryan. Bryan had been born in Goose Creek, South Carolina, and was baptized by Liele in 1782. Bryan eventually purchased his freedom and devoted himself to his ministry. It was a decision not without consequences, as whites who feared an unshackled black man whipped Bryan twice and imprisoned him once. Undeterred, he continued to preach to ever-larger congregations, which often contained both blacks and whites. In 1788, his congregation constituted itself into the Savannah Georgia First Colored Church, commonly called the Savannah Church. At the time, it boasted 575 members and would grow to more than 800 at the time of Bryan's death.

Liele, George, and Bryan stood at the forefront of an important movement among African Americans in the South. Their religious teachings fused the African concepts of a unitary universe where the sacred and profane are not segregated, the European mythologies of heaven, hell, and redemption, and their present reality of slavery. God would help Africans through their travail of slavery and would one day lead them out of bondage. In this melding process, certain African reli-

gious practices were proscribed. The church covenant of Liele's Yama Craw Church specifically banned the consumption of blood and strangled meat of animals offered to idols, which had been a part of some West African religious rituals. Other African practices were given an important place, such as moaning as part of religious singing. This practice originated in ecstatic African religious rituals, and moaning and wailing have been preserved in Southern gospel singing. This hybrid religious ritual did not confine itself to African American communities. The emotional shouts and ritual cadences of African worship affected the rhythms of white discourse as well, especially the sermon form, in which the preacher and congregation engage in something of a dialogue.

Liele, George, and Bryan founded churches and baptized ministers who started other churches. One man converted by George and Liele was Jesse Peter. A slave, he was allowed uncommon liberties and preached around Savannah and Augusta. He helped constitute the Springfield African Church in Augusta in 1793, which was later recognized by white Baptists for its excellent church music. Until the American Civil War, the churches started by these men existed, sometimes tenuously. Often, they had to accept direct white oversight to avoid being shut down, but they clung tenaciously to as much independence as local custom and law would allow.

The careers of Liele, George, and Bryan also illustrate the protean political nature of evangelicalism. The formation of churches operated by African Americans reflects the capacity of blacks to avoid complete organizational enslavement as surely as the forming of a black theology kept African Americans from psychic enslavement. From these organizational and intellectual bases, African Americans could confront slavery in various ways. Both Liele and George fled the South for the British Empire, seeking to continue their ministerial work without the specter of slavery hanging over them. Liele went to Jamaica, establishing the first Baptist churches there. George went to Canada, where he worked with both blacks and whites before organizing a back-to-Africa movement, in which a thousand Canadian blacks went with George to Sierra Leone in 1792. Bryan, however, remained in the South, calling upon African Americans to lead better lives and, sometimes stealthily, urging whites to live out the Golden Rule in dealing with blacks. At his death, he was lauded by blacks and whites alike. By establishing churches that counseled patience while teaching a theology of ultimate deliverance, African American leaders like Liele, George, and Bryan helped African Americans survive slavery by encouraging them to expect freedom soon.

—*Edward R. Crowther*

Additional reading:

Davis, John W. "George Liele and Andrew Bryan: Pioneer Negro Baptist Preachers." *Journal of Negro History* 3 (1918): 119-127. This brief pioneering account contains complete sketches of Liele and Bryan.

Fitts, LeRoy. *A History of Black Baptists*. Nashville, Tenn.: Broadman Press, 1985. A sympathetic and readable account of black Baptist leaders and churches.

Lincoln, C. Eric, and Lawrence H. Mamiya. *The Black Church in the African American Experience*. Durham, N.C.: Duke University Press, 1990. A well-written survey of African American churches since their earliest times and their meaning in the African American struggle in the United States.

Sernett, Milton C. *Afro-American Religious History: A Documentary Witness*. Durham, N.C.: Duke University Press, 1985. Contains letters from Bryan and Liele and many other representative documents of the African American religious experience.

Sobel, Mechal. *Trablin' On: The Slave Journey to an Afro-Baptist Faith*. Westport, Conn.: Greenwood Press, 1979. Emphasizes the hybrid quality of African American Baptist religion.

Wilmore, Gayraud S., ed. *African American Religious Studies: An Interdisciplinary Anthology*. Durham, N.C.: Duke University Press, 1989. This series of essays may assist one in interpreting the fragmentary documentary record of early African American religious life.

SEE ALSO: 1730's, First Great Awakening; 1768, Methodist Church Is Established; 1775, Pennsylvania Society for the Abolition of Slavery Is Founded; 1777, Northeast States Abolish Slavery; 1784, Hall's Masonic Lodge Is Chartered; 1786, Virginia Statute of Religious Liberty; 1789, Episcopal Church Is Established; 1790's, Second Great Awakening.

1773 ■ BOSTON TEA PARTY: *symbolic protest against British exploitation of the colonies, one step short of armed rebellion*

DATE: December 16, 1773
LOCALE: Boston, Massachusetts
CATEGORIES: Economics; Government and politics; Wars, uprisings, and civil unrest
KEY FIGURES:
Samuel Adams (1722-1803) and
John Hancock (1737-1793), patriots who aroused Bostonians against the continued presence of the tea ships
Thomas Hutchinson (1711-1780), governor of Massachusetts
Frederick North, second earl of Guilford (1732-1792), prime minister of Great Britain

SUMMARY OF EVENT. On the evening of December 16, 1773, three vessels lay at anchor in Boston Harbor. They carried 342 chests containing more than ninety thousand pounds of dutiable tea worth about nine thousand pounds sterling. Shortly after 6:00 P.M., between thirty and sixty men, calling themselves "Mohawks" and roughly disguised as Indians, boarded the ships. Hundreds of silent onlookers at the wharf saw the "Mohawks," organized into three groups, swiftly and systematically break open the tea chests and pour their contents into the sea. Because the water was only two or three feet deep, the tea began to pile up, forcing the men to rake it aside to allow room for the rest. In less than three hours, they had completed their work and disappeared into the darkness; to this day, the identities of most remain unknown. The "Destruction of the Tea," exclaimed John Adams the next day, "is so bold, so daring . . . it must have so important Consequences and so lasting, that I cannot but consider it as an Epocha [*sic*] in History." Eighteen months later, the colonists were locked in military combat with Great Britain. The Boston Tea Party had ushered in a series of events that led directly to war and, eventually, independence.

The origins of the famous Tea Party are to be found in Parliament's repeal, in 1770, of all the external taxes embodied in the controversial Townshend Revenue Act, except the tax on tea, which was to remain principally as a symbol of Great Britain's right to extract cash from American purses. Although the colonists had won only a partial victory in their battle against the second British program of taxation, compared to a complete repeal of the earlier Stamp Act, the chances for an improvement in Anglo-American relations seemed fairly bright in the years 1771-1773. The secretary of state for the colonies, Wills Hill, earl of Hillsborough and marquis of Downshire, soothed American tempers by announcing that the British government did not intend to propose any new taxes for the colonists.

These were years of renewed commercial prosperity, during which countless Americans drank the dutied brew, when all but a few ignored the frantic schemes of Samuel Adams and a radical minority to keep alive the old flames of resentment. There were, to be sure, occasional events that generated fresh ill will, such as the burning by Rhode Islanders of the royal revenue cutter *Gaspee* and the clandestine publication of Massachusetts governor Thomas Hutchinson's correspondence expressing stern criticism of the colony's patriot leaders. But it was Parliament's Tea Act of 1773 that brought the period of quiescence to an abrupt end throughout North America. Ironically, British politicians acted not with the purpose of disciplining the Americans but with the intention of boosting the sagging fortunes of the giant East India Company. After unsuccessful attempts to help the ailing corporation with huge investments in India, the prime minister of Great Britain, Lord North, earl of Guilford, secured passage of the Tea Act. This allowed the East India Company to sell tea directly to America for the first time, and to do so through its own agents; previously, it had sold its product to English wholesale merchants, from whom the tea passed into the hands of American wholesalers and retailers. By removing the profits formerly obtained by English and American middlemen, and by the added provision eliminating English duties on tea exported to the New World possessions, the company hoped to undersell Dutch-smuggled leaves in America, even though the provincials would have to pay the remaining Townshend tax of three pence on each pound.

Everywhere in North America, Lord North's move met stiff resistance. Merchants accused the ministry of giving the East India Company and its agents a monopoly on the local tea market, which would be followed in time by other monopolies in the American trade. More frightening to Americans was the constitutional threat; they were vulnerable already since the taxed herb had been purchased in America after 1770. Now, if they consumed even more of the duted drink, they would implicitly admit the authority of Parliament to tax them. In fact, they saw in Lord North's undertaking a cynical endeavor to get them to "barter liberty for luxury." Consignees in New York, Philadelphia, and Charleston were persuaded to resign their commissions, as the stamp tax collectors previously had been made to do. The outcome was different in Boston, where Governor Hutchinson backed the consignees and refused to let the tea ships return to England without first unloading their cargo.

The Tea Party was a form of symbolic protest—one step beyond random violence, one step short of organized, armed rebellion. The tea dumpers chose their symbols with utmost care. As the imported tea symbolized British tyranny and taxation, so the image of the Indian, and the Mohawk disguise, represented its antithesis: a trademark of an emerging American identity and a voice for liberty in a new land. The image of the Indian was figured into tea-dumpers' disguises not only in Boston but also in cities all along the Atlantic Seaboard. The Mohawk symbol was not picked at random. It was used as a revolutionary symbol, counterpoising the tea tax.

The image of the Indian (particularly the Mohawk) also appeared at about the same time, in the same context, in revolutionary songs, slogans, and engravings. Paul Revere, whose midnight rides became legendary in the poetry of Henry Wadsworth Longfellow, played a crucial role in forging this sense of identity, contributing to the revolutionary cause a set of remarkable engravings that cast as America's first national symbol an American Indian woman, long before Uncle Sam came along.

Boston's patriots were not known for their civility in the face of British authority, and it was Boston's "Mohawks" who sparked physical confrontation over the tea tax. As they dumped the tea, the "Mohawks" exchanged words in a secret sign language using Indian hand symbols, and sang:

> Rally Mohawks, and bring your axes
> And tell King George we'll pay no taxes
> on his foreign tea;
> His threats are vain, and vain to think
> To force our girls and wives to drink
> his vile Bohea!
> Then rally, boys, and hasten on
> To meet our chiefs at the Green Dragon!
> Our Warren's here, and bold Revere
> With hands to do and words to cheer,
> for liberty and laws;
> Our country's "braves" and firm defenders
> shall ne'er be left by true North Enders
> fighting freedom's cause!
> Then rally, boys, and hasten on
> To meet our chiefs at the Green Dragon.

After the "Mohawks" had performed the task of unloading, Parliament's response was one of unparalleled severity. It passed the Coercive Acts in 1774 in order to bring rebellious

Massachusetts to its knees, by closing the port of Boston, altering the structure of government in the colony, and allowing British officials and soldiers accused of capital offenses to be tried in England or, to avoid a hostile local jury, in a colony other than the one where the offense had occurred. The Coercive Acts also provided for the quartering of troops once more in the town of Boston, stoking the smoldering resentment of its citizens.

The Boston Tea Party is regarded by some as the first battle of the American Revolution, an economic one: In 1773, Britain exported 738,083 pounds of tea to the colonies. In 1774, the figure had fallen to 69,830. Imports of tea fell all along the seaboard: from 206,312 pounds to 30,161 in New England; 208,385 to 1,304 pounds in New York; and 208,191 pounds to none in Pennsylvania.

—*R. Don Higginbotham, updated by Bruce E. Johansen*

ADDITIONAL READING:

Brant, Irving. *James Madison: The Virginia Revolutionist.* Indianapolis: Bobbs-Merrill, 1941. Provides one of the best accounts of the tea crisis in Virginia.

Grinde, Donald A., Jr., and Bruce E. Johansen. "Mohawks, Axes, and Taxes." In *Exemplar of Liberty: Native America and the Evolution of Democracy.* Los Angeles: American Indian Studies Center, University of California, Los Angeles, 1991. Describes the use of American Indian images at the Boston Tea Party, and in revolutionary propaganda of the American Revolution.

Griswwold, Wesley S. *The Night the Revolution Began: The Boston Tea Party, 1773.* Brattleboro, Vt.: S. Greene Press, 1972. An outline account of the Tea Party and its context, published for its bicentennial.

Labaree, Benjamin W. *The Boston Tea Party.* New York: Oxford University Press, 1964. Has remained the seminal work on the Tea Party and its political and economic context.

Thomas, Peter David Garner. *Tea Party to Independence: The Third Phase of the American Revolution, 1773-1776.* Oxford, England: Clarendon Press, 1991. Describes events from the Tea Party to the Declaration of Independence.

SEE ALSO: 1765, Stamp Act Crisis; 1767, Townshend Crisis; 1770, Boston Massacre.

1774 ■ LORD DUNMORE'S WAR: *frontier Virginians and Marylanders battle Shawnees, resulting in relocation of the latter as settlers moved into Kentucky*

DATE: April 27-October 10, 1774
LOCALE: Ohio River region
CATEGORIES: Expansion and land acquisition; Native American history; Wars, uprisings, and civil unrest
KEY FIGURES:
John Connolly (c. 1743-1813), Virginia's administrator for the Monongahela region

Cornstalk (c. 1720-1777), Shawnee leader who tried to negotiate with Dunmore

Michael Cresap (1742-1775), colonist who was developing land for future settlement

John Logan, also known as *Tachnechdorus*, the *Great Mingo* (c. 1723-1780), Mingo war chief

John Murray, fourth earl of Dunmore (1732-1809), royal governor of Virginia

SUMMARY OF EVENT. Lord Dunmore's War was a struggle between the Shawnees and Virginians in the spring and summer of 1774. It represents the culmination of events dating back to Pontiac's Resistance (1763-1766). For both the American Indians and the colonists, the war carried important ramifications. The victor would control what is now Kentucky. In order to understand how the conflict arose, one must understand the unsettled state of Anglo-Indian relations after 1763.

Following Pontiac's Resistance, British officials had tried to create an alliance with the natives of the Ohio and Illinois region. Using the French model, Britain's Indian superintendent for the northern colonies, Sir William Johnson, tried to create a mutually intelligible world that would allow colonists and American Indians to conduct diplomatic and economic activities. Two problems undermined the superintendent's efforts. The first problem confronting the relationship was the emergence of colonial communities west of the Appalachian Mountains. Colonists had settled the region in direct violation of the Proclamation of 1763. Although British soldiers often drove them back across the mountains, the settlers often returned. Outside the range of governmental control, these settlers caused tensions with the native communities of the region. The second problem was the British government's desire to curtail expenditures relating to Indian affairs. The Crown first tried to reduce its commitment by passing some of the costs off on the colonies, but these attempts did not work. As a result, Johnson's office was unable to meet even the basic necessities for conducting Indian affairs after 1770. Taken together, colonial settlement along the frontier and reduced expenditures meant a worsening of Anglo-Indian relations in the years preceding Lord Dunmore's War.

The Shawnees' relationship with the British reached its nadir with the completion of the Treaty of Fort Stanwix in 1768. As a result of this treaty, the Six Nations of the Iroquois ceded much of the territory south and east of the Ohio River to land speculators. The ceded land had belonged to the Shawnees, Lenni Lenapes (Delawares), Cherokees, and Mingos, not the Six Nations. The treaty resulted in a series of confrontations between the Shawnees, who rejected the treaty, and the British. Beginning in 1769, skirmishes between the tribes and the frontier colonists became commonplace. These skirmishes continued not only because of reduced expenditures on American Indian affairs but also because of the withdrawal of British soldiers from the colonial frontier. By 1774, British soldiers were stationed at only Kaskaskia, Detroit, and Michilimackinac. Without British soldiers or Indian agents, the Ohio region became a battleground.

As tensions between the two sides escalated, Sir William Johnson worked to isolate the Shawnees from their allies. By the spring of 1774, he had isolated the Shawnees from their previous confederates, the Hurons, Miamis, and Potawatomis. His activities broke the Shawnee league. Colonists appreciated the importance of Johnson's actions when war broke out in April, 1774. For his part, British commander Thomas Gage expressed no surprise when Dunmore's War began. He had long suspected Virginia's colonial elites of supporting the frontiersmen in their move west.

The war began on April 27, 1774. On this date, Daniel Greathouse and his followers lured an Iroquois hunting party into a trap at the mouth of the Yellow Creek. Greathouse and his men killed nine people. Those killed at Yellow Creek were followers of the Mingo war chief Tachnechdorus, also called John Logan, the Great Mingo. Logan recruited supporters and retaliated. By July, he and his followers had claimed thirteen scalps and the Great Mingo proclaimed himself avenged. Because Virginians were settling on Shawnee lands, Logan focused his reprisals on Virginians in particular rather than colonists (such as Pennsylvanians) in general.

If Logan's actions had been only an isolated response to a massacre, it is doubtful that war would have erupted. However, Logan's actions were not unique. Further down the Ohio River, Michael Cresap and his associates—who were trying to develop land for future settlers—received a message from John Connolly, Virginia's resident administrator for the Monongahela region. Connolly's message implied that a colonial war with the Indians had begun. Situated hundreds of miles beyond colonial settlements, Cresap and his men acted as if war were a reality. They attacked a canoe carrying Lenni Lenape and Shawnee traders. After scalping the Indians, Cresap and his men sought protection in the community of Wheeling.

Following the Yellow Creek Massacre, and while Cresap and his men were seeking the shelter of Wheeling, Connolly participated in a condolence ceremony for the victims of Greathouse's attack. Held at Pittsburgh, the ceremony mollified the Indians' civil leadership. It did not, however, appease the warriors on either side of the cultural divide. Logan continued his attacks against squatters, and Cresap tried to raise a volunteer unit for military service against the natives. Their actions illustrated how young men on both sides of the cultural divide often dictated the actions of their elders.

As late as June, 1774, it was still possible to avert full-scale war. In July, however, Virginia's militia moved westward. Their aims were to destroy the Shawnees and open Kentucky for Virginian settlement. Virginian major Angus McDonald led four hundred Virginians across the Ohio River and destroyed five Shawnee villages, including Wakatomica, in early August. Later that month, Dunmore arrived at Pittsburgh. When Shawnee warriors refused his request to meet with him, Dunmore decided to lead an expedition against the Shawnees located along the Scioto River.

While marching to its new base of operations at Camp Charlotte, a militia detachment burned the Mingo town at the

Salt Licks. In order to prevent the Virginians from invading the Scioto region, nine hundred Shawnees and their allies attacked twelve hundred Virginians at their fortifications at the mouth of the Kanawha River on October 10, 1774. This attack—the Battle of Point Pleasant—resulted in the Shawnees' defeat.

Before the battle at Point Pleasant took place, the traditional leaders of the Shawnee and Lenni Lenape had sought a negotiated settlement with Governor Dunmore. He refused to deal with the Shawnee representative, Cornstalk. Dunmore did meet with Cornstalk's Lenni Lenape counterparts, Captain Pipe and George White Eyes, who tried to mediate the problem. Their efforts resulted only in limiting the war, not preventing it. After the Battle of Point Pleasant, however, Cornstalk again tried to negotiate a settlement with Dunmore. The result was the Camp Charlotte Agreement of 1774.

Governor Dunmore dictated the terms of this agreement. He required the Shawnees to accept Virginia's interpretation of the Treaty of Fort Stanwix. He also required that the Shawnees and Mingos give him hostages as a promise of future good behavior. He demanded that the natives give up their right to hunt on the south side of the Ohio River. In exchange for their promise, Dunmore promised to prohibit Virginians from intruding on Indian lands north of the Ohio River.

While Dunmore and Cornstalk discussed peace terms, Logan refused to attend the council. He did, however, send a statement to the council through the trader John Gibson. "Logan's Lament," as it came to be known after Thomas Jefferson included it years later in his *Notes on the State of Virginia*, justified Logan's actions in the preceding months:

> Col. Cresap, the last spring, in cold blood, and unprovoked, murdered all the relations of Logan. . . . There runs not a drop of my blood in the veins of any living creature. . . . Who is there to mourn for Logan?—Not one.

In response to Logan's speech, Dunmore ordered a detachment of troops to attack the Mingos at Salt Lick Town. The attack resulted in the death of five Indians and the capture of fourteen prisoners.

Following the Virginians' attack, Lord Dunmore's War became fused with the American Revolution. American patriots believed Dunmore really was not interested in claiming Kentucky for settlement; they concluded that Dunmore's real intent was the formation of an army for use against them. By 1775, colonists had turned against Governor Dunmore. As a result, the final treaty ending Lord Dunmore's War, the Treaty of Pittsburgh, was delayed until October, 1775. Following Lord Dunmore's War, Shawnee population centers in the Ohio Valley began to change. Most Shawnees left the Muskingum region and moved southwest toward the Scioto and Mad River areas.   —*Michael J. Mullin*

ADDITIONAL READING:

Jacob, John J. *A Biographical Sketch of the Life of the Late Captain Michael Cresap*. Cincinnati: J. F. Uhlhorn, 1866. John Jacob worked for Michael Cresap and later married Cresap's widow. His book challenges the notion that Cresap was responsible for the Yellow Creek Massacre.

McConnell, Michael N. *A Country Between: The Upper Ohio Valley and Its Peoples, 1724-1774*. Lincoln: University of Nebraska Press, 1992. Discusses colonial expansion from the eighteenth century Native American perspective. McConnell sees the Treaty of Fort Stanwix as a deciding factor in the coming of Lord Dunmore's War.

Mayer, Brantz. *Tah-Gah-Jute, or Logan and Cresap, an Historical Essay*. Albany: Munsell, 1867. The most famous study of the Cresap-Logan controversy written in the nineteenth century.

Tanner, Helen Hornbeck, ed. *Atlas of Great Lakes Indian History*. Norman: University of Oklahoma Press, 1987. This monograph traces Shawnee history through cartographic evidence. Contains a discussion of Lord Dunmore's War.

White, Richard. *The Middle Ground: Indians, Empires, and Republics in the Great Lakes Region, 1650-1815*. New York: Cambridge University Press, 1991. Discusses how both Europeans and American Indians sought accommodation and common meaning. Places Lord Dunmore's War within this context in his analysis of the event.

SEE ALSO: 1763, Pontiac's Resistance; 1763, Proclamation of 1763.

1774 ■ QUEBEC ACT: *Britain grants limited civil rights to Catholics and extends the boundaries of Quebec province into the Ohio Valley*

DATE: May 20, 1774
LOCALE: Province of Quebec
CATEGORIES: Canadian history; Expansion and land acquisition; Laws and acts; Religion
KEY FIGURES:
Guy Carleton, first Lord Dorchester (1724-1808), governor of the Province of Quebec
William Legge, second Lord Dartmouth (1731-1801), secretary of state for the colonies
James Murray (1721-1794), first military and civilian governor of the Province of Quebec
Frederick North, second earl of Guilford (1732-1792), British prime minister
SUMMARY OF EVENT. In 1774, through the efforts of Lord Frederick North, England's prime minister, the British Parliament produced "An Act for Making More Effectual Provision for the Government of the Province of Quebec in North America," the first of several eighteenth and nineteenth century acts to govern the relationship between England and Canada. Among the principal provisions of the act were the assertion of trans-Allegheny power by the Crown, rule of the province through a governor and council, and, most significant, a modicum of religious freedom for the Catholics of Quebec.

QUEBEC ACT, 1774

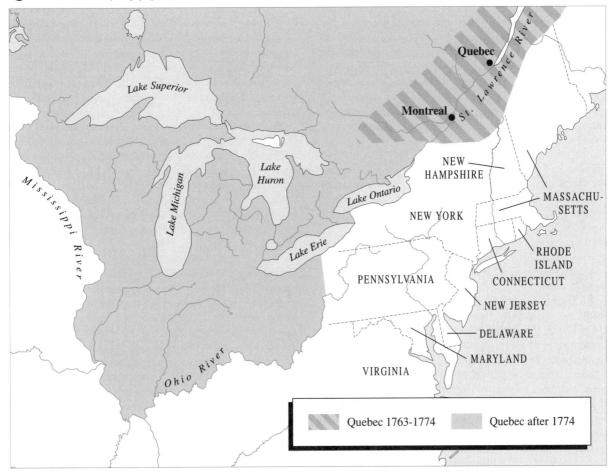

Quebec 1763-1774   Quebec after 1774

When France had ceded New France to Great Britain by the Treaty of Paris in 1763, England suddenly found itself with a province of sixty-five thousand Canadian Catholics. The Articles of Capitulation provided for the continuation of the status quo with regard to religion: Catholics in the province could continue to worship in their traditional way, the French king would still appoint the bishop, and the clergy could continue to receive the tithes of the faithful. However, the treaty also included the proviso, "As far as the laws of Great Britain allow."

During the next ten years, British governors James Murray and Guy Carleton ruled the province with little clear direction from the Parliament. The few English colonists in the province were incensed that French-speaking Catholics not only had freedom to practice their religion but also could take part in civic life, even to sit on juries. In no other part of the empire did such latitude prevail. Clearly, the government had to regularize this anomalous situation. Murray first and then Carleton, even more vigorously, called for a practical toleration of Catholicism in the province, although they hoped that they could attract English colonists in sufficient number so that the

French-speaking colonists would leave Quebec, much as French-speaking settlers had been forced out of Acadia (Nova Scotia) a generation before.

In 1774, Parliament, under the aegis of Lord North and his secretary of state for the colonies, William Legge, Lord Dartmouth, enacted a series of laws that Americans later called the Intolerable Acts. These laws closed the port of Boston, reorganized the administration of Massachusetts, and permitted British troops to commandeer colonists' homes. Americans judged the Quebec Act as just another of the punitive measures enacted that year.

At least three major drafts of the act circulated before the members of Parliament agreed to the final document, largely the work of Carleton as governor of Quebec. The English-speaking colonists in the province agitated for a representative assembly in which they would hold a majority of the seats, although they constituted less than 1 percent of the population. They would have restricted even the minority seats to wealthy French-speaking rural landlords.

There were four principal concerns in the act: geography, Canadian and British law, no representative assembly, and permission for Catholics to practice their religion. First, the Parliament extended the boundaries of the Province of Quebec down through the Ohio Valley, thus effectively keeping the American colonies east of the Alleghenies. There would be no room for the colonies to expand westward into the potentially rich fur-trading area, because this territory would now be a part of Quebec. By spelling out the boundaries of Quebec at the very beginning of the act, Parliament wanted to make it clear that none of the provisions of this act might apply to Newfoundland or any other British territory. This was an expedient for Quebec only.

Administrators in Canada, English-speaking colonists, and members of Parliament all contributed to the discussion about the forms of law to be observed in the new colony. The conclusion was a compromise to appease the non-Canadians without offending the French-speaking too much. Civil law would be governed by traditional French customs, especially regarding properties and family matters. Criminal law, however, would follow the British system of laws. British officers and courts would see to the administration of justice in these matters.

Parliament decided that a government-appointed governor would rule the province, assisted by a council appointed by the governor. In practice, this meant that the taxes would be modest, since no unrepresentative government would be able to command the respect of the populace if it imposed a heavy taxation. To appease the English-speaking colonists, however, there was provision for an eventual representative assembly if Parliament and the governor deemed it expedient in the future. Any future assembly had severely limited powers of taxation.

In order to give French-speaking Canadians freedom to practice their religion, Parliament designed an oath unlike any that could be found elsewhere in the empire. Catholics would be able to swear allegiance to the Crown without having to denounce the papacy. This, in itself, was a major step. The terms of the Treaty of Paris provided that Catholics could practice their faith in conformity with the laws of Great Britain. However, there were no such laws in England that would permit Catholics freedom to practice unimpeded. The proviso of the Quebec Act was the exercise of religion "subject to the King's supremacy." Officially, Parliament asserted the right to appoint a superintendent for Catholics, a deliberately ambiguous title. In fact, however, they settled for a bishop. Catholics could maintain their clergy through a system of tithes, as they were accustomed to doing.

To be considered along with the act itself, however, is the instruction given to the governor in administering the religious affairs of the province. Governors were encouraged to limit French culture and to curb the activity of the Catholic church at every turn by giving preeminence to the Anglican church, or Church of England. It was hoped that this province eventually would become more like Britain's other colonies and that English-speaking Anglicans or, less preferably, other Protestants would prevail.

The Continental Congress, meeting in Philadelphia, immediately perceived this act as a threat and went on record in opposition on September 17, 1774. They objected to the expansion of the provincial boundaries into the Ohio Valley, but they were especially upset about permitting Catholics to exercise their religion. Some historians consider the Quebec Act to be among the most prominent of the colonial grievances that led to war and, eventually, to independence for the American colonies.

Clearly, the Parliament sought to keep the French-speaking Canadians loyal to the Crown and to blunt the westward ambitions of the colonies to the south. They were successful in this regard. By not unduly burdening their Catholic subjects, they were able to avoid serious civil unrest that surely would have followed anything more restrictive. The Catholics of Canada accepted the provisions of the act; however, they thought that they had received in 1774 what they should have received ten years earlier in the Treaty of Paris.

There is every likelihood that Great Britain would have lost Quebec had it imposed harsher terms in the act. As it was, French Canadians were quite aware of the disdain of their southern neighbors for a Catholic enclave in the empire, especially one so close. In April, 1776, an American colonial delegation from the Continental Congress, the first American diplomatic venture to a foreign country, tried to enlist Canadian support for the revolutionary cause. Samuel Chase, Benjamin Franklin, Charles Carroll, and John Carroll received a polite, but chilly, reception. England's policy worked well enough. French Canadians knew they had no other home than in the British Empire. They could not expect any help from their former French sovereign, and the American colonies objected to their very existence. Canada is today what it is, for good or ill, in no small measure as a result of the British policy of expedience in 1774.

—*Daniel A. Brown*

ADDITIONAL READING:

Burt, A. L. *The Old Province of Quebec*. Toronto: McClelland and Steward, 1968. A careful assessment of the economic implications of the enactment.

Coffin, Victor. *The Province of Quebec and the Early American Revolution*. Madison: University of Wisconsin Press, 1896. The earliest study to consider the act's implications to the liberation movement in the thirteen colonies.

Coupland, Reginald. *The Quebec Act: A Study in Statesmanship*. Oxford, England: Clarendon Press, 1925. An almost adulatory study of the diplomatic efforts required to secure parliamentary approval.

Neatly, Hilda. *The Quebec Act: Protest and Policy*. Scarborough, Ont.: Prentice Hall, 1972. Balanced narration of the events surrounding the Quebec Act and its subsequent interpretations by historians and economists.

Thompson, Wayne. *Canada 1995*. 12th ed. Harper's Ferry, W.Va.: Stryker-Post, 1995. A mildly anti-French account that is strong on the military dimensions of the event.

SEE ALSO: 1754, French and Indian War; 1774, First Continental Congress.

1774 ■ FIRST CONTINENTAL CONGRESS:
the beginning of an independent American government, paving the way for separation from Great Britain

DATE: September 5-October 26, 1774
LOCALE: Philadelphia, Pennsylvania
CATEGORY: Government and politics
KEY FIGURES:

John Adams (1735-1826), author of the congressional resolution denying the right of Parliament to tax or legislate for the colonies

Samuel Adams (1722-1803), early advocate of intercolonial assemblages

Joseph Galloway (c. 1731-1803), conservative member of Congress and author of the Plan of Union

Alexander McDougall (1732-1786), patriot who persuaded New York to send delegates committed to a nonimportation agreement

SUMMARY OF EVENT. On September 5, 1774, representatives from all the American colonies, except far-off and thinly settled Georgia, assembled at Carpenter's Hall in Philadelphia to begin the business of the First Continental Congress. The significance that Americans attached to the meeting is revealed in the quality of the men chosen to attend: Peyton Randolph, George Washington, Patrick Henry, and Richard Henry Lee of Virginia; John and Samuel Adams of Massachusetts; John and Edward Rutledge of South Carolina; Roger Sherman of Connecticut; and John Dickinson and Joseph Galloway of Pennsylvania. "There are in the congress," noted John Adams in his diary, "a collection of the greatest men upon this Continent in point of abilities, virtues, and fortune." The greatest potential, as Adams recognized, belonged not to the old and well-tried politicians but to younger men. The future lay with colonial leaders such as John Adams, George Washington, and John Jay, many of whom first became acquainted with one another during the September and October deliberations in Philadelphia.

After Parliament imposed the Coercive Acts upon Massachusetts, the cause of that colony became the cause of all American colonies. If Parliament were permitted to chastise one colony legislatively, it might choose to punish other colonies at any time. The only recourse many colonial leaders saw was united resistance. South Carolina, among the last to hear of Massachusetts' fate, was the first outside New England to send direct aid, dispatching a shipment of rice for the beleaguered Bostonians. Other colonies soon followed South Carolina's lead. Suspicion of Parliament's motives increased after the early summer of 1774, when, with remarkably poor timing, that body passed the Quebec Act. That act gave the province of Quebec a civil government without a representative assembly. It also allowed Quebec's Catholic majority special privileges relative to their religious practices. The Quebec Act

provided further evidence to colonists that a conspiracy against their rights was growing in Parliament. Thoughtful Americans concerned about the prospects of potentially violent local protest recognized the need to coordinate and control efforts to redress grievances against Parliament. With the idea of an intercolonial congress steadily gaining support, Massachusetts, in June, issued a call for a convention of deputies from each colony to be held in Philadelphia. Other colonies soon followed Massachusetts' lead, and in September, the first congress of continental representatives became a reality.

Half the fifty-six delegates who assembled in Philadelphia were lawyers, eleven were merchants, and the rest were farmers. None of the delegates officially represented this assembly. Instead, although acknowledged leaders within their colonies, the delegates were in Philadelphia by their own choice. While the British threat to American commerce was among the delegates' chief concerns, more important was the perceived threat to individual American rights and the British constitution. A majority of the delegates, who would be labeled radicals,

PREMIÈRE ASSEMBLÉE DU CONGRÈS.

A French illustration of the First Continental Congress. "There are in the congress," noted John Adams in his diary, "a collection of the greatest men upon this Continent in point of abilities, virtues, and fortune." (Library of Congress)

embraced an aggressive stance toward recent British actions. Others, identified as "reconciliators" or "conservatives," hoped to pursue a far less confrontational approach.

The intent of Congress to stand resolutely for American rights became obvious early in the proceedings, as the delegates overwhelmingly endorsed the Suffolk Resolves. Adopted by Massachusetts' Suffolk County, these resolutions denounced the Coercive Acts as unconstitutional, urged the people to prepare militarily, and called for an immediate end to trade with the British Empire. In Philadelphia, there was informal talk about setting up a continental army if the crisis deepened, and Charles Lee, a former British officer from Virginia, showed some of his fellow delegates a plan he had drafted for organizing colonial regiments. Congress' adamant position on the Suffolk Resolves alarmed many of the conservative delegates. In response, Joseph Galloway proposed a far more conciliatory approach to the problems with Parliament. He called for the adoption of a Plan of Union that would establish an American Grand Council. Although "an inferior and distinct branch of Parliament," the Grand Council would create a separate American government within the structure of the British Empire by providing colonial representation in all matters involving the American relationship with Great Britain. In a close vote, the Continental Congress rejected the idea and, in so doing, pushed the colonies toward independence from England.

The subject of commercial retaliation, which had been important in bringing about the Congress, took most of the delegates' time. On September 27, Congress adopted a resolution banning importation from Great Britain after December 1, 1774. Three days later, the delegates voted to stop exportation to the various parts of the empire, beginning September 10, 1775, if America's grievances were not redressed by that date. Congress' program of economic coercion, known as the Continental Association, bound each colony to participate in the boycott and created enforcement procedures.

In addition to the formal protest of the Coercive Acts, the Continental Congress pursued a review of colonial America's relationship with Great Britain. Because Parliament had refused to recognize repeated attempts to distinguish between taxation legislation and legislation that regulated trade within the empire but did not generate revenue, many Americans concluded that Parliament had no constitutional justification to maintain authority over the colonies. Thomas Jefferson, in his pamphlet *Summary View*, expressed the thinking of many of his countrymen. He referred to the king as the "chief magistrate" of the empire and denied the authority of Parliament to legislate for the colonies in any case. However, Jefferson went too far for some congressmen. Reluctant to repudiate Parliament completely, conservatives were able to secure approval of a compromise resolution, which stated that by consent, not by right, Parliament could regulate colonial American commerce in the interest of the empire as a whole.

Before adjourning on October 26, Congress scheduled another intercolonial meeting for the following spring and dispatched a series of appeals to the king, to the people of Great Britain, and to the citizens of America. The delegates called for a return to the relationship they had enjoyed with England in the years prior to 1763 and asked for a repeal or withdrawal of policies and laws, beginning with the decision to keep British regulars in colonial America and concluding with the Coercive Acts. In Great Britain, the appeals of Congress went unheeded. As early as November 18, 1774, King George III informed his prime minister, Lord Frederick North, earl of Guilford, that "the New England governments are in a state of rebellion [and] blows must decide whether they are to be subject to this country or independent."

With their work completed and preparations made for a second meeting of the Continental Congress, the delegates returned home. Although most recognized that they had taken important actions in addressing the British threat to American rights, few realized that they had made a significant step toward independence from England and the establishment of an autonomous American government.

—*R. Don Higginbotham, updated by Paul E. Doutrich*

ADDITIONAL READING:

Ammerman, David. *In the Common Cause: American Response to the Coercive Acts*. Charlottesville: University Press of Virginia, 1974. Asserts that the First Continental Congress was the product of popular opposition to British legislation, particularly the Coercive Acts.

Brown, Richard D. *Revolutionary Politics in Massachusetts: The Boston Committee of Correspondence and the Towns, 1772-1774*. Cambridge, Mass.: Harvard University Press, 1970. Examines the role that local protest organizations played immediately preceding the First Continental Congress.

Brown, Wallace. *The King's Friends: The Composition and Motives of the American Loyalist Claimants*. Providence, R.I.: Brown University Press, 1965. Examines the Loyalists, who, between 1777 and 1790, placed claims with the British government for losses suffered in America.

Burnett, Edmund C. *The Continental Congress*. New York: Macmillan, 1941. The first three chapters of this massively detailed book are particularly relevant to the events of 1774.

Jensen, Merrill. *The Founding of a Nation: A History of the American Revolution, 1763-1776*. London: Oxford University Press, 1968. In this fine narrative, the importance of the First Continental Congress is well described.

Meigs, Cornelia L. *The Violent Men: A Study of Human Relations in the First American Congress*. New York: Macmillan, 1949. A fast-paced narrative of the years 1774-1776.

Oliver, Peter. *Peter Oliver's Origin and Progress of the American Rebellion: A Tory View*. Edited by Douglas Adair and John Schutz. San Marino, Calif.: Huntington Library, 1961. Oliver, like most Tory writers, describes the American Revolution as the work of a minority of demagogues who aroused and coerced the people by "every low and dirty art."

SEE ALSO: 1765, Stamp Act Crisis; 1767, Townshend Crisis; 1770, Boston Massacre; 1773, Boston Tea Party; 1774, Quebec Act; 1775, Battle of Lexington and Concord; 1775, Second Continental Congress.

1775 ■ PENNSYLVANIA SOCIETY FOR THE ABOLITION OF SLAVERY IS FOUNDED: *the first antislavery society in America, developing the abolitionist philosophy*

DATE: April 14, 1775
LOCALE: Philadelphia, Pennsylvania
CATEGORIES: African American history; Organizations and institutions; Social reform
KEY FIGURES:
Anthony Benezet (1713-1784), teacher and philanthropist who converted to the Quaker religion
John Woolman (1720-1772), teacher and Quaker leader
SUMMARY OF EVENT. On April 14, 1775, a group of men gathered at the Sun Tavern on Second Street in Philadelphia to establish the first antislavery society in America. After electing John Baldwin their president and adopting a constitution, they named their organization the Society for the Relief of Free Negroes Unlawfully Held in Bondage. Sixteen of the twenty-four founders were members of the Society of Friends, or Quakers. The creation of this antislavery society was instigated when Philadelphia Quakers Israel Pemberton and Thomas Harrison aided Native American Dinah Neville and her children, who were being detained in Philadelphia pending their shipment to the West Indies to be sold as slaves.

Harrison was fined in a Philadelphia court for giving protection to the Neville family. When this incident gained notoriety, members of the Quaker Philadelphia Meeting mobilized to form the antislavery society. At its first meeting, the antislavery society enlisted legal counsel to help the Nevilles and five other victims illegally held in bondage and to form a standing committee to investigate any conditions of slavery in the Philadelphia area.

The Revolutionary War interrupted regular meetings until 1784. At this time, Quaker abolitionist Anthony Benezet revived the antislavery society as members learned that two African Americans had committed suicide rather than be illegally enslaved. Benezet increased the membership to forty, including Benjamin Franklin, James Pemberton, and Dr. Benjamin Rush. The society renamed itself the Pennsylvania Society for Promoting the Abolition of Slavery, for the Relief of Free Negroes Unlawfully Held in Bondage, and for Improving the Condition of the African Race. Since the majority of the members were Friends, the group developed directly from Quaker religious beliefs and within the Quaker social structure. To explore the founding of the Pennsylvania Society for the Abolition of Slavery, it is critical to trace events and movements within the Society of Friends in seventeenth century colonial Pennsylvania.

One of the basic principles espoused by Quaker founder George Fox was that all people are created equal. On a visit to the colonies in 1671, Fox spoke at Friends' meetings and encouraged Quaker slaveholders to free their slaves after a specified period of service. In 1676, Quaker William Edmundson, an associate of Fox, published the first antislavery literature in Rhode Island. While Quakers were formulating an antislavery position early in their movement, German Mennonites migrating to America had vowed that they would not own slaves. Several members of the Mennonite community and Dutch Pietists adopted Quakerism and became members of the Friends' Germantown Meeting. These German Quakers, their minister Pastorius, and other Friends of the Germantown Meeting delivered a petition to the Philadelphia Meeting in 1688 demanding that slavery and the slave trade be abolished. The protest addressed to slave owners of the Philadelphia Monthly Meeting challenged these Friends to explain why they had slaves and how such a practice could exist in a colony founded on the principles of liberty and equality.

Representing the radical leadership of Philadelphia Friends, George Keith published a tract entitled *An Exhortation and Caution to Friends Concerning Buying or Keeping of Negroes.* He gave several directives: that Friends should not purchase African slaves except for the express purpose of setting them free, that those already purchased should be set free after a time of reasonable service, and that, while in service, slaves should be given a Christian education and taught how to read.

During the early eighteenth century, the conservative, wealthy membership of the Philadelphia Meeting took a somewhat confusing position on slavery. Their inconsistent policies included a separate meeting for African Americans, a request that Quakers in the West Indies stop shipping slaves to Philadelphia, and disciplinary measures for members of the meeting who were engaged in antislavery activity. Many prominent Quakers, such as James Logan, Jonathan Dickinson, and Isaac Norris, continued to purchase and own slaves.

The customary procedure of resolving issues at Friends' meetings was to achieve a consensus by gaining a sense of the meeting. Thus, the Quaker drift toward an antislavery sentiment gained momentum with the efforts of a few radicals but achieved success only when the majority bowed to the principles of Quaker conscience.

Unpopular radical member Benjamin Lay was unwelcome at the Philadelphia Meeting because of his unorthodox promotion of the antislavery cause. For example, Lay once had kidnapped a Quaker youth in order to illustrate the tragedy of abduction of African children for the slave trade. In 1738, he outdid himself at the Philadelphia Yearly Meeting, wearing a military uniform to emphasize the connection between slavery and war and concealing under his cloak an animal bladder that he had filled with red juice. Delivering an inflamed speech on the evils of slavery, he concluded by saying that slavery took the very lifeblood out of the slave, simultaneously piercing the bladder and splashing the horrified audience with simulated blood.

By the 1730's, the effects of the antislavery movement were evident among Quakers as more Friends provided for the manumission of their slaves in their wills. In addition, the increased immigration of Germans in need of work eliminated the demand for slave labor in the Middle Colonies.

Much of the credit for the success of the antislavery movement among Quakers must be given to New Jersey Quaker John Woolman. Known for his gentle, persuasive approach as a Quaker minister, he began a series of visitations to Quaker slaveholders in New England, the Middle Colonies, and the South in 1743. In 1754, he published *Some Considerations on the Keeping of Negroes*, which proclaimed the evils of slavery and the absolute necessity for Friends to free their slaves. Meetings throughout the colonies and England effectively used his visitations to pressure Quakers to free their slaves. By 1774, Quaker meetings in England, New England, and Pennsylvania had adopted sanctions to disown any member for buying slaves or for serving as executor of an estate that included slaves. It also required slaveholders to treat their slaves humanely and to emancipate them as soon as possible.

Some have argued that Quakers were willing to emancipate their slaves because slavery was not profitable in Pennsylvania in the absence of labor-intensive agriculture. Others claim that Quaker sensitivity to antislavery was aroused not by their own religious ideals but rather by eighteenth century Enlightenment philosophy, which held that liberty is a natural human right. These may be considered arguments; nevertheless, it was the Quakers who first championed the antislavery cause and who organized the first antislavery group in America. The Pennsylvania Society for the Abolition of Slavery served as a model for other antislavery groups. As early as 1794, other states that had formed antislavery societies were asked to send representatives to Philadelphia for annual meetings. As new associations were formed, Friends constituted a majority of the membership. Statesmen such as Franklin, Rush, Alexander Hamilton, John Jay, and Thomas Paine believed that the institution of slavery contradicted the ideals of the Declaration of Independence and joined in support of the Friends' antislavery campaign. —*Emily Teipe*

ADDITIONAL READING:

Davis, David Brion. *The Problem of Slavery in the Age of Revolution, 1770-1823.* Ithaca, N.Y.: Cornell University Press, 1975. An exhaustive study of the slave question immediately before the American Revolution and in the succeeding federal period, which includes the pioneering efforts of the Quakers.

Frost, J. William, ed. *The Quaker Origins of Antislavery.* Norwood, Pa.: Norwood Editions, 1980. A history of the Quaker antislavery cause that includes a comprehensive collection of Quaker documents.

James, Sydney V. *A People Among Peoples: Quaker Benevolence in Eighteenth Century America.* Cambridge, Mass.: Harvard University Press, 1963. This classic work discusses antislavery as an outreach of Quaker religious piety, along with the Quakers' other efforts for the good of the social order.

Nash, Gary B. *Quakers and Politics: Pennsylvania 1681-1726.* Princeton, N.J.: Princeton University Press, 1968. Places the antislavery cause within the larger framework of troubled politics in colonial Pennsylvania.

Soderlund, Jean R. *Quakers and Slavery: A Divided Spirit.* Princeton, N.J.: Princeton University Press, 1985. A study of the Philadelphia Yearly Meeting and its progression to an antislavery philosophy. Draws parallels with the Civil Rights movement of the 1960's.

SEE ALSO: 1777, Northeast States Abolish Slavery; 1784, Hall's Masonic Lodge Is Chartered; 1787, Free African Society Is Founded; 1804, First Black Codes; 1807, Congress Bans Importation of African Slaves.

1775 ■ BATTLE OF LEXINGTON AND CONCORD: *the opening of hostilities in what became America's Revolutionary War*

DATE: April 19, 1775
LOCALE: Lexington and Concord, Massachusetts
CATEGORY: Wars, uprisings, and civil unrest
KEY FIGURES:

Thomas Gage (1721-1787), governor of Massachusetts and commander in chief of British forces in North America

George III (1738-1820), king of Great Britain

William Legge, second Lord Dartmouth (1731-1801), secretary of state for the colonies

John Parker (1729-1775), veteran militia officer who commanded the Minuteman company on the Lexington green

John Pitcairn (1722-1775), Smith's second in command

Paul Revere (1735-1818), silversmith-engraver and active patriot who aroused the Massachusetts countryside

Francis Smith, who headed the royal detachment sent to Concord

SUMMARY OF EVENT. In the early-morning hours of April 19, 1775, Captain John Parker, forty-five-year-old veteran of the French and Indian War, stood with his single company of Minutemen on the village green at Lexington, Massachusetts. Several hours had passed since Paul Revere's word of an approaching column of redcoats had brought them tumbling out of their beds. Revere had been unsure as to how General Thomas Gage would lead his men, quartered in Boston, toward Lexington. The land route across the isthmus to the mainland was long and more obvious; the Charles River was not frozen, and the river route was shorter. A signal from the steeple of Christ's Church provided the answer; the British were coming by sea. Now a messenger reported that the royal troops were almost within sight. Earlier, the Minutemen and their neighbors had adopted a resolution that the presence of a British Army in their province constituted an infringement upon their "natural, constitutional, chartered rights." They had pledged their "estates and every thing dear in life, yea and life itself" if necessary in opposing the Coercive Acts. The British were correct in their suspicions that the Americans had hidden arms; gunpowder and shot had been stored all winter for such a moment as this.

The seventy-seven men who answered Parker's call, including sixteen-year-old drummer William Diamond, were hopelessly outnumbered by the approaching British. Many were old for such work; fifty-five were more than thirty years of age. Most of the town's men hoped not to provoke the British. Parker kept his men on the green and away from the nearby road the British would follow to the next town of Concord. The captain of the Minutemen intended their presence to serve only a symbolic purpose, an expression of their displeasure at the redcoats' intrusion. British major John Pitcairn nevertheless led his advance companies onto the green. As the British approached, Pitcairn ordered his men to hold their fire. He told the Minutemen to leave their arms and disperse. Seeing they had made their point, some of the Americans broke ranks and walked away, but a shot rang out, its origin unknown. The British immediately returned volleys of fire, beyond control of their officers. The Americans were quickly driven from the field, leaving eight dead and ten wounded. Lexington was hardly a battle, and yet a war had begun. The United States was born in an act of violence lasting but fifteen to twenty minutes.

British troops had returned to Boston following the Tea Party and the Coercive Acts. With them came a new governor of Massachusetts, General Thomas Gage, longtime military commander in chief in North America. In retaliation, the Massachusetts Assembly, now calling itself the Provincial Congress and sitting as an extralegal body, took control of the militia, appointed general officers, and ordered the organizing of one-fourth of all the militia into Minute companies. Massachusetts' firm resolution to fight if pressed was duplicated throughout New England, as well as in the Middle Colonies and in far-off Virginia, where on March 9, the Virginia convention sat transfixed by the eloquence of Patrick Henry: "The war is inevitable. . . . The war is actually begun. . . . Our brethren are already in the field! Why stand here idle?" The potentially explosive situation was heightened by the struggle over gunpowder in the colonies. In London, the ministry imposed an embargo on the shipment of munitions to America, except for quantities headed for Gage's army. Armed clashes were narrowly averted in Rhode Island, New Hampshire, and Virginia, as patriots and British authorities sought to monopolize the critically short amounts of powder. The capture or destruction of the Massachusetts Provincial Congress' military stores was the assignment of Lieutenant Colonel Francis Smith as he headed down the silent country road that ran through Lexington and on to Concord on the night of April 18, 1775.

Long before reaching Lexington, Smith realized that his assignment was known to the patriots, whose church bells and signal guns were audible to the marchers. Consequently, Smith dispatched Major Pitcairn ahead with six companies to occupy the bridges over the Concord River, at the same time that he wisely sent a courier to ask General Gage for reinforcements. After routing the Lexington Minutemen, Pitcairn continued on the additional five miles to Concord, entering the village at eight o'clock in the morning. The patriots had managed to cart away part of their supplies. When the British had burned several gun carriages and destroyed flour, they set out about noon on their return journey.

The sixteen miles back to Boston were a nightmare for Smith and Pitcairn. The scarlet column proved an inviting target for the swarms of militia and Minute companies that had converged on Concord and Lexington. From trees, rocks, and stone walls, they kept up a steady fire. Smith's force may well have escaped annihilation only because at Lexington they received a reinforcement of nine hundred men under General Hugh, Earl Percy. Even so, the combined column might have been destroyed had the efforts of the various American detachments been coordinated. As it was, the wild, unorthodox battle continued until the British reached Charleston, across the harbor from Boston, where dusk and the protecting guns of the Royal Navy brought an end to the mauling.

British losses came to 73 killed, 174 wounded, and 26 missing, while American casualties in all categories totaled 93. The colonists remained to besiege the enemy in Boston. The *Newport Mercury* described the day's events as the beginning of "the American Civil War, which will hereafter fill an important page in History." At least some British papers also reflected the American viewpoint. For example, forty-one days after the fighting, the *London Chronicle* carried a detailed description of the events that had transpired at Lexington. The account included statements from witnesses who reported that the British had indeed fired first, clearly favoring the American version of events. This was followed some weeks later with General Gage's account of the affair. Gage also alluded to the Americans having returned fire, the implication being that the British had fired the first shots.

The British had badly misjudged the extent of American resistance. While at no point in the war were the Americans united in their stand against England, events that transpired at Lexington and Concord had lit a fire in the "belly of the beast." It would be a short time before the patriots would be unsatisfied with anything but independence.

—R. Don Higginbotham, updated by Richard Adler

ADDITIONAL READING:

Commager, Henry, and Richard Morris. *The Spirit of Seventy-Six*. 1975. Reprint. New York: Da Capo Press, 1995. Provides an excellent account of events in the war as seen by the participants.

Fischer, David. *Paul Revere's Ride*. New York: Oxford University Press, 1994. Although centered on the famous ride of Paul Revere, the book provides a fine account of the opening engagements at Lexington and Concord.

Forbes, Esther. *Paul Revere and the World He Lived In*. Boston: Houghton Mifflin, 1942. Pulitzer Prize-winning biography and history of events unfolding around the early fighting.

Langguth, A. J. *Patriots: The Men Who Started the American Revolution*. New York: Touchstone, 1988. Illuminating account of the prominent figures in the war and their evolving role as the revolution proceeded. Takes a humanistic approach.

Tourtellot, Arthur. *William Diamond's Drum: The Beginning of the War of the American Revolution*. Garden City, N.Y.: Doubleday, 1959. An account of the opening engagements of the war, which led to the creation of the Continental Army.

HIGHLIGHTS OF THE AMERICAN REVOLUTIONARY WAR

Apr. 19, 1775   BATTLE OF LEXINGTON AND CONCORD: American Minute Men confront British troops in Lexington Common. When someone fires "the shot heard round the world," both Americans and British open fire and the war begins. *See* **1775, Battle of Lexington and Concord.**

June 17, 1775   BATTLE OF BUNKER HILL: Americans engage British at Breed's Hill near Boston; British win but sustain heavy losses.

Aug.-Dec., 1775   EXPEDITIONS AGAINST QUEBEC: Americans mount two offensives against British Canada but are defeated.

Mar. 17, 1776   BRITISH EVACUATE BOSTON, retreating to Halifax, Nova Scotia.

July 4, 1776   DECLARATION OF INDEPENDENCE approved by Congress. *See* **1776, Declaration of Independence.**

Aug. 27, 1776   BATTLE OF LONG ISLAND: Leading the British, General William Howe and Admiral Richard Howe enter New York harbor, land twenty thousand troops on Long Island, and establish a base of operations. General George Washington retreats to Manhattan Island. British occupy New York City by September.

Oct. 11, 1776   BATTLE OF VALCOUR BAY: British commander Guy Carleton attacks American general Benedict Arnold at Lake Champlain, routing the American flotilla.

Oct. 28, 1776   BATTLE OF WHITE PLAINS: British defeat Americans, who take heavy losses. Washington's troops retreat to Peekskill, Ft. Lee, and Trenton, New Jersey.

Dec. 26, 1776   BATTLE OF TRENTON: Washington defeats the British after crossing the icey Delaware River in a surprise attack.

Jan. 3, 1777   PRINCETON COUP: Washington routs British general near Princeton, New Jersey, and then establishes headquarters in Morristown.

June-July, 1777   BRITISH ADVANCE FROM LAKE CHAMPLAIN: General John Burgoyne leads British forces up the Hudson River, taking strategic points at Fort Ticonderoga, Mt. Defiance, and Fort Anne.

MAJOR SITES IN THE AMERICAN REVOLUTIONARY WAR

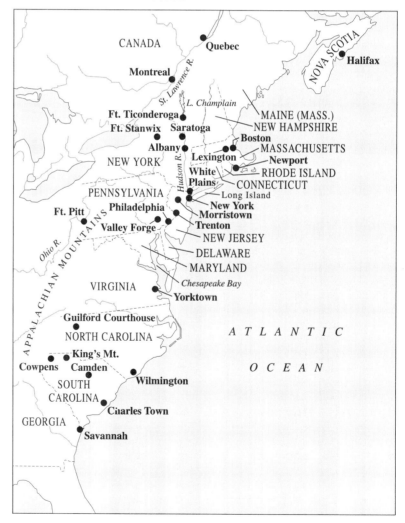

Aug. 6, 1777	BATTLE OF ORISKANY CREEK: Southeast of Lake Ontario and Fort Stanwix, an Indian force fighting for the British under Chief Joseph Brant ambushes Americans under General Nicholas Herkimer. Native American losses and renewed American efforts force the British to retreat. *See* **1777, Battle of Oriskany Creek.**
Aug. 16, 1777	BATTLE OF BENNINGTON: In Vermont, a German contingent fighting for the British under orders of Burgoyne is routed by Americans under General John Stark.
Sept. 11, 1777	BATTLE OF BRANDYWINE CREEK: In Pennsylvania, the British force Washington and his men to retreat to Philadelphia, occupying that city by September 26.
Oct. 4, 1777	BATTLE OF GERMANTOWN: Washington's attack on British forces fails when fog confuses his troops. Americans retreat to Valley Forge, where they will spend a harsh winter.
Oct. 8-17, 1777	BATTLE OF SARATOGA: Burgoyne's campaign to capture Albany, New York, is foiled when Benedict Arnold assaults British forces at Bemis Heights; Burgoyne retreats. One week later, Burgoyne and his British forces surrender. *See* **1777, Battle of Saratoga.**
Nov., 1777	ARTICLES OF CONFEDERATION SUBMITTED TO THE STATES: After a year of debate, the Continental Congress devises a plan of government and submits it to the states for ratification, achieved in March, 1781. *See* **1781, Articles of Confederation.**
Feb. 6, 1778	FRANCO-AMERICAN TREATIES: France agrees to assist Americans against British. *See* **1778, Franco-American Treaties.**
June 28, 1778	BATTLE OF MONMOUTH: After a severe winter at Valley Forge, George Washington and the Americans pursue General Henry Clinton, who had commanded the British campaign in Philadelphia. Under General Charles Lee, the Americans rout the British; Washington later engages Clinton in an ensuing battle, forcing a British retreat.
July-Aug., 1778	ATTACK AT NEWPORT: In Rhode Island, combined American and French forces are repelled after attempting to take a British garrison.
Dec. 29, 1778	FALL OF SAVANNAH: British under General Clinton take Savannah.
July 15, 1779	BATTLE OF STONY POINT: American general Anthony Wayne takes Stony Point, on the Hudson River, from Clinton.
Aug. 29, 1779	BATTLE OF NEWTOWN: At modern-day Elmira, New York, Americans under John Sullivan defeat British loyalists and Indians who had been terrorizing frontier settlements of Pennsylvania and New York.
Sept.-Oct., 1779	SAVANNAH CAMPAIGN: In Georgia, American and French forces fail to take Savannah from the British, suffering heavy casualties.
Feb.-May, 1780	FALL OF CHARLES TOWN: General Clinton assaults Charles Town (Charleston), South Carolina, capturing the American garrison and four ships—the greatest American losses of the war.
Aug. 16, 1780	BATTLE OF CAMDEN: In South Carolina, Americans under General Horatio Gates move against the British under Lord Cornwallis but are routed, opening the way for a British advance into North Carolina, where on Oct. 7 British troops are repelled by Carolina backwoodsmen.
Sept., 1780	TREASON OF BENEDICT ARNOLD: After supplying the British with information for more than a year, Arnold is exposed in a plot to hand over the American garrison at West Point. He becomes a British officer and conducts British assaults on Virginia and Connecticut in 1781.
Jan. 17, 1781	BATTLE OF COWPENS: In South Carolina, American general Daniel Morgan repels the British forces of General Banastre Tarleton.
Mar. 15, 1781	BATTLE AT GUILFORD COURTHOUSE: American general Nathanael Greene engages Cornwallis in North Carolina; Americans are defeated but seriously weaken the British, forcing their retreat.
Oct. 19, 1781	SURRENDER AT YORKTOWN: Having abandoned the Carolinas for Virginia, Cornwallis and the British establish a base at Yorktown but French ground and naval forces join with the Americans to hem him in, forcing surrender. Despite General Clinton's remaining forces in New York, the British are essentially defeated. *See* **1781, Cornwallis Surrenders at Yorktown.**
Sept. 3, 1783	TREATY OF PARIS: British and Americans negotiate a peace settlement. *See* **1783, Treaty of Paris.**

SEE ALSO: 1765, Stamp Act Crisis; 1767, Townshend Crisis; 1770, Boston Massacre; 1773, Boston Tea Party; 1774, First Continental Congress; 1775, Second Continental Congress; 1776, Indian Delegation Meets with Congress; 1776, Declaration of Independence; 1776, First Test of a Submarine in Warfare; 1777, Battle of Oriskany Creek; 1777, Battle of Saratoga; 1778, Franco-American Treaties; 1781, Articles of Confederation; 1781, Cornwallis Surrenders at Yorktown; 1783, Treaty of Paris.

1775 ■ SECOND CONTINENTAL CONGRESS:
early patriots manage the Revolutionary War and form the core of a federal government for the United States of America

DATE: May 10-August 2, 1775
LOCALE: Philadelphia, Pennsylvania
CATEGORIES: Government and politics; Wars, uprisings, and civil unrest
KEY FIGURES:

John Adams (1735-1826), delegate from Massachusetts who urged Washington's election

Benjamin Franklin (1706-1790), delegate from Pennsylvania, experienced in military affairs

John Hancock (1737-1793), delegate from Massachusetts and first president of the Second Continental Congress

Thomas Jefferson (1743-1826), delegate from Virginia and coauthor of the Declaration of Causes of Taking up Arms

George Washington (1732-1799), delegate from Virginia who was appointed commander in chief of the Continental Army

SUMMARY OF EVENT. The Second Continental Congress began its deliberations at the State House in Philadelphia on May 10, 1775. It was, like the First Continental Congress, an extralegal body, until the ratification of the Articles of Confederation in 1781. However, it continued to meet throughout the Revolutionary War, exercising whatever authority the colony-states permitted. Although it was weak in terms of legal jurisdiction and state pressures, and lacked material resources for waging war, the Second Continental Congress accomplished much. Out of a bond forged by a common threat from Great Britain, a bond often frustrated by local politicians more interested in state sovereignty than wartime efficiency, there emerged a cluster of American political leaders, nationalists who echoed the plea of New York's John Jay that the "Union depends much upon breaking down provincial Conventions."

Forging a national identity was a delicate task that was much discussed among the delegates. Wary of a strong national government that had plagued the colonies, pushing them into war with the mother country, the delegates recognized that a united effort would be the only solution to the problems with Great Britain. The delegates to the congress knew also that a central government would be necessary long after the current feud and revolution ended, and that actions taken at the congress would dictate whether a central government could be formed and survive. Through the judicious coordination of individual events and the selection of military commanders from one section of the colonies to lead in other sections, the delegates at the Second Continental Congress were able to form a central government that bound the individual states in common cause and made the idea of a federal government acceptable to independent-minded Americans.

Delegates came to Philadelphia from all the colonies except Georgia, which was not represented until the second session of the Congress, held that fall. An extraordinary task faced the delegates: The First Continental Congress had hammered out agreements on constitutional principles, but the Second Continental Congress had to unite for military action. Fortunately, the new congress contained men of distinction, such as John Hancock, who became its president. There were familiar faces from the preceding year, including the Adams cousins of Massachusetts, George Washington and Richard Henry Lee of Virginia, Edward Rutledge of South Carolina, John Jay of New York, and John Dickinson of Pennsylvania. They were joined by talented newcomers, such as the youthful Thomas Jefferson, the venerable Benjamin Franklin, and the scholarly James Wilson of Pennsylvania. Although realizing that the chances of securing an amicable reconciliation might suffer if the delegates involved themselves in the confrontation between New England and General Thomas Gage's redcoats, this congress was in no mood to turn the other cheek. In their Declaration of Causes of Taking up Arms, the legislators solemnly announced that the American people had two choices: submission to tyranny or resistance by force. They preferred the latter. The colonies, moreover, looked to the Continental Congress for advice and direction. Connecticut asked what should be done with munitions captured at Ticonderoga and Crown Point. New York inquired whether it should resist a landing by British troops. Massachusetts sought approval for establishing a civil government and urged the congress to assume responsibility for the New England forces besieging Boston. "Such vast Multitude of Objects, civil, political, commercial and military, press and crowd upon us so fast, that we know not what to do first," exclaimed John Adams.

The congress nevertheless moved resolutely to put America in a state of defense, calling upon the colonies to prepare themselves and voting to take charge of the New England troops outside Boston. In selecting a commanding general, the congress rejected Massachusetts' ranking officer, General Artemas Ward, as well as John Hancock, both of whom desired the post. It was "absolutely Necessary in point of prudence," wrote Eliphalet Dyer of Connecticut, "to pick a non-New Englander to head the Continental army; it removes all jealousies [and] more firmly Cements the southern to the Northern" colonies. One important reason for the subsequent appointment of George Washington as commander in chief was to demonstrate to Americans everywhere that the war transcended the interests of a particular section, a step that would arouse support for the military effort in the middle and southern parts of America. Washington, bearing the proper regional credentials, also hailed from the "right" colony, prosperous and populous Virginia. Equally or more important, Washington possessed certain qualities as a man, a patriot, and a soldier requisite for the high office bestowed upon him. The congress, in picking a ranking general, had taken an accurate measure of its man. Aware of the congress' limitations and cognizant of state jealousies, he remained unflinchingly deferential to the civil authority. Washington was a rare combination of soldier and statesman who understood, however maddening it might be at times, that the revaluation was a peculiar kind of coalition war. It is doubtful whether his accomplishments could have been equaled by any other general officer appointed at the time—men such as Major Generals Artemas Ward, Charles Lee, Philip Schuyler, and Israel Putnam, or Brigadier Generals Seth Pomeroy, William Heath, John Thomas, David Wooster, Joseph Spencer, John Sullivan, Nathanael Greene, and Richard Montgomery.

Along with problems of state, the conduct of war, and the development of philosophies for a new kind of nation, the delegates to the congress dealt with the problems of personalities and special interests. Strong personalities such as John Adams, Richard Henry Lee, and Thomas Jefferson often conflicted with more tempered personalities such as Benjamin Franklin, James Wilson, and John Hancock. Only because of their strong sense of duty and their belief in the future of a new nation could such men as Jefferson withstand the constant haggling over committee reports that had been laboriously written or the parliamentary tactics that were used to give one group an advantage in the various debates. Regional squabbles, especially over the issues of trade and slavery, were obstacles to the formation of a central government that would be capable of leading yet flexible enough to accommodate turning over many powers and privileges to individual states.

The first session of the Second Continental Congress came to an end on August 2, with the legislators agreeing to reconvene six weeks later. The delegates had accomplished much in less than three months. Besides calling the colonies to defensive preparations, adopting an army, providing for its regulation, and appointing its general offices, they had taken steps to issue paper money, encourage limited foreign trade, and bolster the militias. The congress was no longer a temporary council of American dignitaries sitting to articulate constitutional doctrines and draft remonstrances; it was the central government of a people at war, a revolutionary body in the fullest sense.—*R. Don Higginbotham, updated by Kay Hively*

ADDITIONAL READING:

Burnett, Edmund C. *The Continental Congress.* New York: Macmillan, 1941. A chronological look at the day-to-day events of the Continental Congress. Strongly supports the theory that the congress was the federal governing body of the colony-states.

French, Allen. *The First Year of the American Revolution.* Boston: Houghton Mifflin, 1934. Looks beyond the congres-

sional sessions and demonstrates the effectiveness of the actions in Philadelphia.

Levin, Phyllis Lee. *Abigail Adams.* New York: St. Martin's Press, 1987. Uses Adams' letters and diaries to present the unique view of an American woman who was privileged to have access to the inner activities of the Second Continental Congress.

Montross, Lynn. *The Reluctant Rebels: The Story of the Continental Congress, 1774-1789.* New York: Harper & Row, 1950. A readable work filled with quotations and characterizations of the early patriots.

Randall, Willard Sterne. *Jefferson: A Life.* New York: Henry Holt, 1993. A close look at the public and private life of the man who put into words many of the great ideas and ideals of the Second Continental Congress.

SEE ALSO: 1765, Stamp Act Crisis; 1767, Townshend Crisis; 1770, Boston Massacre; 1773, Boston Tea Party; 1774, First Continental Congress; 1775, Battle of Lexington and Concord; 1776, Indian Delegation Meets with Congress; 1776, Declaration of Independence; 1776, First Test of a Submarine in Warfare; 1777, Battle of Oriskany Creek; 1777, Battle of Saratoga; 1778, Franco-American Treaties; 1781, Articles of Confederation; 1781, Cornwallis Surrenders at Yorktown; 1783, Treaty of Paris.

1776 ■ INDIAN DELEGATION MEETS WITH CONGRESS: *the Six Nations of the Iroquois Confederacy attempt to secure neutrality during the Revolutionary War but ultimately dissolve, losing control of the Northeast riverine trade*

DATE: May 24 and June 11, 1776
LOCALE: Finger Lakes Region, Mohawk River Valley, Albany, Boston, Philadelphia
CATEGORIES: Native American history; Wars, uprisings, and civil unrest
KEY FIGURES:
Joseph Brant, also known as *Thayendanegea* (1742-1807), principal warrior chief of the Mohawks
William Johnson (1715-1774), British Commissioner of Indian Affairs, who significantly influenced the Six Nations
Samuel Kirkland (1741-1808), first American-born missionary to the Iroquois

SUMMARY OF EVENT. The withdrawal of the French in 1763 from the New World was a watershed event for the Six Nations (the Iroquois Confederacy). Between 1640, when the Iroquois established their hegemony over the fur trade, and the end of the French and Indian War in 1763, the Iroquois were profoundly involved in the imperial rivalries between the English and the French and were pivotal in the balance of power in the

New World. When the French left, the Iroquois lost the fulcrum on which they kept the balance.

The British government's Proclamation of 1763 provided that all territory between the crest of the Alleghenies and the Mississippi River and from Florida to 50° north latitude were closed to settlers and land speculators and reserved "for the present" to American Indians. This proclamation, however, served the British agenda, not the needs of either natives or settlers. Britain wished to protect the valuable furbearing animals' habitate from encroaching colonists. Guaranteeing boundaries, moreover, did not guarantee sovereignty.

In fact, the British were less accommodating of the Indians than the French had been. Native resistance flared with Pontiac's Resistance (1763-1766), in which the Six Nation Senecas fought on the side of Pontiac, while the Mohawks supported the British. When that rebellion failed, the Senecas were punished by William Johnson and were forced to cede some of their land to the British. In 1775, the Senecas successfully negotiated with the Americans at Pittsburgh to remain neutral in the frontier battles and the impending Revolutionary War, as long as the Americans stayed out of Iroquois territory. This negotiation was approved by the full governing council of the Six Nations. It was the last significant action that exhibited that the council still had control of its warriors.

In that Pittsburgh agreement, American settlers who encroached on Mohawk territory were supposed to be punished by Americans. However, encroachment of the farmers and frontiersmen called the Albany Group near the Mohawk River Valley never abated; thus the Mohawks, led by Joseph Brant, grew more dependent on the British to help defend against American encroachment.

During 1775 and into the spring of 1776, the British expended considerable effort to create military allegiances with all the tribes of the Six Nations. So great was their influence among the Mohawks that Joseph Brant and several other warrior chiefs sailed to England in November, 1775, professedly to secure Iroquois sovereignty in exchange for allegiance to the British during the war. By 1776, the American Congress wanted desperately for the Iroquois to join the fight on the side of the colonies, but did not have the financial ability to dispense the gifts of food, ammunition, clothing, and other necessities that the Iroquois expected when asked to fight as mercenaries. The American alternative was a proclamation of friendship and the stated desire that the Six Nations remain neutral.

In England, King George guaranteed Joseph Brant the boundaries of the Iroquois homelands, but this was no concession to the key word, "sovereignty." It is believed that Joseph Brant misunderstood the British attitude toward territorial *sovereignty* and territorial *occupancy*. It is known that Brant believed the Americans' goal was to overrun the continent at the expense of all American Indians. Brant decided the Iroquois' future lay with the British. In England, Joseph Brant was commissioned a colonel in the British colonial militia.

Up to this time, the Americans had done no violence to the Iroquois and, with the exception of the Albany Group, were careful to avoid trespassing on Iroquois territory. After acting Indian Commissioner John Johnson attempted to arrest the patriot missionary Samuel Kirkland at Oriskany, the Oneida stronghold, the Albany Group entered Mohawk territory to arrest Johnson. Both actions failed in their objectives, although Kirkland was momentarily muzzled and Johnson had to flee to Canada with a significant force of Mohawk warriors.

With this backdrop, an Iroquois delegation of twenty-one members representing four of the Six Nations traveled to Philadelphia to be presented to Congress on May 24 and again on June 11. Brant was still in England. The delegates were presented to "the great warrior chief" George Washington on May 24 and to the full Congress on June 11. While in Philadelphia, they boarded in a room directly above the meeting room of the Congress. Washington had spent the previous two weeks persuading the Continental Congress to break the Pittsburgh agreement and allow him to recruit an Indian militia. On May 25, the Congress resolved that it would be expedient to engage American Indians in the service of the colonies. The significance of this was twofold: Congress was ignoring or nullifying the sovereignty of the Council of the Confederacy that had approved the Pittsburgh agreement, and Congress was ignoring the purpose of the Iroquois delegation, which was to assure the sincere and serious effort by the Iroquois to hold fast to the neutrality agreement.

George Washington knew the path to either a British or American victory led through Iroquois land. The strategic importance of that land could not be ignored. Congress was clever enough not to tell the Iroquois delegates that Washington was about to recruit Iroquois as soldiers; as the minutes of June 11 show, "We shall order our warriors not to hurt any of your kindred, and we hope you will not allow any of your young brothers to join with the enemy . . . we desire you accept these few necessaries as tokens of our good-will . . . we hope the friendship between us will be firm as long as the sun shall shine and the waters run, that we be as one people." While saying these words, Congress did not understand the disastrous implications of their conniving efforts to recruit American Indians.

The word to recruit was passed through patriot channels to the Reverend Kirkland and the Oneida and Tuscarora, and also to General Philip Schuyler of the Albany Group. Schuyler was asked to recruit two thousand Iroquois to be paid a reward of one hundred dollars for every British officer killed or taken prisoner and thirty dollars for every enlisted man. Schuyler was dubious not only of the policy but also of the numbers—there were not two thousand Iroquois men available, much less warriors, who were not already aiding the British. The Oneida, however, decided to send five hundred warriors to help protect the American Fort Stanwix near Utica, New York. This action would breach the Iroquois Confederacy.

The Revolutionary War brought what was thought to be impossible to the Iroquois nations: Their Covenant Chain broke. In 1777, the league chiefs "covered their fire." For the first time within living memory, Iroquois fought and killed Iroquois, and their league shattered. The Treaty of Paris in 1783 said nothing about the American Indians. Those who allied with Britain were abandoned to the care of the Americans. Joseph Brant's pledge to the king in exchange for Brant's understanding of a pledge of sovereignty was particularly bitter when he discovered that the British had ceded all Mohawk land to the Americans. That the Mohawks were given a reserve in Canada was little consolation. —*Glenn Schiffman*

ADDITIONAL READING:

Graymont, Barbara. *The Iroquois.* New York. Chelsea House Publishers. 1988. A useful book by a recognized expert on the subject.

_____. *The Iroquois in the American Revolution.* Syracuse, N.Y.: Syracuse University Press. 1972. The author is considered to be the foremost authority on the subject matter of this work.

Jennings, Francis. *The Founders of America.* New York: W. W. Norton, 1993. This exceptional history of the events around the American Revolution is accessible to both casual readers and scholars.

Josephy. Alvin M., Jr. *500 Nations: An Illustrated History of North American Indians.* New York: Alfred A. Knopf, 1994. Companion book to the CBS television series *500 Nations,* written by one of America's foremost authorities on American Indian culture.

Stone, William L. *Life of Joseph Brant.* Albany, N.Y.: J. Munsell, 1864. A source for quotations of early colonial documents. Contains some historical inaccuracies; for example, this is the source of the erroneous information that Brant was in North America at the time of the Philadelphia meeting.

Wise, Jennings C. *The Red Man in the New World Drama,* edited by Vine Deloria, Jr. New York: Macmillan, 1971. The key words "new world drama" provide a clue to the American Indian perspective of this author and editor.

SEE ALSO: 1500, Iroquois Confederacy; 1763, Pontiac's Resistance; 1763, Proclamation of 1763; 1777, Battle of Oriskany Creek; 1783, Treaty of Paris; 1784, Fort Stanwix Treaty.

1776 ■ NEW JERSEY WOMEN GAIN THE VOTE: *more than a century before secur-ing national woman suffrage, women in New Jersey briefly exercise the right to vote*

DATE: July 2, 1776
LOCALE: New Jersey
CATEGORIES: Civil rights; Women's issues
KEY FIGURES:
Elias Boudinot (1740-1821), lawyer and Federalist orator
John Cooper, Quaker and Federalist legislator in the New Jersey Provincial Congress

SUMMARY OF EVENT. New Jersey was unlike other states of the early republic in that its first constitution allowed its female inhabitants the right to vote. It has been said that this instance was one of the most important opportunities women have had to vote in the United States. After thirty-one years of being the center of a political struggle, women lost the vote and did not regain it again until the Nineteenth Amendment to the U.S. Constitution was ratified in 1920.

On the recommendation of the Second Continental Congress, several New Jersey legislators of the Provincial Congress met from May 26 to July 2, 1776, to draft their first constitution to formalize their revolutionary government. That first draft of the New Jersey Constitution included the clause that allowed women the right to vote, stating that all

> . . . Inhabitants of the colony, of full age, who are worth fifty pounds proclamation money, clear estate in the same, and have resided within the country in which they claim a vote for twelve months immediately preceding the election, shall be entitled to vote for Representatives in Council and Assembly; and also for all other public officers, that shall be elected by the people of the county at large.

Few records remain from the eight days it took to draft the document at the highly secretive forum, making it difficult to determine the drafters' motives. Scholars have debated whether it was the Framers' intention from the beginning to include women or if, in their haste to draw up the document, they inadvertently included the rights of some women to vote. Such women would have included young ladies not yet married and women who were widowed, as well as African Americans of both sexes; few in the latter group, however, would have been able to the other qualifications.

The Quakers, a religious group known for embracing sexual equality, likely played a substantial role in the drafting of New Jersey's constitution. In their own religion, women were able to hold positions of power, although they could not hold all the positions men could hold. John Cooper, a Quaker, created a draft of the constitution that entitled women to vote, a move of which many members approved. It was not until 1790 that Cooper openly expressed his belief that women should be able to vote and that a law was drafted to specifically include women. The law became effective November 18, 1790, and it cleared up any misconceptions of the suffrage clause by replacing "he" with "he or she" in the clause.

The year 1790 also marks the point when Federalists, many of whom were Quakers, wanted to expand their electorate in hope of gaining control of the legislature. In 1790, east Jersey controlled the legislature and west Jersey needed to find more support, and women were an eligible group. The pinnacle of the Federalist campaign to include women in the electorate came in 1793. On July 4 of that year, Elias Boudinot, a friend of Federalist Alexander Hamilton, gave a speech expressing his desire for more women to take opportunities to become involved in public affairs. Boudinot, aware of the criticisms women would receive, reminded the audience that if it were not for Queen Isabella, Columbus would not have been able to make his discoveries.

As the decade progressed, the Federalists began to change their opinion of woman suffrage because of the influence of French émigrés who were strongly affected by the French Revolution. These émigrés believed New Jersey was giving women too much credit in the political scene. The emergence of the Republican Party also created concern for women voting. Despite their hesitancy, the Federalists continued to seek the support of women voters in the elections.

In Essex County, New Jersey, in October, 1797, John Condit, a Republican from Newark, and William Crane, a Federalist from Elizabethtown, were both candidates for the legislature. John Condit was able to win by a narrow margin, but only after a large group of women went to the polls to vote in the last hours, swaying the outcome. Immediately after the election, the local newspaper reported the seemingly rare occurrence of women voting. For the first time, women voting became a fiercely debated issue for many people of New Jersey.

The Federalists had needed the votes of women to win the elections of 1797 and 1798. At the same time they sought the women's vote, however, they feared that women's votes would benefit the Republican cause more than their own; therefore, they altered their position on woman suffrage and began to discourage women from voting. Also, it became increasingly necessary to revise the constitution of New Jersey so that it reflected the federal Constitution, which many believed did not allow for woman suffrage.

The next several years saw continued debate over whether the Constitution actually provided for the franchise for women. In 1800, a presidential election year, Republican officials suggested an amendment to the election law to guarantee the rights of women to vote at the polls. The amendment was rejected on the basis that the constitution already provided the right. Republican politicians advertised this ruling prior to the election.

With the Republican politicization of women, the Federalists were again forced to seek the female vote. The Republican politicization did not help in the 1800 election, because more women supported the Federalist candidate than the Republican candidate. Republicans made a swift change of position and presented a bill to Congress that would allow only free white males to vote. At this time, the Federalists saw no need to support the plan when the votes were already on their side.

In 1804, a third party of liberal Republicans emerged. The party succeeded in placing itself directly in the middle of Republican and Federalist ideology, gaining support from both sides, with the larger share coming from the more moderate Republicans. The 1806 election for the building of a new courthouse in the heavily populated Republican county of Essex created a great deal of intraparty conflict. The moderate Republicans lost the fraudulent election and petitioned for its annulment. The Republican leadership saw the strain and embarrassment the third party was creating so close to the

1808 presidential elections and began to make amends. Newark would receive the courthouse in return for the vote of moderate Republicans on the bill to limit the vote to white, taxpaying, male citizens. Federalists also agreed to the passage of the bill.

In 1807, the state legislature of New Jersey changed the suffrage clause to include only adult taxpaying white males. As 1808, a presidential election year, approached, it became necessary to create a unified Republican Party in order to win the election in light of President Thomas Jefferson's unpopular embargo in New Jersey. Little was heard from the women who lost their right to vote. They were not able to arrange a formidable group as a result of laws that denied married women, the largest single group of women, a voice in politics. The young Federalist women who could vote declined to speak out for fear of association with African Americans and aliens, groups that many of them considered to be beneath themselves. The law of 1807 eliminated female representation for political reasons, much as women had been granted suffrage for political reasons. It would be more than a century before women gained the right to vote on a national level. —*Jeri Kurtzleben*

ADDITIONAL READING:

Baker, Paula. "The Domestication of Politics: Women and American Society, 1780-1920." *American Historical Review* 89 (June, 1984): 620-647. Discusses the politicization of women for the advancement of men's political parties.

Flexnor, Eleanor. *Century of Struggle*. Cambridge, Mass.: The Belknap Press of Harvard University Press, 1959. Demonstrates the importance of New Jersey women in the suffrage movement.

Klinghoffer, Judith Apter, and Lois Elkis. "The Petticoat Electors: Women's Suffrage in New Jersey, 1776-1807." *Journal of the Early Republic* 12, no. 2. (Summer, 1992): 158-193. Sheds new light on what once was considered a hastily drawn draft of New Jersey's first constitution.

Pomfret, John. *Colonial New Jersey: A History*. New York: Charles Scribner's Sons, 1973. Describes in detail the events surrounding the drive to gain votes for representation.

Trager, James. *The Women's Chronology*. New York: Henry Holt, 1994. Demonstrates the activities of women in the early republic.

Turner, Edward Raymond. "Women's Suffrage in New Jersey: 1790-1807." *Smith College Studies in History* 1 (1916): 165-187. Explores the early conception of the anomaly concerning women voting in New Jersey.

SEE ALSO: 1801, Jefferson Is Elected President; 1848, Seneca Falls Convention; 1851, Akron Woman's Rights Convention; 1866, Suffragists Protest the Fourteenth Amendment; 1869, Rise of Woman Suffrage Associations; 1869, Western States Grant Woman Suffrage; 1872, Susan B. Anthony Is Arrested; 1876, Declaration of the Rights of Women; 1890, Women's Rights Associations Unite; 1916, National Woman's Party Is Founded; 1917, Canadian Women Gain the Vote; 1920, League of Women Voters Is Founded; 1920, U.S. Women Gain the Vote.

1776 ■ DECLARATION OF INDEPENDENCE:
the document that marked the beginning of the United States of America, embodying the philosophies of the republic

DATE: July 4, 1776

LOCALE: Philadelphia, Pennsylvania

CATEGORIES: Civil rights; Cultural and intellectual history; Government and politics

KEY FIGURES:

Abigail Adams (1744-1818), John Adams' wife, who urged him to "remember the ladies" in the declaration

John Adams (1735-1826), Massachusetts delegate

Benjamin Franklin (1706-1790), Pennsylvania delegate

Thomas Jefferson (1743-1826), Virginia delegate and principal author of the declaration

Richard Henry Lee (1732-1794), Virginia delegate

Thomas Paine (1737-1809), English-born colonist whose pamphlet *Common Sense* crystalized thoughts of independence

SUMMARY OF EVENT. The Declaration of Independence was the culmination of a ten-year drift by the colonies from active participants in the British Empire to rebellious advocates of a total break with the mother country. This decade of accelerating estrangement was fueled by fundamental disagreement over the Proclamation Line of 1763, the Sugar Act and Currency Act (1764), the Stamp Act and Quartering Act (1765), the 1766 Declaratory Act, the 1767 Townshend Acts, the Boston Massacre (1770), the Tea Act and Boston Tea Party (1773), the 1774 Coercive Acts, and the 1775 clash at Lexington and Concord.

In the opening months of 1776, the colonists faced a momentous decision. Should they content themselves with a return of British authority as it existed prior to 1763, or should they irrevocably sever all political ties with, and dependence upon, Great Britain? Since Great Britain was unwilling to give them that choice, offering instead only abject surrender to parliamentary sovereignty, Americans in increasing numbers concluded that complete independence, not merely autonomy within the British Empire, must be their goal. Many of the undecided were won over to defiance of the Crown as a result of Parliament's Prohibitory Act, which called for a naval blockade of the colonies, the seizure of American goods on the high seas, and the dragooning of captured provincial seamen into the royal navy. For many colonists, news of the British ministry's decision to employ German mercenaries for use in America was the last straw. The requirements of the struggle itself lent weight to the idea of complete separation. People would not do battle wholeheartedly for vaguely defined purposes, nor would French or Spanish aid, deemed essential to military success, be forthcoming if the colonies fought merely for a greater freedom within the empire.

In January, 1776, these colonial issues were the subject of Thomas Paine's *Common Sense*. Although it may be doubted that Paine's widely read pamphlet was the immediate impetus for the break, and although he advanced no new arguments, Paine expressed cogent and compelling arguments for a free America that would pursue its own destiny. Although Americans of almost every persuasion were already disputing the right of Parliament to rule over the colonies, there remained among the colonists a strong attachment to the British crown and to King George III. Monarchy in general, and the Hanoverian king in particular, received scathing denunciation from Paine, who asserted that kings were frauds imposed upon people capable of governing themselves. George III, Paine reasoned, was no exception and had engaged in oppressive acts that had destroyed every claim upon American loyalties. Paine held that the break should come immediately, while Americans were in arms and sensitive to their liberties. Independence, he argued, was inevitable for a wealthy, expanding continent that could not long be tied to a small and distant island controlled by "a Royal Brute."

One by one, the Southern and New England colonial assemblies authorized their delegates to the Continental Congress, meeting in Philadelphia, to vote for independence. On June 7, 1776, Richard Henry Lee, obeying instructions from Virginia, introduced at the congress a resolution declaring the colonies independent. Temporarily, the Middle Colonies hesitated to make such a drastic decision, causing a delay in acting on the matter; but on July 2, with only New York abstaining, the vote was twelve to nothing in favor of Lee's resolution declaring that "the United colonies are, and of right ought to be, free and independent States." Anticipating the outcome, Congress had earlier formed a committee, composed of Thomas Jefferson, John Adams, Benjamin Franklin, Robert R. Livingston, and Roger Sherman, to prepare a statement concerning independence. The now famous document was drafted by Jefferson with some assistance from Adams and Franklin. Congress, after first making some revisions, such as deleting Jefferson's passage denouncing the king for not ending the slave trade, adopted it on July 4.

The purpose of the Declaration of Independence was not to change the legal status of America; on July 2, Congress had voted to sever the colonies from the British Empire. The intent of Jefferson and his colleagues was rather to explain and justify the action of Congress in terms meaningful to Americans and Europeans alike. In doing so, Jefferson drew heavily upon the general cluster of ideas associated with the eighteenth century philosophies collectively known as the Enlightenment. Besides a preface and a conclusion, the Declaration of Independence consists of a statement of the right of revolution based upon the philosophy of natural rights, a list of grievances against the king, and an account of the colonists' inability to obtain redress of grievances within the structure of the British Empire.

Some modern scholars consider the barrage of accusations heaped upon the king to be lacking in dignity and significance in relation to the rest of the document. They point out that George III was a strict constitutionalist whose conduct in the

The Declaration of Independence. (National Archives)

political arena was in accord with the practices and traditions of the earlier Hanoverian monarchs. Moreover, most of the programs and policies held to be reprehensible by the colonists hardly originated in the mind of the king. Still, George III favored a rigid policy of government, and he consistently turned a deaf ear to the remonstrances from the American assemblies and congresses. To counter the public mood of the times, it was essential for Jefferson to lay America's troubles at the feet of the king. Since the time of the First Continental Congress in 1774, patriot leaders had denied that there was any legitimate parliamentary authority to cast off; it was this lingering loyalty to the Crown that held many to the empire.

The enduring significance of the Declaration of Independence transcends the Anglo-American conflict. The statement that "all men are created equal"—that they have certain unalienable rights under God that governments may not destroy—not only inspired people in that day but also has moved people in the United States and elsewhere ever since. The phrase, applied narrowly at first, came to be the focus of debate as women, people of color, the young, and the poor—excluded *de facto* from the document's guarantees—began to fight for full equality. Women were denied the right to vote in federal elections until ratification of the Nineteenth Amendment in 1920; African American men received this right in the Fifteenth Amendment, ratified in 1870; persons between eighteen and twenty-one years of age were given the right to vote by the Twenty-sixth Amendment in 1970. Rights and liberties other than voting—due process of law, fair housing and public accommodations, equal opportunity in employment and college admissions—have all been fought for and gradually won by groups previously discriminated against. The force that sparked the emergence of this powerful movement was the burning desire of the supporters of the Declaration of Independence to be free to shape their own destiny. The message they conveyed has left a lasting imprint on the conscience of the world.

—*R. Don Higginbotham, updated by Joseph Edward Lee*

ADDITIONAL READING:

Bailyn, Bernard. *The Ideological Origins of the American Revolution.* Cambridge, Mass.: The Belknap Press of Harvard University Press, 1967. An intellectual history of the Revolution based on a close reading of the ideas that found their way into the era's pamphlets.

Becker, Carl L. *The Declaration of Independence: A Study in the History of Political Ideas.* 2d ed. New York: Harcourt, Brace, & World, 1951. The classic study of the power of the ideas embodied in the document.

Maier, Pauline. *From Resistance to Revolution.* New York: Alfred A. Knopf, 1972. A close examination of the decade prior to 1776, when the colonies slid toward rebellion.

Middlekauf, Robert. *The Glorious Cause: The American Revolution, 1763-1789.* New York: Oxford University Press, 1982. A comprehensive, readable history of the revolution.

Norton, Mary Beth. *Liberty's Daughters: The Revolutionary Experience of American Women, 1750-1800.* Boston: Little, Brown, 1980. A pioneering study of women's contributions to the revolution.

Wills, Garry. *Inventing America: Jefferson's Declaration of Independence.* Garden City, N.Y.: Doubleday, 1978. Links Jefferson to the ideas argued by the Scottish Enlightenment figures.

Wood, Gordon S. *The Radicalism of the American Revolution.* New York: Alfred A. Knopf, 1992. Asserts that the move toward independence was radical in nature.

SEE ALSO: 1781, Articles of Confederation; 1786, Virginia Statute of Religious Liberty; 1787, U.S. Constitution Is Adopted; 1787, *Federalist* Papers Are Published; 1791, U.S. Bill of Rights Is Ratified.

1776 ■ FIRST TEST OF A SUBMARINE IN WARFARE: *technology is driven and advanced by the need to succeed in revolutionary combat*

DATE: September 6-7, 1776
LOCALE: New York
CATEGORIES: Science and technology; Wars, uprisings, and civil unrest
KEY FIGURES:
David Bushnell (1742-1824), inventor of the first submarine used under combat conditions
Ezra Bushnell, David's brother, who assisted him in building the *Turtle*
Benjamin Gale (1715-1790), Bushnell's friend who introduced him to Benjamin Franklin
Richard Howe (1726-1799), admiral of the English fleet
Ezra Lee, sergeant who piloted the first combat submarine attack in history
Israel Putnam (1718-1790), major general of the Continental Army, who cooperated in Bushnell's endeavor
Jonathan Trumbull (1710-1785), governor of Connecticut
SUMMARY OF EVENT. David Bushnell was known throughout his native Connecticut for his inventive mind. While on his father's farm, he had developed a harrow with flexible teeth, which farmers could use in the stony New England fields without the teeth's breaking constantly. As a student at Yale College, he became interested in the possibilities of exploding kegs of black powder under water. Traditional theories of the time held that such an explosion would not work, because the water would dissipate its force. Through experiments, Bushnell proved that this theory was wrong and developed the forerunner of the naval mine.

With the onset of the American Revolution, Bushnell decided that his mine would be useful against the blockading British fleet, but he needed an accurate method of placing his explosives under a ship's keel without being seen by naval gunners. His solution was a submarine vessel called the *Turtle*, which he designed early in 1775 while still a student at Yale.

During the college's spring vacation that year, Bushnell went home to Saybrook, Connecticut, where he and his brother Ezra spent more than a month constructing the world's first submarine. They built no model; the *Turtle* was built full-sized from the start.

According to its inventor, the submarine "bore some resemblance to two upper tortoise shells of equal size joined together." The boat was seven and a half feet long, four feet wide, and eight feet deep. Made of carefully fitted oak timbers caulked with cork and tar, Bushnell's craft was driven by a screw propeller, the first one ever used to power a ship. The contraption included a short, primitive "snorkel," through which the one-person crew could obtain fresh air. The tube was equipped with valves that automatically closed when the submarine submerged to greater depths. The operator navigated the vessel by looking through a glass conning tower and by checking his compass and depth gauge, which were illuminated by fox fire.

Although many accounts of David Bushnell and his *Turtle* do not indicate that he piloted the vessel, Robert F. Burgess in *Ships Beneath the Sea* (1975) reveals that he did. Once Bushnell graduated from Yale in June, 1775, he returned to Saybrook to make some adjustments to the boat. The maiden voyage of the *Turtle* took place in Long Island Sound, where David Bushnell stayed submerged for a rather uneventful forty-five minutes. He nearly fainted, however, and based on this initial experience, realized he was not physically capable of piloting the submarine for extended periods. From then on, his brother, Ezra, practiced maneuvering the *Turtle* in the sound and prepared for its ultimate mission.

In subsequent months, several devices were added to assist in navigation, including a compass and a barometer. At this point, Dr. Benjamin Gale, a family friend of the Bushnells, brought Benjamin Franklin to see the *Turtle*. Franklin encouraged Bushnell to take his vessel to New York, where the British fleet had set up a blockade. Franklin then told General George Washington about the submarine. Washington was doubtful, however, about the boat's potential in his endeavors.

Through the influence of Governor Jonathan Trumbull of Connecticut in late 1775, Bushnell demonstrated the *Turtle* for Major General Israel Putnam of the new Continental Army. Putnam was impressed and secured government financing for further development of the submarine. The army wanted to use the submersible to break the British blockade of Boston, but the British squadron departed before Bushnell could fully assemble the ballast pumps.

The next opportunity to strike at the British fleet was in 1776 at New York City. The *Turtle* was hauled overland and launched into the harbor from Manhattan Island. Ezra Bushnell was to have navigated the submarine in its first real combat mission; he was well prepared after a year's training in the sound. Unfortunately, he became seriously ill with a fever and had to be hospitalized for several weeks. The mission could not wait. General Putnam provided three volunteers, whom Bushnell trained to navigate the vessel. It was twenty-

seven-year-old Sergeant Ezra Lee who proved to be the most capable replacement.

Just after midnight on the night of September 6, 1776, Lee slipped into the *Turtle* and, after two hours of tediously maneuvering the boat with hand cranks, guided it under the sixty-four-gun HMS *Eagle*, the British flagship. Lee was supposed to attach an explosive charge to the flagship by screwing it to the hull. Some historians speculate that Lee might have hit an iron bar connecting a part of the rudder to the stern, because each time he attempted to twist the bit into the metal of the ship, it would not engage. The hull of the *Eagle* was sheathed in copper, but Bushnell had anticipated this and had made the auger strong enough to penetrate the weaker metal. While Lee tried to maneuver the submarine to another spot on the hull, the *Turtle* rose to the surface in broad daylight.

At the mercy of the tide and without the aid of a compass—which, for some reason, was not working—Lee remained four miles from safety. Although he submerged every few minutes, he finally had to remain on the surface to see his way. Lee's craft was spotted by English sentries on Governor's Island, and the sentries quickly launched their own boat in a chase. Lee reported that the sailors came within fifty yards of the *Turtle* but were frightened of what they saw and turned away. Lee released the keg of powder, which drifted harmlessly into the bay and later exploded. Heading back to New York Harbor, Lee was spotted by his own people and towed to shore by a whaleboat.

Lee made several other attempts to destroy British ships in New York Harbor, but all were unsuccessful. When the British advanced up the Hudson River in October, 1776, Bushnell placed his invention aboard a small sloop. A British warship sank the sloop as it fled up the river in an effort to avoid capture. Although Bushnell reportedly recovered his submarine from the depths, its actual fate remains unknown. After the loss of the *Turtle*, Governor Trumbull had Bushnell commissioned as an officer in the Sappers and Miners Corps of the Continental Army, and Bushnell served during the remainder of the war as a demolition expert. After the American Revolution, the reticent inventor moved to Georgia, where he practiced medicine, taught school, and died in obscurity in 1824.

Although David Bushnell's submarine failed to sink any enemy vessels, he was responsible for several notable achievements. He was the first to prove that gunpowder could explode underwater with sufficient force to disable and sink a surface ship. He also developed floating and submerged mines and invented the first practical submarine. In so doing, Bushnell solved several basic engineering and nautical problems: constructing a watertight and pressure-proof hull with vertical and horizontal propulsion mechanisms; achieving vertical stability and steering control; and developing the means of using variable ballast systems. Bushnell's inventions were rapidly improved upon by other U.S. inventors who continued to develop the submarine for use in subsequent U.S. naval conflicts.   —*William L. Richter, updated by Liesel Ashley Miller*

ADDITIONAL READING:

Abbot, Henry L. *Beginning of Modern Submarine Warfare Under Captain Lieutenant David Bushnell*. Edited by Frank Anderson. Hamden, Conn.: Archon Books, 1966. A facsimile reproduction of the 1881 pamphlet. The collection contains the earliest accounts and descriptions of the *Turtle*, Bushnell, and Sergeant Ezra Lee. Biographical appendices and bibliography by the editor.

Burgess, Robert Forrest. "The *Eagle* and the *Turtle*." In *Ships Beneath the Sea: A History of Subs and Submersibles*. New York: McGraw-Hill, 1975. A superior description of Bushnell, his design, and the construction of the *Turtle*. One of the most thorough accounts of the events surrounding the first combat submarine attack in history.

Coggins, Jack. *Ships and Seamen of the American Revolution*. Harrisburg, Pa.: Stackpole Books, 1969. A colorful, well-illustrated book on virtually all aspects of the numerous naval engagements of the Revolutionary War.

Hoyt, Edwin P. *Submarines at War: The History of the American Silent Service*. Briarcliff Manor, N.Y.: Stein & Day, 1983. Commencing with the unsuccessful attack of Bushnell's *Turtle* on the British Royal Navy, chronicles the development of U.S. submarines and submarine warfare into the 1980's.

Macintyre, Donald G. F. W. "The Pioneers." In *Fighting Under the Sea*. New York: W. W. Norton, 1966. One of the most complete accounts of the *Turtle*'s attempt to sink the English warship *Eagle*. Proves details of Ezra Lee's efforts, using Lee's own words.

Perlmutter, Tom, ed. *War Machines: Sea*. London: Octopus Books, 1975. Contains one of the few detailed diagrams of the *Turtle*, but is otherwise of limited use.

Van der Vat, Dan. *Stealth at Sea: The History of the Submarine*. Boston: Houghton Mifflin, 1995. An invaluable reference source on the history of submarines and submarine warfare. Illustrations, bibliography, and index.

SEE ALSO: 1807, Voyage of the *Clermont*; 1845, Era of the Clipper Ships; 1862, *Monitor* vs. *Virginia*; 1940, United States Builds a Two-Ocean Navy.

1777 ■ NORTHEAST STATES ABOLISH SLAVERY: *eight northeastern states take action to emancipate slaves and end slavery during the American Revolution*

DATE: July 2, 1777-1804
LOCALE: Northeastern United States
CATEGORIES: African American history; Social reform
KEY FIGURES:
Moses Brown (1738-1836), opponent of slavery in Rhode Island
Aaron Burr (1756-1836), leader of the fight against slavery in New York

Caleb Cushing (1800-1879), judge who ruled slavery illegal in Massachusetts
Quork Walker, slave who successfully sued for freedom in Massachusetts

SUMMARY OF EVENT. In 1775, Pennsylvania's Provincial Congress called for an end to the importation of slaves and the gradual emancipation of all slaves in the colony. Two years later, Vermont, on July 2, 1777, became the first state to abolish slavery fully. Its 1777 Constitution outlawed "holding anyone by law to serve any person" as a servant, slave, or apprentice after he or she reached twenty-one years of age. Pennsylvania did not pass a law gradually ending the slave system until 1780, because opponents argued that abolishing slavery during the war for independence from England would break up the Union. Any radical attack against human bondage would antagonize the South, where slavery was a deeply embedded institution. Pennsylvania, like the other Northern states, had allowed slavery since its beginning as a colony, but slaves had never become an important part of the workforce. In 1780, only 3,761 of Pennsylvania's 435,150 people were slaves, and most of them were household servants. White workers argued successfully that free labor cost less than slavery, because slave masters had to take care of their slaves even if they were not working. Such was not the case with free workers.

Pennsylvania's law called for a gradual end to slavery. Property rights were respected and children born slaves in 1780 would remain in service to their owners until they were twenty-eight years of age. This length of service was to compensate masters for the cost of raising slave children. The law required owners to register their slaves by the end of the year. Any African Americans not registered would be freed immediately. The law also ended years of discrimination against blacks: They could now testify against whites in courts, the separate courts established for them were abolished, and interracial marriage became legal. Pennsylvania became the only Northern state to provide for this kind of equality. Conservatives, who could not accept the idea of equality for African Americans, resisted all these measures and successfully defeated a proposal granting freed slaves the right to vote.

Massachusetts acted slowly on the slavery question. In 1777, opponents defeated a gradual emancipation bill, arguing that it would divide the new nation by antagonizing the South. Three years later, voters turned down a new constitution that declared all men free and equal and provided voting rights for free blacks. In 1781, however, a slave named Quork Walker sued for his freedom in a state court because his owner had severely abused him. The trial judge, Caleb Cushing, instructed the jury that the idea of slavery conflicted with state law, so Walker was ordered freed. Although the legislature refused to act, by 1790, slavery no longer existed in Massachusetts because of similar court actions in dozens of other cases.

More than six hundred slaves lived in New Hampshire prior to the American Revolution. During the war, the legislature gave freedom to any slave who volunteered for the militia. Other slaves gained their liberty by running away and joining the British, who also promised freedom to slaves who joined their military. Thus, when the 1783 Constitution declared all men equal and independent from birth, only fifty slaves remained the property of masters in New Hampshire. Although slavery was never abolished legally, slave property was removed from tax roles in 1789 and eleven years later, only eight slaves remained in the state.

Rhode Island acted in 1783, after Moses Brown and five other Quakers petitioned its assembly for immediate liberation for all human beings kept as property. The cautious legislators passed a gradual emancipation bill instead. Under its provisions, all slave children born after March 1 would be apprentices. Girls became free at the age of eighteen years, while boys could be kept until they reached twenty-one years of age. Until then, the apprentices would get food and economic support from the towns in which they lived. After slaves were freed, their masters were required to post bonds with the state guaranteeing that the former slaves would never require public assistance.

Connecticut, the New England state with the largest population of African Americans, granted freedom to slaves who fought against England, but three times—in 1777, 1779, and 1780—the legislature rejected gradual emancipation. Some lawmakers feared a race riot if blacks were freed. In 1784, however, the legislature declared an end to slavery. The law declared that black and mulatto (mixed race) children would become free at twenty-five years of age. Persons being held as slaves at the time would be freed by the end of the year. At the same time, discriminatory colonial laws similar to those found in Massachusetts became part of the state legal code. Free blacks could not vote, could not serve on juries, and could not marry whites. African Americans were free but not equal.

New York and New Jersey were the last Northern states to act on the slavery question. Both of these states freed African Americans who served in the army, but opponents of emancipation warned against doing anything more, so as to respect property rights. Some opponents used openly racist arguments, saying that free blacks would not work unless forced to do so. They argued that Africans were lazy, ignorant, and criminal, and that slavery protected whites from an onslaught of savagery. New York's legislature rejected gradual emancipation in 1777. Eight years later, a freedom bill supported by the New York Manumission Society, whose membership included Alexander Hamilton, John Jay, and Aaron Burr, went down to defeat. Although proposals to discriminate legally against blacks failed, the legislature did agree to deny African Americans the right to vote. In 1785, New York prohibited the sale and importation of slaves and allowed masters to manumit (free) their slaves, but only if they guaranteed that they would not require public assistance. The next year, New Jersey passed similar laws. In 1788, New York declared that slaves would no longer be judged or punished under standards different from those used to judge whites.

Still, freedom did not come. In the 1790's, the New York Manumission Society fought a constant war against the slave system. It sent petitions with thousands of signatures to the state legislature. The Society for Promoting the Abolition of Slavery in New Jersey conducted a similar campaign. In both states, the antislavery groups organized boycotts of businesses that had any connection with slavery, such as newspapers that advertised slave auctions and companies that built slave ships. Auctions for slaves ended in both states by 1790. Only in 1799, however, did New York pass an emancipation bill. Owners could free their slaves regardless of age or condition, although children could still be kept as property—boys until twenty-eight years of age and girls until the age of twenty-five years. In 1804, New Jersey became the last of the original Northern states to end slavery legally. Neither New York nor New Jersey allowed free African Americans the right to vote.

The 1810 census found that the five New England states—Vermont, New Hampshire, Massachusetts, Connecticut, and Rhode Island—had 418 slaves in an African American population totaling more than twenty thousand. New York and New Jersey, on the other hand, had nearly eighteen thousand slaves, because their laws provided longer time periods for emancipating children and were passed much later. Pennsylvania, the first state to provide for gradual emancipation, had fewer than fifty slaves.

Thus, despite racist attitudes and the desire of many legislators to protect property rights, slavery was close to an end in the North. It would take a bloody civil war to end slavery in the South fifty years later. Emancipation in the North did not mean equality for African Americans, however. Laws discriminating against free blacks were passed, usually with or shortly after bills calling for the end of slavery. Prejudice remained high in Northern states, although they had very small African American populations, less than 1 percent in most cities and towns. Efforts to end slavery did not eliminate racism and feelings of white supremacy.

—*Leslie V. Tischauser*

ADDITIONAL READING:

Litwack, Leon F. *North of Slavery: The Negro in the Free States: 1790-1860*. Chicago: University of Chicago Press, 1961. Describes prejudice against African Americans in the Northeast, but points out that free blacks, despite second-class status in the North, were at least free and not someone's property.

Nash, Gary B., and Jean R. Soderlund. *Freedom by Degrees: Emancipation in Pennsylvania and Its Aftermath*. New York: Oxford University Press, 1991. Describes the movement toward gradual freedom for slaves; discusses the racism underlying opposition to complete abolition.

White, Shane. *Somewhat More Independent: The End of Slavery in New York City, 1770-1810*. Athens: University of Georgia Press, 1991. Demonstrates that freedom did not lead to equality.

Zilversmit, Arthur. *The First Emancipation: The Abolition of Slavery in the North*. Chicago: University of Chicago Press, 1967. An excellent general survey, which provides a state-by-state account of the movement toward abolition. Describes supporters and opponents of abolition.

SEE ALSO: **SEE ALSO:** 1641, Massachusetts Recognizes Slavery; 1661, Virginia Slave Codes; 1775, Pennsylvania Society for the Abolition of Slavery Is Founded; 1784, Hall's Masonic Lodge Is Chartered; 1787, Free African Society Is Founded; 1793, First Fugitive Slave Law; 1804, First Black Codes; 1807, Congress Bans Importation of African Slaves; 1820, Missouri Compromise; 1830, Proslavery Argument; 1833, American Anti-Slavery Society Is Founded; 1850, Second Fugitive Slave Law.

1777 ■ BATTLE OF ORISKANY CREEK:
British forces retreated west, leaving American forces free to concentrate against Burgoyne

DATE: August 6, 1777
LOCALE: Oriskany Creek, New York
CATEGORY: Wars, uprisings, and civil unrest
KEY FIGURES:

Joseph Brant, also known as *Thayendanegea* (1742-1807), Mohawk Indian leader and commander of Iroquois forces fighting with the British

John Burgoyne (1722-1792), British general and commander of forces that invaded New York State from Canada

Horatio Gates (c. 1728-1806), commander of American forces that opposed those of Burgoyne during the New York campaign

Nicholas Herkimer (1728-1777), general of the American militia at the Battle of Oriskany

Barry St. Leger (1737-1789), British commander of forces that accompanied those of Burgoyne during the invasion of New York State

SUMMARY OF EVENT. British strategy for suppressing the rebellion in their American colonies during 1776 and 1777 was twofold: a defeat of George Washington's rebel army and an invasion through New York State to cut the colonies in two. If they succeeded in their strategy, the British would cut off New England, the center of the rebellion, allowing for its occupation and submission by British troops. The remaining colonies, bereft of leadership, would fall under British control. In the summer of 1776, a British army of thirty thousand soldiers, under General William Howe, was to move west from New York City, to be met by a smaller force advancing from Canada under Guy Carleton, British general and governor of Canada. Although an American initiative into Canada, led by Colonel Benedict Arnold and General Richard Montgomery, was stopped at the gates of Quebec, it disrupted this strategy. Carleton, knighted for his success at Quebec, was unable to press on into New York.

Lieutenant General "Gentleman Johnny" Burgoyne, so named for his appearance and manner, had been in the colonies since the beginning of the revolution. Burgoyne had accompanied Carleton in the attempt to invade New York during the summer of 1776. Returning to England the following winter, Burgoyne presented to King George a paper called "Thoughts for Conducting the War from the Side of Canada," arguing the soundness of the strategy for an invasion from Canada. Burgoyne felt that more aggressive leadership (provided by himself) would prove more successful than the earlier attempt. The invasion would begin from Montreal, cross Lake Champlain, and follow the Hudson River. A second force would proceed from Oswego down the Mohawk Valley, along a tributary of the Hudson River; a third force, under Howe, would move from New York City up the Hudson River. The three armies would converge at Albany, cutting off the northern colonies and isolating Washington's army.

The British ministry accepted Burgoyne's plan as its war strategy for the following year, and in March, 1777, Burgoyne was given command of the forces from Canada. Lieutenant Colonel Barry St. Leger was given the temporary rank of brigadier and command of the force moving down the Mohawk Valley.

On May 6, 1777, Burgoyne arrived in Quebec, where he was met by Carleton. Burgoyne's army of eighty-three hundred men included thirty-seven hundred regulars and four hundred men from the Six Nations of the Iroquois Confederacy. On June 20, Burgoyne and his forces assembled and set sail from Lake Champlain, heading for Crown Point, eight miles north of Fort Ticonderoga. The second arm of the British strategy, four hundred troops under St. Leger, arrived at Oswego in western New York on July 25. There St. Leger was joined by a thousand Iroquois under the command of Thayendanegea, known as Joseph Brant. St. Leger planned on advancing along the Mohawk River to the Hudson River, brushing past Fort Schuyler on the way.

Opposing the British was the Northern Department of the Continental Army. Ostensibly under the leadership of General Philip Schuyler, the Americans actually regarded Horatio Gates as their commander. Schuyler was a New York patroon, autocratic, and less than successful in earlier campaigns. Many of his troops were New Englanders. They had not excelled as soldiers to date, and Schuyler despised them for it. Gates, although a plantation-owning Virginian, was much like the New Englanders he hoped to lead. He was a man of plain appearance and, although a veteran of the French and Indian War, not a strict disciplinarian. He admired the New Englanders and was admired in return.

Burgoyne's first target was Fort Ticonderoga. The fort had been seized two years earlier by Americans under the command of Benedict Arnold and Ethan Allen. The fort straddled the northern tip of Lake George and was virtually indefensible if the British occupied a nearby hill. This they did on July 5, and the commander at Fort Ticonderoga, General Arthur St. Clair, evacuated his army south. Burgoyne spent the next three weeks advancing toward the Hudson River, which he reached on July 30. On August 4, Gates replaced Schuyler as commander of the northern Continental Army.

Meanwhile, St. Leger was about to march toward the Hudson River, 150 miles east. Only Fort Schuyler stood in the way. Built during the French and Indian War, the fort had only recently been reoccupied. Its commander, Colonel Peter Gansevoort, had strengthened its defenses the previous three months. When his allies, local Oneidas, warned him of St. Leger's approach, Gansevoort evacuated the women and children, leaving about 750 men to oppose St. Leger. The British commander began an encirclement of the fort, preparing to lay siege. Coming to the fort's relief were General Nicholas Herkimer and eight hundred volunteers of the Tryon County militia. On August 5, Herkimer approached Oriskany Creek, eight miles from the fort.

That night, Herkimer sent messengers to the fort requesting that guns be fired as a diversion to cover his men. However, St. Leger was well aware of his arrival. Herkimer's column included four hundred oxcarts of supplies, strung out for more than a mile. In addition, Molly Brant, Joseph Brant's sister, had learned of Herkimer's approach and warned St. Leger.

St. Leger laid a trap along a ravine on the road to the fort. At ten o'clock Herkimer reached the ravine, where a waiting Tory detachment, and Native Americans commanded by Brant, opened a cascade of fire. Racing toward the firing, Herkimer was badly wounded in the leg. Herkimer propped himself by a tree, lit his pipe, and directed his men in the battle.

Refusing to panic, the officers assembled the men into a defensive perimeter from which they held off the British and their Native American allies for an hour, until rain interrupted the battle. Wet powder then prevented the guns from firing. When fighting resumed, Herkimer directed his men to fight in pairs, so natives could not tomahawk a man while he was reloading. Brant was reinforced by troops participating in the siege at Fort Schuyler. Hoping to fool the Americans, they disguised themselves as fellow militia. However, a militiaman recognized one as his neighbor, a Tory who sided with the British, and the ruse failed.

The battle continued for six hours, evolving into bitter hand-to-hand combat. Losses among the attacking force approached 25 percent, and finally they withdrew. More than two hundred Americans were killed or wounded. Herkimer was carried to his home and died ten days later.

Despite Herkimer's failure to relieve the fort, casualties among St. Leger's Native American allies were so heavy that they lost interest in the campaign. Furthermore, General Schuyler was determined that the Americans would retain control of the Mohawk Valley; he directed reinforcements under General Arnold to come to Gansevoort's aid. When St. Leger learned of the column's approach, he lifted the siege, ending his role in Burgoyne's campaign. Burgoyne himself would receive no reinforcements. Trapped by General Gates in Saratoga a month later, he surrendered his army.

Following the Battle of Oriskany and the defeat of Burgoyne, fighting became increasingly bitter, as each side revenged itself on its opponent's allies. In July, 1778, Colonel John Butler, leading four hundred Tories and five hundred Senecas, burned and murdered his way through Pennsylva-

nia's Wyoming Valley. In response, Washington ordered General John Sullivan to destroy the country of the Six Nations, comprising much of western New York and northern Pennsylvania. During the spring and summer of 1779, Sullivan's four thousand men marched through the Mohawk Valley. Although he met little opposition, Sullivan destroyed more than forty Seneca, Cayuga, Onondaga, and Mohawk towns. Similarly, Iroquois warriors under Joseph Brant worked devastation on American allies, burning Oneida and Tuscarora villages. This period not only marked an escalation in the bitterness and the extent of fighting but also heralded the disintegration of the once neutral Iroquois Confederacy. The union of the Six Nations did not survive the revolution.   —*Richard Adler*

ADDITIONAL READING:

Hibbert, Christopher. *Redcoats and Rebels: The American Revolution Through British Eyes*. New York: W. W. Norton, 1990. Presents the revolution from the British perspective.

Middelkauff, Robert. *The Glorious Cause: The American Revolution, 1763-1789*. New York: Oxford University Press, 1982. An excellent general narrative on the history of the American Revolution.

Scheer, George, and Hugh Rankin. *Rebels and Redcoats*. New York: World Publishing, 1957. A scholarly account of the American Revolution, with emphasis on first-person accounts.

Smith, Page. *A New Age Now Begins: A People's History of the American Revolution*. New York: Penguin Books, 1976. 2 vols. Depicts the revolution as a people's rebellion; analyzes actions and feelings.

Wood, W. J. *Battles of the Revolutionary War, 1775-1781*. New York: Da Capo Press, 1995. A detailed history of the major campaigns and skirmishes of the war.

SEE ALSO: 1775, Battle of Lexington and Concord; 1776, Indian Delegation Meets with Congress; 1777, Battle of Saratoga; 1781, Cornwallis Surrenders at Yorktown; 1784, Fort Stanwix Treaty.

1777 ■ BATTLE OF SARATOGA: *Britain's defeat marks the end of any prospect of British victory in the Revolutionary War*

DATE: October 8-17, 1777
LOCALE: Upper New York State
CATEGORY: Wars, uprisings, and civil unrest
KEY FIGURES:
Benedict Arnold (1741-1801), subordinate commander of American troops at Saratoga
John Burgoyne (1722-1792), British commander of the expedition from Canada
Henry Clinton (1738?-1795), commander of the British garrison in New York
Horatio Gates (1728?-1806), named by Congress to command the American troops at Saratoga shortly before the battle

William Howe (1729-1814), commander in chief of the
British forces in America in 1777

George Sackville Germain, Viscount Sackville (1716-1785),
British secretary of state for the colonies

SUMMARY OF EVENT. For the campaign of 1777 of the American Revolution, the British devised a bold strategy designed to bring the war to an immediate end. It involved military action in three different locales: the capture of Philadelphia, the seat of the American Congress, by an army led by William Howe and transported to the vicinity by the British Navy; an attack from Canada down the Lake Champlain-Lake George waterway, under the command of General John Burgoyne, to assault and seize Albany; and a movement of British forces from their base in New York City up the Hudson River, to meet Burgoyne at Albany. The effect would be to split the colonies in two—in particular to seal off New England, where revolutionary fervor was greatest, from the colonies to the south. Although all participants agreed on the plan, the exact role each was to play, and especially their coordination with one another, was never made clear.

George Washington, the American commander in chief, realized early the nature of the British plan but was powerless to do much about it. He felt compelled to try to protect Philadelphia, but his efforts led only to defeat by Howe. Recognizing the significance of the Burgoyne expedition, Washington sent Colonel Daniel Morgan's detachment of sharpshooters north to join the American army defending Albany. Morgan's unit at Saratoga helped to neutralize the Native American forces fighting on the British side and played a vital role in overcoming the British officers.

General Burgoyne's army, about eight thousand strong, was successfully advancing toward Albany. A large flotilla had been assembled, able to proceed by water down the Richelieu River to Lake Champlain, where it defeated American attempts to halt it. The British disembarked at the foot of Lake George and successfully seized the lightly guarded fort at Ticonderoga, from which the American force was compelled to withdraw. Burgoyne then proceeded overland toward the Hudson River, but the terrain, the weather, and the lack of adequate oxen and horses to draw his supplies slowed his advance substantially. Foreseeing the need for more supplies and especially more animals, Burgoyne detached a force of Germans serving under him to invade Vermont and capture any supplies and animals they could find. This force was wiped out by the Americans at the Battle of Bennington on August 16. The American victory did much to enhance American morale and to motivate recruits to join the American army defending Albany.

The American army, previously under the command of General Philip Schuyler, was now turned over to the command of General Horatio Gates. Gates's talent was organization, not battlefield tactics, and he has been much criticized for taking a defensive posture against Burgoyne's advancing army. However, he did realize the importance of a strong defensive position, and this led him to move the American forces north-

ward, to a position above Stillwater on the heights overlooking the Hudson River. The American forces heavily fortified their position.

On September 19, 1777, the opposing forces came face to face with each other. Burgoyne, recognizing the folly of attempting to advance further on the road to Albany, deployed his forces, now down to about five thousand. His plan was to attack the American left wing, on the heights, with his British troops, leaving the Germans to anchor the position on the road and along the river. The attack on the heights was fought largely in the woods, but partly in a clearing around an isolated farm called Freeman's Farm. The American sharpshooters shot down the officers; the British suffered heavy casualties.

Burgoyne regrouped his forces to consider what to do next. He had received little news of the cooperating army, under Henry Clinton, that was supposed to advance up the Hudson River and meet him at Albany. He did learn that many of the supplies he had left behind at Ticonderoga had been seized by American forces, leaving him with only enough supplies to last until mid-October. Burgoyne therefore staged a second, hotly contested attack on the American positions on October 7. Benedict Arnold again led the Americans in battle, and the British were unable to overcome the American forces. Unable to advance, Burgoyne on October 8 ordered his army to retreat toward Saratoga.

Meanwhile, American forces had seized more of the line of retreat toward Canada. Burgoyne's army was effectively surrounded. On October 13, Burgoyne began to negotiate terms of surrender with Gates, negotiations that were completed on October 16. Under the terms of the Convention of Saratoga, the British troops laid down their arms on October 17. They were to be marched to a port of embarkation and sent back to Europe, on condition that they would take no further part in the conflict. In the end, Congress reneged on this commitment and the captured troops spent the rest of the war in prisoner-of-war camps in America.

The defeat of Burgoyne's expedition meant the failure of the British strategy to end the war in 1777. France took steps to support the Americans, and this cooperation led eventually to the American victory at Yorktown. —*Nancy M. Gordon*

ADDITIONAL READING:

Fuller, J. F. C. *The Decisive Battles of the Western World.* Vol. 3. London: Eyre & Spottiswode, 1955. Chapter 9 discusses Saratoga. Credits Burgoyne for honesty and courage and notes his popularity with his troops, but blames him for some tactical errors. Asserts that Benedict Arnold, Gates's subordinate, should receive credit for the U.S. victory.

Glover, Michael. *General Burgoyne in Canada and America: Scapegoat for a System.* London: Gordon & Cremonesi, 1976. An exoneration of Burgoyne that lays the blame for Burgoyne's defeat on General Clinton, for his failure to communicate effectively with Burgoyne, and on the British ministers.

Hargrove, Richard J., Jr. *General John Burgoyne.* Newark: University of Delaware Press, 1983. A balanced judgment, noting Burgoyne's virtues and his weaknesses. Contains a first-rate account of the battles of Bennington and the two at Saratoga, making clear the reasons for the outcome.

Howson, Gerald. *Burgoyne of Saratoga: A Biography*. New York: Times Books, 1979. A scholarly attempt to rescue Burgoyne's reputation. Asserts that Burgoyne was a competent, careful officer. Attributes Burgoyne's defeat to inadequate appreciation of American capabilities and terrain, coupled with poor strategic planning and coordination on the part of the British military authorities.

Lunt, James. *John Burgoyne of Saratoga*. New York: Harcourt, Brace, Jovanovich, 1975. A popular, readable account, with a balanced judgment on Burgoyne. Describes Burgoyne's attempt to rescue his reputation and transfer the blame to the contemporary British ministry and, to some degree, to Howe.

Mintz, Max M. *The Generals of Saratoga*. New Haven, Conn.: Yale University Press, 1990. Depicts the Saratoga battle as a competition between Generals Burgoyne and Gates, and asserts that Gates was the hero. Stresses the numerical superiority of the American army.

SEE ALSO: 1775, Battle of Lexington and Concord; 1775, Second Continental Congress; 1776, Declaration of Independence; 1776, First Test of a Submarine in Warfare; 1777, Battle of Oriskany Creek; 1778, Franco-American Treaties; 1781, Cornwallis Surrenders at Yorktown.

1778 ■ FRANCO-AMERICAN TREATIES:
long-standing enmity between France and Britain gains French assistance for the emerging nation

DATE: February 6, 1778
LOCALE: Paris
CATEGORY: Treaties and agreements
KEY FIGURES:
Pierre Augustin Caron de Beaumarchais (1732-1799), playwright and French secret agent
Silas Deane (1737-1789),
Benjamin Franklin (1706-1790), and
Arthur Lee (1740-1792), American commissioners at the French court
Charles Gravier, comte de Vergennes (1717-1787), French minister of foreign affairs
Anne César, Chevalier de La Luzerne (1741-1791), French minister to the United States, 1778-1784
Louis XVI (1754-1993), king of France, 1774-1792
José Moñino y Redondo, conde de Floridablanca (1728-1808), prime minister of Spain and minister of foreign affairs
SUMMARY OF EVENT. The American revolutionaries did not believe that their war of independence would go unnoticed by the outside world. In 1763, the balance of power in Europe had swung decisively toward Great Britain, largely because of its defeat of France and Spain in the Western Hemisphere. Ameri-

cans and Europeans agreed that the scales would remain tipped in favor of the island kingdom only so long as it retained its New World possessions. At first, colonial writers warned that the Bourbon monarchies might attempt to seize several of George III's American provinces while his house was divided against itself, and that such storm warnings might offer the most compelling reasons for the colonies and the mother country to patch up their quarrel. As the imperial crisis deepened, American opinion of the Catholic states gradually shifted from fear to the hope that they would assist America in case of war with Great Britain.

That change of sentiment was one of the radical features of the American Revolution. Bred on a hatred of Catholicism and political absolutism associated especially with France, American publicists for decades had shrilled for the permanent removal of the French peril from North America. The elimination of France from Canada in 1763, however, meant that France was no longer the threat it had been previously. France and its ally, Spain, were now more tolerable from afar than in the day when the *fleur-de-lis* loomed over the back door of the mainland settlements. Moreover, France's nearly total elimination from mainland North America did not mean that the striving colonies were destined to lose a potentially valuable international trading partner. A thriving market for import-export trade had grown between Atlantic seaboard ports and the Spanish and French colonial possessions in the Caribbean area. The American colonists' desire to keep this trade free from British control was as much a factor in their feelings toward France as was their interest in political independence.

The need for foreign assistance, so ably expressed in Thomas Paine's *Common Sense* (1776), was a powerful catalyst for independence. Anticipating the final break, Congress in March, 1776, dispatched Silas Deane to Paris to purchase military stores and to explore the possibilities of a commercial alliance. Even before Deane's arrival, French leaders decided to provide the patriots with covert aid. The Anglo-American war gave France the long-awaited opportunity to gain revenge for its humiliation in 1763. However, the comte de Vergennes, French minister of foreign affairs, was cautious and prudent, a tough-minded career diplomat, and no messenger of Enlightenment idealism. Fearful of American defeat or a compromise settlement between the colonies and Great Britain, Vergennes plotted a judicious course until the picture cleared. The attitude of Spain, which feared an independent America as a threat to its overseas dominions, also served to restrain Vergennes and his countrymen. Nevertheless, the year 1777 marked France's increasing commitment to the American patriots. The growing stream of supplies bought with royal funds or taken surreptitiously from military arsenals, the opening of French ports to rebel privateers and warships, the procession of French officers bound for Washington's army, the unremitting pressures of Silas Deane, and the subtler blandishments of his colleague, Benjamin Franklin, all combined to move France toward the patriots' orbit. News of the British capitulation of General John Burgoyne at Saratoga in October, 1777, dispelled any lingering doubts as to the patriots' ability to continue the struggle. Vergennes now feared that the American victory might give rise to a spirit of conciliation in Great Britain, leading to some form of reunion between the English-speaking people on opposite sides of the Atlantic. The French minister of foreign affairs notified Franklin and his fellow commissioners that the government of Louis XVI was ready to establish formal ties with the United States.

Prior to and after final agreement on the treaties that were signed in 1778, Vergennes had French agents in America contact (and contract) willing propagandists to support a Franco-American Alliance. The best-known of these, until American leaders' political differences led to his alienation, was Thomas Paine. Another supporter of the French, in Massachusetts, was the Reverend Samuel Cooper, whose brother was active in the politics of independence both before and after 1776. Cooper not only wrote articles calling for closer Franco-American relations but also gathered key information from the American emissary in Paris, Benjamin Franklin. His activities actually earned for him a salary from the French foreign ministry. Shortly after the French and Americans signed the 1778 treaties, he and a number of other Francophiles opened a literary and social salon in Boston, to which French officers, including the famous marquis de Lafayette, were invited. Although Cooper was among a small number of American patriots who corresponded regularly with French officials (including Foreign Minister Vergennes and France's chief minister in America, Chevalier de La Luzerne), Lafayette did not know of their semi-official propagandistic functions. Lafayette even wrote to Vergennes in May, 1780, urging Paris to "especially put Dr. Cooper at the head of the list of our friends." Cooper's service to the cause of closer Franco-American relations continued until he died in 1784. Another patriot propagandist who maintained close ties with La Luzerne was Hugh Henry Brackenridge, a Philadelphia Presbyterian minister and attorney who in 1779 edited *United States Magazine*. Although the magazine did not print specific articles backing the French treaties, it was assumed that French pay for other propagandistic pieces helped finance Brackenridge's publication.

For both parties, the Franco-American Alliance was the child of necessity. If the patriots in the beginning hoped for massive French aid and the entrance of the Bourbon nation into the war, they wanted only a temporary relationship; too intimate a formal connection would mean becoming involved in the future strife of the Old World, whose peoples mirrored a society and way of life incompatible with free, republican institutions. While the patriots offered only a commercial treaty to France, Vergennes successfully demanded more: a "conditional and defensive alliance." The French minister of foreign affairs and his sovereign were not enthusiastic about revolution against kings. Their willingness to recognize the United States of America and to sign treaties with the infant nation on February 6, 1778, was based upon a desire to humiliate France's ancient foe. The Treaty of Amity and Commerce contained most of the proposals made by Congress for liber-

alization of trade along principles foreign to mercantilism. The Treaty of Alliance stipulated that, in case of war between Great Britain and France—which the two treaties made inevitable—neither America nor France would make peace without the approval of the other. France renounced forever any claims to British territory on the continent of North America and agreed to recognize the United States' right to any such territory seized by patriot armies. The two nations also guaranteed each other's territorial boundaries in the New World as they would be drawn at the end of hostilities.

Once news of the Franco-American treaties spread, an inevitable division of opinion over their presumed positive or negative significance appeared among American clerics. Although not all Anglican and Methodist ministers denounced the treaties, their denominational closeness to England caused schisms among parishioners. Many loyalists among the clergy had already left their pulpits as early as 1775 and 1776. The dissenting clergy that took over such ministerial posts tried to combine support for independence with some form of justification for the expediency of a formal alliance between the secularist Continental Congress and monarchical Catholic France. Among non-Anglicans, some pastors, such as the Reverend Cooper (already committed, for pay, to the French cause), defended the treaties openly. Others, including James Dana of Wallingford, Connecticut, recognized the necessity of international political alliances to help the struggling former colonies defeat Great Britain, but insisted that more extensive ties with "popery" would run counter to American principles of free government. A striking example of denunciation of the alliance as camouflage to hide presumed French Catholic propagandistic intentions came from John Zulby, a Swiss-born cleric and anti-independence member of the Continental Congress. Zulby was ultimately banished for referring to American patriots as preferring "Independancy and papist Connections" over "the Gospel and . . . former acknowledged happy Connections" with Great Britain.

Great Britain's international difficulties continued to mount after hostilities opened with France in the summer of 1778. The next year, Spain entered the fray after securing a promise from Vergennes to continue hostilities until Gibraltar was regained. Although Spain did not join the Franco-American Alliance, the United States, through its tie with France, found itself committed to fight until Gibraltar fell to Spain. In 1780, Anglo-Dutch commercial friction brought the Netherlands into the war. Great Britain was also confronted by the League of Armed Neutrality, organized by several nonbelligerent nations in protest against British practices of search and seizure on the high seas. Unlike in earlier wars of the eighteenth century, Great Britain was isolated both diplomatically and militarily.

—*R. Don Higginbotham, updated by Byron D. Cannon*

ADDITIONAL READING:

Corwin, Edward S. *French Policy and the American Alliance of 1778*. Princeton, N.J.: Princeton University Press, 1916. A revisionist and realistic look at the motives of France in supporting the American Revolution, concluding that the alliance reflected a desire to reverse the effects of France's defeat in 1763 and reestablish its position as an international power.

Gottschalk, Louis. *Lafayette Comes to America*. Chicago: University of Chicago Press, 1935. This first installment of Gottschalk's multivolume biography tears away much of the myth surrounding Lafayette and reveals attitudes of the French Court toward America.

Kennedy, Roger G. *Orders from France: The Americans and the French in a Revolutionary World, 1780-1820*. New York: Alfred A. Knopf, 1989. An excellent study of repercussions—social, economic, and cultural (particularly in art and architectural styles)—that followed the political and military aid links between France and the United States during the American Revolution. Concentrates on major biographies.

Liss, Peggy K. *Atlantic Empires: The Network of Trade and Revolution, 1713-1826*. Baltimore: The Johns Hopkins University Press, 1983. Ties North and South America to eighteenth century European commerce. The chapter on the thirteen colonies shows a number of economic links between the North American colonists and French colonies in the Caribbean just before and during establishment of the Franco-American Alliance.

Morris, Richard B. *The American Revolution Reconsidered*. New York: Harper & Row, 1967. Explores misconceptions about the diplomatic history of the American Revolution.

Stinchcombe, William C. *The American Revolution and the French Alliance*. Syracuse, N.Y.: Syracuse University Press, 1969. A comprehensive examination of the process that led to the Franco-American Alliance, beginning with the conclusion of the Seven Years' War and the Treaty of Paris in 1763. Valuable, extensive bibliography.

Varg, Paul A. *Foreign Policies of the Founding Fathers*. East Lansing: Michigan State University Press, 1963. A provocative book that deals with the relationship between commerce and foreign policy, a factor that many historians believe operated in the Franco-American Alliance.

SEE ALSO: 1775, Battle of Lexington and Concord; 1775, Second Continental Congress; 1776, Declaration of Independence; 1776, First Test of a Submarine in Warfare; 1777, Battle of Oriskany Creek; 1777, Battle of Saratoga; 1781, Cornwallis Surrenders at Yorktown.

1781 ■ ARTICLES OF CONFEDERATION:
creation of a cooperative central administration for the thirteen new American states paves the way for a new nation

DATE: March 1, 1781
LOCALE: Philadelphia, Pennsylvania
CATEGORIES: Government and politics; Laws and acts

KEY FIGURES:
Thomas Burke (1747?-1783), North Carolina delegate who won acceptance for Article 2, a strong statement in favor of states' rights and limited government
Chevalier de la Luzerne, French envoy to the United States
John Dickinson (1732-1808), principal author of the first draft of the Articles of Confederation
Thomas Jefferson (1743-1826), statesman who led Virginia into ceding most of its western lands to the Confederation

SUMMARY OF EVENT. The American experience with nationalism ran counter to developments that had led to nationhood throughout much of the modern world. A sense of American nationalism scarcely existed during the colonial period. Nor did nationalism produce a revolution aimed at the creation of a single, unified American government. Slowly, almost imperceptibly, Americans' sense of oneness grew as the colonies stood together in opposition to Great Britain's post-1763 imperial program. As Americans traveled the long road to 1776 and became more aware of their shared principles and interests, they began to think simultaneously about independence and union. Because the independent states realized they must work cooperatively or perish, American patriots turned to the task of creating a confederacy of states.

In June, 1776, while Thomas Jefferson and his committee worked at a statement that justified independence, a second committee was appointed by the Continental Congress. Including one representative from each colony, the committee was instructed to draft a series of articles that would form a cooperative union of states, thus linking the thirteen self-governing states into a "league of friendship." With John Dickinson from Pennsylvania as chairman, the committee quickly proposed a plan for union, but in late July, opponents of such a union convinced the Continental Congress to reject Dickinson's document.

Nearly five years elapsed before all agreements and compromises could be reached within the Continental Congress and at state level. The exigencies of the war slowed the process as the Continental Congress grappled with enlistments, supplies, finances, and foreign aid. Lawmakers also twice fled, once to Baltimore and once to York, Pennsylvania, from approaching British armies. State governments were similarly distracted, which further slowed the process. Political clashes in and out of the Continental Congress about the contents of the proposed document added yet another obstacle to approval of the Articles. Historians have differed sharply over the nature of the struggles. Some contend that they were ideological in substance, between so-called radicals and conservatives; others contend that they were rivalries between the small and large states. However, few scholars deny that the conflicts over questions concerning local authority versus central authority were conditioned by the colonists' previous experience with remote, impersonal government control from London. Nor should it be forgotten that creating a central administrative authority for all thirteen states and participating in government beyond the colony level were experiences largely foreign to Americans.

Although the committee report, of which John Dickinson was the primary architect, was placed before the Continental Congress as early as July 12, 1776, it languished as attention was focused on questions about administering the West and apportioning representation and financial burdens among the states. Most delegates favored a loose confederation, as opposed to a highly centralized and powerful national government. Sometimes explicitly, but more often implicitly, it seemed that the Dickinson draft left too much authority in the hands of Congress. Finally, in November, 1777, the Continental Congress agreed upon the Articles of Confederation and submitted the agreement to the states for ratification.

Under the Articles, the confederated Congress became the only branch of the central government. Each state would have one vote to cast, regardless of population, by delegates selected by the various state legislatures. A simply majority of states could decide issues, except for specified matters that required the consent of nine. Each state had the sole power to tax its population, although each state also was expected to contribute its share of money (based upon improved lands) to the upkeep of the Confederation. States also retained exclusive power to regulate their own commercial activities. Each state claiming territory in the trans-Appalachian region was allowed to keep its possessions instead of turning them over to the United States. Individually, the states were to retain their sovereignty, freedom, and independence, and the rights not specifically granted to Congress. In turn, the Articles gave the confederated Congress the authority to make war and peace, make military appointments, requisition men and money from the states, send out and receive ambassadors, and negotiate treaties and alliances. Management of postal affairs and the authority to coin money, decide weights and measures, and settle disputes between states were also responsibilities that the Articles gave to the confederated administration.

Although the Articles of Confederation vested momentous responsibilities in Congress, the agreement did not give the confederated Congress the authority to discharge those responsibilities. Without the ability to tax or regulate trade and lacking powers of enforcement, Congress could only hope that the states would meet their assigned requisitions and cooperate with the confederated administration in other vital areas. Despite the limits on power built into the Articles of Confederation, some states were reluctant to give their consent to the proposed confederated Congress. Opponents continued to question jurisdictional responsibilities assigned to the central government.

By 1779, all states except Maryland had endorsed the Articles. Maryland's continuing opposition was driven largely by avaricious land speculators. Colonial charters had given Connecticut, Massachusetts, and all states south of the Potomac River land grants extending westward to the Pacific Ocean. Many people from the "landless" states felt that regions beyond the settled areas should be turned over to the Confederation, so that states with extensive western claims would not enter the union with distinct natural advantages over states without western claims. Likewise, "landless" representatives maintained that the West eventually would be won through the combined military efforts of all.

If Maryland land speculators (who hoped to fare better from Congress than from the Commonwealth of Virginia in having prewar claims recognized) had exercised a decisive role in their state's refusal to ratify, their stand did not invalidate the reasoning of others who demanded an equitable solution to the western land problem. To break the impasse, Congress reversed itself and recommended that the landed states relinquish generous portions of their transmontane territories. Virginia, with vast claims, held the key. Prompted by Thomas Jefferson, on January 2, 1781, Virginia offered the Confederation its rights to all lands north of the Ohio River. Equally important and far-reaching were Virginia's stipulations (ultimately accepted) that speculators' claims be canceled and that new states be created and admitted to the union on terms of equality with the original thirteen. New York also responded, abandoning its tenuous claims, as Connecticut abandoned its more solid ones. In time, the remaining landed states followed suit. Maryland, which had requested French naval protection, was prodded into ratification by the French envoy, the Chevalier de la Luzerne, and on March 1, 1781, Congress announced the formal creation of a "perpetual union."

Characterized as a league of friendship, the Confederation created a union of thirteen sovereign states. Time and circumstances during the 1780's, however, would demonstrate the inherent flaws in the Articles of Confederation. By the end of the decade, it had become apparent to many Americans that the Articles were not adequate for the needs of the thirteen member states. Instead, the states consented, for the first time, to create a national government.

—*R. Don Higginbotham, updated by Paul E. Doutrich*

ADDITIONAL READING:

Douglas, Elisha P. *Rebels and Democrats: The Struggle for Equal Political Rights and Majority Rule During the American Revolution*. Chapel Hill: University of North Carolina Press, 1955. Demonstrates that the fortunes of the pre-Revolutionary ruling class varied from state to state.

Henderson, H. James. *Party Politics in the Continental Congress*. New York: McGraw-Hill, 1974. Focuses on the various interests that separated and then united members of the Continental Congress.

Jameson, J. Franklin. *The American Revolution Considered as a Social Movement*. Princeton, N.J.: Princeton University Press, 1926. Stimulating and suggestive, although the degree of immediate change produced by the American Revolution may be exaggerated.

Main, Jackson T. *The Social Structure of Revolutionary America*. Princeton, N.J.: Princeton University Press, 1965. Describes the era as one of relatively little social change, although few Americans were frozen in a lower-class status.

Miller, John C. *Triumph and Freedom: 1775-1783*. Boston: Little, Brown, 1948. Provides a somewhat detailed account of the events involved in the American Revolution.

Morris, Richard B. *Forging of the Union, 1781-1789*. New York: Harper & Row, 1987. The evolution of U.S. national government is described in some detail.

Wood, Gordon. *The Creation of the American Republic, 1776-1787*. New York: W. W. Norton, 1969. Presents a thorough analysis of the motives and goals of American political theory between independence and the creation of the nation in 1787.

SEE ALSO: 1774, First Continental Congress; 1775, Second Continental Congress; 1776, Declaration of Independence; 1778, Franco-American Treaties; 1783, Treaty of Paris; 1787, U.S. Constitution Is Adopted.

1781 ■ CORNWALLIS SURRENDERS AT YORKTOWN: *the entire British field army surrenders to combined American and French forces, marking the military end to the Revolutionary War*

DATE: October 19, 1781
LOCALE: Yorktown, Virginia
CATEGORY: Wars, uprisings, and civil unrest
KEY FIGURES:
Henry Clinton (1738?-1795), British commander in chief in America, 1778-1781
Charles Cornwallis (1738-1805), ranking British general in the South
Nathanael Greene (1742-1786), commander of the American Southern Department
Benjamin Lincoln (1733-1810), American officer who accepted the British surrender at Yorktown
Jean Baptiste Donatien de Vimeur, comte de Rochambeau (1725-1807), commander of French land forces at Yorktown
George Washington (1732-1799), commander in chief of the Continental Army

SUMMARY OF EVENT. The surrender of Lord Charles Cornwallis in 1781 at Yorktown made immortal the name of that sleepy village at the tip of a Virginia peninsula. The roots of the Yorktown debacle are to be found in a train of events that followed the decision of the Ministry in London in 1778 to shift the focus of the war to the region below the Potomac. French intervention and failure to win in the North led to the British campaign in the South. Although such a campaign would see royal military forces dispersed from Manhattan to the West Indies, the policymakers at Whitehall based their decision on two crucial assumptions: first, that the Southern Loyalists were exceedingly numerous; and second, that on the sea, Great Britain could maintain naval superiority against its combined Bourbon enemies of France and Spain.

Although the Loyalists were not so numerous as anticipated, and a British garrison at Savannah almost fell to French admiral Jean-Baptiste-Charles-Henri-Hector d'Estaing in October, 1779, when he caught the British fleet napping, the basic assumptions in London never were altered. Indeed, the war in

the South went extremely well for the home government until 1781. Georgia fell in 1779 and South Carolina in 1780. In major actions in the latter state, at Charleston on May 12, 1780, and at Camden on August 16, 1780, the Continental Congress entrusted to Major General Nathanael Greene, a former Quaker from Rhode Island, the task of rallying the scattered and dispirited American forces. His antagonist was Major General Lord Charles Cornwallis, who headed the British field army when Lieutenant General Sir Henry Clinton returned to New York. Cornwallis displayed none of the caution or timidity that many of the British senior officers had shown during the American Revolution. Determined to overrun North Carolina and, he hoped, Virginia as well, he refused to allow the annihilation of two of his detached units, at King's Mountain on October 7, 1780, and at Cowpens on January 17, 1781, to dampen his ambitions. Nor did the failure of the Loyalists, whose numbers he exaggerated, alter his thinking. Greene, a master of harassment tactics, severely mauled still more of Cornwallis' irreplaceable redcoats at Guilford Court House, North Carolina, on March 15, 1781. In April, Greene and Cornwallis went opposite ways—Greene south to pick off British outposts in South Carolina, Cornwallis north to invade Virginia.

Greene's brilliant campaign eventually cleared the enemy from all points except Charleston, South Carolina, and Savannah, Georgia, while Cornwallis, far from his supply depots, took the road to disaster. Although Clinton had favored the establishment of a naval base on the Chesapeake and had sent turncoat Brigadier General Benedict Arnold to Virginia on a raiding expedition, he had been more concerned about the welfare of British interests in the lower South. Consequently, he had instructed his restless subordinate to undertake nothing that might endanger "the tranquility of South Carolina." After limping to Wilmington, North Carolina, to rest his troops, Cornwallis wrote to Clinton, who previously had been in the dark as to Cornwallis' whereabouts, that "a serious attempt upon Virginia . . . would tend to the security of South Carolina and ultimately to the submission of North Carolina." On May 20, Cornwallis joined Arnold at Petersburg, Virginia, and assumed direction of the combined force of seventy-two hundred men. Apprehensive about the possible arrival of a French fleet in the Chesapeake Bay, Clinton disapproved of Cornwallis' abandoning South Carolina and voiced reluctance at turning Virginia into a prime military theater. Clinton, an able strategist but an insecure commander in chief, failed to deal decisively with Cornwallis, a personal rival who, he feared, might be appointed to succeed him at any moment. Cornwallis, meanwhile, idled away vital weeks skirmishing in the Old Dominion before retiring to Yorktown in the late summer to erect fortifications.

In New York, Clinton fretted and Washington awaited a large French fleet. Approximately five thousand French troops under Brigadier General Comte de Rochambeau were already at Newport, Rhode Island, but the comte de Barras' escorting ships had been quickly blockaded inside the harbor by a superior British squadron. Finally, word came of Admiral Françoise-Joseph-Paul de Grasse's sailing from France to the

West Indies with plans to detach part of his fleet later to assist a mainland campaign. Although Washington preferred to attack New York City, after hearing on August 14 that Grasse was bound for the Chesapeake, he recognized that his better prospect would be to trap Cornwallis. Accordingly, Washington and Rochambeau hurried southward with seven thousand men, while Barras, loaded with the siege guns for the allied armies, slipped out of Newport. It was scarcely the British Navy's finest hour; not only had the navy permitted Barras to elude the Newport blockade, but the West Indian squadron also had been equally lax, because Admiral Sir George Rodney had assumed erroneously that Grasse would not sail to the Virginia coast with his entire fleet of twenty-eight ships. Rodney consequently sent only fourteen vessels northward under Admiral Sir Samuel Hood, who united with the seven ships of Admiral Sir Thomas Graves at New York. Unaware of Grasse's strength, Graves hastened down the coast and met the French admiral at the mouth of Chesapeake Bay on September 5. The ensuing contest was indecisive, but Graves felt compelled to return to New York, leaving the French in control of the ocean approaches to the Middle Colonies. The fate of Cornwallis at Yorktown was then all but sealed.

Franco-American land operations began on September 7, when soldiers carried by Grasse and Lafayette's Americans took up positions on the land side of Yorktown. By September 28, after the arrival of Washington and Rochambeau, the entire allied force was in siege position. It numbered more than sixteen thousand men, about half of it French and half American. Once the first parallel was opened and allied siege guns were emplaced, the firing was incessant, forcing the British to withdraw to their inner fortifications. At this point, the British were closely invested by land and completely isolated by sea. With their supplies and morale dangerously low, the British recognized the hopelessness of their position. On October 17, when Cornwallis asked for terms, the allies demanded complete surrender. Two days later, his seven thousand scarlet-uniformed veterans marched out between rows of white-coated Frenchmen and ill-clad Americans and stacked their arms, while the British bands played "The World Turned Upside Down." News of Yorktown convinced responsible leaders on both sides of the Atlantic that Great Britain's American empire had been permanently rent asunder.

The defeat of Cornwallis and the surrender of his army by no means ended the American Revolution in a single blow. In fact, had the British Empire chosen to do so, it could have mounted renewed thrusts against the rebellious colonies, either from forces in New York or with reinforcements from the British Isles. However, the effect of a major military setback in the Americas, in conjunction with Great Britain's precarious position in a worldwide struggle against Spain, France, and Holland, as well as the newly formed United States, combined to force George III and his ministers to accept peace with American independence as the best possible solution left to them under the circumstances.

—*R. Don Higginbotham, updated by Michael Witkoski*

ADDITIONAL READING:

Cook, Don. *The Long Fuse: England and America, 1760-1785.* New York: Atlantic Monthly Press, 1995. Because it covers the entire period of the American Revolution, including the gradual but persistent growth in favor of independence among the colonies, this work is especially helpful in explaining why Cornwallis' surrender proved such a devastating blow to the British will to continue the contest.

Hibbert, Christopher. *Redcoats and Rebels: The American Revolution Through British Eyes.* New York: W. W. Norton, 1990. Presents a subtler and more complicated story than is often told. Places Cornwallis' surrender, and its impact, in a fresh light.

Lumpkin, Henry. *From Savannah to Yorktown: The American Revolution in the South.* Columbia: University of South Carolina Press, 1981. Persuasively advances the thesis that the American Revolution was actually won during the Southern phase of the struggle, and that Greene's campaigns against Cornwallis—along with the efforts of partisans such as Francis Marion—were the decisive factor in gaining American independence.

Mackesy, Piers. *The War for America, 1775-1783.* Cambridge, Mass.: Harvard University Press, 1964. For the British, the struggle in America was part of a worldwide war that ranged from the colonies to the West Indies to Europe and India. For example, troops under Clinton in New York were also expected to defend British possessions in the Caribbean. Reveals the larger pattern of which Cornwallis' surrender was but a part.

Tebbel, John. *Turning the World Upside Down: Inside the American Revolution.* New York: Orion Books, 1993. An excellent introduction that underscores how the decision at Yorktown was a final blow to Great Britain's efforts to subdue the rebellious colonies while simultaneously maintaining a global conflict.

Tuchman, Barbara. *The First Salute: A View of the American Revolution.* New York: Alfred A. Knopf, 1988. An excellent historian presents a survey of the entire struggle, placing Yorktown and its impact into its contemporaneous setting and significance. Invaluable in helping the reader understand the causes as well as the events of the American Revolution.

SEE ALSO: 1775, Battle of Lexington and Concord; 1775, Second Continental Congress; 1776, Declaration of Independence; 1776, First Test of a Submarine in Warfare; 1777, Battle of Oriskany Creek; 1777, Battle of Saratoga; 1778, Franco-American Treaties; 1783, Treaty of Paris.

1783 ■ TREATY OF PARIS: *the formal close to the American Revolution, in which the United States is recognized as a sovereign nation*

DATE: September 3, 1783
LOCALE: Paris
CATEGORY: Treaties and agreements

Pedro Pablo Abarca de Bolea, conde de Aranda
 (1718-1798), Spanish ambassador to France
John Adams (1735-1826), U.S. minister to the Netherlands
 and commissioner in the peace negotiations with the
 British
Benjamin Franklin (1706-1790), U.S. minister to France and
 the senior U.S. negotiator with the British
Charles Gravier, comte de Vergennes (1719-1787), French
 minister of foreign affairs
John Jay (1745-1829), U.S. minister to Spain and a member
 of the U.S. delegation negotiating with the British
Frederick North (1732-1792), prime minister of Great
 Britain, 1770-1782
Richard Oswald (1705-1784), major British negotiator with
 the United States
William Petty, earl of Shelburne (1737-1805), British prime
 minister, 1782-1783
Gérard de Rayneval (1746-1812), Vergennes' secretary and
 diplomatic courier
Charles Watson Wentworth, Lord Rockingham (1730-1782),
 British prime minister, 1782

Summary of event. The United States' ultimate success in winning the Revolutionary War did not immediately translate into an easy peace. The new nation's primary objective was to gain formal recognition of its independence from Great Britain; it also needed agreements related to tangential issues, such as boundaries and fishing rights off Newfoundland and Nova Scotia. It quickly became evident that the United States could not expect altruistic generosity from either its friends or its former adversaries. France, an ally of Spain, hesitated to support U.S. interests against the wishes of its Bourbon neighbor. Madrid also objected to any new rising empire in the Western Hemisphere, fearing possible instability within its own Latin American colonies. If Great Britain appeared conciliatory toward the United States, its motives were dictated by a desire to weaken the Franco-American Alliance and maintain remaining North American interests. At the same time, as events later revealed, Great Britain and France were willing to cooperate surreptitiously to limit the territorial aspirations of the United States when it proved to be in the interest of either power.

The U.S. diplomats at the peace conference were a match for their French and English counterparts, despite problems in undertaking their important task. Of those appointed by the Continental Congress to negotiate a peace, Thomas Jefferson did not serve because of the fatal illness of his wife, and Henry Laurens was a prisoner in England during the most crucial period of the peacemaking discussions. Two other appointees were serving in previous diplomatic assignments—John Jay at Madrid and John Adams at the Hague—and did not reach Paris until months after Benjamin Franklin began discussions with the British in April, 1782. (Jay reached Paris in late June, while Adams did not arrive until the end of October.)

In London, Lord North had been prime minister through-

out the entire war, but King George III largely had dictated government policy. The revolt of the American colonies and their probable loss from the British Empire led to North's resignation in March, 1782. Lord Rockingham succeeded him but died several months later. William Petty, the earl of Shelburne, the home secretary in Rockingham's cabinet, had been assigned the responsibility of dealing with the Americans. Shelburne sent to Paris a Scottish merchant named Richard Oswald, an elderly acquaintance of Franklin, to start conversations aimed at luring the venerable commissioner away from France.

Oswald argued that the former British colonies in America could gain more by dealing separately with the mother country, but while Franklin revealed a willingness to speak with the British representatives, he remained firmly committed to the Franco-American military alliance created in 1778. He did, however, assure Oswald that a generous peace would go far toward rebuilding ties between the English-speaking nations. When Lord Rockingham died in July, Shelburne became prime minister but was reluctant to concede total independence to the former colonies.

When Jay finally arrived in Paris in June, he expressed his deep suspicion of French intentions, correctly believing that the comte de Vergennes, French minister of foreign affairs, favored Spanish ambitions in the disputed region between the Appalachian mountains and the Mississippi River. The conde de Aranda, Spanish ambassador to France, informed Jay of the unwillingness of Charles III, the Bourbon king of Spain, to recognize the United States' western claims to all lands to the east bank of the Mississippi River north of 31° north latitude and to free navigation of the entire river. Subsequently, Aranda and Gérard de Rayneval, Vergennes' secretary and diplomatic courier, proposed that the region between the Great Lakes and the Ohio River remain in British hands and that much of the Southwest should become a Spanish protectorate. When he learned that Rayneval had slipped away to London, Jay suspected that the Bourbons might negotiate with Great Britain at U.S. expense.

Led by Jay, who personally took the initiative in August, the U.S. commissioners assured Shelburne of their willingness to deal directly with the British if London would change Oswald's instructions to permit him to negotiate openly and with full authority with the representatives of the United States. This would be an implicit recognition of U.S. sovereignty, which Great Britain had hitherto refused to acknowledge. Shelburne now responded positively, believing that the patriots could be separated from France and would be more cooperative with Great Britain in the future. Oswald received his increased authority in September, and the negotiations rapidly clarified the details of an agreement.

Franklin was disappointed at not gaining Canada, one of his personal objectives in the negotiations, but the boundaries agreed upon in the preliminary treaty did meet the United States' aspirations in the northwest and southwest. The Mississippi River was designated as the primary western boundary of

TERRITORY OF THE UNITED STATES IN 1783

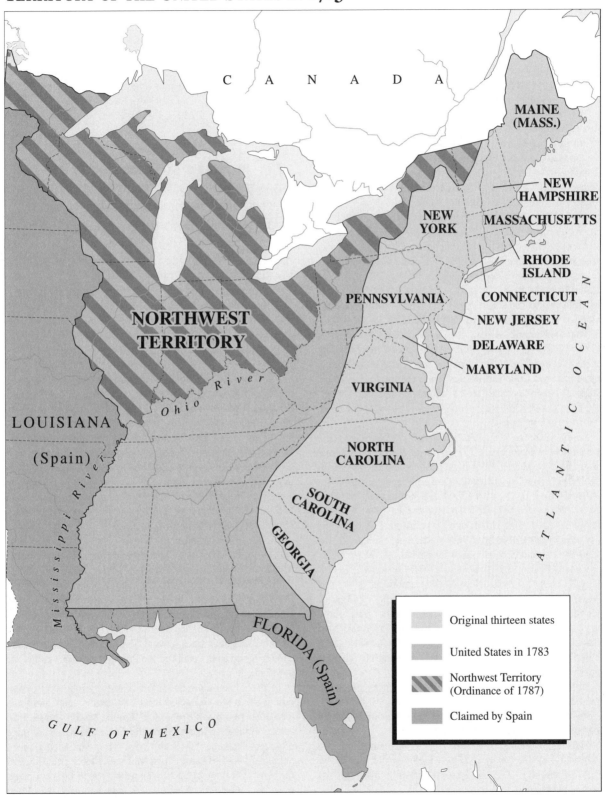

CANADA

MAINE
(MASS.)

NEW
HAMPSHIRE

MASSACHUSETTS

NEW
YORK

RHODE
ISLAND

CONNECTICUT

PENNSYLVANIA

NEW JERSEY

DELAWARE

NORTHWEST
TERRITORY

MARYLAND

VIRGINIA

Ohio River

LOUISIANA

NORTH
CAROLINA

(Spain)

SOUTH
CAROLINA

GEORGIA

Mississippi River

ATLANTIC OCEAN

FLORIDA (Spain)

GULF OF MEXICO

Original thirteen states

United States in 1783

Northwest Territory
(Ordinance of 1787)

Claimed by Spain

the United States. In addition, the new nation was given access to the Canadian fishing grounds, and British forces would be evacuated from U.S. soil. In return, the U.S. commissioners agreed to validate prewar debts owed to British subjects and to recommend to the states that they return confiscated Loyalist property. On balance, the United States gained more than the British in the concessions each side made to reach a satisfactory conclusion.

The preliminary articles, signed on November 30, 1782, although without the advice or consent of Vergennes, did not technically violate the letter of the Franco-American Alliance, for the treaty was not to go into effect until France and Great Britain also had come to terms. What the commissioners had violated, however, were the instructions given by Congress in June, 1781, that they do nothing without the knowledge and consent of France. At that time, Congress had even withdrawn the requirement that the Mississippi River be the nation's western boundary, ordering its commissioners to insist only upon independence. The negotiators' coup enabled Vergennes, never really eager to keep fighting until Spain recovered Gibraltar from the British, to persuade Charles III's ministers to settle instead for the acquisition of the island of Minorca in the Mediterranean Sea, as well as the two Floridas.

The final treaties were signed at Paris on September 3, 1783, confirming the detailed Anglo-American understanding of the previous November. With the acceptance of the formal agreement and Congress' ratification of the treaty, the United States of America entered the community of nations.

—*R. Don Higginbotham, updated by Taylor Stults*

ADDITIONAL READING:

Bemis, Samuel Flagg. *The Diplomacy of the American Revolution.* Washington, D.C.: American Historical Association, 1935. Reprint. 1957. A pioneering assessment by one of the United States' most distinguished diplomatic historians.

Burt, Alfred L. *The United States, Great Britain, and British North America from the Revolution to the Establishment of Peace After the War of 1812.* New Haven, Conn.: Yale University Press, 1940. Reprint. 1968. A detailed account of the controversies and negotiations of the period.

Cohen, Warren, ed. *Cambridge History of American Foreign Relations.* 4 vols. New York: Cambridge University Press, 1993. Volume 1, which discusses the 1782-1783 peace negotiations, is highly critical of Jay's role in the affair.

Darling, Arthur B. *Our Rising Empire, 1763-1803.* New Haven, Conn.: Yale University Press, 1940. Reprint. 1972. Contributes sound chapters on the peacemaking negotiations and the postwar period.

Dull, Jonathan R. *A Diplomatic History of the American Revolution.* New Haven, Conn.: Yale University Press, 1985. Places the Revolutionary War and subsequent peacemaking in the context of European power politics.

Hoffman, Ronald, and Albert, Peter J., eds. *Peace and the Peacemakers: The Treaty of 1783.* Charlottesville: University Press of Virginia, 1986. Essays cover specific diplomatic issues of the period.

Morris, Richard. *The Peacemakers: The Great Powers and American Independence.* New York: Harper & Row, 1965. Reprint. 1983. Widely respected as a comprehensive description and analysis of this subject.

SEE ALSO: 1775, Battle of Lexington and Concord; 1775, Second Continental Congress; 1776, Declaration of Independence; 1776, First Test of a Submarine in Warfare; 1777, Battle of Oriskany Creek; 1777, Battle of Saratoga; 1778, Franco-American Treaties; 1781, Cornwallis Surrenders at Yorktown.

1784 ■ HALL'S MASONIC LODGE IS CHARTERED: *establishment of a pillar organization in the African American middle-class community*

DATE: September 29, 1784
LOCALE: Boston, Massachusetts
CATEGORIES: African American history; Organizations and institutions
KEY FIGURES:
Prince Hall (1735?-1807), former slave, leather worker, and Boston community leader
John Marrant (1755-1791), African American minister, missionary to American Indians, and an early exponent of pride in African culture

SUMMARY OF EVENT. Prince Hall, a former slave living in Boston, perceived the many benefits of belonging to the fraternal group called the Freemasons. In the thirteen colonies, many of the most prominent and respected citizens were Masons, including George Washington, Samuel Adams, and Benjamin Franklin. As in the mother country, Masonic lodges in America stressed religion, morality, and charity to members in need and to all humankind. Many members developed business ties with their Masonic associates.

Prince Hall was born a slave in 1748. When Hall was twenty-one years of age, he was granted his freedom by his master. Hall entered into the trade of leather work. He pursued this calling for the rest of his life, although later, his Masonic leadership and his catering business occupied increasing amounts of his time. Tradition holds that Prince Hall fought against the British in the American Revolution. This is almost certainly true, but since several Massachusetts soldiers were named Prince Hall, details of this Prince Hall's army career are not clear.

In 1775, just before the outbreak of the American Revolution, a white Mason named John Batt initiated Hall and fourteen other free black Bostonians into the Masonic order. The fifteen initiates soon organized the first black Masonic lodge in America, calling it African Lodge. They continued to meet, but under the strict hierarchy of Masonry, a local group such as the African Lodge must be subordinate to a Grand Lodge, making regular reports as well as payments into the Grand

Born a slave, Prince Hall gained his freedom at twenty-one and became a leather worker by trade. His involvement with Boston's Freemasons soon persuaded him that he and fellow African Americans could make greater strides toward black rights by working together in a separate African Lodge. (Schomburg Center for Research in Black Culture, New York Public Library)

Lodge charity fund. The American Masonic hierarchy was still evolving, and Prince Hall and his associates knew that many white Masons in the new country did not approve of black lodges or even black members.

On March 2, 1784, and again on June 30 of that year, Prince Hall wrote to the Grand Lodge of England asking for an official charter. This charter would confer added legitimacy on African Lodge and would give it a powerful ally. Difficulties in getting letters and money between Boston and England slowed the process of obtaining the charter, but Hall's group finally got the requisite fees to the Grand Lodge of England, and in 1787 African Lodge received its charter. The document, dated September 29, 1784, gave African Lodge the right to initiate new members and the duty of reporting regularly to the English Grand Lodge.

Some of the activities of African Lodge related directly to race. In 1787, three free African Americans from Boston were kidnapped by men who took them to the Caribbean island of St. Bartholomew and prepared to sell them into bondage. One of the three was a member of African Lodge. Prince Hall and the other black Masons of Boston agitated actively for release of their brother Mason, and for law enforcement officers to protect free African Americans from kidnapping. The petition circulated by Prince Hall helped goad the Massachusetts legislature into passing a law to punish slave traders and kidnappers. The three men won their release when the one who was a member of African Lodge gave a Masonic sign that was recognized by a white Mason living on St. Bartholomew, and the white Mason had the captors arrested and the three men returned to Boston.

Although the records of the early meetings of African Lodge are scarce, copies of two addresses by Prince Hall and one sermon by the lodge chaplain have survived. All three documents exhibit a strong degree of racial pride and solidarity. In his first charge to the African Lodge, delivered and published in 1792, Hall chided white Masons who claimed that the existence of black Masons would somehow make the order too common. He pointed out that that had not been the feeling during the recent Revolutionary War, when white and black soldiers had fought shoulder to shoulder. Prince Hall concluded by saying that any man who rebuked an African American man because of his skin color actually was rebuking God, who had made all people in his own image.

Hall's second charge to his lodge was delivered and published in 1797. In this address, the Masonic leader painted a baleful picture of the barbaric cruelties of slavery, and used the Bible to prove that the institution was not part of God's will. On a more optimistic note, Hall lectured his brother Masons about the nation of Haiti, where six years earlier the slaves had revolted and thrown off the yoke of French government and of slavery itself. Hall saw the revolt in Haiti as a first step by African Americans in ending the hated system of slavery.

John Marrant, a free African American minister living in Boston, became the chaplain of African Lodge. One of Mar-

rant's sermons to the lodge was delivered and printed in 1789. As was the case with Hall's addresses, Marrant's sermon stressed what later writers would call black pride. Marrant said that African Americans should not be ashamed that their race was enslaved, since nearly every great people had been enslaved at one time or another, and such enslavement had often been the prelude to a great flourishing of that people. Marrant dipped into the Bible and into ancient history to prove that Africa had produced at least as many great civilizations as had any other region on earth. On at least one occasion, members of the African Lodge put their pride in Africa into action. In 1787, Prince Hall circulated a petition asking the Massachusetts government to aid in returning men and women of color to Africa. Seventy-three persons signed the petition, including most members of African Lodge. The petition is one of the earliest documents in American history associated with a back-to-Africa movement. On most other occasions, however, members of African Lodge preferred to work to improve their standing within the United States.

As the free black population in the northern states continued to grow, African Lodge responded to requests to bring Masonry to African Americans in other areas. A number of residents of Providence, Rhode Island, were initiated into African Lodge and later began their own lodge with the blessings of Prince Hall and his followers. African Lodge also helped found new lodges in Philadelphia and New York. Meanwhile, all the Masonic lodges in the United States that were chartered by one of the British Grand Lodges began to have less contact with the Grand Lodges across the ocean. African Lodge was no exception. In 1827, African Lodge declared its independence of the English Grand Lodge and of any other Grand Lodge. It became the Grand Lodge for all chapters of African American Masons it founded in the United States.

The so-called Prince Hall Masonry continued to flourish long after the death of Hall in 1807. In 1995, the order boasted three hundred thousand members in the United States. For more than two hundred years, Prince Hall Masonry has provided moral teachings, aid to members in need, and even business contacts for the millions of African American men who passed through the ranks of the order. For most of that time, white Masons attacked the Prince Hall Masons for claimed irregularities in the latter's organizational history, including the history of the Prince Hall Masons' charters. Yet any alleged irregularities were also part of the history of early white lodges in the United States. While attacks on Prince Hall Masonry are less common today than they were previously, Masonry remains a highly segregated area of American life.

—*Stephen Cresswell*

ADDITIONAL READING:

Crawford, George W. *Prince Hall and His Followers*. 1914. Reprint. New York: AMS Press, 1971. The classic defense of Prince Hall Masons to the charges of irregularity made by white Masonic groups.

Dillard, Thomas Henry. "History of Calumet Lodge #25 Free and Accepted Masons, Prince Hall Affiliation." *Journal of the Afro-American Historical and Genealogical Society* 10, no. 1 (1989): 22-28. A rare glimpse into the history of a single lodge of Prince Hall Masons.

Grimshaw, William H. *Official History of Freemasonry Among the Colored People in North America*. 1903. Reprint. Freeport, N.Y.: Books for Libraries Press, 1971. For many years, this book was considered the basic history of Prince Hall Masonry. Readers should be aware that it contains a vast number of unsubstantiated statements and should be used with care.

Muraskin, William A. *Middle-Class Blacks in a White Society: Prince Hall Freemasonry in America*. Berkeley: University of California Press, 1975. Sociological and historical examination of Prince Hall Masonry as a foundation of the African American middle class.

Wesley, Charles H. *Prince Hall: Life and Legacy*. 2d ed. Washington, D.C.: United Supreme Council, 1983. A careful history that does a good job of separating earlier myths about the origins of Prince Hall Masonry from documented fact.

SEE ALSO: 1775, Pennsylvania Society for the Abolition of Slavery Is Founded; 1777, Northeast States Abolish Slavery; 1787, Free African Society Is Founded; 1804, First Black Codes; 1807, Congress Bans Importation of African Slaves.

1784 ■ FORT STANWIX TREATY: *Iroquois tribes cede lands to the United States and are forced to move westward*

DATE: October 22, 1784
LOCALE: Fort Stanwix, New York
CATEGORIES: Expansion and land acquisition; Native American history; Treaties and agreements
KEY FIGURES:
Joseph Brant, also known as *Thayendanegea* (1742-1807), Mohawk leader who fought with the British during the Revolutionary War
Samuel Kirkland (1741-1808), minister who influenced the Oneida and Tuscarora to fight on the American side during the Revolutionary War
James Madison (1751-1836), statesman who supported the supremacy of Congress over New York State in Indian affairs
Arthur St. Clair (1736-1818), governor of the Northwest Territory and negotiator of the Treaty of Fort Harmar
SUMMARY OF EVENT. The Treaty of Fort Stanwix, signed in 1784, was a product of the American Revolution that involved colonists and the Iroquois nations. Because several Iroquois tribes had fought alongside the British during the war, victorious Americans maintained that they had won lands occupied by "defeated" Iroquois. The Treaty of Fort Stanwix marked the beginning of negotiations with Native Americans that dealt with them as a conquered people rather than as equals. The

Revolutionary War and resulting treaty negotiations irreparably split the Iroquois Confederacy.

At the outbreak of the American Revolution, the Six Nations of the powerful Iroquois Confederacy were divided over whether to support the English, to side with the American rebels, or to remain neutral. The confederation had traded and fought alongside the English for many years and considered the English and colonists as the same. Both British and American Indian agents encouraged Native Americans throughout the colonies to remain neutral. Initially, the Iroquois remained nonpartisan. This allowed the Iroquois to deal with both the British in Canada and the Americans in the colonies, playing one against another as they had the French and British prior to the French and Indian War.

As the Revolutionary War progressed, however, both the British and the Americans saw the advantages of including American Indians in their ranks and urged Native Americans to ally themselves. The pressure to choose sides exerted by British and American agents split the six-nation Iroquois Confederacy into two groups. Unable to agree on which side to support, the confederation decided to allow each nation to choose which side, if either, to endorse. The Oneidas and Tuscaroras fought for the rebels. American attacks on Mohawk settlements encouraged the Mohawks to support the British; they were joined by the Onondagas, Cayugas, and Senecas. These tribes were effective in British attacks on frontier locations, especially in the Mohawk Valley around Fort Stanwix.

During the war, British officers had made promises of land to Native Americans who fought with them, but during the peace negotiations in Paris, the defeated British ignored the interests of their Native American allies. The Treaty of Paris surrendered all the land east of the Mississippi River to the former colonists. Some of this land belonged to various Native American tribes and was not England's to grant.

New York State granted Iroquois lands to Revolutionary War soldiers as compensation for services during the war. New York tried to negotiate land sales with the Iroquois that would directly benefit the state. The United States Congress, under the Articles of Confederation, admonished New York officials and appointed Indian commissioners Oliver Wolcott, Richard Butler, and Arthur Lee to negotiate peace and land cessions for the United States with the Mohawks, Onondagas, Cayugas, and Senecas. A peace conference was called and held in New York at Fort Stanwix near Oneida Lake. A number of Iroquois could not attend because of illness and other factors, and only a quickly formed irregular group of Iroquois representatives was present. The commissioners arrived at Fort Stanwix with an intimidating military escort. Rather than negotiating with the Iroquois as equals, as the English had done previously, American commissioners asserted political sovereignty over all tribal natives on American soil. Iroquois speeches were cut short and credentials challenged.

The commissioners insisted that the Iroquois tribes that fought on the side of the British were a conquered people. All lands held by those tribes, therefore, were forfeit to the United States as spoils of war. America would allow them to retain some of their lands but demanded land cessions in reparation for injuries inflicted on Americans during the war. The Iroquois contended (1) that England had had no right to cede tribal lands to America, (2) that if the Iroquois were to surrender their lands to Americans, they expected something in return, and (3) that they had not, in any event, been defeated in battle and therefore were not party to peace negotiations.

As part of the resulting Treaty of Fort Stanwix, the attending Iroquois ceded a strip of land that began at the mouth of Oyonwaye Creek on Lake Ontario four miles south of the Niagara portage path. The boundary line ran south to the mouth of the Tehosaroro, or Buffalo Creek, to the Pennsylvania line, and along its north-south boundary to the Ohio River. In effect, the treaty took all Iroquois lands west of New York and Pennsylvania and all of Ohio.

The United States released any claim it may have had by right of conquest to tribal lands west of that boundary. Iroquois property in the western region of New York state east of the Oyonwaye remained unaffected. The treaty assured the Oneida and Tuscarora who had fought on the side of the Americans continued peaceful possession of their lands. The United States agreed to protect the remaining Iroquois territories against encroachments, seizures, and other possible violations, and guaranteed the right of the Six Nations of the Iroquois Confederacy to independence.

Representatives for the Iroquois Confederacy agreed to peaceful relations with the United States. The tribes who had fought against the colonies promised to deliver up all prisoners, black and white, whom they had taken during the war. As guarantee of that promise, six Iroquois would be taken as hostages to Fort Harmar by General Arthur St. Clair, governor of the Northwest Territory.

Immediately after the congressional commissioners concluded their negotiations, commissioners from Pennsylvania negotiated for large land grants in their state. In return, the Iroquois received five thousand dollars in goods and supplies. Soon after, New York State, in defiance of Congress, negotiated land sales with the Oneida and Tuscarora. Additional land treaties quickly ensued. Congress' inability to prevent New York State from negotiating separate land sales and to uphold other aspects of the Treaty of Fort Stanwix highlighted the weaknesses in central government under the Articles of Confederation and served as a reminder that each state considered itself a sovereign nation.

In 1786, the Iroquois Confederacy held a council meeting at Buffalo Creek, New York. Disappointed and upset with their delegates, they refused to ratify the Treaty of Fort Stanwix and offered to return gifts presented to the delegates at the negotiations. Congress, however, considered the terms of treaty to be valid and acted on them accordingly.

After the American Revolution, British officials did little to discourage continued relations with northern Native American tribes. The English traded with and provided provisions to local tribes and allowed large councils to be held at British-held forts. After the council of Buffalo Creek, the Iroquois sought support from the British in their effort to denounce the treaty and continue their war against the United States. The Iroquois Confederacy soon discovered that the British had no intention of militarily supporting their former allies in defense of their land rights. Lacking the desire to go to war against the Americans alone, the Iroquois let the treaty stand.

On January 9, 1789, St. Clair negotiated the Treaty of Fort Harmar with a group of Senecas. The treaty reaffirmed the terms and boundaries set forth in the Treaty of Fort Stanwix. The Iroquois were given permission to hunt in their old lands "as long as they were peaceful about it."

The treaties of Fort Stanwix and Fort Harmar further fractionalized the confederation's six tribes, a process that had begun in 1777, when the Six Nations had split in choosing sides during the Revolutionary War. Joseph Brant led a group of Mohawk, Cayuga, and other tribe members out of the country and into Ontario, Canada, thereby splitting the confederacy in half. Those who remained in the United States were divided over other issues between the American Indians and the settlers. There was no single chief or council that could speak for the entire Iroquois Confederacy, and the Iroquois Confederacy was never again united.   —*Leslie Stricker*

ADDITIONAL READING:

Downes, Randolph C. *Council Fires on the Upper Ohio: A Narrative of Indian Affairs in the Upper Ohio Valley Until 1795.* Pittsburgh: University of Pittsburgh Press, 1940. Discusses the relations between settlers and various tribes in the Ohio Valley, including those at Fort Stanwix.

Graymont, Barbara. *The Iroquois in the American Revolution.* Syracuse, N.Y.: Syracuse University Press, 1972. Chapters 6 and 7 describe Iroquois warfare, diplomacy, decline, and removal.

Jennings, Francis, ed. *The History and Culture of Iroquois Diplomacy: An Interdisciplinary Guide to the Treaties of the Six Nations and Their League.* Syracuse, N.Y.: Syracuse University Press, 1985. Extensive discussion of treaty negotiations, terms, and results.

Trigger, Bruce G., ed. *Northeast.* Vol. 15 in *Handbook of North American Indians,* edited by William C. Sturtevant. Washington, D.C.: Smithsonian Institution, 1978. Discusses Native Americans from the Northeast in considerable detail, including language, history, customs, culture, and religion.

Washburn, Wilcomb E., ed. *History of Indian-White Relations.* Vol. 4 in *Handbook of North American Indians,* edited by William C. Sturtevant. Washington, D.C.: Smithsonian Institution Press, 1988. Extensive coverage of relations between American Indians and whites across the United States, from first contact to 1987.

SEE ALSO: 1500, Iroquois Confederacy; 1763, Proclamation of 1763; 1776, Indian Delegation Meets with Congress; 1777, Battle of Oriskany Creek; 1783, Treaty of Paris; 1785, Ordinance of 1785; 1787, Northwest Ordinance; 1790, Little Turtle's War.

1785 ■ BEGINNINGS OF STATE UNIVERSI-TIES: *the rise of public support for higher education made it available to a growing middle class*

DATE: 1785
LOCALE: South and Midwest
CATEGORIES: Education; Organizations and institutions
KEY FIGURES:

Abraham Baldwin (1754-1807), state legislator, lawyer, and author of the charter of the University of Georgia

Manasseh Cutler (1742-1823), clergyman and lobbyist before Congress for the Ohio Company

Thomas Jefferson (1743-1826), third president of the United States, 1801-1809, and founder of the University of Virginia

John Marshall (1755-1835), chief justice of the United States and author of the opinion rendered in the Dartmouth College case

Daniel Webster (1782-1852), representative of Dartmouth College to the Supreme Court

SUMMARY OF EVENT. For most Americans, state universities may be defined as publicly supported and controlled nonsectarian, degree-granting institutions of higher learning, designed to discover, conserve, and disseminate knowledge. The concept, if not the realization, is at least as old as the Republic. In 1779 Thomas Jefferson proposed a comprehensive educational plan, part of which involved converting his alma mater, William and Mary College, into the State University of Virginia. Even earlier, North Carolina's founding fathers drafted a constitution which authorized the creation of one or more publicly controlled and endowed universities for that state. They also barred clergymen from holding office in the general assembly. Although neither Jefferson nor the Carolinians succeeded in the 1770's, their schemes to create state universities reflected the strongly republican and secular sentiments prevalent among many of America's revolutionary leaders. They also illustrated the firm conviction of many public men that no self-governing people could long endure without making provision for an informed electorate and an educated leadership.

During the colonial period, the principle of the separation of church and state was not yet widely accepted. After the beginning of the U.S. republic, it thus proved more difficult for legislatures to create universities in states where colonial colleges already existed. The first state universities created in the original thirteen states were concentrated in the South, where only one of the nine sectarian colleges founded in the colonial period was located. Under the leadership of a recent immigrant from Connecticut, Abraham Baldwin, Georgia chartered her state university in 1785, although the institution did not admit students until 1801. By that time, North and South Carolina also boasted state universities. Created in 1789, the University of North Carolina began classes at

Chapel Hill in January, 1795. South Carolina's legislature acted in 1801 and the state university opened its doors four years later. Maryland, Virginia, and Delaware followed Georgia and the Carolinas in chartering state universities. Admitting its first entering class in 1825, the University of Virginia was the only state university founded before the Civil War in a state where a college had existed prior to the American Revolution. On the grounds that any state university needed to reflect basic principles of religious and academic freedom, Jefferson refrained from establishing a professorship of divinity at the university, institutionalized lifetime appointments for the faculty, and gave students more latitude than was customary in deciding which lectures to attend. From the beginning a successful model of nonsectarian education, the University of Virginia operated without interruption or significant change in legal status before the Civil War.

Among the new states added to the Union before 1861, at least a dozen of them chartered state universities, largely as a result of the westward movement and federal largesse. In 1787, lobbying for a group of New England land speculators organized as the Ohio Company of Associates, Massachusetts-born clergyman Manasseh Cutler persuaded Congress to award two free townships to the land company for the purpose of creating a university. Otherwise, Cutler argued, New Englanders would not emigrate. From these grants came Ohio University (1802) and, after another land sale, Miami University at Oxford (1809). By the outbreak of the Civil War, the land grant pattern set by Congress in Ohio had been applied to twenty-one of the twenty-four states admitted to the Union following ratification of the Constitution.

As the American population expanded into the West, the common perception that civic order needed to be established as quickly as possible helped in this region to fuel the rapid growth of state universities. These institutions, it was assumed, would provide their students with an education in civic virtue so, once graduated, they might take on the roles of responsible citizens of a republican nation. They also took the lead in the development of coeducation at the state university level, with the University of Iowa in 1855 becoming the first state university to admit women, followed by the University of Wisconsin in 1863. Early advocates of state-supported, non-sectarian education, despite their initial successes in the South and on the frontier, made almost no headway where denominational schools were well entrenched or where, as in Massachusetts and Connecticut, separation of church and state did not occur until well into the nineteenth century. In any case, by the time Thomas Jefferson had left the Executive Mansion in 1809, the strongly secular spirit regarding higher education, so widespread immediately following the Revolution, had largely disappeared in a wave of evangelicalism that has been called the Second Great Awakening.

Another obstacle to the early establishment of state universities was the Dartmouth College case of 1819. In 1816 the New Hampshire legislature, influenced by the results of a recent election, sought to bring Dartmouth College, a Congregational institution founded in 1769, under state control. The Board of Trustees sued to retain the college's charter as a private institution, but the New Hampshire high court upheld the state law. Undaunted, the board appealed to the United States Supreme Court. Persuaded by the passionate appeal of Daniel Webster, himself a Congregationalist and alumnus of Dartmouth College, to preserve the institution's autonomy, Chief Justice John Marshall reversed the lower court in a precedent-setting opinion, holding that a charter granted to a private corporation constituted a contract, and a contract, under Article I, Section 10 of the Constitution, could not be impaired by the action of a state. Dartmouth College, therefore, was immune from legislative tampering. More important, the Dartmouth decision killed efforts in other states to make public universities out of private colleges. It also unleashed what one authority on higher education has called a Protestant counter-reformation; that is, it spurred the creation of innumerable inferior denominational colleges, all secure in the knowledge that their charters, once obtained, placed them beyond state control.

America's first state universities, never very well supported from public funds, came under increasing attack after the War of 1812. While sectarians accused them of "godless atheism," an upwardly mobile electorate suspected them of promoting aristocratic privilege at the expense of the common man. Timid legislators responded predictably. They refused to support state universities altogether, diverted university funds to the common schools, or parcelled out meager resources among a host of inferior denominational colleges. In some instances, lawmakers blunted popular criticism by naming representatives of the most powerful sects to state university faculties or boards of trustees. The net effect was that true state universities were almost stifled in their infancy. Not until the Civil War would they begin to break free from the crippling effects of sectarianism, local boosterism, political demagoguery, and niggardly legislative appropriations. By that time new forces were active in American society. The Industrial Revolution and the political coming-of-age of the middle and lower classes combined to bring about a concerted drive for what contemporaries called a more "practical education," one which would stress the agricultural and mechanical arts so necessary to a progressive and developing materialist society.

—Germaine M. Reed, updated by Diane P. Michelfelder

ADDITIONAL READING:

Marsden, George M. *The Soul of the American University: From Protestant Establishment to Established Nonbelief.* Oxford: Oxford University Press, 1994. A captivating account of the history of the relationship between church and state in the development of higher education in America, with a focus on the diminishing role of religious values in publicly supported universities.

Pangle, Lorraine Smith and Thomas L. Pangle. *The Learning of Liberty: The Educational Ideas of the American Founders.* Lawrence: University Press of Kansas, 1993. An illuminating study of the beliefs held by George Washington,

Benjamin Franklin, Thomas Jefferson, and others concerning the role of education in a republican nation. Chapter 8, "Higher Education," concentrates on the development of the University of Virginia.

Rudolph, Frederick. *The American College and University: A History.* New York: Alfred A. Knopf, 1962. One of the earliest comprehensive histories of higher education in America. Rudolph draws on numerous histories of specific institutions to create an engaging study ranging over a number of topics, including the development of coeducation in higher education and the movement to create land grant colleges.

Tewksbury, Donald G. *The Founding of American Colleges and Universities Before the Civil War.* New York: Archon Books, 1965. A valuable source of information related to the chronological development of state universities. Includes tables.

Westmayer, Paul. *A History of American Higher Education.* Springfield, Ill.: Charles C Thomas, 1985. While similar to other histories of American higher education in the material and topics covered, this book also covers the relation of the development of America to the development of the colleges and universities within it.

SEE ALSO: 1650, Harvard College Is Established; 1790's, Second Great Awakening; 1820's, Free Public School Movement; 1823, Hartford Female Seminary Is Founded; 1833, Oberlin College Is Established; 1837, Mt. Holyoke Seminary Is Founded; 1857, First African American University; 1862, Morrill Land Grant Act; 1865, Vassar College Is Founded; 1867, Office of Education Is Created.

1785 ■ ORDINANCE OF 1785: *regulation of the sale of the public domain through an orderly framework for land distribution*

DATE: May 20, 1785
LOCALE: New York
CATEGORIES: Expansion and land acquisition; Laws and acts
KEY FIGURES:
Manasseh Cutler (1742-1823), lobbyist for the Ohio Company of Associates
William Duer (1747-1799), secretary of the Confederation's Board of the Treasury
Thomas Hutchins (1730-1789), congressional geographer who surveyed the first eleven ranges of the Ohio country
Thomas Jefferson (1743-1826), leading member of the Confederation Congress committee that drafted the report upon which the ordinance was based
Rufus Putnam (1738-1824), member of the Ohio Company of Associates
Winthrop Sargent (1753-1820), member of the Ohio Company of Associates and later secretary of the Northwest Territory
John Cleves Symmes (1742-1814), organizer of the Symmes Purchase

SUMMARY OF EVENT. By 1779, twelve of the thirteen American states, engaged at that time in the Revolutionary War, had ratified the Articles of Confederation. The recalcitrant state, Maryland, ostensibly refused to ratify the document until the states with land claims in the West ceded those lands to the new government. Pressure from the landless states and the exigencies of the war finally compelled the landed states, particularly New York and Virginia, to cede their western claims to the Revolutionary government. Maryland then ratified the Articles of Confederation early in 1781 and the confederation government came into existence as the owner of a vast public domain. Although little was done by that government to dispose of these lands during the war, in October, 1780, Congress passed an act declaring its intent to sell the public lands and create states out of the new territories.

After the Treaty of Paris had been signed in 1783, the Confederation Congress turned to the formulation of a national land policy. To implement the intentions expressed in the Act of 1780, three problems had to be met. First, security against the natives was necessary before the new lands could be established, and some measure of success in this direction was achieved with General Anthony Wayne's victory at the Battle of Fallen Timbers. Second, some procedure had to be devised for the political organization of the new regions; this problem was resolved with the Northwest Ordinance in 1787. Third, a system for the survey and sale of the lands had to be established, and this was the purpose of the Ordinance of 1785.

The debate over disposal of the public domain brought into view two divergent approaches that persisted into the nineteenth century. There were those who desired rapid settlement of the land and who, therefore, favored a policy that would attract settlers by the cheapness of the land. Others, moved by a variety of motives, advocated less liberal terms to settlers. Some of this latter group were concerned about the grave financial situation of the government. The Articles of Confederation did not provide the government with an independent and reliable source of revenue. Proceeds from the sale of public lands might alleviate this situation. Some from eastern (tidewater) areas feared that the rapid growth of the West would quickly diminish the political power of the older states. Others, interested in the possibilities of land speculation, looked upon liberal policies as dangerous competition.

There was also disagreement as to the method of land disposal. Two basic forms were available. The more systematic approach was the New England practice of township settlement, which provided for concentrated patterns of ownership, security in communities, and such community institutions as schools and churches. The other approach, generally referred to as the southern method, resulted in dispersed settlement with each individual staking out a claim to hitherto unsettled lands. In the New England plan, survey preceded sale and the possibility of conflicting claims was considerably lessened.

The matter was debated through 1784 and 1785, and when the Ordinance of 1785 was passed, it appeared to incorporate the basic features of the New England practice. The principle that survey should precede sale was adopted, as the act provided for rectangular surveys that divided the land into townships of six square miles. Townships were divided into tracts of 640 acres, or sections, which were to be sold at public auction for a minimum price of one dollar per acre. In each township, one lot was set aside for the support of public schools and four for the federal government. A provision giving similar support for religion was narrowly defeated.

This ordinance, with its minimal purchase requirement of 640 acres and its prohibition against indiscriminate settlement, seemed to favor the needs of speculators more than bona fide settlers. Few people of the type willing to carve a farm out of the wilderness in an area open to attack by American Indians had $640 in cash. Moreover, the disposition of the people who moved west was to settle where they lit, regardless of surveys, which were unable to keep up with settlement during the nineteenth century.

Congress itself, in its desperate need for ready money, compromised the intent of the act by disposing of vast tracts of land to private land companies for purposes of sale to settlers at a profit. The most famous of these companies was the Ohio Company of Associates. In 1787, Congress agreed to sell one and a half million acres of land to this group and another three and a half million to the Scioto Company. This latter speculative venture included many of the most important men in Congress, and their inclusion in the speculation made possible the passage of the Ohio Company grant. Also in 1787, the Symmes Purchase of two million acres was made at about sixty-six cents per acre.

The confederation government did not realize much money from these sales, nor did these sales greatly stimulate settlement. Conditions were too precarious in the Ohio country. The Land Act of 1796, which raised the minimum price to two dollars per acre, did little to advance settlement. The change to a more liberal policy began with the Harrison Land Act of 1800.

Nevertheless, the ordinance established an orderly method of disposing of public lands into private hands—a method that solved several problems simultaneously. First, it brought settlers and farmers into the national effort to repay the Revolutionary War debts. Even if the sales did not achieve what Thomas Jefferson hoped, the concept showed that all the nation's citizens would be called upon to shoulder part of the price of independence. Second, the principle of organized and methodical settlement—although, again, far from perfect in reality—reflected a clear understanding about the importance of keeping populations reasonably dense for purposes of defense and development. Third, and perhaps most significant, the ordinance ratified the fundamental property rights that undergirded the entire economic system. Land, once only held by nobility, was available to anyone for a tiny sum. Along with Jefferson's Northwest Ordinance, the Ordinance of 1785 allowed people to settle new land, bring it into the Union, and participate as equals in the polity.

—*John G. Clark, updated by Larry Schweikart*

ADDITIONAL READING:

Atack, Jeremy, and Peter Passell. *A New Economic View of American History*. 2d ed. New York: W. W. Norton, 1994. Contains an excellent chapter on land, land policies, agriculture, and productivity. Another chapter gives a good review of relevant material on the colonial economy.

Harris, Marshall D. *Origin of the Land Tenure System in the United States*. Westport, Conn.: Greenwood Press, 1953. Evaluates the influence of colonial precedents on the Ordinance of 1785.

Hibbard, Benjamin H. *A History of the Public Land Policies*. New York: Peter Smith, 1960. A good treatment of the adoption and implementation of the Ordinance of 1785. Emphasizes political policies more than Robbins' book.

Morris, Richard B. *The Forging of the Union, 1781-1789*. New York: Harper & Row, 1987. Touches only briefly on the ordinance itself, but sets the political stage for land policies under the Articles of Confederation.

Pattison, William D. *Beginnings of the American Rectangular Land Survey System, 1784-1800*. Chicago: University of Chicago Press, 1957. Focuses far more on the principles behind the surveys—such as how land should be divided and what land reserved for public uses—than on the ideals behind Jefferson's acts.

Robbins, Roy M. *Our Landed Heritage: The Public Domain, 1776-1936*. New York: Peter Smith, 1962. A general survey of land laws and their application.

Treat, Payson Jackson. *The National Land System, 1785-1820*. New York: E. B. Treat, 1910. A detailed analysis of the land acts in the early republic. Praises the survey system and details its problems in collecting money for the land.

SEE ALSO: 1783, Treaty of Paris; 1787, Northwest Ordinance; 1794, Battle of Fallen Timbers; 1820, Land Act of 1820.

1786 ■ VIRGINIA STATUTE OF RELIGIOUS LIBERTY: *the first state to legislate religious liberty, which influenced the First Amendment's provision for separation of church and state*

DATE: January 16, 1786
LOCALE: Richmond, Virginia
CATEGORIES: Civil rights; Laws and acts; Religion
KEY FIGURES:
Isaac Backus (1724-1799), leader of the fight for the disestablishment of religion in Massachusetts
Patrick Henry (1736-1799), leader of the effort to enact the General Assessment Bill
Thomas Jefferson (1743-1826), author of the "Bill for Establishing Religious Freedom"
James Madison (1751-1836), leader of the fight to enact Jefferson's bill

Roger Williams (c. 1603-1683), founder of Rhode Island and an early advocate of separation of church and state

SUMMARY OF EVENT. The adoption by the state of Virginia of the Statute of Religious Liberty was a pivotal episode in the long struggle for separation of church and state in the United States. The American colonies had inherited from England an organic concept of society that predominated in the Middle Ages and survived the Protestant Reformation. In England, the church and the state had been regarded ideally as parts of a greater and divinely sanctioned social order and so owed mutual support to each other. While the Puritans and other sects emigrated partly to practice their particular faiths without harassment, few were committed to genuine religious freedom. The legal toleration of all Christians in Maryland and Pennsylvania, and the complete toleration offered in Rhode Island, were exceptional in the seventeenth century, and even those colonies imposed penalties on Catholics by the time of the Revolutionary War. Whereas, in the later colonial period, toleration of dissenting sects was often a practical necessity, connections between the church and state persisted. The Church of England was established legally in the Southern colonies, and Protestant churches were supported by public funds in most of New England. Catholics and Jews remained under civil disabilities in some states until well into the nineteenth century.

During the period of the American Revolution, there was an acceleration of the long-term evolution to a concept of society in which political and religious life existed in separate compartments and in which religion withdrew, theoretically, into the private sphere of activity. Part of the impetus behind the separation of church and state was religious. Some originally radical Protestant sects were committed to separation early, either because of their own experience with persecution or out of more abstract considerations. Some agreed with Roger Williams that a church would be corrupted only by connection with the state. The Baptists were particularly energetic advocates of separation. Isaac Backus, Baptist leader of the fight for religious disestablishment in Massachusetts, has been characterized as the leading American advocate of religious liberty after Williams. In addition to these strains within American Protestantism, the philosophy of the Enlightenment, emphasizing the sanctity of the individual conscience, was influential, most notably among Thomas Jefferson and other leaders of the disestablishment struggle in Virginia. Perhaps the overriding factor in deciding the general issue in the United States, however, was a practical consideration: that because of the extreme multiplicity of sects in the country, in the long run it was not politically feasible to establish any one of them or even a combination.

The American Revolution, bringing new state constitutions and the withdrawal of British support for the Anglican establishment, provided an occasion for the reform of relationships between church and state. Virginia's action in the period following the Declaration of Independence was particularly significant. Virginia—one of the largest and most important states in the new republic and the seat of the most deeply rooted of the Anglican establishments—took the lead in moving toward religious liberty and the complete separation of church and state. Only Rhode Island offered comparable liberty among the original states, although, despite its early toleration, Catholics and Jews had been barred from citizenship there in the late colonial period.

Revolutionary Virginia inherited a strongly antiestablishment sentiment, marked historically by disputes over clerical salaries and the long struggle by Baptists and Presbyterians against Anglican domination. The Declaration of Rights, adopted by the Virginia legislature three weeks before the Declaration of Independence, asserted that "all men are equally entitled to the free exercise of religion, according to the dictates of conscience. . . ." James Madison had suggested this liberal phrasing in preference to a more narrow statement of religious toleration. Later in 1776, penalties against those of dissenting religious persuasion were repealed, and dissenters were exempted from contributing to the support of the still-established Church of England. In 1779, the legislature moved in the direction of disestablishment by discontinuing the payment of salaries to clergy of the Church of England in Virginia.

The conclusive debates in Virginia took place in 1784 and 1785. Patrick Henry led a move in Virginia's legislature to establish a general assessment for the support of Christian worship, which would have substituted a general Christian establishment for the Anglican establishment. Initially passed in November, 1784, this General Assessment Bill was sharply attacked by Madison and defeated on its final reading in October, 1785. Madison followed up this victory by securing a vote on the "Bill for Establishing Religious Freedom," proposed by Thomas Jefferson and originally introduced in the legislature in 1779. It was adopted and became law as the Statute of Religious Liberty in January, 1786. With a preamble asserting that God had "created the mind free" and that attempts to coerce it "tend only to beget habits of hypocrisy and meanness, and are a departure from the plan of the Holy Author of our religion," Jefferson's statute provided "that no man shall be compelled to frequent or support any religious worship, place or ministry whatsoever, nor shall be enforced, restrained, molested, or burthened in his body or goods, nor otherwise suffer on account of his religious opinions or belief. . . ." There remained some vestigial connections between the church and the state, but their separation had been completed by 1802.

Few other states immediately followed Virginia's lead. Officeholders under many of the original state constitutions were required to be believers in God, Christians, or even Protestants. It was not until 1818 that Connecticut did away with compulsory public support of churches, and not until 1833 was a similar establishment completely eliminated in Massachusetts. The First Amendment to the federal Constitution, which prohibited religious establishment or infringement of religious liberty on the national level, helped to commend the example of Virginia to its sister states.

—*Michael D. Clark, updated by Daniel A. Brown*

ADDITIONAL READING:

Drakeman, Donald L. "Religion and the Republic: James Madison and the First Amendment." *Journal of Church and State* 25, no. 3 (1983): 427-445. Provides a historical appraisal of Madison's evolution on this issue.

Howe, Mark De Wolfe. *The Garden and the Wilderness: Religion and Government in American Constitutional History.* Chicago: University of Chicago Press, 1965. Discusses the church and the world in the unfolding drama connecting them.

Noll, Mark A., ed. *Religion and American Politics: From the Colonial Period to the 1980's.* New York: Oxford University Press, 1990. A collection of historical articles with a comprehensive section on the time of the Founding Fathers.

Peterson, Merrill D., and Robert C. Vaughan, eds. *The Virginia Statute for Religious Freedom: Its Evolution and Consequences in American History.* New York: Cambridge University Press, 1988. A rich collection by historians, philosophers, lawyers, and religion scholars on the impact of the Virginia statute in the late eighteenth century and after.

Stokes, Anson P., and Leo Pfeffer. *Church and State in the United States.* Rev. ed. New York: Harper & Row, 1964. A useful abridgment of the standard, monumental survey of legal development of church and state issues in the United States.

Wald, Kenneth D. *Religion and Politics in the United States.* 2d ed. Washington, D.C.: Congressional Quarterly Press, 1992. A reliable primer on the history, law, and sociology involved in the relationship of church and state in the United States.

SEE ALSO: 1649, Maryland Act of Toleration; 1787, U.S. Constitution Is Adopted; 1791, U.S. Bill of Rights Is Ratified.

1787 ■ FREE AFRICAN SOCIETY IS FOUNDED: *the first major secular institution with a mission to aid African Americans*

DATE: April 12, 1787

LOCALE: Philadelphia, Pennsylvania

CATEGORIES: African American history; Organizations and institutions; Social reform

KEY FIGURES:

Richard Allen (1760-1831), freed slave who dedicated his life to religious teaching and social reform for African Americans

Absalom Jones (1746-1818), leader of the Free African Society who disagreed with Allen over denominational priorities

Benjamin Rush (1745-1813), physician and member of the Continental Congress who helped draft the society's bylaws

SUMMARY OF EVENT. Both the origins of the Free African Society and the long-term repercussions of its founding form an essential part of the religious history of African Americans. The original organization itself was of short duration: About seven years after it was organized, it disappeared as a formal body. In its immediate wake, however, closely related institutions emerged that tried to take over its proclaimed mission.

Generally speaking, prior to the 1790's people of African slave origins who managed to obtain their individual freedom had only one option if they wished to practice Christianity: association, as subordinate parishioners, in an existing white-run church. Several churches in the American colonies before independence, including the Quakers and Methodists, had tried to identify their religious cause with that of the black victims of slavery.

Richard Allen, born in 1760 as a slave whose family belonged to Pennsylvania's then attorney general, Benjamin Chew, was destined to become one of the earliest religious leaders of the black segment of the American Methodist church. As a youth, Allen gained extensive experience with Methodist teachings after his family was separated on the auction block in Dover, Delaware. Allen was encouraged by his second owner, Master Stokeley, to espouse the religious teachings of the itinerant American Methodist preacher Freeborn Garrettson. Allen's conversion to Methodism was rewarded when Stokeley freed him at age twenty to follow the calling of religion. His freedom came just as the Revolutionary War ended.

For six years, Allen worked under the influence of Methodist evangelist Benjamin Abbott and the Reverend (later Bishop) Richard Whatcoat, with whom he traveled on an extensive preaching circuit. Allen's writings refer to Whatcoat as his "father in Israel." With Whatcoat's encouragement, Allen accepted an invitation from the Methodist elder in Philadelphia to return to his birthplace to become a preacher. At that time, Philadelphia's religious environment seemed to be dominated by the Episcopal church. This church had been active since 1758 in extending its ministry to African Americans. It was St. George's Methodist Episcopal Church, however, that, in the 1780's, had drawn the largest number of former slaves to its rolls. Once the circumstances of blacks' second-class status became clear to Allen, he decided that his leadership mission should be specifically dedicated to the needs of his people. Within a short time, he joined another African American, Absalom Jones, in founding what was originally intended to be more of a secular movement than a formal denominational movement: the Free African Society.

Absalom Jones was older than Allen and had had a different set of life experiences. Born a slave in Delaware in 1746, Jones served for more than twenty years in his master's store in Philadelphia. He earned enough money to purchase his wife's freedom, to build his own home, and finally, in 1784, to purchase his own freedom. He continued to work for his former master for wages and bought and managed two houses for additional income. His success earned him great respect among other free blacks and opened the way for him to serve as lay leader representing the African American membership of St. George's Methodist Episcopal Church.

Traditional accounts of Jones's role in the founding of the Free African Society assert that, when Jones refused to comply with the announcement of St. George's sexton that African American parishioners should give up their usual seats among the white congregation and move to the upper gallery, he was supported by Richard Allen, in particular. The two then agreed that the only way African Americans could worship in an environment that responded to their social, as well as religious, needs would be to found an all-black congregation. Some sources suggest that Jones's reaction to the reseating order was the crowning blow, and that Allen previously had tried to organize several fellow black parishioners, including Doras Giddings, William White, and Jones, to support his idea of a separate congregation, only to have the idea rejected by the church elders.

Whatever the specific stimulus for Allen's and Jones's actions in 1787, they announced publicly that their newly declared movement would not only serve the black community's religious needs as a nondenominational congregation but also function as a benevolent mutual aid organization. The latter goal involved plans to collect funds (through membership fees) to assist the sick, orphans, and widows in the African American community. Other secular social assistance aims included enforcement of a code of temperance, propriety, and fidelity in marriage. It is significant that a number of the early members of the Free African Society came to it from the rolls

Richard Allen, founder with Absalom Jones of the Free African Society and later of the African Methodist Episcopal Church. (The Associated Publishers, Inc.)

of other Protestant churches, not only St. George's Methodist Episcopal congregation.

The dual nature of the organization's goals soon led to divisions in the politics of leadership. Apparently, it was Allen who wanted to use the breakaway from St. George's as a first step in founding a specifically black Methodist church. Others wished to emphasize the Free African Society's nondenominational character and pursue mainly social and moral aid services. Within two years, therefore, Allen resigned his membership, going on to found, in July, 1794, the Bethel African Methodist Episcopal Church. Although this move clearly marked the beginnings of a specifically African American church with a defined denominational status, Allen's efforts for many years continued to be directed at social and economic self-help projects for African Americans, irrespective of their formal religious orientation.

By 1804, Allen was involved in founding a group whose name reflected its basic social reform goals: the Society of Free People of Color for Promoting the Instruction and School Education of Children of African Descent. Another of Allen's efforts came in 1830, when Allen, then seventy years of age, involved his church in the Free Produce Society in Philadelphia. This group raised money to buy goods grown only by nonslave labor to redistribute to poor African Americans. It also tried to organize active boycotts against the marketing and purchase of goods produced by slave-owning farmers, thus providing an early model for the grass-roots organizations aimed at social and political goals that would become familiar to African Americans in the mid-twentieth century.

The Free African Society passed through several short but key stages both before and after Richard Allen's decision to remove himself from active membership. One focal point was the group's early association with the prominent medical doctor and philanthropist Benjamin Rush. Rush helped the Free African Society to draft a document involving articles of faith that were meant to be general enough to include the essential religious principles of any Christian church. When the organization adopted these tenets, in 1791, its status as a religious congregation generally was recognized by members and outsiders alike. More and more, its close relationship with the Episcopal church (first demonstrated by its "friendly adoption" by the Reverend Joseph Pilmore and the white membership of St. Paul's Church in Philadelphia) determined its future denominational status. After 1795, the Free African Society per se had receded before a new church built by a committee sparked by Absalom Jones: the African Methodist Episcopal Church. This fact did not, however, prevent those who had been associated with the Free African Society's origins from integrating its strong social and moral reform program with the religious principles that marked the emergence of the first all-black Christian congregations in the United States by the end of the 1790's.   —Byron D. Cannon

ADDITIONAL READING:

George, Carol V. R. *Segregated Sabbaths: Richard Allen and the Emergence of Independent Black Churches, 1760-*

1840. New York: Oxford University Press, 1973. A scholarly account that includes discussion of the African American churches' eventual abolitionist activities.

Mukenge, Ida Rousseau. *The Black Church in Urban America.* Lanham, Md.: University Press of America, 1983. A comprehensive historical account, emphasizing changes that came by the nineteenth and twentieth centuries.

Mwadilitu, Mwalimu I. [Alexander E. Curtis]. *Richard Allen: The First Exemplar of African American Education.* New York: ECA Associates, 1985. This short volume focuses on the career of Richard Allen, including his functions after 1816 as the first bishop of the African Methodist Episcopal Church.

Phillips, C. H. *The History of the Colored Methodist Episcopal Church in America.* 1898. Reprint. New York: Arno Press, 1972. Written by the editor of the church's official newspaper.

Raboteau, Albert J. "Richard Allen and the African Church Movement." In *Black Leaders of the Nineteenth Century*, edited by Leon Litwack and August Meier. Urbana: University of Illinois Press, 1988. A scholarly account of the Free African Society's origins, suggesting that Allen and Jones had discussed the special need for a separate African American church well before the "gallery event" so frequently cited.

SEE ALSO: 1768, Methodist Church Is Established; 1775, Pennsylvania Society for the Abolition of Slavery Is Founded; 1784, Hall's Masonic Lodge Is Chartered; 1804, First Black Codes; 1807, Congress Bans Importation of African Slaves; 1816, AME Church Is Founded; 1831, *The Liberator* Begins Publication; 1833, American Anti-Slavery Society Is Founded.

1787 ■ NORTHWEST ORDINANCE: *the rise of federal involvement in the organization of Western lands and the first sectional compromise over the extension of slavery*

DATE: July 13, 1787
LOCALE: New York
CATEGORIES: African American history; Expansion and land acquisition; Laws and acts
KEY FIGURES:
Nathan Dane (1752-1835), Federalist lawyer who prepared the final draft of the ordinance
Timothy Pickering (1745-1829), opponent of a liberal policy regarding the West
Arthur St. Clair (1736-1818), president of the Confederation Congress and first governor of the Northwest Territory
SUMMARY OF EVENT. In March, 1784, the Congress of the Confederation accepted the cession of lands Virginia had claimed west of the Appalachian Mountains. A congressional committee headed by Thomas Jefferson, delegate from Virginia, then took steps to provide for the political organization of the vast area south of the Great Lakes, west of the Appalachians, and east of the Mississippi River. The committee's task

was to draft legislation for the disposal of the land and the government of its settlers. The proposal of Jefferson's committee met the approval of Congress as the Ordinance of 1784.

The Ordinance of 1784 divided the West into eighteen districts. Each district would be admitted to the Union as a state when its population equaled that of the least populous of the original states. In the meantime, when the population of a district reached twenty thousand, it might write a constitution and send a delegate to Congress. As Jefferson envisaged it, as many as ten new states might be carved from the new lands, many of them provided with mellifluous classical names. In Jefferson's original version, slavery was to be excluded after 1800, but this was stricken from the ordinance when it was adopted in 1784. The Ordinance of 1784 was to become effective once all Western lands claimed by the states had been ceded to the government. Before the states ceded their lands, however, a new ordinance was adopted that superseded that of 1784.

The Ordinance of 1787, known as the Northwest Ordinance, was passed, according to some historians, at the insistence of land speculators who opposed the liberality of the Ordinance of 1784. The new ordinance did indeed slow down the process by which a territory might become a state, but it also added certain important features and provided for the more orderly creation of new states. While the Northwest Ordinance may have been less liberal than its predecessor, it was not undemocratic.

The Northwest Ordinance established government in the territory north of the Ohio River. The plan provided for the eventual establishment of a bicameral assembly, the creation of three to five states equal to the original thirteen states, freedom of religion, the right to a jury trial, public education, and a ban on the expansion of slavery. To accomplish these goals, legislation provided that the whole Northwest region should be governed temporarily as a single territory and administered by a governor, a secretary, and three judges appointed by Congress. When the population of the territory reached five thousand free, adult, male inhabitants, the citizens might elect representatives to a territorial assembly. Property qualifications for voting were established, but they were small. The general assembly was to choose ten men, all of whom owned at least five hundred acres, from whom Congress would choose five men to serve as the upper house of the legislature. The governor would continue to be selected by Congress and have an absolute veto over all legislation.

The territory was to be divided into not fewer than three nor more than five districts. Whenever the population of one of the districts reached sixty thousand free inhabitants, it would be allowed to draft a constitution and submit it to Congress. If the constitution guaranteed a republican form of government, Congress would pass an enabling act admitting the district into the Union as a state on an equal basis with those states already in the Union.

The ordinance guaranteed certain basic rights to citizens who moved into the new lands. A bill of rights provided for freedom of religion and guaranteed the benefits of writs of habeas corpus, the right of trial by jury, bail, and the general process of law. The third article read: "Religion, morality and knowledge being necessary to good government and the happiness of mankind, Schools and the means of education shall forever be encouraged. The utmost good faith shall always be observed towards the Indians." The first of these moral injunctions was implemented as the inhabitants obtained the means to do so. The second, regarding the American Indians, has still to be achieved. The fourth article established the basis for relations between the general government and the territories and states that might be formed from them. The fifth article provided for equitable taxation and the free navigation of the waters leading into the Mississippi and St. Lawrence Rivers. The sixth article was epoch-making. It read: "There shall be neither Slavery nor involuntary Servitude in the said territory otherwise than in the punishment of crimes, whereof the party shall have been duly convicted." This provision determined that the society that developed north of the Ohio River would eventually be free. Influenced by the French slaveholders inhabiting the region, the interpretation of Article VI forbade the further introduction of slavery but did not abolish slavery or affect the rights of those holding slaves prior to 1787. No such provision was written into the act establishing the Southwest Territory, in 1790.

The pattern established by the Northwest Ordinance was more or less followed in the later admission of states into the Union. Some, such as Texas and California, came in without a territorial period. Others, such as Michigan, caused trouble because of boundary disputes with neighboring states. As for the Ohio country, Arthur St. Clair, president of the Confederation Congress in 1787, was appointed first governor of the territory. Indiana Territory was organized in 1803, the same year in which Ohio entered the Union. Indiana entered as a state in 1816, Illinois in 1818, Michigan in 1837, and Wisconsin in 1848. Statehood was delayed for Indiana and Illinois territories as a result of their repeated petitions seeking repeal of the restrictions in the ordinance against the expansion of further slavery in the territory. Congress refused to repeal or revise the section, making slaveholders reluctant to move into the area. The predominant settlement by nonslaveholders eventually led to strengthening of the antislavery movement in the region.

The Northwest Ordinance proved to be a crowning legislative achievement of the otherwise lackluster confederation government. However, while Congress was debating the Northwest Ordinance, the Constitutional Convention was occurring in Philadelphia. It has been argued that the antislavery provisions influenced the debates of the constitutional convention over congressional representation. Since each state won two seats in the Senate, Southern states acceded freedom to the Northwest Territory by limiting the number of free states formed from the region. In turn, the Southern states hoped for dominance in the House of Representatives through the three-fifths clause counting slaves for congressional representation.

LAND CESSIONS BY THE STATES AFTER THE REVOLUTIONARY WAR, 1783-1802

Before the end of the Revolutionary War, the original thirteen colonies had laid claim to lands west of the Appalachian Mountains—formerly reserved as Indian Territory in the Proclamation of 1763, although exploited by white settlers. After the revolution, Congress began to organize these western territories for future settlement, passing the Ordinance of 1785 and the Ordinance of 1787 (the Northwest Ordinance). The former colonies gradually, if reluctantly, ceded their claims.

Under the new Constitution, Congress reenacted the Ordinance of 1787 as a model of territorial government.

—*John G. Clark, updated by Dorothy C. Salem*

ADDITIONAL READING:

Berwanger, Eugene H. "Western Prejudice and the Extension of Slavery." *Civil War History* 12 (September, 1966): 197-212. Demonstrates the racial prejudices following the emigration of Europeans westward and how these attitudes influenced the interpretations of the Northwest Ordinance—not forbidding slavery but halting its further introduction.

Cayton, Andrew R. L. *The Midwest and the Nation: Rethinking the History of an American Region.* Bloomington: Indiana University Press, 1990. Provides an overview of the historical significance of the Northwest Ordinance for the Midwest and its influence on that region.

Johnson, Andrew J. *The Life and Constitutional Thought of Nathan Dane.* New York: Garland, 1987. The best biographical account of the major author of the Northwest Ordinance and his place in the history of the new nation.

Konig, David Thomas. *Devising Liberty: Preserving and Creating Freedom in the New American Republic.* Stanford, Calif.: Stanford University Press, 1995. Examines the role of the Northwest Ordinance within the framework shaping modern U.S. freedom.

Onuf, Peter S. *Sovereignty and Territory: Claims Conflict in the Old Northwest and the Origins of the American Federal Republic.* Baltimore: The Johns Hopkins University Press, 1973. Analyzes the land speculation conflicts and their role in shaping the powers of the state.

_____. *Statehood and Union: A History of the Northwest Ordinance.* Bloomington: Indiana University Press, 1987. A comprehensive study of the framing and impact of the Northwest Ordinance and the competing forces that shaped the document.

Swierenga, Robert P. "The Settlement of the Old Northwest: Ethnic Pluralism in a Featureless Plain." *Journal of the Early Republic* 9 (Spring, 1989): 73-105. Describes the settlement of the territory by foreign-born and American-born immigrants who influenced the ethnic pluralism of the region.

SEE ALSO: 1785, Ordinance of 1785.

1787 ■ U.S. CONSTITUTION IS ADOPTED:

the highest law of the United States of America, signaling the creation of the new republic's government

DATE: September 17, 1787

LOCALE: Philadelphia, Pennsylvania

CATEGORIES: Civil rights; Government and politics; Laws and acts

KEY FIGURES:

Benjamin Franklin (1706-1790), oldest and most venerable delegate to the Constitutional Convention

James Madison (1751-1836), generally credited with having designed the blueprint for the proposed national government

Gouverneur Morris (1752-1816), author of the final draft of the Constitution and a vigorous supporter of a strong national government

William Patterson (1745-1806), sponsor of the New Jersey Plan, which favored a weak central government

Roger Sherman (1721-1793), instrumental in forging compromise between advocates of a strong national government and supporters of a weak central government

George Washington (1732-1799), presiding officer at the Constitutional Convention

James Wilson (1742-1798), prominent lawyer who contributed considerably to determining the specific responsibilities of the new national government

SUMMARY OF EVENT. By the middle of the 1780's, much dissatisfaction with government under the Articles of Confederation had became evident throughout the United States. Many of those prominent in the political life of the United States—George Washington, Thomas Jefferson, John Jay, Alexander Hamilton, and Noah Webster, among others—in papers, letters, and conversations criticized the functioning of the Confederation Congress. Specific concerns included Congress' lack of power to tax, to regulate interstate commerce, and to force states to cooperate more effectively with the central government. All efforts to improve the Articles of Confederation seemed doomed to failure, because amendments required unanimous approval by the states. It became evident to many concerned persons that changes might best be accomplished by abandoning the Articles altogether.

In March, 1785, a meeting of delegates from Virginia and Maryland initiated a series of meetings that culminated in the replacement of the Articles. At the March meeting, the two states worked out an agreement involving commercial regulations on the Potomac River. After the success of the meeting, Virginia called for another meeting to be held in Annapolis, Maryland, during the following year. It was hoped that the convention would provide an opportunity for those attending to discuss common problems and possible solutions. Nine states were invited, but only five sent delegates. The most important result of the Annapolis Convention was the publication of a report, probably drafted by Alexander Hamilton, that called for yet another convention. This one, scheduled for Philadelphia in May, 1787, was to include delegates from all states. The purpose of the convention was to address and correct the defects in the Confederation government. Copies of the report were sent to each state legislature with a request that delegates be appointed and sent to Philadelphia.

Every state except Rhode Island honored the request and sent representatives. Seventy-four delegates were appointed to the convention, although only fifty-five attended. Thirty-nine signed the final document. The Virginia delegation was among the first to reach Philadelphia, arriving two weeks before the scheduled start of deliberations. The Virginians brought with

WE, the People of the United States, in order to form a more perfect Union, establish Justice, insure domestic Tranquility, provide for the common Defence, promote the General Welfare, and secure the Blessings of Liberty to Ourselves and our Posterity, do ordain and establish this Constitution for the United States of America.

ARTICLE I.

Sect. 1. ALL legislative powers herein granted shall be vested in a Congress of the United States, which shall consist of a Senate and House of Representatives.

Sect. 2. The House of Representatives shall be composed of members chosen every second year by the people of the several states, and the electors in each state shall have the qualifications requisite for electors of the most numerous branch of the state legislature.

No person shall be a representative who shall not have attained to the age of twenty-five years, and been seven years a citizen of the United States, and who shall not, when elected, be an inhabitant of that state in which he shall be chosen.

Representatives and direct taxes shall be apportioned among the several states which may be included within this Union, according to their respective numbers, which shall be determined by adding to the whole number of free persons, including those bound to service for a term of years, and excluding Indians not taxed, three-fifths of all other persons. The actual enumeration shall be made within three years after the first meeting of the Congress of the United States, and within every subsequent term of ten years, in such manner as they shall by law direct. The number of representatives shall not exceed one for every thirty thousand, but each state shall have at least one representative; and until such enumeration shall be made, the state of New-Hampshire shall be entitled to chuse three, Massachusetts eight, Rhode-Island and Providence Plantations one, Connecticut five, New-York six, New-Jersey four, Pennsylvania eight, Delaware one, Maryland six, Virginia ten, North-Carolina five, South-Carolina five, and Georgia three.

When vacancies happen in the representation from any state, the Executive authority thereof shall issue writs of election to fill such vacancies.

The House of Representatives shall chuse their Speaker and other officers; and shall have the sole power of impeachment.

Sect. 3. The Senate of the United States shall be composed of two senators from each state, chosen by the legislature thereof, for six years; and each senator shall have one vote.

Immediately after they shall be assembled in consequence of the first election, they shall be divided as equally as may be into three classes. The seats of the senators of the first class shall be vacated at the expiration of the second year, of the second class at the expiration of the fourth year, and of the third class at the expiration of the sixth year, so that one-third may be chosen every second year; and if vacancies happen by resignation, or otherwise, during the recess of the Legislature of any state, the Executive thereof may make temporary appointments until the next meeting of the Legislature, which shall then fill such vacancies.

No person shall be a senator who shall not have attained to the age of thirty years, and been nine years a citizen of the United States, and who shall not, when elected, be an inhabitant of that state for which he shall be chosen.

The Vice-President of the United States shall be President of the senate, but shall have no vote, unless they be equally divided.

The Senate shall chuse their other officers, and also a President pro tempore, in the absence of the Vice-President, or when he shall exercise the office of President of the United States.

The Senate shall have the sole power to try all impeachments. When sitting for that purpose, they shall be on oath or affirmation. When the President of the United States is tried, the Chief Justice shall preside: And no person shall be convicted without the concurrence of two-thirds of the members present.

Judgment in cases of impeachment shall not extend further than to removal from office, and disqualification to hold and enjoy any office of honor, trust or profit under the United States; but the party convicted shall nevertheless be liable and subject to indictment, trial, judgment and punishment, according to law.

Sect. 4. The times, places and manner of holding elections for senators and representatives, shall be prescribed in each state by the legislature thereof; but the Congress may at any time by law make or alter such regulations, except as to the places of chusing Senators.

The Congress shall assemble at least once in every year, and such meeting shall be on the first Monday in December, unless they shall by law appoint a different day.

Sect. 5. Each house shall be the judge of the elections, returns and qualifications of its own members, and a majority of each shall constitute a quorum to do business; but a smaller number may adjourn from day to day, and may be authorised to compel the attendance of absent members, in such manner, and under such penalties as each house may provide.

Each house may determine the rules of its proceedings, punish its members for disorderly behaviour, and, with the concurrence of two-thirds, expel a member.

Each house shall keep a journal of its proceedings, and from time to time publish the same, excepting such parts as may in their judgment require secrecy; and the yeas and nays of the members of either house on any question shall, at the desire of one-fifth of those present, be entered on the journal.

Neither house, during the session of Congress, shall, without the consent of the other, adjourn for more than three days, nor to any other place than that in which the two houses shall be sitting.

Sect. 6. The senators and representatives shall receive a compensation for their services, to be ascertained by law, and paid out of the treasury of the United States. They shall in all cases, except treason, felony and breach of the peace, be privileged from arrest during their attendance at the session of their respective houses, and in going to and returning from the same; and for any speech or debate in either house, they shall not be questioned in any other place.

No senator or representative shall, during the time for which he was elected, be appointed to any civil office under the authority of the United States, which shall have been created, or the emoluments whereof shall have been encreased during such time; and no person holding any office under the United States, shall be a member of either house during his continuance in office.

Sect. 7. All bills for raising revenue shall originate in the house of representatives; but the senate may propose or concur with amendments as on other bills.

Every bill which shall have passed the house of representatives and the senate, shall, before it become a law, be presented to the president of the United States; if he approve he shall sign it, but if not he shall return it, with his objections to that house in which it shall have originated, who shall enter the objections at large on their journal, and proceed to reconsider it. If after such reconsideration two-thirds of that house shall agree to pass the bill, it shall be sent, together with the objections, to the other house, by which it shall likewise be reconsidered, and if approved by two-thirds of that house, it shall become a law. But in all such cases the votes of both houses shall them the outline of a plan of government that they intended to offer to the convention. The plan, considered quite controversial at the time, proposed creating a new national government. The Virginians sought a strong government that would include three branches and a sophisticated system of checks and balances. During the days before the convention began, several of the Virginia delegates, particularly James Madison, conferred with other early arrivals to hone their plan.

The convention first met on May 25 and appointed George Washington as the presiding officer. The section was significant, because Washington was held in high regard by the American people. The presence of Benjamin Franklin, who at eighty-one years of age was the oldest delegate, also added prestige to the gathering. With two such notable figures participating, the American public anticipated notable results.

On May 29, with the convention only four days old, the Virginia delegation proposed a series of resolutions that immediately were known as the Virginia Plan. Drafted largely by James Madison and introduced by Edmund Randolph, the plan argued that, rather than merely revise the Articles of Confederation, the convention should discard them altogether and create a constitution that embodied an entirely new frame of government. The proposed government would have far more authority than did the confederated administration, and it would not be subordinate to each state government. The proposals set off a fierce debate that dominated the convention throughout most of June. On one side were delegates who endorsed the Virginia Plan. On the other side were delegates who feared that a powerful national government might jeopardize many of the rights and liberties won during the Revolutionary War.

As the debate intensified, delegates from several of the smaller states devised a series of resolutions designed to counter the Virginia Plan. Introduced by William Patterson from New Jersey, the resolutions became know as the New Jersey Plan. These proposals rejected the need for a new national government and called instead for the convention to retain, but significantly revise, the existing confederated government.

Among the more active delegates in favor of establishing a strong federal government were James Madison and George Mason from Virginia, James Wilson and Gouverneur Morris from Pennsylvania, John Dickinson from Delaware, John Rutledge and Charles Pinckney from South Carolina, and Oliver Ellsworth from Connecticut. In addition to Patterson, the leading supporters of the New Jersey Plan included Roger Sherman from Connecticut, Elbridge Gerry from Massachusetts, and Luther Martin from Maryland.

For almost a month, delegates intensely deliberated over the two plans. In late June, with the convention on the verge of dissolution, Benjamin Franklin implored the delegates to find a common ground. Spurred on by Franklin's pleas, the convention agreed to discard the Articles of Confederation and create a constitution that would embody a strong national government. With the initial differences resolved, other as-

pects of both the Virginia and New Jersey Plans were debated throughout the summer. Central to the discussions was the concern of less populated states, such as Connecticut and Maryland, that they would lose all power and authority to the national government if representation within the new government were determined exclusively according to population. Responding to these concerns, proponents of the national government agreed to create a dual system of representation within Congress: Membership in the House of Representatives would be determined according to population; in the Senate, each state, regardless of the size of its population, would be given two members. It also was agreed that before a bill could become a law, both houses of Congress would have to approve it.

The agreement concerning representation within the legislative branch, sometimes referred to as the Great Compromise, reflected the spirit of concession that marked convention proceedings during the late summer months. Many other issues, including the length of presidential terms, the electoral procedure, the responsibilities of the judicial branch, the amendment process, and slavery within the new nation, tested the delegates' ability to negotiate and cooperate. In the end, the document could not be considered the work of any one group or faction of delegates. It had become a synthesis of the plans of all the delegates.

In September, Gouverneur Morris, an outspoken Pennsylvania delegate, became chair of a committee that was instructed to write a final draft of the Constitution. After some preliminary discussions about style and content, the document was formally presented to the convention on September 17. Although few delegates agreed to all revisions, a large majority found the document as a whole acceptable. Signed by thirty-nine delegates, the Constitution was declared adopted "by unanimous consent." Upon endorsement by the convention, the Constitution was submitted to each state legislature for ratification. In late June, 1788, approval by nine states, the number required for ratification, was reached and implementation of the new national government began.

—Edward J. Maguire, updated by Paul E. Doutrich

ADDITIONAL READING:

Conley, Patrick, and John Kaminski, eds. *The Constitution and the States: The Role of the Original Thirteen in Framing and Adoption of the Federal Constitution.* Madison, Wis.: Madison House, 1988. A unique look at how each state reacted to the proposed Constitutional Convention.

Farrand, Max. *The Records of the Federal Convention of 1787.* 4 vols. New Haven, Conn.: Yale University Press, 1966. The definitive set of primary source documents for the convention.

Jensen, Merrill. *The Making of the American Constitution.* Princeton, N.J.: Van Nostrand, 1964. A brief but excellent account of the creation of the Constitution.

Kammen, Michael. *A Machine That Would Go of Itself.* New York: Alfred A. Knopf, 1986. Examines the cultural impact of the United States Constitution.

McDonald, Forrest. *"Novus Ordo Seclorum": The Intellectual Origins of the Constitution.* Lawrence: University Press of Kansas, 1985. Discusses the traditions and attitudes from which the Constitution was conceived.

Peters, William. *A More Perfect Union: The Making of the United States Constitution.* New York: Crown, 1987. A narrative account of the events involved in the creation of the U.S. Constitution.

Wood, Gordon. *The Creation of the American Republic, 1776-1787.* New York: W. W. Norton, 1969. A definitive work that explores the ideological foundations of the Constitution.

SEE ALSO: 1781, Articles of Confederation; 1787, *Federalist* Papers Are Published; 1789, Judiciary Act; 1791, U.S. Bill of Rights Is Ratified; 1804, Twelfth Amendment; 1865, Thirteenth Amendment; 1868, Fourteenth Amendment; 1913, Sixteenth Amendment; 1920, Prohibition; 1920, U.S. Women Gain the Vote; 1923, Proposal of the Equal Rights Amendment; 1970, U.S. Voting Age Is Lowered to Eighteen.

1787 ■ FEDERALIST PAPERS ARE PUBLISHED: *the clearest exposition of the intentions of the Framers of the constitutional government of the United States*

DATE: October 27, 1787-May, 1788
LOCALE: New York City
CATEGORIES: Cultural and intellectual history; Government and politics
KEY FIGURES:
Alexander Hamilton (1757-1804), author of more than half the essays in *The Federalist*
John Jay (1745-1829), author of five of *The Federalist* essays
James Madison (1751-1836), author or co-author of perhaps twenty essays in *The Federalist*

SUMMARY OF EVENT. *The Federalist* comprises eighty-five essays that were published anonymously by Alexander Hamilton, John Jay, and James Madison between October, 1787, and May, 1788, urging ratification of the United States Constitution. That constitution, drafted by the Philadelphia Convention of 1787, sought to increase the power of the national government at the expense of the state governments. The national debate over ratification began almost immediately after the Philadelphia Convention sent the proposed constitution to Congress on September 10 and its contents became known. Before the document could take effect, it had to be ratified by specially elected conventions in at least nine of the thirteen states. Throughout the nation, critics of the Constitution (Antifederalists) battled its supporters (Federalists) in campaigns to elect men to the state conventions. The debate was particularly tense in New York, which was sharply divided over the Constitution. Federalists dominated New York City and the surrounding areas, but the rural upstate areas were strongly

Antifederalist, as was the state's popular and powerful governor, George Clinton.

Late in September, 1787, the *New York Journal* began printing a series of antifederal essays by "Cato" (who may have been Governor Clinton). In order to refute these and other antifederal tracts, Alexander Hamilton and John Jay, two of New York's most prominent Federalists, agreed to write a series of newspaper essays under the name "Publius." The first, *The Federalist* No. 1, written by Hamilton, appeared in the *New York Independent Journal* on October 27, and in it, Hamilton outlined the purpose of the entire series. The essays would explain the necessity of the union for political prosperity, the "insufficiency of the present Confederation to preserve that Union," the need for a more energetic government than that which existed under the Articles of Confederation, the "conformity of the proposed constitution to the true principles of republican government," and the security that the Constitution would provide to liberty and property.

John Jay wrote the next four installments before ill health forced him to quit. In November, James Madison, who was in New York representing Virginia in Congress, took Jay's place. Madison and Hamilton produced all but one of the remaining eighty essays; Jay wrote No. 64.

Madison's first contribution to the series, *The Federalist* No. 10, is the most famous of all the essays. In it he discussed the origins of parties, or "factions" as he called them, and argued that they sprang inevitably from the unequal distribution of property. "Those who hold, and those who are without property," he continued, "have ever formed distinct interests in society." In any nation, "a landed interest, a manufacturing interest, a mercantile interest, a monied interest, [and] many lesser interests, grow up of necessity" and divide people into different classes. Some Antifederalists had argued that the nation was much too large and too diverse to be governed effectively by a powerful central government without sacrificing people's liberties and freedoms in the process; in *The Federalist* No. 10, Madison used his ideas about factions to reverse their argument. The nation's size, he wrote, and the great variety of its people and their interests were sources of strength, not weakness. There were so many different groups or factions, so many different interests that would be represented in the new government, that no one faction, no one group, no lone demagogue could ever capture control of the national government. Far from inviting tyranny, he argued, the nation's size and diversity, when coupled with the federal republican form of government proposed by the Constitution, would provide a strong check against tyranny.

Addressed to "the People of the State of New York," the essays of *The Federalist* were intended primarily as New York ratification campaign tracts, but they also were reprinted by newspapers in other states and cities, particularly in Philadelphia and Boston. Hamilton had the first thirty-six numbers published as a book in March, 1788, and some of these books were sent to Virginia, where they arrived in time to be useful to Federalists at the Virginia ratifying convention. A second volume, containing the remaining forty-nine essays, appeared the following May.

It is hard to estimate the impact of *The Federalist* on the campaign to ratify the Constitution even in New York, much less nationally. Certainly the articles were not as successful as their authors had hoped, for New York voters sent twice as many opponents of the Constitution to the New York ratifying convention as they sent supporters. By the time the convention balloted, ten states had already ratified, and New York did so too on July 26, 1788, by a narrow three-vote margin. It is unlikely that *The Federalist* contributed much to the result.

Whether or not the essays in *The Federalist* were effective political tracts in 1788, they long have been considered important keys to understanding the intentions of the members of the Philadelphia Convention. Historians and even Supreme Court justices have studied the papers as a guide to the intent of the Framers, even though they were written as election tracts, and in spite of the fact that one author (Jay) did not attend the Philadelphia Convention, another (Hamilton) played a very small role there and was dissatisfied with the Constitution, and the third (Madison) came to have serious doubts about the meaning of the Constitution and the kind of government it created within a few years after he wrote his essays for *The Federalist*.

The reputation of *The Federalist* has grown steadily since 1788. The work has been widely republished around the world in several languages and is regularly reprinted in the United States. The essays have been brought into many public political debates since 1789, particularly during times of constitutional crisis, such as the states' rights debates that preceded the Civil War, the public discussion over the constitutionality of President Franklin Roosevelt's New Deal policies, the debate over states' rights and civil liberties in the 1950's, and the proposals during the 1990's to reduce the federal deficit by shifting to the states the responsibility for—and, often, the financing of—many of the social programs enacted in Washington during and after the New Deal. Apart from its partisan political value, past and present, many historians and political scientists consider *The Federalist* to be the best existing defense of federal republicanism in general and of the American Constitution in particular.

—*Robert A. Becker, updated by Joseph R. Rudolph, Jr.*

ADDITIONAL READING:

De Pauw, Linda G. *The Eleventh Pillar: New York State and the Federal Constitution*. Ithaca, N.Y.: Cornell University Press, 1966. An outstanding examination of *The Federalist* papers in the context of their time and as campaign literature aimed at the citizens of New York.

Dietze, Gottfried. *The Federalist: A Classic on Federalism and Free Government*. Baltimore: The Johns Hopkins University Press, 1960. Still one of the best examinations of the work as a statement of the Framers' thoughts and a part of the constitutional heritage that has continued to affect the political process in the United States.

Epstein, David F. *The Political Theory of the Federalist*. Chicago: University of Chicago Press, 1984. A well-indexed, outstanding analysis of the topic.

Hamilton, Alexander, John Jay, and James Madison. *The Federalist*. Annotated by Jacob E. Cooke. Middletown, Conn.: Wesleyan University Press, 1961. Among the many editions of *The Federalist*, this is one of the best annotated.

Kenyon, Cecelia M., ed. *The Antifederalists*. Indianapolis: Bobbs-Merrill, 1966. An excellent collection of essays illustrating the Antifederalist arguments against the Constitution.

Kesler, Charles, ed. *Saving the Revolution: The Federalist Papers and the American Founding*. New York: Free Press, 1987. Published on the two hundredth anniversary of *The Federalist* papers, these essays are for advanced research.

Lewis, John D., ed. *Anti-Federalists Versus Federalists: Selected Documents*. San Francisco: Chandler, 1967. A well-balanced selection of often hard-to-find documents, including the minority reports from the constitutional convention.

McWilliams, Wilson Carey, and Michael T. Gibbons, eds. *The Federalists, the Antifederalists, and the American Political Tradition*. New York: Greenwood Press, 1992. This brief collection of solid essays provides excellent introductory reading on the constitutional debate.

White, Morton Gabriel. *Philosophy, "The Federalist," and the Constitution*. New York: Oxford University Press, 1987. Focuses on the impact of *The Federalist* on U.S. constitutional history. An excellent work.

SEE ALSO: 1787, U.S. Constitution Is Adopted.

1789 ■ WASHINGTON'S INAUGURATION: *the first president of the United States articulates his concept of the office of head of state in a democratic republic*

DATE: April 30, 1789
LOCALE: Federal Hall, New York City
CATEGORY: Government and politics
KEY FIGURES:
John Adams (1735-1826), vice president of the United States under Washington
Robert R. Livingston (1746-1813), chancellor of the State of New York, who administered the oath of office
Samuel Otis (1740-1814), secretary of the Senate, who held the Bible for Washington
George Washington (1732-1799), first president of the United States, 1789-1797

SUMMARY OF EVENT. Early on the afternoon of April 30, 1789, George Washington took the oath of office of president of the United States as prescribed by the new Constitution. Standing on a small portico at Federal Hall, New York City, Washington repeated the solemn words administered by Robert Livingston, chancellor of the State of New York, and then added his own suffix: "So help me God." Bending forward, the first president of the United States kissed the Bible held for him by Samuel Otis, secretary of the Senate. Livingston then declared, "It is done!" and turning to the multitudes on the rooftops, in the street, and at the windows of Broad and Wall Streets below, he shouted: "Long live George Washington, President of the United States." The crowd roared back, "God bless our President," and the flag was jubilantly raised to the cupola of the great hall while gun salutes and church bells resounded.

The fifty-seven-year-old Washington took office in a newly formed nation of four million people, citizens and noncitizens, living in thirteen states. He came to the presidency without previous experience in any elected executive office, despite a lifetime of dedicated public service. Influenced as were many men of his generation by the principles of the Enlightenment, Washington believed in the republican ideal, with its emphasis on self-sacrifice and the public good. His long career had begun in 1758 with his election to the Virginia Assembly. He served as a colonel in the Virginia militia under the British in the French and Indian War. As commander in chief of the Continental Army, he wielded more authority—and perhaps commanded more respect—than had the Continental Congress that appointed him. In 1787, he was unanimously chosen as president of the Constitutional Convention, which ultimately would produce the new Constitution. In taking office as president of the nation under that new Constitution, Washington provided the fledgling nation with a model of simple dignity—the soul and air of a hero-leader. Earnest and sincere, he evoked memories of the victorious American Revolution and offered unity and confidence to the citizens in their new government. As such, he had been unanimously chosen by the electoral college under the new Constitution.

The anxieties of war, his labor for the Constitution, his desire for retirement from public life, and his love for his family and his home at Mount Vernon made Washington's decision to accept the presidency a difficult one. He wrote: "My movements to the chair of government will be accompanied by feelings not unlike those of a culprit who is going to the place of his execution, so unwilling am I, in the evening of a life nearly consumed in public cares, to quit a peaceful abode for an ocean of difficulties, without that competency of political skills, abilities and inclination which is necessary to manage the helm."

Thus, it was with mixed emotions that Washington set out for New York on April 16, 1789. Acclamations met him on each stage of his journey. In Alexandria, Georgetown, Baltimore, Wilmington, and Philadelphia, grateful citizens welcomed their acknowledged leader, who traveled by carriage, horseback, and flotilla. One week before his inauguration, Washington arrived at the end of Wall Street by barge from Elizabeth Town Point, New Jersey, to be met by thousands of cheering New Yorkers, a great display of boats and festooned ships, and the loud roar of cannon.

Washington represented for the people who cheered him the last great hope for unity. Americans had been made wary by

As the first president of the United States, George Washington felt keenly the responsibility of setting a precedent for presidents to follow. He combined humility and dignity with strong leadership abilities in an effort to create an office that would forgo the privilege of monarchy, support democracy, and place constitutional law above the individual. (Library of Congress)

the revolution, the inadequacy of the Articles of Confederation, and the Federalist and Antifederalist factions that had developed as the Constitution underwent the difficult process of ratification. The young nation looked to the new Constitution for the leadership that would set its government in motion and make it endure. Washington took stewardship of the Constitution, which provided for a strong central government while strictly defining the powers of that government. His calm, purposeful presence during the contentious debates, and his refusal to side with any party, would sound the keynote to his new administration. Washington's inauguration marked the delivery of the Constitution and the start of a new era.

That Washington keenly felt the need for unity was apparent in his inaugural address, although the event was marred somewhat by factional debate over what title Washington should take as president. Federalists were concerned their new president would not receive sufficient respect without a dignified title, especially from emissaries from foreign nations. They proposed "His Most Benign Excellency" and "His Highness, the President of the United States and Protector of their Liberties" as likely titles. These received loud and derisive complaints from the Antifederalist members of Congress, already worried that a too-powerful executive would bring a return of the tyranny many recalled under British rule. Eventually, the designation of "President of the United States" was determined, and Washington was pleased to be addressed simply as Mr. President.

After taking the oath of office, the new president entered the Senate Chamber, where both houses of Congress and various dignitaries took seats. On the canopied dias with the president were Vice President John Adams, Chancellor Livingston, and New York governor George Clinton. President Washington modestly delivered the well-fashioned phrases of his first presidential address. In his opening remarks, he spoke of his inner conflict, his consciousness of his "inferior endowments," and his lack of experience in civil administration. He paid homage to God, whose provident hand had guided the people through their struggles and deliberation. Recognizing his duty under the Constitution to make recommendations to the Congress, he expressed his trust that the legislators would rise above the local pledges or attachments and petty animosities. In the only specific suggestion of the address, Washington urged Congress to quell "inquietude" by deciding to what extent it would advocate constitutional amendments. He expressed confidence in Congress' ultimate wisdom in pursuit of the public good. Washington concluded on the theme of unity, trusting that God had

> been pleased to favor the American people, with opportunities for deliberating in perfect tranquillity, and dispositions for deciding with unparalleled unanimity on a form of government for the security of their Union and the advancement of their happiness; so his divine blessing may be equally conspicuous in the enlarged views, the temperate consultations and the wise measures on which the success of the Government must depend.

From Federal Hall, the president walked triumphantly with congressmen and guests through streets lined with militia to services at St. Paul's Chapel. That day, Washington believed, was the consummation of the revolution. The political experiment should have a fair trial, and the new president vowed to do his best to support it. Deeply conscious that he was setting the pattern that future presidents would follow, Washington brought the same dignity and modesty he had demonstrated throughout his career to the office of the presidency.

—Emory M. Thomas, updated by Kelley Graham

ADDITIONAL READING:

Alden, John R. *George Washington: A Biography*. Baton Rouge: Louisiana State University Press, 1984. A comprehensive, interesting biography that bypasses the common mistake of lionizing the subject.

Schwartz, Barry. *George Washington: The Making of an American Symbol*. New York: Free Press, 1987. An exploration of the iconization of Washington, a process influenced by public events such as Washington's inauguration.

Smith, Richard Norton. *Patriarch: George Washington and the New American Nation*. Boston: Houghton Mifflin, 1993. Beginning with an account of Washington's inauguration, this book explores the ways in which Washington defined the presidency.

Washington, George. *April-June, 1789*. Vol. 2 in *The Papers of George Washington, Presidential Series*, edited by W. W. Abbot and Dorothy Twohig. Charlottesville: University Press of Virginia, 1992-1995. Includes the full text of Washington's address, as well as the fragmentary text discarded.

Zagarri, Rosemarie, ed. *David Humphreys' "Life of General Washington" with George Washington's "Remarks."* Athens: University of Georgia Press, 1991. A newly edited version of the authorized biography of Washington, which includes his feelings about the presidency and the difficulties of life in public office.

SEE ALSO: 1796, Washington's Farewell Address.

1789 ■ EPISCOPAL CHURCH IS ESTABLISHED: *the General Convention adopted a church constitution, canons, and liturgy that shaped a uniquely American Episcopal church, independent of its mother Church of England*

DATE: July 28-October 16, 1789
LOCALE: Philadelphia, Pennsylvania
CATEGORIES: Organizations and institutions; Religion
KEY FIGURES:
Samuel Provoost (1742-1815), bishop of New York and ardent revolutionary
Samuel Seabury (1729-1796), first presiding bishop of the Episcopal church in the United States
William White (1748-1836), architect of the Ecclesiastical Constitution

SUMMARY OF EVENT. Although the Episcopal church in the United States was officially established by the General Convention of 1789, circumstances prior to that event were crucial in laying its foundation. Before the American Revolution, the Anglican church in America (the Church of England) was in a tenuous position. Early in the eighteenth century, the English Society for the Propagation of the Gospel sent out missionaries to establish parishes in the American colonies. The parishes were under state jurisdiction. Each royal governor supported the church financially by taxing all community members, regardless of whether they belonged to the Church of England. Because the majority did not belong to the Church of England, this practice caused resentment among the general population. Also, the church in America had no bishops and was governed by the bishop of London. The close ties between church and state produced mistrust in many colonists.

During the American Revolution, the Anglican church was almost destroyed. Because of their religious practices, Episcopalians were rebel targets. For example, upon ordination, the clergy were required to take a loyalty oath to the king. They also used the English Book of Common Prayer, which contained prayers for the welfare of the monarch. In spite of these customs, many clergy, such as William White, a leading Episcopal priest in Philadelphia and later chaplain to the Continental Congress, sided with the rebels. In New York, all the clergy were loyal to the king except Samuel Provoost. In contrast to White and Provoost, Samuel Seabury from Connecticut, a high churchman and a Tory, represented the sentiments of the majority of the people of his state.

When the revolution ended in 1783, the Episcopal church in America was disestablished and seeking a new direction. The English church no longer provided either economic or spiritual support. Where there had been a unity of sorts with the king as the focal point, there was no single tie to bind the parishes in the various states together. There were no bishops to oversee the church. In order to survive, the church in the United States had to reorganize, address the issue of unity, and establish a U.S. episcopate.

Some efforts were made toward these goals even before the Revolutionary War ended. A conference of clergy and laity met in Maryland in 1780 and adopted the name Protestant Episcopal Church. At a larger convention in Annapolis in 1783, the name was officially embraced and the vision of a United States identity began to be realized. The question of a national church was addressed by William White in his essay "The Case of the Episcopal Churches in the United States Considered," written in 1782. In this document, White proposed a democratic church organized along lines similar to those of the federal Constitution.

The quest for a United States episcopate proved elusive. Because a bishop was considered a state official in England, the church in the United States was ambivalent concerning an American bishop. Because of the separation between church and state mandated by the federal Constitution, U.S. Anglicans were unsure of how the office of bishop would function in their church.

The first step in establishing an American episcopate was taken when the church in Connecticut sent Samuel Seabury to England to be consecrated by English bishops. To retain episcopal succession, it was important that Seabury be consecrated by bishops whose orders were valid. He left America for England in 1783 and attempted to persuade the English church to consecrate him. The English bishops refused, because Seabury was no longer loyal to the king and because he was not a state official approved by the Connecticut legislature. Seabury then went to Scotland and, in 1784, was consecrated by three nonjuring bishops.

Three important events further shaped the church in America before the General Convention of 1789. First, on May 24, 1784, William White led a convention of clergy and laity in Philadelphia that established a set of basic principles that were later incorporated into the final constitution. These precepts dictated that the American church would remain independent of all foreign authority, that its liturgy would conform to that of the Church of England, and that there would be three orders of ministers: bishops, priests, and deacons.

Second, the first General Convention of the Protestant Episcopal Church in the United States of America met on September 27, 1785. This convention addressed the issues of the episcopate, the liturgy, and the church constitution. The delegates decided that they would appeal to the Church of England to reconsider the consecration of U.S. bishops.

Third, in 1786, Parliament passed an act that allowed the English church to consecrate bishops who did not take an oath of loyalty to the king. White and Provoost were elected by their states to travel to England and were consecrated bishops in 1787. The church in the United States then had three bishops, a proposed liturgy, and a constitution, but was not yet unified. Each state (later known as a diocese) was an independent entity. Disagreement resulting from political differences continued to exist between the bishops. There was ill will between Seabury, a former Tory, and Provoost, a former revolutionary. Also, Seabury believed that bishops should control all aspects of church government, while White and Provoost believed that the clergy and laity should have a voice in church affairs.

The General Convention of 1789, held at Christ Church in Philadelphia, was vital in organizing and redefining the Anglican church in the United States. Representatives from New England did not attend the first session, because delegates from other states questioned the validity of Bishop Seabury's Episcopal orders. In order to achieve union with the churches in New England, the delegates voted unanimously to accept Bishop Seabury as equal to Bishops Provoost and White. The absence of Bishop Provoost due to illness was fortuitous. Provoost resented Seabury's political views and would have prevented a decision in Seabury's favor. Another issue addressed during the summer session was the creation of a House of Bishops and a House of Deputies. This structure mirrored the House of Representatives and Senate of the United States government.

The second session of the 1789 General Convention began September 30 and ended October 16. Bishop Seabury, with two clerical deputies plus representatives from Massachusetts and New Hampshire, joined the delegates who had attended the previous session. The House of Bishops, consisting of White and Seabury, met separately without Bishop Provoost. Although he attended the convention, Provoost refused to participate because of Seabury's presence.

Three concerns were addressed during the fall session: the constitution, the prayer book, and canonical law. The church constitution was formally adopted and echoed the democratic principles recently presented in the federal Constitution. The church would consist of a collection of independent dioceses, each headed by a bishop; church policy would be formulated at a triennial General Convention made up of laity and clergy. The central canon of the church was, and still is, that bishops, priests, and deacons make up the three orders of ministry. The constitution also made the use of the American Book of Common Prayer compulsory.

The revision of the prayer book was an important task, which also conveyed a political message. The liturgical committee decided to retain the text of the English Book of Common Prayer with some revisions. The most important change was the deletion of any reference to the king. The preface to the U.S. prayer book made it clear that the intent of the U.S. church was to remain in communion with the English church but retain its independence to govern its own affairs.

—*Pegge A. Bochynski*

ADDITIONAL READING:

Addison, James Thayer. *The Episcopal Church in the United States: 1789-1931*. New York: Charles Scribner's Sons, 1951. A narrative of the search of the Episcopal church in the United States for a new identity during the Convention of 1789. Addison credits both Seabury and White with strong leadership during the proceedings, but calls White "the Madison of the Church's constitution."

Chorley, E. Clowes. *Men and Movements in the American Episcopal Church*. New York: Charles Scribner's Sons, 1950. A brief profile of Bishop Samuel Seabury, capturing the essence of his personality and exploring his career as a priest, his consecration by the Scottish church, and his influence on the early Episcopal church in the United States.

Hatchett, Marion J. *The Making of the First American Book of Common Prayer, 1776-1789*. New York: Seabury Press, 1982. Examines the evolution of the American Book of Common Prayer and details the various editions that eventually led to the revised book of 1789.

Holmes, David L. *A Brief History of the Episcopal Church*. Valley Forge, Pa.: Trinity Press, 1993. A concise account of the sociological, economic, and political factors that shaped the young Episcopal church in the United States.

White, William. "The Case of the Episcopal Churches in the United States Considered." In *Readings from the History of the Episcopal Church*, edited by Robert W. Prichard. Wilton, Conn.: Morehouse-Barlow, 1986. This 1782 document explores the democratic concepts eventually incorporated into the U.S. Episcopal church constitution of 1789. Among its chief ideas is that the laity be given a voice in church government.

SEE ALSO: 1816, AME Church Is Founded.

1789 ■ JUDICIARY ACT: *creation of a federal court system independent of the legislative and executive branches of the U.S. government*

DATE: September 24, 1789
LOCALE: New York City
CATEGORIES: Government and politics; Laws and acts
KEY FIGURES:
Oliver Ellsworth (1745-1807), second chief justice of the United States
John Jay (1745-1829), first chief justice of the United States
William Paterson (1745-1806), associate justice of the United States
Caleb Strong (1745-1819), United States senator from Massachusetts

George Washington (1732-1799), first president of the United States, 1789-1797

SUMMARY OF EVENT. The Constitution of the United States created the basic framework for a national government. It remained for the First Congress, meeting in New York in April, 1789, to implement the document. Few congresses have been of greater importance than the first. Virtually every act set a precedent. The vagueness of the Constitution added to the significance of congressional activity. The document contained many obscure clauses and unanswered questions regarding the powers and responsibilities of the various branches of the federal government. These so-called Silences of the Constitution left Congress with much discretionary power to deal with the problem of judicial authority.

The Constitution, in Article III, Sections 1 and 2, provided for an independent judiciary to consist of a Supreme Court and inferior courts. The general jurisdiction of the court system was defined in Section 2. The Constitution did not deal with the question of judicial review—the power of the federal courts to determine the constitutionality of federal or state legislation. Nor did the Constitution address itself to the responsibility of the federal courts to interpret the meaning of the Constitution.

Most members of the Philadelphia Convention apparently agreed that the judiciary should possess the power to determine the constitutionality of legislation. The convention's members did not intend that the courts should interpret the document. However, neither of these issues was settled definitively, and much was left to the discretion of Congress.

Work on a federal judicial system began in April, 1789, when a Senate committee was formed and directed to bring in a bill. Its fundamental significance to the new nation was evident. Ten senators from ten different states were chosen, ensuring a committee broadly representative of the new nation's divergent points of view on a federal judiciary. The leading role, however, was played by the Federalist senators, Oliver Ellsworth of Connecticut, Caleb Strong of Massachusetts, and William Paterson of New Jersey. To ensure a workable plan, the committee conferred widely with other senators, members of the House of Representatives, and various lawyers and judges.

The principal struggle was over the need for a level of lower federal courts. Antifederalist opponents of a strong central government argued for the use of the state courts as the first instance in federal questions. Federalists contended that lower national courts were necessary in order to safeguard the contract and property rights of merchants engaged in interstate commerce and foreign nationals doing business in the United States.

The First Congress was uncertain as to the proper relationship between the federal courts that they were to create and the already functioning state judicial systems. Although most members of the Congress had been ardent supporters of the Constitution, and therefore nationalist in sentiment, they were fearful that too powerful a federal judiciary would invade the rights of the states. The Judiciary Act of 1789 was a compromise between those who desired a truly national court system and those fearful for the integrity of the state courts. It passed the Senate by a vote of 14 to 6 and the House of Representatives by 29 to 22. President George Washington signed it into law on September 24, 1789.

The Judiciary Act created a Supreme Court, fixing its membership at six justices—a chief justice and five associates. It established a middle tier of three circuit courts, each comprising two Supreme Court justices, who rode circuit, and a district judge from within the circuit. The lowest tier of the federal system was the thirteen district courts, one in each state, with original jurisdiction in both criminal and civil cases. District judges were to be chosen from among residents of the state in which they served. The act also created the office of United States attorney general and provided U.S. attorneys for each federal judicial district. The federal courts were given marshals, serving four-year terms, to attend court, execute precepts directed to them under the authority of the United States, and take custody of prisoners.

The state courts were allowed a limited concurrent jurisdiction with the national courts. Cases arising under the Constitution, laws, and treaties of the United States were first heard in the state courts. The nationalists achieved a significant victory in providing, in Section 25 of the Judiciary Act, for appeals from the state courts to federal courts in all instances where it could be shown that the state courts had failed to give full recognition to the United States Constitution, federal laws, or treaties to which the United States was a party—these three constituting the supreme law of the land, according to the Constitution. This appellate jurisdiction implied the power of the federal courts to review the constitutionality of state and federal legislation. In later years, a great controversy arose over the constitutionality of Section 25 of the Judiciary Act.

The influence and prestige of the Supreme Court grew slowly during the first decade of its existence. Precedents were established that defined the powers of the Court and its relationship with other branches of the government. In 1793, President Washington requested that the Court advise him concerning certain questions of international law. The Court declined to involve itself in extrajudicial or nonjudicial matters. This firmly established the separate and independent existence of the Supreme Court.

In certain decisions, the Supreme Court did assume the power of judicial review. In *Ware v. Hylton* (1796), the Supreme Court invalidated a Virginia statute sequestering the pre-Revolutionary War debts of British creditors. These debts were guaranteed by the Treaty of Paris of 1783. According to the Constitution, treaties were part of the law of the land and therefore superior to state laws. In *Hylton v. United States* (1796), upholding a Virginia law taxing carriages, the Court not only applied the power of judicial review but also, in deciding whether this tax was direct or indirect, interpreted the Constitution. The lower federal courts were also involved in reviewing state laws.

The decision in the case of *Ware v. Hylton* aroused considerable opposition to the Supreme Court from the Republican Party, which accused the Court of being pro-British. Even more serious opposition was engendered by the decision in *Chisholm v. Georgia* (1793). In that case, two citizens of South Carolina, as agents for a British subject, brought suit in the Supreme Court for the recovery of confiscated property. The Court found in favor of the British creditor. Opponents of this decision immediately launched a campaign to curtail the power of the Supreme Court. The result was the Eleventh Amendment, ratified in 1798, which denied to the Court the authority to decide cases "commenced or prosecuted against one of the United States by Citizens of another State, or by Citizens or Subjects of any Foreign State." States could not be brought into federal courts to be sued without their consent.

In spite of the Eleventh Amendment, the Supreme Court was firmly established by 1800. The Supreme Court, under the dynamic leadership of Chief Justice John Marshall of Virginia, survived an attack by the Republican Party on its independence during the Jefferson Administration and definitively asserted its right of judicial review in *Marbury v. Madison* (1803). The Court became the most effective force for nationalism in the federal government.

—John G. Clark, updated by Charles H. O'Brien

ADDITIONAL READING:

Brown, William G. *The Life of Oliver Ellsworth.* 1905. Reprint. New York: Da Capo Press, 1970. The biography of a powerful Federalist leader whose judicial experience in Connecticut helped prepare him to draft the Judiciary Act of 1789.

Corwin, Edward S. *The Doctrine of Judicial Review.* Princeton, N.J.: Princeton University Press, 1914. A classic study, by one of the foremost students of the Constitution, of the intent of the Founding Fathers regarding judicial review.

Goebel, Julius, Jr. *Antecedents and Beginnings to 1801.* Vol. 1 in *History of the Supreme Court of the United States.* New York: Macmillan, 1971. Chapter 11 offers an exhaustive scholarly examination of the act's evolution.

Marcus, Maeva, ed. *Origins of the Federal Judiciary: Essays on the Judiciary Act of 1789.* New York: Oxford University Press, 1992. Nine substantial essays offering a fresh scholarly appraisal of the act.

Ritz, Wilfred. *Rewriting the History of the Judiciary Act of 1789.* Norman: University of Oklahoma Press, 1990. A major study of the act and its significance in its political context, challenging the work of Warren and Goebel on many points.

Schwartz, Bernard. *A History of the Supreme Court.* New York: Oxford University Press, 1993. An excellent narrative history of the Supreme Court, clarifying complex legal issues with engaging style.

Warren, Charles. *The Supreme Court in United States History.* 2 vols. Boston: Little, Brown, 1932. Revised edition of the most influential scholarly work on the evolution of the Supreme Court.

SEE ALSO: 1787, U.S. Constitution Is Adopted; 1803, *Marbury v. Madison.*

1790's ■ FIRST U.S. POLITICAL PARTIES:
philosophical and practical differences cause leaders of the United States to form parties to advance their interests and ideals

DATE: 1790's
LOCALE: Philadelphia, Pennsylvania
CATEGORIES: Government and politics; Organizations and institutions
KEY FIGURES:
John Adams (1735-1826), vice president, 1789-1797; president, 1797-1801
Fisher Ames (1758-1808), congressman from Massachusetts and Federalist leader
John Beckley (1757-1807), Republican organizer and leader in Pennsylvania
Aaron Burr (1756-1836), Republican organizer in New York, later vice president
Albert Gallatin (1761-1849), congressman from Pennsylvania and Republican leader
Alexander Hamilton (1757-1804), secretary of the Treasury, 1789-1795
Thomas Jefferson (1743-1826), secretary of state, 1790-1793, later vice president and president
James Madison (1751-1836), congressman from Virginia and Republican leader, later president
Timothy Pickering (1745-1829), secretary of state under Washington and Adams
George Washington (1732-1799), first president of the United States, 1789-1797
SUMMARY OF EVENT. The Founding Fathers did not anticipate the development of political parties in the United States, and the Constitution made no provision for them. James Madison, in writing *The Federalist* No. 10, discussed factions (parties) in detail and considered them to be a disease in the body politic. Madison feared the rise of factions, stating: "When a majority is included in a faction, the form of popular government . . . enables it to sacrifice to its ruling passion or interest both the public good and the rights of other citizens." He clearly believed that parties were sources of turbulence, oppression, and corruption. Madison argued that one of the blessings of the Constitution would be its applicability to the control of factions. He believed that a federal and representative form of government operating in a country of vast size would make it impossible for permanent majorities to form. Ironically, within four years Madison became the congressional leader of one of the two political parties contending for power in the United States.

Parties arose in the United States in response to the economic and foreign policies of the Washington Administration. By the end of the debate over Jay's Treaty in 1796, parties were operating. In tracing their origin, it is necessary to begin with the debate over ratification of the Constitution.

Although there are certain exceptions, those who supported ratification of the Constitution generally became Federalists, and those who opposed the Constitution became Republicans. The most important exception was Madison himself, the "father of the Constitution" and also a founder of the Republican (now Democratic) Party. Patrick Henry, who opposed the Constitution, became a firm Federalist during the Washington Administration. For the most part, Washington appointed men who had strongly advocated ratification, while congressional support for Washington's programs derived from the same source.

The debates over Alexander Hamilton's economic programs provided the first serious indication that a strong and vocal opposition existed in Congress. The nucleus for a party was to be found in this opposition, composed mainly of men from the South. Madison opposed the funding of the national debt, the assumption by the federal government of the states' war debts, and the creation of a national bank for two reasons: The legislation favored the North more than it did the South; and, because the power to charter the bank was not one of the enumerated powers of Congress in the Constitution, it was unconstitutional. Madison and others were able to unite their sectional fears with strict construction of the Constitution into a general states' rights philosophy that became the ideological arm of the Republican Party. At this stage of development, although factions existed in Congress supporting or opposing Hamilton's program, parties in a national sense did not exist.

Progress in the organization of parties at the national level and the growth of support at the local level came basically from two sources: implementation and funding of Hamilton's program, and divisions arising from the outbreak of the French Revolution and the ensuing revolutionary wars.

First, paying off the national debt placed an enormous burden on the nation, requiring a tax policy that caused complaints. In particular, the excise tax on whiskey sparked a small uprising in western Pennsylvania. Troops were sent in to crush the rioting, men were arrested, and popular indignation drew many into opposition to Washington's Administration. The government was criticized as oppressing the poor to aid the rich.

Second, these domestic tensions were coupled with differences that appeared as the French Revolution emerged in Europe and soon plunged the Continent into war. Americans, while basically neutral, openly expressed preferences for either the French or the British. Many people in the United States immediately experienced a psychological association with the idealism of the French Revolution. Others, more conservative, looked to Great Britain as the last bulwark of stability and order against the turbulence of the democratic masses. Hamilton, for example, was outspoken in his preference for Great Britain and his abhorrence of the French Revolution. Thomas Jefferson, on the other hand, openly sympathized with the French. The coincidence of his opposition to Hamilton's economic policies, his attitudes toward the French Revolution, and his sectional residence was striking. New Englanders were generally pro-British and pro-Hamilton. Southerners were generally pro-French and anti-Hamilton. In

FEDERALISTS VS. ANTIFEDERALISTS, 1788

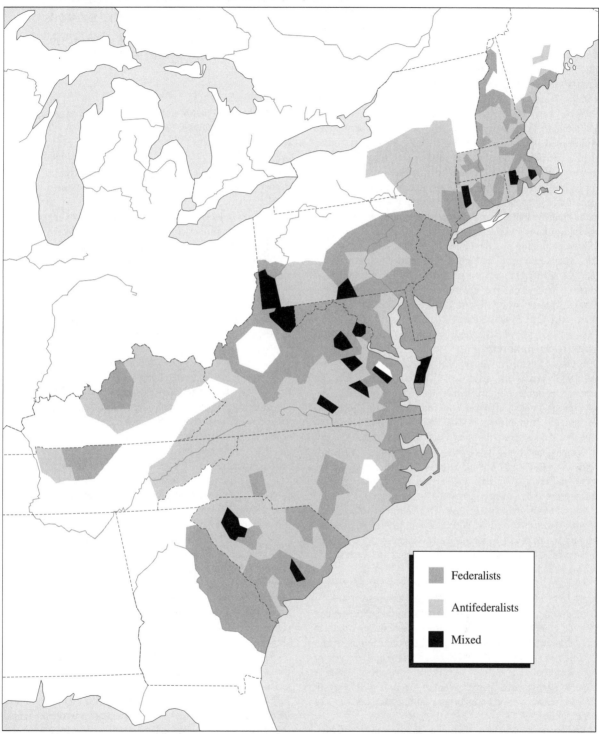

Federalists

Antifederalists

Mixed

The ratification of the U.S. Constitution was controversial, splitting Federalists—those in favor of a strong central government and ratification of the Constitution—and Antifederalists—those who preferred a weaker central government and greater state powers. This division laid the groundwork for the first political parties in the United States: Federalists versus Jeffersonian, or Democratic, Republicans. Former Antifederalists provided the base for the Democratic Republicans' constituency.

the middle states, where sectional feeling was less strong, the division was often East-West rather than North-South. Men from western Pennsylvania, such as Albert Gallatin, fell into the anti-administration ranks, as did western New Yorkers, while the seaboard was pro-administration. The divisions were much less clear-cut, however, in the middle states than in the South or in New England.

Jay's Treaty was the catalyst of party formation. All the elements were present. A momentous issue was necessary for the bonding. The reaction to the treaty was sharp and violent. Widespread opposition appeared at both national and local levels. The debate raged in the year prior to the presidential election. Washington's decision to step down provided the opportunity for men opposed to his administration to gather their forces in an effort to replace those in power. Opposition to the great Washington was dangerous and almost impossible, but John Adams presented no such problems. In 1796, Thomas Jefferson, running as a Republican, contested with Adams for the nation's first position. Parties were formed but, as the next four years would prove, their permanency was not guaranteed. A two-party system was not yet customary, and there were men in power who preferred the existence of a single party—the party to which they belonged.

—*John G. Clark, updated by Michael Witkoski*

ADDITIONAL READING:

Brenner, Lenni. *The Lesser Evil*. Secaucus, N.J.: Lyle Stuart, 1988. Traces the history of the Democratic Party, the oldest continuous political institution in the world, from its beginnings under Jefferson and Madison during the first Washington Administration. The study is not entirely favorable, but it does reveal the party's enduring strengths.

Cunningham, Nobel. *In Pursuit of Reason: The Life of Thomas Jefferson*. New York: Ballantine Books, 1988. The public career of Jefferson, founder of the Democratic Party, is explored and presented in a manner accessible to the general reader.

Ellis, Joseph. *Passionate Sage: The Character and Legacy of John Adams*. New York: W. W. Norton, 1993. John Adams, leading figure of the Federalist Party, is one of the enigmatic figures of U.S. history. This work presents his career in a sympathetic light.

Hoadley, John F. *Origins of American Political Parties, 1789-1803*. Lexington: University Press of Kentucky, 1986. An evenhanded, comprehensive review of the turbulent period that saw the emergence of political parties (factions, as Madison termed them) and their enduring influence on U.S. public life.

Reichley, A. James. *The Life of the Parties: A History of American Political Parties*. New York: Free Press, 1992. A popular review of the party system in the United States with an informative section on its origins during the early years of the republic.

SEE ALSO: 1787, U.S. Constitution Is Adopted; 1787, *Federalist* Papers Are Published; 1790, Hamilton's *Report on Public Credit*; 1794, Whiskey Rebellion; 1794, Jay's Treaty; 1796, Washington's Farewell Address; 1797, XYZ Affair; 1798, Alien and Sedition Acts; 1801, Jefferson Is Elected President.

1790's ■ SECOND GREAT AWAKENING: *a spiritual reawakening giving expression to the new social, political, and economic realities of the eighteenth century*

DATE: 1790's-1830's
LOCALE: United States, particularly the Western frontier
CATEGORIES: Religion; Social reform
KEY FIGURES:

Francis Asbury (1745-1816), Methodist bishop who helped establish the circuit system in the United States
Peter Cartwright (1785-1872), most famous of the Methodist circuit riders
Timothy Dwight (1752-1817), president of Yale College and catalyst for spiritual awakening in New England
Charles Grandison Finney (1792-1875), leading evangelist, who helped create the style of modern evangelism
James McGready (1758?-1817), Presbyterian minister and leader of the revival in Kentucky
Barton Stone (1772-1844), revival minister
Nathaniel William Taylor (1786-1858), member of the Yale Divinity School who taught a modified Calvinism
Theodore Dwight Weld (1803-1895), American Anti-Slavery Society's most powerful figure in spreading abolitionist sentiment among evangelicals

SUMMARY OF EVENT. The upsurge of religious feeling that began at the end of the eighteenth century constituted one of several major revivals in U.S. history. Designated the "Second Awakening" in reference to the Great Awakening of the 1730's and 1740's, the revival of 1800 followed a period of relative religious laxity. The Protestant clergy complained of the decay of morality, particularly in the West, where access to organized religion was difficult. The spread of Deism, not entirely an elite doctrine in the United States, was viewed as a dangerous threat by orthodox believers.

By the late 1790's, stirrings of revived religious consciousness were apparent in all regions of the United States. Revival among the Congregationalists (Puritan denominations) of New England was precipitated in 1802 by a series of chapel sermons by Yale's president, Timothy Dwight, who sought to arrest "freethinking" among the students at his college. The results were impressive, and revival soon spread to other colleges in New England and then to villages and towns. Lyman Beecher, Nathaniel W. Taylor, and others soon were enlisted in the cause of revival faith. To the south, in Virginia, the Presbyterian colleges of Hampden-Sidney and Washington had already experienced renewed religious concern and would provide a significant part of the Congregationalists' evangelical leadership during the Second Awakening. Western New York, which became one of the most fertile areas of spiritual zeal, knew the winter of 1799-1800 as the time of the Great Revival.

The most spectacular of the early manifestations came on the Western frontier. James McGready, a Presbyterian minister, played the leading role in bringing about the Logan County, or Cumberland, revival in Kentucky, which culminated in 1800, and helped spark revivalism throughout the West. The Cane Ridge, Kentucky, camp meeting that attracted between ten and twenty-five thousand people in the following year has been described as the largest and most emotional revival of early U.S. history.

The Second Awakening affected all the major Protestant denominations, although the more evangelical among them gained the most in strength. The Congregationalists and Presbyterians contributed some of the outstanding revivalists, but their participation in the more emotional phases of the revival was inhibited by their more staid Calvinist traditions. Working together in their Western endeavors, the two sects sanctioned "rational" revivalism, a stand that was rejected by such schismatic groups as the Stonite, or New Light Presbyterian, church. Frontier awakening also saw the birth of new churches such as the Disciples of Christ, a church that advocated Christian unity, a radical doctrine of free grace, and a restoration of New Testament Christianity. Mormonism and Adventism also arose in connection with the Great Revival.

Quantitatively, Baptists and Methodists dominated the Second Awakening, being the leaders of frontier revivalism. The Methodists, however, were most successful in the West, and by the 1830's constituted the largest religious group in the United States. The Methodists saw notable growth among African Americans and Native Americans, whose membership in the church by the 1930's numbered fifteen thousand and two thousand, respectively. Like the Baptists, whose numbers also swelled dramatically during the Second Awakening, Methodists were advocates of a free-will theology that complemented the frontier's independent and optimistic character. Emphasis on a simple gospel and comfort with an uneducated clergy also contributed to this remarkable growth. However, the circuit rider, a familiar frontier figure adapted to the American scene by the United States' first Methodist bishop, Francis Asbury, and by charismatic preachers such as Illinois' Peter Cartwright, may have equipped Methodism best to minister to a population at once widely scattered and in motion. The Methodists also enthusiastically adopted the system of protracted outdoor revival service known as camp meetings. By 1825, the camp meeting had become almost exclusively a Methodist institution.

Methodist acceptance of the doctrine that individuals have free will to attain salvation was in accord with a general shift of theological emphasis within American Protestantism in the early nineteenth century. Calvinist sects, including Congregationalists, Presbyterians, and certain Baptists, had traditionally adhered to the doctrine of predestination. In the early phase of the Second Awakening, predestinarian Calvinism and free-will Arminianism were preached side by side. After 1810, Calvinism was modified by such theologians as Timothy Dwight and Nathaniel William Taylor; later, the revivalist Charles Grandison Finney took the lead in establishing what was clearly an Arminian brand of evangelism within the traditionally Calvin-

ist sector of U.S. Protestantism. The ascendancy of Arminianism appears to have reflected the social and political climate of the country. Although historians have found affinities between Calvinist revivalism and political radicalism in the eighteenth century, by the Jacksonian period the message of free will seemed to many the spiritual counterpart of suffrage and laissez-faire.

Perhaps more significant for the future of revivalism in the United States was the conviction that revivals could be provoked and that methods for creating religious conviction could be cultivated by revivalist preachers, whose ministry shifted from that of a pastor to a winner of souls. Unlike the revivalists of the Great Awakening—who believed that revivalism was the consequence of a gracious outpouring of God's Spirit, patiently to be awaited—the new revivalists tended to regard revivalism instrumentally as a means or a technique for precipitating religious conviction, inculcating moral principles, or even the restitution of civic life. At their most successful, these soul-winners became professional mass evangelists, such as Finney, who did much to create the style of modern revivalism represented subsequently by Dwight L. Moody, Billy Sunday, and Billy Graham. With Finney, the preoccupation with theology (exemplified in the Great Awakening by Jonathan Edwards) began to yield to a more one-sided concern with religious experience; revivalism increasingly purveyed a simple religion of the heart.

Another consequence of this emphasis on method and experience was its empowerment of women. Women at revival meetings were encouraged to testify and pray in public. They were emboldened to speak openly of the preacher's opinions and to quote scripture. They formed themselves into voluntary societies that organized and promoted the work of revivalism. In short, revivalism created a psychological and social space for women, within which they could validate their own experience, give voice to their own views, become practiced in organizational ability, and exercise leadership.

The tide of religious feeling had begun to ebb by the early 1830's, but the social effects of the Second Awakening were pervasive and lasting. Voluntary societies had been formed to promote religious education and Sunday schools, distribute Bibles, and advance charitable efforts. Moral and humanitarian crusades were launched. A crusade for the abolition of slavery was entered upon by revivalists such as Theodore Weld, who employed Finney's revival techniques in opposing slavery. Colleges and seminaries were founded which, like Oberlin in Ohio, were dedicated to "universal reform" and the education of women and African Americans. Thus, despite the inherent revivalist concern with individual salvation and the reluctance with which evangelists such as Finney embraced social causes, Finney's own "postmillennialism" involved the belief that the world could be made better in preparation for the Second Coming of Christ.

—Michael D. Clark, updated by Thomas E. Helm

ADDITIONAL READING:

Cleveland, Catherine C. *The Great Revival in the West, 1797-1805.* 1916. Reprint. Gloucester, Mass.: Peter Smith, 1959. A significant study of the early phase of the revival, with discussion of the social, economic, and psychological factors that shaped it.

Cross, Whitney W. R. *The Burned-Over District: The Social and Intellectual History of Enthusiastic Religion in Western New York, 1800-1850*. Ithaca, N.Y.: Cornell University Press, 1950. Examines the revivals that swept western New York State, with attention to social and religious factors.

Johnson, Charles A. *The Frontier Camp Meeting: Religion's Harvest Time*. Reprint. New introduction by Ferenc M. Szasz. Dallas: Southern Methodist University Press, 1985. The first major scholarly study on the frontier camp meeting, with a balanced description of the camp meeting's character, development and role as a social and religious institution.

Luchettik, Cathy. *Under God's Spell: Frontier Evangelists, 1722-1915*. New York: Harcourt Brace Jovanovich, 1989. Captures the flavor of frontier evangelists' experience with excerpts from diaries and journals of eighteenth and nineteenth century evangelists. Includes selections from women and African Americans.

McLoughlin, William G. *Revivals, Awakenings, and Reform: An Essay on Religion and Social Change in America, 1607-1977*. Chicago: University of Chicago Press, 1978. Examines the relationship between the United States' religious awakenings, periods of cultural stress, and social reform.

Posey, Walter B. *Frontier Mission: A History of Religion West of the Southern Appalachians*. Lexington: University Press of Kentucky, 1966. Explores Southwestern revivalism and discusses African Americans, Native Americans, and Roman Catholic expansion.

Thomas, George W. *Revivalism and Cultural Change: Christianity, Nation Building and the Market in Nineteenth-Century United States*. Chicago: University of Chicago Press, 1989. Explores the structural consequences and causal links among revival religion, Republican politics, Prohibition morality, and economic realities. Decided sociological orientation.

SEE ALSO: 1630, Great Puritan Migration; 1730's, First Great Awakening; 1768, Methodist Church Is Established; 1773, African American Baptist Church Is Founded; 1789, Episcopal Church Is Established; 1814, New Harmony and the Communitarian Movement; 1816, AME Church Is Founded; 1819, Unitarian Church Is Founded; 1820's, Social Reform Movement.

1790 ■ HAMILTON'S REPORT ON PUBLIC CREDIT: *the basis for the federal government's economic policy, giving high priority to paying interest and principal on the securities constituting the national debt*

DATE: January, 1790
LOCALE: Philadelphia
CATEGORIES: Economics; Government and politics

KEY FIGURES:
William Duer (1747-1799), New York merchant, assistant secretary of the Treasury
Alexander Hamilton (1757-1804), secretary of the Treasury
Thomas Jefferson (1743-1826), secretary of state
George Washington (1732-1799), first president of the United States, 1789-1797

SUMMARY OF EVENT. The United States government, operating under the Articles of Confederation, had incurred large debts in the successful Revolutionary War, but the Articles of Confederation provided no tax resources for the national government. The securities issued to borrow money declined in value after the war. Desire to provide a stronger fiscal system and pay off these securities was one of the motives for adopting the new federal Constitution. When the newly formed Congress convened, one of its first acts was a resolution in September, 1789, instructing the secretary of the Treasury to "prepare a proper plan for the support of the Public Credit." Secretary of the Treasury Alexander Hamilton submitted his plan in January, 1790. The *Report on Public Credit* touched off a vigorous congressional debate and was the basis for the Funding Act of August, 1790. This act gave high priority to the payment of the principal of and the interest on the securities constituting the public debt. As a result, investors came to regard United States government securities as a high-grade investment with no significant risk of default.

The *Report on Public Credit* was the first of three classic reports emanating from Hamilton's fertile mind. In December, 1790, he submitted his *Report on a National Bank*, virtually an auxiliary to the funding program. A year later came his *Report on Manufacturers*. Taken together, the reports outlined a comprehensive system of economic nationalism. They were intended to strengthen the newly formed federal government by enlisting the political support of wealthy entrepreneurs and to promote the economic and industrial development of the new nation.

It was urgent that the new government take steps to provide for the government debt, which amounted, according to Hamilton's calculations, to seventy-seven million dollars. This included debts incurred by individual state governments of twenty-five million dollars and interest in arrears of more than fourteen million dollars. Hamilton proposed that holders of securities and claims against the government could turn them in and receive new securities in exchange. (At the time, these were called stocks; in the twentieth century, they would be called bonds.) Payment of the interest and, ultimately, principal of the new securities would be given high priority in the government's fiscal program.

The funding of this enormous debt would serve several purposes, according to Hamilton. The credit of the nation would be restored at home and abroad, security prices would increase, and the government would able to borrow on favorable terms in the future, if necessary. Interest rates would be lowered, which would promote investments in land, commerce, and industry. Hamilton believed the new securities would serve somewhat as money, stimulating business.

Hamilton's credit proposals ran into immediate opposition in Congress. Leading the opposition was Hamilton's former ally, James Madison of Virginia. There was no opposition to the funding of the foreign debt, amounting to $11,700,000. It was also agreed that the debt contracted by the Continental Congress and Confederation should be funded. There was considerable debate, however, about Hamilton's proposal to pay off the holders of this debt at its full specie value. Most of the original holders of the debt had sold their holdings to speculators such as William Duer, often at greatly depreciated prices. If Hamilton's proposal were carried, speculators would receive large benefits. Some members of Congress believed that part of this windfall should go to the original owners. The secretary of the Treasury rejected this idea, arguing that such discrimination violated the terms of the implied contract between the government and those who had sufficient faith in it to buy its bonds.

Hamilton's plan for the assumption of the states' debts encountered even more strenuous opposition. Southern states were especially hostile, because many of them had made substantial progress toward paying their debts. New England states, in contrast, had large debts outstanding. Furthermore, large portions of the remaining debts of Southern states were owned in the North. For the states of Virginia, North Carolina, and South Carolina, it has been estimated that nonresident owners, largely Northern, held 53 percent of the total combined debt.

Because of such opposition, Hamilton's measures suffered four successive defeats in Congress. Then occurred one of the classic political deals in U.S. history. Hamilton agreed to support locating the new national capital on the Potomac River. In turn, Secretary of State Thomas Jefferson promised to use his influence to gain Madison's support for the Funding Act, which passed by a narrow margin and was signed into law August 4, 1790. The law authorized issue of three new types of federal securities in exchange for old ones. One component would pay 6 percent interest immediately, while a second (deferred stock) also would pay interest only from 1801. Owners of these securities would receive redemption payments by scheduled installments. A third issue of securities would pay only 3 percent a year and could not be redeemed until all other parts of the national debt were paid off.

A crucial question concerned the willingness and ability of the government to make the payments that the Funding Act promised. One important step was creating a federal tax system, the most important part of which was achieved by imposing tariff duties on imports beginning in 1789. The second step was the consistent commitment of Congress and the successive administrations to scrupulous dedication of federal funds to debt service as promised, even when this required new borrowing, and even when some of the bondholders resided in enemy countries (as during the War of 1812).

In December, 1790, as the funding program was getting under way, Hamilton proposed that the federal government charter a national bank. The proposal was designed in part to make the newly issued federal securities more attractive to investors. Those securities could be used to buy stock in the new bank, stock that was expected (correctly) to pay generous dividends. Thus began a pattern whereby United States government securities became a customary investment for banks, providing them with a low-risk asset that could be sold to raise cash if necessary—a pattern that has continued to exist.

The political accommodation between Hamilton and the two Virginia statesmen, Madison and Jefferson, soon dissolved. Within a year, Jefferson and Hamilton were embroiled in a dispute without hope of compromise over the constitutionality of Hamilton's proposed national bank. Ironically, one of Jefferson's greatest achievements, the purchase of Louisiana Territory in 1803, was made financially possible by the excellent credit standing of the United States government resulting from adoption of Hamilton's funding plan.

—*John G. Clark, updated by Paul B. Trescott*

ADDITIONAL READING:

Beard, Charles A. *Economic Origins of Jeffersonian Democracy.* New York: Macmillan, 1915. A provocative study that tries to identify the roots of the political split between Hamilton and Jefferson in the economic interest groups strongly affected by policies regarding the national debt and national bank.

Ferguson, E. James. *The Power of the Purse: A History of American Public Finance 1776-1790.* Durham: University of North Carolina Press, 1961. Corrects many of Beard's errors and shows how important were Hamilton's measures in saving the country from "currency finance" and creating an environment favoring economic growth and stability.

Mitchell, Broadus. *Alexander Hamilton.* 2 vols. New York: Macmillan, 1957-1962. Hamilton's colorful life and political career are fully explored. Volume 2 contains extensive discussion of public debt policy.

Nettels, Curtis P. *The Emergence of a National Economy, 1775-1815.* New York: Holt, Rinehart and Winston, 1962. Chapters 5 and 6 of this traditional economic history present Hamilton's program in economic and political contexts.

SEE ALSO: 1785, Ordinance of 1785; 1787, *Federalist* Papers Are Published; 1801, Jefferson Is Elected President; 1803, Louisiana Purchase; 1832, Jackson vs. the Bank of the United States.

1790 ■ NOOTKA SOUND CONVENTION:

after a prolonged dispute over competing Spanish and British claims to the region, Spain abandoned all settlements there

DATE: October, 1790

LOCALE: Vancouver Island, off the western coast of Canada

CATEGORIES: Canadian history; Expansion and land acquisition; Native American history; Treaties and agreements

KEY FIGURES:

Juan Bodega y Quadra (c. 1740-1794), Spanish explorer
James Cook (1728-1779), British explorer
Maquinna (fl. 1778-1806), chief of the Nootkas
Esteban Martinez (1742-1798), Spanish commander in 1790
John Meares (c. 1756-1809), British trader
Juan Pérez (c. 1725-1775), Spanish explorer
George Vancouver (1757-1798), British navigator and
  explorer

SUMMARY OF EVENT. Nootka Sound is an inlet on the western coast of Vancouver Island, approximately 170 miles northwest of Vancouver, British Columbia. Native peoples have inhabited the island for several thousand years. The first European expedition known to have entered the sound was under the command of Juan Pérez, a Spanish explorer who had made his way north from California in 1774. Pérez's mission was to challenge Russian claims in the northwest. The Russians, who had staked claims in Alaska, had begun exploring down the northwest coast, and the Spanish feared they would encroach on Spanish territories. Pérez traded with Native Americans who came out to meet his ship, but did not land.

Captain James Cook of England was sent to the Pacific northwest coast in 1778 to try to find the elusive Northwest Passage, a hypothetical all-water route through North America. Cook gave the excellent natural harbor on Vancouver Island the name King George's Sound, but later changed it to Nootka, which he believed was the natives' name for the place. Cook landed and spent almost a month trading for furs with the local people. He did not take formal possession of the area for his king. Captain Cook was killed in 1779 while his expedition was in the Sandwich Islands (Hawaii), but his crew transported the sea-otter furs they had obtained at Nootka to China, where they traded them for enormous prices. For the next several years, traders from many countries sailed the northwest coast and traded with the natives for beaver and sea-otter pelts.

As trade expanded, British businessmen desired a trading base on the northwest coast. In 1788, Captain John Meares, a British trader, obtained permission from a local tribal chief to erect a small building to be used as a house and trading post. Joining him that year at Nootka were several U.S. ships, as well as other English ships. Meares took his furs to China and returned to Nootka in 1789.

Meanwhile, French traders had informed the Spanish government in Mexico of the English presence at Nootka Sound. Esteban Martinez was sent to assert the Spanish claim to the region. He entered Nootka Sound in May of 1789 and took possession of the region in the name of the king of Spain, with "visible demonstrations of joy" from the local people. He negotiated with them and purchased land on which to build his fort.

The U.S. and Portuguese ships at Nootka quickly agreed they would acknowledge Spanish sovereignty as long as they were allowed to leave with their furs. However, the English ships that Meares had left at Nootka refused to accept the Spanish claims. Martinez promptly seized two of them and sailed them, with their crews, to Mexico.

When Meares learned, early in 1790, of the seizure of his ships by the Spanish, he called immediately for his government to protest the action and asked for $500,000 in compensation for his losses. Spain was prepared to pay restitution, but the British government chose to demand more and to challenge exclusive Spanish claims to territory in the northwest. The British government prepared for war. Spain sought help from France, but the French were embroiled in a revolution and refused to come to Spain's aid. This potential conflict between Britain and Spain was the occasion for the first foreign policy debate of the government of the United States under its new constitution. President George Washington and his cabinet decided not to interfere. Because they were in no position to fight a war with the British, the Spanish soon pressed for a diplomatic settlement. The document resulting from their negotiations, the Nootka Sound Convention, was signed in October, 1790.

The Nootka Sound Convention favored British interests. The British government agreed to forbid British subjects to trade with Spanish settlements or to fish in Spanish waters. Spain agreed to give the British rights to trade freely at Nootka and to restore Meares's property. It also recognized Britain's right to explore, trade, and settle "in the Pacific Ocean or in the South Seas." Both sides agreed to send commissioners to meet at Nootka Sound and work out details for the conduct of trade at Nootka.

Early in 1790, the Spanish sent ships with supplies, soldiers, and artillery to set up a trading settlement and fort at Nootka. By 1792, Cala de los Amigos (Friendly Cove) had about fifty houses and two hundred Spanish inhabitants. During the summer of 1792, Spanish, English, Portuguese, French, and U.S. ships all stopped to trade at Nootka. In August, Juan Bodega y Quadra, the Spanish representative, and George Vancouver, the British representative, met in the Spanish village on the sound and conducted diplomatic negotiations. Bodega y Quadra entertained the many captains of the various trading vessels lavishly. On one occasion, fifty-four people sat down to a dinner served on solid silver plates. Vancouver got along well with the Spanish representative; together they charted the island, which they agreed to call Quadra and Vancouver Island.

In spite of the fact that the two men got along well personally, they could not agree on terms for the formal settlement of the rival claims. Vancouver understood that Spain was to give up all its claim to Nootka Sound, while Bodega y Quadra understood that Spain was to cede only the plot of land on which Meares's building had stood. Bodega y Quadra continually stressed the fact that the Spanish had been given complete title to the land by the local chief.

The two commissioners made some effort to make the great chief of the Nootka, Maquinna, feel that he was a part of the negotiations. They received him on board their ships, invited him to dinner, and made an elaborate state visit to his home.

Maquinna's people entertained the Europeans with demonstrations of dancing. The mysterious death of a young Spanish sailor caused a rift between the Europeans and Maquinna's people. The Nootkas withdrew and took no further part in the negotiations. Vancouver and Bodega y Quadra completed their talks and parted as friends, but the real issues between their two governments remained unresolved.

Negotiations between Spain and Britain continued in Europe. In February, 1793, another document, the Nootka Claims Convention, was signed. This gave Meares $210,000 in compensation, and both Spain and Britain agreed to give up exclusive claim to trade in the northwest. In January of 1794, the third Nootka Convention tied up loose ends and both sides agreed not to establish any permanent settlements at Nootka. In 1795, commissioners from both countries once again arrived at Nootka Sound to oversee the withdrawal of the settlements. By that time, the Spanish had already decided to abandon all claim to the northwest and concentrate their efforts in California and Mexico. Both countries had abandoned their settlements by March of 1795. While they continued to trade with the natives of Nootka, neither country again attempted settlement there. This withdrawal marked the end of Spanish dominance in the Pacific and the beginning of the end of their great empire.

The British government eventually gave exclusive trading rights in the northwest to the Hudson's Bay Company, which competed with various U.S. commercial enterprises for the furs of the northwest. By 1840, the furbearing animals were virtually gone from coastal waters and interior areas. In 1846, after thirty years of joint occupation of the northwest by U.S. and British interests, the Oregon Treaty formally gave possession of Vancouver Island to the British, and it has remained part of the Canadian province of British Columbia.

—*Deborah D. Wallin*

ADDITIONAL READING:

Hays, H. R. *Children of the Raven: The Seven Indian Nations of the Northwest Coast.* New York: McGraw-Hill, 1975. Gives history, culture, stories, and legends of the natives of the northwest coast, including the Nootka. Many photographs.

Johansen, Dorothy O. *Empire of the Columbia: A History of the Pacific Northwest.* New York: Harper & Row, 1967. Presents a detailed account of the Nootka controversy.

Meany, Edmond S. *Vancouver's Discovery of Puget Sound.* 1935. Reprint. Portland, Oreg.: Binfords & Mort, 1957. An annotated transcription of a portion of Vancouver's journals from 1792. Provides an account of his time at Nootka.

Moziño, José Mariano. *"Noticias de Nutka": An Account of Nootka Sound in 1792.* Seattle: University of Washington Press, 1991. An extensively annotated translation of the account of a member of Bodega y Quadra's expedition. Contains a wealth of information about the Nootka people, including a brief dictionary of the Nootka language. Illustrations.

Pethick, Derek. *The Nootka Connection: Europe and the Northwest Coast, 1790-1795.* Vancouver, B.C.: Douglas & McIntyre, 1980. Gives a detailed account of the events and controversies of the time. Maps, illustrations, notes, bibliography, and a detailed chronology.

SEE ALSO: 1579, Drake Lands in Northern California; 1728, Russian Voyages to Alaska; 1804, Lewis and Clark Expedition; 1808, American Fur Company Is Chartered; 1810, Astorian Expeditions; 1846, Oregon Settlement; 1959, Alaska and Hawaii Gain Statehood.

1790 ■ LITTLE TURTLE'S WAR: *Native Americans inflict the worst battlefield defeat on U.S. Army troops during the Indian wars*

DATE: October 18, 1790-July, 1794
LOCALE: Ohio Valley
CATEGORIES: Expansion and land acquisition; Native American history; Wars, uprisings, and civil unrest
KEY FIGURES:
Blue Jacket, also known as *Weyapiersenwah* (1764?-1810), chief who rejected Little Turtle's caution and led the native troops against General Wayne
Josiah Harmar and
Arthur St. Clair (1736-1818), generals defeated by Little Turtle's alliance
Little Turtle, also known as *Michikinikwa* (c. 1752-1812), leader of a Native American alliance that defeated St. Clair's troops, then advised suing for peace
Tecumseh (1768-1813), advocate of a Native American alliance to stop the European advance in the Ohio Valley and nearby areas
Anthony Wayne (1745-1796), general who defeated the native alliance in the Ohio Valley
SUMMARY OF EVENT. On November 4, 1791, Little Turtle was one of the principal chiefs among a coalition of Shawnees, Miamis, Lenni Lenapes (Delawares), Potawatomis, Ottawas, Chippewas, and Wyandots in the Old Northwest (Ohio Country) that defeated an army of fourteen hundred soldiers under General Arthur St. Clair. About 1,200 warriors rallied by Little Turtle, aided by the element of surprise, killed or wounded nearly 950 of St. Clair's force, the largest single battlefield victory by an American Indian force in U.S. history. The victory was short-lived, however; in 1794, "Mad Anthony" Wayne's forces defeated Little Turtle and his allies at the Battle of Fallen Timbers. On August 3, 1795, the American Indians gave up most of their hunting grounds west of the Ohio River, by signing the Treaty of Greenville.

Little Turtle was known as a master of battlefield strategy. Born to a Miami chief and a Mahican (or Mohican) mother, Little Turtle became a war chief of the Miamis because of his extraordinary personal abilities; under ordinary circumstances, the matriarchal nature of the culture would have prohibited a leadership role for him. In 1787, the hunting grounds of the Miamis and their allies had been guaranteed in perpetuity by the U.S. Congress. The act did not stop an invasion of settlers, and by the early 1790's, Little Turtle had cemented an alliance that foreshadowed later efforts by Tecumseh, who assembled an alliance of several native nations a generation later.

Little Turtle's principal allies in this effort were the Shawnee Blue Jacket and the Lenni Lenape Buckongahelos. This alliance first defeated a force of a thousand troops under Josiah Harmar during October, 1790. Harmar dispatched an advance force of 180 men, who were drawn into a trap and annihilated on October 18. On October 19, Harmar dispatched 360 more troops to punish the natives, but the Americans were drawn into a similar trap, in which about a hundred of them were killed. The remainder of Harmar's force then retreated to Fort Washington, on the present-day site of Cincinnati.

Harmar's defeat stunned the Army, whose commanders knew that the Old Northwest would remain closed to settlement as long as Little Turtle's alliance held. General Arthur St. Clair, who had served as president of the Continental Congress in the mid-1780's, gathered an army of two thousand troops during the summer of 1791 and marched into the Ohio Country. About a quarter of the troops deserted en route; to keep the others happy, St. Clair permitted about two hundred soldiers' wives to travel with the army.

On November 4, 1791, Little Turtle and his allies lured St. Clair's forces into the same sort of trap that had defeated Harmar's smaller army near St. Mary's Creek, a tributary of the Wabash River. Thirty-eight officers and 598 enlisted men died in the battle; 242 others were wounded, many of whom later died. Fifty-six wives also lost their lives, bringing casualties close to 950—nearly four times the number killed at the Little Bighorn in 1876 and the largest defeat of a U.S. Army force in all of the Indian wars. After the battle, St. Clair resigned his commission in disgrace. Dealing from strength, Little Turtle's alliance refused to cede land to the United States.

In 1794, General "Mad Anthony" Wayne was dispatched with a fresh army, which visited the scene of St. Clair's debacle. According to Wayne, "Five hundred skull bones lay in the space of 350 yards. From thence, five miles on, the woods were strewn with skeletons, knapsacks, and other debris." Little Turtle had more respect for Wayne than he had had for Harmar or St. Clair, calling Wayne "the chief who never sleeps." Aware that Wayne was unlikely to be defeated by his surprise tactics, Little Turtle proposed that the Indian alliance talk peace. A majority of the warriors rebuffed Little Turtle, so in late June or early July he relinquished his command to a Shawnee, Blue Jacket (although some scholars say it was Turkey Foot). In April, 1790, Blue Jacket had refused to attend treaty councils that he feared would cost his people their lands. His forces were defeated by Wayne at the Battle of Fallen Timbers. Afterward, Blue Jacket signed the Treaty of Greenville (1795) and the Treaty of Fort Industry (1805), ceding millions of acres of native land.

Stripped of their lands, many of Little Turtle's people sank into alcoholic despair. The aging chief continued to lead them as best he could. In 1802, Little Turtle addressed the legislatures of Ohio and Kentucky, urging members to pass laws forbidding traders to supply natives with whiskey. He said that whiskey traders had "stripped the poor Indian of skins, guns, blankets, everything—while his squaw and the children dependent on him lay starving and shivering in his wigwam." Neither state did anything to stop the flow of whiskey, some of which was adulterated with other substances, such as chili peppers and arsenic.

Little Turtle died July 14, 1812, at his lodge near the junction of the St. Joseph River and St. Mary Creek. He was buried with full military honors by Army officers who knew his genius. William Henry Harrison, who had been an aide to Wayne and who later defeated Tecumseh in the same general area, paid Little Turtle this tribute: " 'A safe leader is better than a bold one.' This maxim was a great favorite of [the Roman] Caesar Augustus . . . who . . . was, I believe, inferior to the warrior Little Turtle."

For almost two centuries, local historians placed the site of the Battle of Fallen Timbers along the Maumee River floodplain near U.S. Highway 24, near present-day Toledo, Ohio. A monument was erected at the site, even as Native Americans contended that the battle had really occurred a mile away, in what had become a soybean field. In 1995, to settle the issue, G. Michael Pratt, an anthropology professor in Ohio, organized an archaeological dig in the soybean field. Teams of as many as 150 people excavated the site, which yielded large numbers of battlefield artifacts, indicating conclusively that the Native American account of the site was correct.

—*Bruce E. Johansen*

ADDITIONAL READING:

Carter, Harvey Lewis. *The Life and Times of Little Turtle: First Sagamore of the Wabash*. Urbana: University of Illinois Press, 1987. Includes a detailed description of the battle with St. Clair's troops from Little Turtle's perspective.

Hamilton, Charles, ed. *Cry of the Thunderbird*. Norman: University of Oklahoma Press, 1972. Extensive quotations from some of Little Turtle's speeches.

Porter, C. Fayne. *Our Indian Heritage: Profiles of Twelve Great Leaders*. Philadelphia: Chilton Books, 1964. Little Turtle is one of the twelve leaders discussed.

Sword, Wiley. *President Washington's Indian War: The Struggle for the Old Northwest, 1790-1795*. Norman: University of Oklahoma Press, 1985. Discusses the battles that the U.S. Army fought with Little Turtle's alliance, in the context of United States politics of the time.

Winger, Otho. *Last of the Miamis: Little Turtle*. North Manchester, Ind.: O. Winger, 1935. Concise sketch of Little Turtle's life and his attempts to forge a Native American confederation in the Ohio Valley.

Young, Calvin M. *Little Turtle*. 1917. Reprint. Fort Wayne, Ind.: Public Library of Fort Wayne and Allen County, 1956. A sketch of Little Turtle's life, including the St. Clair battle.

SEE ALSO: 1794, Battle of Fallen Timbers.

1790 ■ SLATER'S SPINNING MILL: *introduction to America of modern textile manufacturing and business management*

DATE: December 20, 1790
LOCALE: Pawtucket, Rhode Island
CATEGORIES: Business and labor; Economics; Science and technology
KEY FIGURES:
Richard Arkwright (1732-1792), English inventor and developer of modern textile manufacturing
Moses Brown (1738-1836), Rhode Island merchant-manufacturer
Samuel Slater (1768-1835), English mechanic who built and operated the first successful cotton spinning mill in America
Jedediah Strutt (1796-1797), English textile manufacturer and former partner of Arkwright

SUMMARY OF EVENT. On December 20, 1790, the waters of the Blackstone River surging through Sargeant's Trench in the tiny village of Pawtucket, Rhode Island, began to turn a waterwheel outside Ezekiel Carpenter's clothier shop. The wheel transmitted power to America's first successful textile machinery built on the Arkwright pattern. A new style of doing business, as well as a great American industry, had been established.

Both were imported from England, results of the ambitious plans of Samuel Slater and Richard Arkwright. Born in 1768 in Belper, Derbyshire, England, Slater grew up near the banks of the Derwent, a river that powered the world's first water-driven spinning mill. In the same year, Richard Arkwright finally succeeded in organizing the elements of cotton preparation for the spinning industry that was destined to change the course of world history. Within the next two years, Arkwright received patents for his various machines and built his first mill. When one of Arkwright's partners, Jedediah Strutt, required land and a water privilege to build a new mill in nearby Milford, it was William Slater, Samuel's father and well-to-do farmer and landowner, who arranged the deal. As a result, Samuel was apprenticed to Strutt for the usual seven-year indenture. Because of his father's position and his own aptitude, however, Samuel's apprenticeship was not as a laborer or mechanic but as a trainee in bookkeeping, mathematical calculations, and administration. From Strutt, Samuel learned that the secret to proper management of a water-powered mill was to establish and maintain a continuous flow of materials at the pace at which machines could process them, and to maintain the proper configuration of machines so that no part of the manufacturing process created a bottleneck to hinder that flow.

During this period, England was depending on the American colonies to provide many of the raw materials used in cloth-making; the colonies were not seen as a site for the manufacturing process itself. However, during this period America was acquiring mechanics and a nucleus of small industries centered on shipbuilding. A number of skilled American craftsmen were experimenting in building textile machines, including versions of the Arkwright models. By 1786, two brothers from Scotland, Thomas and Alexander Barr, had produced a carding machine and a spinning frame of the Arkwright design through a subsidy from the Massachusetts General Court, the state's general assembly. Although most of these early machines were never productively operated, they were placed on display in East Bridgewater, Massachusetts, to serve as teaching models. Merchants in adjoining Rhode Island were among those experimenting in textile manufacturing.

Meanwhile, in England, Samuel Slater came to the end of his apprenticeship. Seeing that his country was rapidly becoming saturated with textile manufacturers, he determined that his chances for success would be better in the young United States. On September 1, 1789, Slater left Derbyshire for London, and in November he landed in New York. He secured employment immediately with the New York Manufacturing Company in lower Manhattan, but he was soon disillusioned and sought out Moses Brown, a Rhode Island Quaker who had been experimenting for some years, without success, to mechanize textile production. In January, 1790, Slater inspected the Pawtucket works of Moses' nephew Smith Brown and Moses' son-in-law William Almy and advised the partners that their machinery was unworkable. After some negotiations and a trial period, Slater signed a partnership agreement with Almy and Smith Brown, persuaded them and Moses to write off the machinery they had optimistically collected, and with other craftsmen either rebuild the machinery or build new units. Among those involved were Sylvanus Brown (no relation to Moses), who cut the wooden parts, and David Wilkinson, who did the metal work, assisted by Pliny Earle, a Quaker from Leicester, Massachusetts, who made the hand cards, and an elderly African American named Samuel Brunius Jenks. By the end of the year, the machinery was installed in Ezekiel Carpenter's fulling mill.

The next several years were a time of frustration for Slater, who tried unsuccessfully to introduce modern management methods into the new concern. He considered his responsibility to deliver the most yarn possible and that of his partners to develop markets in which to sell this yarn. Slater's partners, however, were reluctant to manufacture anything until orders had been secured. In 1793, a 49-by-29-foot building containing two floors and an attic was constructed about 20 rods up the Blackstone River from Carpenter's mill, and there Slater organized the machinery for maximum production. Slater also encouraged narrowing the scope of manufacture so that the mill specialized in producing a great volume of a few basic items, thereby functioning as a wholesale outlet for shops along the entire eastern seaboard.

Still frustrated by his partners' conservatism, Slater in 1797 constructed the "White Mill," directly across the river from the "Old Slater Mill," in partnership with his father-in-law and several brothers-in-law. By 1827, Slater held no fewer than thirteen separate partnerships throughout New England. Soon, some 165 cotton mills were working to full capacity in New England. America had entered the Industrial Age, and Samuel Slater's contribution fully justified the title bestowed on him by Andrew Jackson: Father of American Manufactures.

—*James E. Fickle, updated by Erika E. Pilver*

ADDITIONAL READING:

Cameron, Edward H. *Samuel Slater, Father of American Manufactures*. Freeport, Maine: Bond Wheelwright, 1960. Poorly organized and uncritical, this work is nevertheless of interest because it was based on the efforts of a great-grandson to honor his ancestor.

Rivard, Paul E. *Samuel Slater: A Short, Interpretive Essay*. Pawtucket, R.I.: Slater Mill Historic Site, 1974. Reprint. Providence, R.I.: Jo-Art Copy Service, 1988. Although brief (twenty-nine pages), this booklet provides a comprehensive interpretive essay on Slater's role in the birth of the American textile industry.

Thompson, Mack. *Moses Brown: Reluctant Reformer*. Chapel Hill: University of North Carolina Press, 1962. Contains a chapter on the Pawtucket story, with emphasis on Moses Brown.

White, George S. *Memoir of Samuel Slater: The Father of American Manufactures*. 1836. Reprint. New York: Augustus M. Kelley, 1967. Still the most definitive source of factual information, White's work assembles and preserves much personal detail, including a wide selection of Slater's correspondence and other primary documents concerning his life and career.

SEE ALSO: 1793, Whitney Invents the Cotton Gin; 1807, Voyage of the *Clermont*; 1831, McCormick Invents the Reaper; 1846, Howe's Sewing Machine.

1791 ■ CANADA'S CONSTITUTIONAL ACT:
one of a series of acts that created a constitution for Canada

DATE: 1791

LOCALE: Great Britain and Canada

CATEGORIES: Canadian history; Government and politics; Laws and acts

KEY FIGURES:

Guy Carleton, first Lord Dorchester (1724-1808), governor in chief in Canada

William Pitt the Younger (1759-1806), British prime minister

SUMMARY OF EVENT. England's defeat of France during the Seven Years' War (known in North America as the French and Indian War) resulted in Great Britain's acquisition, in 1763, of New France, the former holdings of France on the North American continent. This acquisition posed an immediate problem for Britain: how to govern the newly acquired territory. After a series of failed experiments, the British Parliament adopted the Canada Constitutional Act of 1791.

The principal difficulty in governing the new acquisition of the British Empire was that the two primary groups of inhabitants, the French colonists and the American Indians, had no previous experience with British methods of government of colonial holdings, had cultures that differed profoundly from that of the British, and had been at war intermittently for two centuries with the inhabitants of the British colonies to the south. For France, Canada had been a colony of exploitation; for Great Britain, direct governance of colonies of exploitation had not been practiced—the British favored privatization of colonies of exploitation, as was the case in India.

The task of governing Canada was profoundly influenced by developments in the British colonies to the south. These were colonies of settlement, and under British rule, Canada became converted from a colony of exploitation to a colony of settlement. Britain's task, then—at least as it appeared to the governmental leaders in Great Britain—was how to assimilate the new acquisition, so different from those colonies to the south that had been British from the outset (or almost so, in the case of New York). The constitutional development of Canada in this period was an outstanding example of the famous British pragmatism at work.

The first Canadian constitutional document, the Proclamation of 1763, had been issued as a royal proclamation following earlier precedent that government of the colonies arose from royal prerogative. It separated Quebec from the other conquests of 1763. For Quebec, it established a rudimentary system of government by a royal governor assisted by a general assembly to be drawn from the inhabitants. Such an assembly would have the authority to pass laws, which, subject to approval by the governor and the government in Great Britain, were to be in conformity with existing British law as far as possible. Such an assembly never met; nevertheless, this attempt to assimilate the new conquests to the prevailing system of government in the older British colonies to the south proved unworkable. It took no account of the profound cultural differences between the inhabitants of Quebec, the French-speaking "habitants," and their semifeudal superiors, the seigneurs. Roman Catholics could not participate in any general assembly, because they would have had to deny their adherence to the Roman Catholic church. All disputes among the French Canadians previously had been settled by French civil law; laws similar to British common law were wholly unfamiliar and unacceptable.

Accordingly, the British Parliament intervened with the Quebec Act of 1774, in the process ending the old concept that government in the colonies arose from royal prerogative. This act (heavily promoted by the governor, Guy Carleton) recognized the right of the French inhabitants to continue to practice their religion; their priests were to continue to receive the payments to which they had formerly been entitled. French civil law was to govern in the province, but English criminal law was to prevail. The act pacified the French Canadians but infuriated the colonists to the south and played its part in arousing the Americans to declare independence.

Meanwhile, the American Revolution intervened. The Canadians did not join the dissidents to the south, perhaps because their right to continue in the old ways had been recognized by the Quebec Act. The American Revolution nevertheless had a profound effect on Canada, for it brought a large influx of loyalists into Canada, individuals whose background was wholly British. Although these settlers refused to renounce their allegiance to Great Britain, many shared the same desire for self-government as the American revolutionaries. The need to meet this aspiration created the third British constitutional document, the Constitutional Act of 1791, passed by the ministry of William Pitt the Younger.

This act began by recognizing the difficulty of having the same system of government for the French Canadians as for settlers of British origin. Quebec was divided into two parts: Lower Canada, comprising the lower St. Lawrence lands inhabited by the French Canadians, and Upper Canada, the upper St. Lawrence Valley together with a corridor west to Lake Huron. Upper Canada's inhabitants were overwhelmingly of British origin. The French Canadians again were guaranteed the free exercise of their religion, and, as in the Quebec Act, were provided with an oath to be administered upon taking public office that did not violate their adherence to the Roman Catholic church.

The act provided that both provinces would be governed by an executive appointed by the British government, with the advice of a legislative council and a legislative assembly. The council was to be appointed by the British government on the advice of the governor, and those appointed would hold office for life. The legislative assembly was to be elected by the inhabitants. The legislative assembly passed all laws, which, with the assent of the governor, the council, and the British government, became operative.

The act retained for the British government the final authority to approve or disapprove legislation passed by the assembly. The executive remained wholly independent of the legislature, even though in Great Britain at that time the executive was formed by the majority in Parliament. Although the act went part of the way toward satisfying the demands of the settlers of British or American origin for self-government, as the numbers of this group increased, it became less and less acceptable. Not a few settlers were Americans who took advantage of the favorable terms on which land could be acquired in Canada but who brought with them the same attitudes toward self-government as prevailed in the United States they had left. They demanded full self-government.

In Lower Canada, as the number of inhabitants of British origin increased, the division between those settlers and the French Canadian majority became more evident. The governor and legislative council were almost entirely of British origin, although some governors, such as Guy Carleton, sought to balance the picture by protecting the interests of the French Canadians against economic exploitation by the British contingent. The legislative assembly, by contrast, was almost wholly French Canadian in its makeup.

Perhaps one of the most divisive issues in the years following 1791, until this Constitutional Act was suspended in 1840, was the access, on the part of the executive, to funds not controlled by the legislative assembly. This lack of the "power of the purse" meant that the popular representatives in the legislative assembly lacked the ultimate weapon to control the actions of the executive. It represented the continued refusal of the British government to allow all taxation to be based on the consent of the governed. In time, it sparked the revolt of 1837, which shook Canada to its roots and brought about the replacement of the Constitution of 1791 by a system of genuine self-government. —Nancy M. Gordon

ADDITIONAL READING:

Creighton, Donald Grant. *Dominion of the North: A History of Canada*. Cambridge, Mass.: Riverside Press, 1944. A history of Canada from the earliest French explorations to 1940. Although it treats constitutional developments only as they arise historically, it gives a good overall view.

Lower, Arthur M. *Colony to Nation: A History of Canada*. Toronto: Longmans, 1946. One of the best accounts of Canadian history. The background of constitutional developments is explored in greater detail than in Creighton.

Mallory, J. R. *The Structure of Canadian Government*. Toronto: Gage, 1984. Although this is a description of modern Canadian government, the introduction provides historical background.

Manning, Helen Taft. *British Colonial Government After the American Revolution*. 1933. Reprint. Hamden, Conn.: Archon Books, 1966. Sets Canadian developments in the broader picture of an evolving system of imperial governance.

Tanguay, J. Fernand, ed. *Canada 125: Its Constitutions, 1763-1982*. Introduction by Gerald A. Beaudoin. Montreal: Editions Meridien, 1992. The primary source for Canadian constitutions; the texts of all of them are reprinted. The introduction is by Canada's primary constitutional scholar.

SEE ALSO: 1754, French and Indian War; 1763, Proclamation of 1763; 1774, Quebec Act; 1815, Treaty of Ghent; 1837, Rebellions in Canada; 1841, Upper and Lower Canada Unite.

1791 ■ HAITIAN INDEPENDENCE: *a massive slave revolt initiated an anticolonial struggle and resulted in the first black republic in modern times*

DATE: August 22, 1791-January 1, 1804
LOCALE: Haiti (Western Hispaniola)
CATEGORIES: African American history; Wars, uprisings, and civil unrest
KEY FIGURES:
Henri Christophe (1767-1820), Toussaint L'Ouverture's lieutenant, who crowned himself king of Haiti
Jean-Jacques Dessalines (1758-1806), Toussaint

L'Ouverture's lieutenant and first ruler of an independent Haiti

Charles Le Clerc (1772-1802), commander of the French expeditionary force that invaded Haiti

Alexandre Pétion (1770-1818), mulatto leader who became president of southern Haiti

André Rigaud (1761-1811), mulatto leader whose forces were crushed by Toussaint L'Ouverture

Pierre Dominique Toussaint L'Ouverture (1743-1803), revolutionary military and political leader who fought for Haitian independence

SUMMARY OF EVENT. On August 22, 1791, a major slave uprising ignited a long, bloody rebellion in Haiti that would ultimately break both the shackles of slavery and the constraints of French colonial rule. Following more than twelve years of continuous revolt, including attacks directed at the might of Napoleon's forces, Haiti became the first independent nation in Latin America. Having concluded the second successful revolution in the Western Hemisphere, the Haitians established the first black republic in modern times.

In 1697, France had gained control of the western third of Hispaniola (now Haiti) from Spain as part of the Treaty of Ryswick. Long neglected as a backwater area by Spain, Haiti rapidly became France's most productive colony. During the eighteenth century, economic activity accelerated, as Haiti became a major exporter of sugar, coffee, indigo, cocoa, and cotton. The high productivity was based on a slave plantation economy. By 1789, more than five hundred thousand African slaves, often working under abysmal conditions, provided prosperity for approximately forty thousand white planters and twenty-five thousand people of mixed ancestry (mulattoes) who, although officially accorded French citizenship rights, were subject to social and political inequalities.

Brutal plantation conditions led to a high mortality rate and the need to replace slaves, on an average, after twenty years. To escape the ravages of the plantation, many slaves fled to the remote forests and mountains of Haiti to attempt to find freedom by founding their own communities. From these scattered bases the runaways, called marrons, launched attacks on the hated plantations to secure supplies and weapons. The most intensive marron attacks (1751-1757) were led by François Macandal and were only repressed after concerted efforts of the white planter and mulatto classes. To set an example, Macandal was burned at the stake in 1758, yet Macandal's revolt was, in many respects, a harbinger of what was to occur in 1791.

The French Revolution of 1789, and its rationale of "Liberty, Equality, Fraternity," shook the already unstable political foundations of Haiti and led to a series of events that culminated in the slave rebellion of 1791. For the white planter class, the French Revolution opened strong possibilities for greater local autonomy. For the mulattoes, it offered hopes of greater social equality and a share in the political power structure. The decision of the National Assembly to grant voting rights to all landed taxpaying mulattoes, and the efforts of the white colonists to repeal these rights, set into motion tensions

between the two top classes. A mulatto demonstration for voting rights in March, 1791, led to the seizure of two demonstration leaders, who soon were executed publicly by being broken on the wheel. Also broken were any hopes for peaceful resolution of differences. Ironically, in their dispute, both sides were blind to the revolutionary storm brewing among the 85 percent of the population that formed the slave class.

On August 22, 1791, more than one hundred thousand slaves rose to make their own nonnegotiable demands for liberty. After a weeklong planning session in the Bois Cayman (Alligator Woods), presided over by a voodoo priest named Boukman, marron and slave leaders decided to unleash the pent-up fury of the exploited majority. In the ensuing carnage, an estimated thousand plantations were burned and two thousand white settlers were killed. Destruction in the northern settlements was particularly widespread. Survivors fled to the heavily armed and fortified port city of Cap Français to make a stand. Using superior firepower against a motivated attacking force of superior numbers, they fought a fierce battle that exacted a heavy toll from the attackers. It is estimated that ten thousand blacks were killed during the rebellion. However, what might have appeared to be a terminal event to the colonial militia was the initial phase of a thirteen-year revolution for independence and majority rule.

As black forces began to regroup under new, although often divided, leadership, the mulattoes, led by André Rigaud and Alexandre Pétion, continued sporadic action against the colonial militia. Meanwhile, in France, the Bourbon king was deposed. The newly formed French Republic soon found itself involved in a European war with two of its adversaries, Spain and Great Britain, eager to intervene in Haitian affairs.

In a highly factionalized and complex political atmosphere, leadership of the black forces was established by Pierre Dominique Toussaint L'Ouverture, an educated slave and remarkable revolutionary leader who had served as a strategist in the 1791 revolt. He decided to side with Republican France after the February, 1794, decree abolishing slavery in French territory. Toussaint L'Ouverture's main goal was the creation of an independent state under black leadership; to achieve this end, he struggled against all foreign parties during the succeeding decade. Lack of mulatto cooperation with his nationalist plans led to open conflict and ultimately to the defeat of Rigaud's forces in 1800.

By 1800, Toussaint L'Ouverture had emerged as undisputed leader of a Haiti still technically under French control. By the Constitution of 1801, he became governor general for life. Attempting to reverse a decade of anarchy and destruction, he reinstituted the plantation system and ruled through a military dictatorship. To achieve his goal of prosperity, Toussaint L'Ouverture needed a period of peace. However, revolutionary France had fallen under the command of an individual who favored military dictatorship and a militant colonial policy.

Late in 1801, Napoleon Bonaparte, then first consul of France, decided to return Haiti to more direct French control.

Pierre Dominique Toussaint L'Ouverture, liberator of Haiti, proclaims the Constitution of the new Haitian republic. (Library of Congress)

In January, 1802, he sent an expedition of between sixteen and twenty thousand troops under the command of his brother-in-law, General Charles Le Clerc. The invading force was joined by both white colonists and mulatto forces under Pétion. Toussaint L'Ouverture's armies were equal in size to the French forces, a situation that may have caused him to decide not to arm the general populace, who could have wreaked havoc on the French in a guerrilla war. Because Napoleon had already reinstituted slavery on Martinique, it would not have been difficult to rally the populace by manipulating the fear that Haiti would be next.

Within three months, Le Clerc was able to wear down Toussaint L'Ouverture's forces. After two of his lieutenants, Jean-Jacques Dessalines and Henri Christophe, deserted his cause, on May 5, 1802, Toussaint L'Ouverture was forced to surrender to Le Clerc. Promised a peaceful retirement, he instead was seized and shipped in chains to a French prison, where he died on April 7, 1803. Le Clerc, his betrayer, died of yellow fever in November, 1802, a victim of the disease that would decimate French forces.

Anger over the betrayal of Toussaint L'Ouverture and the French restoration of slavery caused Dessalines, Christophe, and Pétion to unite with other leaders to drive out the French. Their combined strength, and the tremendous toll taken by yellow fever, undermined Napoleon's efforts to maintain control. Moreover, the resumption of war with Britain in 1803, and the decision to sell Louisiana to the United States, made continuation of the Haitian campaign no longer feasible.

On January 1, 1804, Haitian independence was proclaimed with Dessalines—a former field slave and military commander of Haitian forces during the last phases of the war—as its first leader. The successful revolution stands as a symbol of the power of antislave sentiment and the desire for independent self-government. Yet after 1804, Haiti continued to suffer from continued factional struggles between Dessalines, Christophe, and Pétion. Succeeding decades of unstable and ineffective government continued to cloud Toussaint L'Ouverture's vision of a stable, prosperous, and independent state.   —*Irwin Halfond*

ADDITIONAL READING:

Bellegarde-Smith, Patrick. *Haiti: The Breached Citadel*. Boulder, Colo.: Westview Press, 1990. A highly readable presentation of major themes and events in the historical development of Haiti.

Fick, Carolyn E. *The Making of Haiti: The Saint Domingue Revolution from Below*. Knoxville: University of Tennessee Press, 1990. A detailed study of the influence of popular movements on the course of the Haitian revolution.

James, Cyril L. R. *The Black Jacobins: Toussaint L'Ouverture and the San Domingo Revolution*. New York: Vintage Books, 1989. A recent revision of the classic study of the leadership of the Haitian revolution.

Moran, Charles. *Black Triumvirate: A Study of Louverture, Dessalines, Christophe, the Men Who Made Haiti*. New York: Exposition Press, 1957. A short, highly readable study of the roles of the three revolutionary leaders.

Nicholls, David. *Haiti in the Caribbean Context: Ethnicity, Economy, and Revolt*. New York: St. Martin's Press, 1985. A major work in comparative history, which provides an understanding of Haitian affairs from the wider context of Caribbean developments.

Ott, Thomas O. *The Haitian Revolution, 1789-1804*. Knoxville: University of Tennessee Press, 1973. A well-researched, detailed study of the events involved in the Haitian revolution.

SEE ALSO: 1495, West Indian Uprisings.

1791 ■ U.S. BILL OF RIGHTS IS RATIFIED: *the placing of limits on the powers of the federal government to ensure civil rights*

DATE: December 15, 1791
LOCALE: United States
CATEGORIES: Civil rights; Government and politics; Laws and acts
KEY FIGURES:
Elbridge Gerry (1744-1814), leader from Massachusetts who demanded a bill of rights
Richard Henry Lee (1732-1794), Virginian whose writings advocated a bill of rights
James Madison (1751-1836), Federalist and staunch supporter of the Constitution who guided amendments through Congress
George Mason (1725-1792), Virginia delegate to the Constitutional Convention and an early advocate of a bill of rights
Roger Sherman (1721-1793), American jurist and statesman, author of the first draft of the Bill of Rights
James Wilson (1742-1798), Federalist who saw no need for a bill of rights
SUMMARY OF EVENT. The first ten amendments to the United States Constitution are known as the Bill of Rights. These amendments were added two years after the adoption of the Constitution because of demand from prominent people in the states. Their omission from the original document was not a mistake or an oversight. No such list of rights or privileges was included in the original Constitution because majority opinion held that it was unnecessary to guarantee rights that were already commonly accepted and, in most cases, were already guaranteed by the various state constitutions.

When the Constitution was approved by the Constitutional Convention in Philadelphia in 1787 and sent to the states for ratification, a movement to append a bill of rights immediately was evident. Richard Henry Lee, George Mason, Patrick Henry, Elbridge Gerry, and many other prominent state leaders announced opposition to the ratification of the Constitution because it contained no bill of rights. There is no doubt that these Antifederalists objected to several different parts of the document. They chose, however, to concentrate their attack on the absence of a bill of rights. They correctly reasoned that this issue would bring them popular support.

As the various state conventions met to discuss ratification of the Constitution, it became apparent that the Antifederalists had gathered support for their demands for a bill of rights. The Federalists, who staunchly supported the Constitution, began to show concern and worry. James Madison from Virginia, Alexander Hamilton from New York, James Wilson from Pennsylvania, Roger Sherman from Connecticut, and many other Federalist leaders stepped up their campaign for a quick ratification. Better organized than the Antifederalists and equipped with power and persuasive arguments favoring ratification, Federalists in all states put party machinery into operation and worked hard to promote their cause. A study of the ratification struggle state by state shows that the Federalists prevailed, but the demand for some kind of a bill of rights remained strong.

Pennsylvania, the second state to ratify the Constitution, did so by a vote of forty-six to twenty-three. However, twenty-one of the opponents met afterward and drew up a manifesto demanding the addition of a bill of rights. In Massachusetts, a close vote favoring ratification was preceded by a heated debate on the question of a bill of rights. A compromise was reached by which the state's ratification was accompanied by a recommendation for the addition of a bill of rights. Ratification passed narrowly in Virginia (eighty-nine to seventy-nine) and in New York (thirty to twenty-seven), and both states sent with their ratifications strong demands for changes in the Constitution that would protect personal liberties. Several other states followed this pattern, and by the time that Constitution was ratified, it was admitted by all but a few die-hard Federalists that a bill of rights would have to be adopted.

A Federalist in 1788 and a strong supporter of the Constitution from the beginning, James Madison was at first only lukewarm toward a bill of rights, but he assumed leadership of the Antifederalists, who were determined that the first Congress should produce a bill of rights. Although it was believed for many years that Madison himself was the author of the first draft of the Bill of Rights, opinion changed in 1987 as the result of the discovery of a handwritten letter to Madison from Representative Roger Sherman of Connecticut. This manuscript, which was found in the Library of Congress' collection of Madison's papers, actually contains the first draft of the Bill of Rights.

The House of Representatives assembled early in April, 1789, and soon turned its attention to the problem of raising money for the operation of the new government. Madison announced that he would introduce the subject of amendments before the congressional session ended, which he did early in June. Up to that point, a wide variety of opinions had been expressed concerning the manner in which a bill of rights could be incorporated into the Constitution. Some had suggested that the body of the Constitution be amended in different places in order to weave a bill of rights into the original document. Others preferred a declaration of rights as a preface. Still others thought one inclusive amendment would solve the problem. As a result of Madison's introduction of separate amendments (slightly modified from Sherman's draft), it was agreed to place the Bill of Rights in a series of amendments. There followed more discussion concerning the subject matter of the amendments. In September, 1789, a conference committee composed of three senators and three representatives worked out a compromise agreement consisting of twelve amendments. The Senate and the House of Representatives both passed these amendments and sent them to the president to be presented to the states for ratification. Two of the twelve amendments were rejected by the states, but the other ten were ratified by the necessary three-fourths of the states by December 15, 1791. In March, 1792, Secretary of State Thomas Jefferson announced to the governors that these amendments, now known as the Bill of Rights, were in effect.

The ten amendments that were accepted by the states constitute a powerful charter of liberties, although their effect on many of the most important relations of individuals and government was not potentiated fully until the last third of the twentieth century. It is important to note that the Bill of Rights was designed to limit only the federal government's powers. Because it did not pertain to state governments, it did not provide protection for people in such domains as slavery, domestic relations, law, discrimination, or state criminal procedures. Only with the ratification of the Fourteenth Amendment in 1868, just after the Civil War, did it become possible for courts to apply the Bill of Rights to state and local legal questions. —*Edward J. Maguire, updated by Robert Jacobs*

ADDITIONAL READING:

Broadus, Mitchell, and Louise P. Mitchell. *A Biography of the Constitution of the United States: Its Origin, Formation, Adoption, Interpretation*. New York: Oxford University Press, 1965. Strongly emphasizes the role of public demand in forcing a not altogether enthusiastic Congress to move ahead with the Bill of Rights.

Jensen, Merrill. *The Making of the American Constitution*. Princeton, N.J.: Van Nostrand, 1964. Includes a section on the Bill of Rights and a copy of the Virginia amendments of June 27, 1788, which show the kind of rights that were being demanded by the states.

Levy, Leonard W., and Dennis J. Mahoney. *The Framing and Ratification of the Constitution*. New York: Macmillan, 1987. Useful essays describing the intent and politics of the Constitution and Bill of Rights.

Rutland, Robert A. *Birth of the Bill of Rights, 1776-1791*. Chapel Hill: University of North Carolina Press, 1955. Complete history of the Bill of Rights. Excellent except for the omission of Roger Sherman's contribution, which was not known when this book was written.

Weinberger, Andrew D. *Freedom and Protection: The Bill of Rights*. San Francisco: Chandler, 1962. Takes a broader view of the Bill of Rights than most books. Includes in the Bill of Rights the first ten amendments, amendments Thirteen, Fourteen, Fifteen, and Nineteen, and those parts of the original Constitution that deal with personal liberty.

SEE ALSO: 1776, Declaration of Independence; 1781, Articles of Confederation; 1787, U.S. Constitution Is Adopted; 1790's, First U.S. Political Parties; 1865, Thirteenth Amendment; 1868, Fourteenth Amendment; 1920, U.S. Women Gain the Vote; 1970, U.S. Voting Age Is Lowered to Eighteen.

1793 ■ WHITNEY INVENTS THE COTTON GIN: *a new technology revolutionizes methods of agricultural production and consumption, increasing the use of slave labor in the South*

DATE: 1793

LOCALE: Georgia

CATEGORIES: African American history; Business and labor; Economics; Science and technology

KEY FIGURES:

Richard Arkwright (1732-1792), inventor of the water frame for spinning cotton

Edmund Cartwright (1743-1823), inventor of the power loom

Samuel Crompton (1753-1827), inventor of the spinning mule

J. D. B. DeBow (1820-1867), editor of *DeBow's Review* in New Orleans and apostle of Southern diversification

Catherine Greene (1753-1814), friend of Whitney

James Hargreaves (died 1778), inventor of the spinning jenny

Phineas Miller (1764-1803), Whitney's business partner

Edmund Ruffin (1794-1865), advocate of scientific farming

James Watt (1736-1819), inventor of the steam engine

Eli Whitney (1765-1825), inventor of the cotton gin

SUMMARY OF EVENT. Eli Whitney was born December 8, 1765, in Westborough, Massachusetts. The eldest of four children in a middle-class farming family, he had exceptional manual dexterity and a very inquisitive mind. The young Whitney particularly enjoyed dismantling mechanical devices and putting them back together. He also liked to build things in his father's workshop. This early curiosity continued to manifest itself throughout his teenage years and led to a degree from Yale College in 1792.

Following his graduation from Yale, Whitney decided to take a position in South Carolina as a tutor. On his journey south, he became acquainted with Catherine Greene, who persuaded him to visit her home near Savannah, Georgia. Whitney decided to stay at the Mulberry Grove plantation. It was there that Greene first suggested to Whitney that he invent a machine to clean the seeds from cotton. According to Whitney's personal account, he built that first small-scale model of the cotton gin in about ten days. He showed it to Greene and her plantation manager, Phineas Miller, who encouraged Whitney and financed the gin's development. Whitney made several adaptations to the already existing machines (which he had never seen), and the completed model of the cotton gin took months to finish.

Whitney's genius did not bring him the financial rewards he expected. The gin was of such great general utility that the South refused to allow anyone a monopoly on production of the machine and, as a result, there was much pirating. Whitney's problems with the gin and the patent struggles in which he engaged affected his approach to the rest of his industrial career. He was willing to improve the efficiency of his shop only if it did not threaten his security. He conceived the design of a musket-barrel-turning machine, for example, but did not build it for fear that competitors would use it to lure away his trained workmen. Whitney's business abilities were not outstanding. He was primarily interested in the mechanics and efficiency of production, but in those early days an entrepreneur had to be his own chief engineer, foreman, salesman, and public relations expert. Only in the latter part of the nineteenth century did industrial specialization become common.

The invention of the cotton gin by Whitney was one of several important technological advances during the eighteenth century that revolutionized methods of production and habits of consumption throughout Europe and the United States. Whitney did for the cotton planter what Sir Richard Arkwright, James Hargreaves, and Samuel Crompton had done for the cotton manufacturer in Great Britain. The cumulative result of the water frame, the spinning jenny, and the spinning mule was to increase the demand in England for raw cotton, and the cotton gin made it possible for U.S. planters to meet that demand. The application of steam to these machines greatly increased the output of yarn and cloth, thus serving to intensify the demands made upon cotton plants in the United States.

The growth of the cotton industry in the United States was a major force in the rapid economic development of the nation, and much credit for this fact must go to the invention of the cotton gin. The period of the industry's greatest growth followed hard upon the end of the War of 1812, in 1815. Cotton production in the United States rose from 364,000 bales in 1815, of which 82 percent was exported, to 4,861,000 bales in 1860, of which 77 percent was exported. By 1860, Great Britain was consuming one quarter of the entire U.S. crop. Cotton was the United States' leading domestic export. In 1860, the total value of U.S. exports reached $334 million, 57 percent of which was from cotton. If the value of exports of other Southern staples, notably tobacco, sugar, and rice, is added to this figure, the contribution of the South to the nation's export trade approached 65 percent. In spite of these impressive statistics, Southerners complained that the fruits of their labor were gathered by other sections of the country.

To a large degree, this charge was accurate. Southern planters sold their crops abroad or to the Northeastern states. The market was erratic, varying according to demand and supply; it was sensitive to international incidents and almost impossible to predict. Communications were slow. Planters shipped according to one set of prices, only to find a different set of prices operative when their cargoes arrived in port. Risks at sea were great. The costs of shipment were large and paid in the form of commissions to agents of the planters. These men, called factors, handled every detail of the shipment, in addition to making purchases for, and offering credits to, the planters.

These problems were common to all the participants of the staple trade, but they fell with greater impact, especially after 1830, on the older cotton-producing regions along the South Atlantic coast. There, constant plantings without attention to soil conservation reduced yields per acre while increasing costs of production per unit of crop. South Carolina planters found it extremely difficult to compete with planters on Mississippi's lush and virgin lands. Economic stagnation and nullification inevitably followed. Another result was an effort on the part of some farsighted Southerners to stimulate economic diversification in the region. J. D. B. DeBow of New Orleans and Edmund Ruffin of Virginia were among those who preached the virtues of scientific agriculture, industrialization, and transportation improvements.

The dramatic growth of the cotton plantation was more than a matter of production statistics and marketing problems. It was the story of great movements of population into the lush lands of the lower Mississippi River Valley. It was also the story of the master and the slave. To some historians, particularly those from the South, it was the story of the evolution of a culture distinct from that of other regions. Most historians, including those who deny the concept of cultural distinctiveness, agree that by the 1850's—according to most economic indices—the South was in a manifestly inferior position, perhaps in a colonial position, relative to the North. Most also would agree that the institution of slavery was a major cause of this inferiority.

The North was not an industrial area in 1860, although strong beginnings had been made in some parts. The North was basically agrarian but was more industrialized than the South. This meant that the North offered more nonagricultural opportunities for economic advancement. The agricultural sector in the North was based on the small farm. In the South, by contrast, small farmers found it increasingly difficult to compete with the plantation. The size of individual landholdings increased markedly in the South after 1840, while farms became smaller in the North. The population of the North was compact; the plantation system dispersed population in the South, retarding Southern town and city development. Fewer urban areas meant there were fewer commercial and banking facilities in the South, which, in turn, meant a slow rate of capital formation and presented difficulties to those wishing to diversify or undertake transportation improvement. Fewer inducements were available to attract skilled labor, and the fear of competing with slaves was also an obstacle. At the same time, the need for unskilled labor—specifically African American slave labor—was increasing as the South struggled to meet the growing demand for cotton made possible by the new technology.

The effect of all these factors was to make the South economically weaker than the North, although the South was integrated in the budding national economy. The South was neither distinct nor unique, but as pressures on, and criticism (particularly abolitionist criticism) of, the South accumulated, Southerners created the myth of their cultural uniqueness. Whitney's invention had done much to make this myth—and a growing North-South schism—possible.

—John G. Clark, updated by Liesel Ashley Miller

ADDITIONAL READING:

Aitken, Hugh G. J., ed. *Did Slavery Pay? Readings in the Economics of Black Slavery in the United States*. Boston: Houghton Mifflin, 1971. Essays consider the effects of slavery on the Southern economy. Provides examples of the traditional perspective on the economic dimensions of slavery.

Andrews, Mildred Gwin. *The Men and the Mills: A History of the Southern Textile Industry*. Macon, Ga.: Mercer University Press, 1987. Chronicles the development of the Southern textile industry from the 1800's to the later 1980's. Glossary of terms, illustrations, photographs, and comprehensive bibliography.

Batchelder, Samuel. *Introduction and Early Progress of the Cotton Manufacture in the United States*. Boston: Little, Brown, 1863. Reprint. Clifton, N.J.: August M. Kelley, 1972. This study is considered to be an economic classic.

Fogel, Robert William. *Without Consent or Contract: The Rise and Fall of American Slavery*. New York: W. W. Norton, 1989. A thorough interpretation of the institution of slavery in the United States. Fogel supports his analyses with almost one hundred pages of notes and references.

Fogel, Robert William, and Stanley L. Egnerman. *Time on the Cross: The Economics of American Negro Slavery*. Boston: Little, Brown, 1974. A controversial but important revisionist look at the economic and social foundations of slavery in the U.S. South, using quantitative methods and previously neglected sources of information.

Green, Constance McLaughlin. "The Invention of the Cotton Gin." In *Eli Whitney and the Birth of American Technology*. Boston: Little, Brown, 1956. One of the best accounts of the events leading up to and surrounding Whitney's invention of the cotton gin.

Stapleton, Darwin H. "Eli Whitney and the American System of Manufacturing." In *Technology in America: A History of Individuals and Ideas*, edited by Carroll W. Pursell. 2d ed. Cambridge, Mass.: MIT Press, 1990. Summarizes Whitney's contributions to U.S. technology.

SEE ALSO: 1790, Slater's Spinning Mill; 1807, Voyage of the *Clermont*; 1831, McCormick Invents the Reaper.

1793 ■ FIRST FUGITIVE SLAVE LAW:
federal procedure for slave owners to recover slaves who have fled north, aggravating sectional conflict between free and slave states

DATE: February 12, 1793
LOCALE: Philadelphia
CATEGORIES: African American history; Laws and acts

KEY FIGURES:

George Cabot (1752-1823), senator and chair of the committee that reported a fugitive slave bill

Samuel Johnston (1733-1816),

George Read (1733-1798),

Roger Sherman (1721-1793), and

John Taylor (1753-1824), senators and members of the committee on fugitives

Theodore Sedgwick (1746-1813), chair of the committee of the House of Representatives that considered the fugitive slave bill

George Washington (1732-1799), first president of the United States, 1789-1797

SUMMARY OF EVENT. In colonial America, the return of fugitives within and between jurisdictions was a common practice. These fugitives were usually felons escaping from jails; persons charged with crimes; apprentices and indentured servants fleeing from their employers; or black, white, or Native American slaves running away from their masters. Their rendition between jurisdictions depended on comity among colonial authorities. The articles of the New England Confederation of 1643 included a provision for the return of fugitive slaves and servants. Like all subsequent American legislation on the topic, it did not provide for a trial by jury.

In the late eighteenth century, with the growth of antislavery sentiment in the North and the settlement of territory west of the Appalachian Mountains, a uniform method for the return of fugitive slaves became necessary. Article VI of the Northwest Ordinance of 1787 excluding chattel slavery provided that persons escaping into the territory from whom labor or service was lawfully claimed in any one of the original states might be returned to the person claiming their labor or service. The provision did not distinguish between slaves and indentured servants.

The United States Constitution of the same year incorporated the provision, without limiting the claimants to residents of the original states of the union. One of several concessions intended to win support from the slaveholding states, Article IV, Section 2, states that "no person held to service or labor in one state, under the laws thereof, escaping into another, shall, in consequence of any law or regulation therein, be discharged from such service or labor, but shall be delivered up on claim of the party to whom such service or labor may be due."

In 1793, Congress decided to set federal rules for the rendition of alleged fugitives. This action was prompted by Pennsylvania's attempt to recover from Virginia several men accused of having kidnapped John Davis, a free black man. Unable to receive satisfaction, the governor of Pennsylvania brought the matter to the attention of President George Washington, who referred it to the Congress.

A committee of the House of Representatives, led by Theodore Sedgwick of Massachusetts, reported a rendition bill on November 15, 1791, but no action was taken. A special Senate committee, consisting of George Cabot of Massachusetts, Samuel Johnston of North Carolina, and George Read of Delaware, submitted a bill on December 20, 1792, establishing a ministerial procedure for the extradition of judicial fugitives. It also provided a system for the recovery of fugitives from labor or service. A claimant had to present a written deposition from one or more credible persons to a local magistrate who would order officers of the court to seize the fugitive and turn him or her over to the claimant. The bill set penalties for harboring a fugitive, neglecting a duty, or obstructing an arrest. After debate, the bill was recommitted with instructions to amend, and John Taylor of Virginia and Roger Sherman of Connecticut were added to the committee.

January 3, 1793, a revised bill was reported to the Senate by Johnston, allowing the claimant or his agent to seize a fugitive and bring that person to a federal court or a local magistrate. Oral testimony or an affidavit certified by a magistrate of the master's state sufficed to establish a claim. To guard against the kidnapping of free African Americans, residents of the territory or state in which they were seized, the new bill included a proviso assuring them their rights under the laws of that territory or state. This meant they were entitled to a judicial inquiry or a jury trial to determine their status. They were also to be presumed free, until proven otherwise, and allowed to testify on their own behalf.

After two debates, during which the proviso was dropped, the bill passed the Senate on January 18. It was entitled "An act respecting fugitives from justice and persons escaping from their masters." The House passed it with little discussion, February 5, by a vote of forty-eight to seven. Seven days later, President Washington signed the bill into law.

The first two sections of the act, known popularly as the Fugitive Slave Act of 1793, dealt with the interstate rendition of fugitives from justice. The third section provided that when a person held to labor escaped into any state or territory of the United States, the master or a designated agent could seize that individual and bring him or her before a judge of the federal courts in the state or before any magistrate of a county, city, or incorporated town. Title was proven by the testimony of the master or the affidavit of a magistrate in the state from which the escapee came, certifying that the person had escaped. The judge or magistrate then had to provide a certificate entitling the petitioner to remove the fugitives.

The act applied to fugitive apprentices or indentured servants as well as to slaves, a provision important at that time to representatives of the northern states. The act did not admit a trial by jury, and it contained no provisions for the alleged fugitives to offer evidence on their own behalf, although they were not prevented from doing so if the presiding judge or magistrate agreed.

Section 4 provided criminal penalties, a fine of five hundred dollars, in addition to any civil action the owner might have under state law, for obstructing the capture and for rescuing, harboring, aiding, or hiding fugitives.

Although many attempts were made to amend the act, it remained the law of the land until the abolition of slavery, its constitutionality repeatedly upheld by the Supreme Court.

It was amended and supplemented, not replaced, by the Second Fugitive Slave Law of 1850, part of the Compromise of 1850.

The statute contributed significantly to acerbating the growth of sectional conflict within the United States. Efforts to enforce its provisions encountered immediate resistance in Northern states, isolated and scattered at first but increasingly well-organized and vigorous (for example, the Underground Railroad), as slavery prospered in the Old South and spread to western lands. Many Northern states passed personal liberty laws (Indiana in 1824, Connecticut in 1828, New York and Vermont in 1840). Designed to prevent the kidnapping of free African Americans, these laws provided for trial by jury to determine their true status. The effectiveness of the statute was further diminished by the Supreme Court's decision in *Prigg v. Commonwealth of Pennsylvania* (1842) that state authorities could not be forced by the national government to act in fugitive slave cases. Subsequently, Massachusetts (1843), Vermont (1843), Pennsylvania (1847), and Rhode Island (1848) forbade their officials to help enforce the law and refused the use of their jails for fugitive slaves. Because the Fugitive Slave Act of 1793 provided no federal means of apprehending fugitive slaves, owners had to rely on the often ineffectual and costly services of slave catchers. With the outbreak of the Civil War, the law ceased to apply to the Confederate States. It was considered valid in the loyal border states until it was repealed June 28, 1864.   —*Charles H. O'Brien*

ADDITIONAL READING:

Campbell, Stanley. *The Slave Catchers: Enforcement of the Fugitive Slave Law, 1850-1860.* Chapel Hill: University of North Carolina Press, 1970. Chapter 1 deals with attempts to enforce the Fugitive Slave Act of 1793.

Finkelman, Paul. "The Kidnapping of John Davis and the Adoption of the Fugitive Slave Law of 1793." *The Journal of Southern History* 56, no. 3 (August, 1990): 397-422. Discusses the incident that led the Congress to take up the issue of fugitive slaves; thoroughly examines the legislative progress of the law.

_____. *Slavery in the Courtroom: An Annotated Bibliography of American Cases.* Washington, D.C.: Library of Congress, 1985. Presents a detailed description of judicial decisions, as well as other documents pertaining to the enforcement of the Fugitive Slave Act of 1793.

McDougall, Marion G. *Fugitive Slaves, 1619-1865.* 1891. Reprint. New York: Bergman, 1969. Appendix includes the text of the Fugitive Slave Act of 1793 and many other relevant legislative and judicial documents.

Morris, Thomas D. *Free Men All: The Personal Liberty Laws of the North, 1780-1861.* Baltimore: The Johns Hopkins University Press, 1974. A definitive account of the efforts of Northern states to secure individual liberty against the harsh implications of the Fugitive Slave Law of 1793.

Wiecek, William M. *Liberty Under Law: The Supreme Court in American Life.* Baltimore: The Johns Hopkins University Press, 1988. Discusses the Supreme Court's interpreta-

tion of the Fugitive Slave Act of 1793 in *Prigg v. Commonwealth of Pennsylvania* (1842).

_____. *The Sources of Antislavery Constitutionalism in America, 1760-1848.* Ithaca, N.Y.: Cornell University Press, 1977. Detailed exposition of the fugitive slave provisions of the Northwest Ordinance and the United States Constitution, 1787.

SEE ALSO: 1787, Northwest Ordinance; 1804, First Black Codes; 1807, Congress Bans Importation of African Slaves; 1820, Missouri Compromise; 1830, Proslavery Argument; 1850, Compromise of 1850; 1850, Second Fugitive Slave Law; 1854, Kansas-Nebraska Act; 1856, Bleeding Kansas.

1793 ■ MACKENZIE REACHES THE ARCTIC OCEAN: *a search for an inland water route to the Pacific Ocean leads to the Arctic coast of North America*

DATE: July 22, 1793
LOCALE: Near present day Inuvik, Northwest Territories, Canada
CATEGORIES: Canadian history; Expansion and land acquisition; Exploration and discovery; Native American history
KEY FIGURES:
Aw-gee-nah, also known as the *English Chief* (fl. 1771-1821), Chipewyan guide to Mackenzie's 1789 expedition
Samuel Hearne (1745-1792), British explorer and the first European to reach the mouth of the Coppermine River.
Alexander Mackenzie (c. 1764-1820), North West Company trader and explorer
Peter Pond (1740-1807), Connecticut-born trader and explorer, and one of the founders of the North West Company.

SUMMARY OF EVENT. At the close of the eighteenth century, three hundred years after European discovery of the North American continent, very little was known of the geography of its western reaches. Both commercial interests and empire builders wanted to find a water route across the continent from the Atlantic to the Pacific Ocean. The British government had offered a prize of twenty thousand pounds to the first person to discover such a passage. It was well known that in the eastern half of the continent, the rivers that flowed west from the Appalachian Mountains to the Mississippi River had sources close to those of the rivers emptying into the Atlantic Ocean. Geographers theorized that a similar arrangement of river systems existed for the west; therefore, it should be possible to discover a transcontinental waterway. This theory was supported by information garnered by explorers. Samuel Hearne, the first European to travel north across the continent to the Arctic coast, reported that there were mountains in the West beyond which all rivers flowed to the Pacific.

MACKENZIE'S NORTHWESTERN EXPLORATIONS, 1789-1793

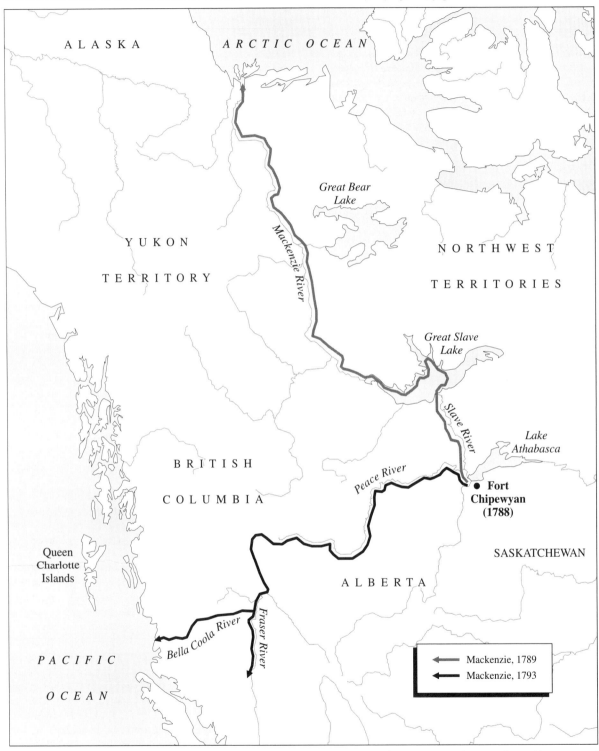

ALASKA

ARCTIC OCEAN

Great Bear Lake

Y U K O N

T E R R I T O R Y

Mackenzie River

N O R T H W E S T

T E R R I T O R I E S

Great Slave Lake

Slave River

Lake Athabasca

B R I T I S H

C O L U M B I A

Peace River

● **Fort Chipewyan (1788)**

SASKATCHEWAN

Queen Charlotte Islands

A L B E R T A

Bella Coola River

Fraser River

P A C I F I C

O C E A N

Mackenzie, 1789
Mackenzie, 1793

Alexander Mackenzie made two river expeditions, one to the Arctic Ocean up the great river that now bears his name, and the other down the Peace River, across the Rocky Mountains, and down the Fraser and Bella Coola Rivers to the Pacific Ocean.

In 1787, a twenty-three-year-old, Scottish-born fur trader, Alexander Mackenzie, traveled west from Montreal to a remote North West Company post in what is now northern Alberta. There, at Fort Chipewyan, he met a veteran of the wilderness, Peter Pond.

Pond had spent more than a decade as a fur trader in the northern prairies and had a better-than-average understanding of the geography of the region. He shared with Mackenzie his knowledge of a great river flowing west from Great Slave Lake. Pond had not traveled this river himself and most likely learned of it from the natives with whom he traded. Pond speculated that the Rocky Mountains ended well south of the Arctic coast, and that this great river, therefore, emptied into the Pacific Ocean.

On June 3, 1789, Alexander Mackenzie set off from Fort Chipewyan to find and follow this river to its mouth. His party included a German, four voyagers and two of their wives, three Chipewyan Indian men, and two Indian women. Serving as guide and translator was the leader of the Chipewyans, a man dubbed the English Chief.

From Fort Chipewyan on Lake Athabasca, this small party descended the Slave River in four birchbark canoes. Nearly a week later, they reached Great Slave Lake and found it too icy for them to proceed by canoe. They portaged along the southwest shore of the lake for twenty days and found the entrance to the "Big River" on June 29, 1789.

At first the river flowed west, raising hopes that they would soon reach the Pacific, but then its course turned north and continued in that direction. Mackenzie realized that this was not the route he wanted and wrote in his journal that "it was evident that these waters emptied themselves into the Hyperborean Sea [Arctic Ocean]."

Rain, cold, and mosquitoes plagued the expedition. Native Americans whom they met along the way (first Slave and Dogrib, later Loucheaux and Hare) reported that it would take several years to reach the ocean. They told tales of dangerous waterfalls, monsters, murderous Inuit, and a shortage of game downstream. A Dogrib man was unwillingly employed to guide the party. He was extremely fearful and repeatedly tried to escape. By July 10, Mackenzie's companions were so discouraged that they begged him to turn back, and he promised to do so if they did not reach the ocean within a week.

On July 12, 1789, the party came to what they thought was another large lake covered with ice. They camped on an island in the mouth of the river and were awakened the next day by the rising tide. Soon afterward, they noticed beluga whales in the water and knew then that they had reached the Arctic Ocean.

The return trip upstream was even more difficult than had been the one downstream, often requiring a great deal of walking while towing the canoes. Although members of the party saw many Inuit campsites throughout the river delta, they encountered no Inuit. Through the English Chief, Mackenzie encouraged the natives he met to begin trading beaver, marten, and other furs. He continued to inquire about a great river flowing west beyond the Rocky Mountains. The reports he received were that such a river existed, but that it was protected by giants and other monsters. Mackenzie soon realized that the English Chief, in his desire to conclude the journey, was withholding information. This led to an argument between Mackenzie and the English Chief, in which the latter threatened to leave the expedition. Realizing he could not continue without his guide and interpreter, Mackenzie was forced to back down. They reached Fort Chipewyan on September 12, 1789. They had traveled more than three thousand miles by canoe and on foot in 102 days.

The discovery of the Mackenzie River, as it is now called, received scant notice at the annual meeting of the North West Company traders the following year at Grand Portage. Mackenzie prepared to undertake another exploration. After a sojourn in England to study surveying and navigation, Mackenzie mounted an expedition across the Rocky Mountains and down the Fraser River, which he mistakenly thought was the Columbia River. The group then proceeded on foot to the Bella Coola River and the Pacific Ocean, arriving there on July 22, 1793. The route traversed steep ridges and dangerous cataracts. Food was difficult to obtain, and the single large canoe with which the expedition started the journey was smashed on rocks in the white water of the Fraser River. Mackenzie had made it to the Pacific Ocean, but his journey did not present obvious opportunities to expand the fur trade. Mackenzie left Fort Chipewyan and retired from the North West Company the following year.

Mackenzie's voyages greatly increased knowledge of the geography of the West, and for this he was knighted by King George III. His journals, which were published in 1801, may have provided the United States Congress and President Thomas Jefferson with the impetus to fund the Lewis and Clark expedition, lest the territory of the west be lost to Great Britain.

Although Alexander Mackenzie was the first European known to travel from east to west across the North American continent, his experience helped prove that no commercially viable overland route existed. A dozen years later, Merriweather Lewis and William Clark confirmed this finding. Mackenzie referred to the river that bears his name as the "River of Disappointment" and considered it to have little commercial potential. It was not until years later that the Mackenzie River became a primary route of travel and commerce between the sub-Arctic and the Arctic. The search for a Northwest Passage to Asia shifted back to the Arctic waters abandoned two centuries earlier. —*Pamela R. Stern*

ADDITIONAL READING:

Allen, John L. "To Unite the Discoveries: The American Response to the Early Exploration of Rupert's Land." In *Rupert's Land: A Cultural Tapestry*, edited by Richard C. Davis. Waterloo, Ontario: Wilfred Laurier University Press, 1988. Interesting analysis of the relationship between Mackenzie's explorations and the funding of the Lewis and Clark Expedition.

Francis, Daniel. *Discovery of the North: The Exploration of Canada's Arctic*. Edmonton, Canada: Hurtig, 1986. Chapter 3 discusses the explorations of Hearne and Mackenzie.

Mackenzie, Alexander. *Voyages from Montreal on the River St. Laurence Through the Continent of North America, to the Frozen and Pacific Oceans in the Years 1789 and 1793*. Ann Arbor, Mich.: University Microfilms, 1966. Facsimile edition of the explorer's 1801 description of the fur trade and his travels.

Newman, Peter C. *Caesars of the Wilderness*. Vol. 2 in *Company of Adventurers*. New York: Penguin Books, 1988. Rich description of the history of the fur trade in Canada. Chapter 3 is devoted to Mackenzie.

Sloan, W. A. "Aw-gee-nah (English Chief)." In *Dictionary of Canadian Biography*. Vol. 6. Edited by Francess G. Halpenny. Toronto: University of Toronto Press, 1987. Brief but comprehensive discussion of the available information on Mackenzie's guide.

SEE ALSO: 1804, Lewis and Clark Expedition; 1808, American Fur Company Is Chartered; 1810, Astorian Expeditions.

1794 ■ WHISKEY REBELLION: *demonstrates the authority of the new U.S. federal government to tax and collect taxes, even if military force becomes necessary*

DATE: July-November, 1794
LOCALE: Western Pennsylvania
CATEGORIES: Government and politics; Wars, uprisings, and civil unrest
KEY FIGURES:
David Bradford and
Albert Gallatin (1761-1849), members of the Pennsylvania Assembly
Alexander Hamilton (1755-1804), secretary of the Treasury
Thomas McKean (1734-1817), Republican who was elected governor of Pennsylvania in 1799
James Marshall, anti-excise leader in Pennsylvania
Thomas Mifflin (1744-1800), governor of Pennsylvania
George Washington (1732-1799), first president of the United States, 1789-1797

SUMMARY OF EVENT. Two of the more pressing and difficult problems that confronted George Washington's administration involved paying the nation's debt and maintaining the loyalty of the West to the United States. These two issues became one during the Whiskey Rebellion crisis.

Problems in the West were largely the product of inadequate security and defense against the resident Native American nations and their European allies. Prior to Jay's Treaty with Great Britain and Pinckney's Treaty with Spain in the mid-1790's, much of the Ohio and Mississippi River Valleys was claimed or occupied by Great Britain and Spain. Both nations apparently encouraged constant Native American attacks against American settlers in the vast region, and Washington's government seemed incapable of containing the hos-

tilities. Settlement was thus retarded, western dissatisfaction was aggravated, and foreign powers were encouraged to bring about the separation of the American West from the United States.

Economic conditions also played an important role in the western problems. High transportation costs compelled western farmers to ship their bulky produce down the Ohio and Mississippi river systems to the Gulf of Mexico. The overland freight rates charged for hauling goods eastward over the mountains were prohibitive. If the western portions of the nation were to grow economically, not only would the federal government have to exert itself militarily against the Native Americans but also it would have to secure from European governments free navigation as far as the mouth of the Mississippi River.

The economic program proposed by Alexander Hamilton, secretary of the Treasury, compounded the western problems. His plan called for the national government to assume and fund all remaining federal and state Revolutionary War debts. Despite stiff Southern opposition, Hamilton successfully steered his program through Congress. However, upon assuming the debt, Hamilton had to devise a way to pay the enormous new liability. The solution included levying a tax. Upon Hamilton's advice, one of the first taxes legislated was an excise tax on distilled whiskey.

Although the excise legislation was quickly approved by Congress, Hamilton's political adversaries immediately launched a campaign against the tax. Southern reaction was particularly negative. Critics of the plan, including Thomas Jefferson, protested that the tax would reward special interests at the expense of small farmers in the West. One Georgia congressman predicted that violence would follow if federal officials attempted to collect the tax.

The proposed tax also was vigorously censured by many settlers west of the Appalachians. Whiskey was an important source of income and a major export product in the West, especially in western Pennsylvania. Farmers found it almost impossible to haul grain to eastern markets because of transportation costs. Instead, grain had to be converted into a form less bulky and more valuable in proportion to its weight. One such form was livestock, which could be driven to market, but this was an arduous and risky business. Another less difficult form to transport was grain converted into distilled spirits. Whiskey could be carried profitably from western farmsteads to eastern markets. For many west of the Appalachians, Hamilton's tax threatened to eliminate whiskey profits. The excise equaled 25 percent of whiskey's retail value, which was more than enough to wipe out a frontier farmer's whiskey earnings.

Western resentments were further aroused by the appointment of federal tax collectors. Of particular concern were stipulations within the tax legislation that distillers charged with evading the excise were to be tried in federal courts located in the East. Westerners resented the interference in their economic life and were especially antagonistic toward the excise agents. Western settlers placed no special trust or faith in the national government, located as it was in the East and representing, in the minds of many Westerners, a challenge to individual freedoms won during the Revolutionary War.

The most threatening protest to the legislation came in western Pennsylvania. Upon learning that the whiskey tax had been passed by Congress, some western Pennsylvanians initiated a series of meetings designed to organize resistance. Local protest groups similar to those created during the American Revolution soon were established. Although most opposition was limited to petitions and demonstrations, in a few instances violence erupted. In one episode in September, 1791, shortly after passage of the tax, an eager excise inspector in the Pittsburgh area was tarred and feathered by a mob of protesters. Several other states also encountered minor disturbances during the first months after passage of the whiskey tax. However, between late 1791 and mid-1794, the resistance, for the most part, remained peaceful.

In July, 1794, after almost three years of protest, peaceful resistance erupted into open rebellion. In one encounter, an armed mob, after a shoot-out with federal troops, attacked and burned the home of the excise inspector of Allegheny County, Pennsylvania. This act of defiance was followed in August by a mass meeting at Braddock's Field and a march to Pittsburgh. In another incident, approximately one hundred angry farmers assaulted a U.S. marshal as he attempted to serve summonses to delinquent taxpayers. In the days that followed, other tax collectors were assaulted, several buildings were burned, and mobs openly roamed through the western Pennsylvania countryside, threatening all who supported the tax.

The turmoil in western Pennsylvania was of grave concern to many, but especially to President Washington. Adding to his alarm was his government's general ineffectiveness at resolving other western problems. Federal efforts to pacify local Native Americans had usually been thwarted, while the British and Spanish influence over the tribes grew stronger. The United States remained no closer to securing the evacuation of the British from the Northwest than it had been immediately after the Revolutionary War. Nor was Washington's administration any closer to freeing navigation along the Mississippi River than it had been five years earlier. With so little success at resolving the western issues, some feared that if left unattended, the West might attempt to leave the union of states and create a country of its own. Such a turn of events would be disastrous for the nation as a whole.

To end the rebellion, President Washington, acting upon reports from state and federal authorities in Pennsylvania, moved swiftly. After issuing a presidential proclamation, Washington called upon several neighboring states to furnish the federal government with a combined force of more than twelve thousand men. Leading the army as far as the Appalachians, the president prepared to do battle with the rebels if necessary. However, the anticipated opposition disappeared at the sight of Washington's troops. The army encountered only citizens who pronounced themselves loyal to the United States. Even a few known protest leaders reversed themselves when confronted by Washington and his men. With the situation apparently under control, the president placed Alexander Hamilton in command and returned east. In short order, Hamilton rounded up 150 suspected rebels and sent 20 back to Philadelphia for trial. Two of Hamilton's captives were convicted of high treason, but both soon were pardoned by the president.

While the potentially explosive episode ended with a whimper, effects of the rebellion were profound. For the first time in the nation's history, the federal government had used force to ensure that its laws were obeyed. The rebellion also generated important philosophical opposition to the Washington Administration and to Federalists, specifically. By 1796, Jefferson's Democratic-Republican Party was deeply entrenched in western Pennsylvania.

—*John G. Clark, updated by Paul E. Doutrich*

ADDITIONAL READING:

Brunhouse, Robert L. *The Counter-Revolution in Pennsylvania, 1776-1790*. Harrisburg: Pennsylvania Historical and Museum Commission, 1942. Writing from an economic perspective, the author describes the partisan struggles within Pennsylvania immediately prior to the Whiskey Rebellion.

Ferguson, Russell J. *Early Western Pennsylvania Politics*. Pittsburgh: University of Pittsburgh Press, 1938. Describes Pennsylvania politics and party development.

McDonald, Forrest. *Alexander Hamilton: A Biography*. New York: W. W. Norton, 1979. Focuses on the Hamiltonian and Jeffersonian philosophies as they applied to the Whiskey Rebellion.

Miller, John. *The Federalist Era, 1789-1801*. New York: Harper and Brothers, 1960. Provides a concise description of the Whiskey Rebellion, paying particular attention to the effects of U.S. foreign policy.

Slaughter, Thomas. *The Whiskey Rebellion: Frontier Epilogue to the American Revolution*. New York: Oxford University Press, 1986. Provides a thorough analysis of the events and motives involved in the Whiskey Rebellion.

SEE ALSO: 1785, Ordinance of 1785; 1787, Northwest Ordinance; 1789, Washington's Inauguration; 1790, Hamilton's *Report on Public Credit*; 1794, Jay's Treaty; 1795, Pinckney's Treaty.

1794 ■ BATTLE OF FALLEN TIMBERS: *the resulting Treaty of Greenville secures U.S. control over much of Ohio and ousts its resident Native Americans*

DATE: August 20, 1794
LOCALE: South of present-day Toledo, Ohio
CATEGORIES: Expansion and land acquisition; Native American history; Wars, uprisings, and civil unrest

KEY FIGURES:

Blue Jacket, also known as *Weyapiersenwah* (1764?-1810), Shawnee war chief

Little Turtle, also known as *Michikinikwa* (c. 1752-1812), Miami war chief

Charles Scott (1739-1813), brigadier general commanding the Kentucky militia

Anthony Wayne (1745-1796), major general and commander of the Legion of the United States

James Wilkinson (1757-1825), brigadier general and Wayne's second in command

SUMMARY OF EVENT. In the 1783 Treaty of Paris, which ended the Revolutionary War, the British acknowledged the United States' claims to territory west of the Appalachians and made no effort to protect American Indian lands in the Ohio Valley. Incursions by settlers there led to serious problems, because American Indian leaders refused to acknowledge U.S. authority north of the Ohio River. Between 1784 and 1789, U.S. government officials persuaded some chiefs to relinquish lands in southern and eastern Ohio, but most American Indians refused to acknowledge the validity of these treaties.

Encouraged by the British, the Miami and Shawnee tribes insisted that the Americans fall back to the Ohio River. When the settlers refused, the Miami attacked them. In 1790 and again in 1791, U.S. troops and militia were sent against American Indians along the Maumee River.

The 1790 expedition, the first for the U.S. Army, ended in disaster. In October, Brigadier General Josiah Harmar set out with a poorly trained force of some 1,200 men. Harmar divided his troops into three separate columns, enabling the Miami and Shawnee, led by Miami chief Little Turtle, to win the battle, inflicting three hundred casualties on U.S. troops.

In November, 1791, Arthur St. Clair, governor of the Northwest Territory and a commissioned major general, led a second expedition, which included the entire six-hundred-man regular army and fifteen hundred militiamen. At present-day Fort Recovery, Ohio, Little Turtle and his warriors administered the most overwhelming defeat ever by American Indians on the British or Americans. Some 650 U.S. troops and 250 civilians died; another 300 were wounded. American Indian losses were reported as twenty-one killed and forty wounded.

In December, 1792, Congress authorized establishment of a five-hundred-man Legion of the United States. Despite misgivings, Washington recalled General "Mad Anthony" Wayne from retirement to command the legion. Wayne found his first training camp, near Pittsburgh, too distracting and marched his men twenty-five miles downriver to a site he named Legionville. Utilizing Baron Friedrich von Steuben's Revolutionary War drill manual, Wayne carried out rigorous training. In May, Wayne moved the legion to Cincinnati and then a few miles north to a new camp, Hobson's Choice.

Wayne issued a call for Kentucky mounted militia and in early October, moved north to Fort Jefferson with two thousand regulars. When Kentucky militiamen arrived, Wayne moved a few miles farther north and began a camp to accom-

modate his larger force. He named it Fort Greeneville (now Greenville, Ohio) in memory of his Revolutionary War commander, Nathaniel Greene. In December, 1793, Wayne ordered a detachment to the site of the previous massacre. On Christmas Day, 1793, U.S. troops reoccupied the battlefield. After burying human remains still in evidence, they constructed a fort on high ground overlooking the Wabash.

Wayne's timetable for the campaign was delayed because of unreliable civilian contractors, attacks on his supply trains, the loss of some of his men to other campaigns, and a cease-fire that led him to believe peace might be at hand. Little Turtle, Blue Jacket, and other tribal chiefs rejected peace negotiations, however.

In February, the British commander ordered construction of Fort Miamis, a post on the Maumee River, to mount cannons larger than those that Wayne might be able to bring against it. By mid-April, work on the fort was well along. This further delayed Wayne's advance, then rescheduled for June.

On June 29, Little Turtle struck first, at Fort Recovery, Wayne's staging point for the invasion. A supply train had just arrived and was bivouacked outside the walls when two thousand warriors attacked. They hoped to take both the supplies and fort in one bold stroke, but Fort Recovery's commander, Captain Alexander Gibson, was ready. Although many soldiers were killed outside the walls, the attackers were beaten back with heavy casualties. After two days with no success, the tribal warriors withdrew. The attack was the high-water mark of their cause; never again would they be able to assemble that many warriors. Defeat at Fort Recovery led some of the smaller tribes to quit the coalition and also caused the eclipse of Little Turtle, who was replaced as principal war leader by the less effective Blue Jacket.

Wayne now had two thousand men. In mid-July, the Kentucky militia, ultimately sixteen hundred men, began to arrive. Wayne also had a hundred American Indians, mostly Choctaws and Chickasaws. On July 28, the men left Fort Greenville for Fort Recovery. Much was at stake, and Washington had warned that a third straight defeat would be ruinous to the reputation of the government.

The two principal American Indian concentrations were Miami Town, the objective of previous offensives, and the rapids of the Maumee River around Fort Miamis. The two were connected by a hundred-mile Maumee River Valley road. Wayne vowed to cut it at midpoint, forcing his enemy to split his forces and defend both possible objectives. By August 3, he had established both Fort Adams and Fort Defiance. Wayne then sent the chiefs a final offer for peace. Little Turtle urged its acceptance, pointing out the great numbers of the enemy and expressing doubts about British support. Blue Jacket and British agents urged war, however, which a majority of the chiefs approved.

Having learned that the American Indians were congregating near Fort Miamis, Wayne decided to move there first. On August 15, Wayne's men still were ten miles from the British fort. Sensing an impending fight, Wayne detached unnecessary elements from his column at a hastily constructed position, Fort Deposit. Manned by Captain Zebulon Pike and two hundred men, it would serve as a refuge in case things did not go well.

On August 20, Wayne again put his column in motion. More than a thousand American Indian warriors, along with some sixty Canadian militiamen, were lying in wait. They hoped to ambush the U.S. troops from the natural defenses of what had been a forest before it had been uprooted by a tornado. The attack plan was sound but based on the assumption that their enemy would either remain in place or run away. Not expecting the daylong delay to build Fort Deposit, Blue Jacket had thought that Wayne would arrive on August 19. The natives had begun a strict fast on August 18 and continued it the next day. When the Americans did not arrive, many of the natives, tired and half-starved, left for Fort Miamis.

Wayne marched his men so as to be ready to meet an attack from any quarter. His infantry were in two wings; well out in front was a select battalion, led by Major William Price, to trigger the enemy attack and allow Wayne time to deploy the main body. When the American Indians opened fire, Price's men fell back into Wilkinson's line. Wayne's troops shattered the ambush with an infantry frontal attack driven home with the bayonet, while cavalry closed in on the flanks. The killing went on to the very gates of the fort, while the British looked on. Of Wayne's troops, only thirty-three were killed and one hundred wounded (eleven of whom later died of their wounds); tribal losses were in the hundreds.

Wayne disregarded Fort Miamis but destroyed American Indian communities and British storehouses in its vicinity. His troops then marched to Miami Town, occupied it without opposition on September 17, and razed it. They then built a fort on the site of Harmar's 1790 defeat, naming it Fort Wayne.

On August 3, 1795, after six weeks of discussions, chiefs representing twelve tribes signed the Treaty of Greenville. The treaty set a definite boundary in the Northwest Territory, forcing the American Indians to give up most of the present state of Ohio and part of Indiana. All hostilities were to cease, prisoners were to be exchanged, and the United States agreed to pay an eight-thousand-dollar-per-year annuity for the loss of hunting lands and twenty thousand dollars in commodities.

The brief Battle of Fallen Timbers broke forever the power of the American Indians in the eastern region of the Northwest Territory. It also led the British to evacuate their garrisons below the Great Lakes. The victory did much to restore the prestige of the U.S. Army; Wayne, justifiably, is known as its father.   —Spencer C. Tucker

ADDITIONAL READING:

Dowd, Gregory Evans. *A Spirited Resistance. The North American Indian Struggle for Unity, 1745-1815.* Baltimore: The Johns Hopkins University Press, 1991. A useful short survey of American Indian affairs.

Nelson, Paul D. *Anthony Wayne: Soldier of the Early Re-*

public. Bloomington: Indiana University Press, 1985. The best biography of Wayne to date.

_____. "Anthony Wayne's Indian War in the Old Northwest, 1792-1795." *Northwest Ohio Quarterly* 56 (1984): 115-140. An excellent short account of this war.

Palmer, Dave R. *1794. America, Its Army, and the Birth of the Nation.* Novato, Calif.: Presidio Press, 1994. A helpful study of early U.S. military policy.

Smith, Dwight L. "Wayne and the Treaty of Green Ville." *Ohio State Archaeological and Historical Quarterly* 63 (January, 1954): 1-7. Careful analysis of the treaty.

Sword, Wiley. *President Washington's Indian War: The Struggle for the Old Northwest, 1790-1795.* Norman: University of Oklahoma Press, 1985. Discusses the struggle for the northwest frontier.

Tebbel, John W. *The Battle of Fallen Timbers, August 20, 1794.* New York: Franklin Watts, 1972. Useful history of the battle.

Wilson, Frazer. *The Treaty of Greenville.* Pigua, Ohio: Correspondent Press, 1894. The only work specifically devoted to the treaty ending the campaign.

SEE ALSO: 1783, Treaty of Paris; 1787, Northwest Ordinance; 1790, Little Turtle's War.

1794 ■ JAY'S TREATY: *a resolution to outstanding conflicts between Britain and the United States leads to large-scale settlement of the Northwest Territory but opens a rift with France*

DATE: November 19, 1794
LOCALE: Philadelphia, Pennsylvania, and London, England
CATEGORIES: Diplomacy and international relations; Expansion and land acquisition; Treaties and agreements
KEY FIGURES:
William Wyndham Grenville (1759-1834), foreign secretary of Great Britain
Alexander Hamilton (1755-1804), secretary of the Treasury
George Hammond (1763-1853), British minister to the United States
John Jay (1745-1829), U.S. negotiator with the British government
Thomas Jefferson (1743-1826), secretary of state
James Madison (1751-1836), anti-administration leader in the House of Representatives
James Monroe (1758-1831), U.S. minister to France
Thomas Pinckney (1750-1828), U.S. minister to Great Britain
William Pitt the Younger (1759-1806), prime minister of Great Britain
George Washington (1732-1799), first president of the United States, 1789-1797

SUMMARY OF EVENT. After Great Britain's recognition of the United States as an independent nation in the 1783 Treaty of

Paris, the United States had to make that independence meaningful and permanent. For the next three decades, the new nation struggled to maintain its integrity by achieving security against hostile forces facing it to the north and south. The southern and western boundaries were in dispute with Spain. There also existed many outstanding problems in Anglo-American relations after 1783, a number of which stemmed from the apparent unwillingness of either side to abide fully by the Treaty of Paris. The British in Canada, for example, refused to evacuate military posts in the Northwest Territory, which the Treaty of Paris recognized as belonging to the United States. Disputes over exact boundaries and fishing rights of Americans along the Grand Banks created further tensions.

To compound this unstable situation, Britain and other European powers went to war in 1793 with France to put down the subversive doctrines evolving from the French Revolution and the later military ambitions of Napoleon Bonaparte. The war between France and the rest of Europe continued from 1793 to 1815, with only brief pause, and the United States was buffeted first by one belligerent and then by the other. The 1794 treaty negotiated by John Jay of New York is an episode in the struggle of the United States to cope with these difficulties.

The United States and Great Britain by 1793 found themselves competing in commercial affairs. In an effort to secure trade for British vessels, Great Britain prohibited American vessels from carrying goods to British colonial ports. At the same time, Great Britain enjoyed a virtual monopoly of American markets for manufactured goods. Even though it became evident that Great Britain could best supply credit and merchandise to the United States, many Americans resented their economic subservience to Great Britain. The administration of President George Washington only with difficulty prevented the passage of commercial legislation designed to retaliate against alleged British discriminatory practices. The United States therefore attempted to increase its trade with France.

When war between France and Great Britain broke out in 1793, new grievances added to the old, and relations between Great Britain and the United States took a rapid turn for the worse. The position of the United States as the major maritime neutral was critical. There was also residual hostility toward Great Britain in contrast to a generally favorable attitude toward France, the United States' important military ally during the Revolutionary War.

The British quickly gained mastery of the oceans, which substantially isolated the French West Indies. These islands could no longer trade with France in French ships. Into this vacuum flowed the merchant fleet of the United States, which gained great profits from this opportunity. The British realized that their naval and commercial supremacy was being weakened. In November, 1793, a British Order in Council ordered British naval commanders to seize all neutral vessels trading with the French islands. So suddenly was this

order implemented that approximately 250 U.S. ships were seized and about half of them condemned to be sold as lawful prizes.

Such action led to widespread anti-British opinion in the United States. James Madison, congressman from Virginia, led a vigorous campaign to pass retaliatory legislation. Secretary of the Treasury Alexander Hamilton successfully thwarted this effort, with Washington's blessing. To blunt Madison's attack further, the president sent John Jay to London as envoy extraordinary to negotiate with the British government. Washington apparently believed that war with Britain was inevitable unless Jay, at that time chief justice of the United States, returned with an acceptable settlement.

The treaty that Jay negotiated in London struck many contemporary observers as barely acceptable. Nevertheless, parts of the agreement do show Jay's success. It required the British to surrender the military posts which they held on American soil in the Northwest Territory, by June of 1796. It also provided for the creation of a joint commission to settle the claims of British citizens for unpaid prerevolutionary U.S. debts, to settle the claims of Americans for the illegal seizures of their ships, and to determine the disputed boundary between Maine and Canada. The rest of the treaty dealt with commercial matters and was to be in force for twelve years. It stated that the "most favored nation" principle was to operate between the United States and the United Kingdom. American vessels were promised the same privileges as British in both Great Britain and the East Indies.

Jay failed, however, to gain British acceptance of several important U.S. objectives. American trading rights with the British West Indies were so restricted that the United States struck out that part of the treaty when it was submitted to the Senate. The agreement included a broad definition of contraband, but said nothing on the important matters of the rights of visit and search and impressment. Other issues were not resolved or included. A number of these issues later contributed to the underlying causes of the War of 1812.

The agreement was signed on November 19, 1794, in London, and Jay returned to the United States satisfied with his efforts. When the terms of the treaty became known, however, advocates of U.S. commercial rights and anti-British opinion criticized Jay for his apparent failure to obtain complete success in the London negotiations. The Republicans charged the Washington Administration with selling the nation out to the British. Effigies of Jay were burned throughout the country. Political pamphleteers and journalists entered the fray.

Congress debated the controversial treaty. The Senate ratified it June 24, 1795, by a vote of 20 to 10, barely meeting the two-thirds minimum required under the Constitution. After ratification by the Senate in a strictly partisan vote (Federalists for, Republicans against), the arguments continued both in Philadelphia and elsewhere. Secretary of State Edmund Randolph was forced to resign in a scandal related to the treaty's adoption. Washington, disappointed by the unevenness of the treaty, reluctantly signed it because he believed its acceptance the only alternative to war. Only an intense effort by his administration prevented the Republicans in the House of Representatives from undercutting the treaty by their threat to refuse to appropriate the funds necessary for its implementation. The essential legislation passed the House in 1796 by a narrow margin of only three votes (51 to 48).

The effects of Jay's Treaty were significant. Most important, it kept the peace between the United States and Great Britain. It also induced Spain to conclude a treaty the following year (Pinckney's Treaty) that was very favorable to the United States, and it prepared the way for the large-scale settlement of the Northwest Territory. The disagreements over the treaty completed the organization of the opposition Republican Party, intensified by Jefferson's and Madison's antagonism to Hamilton and his policies. The Federalists also were divided and weakened. Washington's invulnerability to political attack was breached.

The restraining influence of the British on the Indians along the northwestern frontier was withdrawn, creating further problems in that region. Most significant, the French First Republic was incensed at this apparent repudiation by the United States of the Franco-American Treaty of 1778. While relations with Great Britain improved temporarily, the United States and France drifted apart. This rift between the only republican governments in the world culminated in an undeclared war and proved to be the dominant issue during the administration of President John Adams (1797-1801). Positive relations with Great Britain eventually deteriorated, culminating in the War of 1812.

—*John G. Clark, updated by Taylor Stults*

ADDITIONAL READING:

Bemis, Samuel F. *Jay's Treaty: A Study in Commerce and Diplomacy.* 2d ed. New Haven, Conn.: Yale University Press, 1962. The classic account of the treaty.

Cohen, Warren, ed. *Cambridge History of American Foreign Relations.* New York: Cambridge University Press, 1993. Volume 1 contains coverage of Jay's Treaty in the context of the diplomacy of the 1790's.

Combs, Jerald A. *The Jay Treaty: Political Battleground of the Founding Fathers.* Berkeley: University of California Press, 1970. Covers the domestic debate.

McColley, Robert, ed. *Federalists, Republicans, and Foreign Entanglements, 1789-1815.* Englewood Cliffs, N.J.: Prentice-Hall, 1969. Includes the text of Jay's March, 1795, statement defending the agreement.

Monaghan, Frank. *John Jay.* 1935. Reprint. Indianapolis: Bobbs-Merrill, 1972. An old but solid biography.

Reuter, Frank T. *Trials and Triumphs: George Washington's Foreign Policy.* Fort Worth: Texas Christian University Press, 1983. Admiring assessment of Washington's leadership.

SEE ALSO: 1778, Franco-American Treaties; 1783, Treaty of Paris; 1787, Northwest Ordinance; 1790's, First U.S. Political Parties; 1795, Pinckney's Treaty; 1797, XYZ Affair; 1798, Alien and Sedition Acts; 1803, Louisiana Purchase; 1812, War of 1812.

1795 ■ PINCKNEY'S TREATY: *wars in Europe prompt Spain to recognize the United States' western boundary claims, ensuring free navigation of the Mississippi River*

DATE: October 27, 1795
LOCALE: Spain
CATEGORIES: Economics; Expansion and land acquisition; Treaties and agreements
KEY FIGURES:

Francisco Luís Héctor de Carondelet (c. 1748-1807), Spanish governor of Louisiana, 1795-1797
Diego de Gardoqui, Spanish minister to the United States
Manuel de Godoy y Álvarez de Faria (1767-1851), Spanish minister to the United States
John Jay (1745-1829), American statesman sent to Great Britain to secure the Treaty of Amity, Commerce, and Navigation with Great Britain (Jay's Treaty)
Thomas Pinckney (1750-1828), Minister to Great Britain and Envoy Extraordinary to Spain
George Washington (1732-1799), first president of the United States, 1789-1797
James Wilkinson (1757-1825), major-general in the U.S. Army

SUMMARY OF EVENT. The negotiation of Pinckney's Treaty clearly demonstrates how European conflicts contributed to American diplomatic success and facilitated the nation's territorial growth and expansion during its formative years. With Spain, France, and Great Britain involved in yet another series of wars during the French Revolution, the European powers found it extremely difficult to maintain control over their empires in North America. Further complicated by the expanding westward moving population of the United States, Spain quickly realized that it needed to settle its dispute with the United States in the West in order to sufficiently mobilize all of their resources for the European war. Once again, as the historian Samuel Flagg Bemis concluded, the United States benefited from European distress.

One of the most pressing diplomatic problems facing the United States after 1783 was Spanish occupation of, and claims to, a large portion of the southern and southwestern United States. The Spanish had enjoyed undisputed possession since 1763 of the territory that had been French Louisiana. They had also regained Florida in 1783, after Great Britain had temporarily obtained control over this region between 1763 and 1783. Spanish power rested solidly along the entire Gulf Coast of North and Central America, both banks of the Mississippi River from its mouth to a point midway between present-day Baton Rouge, Louisiana, and Natchez, Mississippi, and the west bank of the river north to the Missouri River and west to the Pacific Ocean. In addition to these vast holdings, the Spanish claimed by right of conquest during the American

Revolution a large portion of the present-day states of Alabama, Mississippi, and Tennessee. In other words, Spain held or claimed both banks of the Mississippi from its mouth to the mouth of the Ohio River and east to the western slopes of the Appalachian Mountains. Yet with American settlers and commerce expanding rapidly into this disputed territory, a potentially volatile diplomatic dispute erupted between the Washington Administration and Spain.

The United States had received the right to navigate the Mississippi from Great Britain in the Treaty of Paris in 1783. Since Spain, however, had not been a party to this treaty, it refused to accept this settlement and closed the Mississippi to all but Spanish commerce. This action directly threatened both the commercial and political success of the American settlers crossing the Appalachians.

In an attempt to thwart American westward expansion, the Spanish, as did the English in the north, manipulated Native American antagonism toward the settlers and encouraged Indian raids in this region. At the same time, the Spanish, intermittently schemed with dissident western Americans who were dissatisfied with the lackluster western policies of the federal government. Looking to strengthen its position within the southeastern region of North America, Madrid tried to convince the settlers to abandon their ties with the United States and form a new republic aligned with Spain. The Spanish were desperately seeking a face saving solution to its problem in America due to its inability to control and manage its affairs in the region. Aggressive and lawless in nature, the frontiersmen threatened the Spanish with an invasion because of the closure of the Mississippi River and Spanish sponsored Indian raids on American settlements.

Military conflicts, separatist sentiments, and navigation rights posed grave problems for the United States. The Washington Administration, fearful over the potential establishment of an independent republic on its southern border, recognized that the right to free navigation of the river was an absolute necessity to the west, since the river was the only economically feasible route to the market. The federal government was also under pressure by western speculative interests whose landholdings suffered in value as a result of Spanish-supported Indian attacks. Washington realized that if he failed to mollify western interests, it could significantly undermine American territorial growth.

Little progress was made in solving the disputes until 1794. Until that time western intrigues, Spanish fears of a Franco-American invasion, and Indian wars were recurrent themes along the southern border. The Spanish attempted, with the aid of the American Major-General James Wilkinson and others, to stimulate disunion in the West. The Spanish, in an attempt to generate momentum for the separatist movement, opened up trade on the Mississippi to Americans on payment of a 15 percent duty. This somewhat mollified the West but failed to produce any meaningful support for separation. Then, in 1794-1795, the French revolutionary wars brought relations to a crisis. In this instance, as has often been the case throughout American history, European wars provided the United States with the opportunity of achieving a striking diplomatic victory without surrendering any of its initial demands.

Spain had joined with Great Britain in the war against the French First Republic. In 1794-1795, when the war turned against Spain, it began to look for a way out. In 1794, even before Spain made its decision relative to the war, it indicated willingness to negotiate with the United States. As a result of this offer, President Washington dispatched Thomas Pinckney, Minister to Great Britain, as Envoy Extraordinary and Minister Plenipotentiary to Madrid. Pinckney arrived in 1795, and since Spain's military position had so deteriorated that it had decided to make a separate peace with France, the delay worked to America's advantage. Spain was also apprehensive concerning John Jay's diplomatic mission to Great Britain. These negotiations convinced the Spanish foreign minister, Don Manuel de Godoy, that a possible Anglo-American rapprochement was about to take place, and that a joint attack on Spain's overseas empire might coincide with the signing of Jay's Treaty. Furthermore, Spain was about to abrogate its alliance with Great Britain and reenter the war allied with France. Thus de Godoy feared British retaliation.

Pinckney was able to capitalize on Spain's anxieties in negotiating the Treaty of San Lorenzo, or Pinckney's Treaty, signed on October 27, 1795. The Spanish conceded point after point, while the United States gave up virtually nothing in return. Spain recognized American sovereignty to the east bank of the Mississippi north of the 31st parallel; granted permission to Americans to navigate the river; established a place to deposit American goods for transfer to oceangoing vessels; and recognized the American definition of neutral rights. Both powers promised to restrain the Native Americans. This was a tacit admission by Spain that it had incited them in the past. In addition, the treaty did not affect the drive of westward expansion.

The Spanish implementation of the treaty came slowly. But due to Spain's unfavorable situation in Europe, de Godoy's government had little choice but to acquiesce to Washington's demands. Spain pulled out of the disastrous war with the French First Republic in the secret Treaty of Basel in 1795. The following year, in the secret Treaty of San Ildefonso, Spain plunged into an equally disastrous war as an ally of the French against Great Britain. With Spain preoccupied with the war in Europe, the United States emerged from Pinckney's negotiations completely victorious. Thus, as Samuel Flagg Bemis concluded, this treaty represents an excellent example of how "America's advantage" resulted from "Europe's distress."

For the second time the possibility of an Anglo-American alliance against Spain compelled Spain to placate the United States. The Treaty of San Lorenzo was executed in full by 1798. In negotiating the Treaty of Greenville (1795) with the Indians, Jay's Treaty, and Pinckney's Treaty, the Washington Administration had achieved much in the field of diplomacy.

The separatist movement was dead, and the West was secured to the Union.

—*John G. Clark, updated by Robert D. Ubriaco, Jr.*

ADDITIONAL READING:

Bemis, Samuel Flagg. *Pinckney's Treaty: A Study of America's Advantage from Europe's Distress.* Baltimore: The John Hopkins University Press, 1926. This classic work in American diplomacy reveals how the United States was able to secure favorable concessions from Spain due to Spanish fears over an Anglo-American alliance and a potential French invasion.

Darling, Arthur B. *Our Rising Empire, 1763-1803.* New Haven, Conn.: Yale University Press, 1940. A readable synthesis of American diplomatic history from the French Alliance of 1778 to the Louisiana Purchase.

DeConde, Alexander. *Entangling Alliances: Politics and Diplomacy Under George Washington.* Durham, N.C.: Duke University Press, 1958. This source outlines how foreign trade issues and the American relationship with Great Britain shaped American diplomacy during the Washington Administration.

Tucker, Robert W., and David C. Hendrickson. *Empire of Liberty: The Statecraft of Thomas Jefferson.* New York: Oxford University Press, 1990. This text places Pinckney's Treaty within the context of the Hamiltonian-Jeffersonian debate over the direction of American foreign policy during the early national period.

Young, Raymond A. "Pinckney's Treaty: A New Perspective." *Hispanic American Historical Review* 43:4 (1963): 526-535. This article highlights Pinckney's decisive role during the negotiations.

SEE ALSO: 1783, Treaty of Paris; 1794, Battle of Fallen Timbers; 1794, Jay's Treaty; 1797, XYZ Affair; 1798, Alien and Sedition Acts; 1803, Louisiana Purchase; 1812, War of 1812; 1819, Adams-Onís Treaty.

1796 ■ WASHINGTON'S FAREWELL ADDRESS: *a retiring senior statesman articulates foreign and domestic policy for the United States*

DATE: September 19, 1796
LOCALE: Philadelphia, Pennsylvania
CATEGORIES: Diplomacy and international relations; Government and politics
KEY FIGURES:
John Adams (1735-1826), vice president of the United States
Pierre Adet, French minister to the United States in 1796
Edmond-Charles "Citizen" Genêt (1763-1834), French minister to the United States
Alexander Hamilton (1757-1804), secretary of the Treasury and principal adviser to Washington

John Jay (1745-1829), Federalist who negotiated the unpopular Jay's Treaty with Great Britain
Thomas Jefferson (1743-1826), leading Anitfederalist; former secretary of state, elected president in 1800
James Madison (1751-1836), leading Federalist who prepared a farewell address for Washington in 1792
George Washington (1732-1799), first president of the United States, 1789-1797

SUMMARY OF EVENT. On September 19, 1796, Claypoole's *Daily American Advertiser,* a Philadelphia newspaper, published the valedictory remarks of retiring President George Washington. The speech promptly became known as Washington's Farewell Address. In publishing the address rather than reading it before Congress, Washington demonstrated that his words were intended for the entire nation. These were not merely the concluding remarks of an outgoing politician, but the final advice of a much beloved and respected leader of more than twenty years, now retiring to private life. As such, the words of the Farewell Address had great impact and weight, and have been recalled by politicians and policymakers into the twentieth century.

Four years earlier, when Washington had thought seriously of retiring from office, James Madison had prepared a final address for him. In 1796, however, Washington asked Alexander Hamilton, his closest adviser and a leading Federalist theorist, for assistance in writing a final political testament. Historians differ over the nature of Washington's contribution, but it is generally agreed that the Farewell Address represents the joint labor of Hamilton and Washington. It embodies ideas to which Washington had long subscribed, but it is written in an elegant fashion that was Hamilton's special talent.

Washington's Farewell Address is remembered as a classic statement of U.S. foreign policy, but, in fact, it concerned mostly domestic issues rather than foreign affairs. Although Washington deeply desired retirement for personal reasons, he seems to have felt keenly that the nation was potentially facing a crisis. In particular, Washington feared that sectionalism and extreme allegiance to political parties would wreck the national unity that he had worked so long to achieve. Washington had entered the presidency when there were no identifiable political parties in the United States. By 1796, he was witnessing the formation of opposing factions in U.S. politics, a development he felt boded ill for the future. The "baneful effects of the spirit of party generally," he warned, "open the door to foreign influence and corruption." Clearly, Washington was upset by the formation of organized opposition to the policies of his own administration, in particular Thomas Jefferson's Antifederalists. His Farewell Address was intended in part to explain the necessity of a Federalist victory in the upcoming presidential election of 1796, which would, he felt, preserve the unity of the nation.

Washington's remarks about a suitable foreign policy for the United States have come to be known as his "Great Rule of Conduct." His general comments were based on recent se-

Washington's Farewell Address had the weight and impact of a political testament, promoting union against sectionalism and neutrality against foreign influence. (Library of Congress)

vere problems in Franco-American relations. In 1778, the United States had concluded a Treaty of Amity and Commerce with France, providing support that would be vital to American success in the revolution against Great Britain. In 1789, as Washington began his first term as president, France began its own revolution, receiving widespread approval from the United States. By 1793, however, successive revolutionary governments in France had replaced the monarchy and executed the king, who had approved funding for the American Revolution in 1778. France was at war with most of Europe and demanded U.S. assistance, just as the French king had aided the colonies during their revolution against Great Britain. Events in France and the wars in Europe inspired partisanship in the United States. The Federalists, with their heavy commercial ties to Great Britain, had grave reservations about supporting the French in a European war. Jefferson and the Antifederalists charged that Washington had an obligation to support revolution in France because of the treaty of 1778. The arrival in 1793 of the French minister, Citizen Edmond Genêt, initially produced a wave of popular support for the French Revolution. For a time, Genêt even actively recruited soldiers for the French Revolution. As a Federalist, Washington issued a proclamation of neutrality—which renounced U.S. obligations to France as having been contracted under a former government—and supported Jay's Treaty, which was quite favorable to France's bitter enemy, England.

Thus when Washington, in his address, warned "against the insidious wiles of foreign influence [to which] the jealousy of a free people ought to be constantly awake," his readers knew it was France that he had in mind. When the president, in the most frequently quoted passage from the address, suggested that "the great rule of conduct for us in regard to foreign nations is, in extending our commercial relations to have with them as little political connection as possible," he justified his decision that the United States should not honor its obligation to France. The dispassionate tone of his remarks may obscure their unmistakable Federalist bias from the unwary modern reader. Washington considered some political alliances, such as Jay's Treaty, to be legitimate: "So far as we have already formed engagements let them be fulfilled with perfect good faith." The 1778 treaty with France was, quite simply, no longer valid: "Here let us stop."

While the Farewell Address spoke to the political passions of the moment, it also seemed to offer advice about the future. It is here that the ambiguous language of the address has caused so much confusion. Washington wanted both commercial relations and political isolation. Although such a goal may have seemed desirable, the United States has never been able to avoid political involvement with other countries when it gains commercial ties to them. In 1796, the United States was a fairly weak nation, which relied considerably on Europe for trade and commerce. Washington did not rule out all political alliances, nor did he say that political alliances would never become a necessity in the future. He seemed, rather, to support a policy of isolationism by advocating separation of the interests of the United States from those of Europe.

The ambiguity of the Farewell Address, widely to be considered a statement of political isolationism in political debates over foreign policy as recently as 1940-1941, can nevertheless be construed as supporting diverse schools of thought. It was republished in 1809 and 1819 to support the soundness of neutrality in the Anglo-French wars. Echoes of Washington's Farewell Address would be heard in later statements of U.S. foreign policy, beginning with the Monroe Doctrine in 1823. While it has been used primarily by politicians and policymakers as proof of the desirability of isolationism, it should be remembered that the Farewell Address was a message to the U.S. people of 1796. Furthermore, Washington's concern was as much to bring about a Federalist victory in the upcoming election as it was to guide foreign policy for the nation for the next two centuries. The words of great leaders may be repeated and interpreted to serve a variety of political purposes, as the republication of Washington's Farewell Address in the early nineteenth century demonstrates.

—David H. Culbert, updated by Kelley Graham

ADDITIONAL READING:

Bowman, Albert Hall. *The Struggle for Neutrality: Franco-American Diplomacy During the Federalist Era.* Knoxville: University of Tennessee Press, 1974. A detailed study that places the Farewell Address in the larger context of Franco-American relations.

Flexner, James Thomas. *Washington: The Indispensable Man.* Boston: Little, Brown, 1974. Biography that discusses the conflict at the end of Washington's second term: his deep sense of responsibility for the nation and his strong desire to return to private life.

Gilbert, Felix. *To the Farewell Address: Ideas of Early American Foreign Policy.* Princeton, N.J.: Princeton University Press, 1961. An intellectual study of the Farewell Address as the culmination of eighteenth century political thought.

Kaufman, Burton Ira, ed. *Washington's Farewell Address: The View from the Twentieth Century.* Chicago: Quadrangle Books, 1969. A collection of articles on the Farewell Address and U.S. foreign policy through 1941, as well as the text of the address itself.

Paltsits, Victor Hugo, ed. *Washington's Farewell Address, in Facsimile, with Transliterations of All the Drafts of Washington, Madison, and Hamilton.* New York: New York Public Library, 1935. All the important drafts of the address and related correspondence are included, along with a history of its origin, its public reception, and a bibliography.

Schwartz, Barry. *George Washington: The Making of an American Symbol.* New York: Free Press, 1987. An exploration of the iconization of Washington, which is the key to understanding the lasting impact of his Farewell Address.

SEE ALSO: 1778, Franco-American Treaties; 1789, Washington's Inauguration; 1790's, First U.S. Political Parties; 1794, Jay's Treaty; 1797, XYZ Affair; 1798, Alien and Sedition Acts; 1823, Monroe Doctrine.

1797 ■ XYZ AFFAIR: *a request for a bribe leads to an undeclared war between France and the United States*

DATE: October 4, 1797-September 30, 1800

LOCALE: Paris, France; Philadelphia, Pennsylvania; Washington, D.C.

CATEGORIES: Diplomacy and international relations; Wars, uprisings, and civil unrest

KEY FIGURES:

John Adams (1735-1826), second president of the United States, 1797-1801

Elbridge Gerry (1744-1814), Massachusetts Republican, member of Adams' first mission to France

Alexander Hamilton (1757-1804), Federalist Party leader

John Marshall (1755-1835), Virginia Federalist, one of the delegates sent to deal with the Directory

Timothy Pickering (1745-1829), secretary of state, 1795-1800

Charles-Maurice de Talleyrand-Périgord, prince de Bénévent (1754-1838), French minister of foreign affairs under the Directory and the Consulate

SUMMARY OF EVENT. The presidency of John Adams of Massachusetts was not a happy one. Adams inherited all the problems of George Washington but none of his prestige. Franco-American relations with the French First Republic progressively worsened. Adams also faced dissension within his own party. Not all Federalists were satisfied when he was chosen as Washington's successor. Alexander Hamilton was known to have opposed Adams and would do so again in 1800. Adams did not help himself by retaining the Washington cabinet, composed of men with no particular loyalty to the new president. The overriding issue was the question of war or peace with France, but hardly less critical was the question of Adams' ability to control his own administration.

In the eyes of the French government, the United States, in signing Jay's Treaty (1795), had repudiated the Franco-American Alliance of 1778. The French charged that the acceptance of the treaty was an unneutral act, inasmuch as the United States had obviously accepted the British definition of neutral rights at sea. The French decided to break off normal relations with the United States. To give force to this action, the French subjected American vessels on the high seas to the same indignities so recently experienced at the hands of the British. In the year following July, 1796, the secretary of state, Timothy Pickering of Massachusetts, reported that the French had seized 316 U.S. vessels.

In an effort to forestall a complete break between the two nations, President Adams sent a three-man delegation to negotiate with the French. At the time of the mission there was no recognized American representative in France because the French had refused to receive Charles Cotesworth Pinckney (brother of Thomas), whom Washington had sent to France as the successor to James Monroe. Adams chose two distinguished Americans—Elbridge Gerry, a Massachusetts Repub-

lican, and John Marshall, a Virginia Federalist—to join with Pinckney in presenting the U.S. position to the French government. The three Americans were in Paris by October 4, 1797.

While Adams and the Federalists were determined to avoid war if at all possible, Adams called upon Congress to look to the defenses of the nation. Bills were introduced calling for the enlargement of the regular army, the creation of a provisional army of fifteen thousand men, the construction of three new frigates for the navy, and tax measures to pay for the preparedness program. The program ran into stiff opposition. The Republicans accused Adams and his party of warmongering and succeeded in defeating the army and tax bills.

The three Americans in Paris made no progress in their negotiations during several weeks in the city. When they were convinced that their mission was a failure, three representatives (the notorious Messrs. X, Y, and Z) from Charles-Maurice de Talleyrand-Périgord, the French minister of foreign affairs, approached them with certain demands as prerequisites to negotiation: President Adams was to apologize for certain statements in his last message to Congress, and the United States was to pay a sum of 1.2 million livres and make a loan of 32 million florins to the French, which was simply a demand for a bribe. The Americans, with no instructions relative to the payment of such a hugh sum of money, could do nothing but refuse. Pinckney and Marshall, convinced of the futility of remaining in France, took their departure. Gerry lingered in Paris in the hope of achieving something, but was soon recalled.

When news of this attempt by the French to dishonor the name of the United States was made public, Americans of virtually all political persuasions were united in condemning the insolence of the French. There were demands that the United States take immediate steps to defend its integrity. Some called for war; most shouted the slogan, "Millions for defense but not one cent for tribute." Congress declared that the treaties of alliance and friendship of 1778 with France were void and authorized public and private vessels of the United States to capture French armed ships on the high seas. The United States and France were dangerously close to war. In the spring of 1798, Congress created a Department of the Navy and appropriated funds to build warships. Preparations were made to raise an army of fifteen thousand men. During the next two years an undeclared war, or Half-War, as Adams called it, was waged against France. By 1800, the United States Navy, with the aid of hundreds of privateers, had successfully cleared U.S. waters of French cruisers and had even carried the naval warfare into the seas surrounding the French West Indies.

President Adams soon found himself in a difficult position. He was rapidly losing control of his own administration. Alexander Hamilton seemed to have more influence with Congress and the cabinet than did the president. Adams, a good New Englander, was basically opposed to the creation of a large standing army. He emphasized the navy as the United States' first line of defense. Hamilton and his supporters pushed army

John Adams, second president of the United States, inherited George Washington's foreign and domestic problems yet none of his prestige. A Federalist, Adams believed in a strong executive office that stood above, not in balance with, the legislative and judicial branches of government. In the wake of the XYZ affair Adams did manage to keep peace with France—though he split the Federalist Party in doing so. (Library of Congress)

legislation through Congress. The army was to be commanded by Washington, but until he actually took the field, Hamilton was to be in charge. Adams opposed Hamilton but could do nothing, since Washington made it clear that he would accept command only on his own terms. Adams, finally recognizing that his cabinet was disloyal, ultimately forced the resignations of Pickering and James McHenry, secretary of war. Adams also learned that the French government was then willing to negotiate seriously. With war fever high among certain Federalists, Adams opted for peace. Without consultation with his cabinet or the Federalist leadership, Adams submitted the name of an envoy to France.

This action precipitated a split in the Federalist Party. Adams did succeed in reopening negotiations with the French, although he was forced to accept a commission of three Federalists rather than the one individual he had nominated. By the time that the three commissioners reached France, Napoleon was First Consul. The settlement reached on September 30, 1800, in the Convention of 1800 (also known as the Treaty of Morfontaine) provided for the mutual abrogation of the Franco-American treaties of 1778, but that the United States was to receive no indemnity for the French seizures of U.S. merchant shipping. Although not entirely satisfactory to the United States, the agreement did end the undeclared war. The peace was popular with most Americans, but the rift that it caused between the supporters of the president and those of Hamilton seriously injured Adams' chances of reelection in 1800.

The XYZ affair would not have achieved the prominence it did had it not become enmeshed in U.S. party politics. Although the XYZ affair is often presented as a case study of U.S. virtue as opposed to Old World corruption, there is evidence that the Americans contributed to the sordidness of the affair. After having supported the Americans in their struggle for independence, the French had reason to be offended by Jay's Treaty, which favored the British in the war against France. The Federalist Party of President Adams was the party of property. The party as a whole despised and feared revolutionary France. Therefore, some Federalists saw an advantage to keeping the animosity toward France alive, even to the extent of war.

There is reason to question how serious the delegates, all Federalist appointees, were in seeking an accommodation with the French Directory. Were the Americans really surprised by the bribes? Some historians maintain that they were prepared to pay handsomely and that it was merely the greediness of the Directory's agents that offended them. Did the delegates, as Talleyrand later maintained, shut themselves in their hotel rooms and leave before they could be officially received? Were the dispatches written by Federalist John Marshall, released to Congress and the press in April of 1798, deliberately intended to inflame public opinion?

If the Federalists wanted war, Talleyrand was not willing to oblige. The last thing France needed, he warned the Directory, was another enemy. By the fall of 1798, the bribes had been forgotten and French vessels were ordered to respect American neutrality. The relieved Republicans saw the whole affair as a Federalist hoax. Adams was swept from power in the "Revolution of 1800"; the French Directory had suffered the same fate the year before at the hands of Napoleon Bonaparte. The XYZ affair was relegated to history, remembered only by a ringing slogan.   —*John G. Clark, updated by Nis Petersen*

ADDITIONAL READING:

Chinard, Gilbert. *Honest John Adams*. Boston: Little, Brown, 1933. A detailed short biography of the second U.S. president, discussing his efforts to deal with an almost treasonable cabinet and the support he received from his wife, Abigail.

DeConde, Alexander. *The Quasi-War: The Politics and Diplomacy of the Undeclared War with France, 1797-1801*. New York: Charles Scribner's Sons, 1966. Summarizes the war in the light of efforts of both the Americans and French to save face.

Elkins, Stanley, and Eric McKitrick. *The Age of Federalism*. New York: Oxford University Press, 1993. A thorough, understandable treatment of the XYZ affair.

Morison, S. E., H. S. Commager, and W. E. Leuchtenburg. "John Adams' Administration." In *The Growth of the American Republic*. 2 vols. 7th ed. New York: Oxford University Press, 1980. The authors, considered authorities on U.S. history, place the affair in historic perspective and offer some fresh insights.

Stinchcombe, William. *The XYZ Affair*. Westport, Conn.: Greenwood Press, 1980. A detailed, documented, standard account of the affair.

SEE ALSO: 1778, Franco-American Treaties; 1794, Jay's Treaty; 1798, Alien and Sedition Acts; 1801, Jefferson Is Elected President.

1798 ■ ALIEN AND SEDITION ACTS: *in the wake of the XYZ affair, Federalists exploit xenophobia to suppress dissent*

DATE: June 25-July 14, 1798

LOCALE: Philadelphia, Pennsylvania

CATEGORIES: Diplomacy and international relations; Immigration; Laws and acts

KEY FIGURES:

John Adams (1735-1826), second president of the United States, 1797-1801

William Duane (1760-1835), Republican editor of the Philadelphia *Aurora*, prosecuted under the Sedition Act

Albert Gallatin (1761-1849), Republican congressman from Pennsylvania who opposed the Alien and Sedition Acts

Thomas Jefferson (1743-1826), vice president of the United States and author of the Virginia Resolutions

Matthew Lyon (1750-1822), Republican congressman who was prosecuted under the Sedition Act

Timothy Pickering (1745-1829), secretary of state and chief enforcement officer of the Alien and Sedition Acts

Harrison Gray Otis (1765-1848), Federalist senator from Massachusetts, one of the chief architects of the Alien and Sedition Acts

SUMMARY OF EVENT. News of the XYZ affair descended upon the American people and their representatives in Congress like a thunderbolt. It galvanized the government into action on the high seas; it helped unite Americans against the French, just as the initial news of British seizures had united them against Great Britain; it seriously weakened the infant Republican Party, which was associated with Francophilism; and it firmly entrenched the Federalists in power. Even President John Adams, for a time, seemed to relish the thought of leading the United States against its newest antagonist, but Adams regained his sense of moderation in time to prevent a catastrophe. The same cannot be said of certain elements of the Federalist Party, which exploited the explosive situation to strike out at their political opponents.

The Federalist Party, or at least its old guard, deeply resented gains made by the Republican opposition. Many of the Federalist leaders resented the very existence of the other political party. The High Federalists were by no means committed to a two-party system and rejected the idea of a loyal opposition. With the Republican tide at low ebb, these Federalists intended to strike a killing blow at two sources of Republican strength: the immigrant vote and the manipulation of public opinion through the use (and abuse) of the press. In selecting these targets, the Federalists demonstrated an acute awareness of the impact of the press on the growth of political parties, and they intended to use their political power to muzzle the Republican press, while leaving the Federalist press intact. Furthermore, Federalists expressed a deep xenophobia, as they viewed people of foreign birth as threats to the fabric of ordered liberty they believed the Federalists had built and must preserve.

Many Federalists had a long history of antiforeign sentiment. With the United States on the verge of war with France, the Federalists were apprehensive over the loyalty of thousands of French West Indian refugees who had flocked to the United States in an effort to escape the ferment of the French Revolution and its accompanying "Terror." The Federalists were further concerned by the fact that the refugees who became U.S. citizens generally aligned themselves with the Republican Party. Much the same was true of the Irish, who supported anyone who opposed the English. Such conditions threatened the continued hold of the Federalists on political power in the national government. To deal with such potential subversives, foreign and domestic, the Federalist-controlled Congress passed a series of four acts, known collectively as the Alien and Sedition Acts.

Three of the acts dealt specifically with aliens or immigrants. The Sedition Act declared speech or writing with the intent to defame the president or Congress to be a misdemeanor. The Alien Act permitted the president to deport allegedly dangerous aliens during times of peace. Neither act was enforced, however. The Naturalization Act struck at the immigrant vote. Previously, aliens could become naturalized citizens after residing for five years in the United States. The new act raised the probationary period to fourteen years.

The Sedition Act was by far the most notorious. It imposed heavy fines and imprisonment as punishment on all those found guilty of writing, publishing, or speaking against the federal government. By allowing a defendant to prove the truth of statements as a defense, the Sedition Act was a definite improvement over the English laws of sedition libel. The fact remains, however, that its intent was the repression of political opposition and the annoying Republican press, and the Sedition Act seemed plainly to ignore the First Amendment. Under the law, suits were initiated against the editors of eight major opposition presses. The principal target was the Philadelphia *Aurora*, whose editor, William Duane, was prosecuted under the act. Congressman Matthew Lyon of Vermont received a jail sentence of four months and was fined one thousand dollars for disparaging remarks he made about President Adams. Some of these suits gave a comic air to the gross abuse of power. One gentleman was fined one hundred dollars for wishing out loud that the wadding of a salute cannon would strike President Adams in his backside.

Republican opposition to these laws was immediate. Vice President Thomas Jefferson, himself a Republican, believed that the Alien and Sedition Acts were designed to be used against such leading Republicans as the Swiss-born congressman from Pennsylvania, Albert Gallatin. Republicans were convinced that the Sedition Act was designed to destroy them as an organized political party. The act had passed the House strictly along sectional-party lines. The vote was forty-four to forty-one, with only two affirmative votes coming from south of the Potomac River, where the Republicans were strongest.

From the Federalist point of view, the acts were completely unsuccessful in suppressing the opposition. They were resented by many, and it soon became obvious even to those who first supported the new laws that they were as unnecessary as they were ineffective. The handful of "subversives" prosecuted under the Sedition Act hardly compensated for the fact that its existence gave the Republicans another campaign issue. Jefferson through the Kentucky legislature, and Madison through the Virginia legislature, penned immediate responses to the Alien and Sedition Acts. These remonstrances, known as the Virginia and Kentucky Resolves, aroused little enthusiasm at the time but did point out not only some of the basic principles of the Republican Party but also some striking differences between two streams of thought within the party.

Both resolutions maintained that the Constitution was a compact between sovereign states that granted to the federal government certain narrowly defined powers, while retaining all other enumerated powers. If the states created the Constitution, they had the power to decide when the federal government had overstepped its proper bounds. Jefferson, in the Kentucky Resolves, went much further than Madison in assigning to the states the power to nullify a federal law—to declare it inoperable and void within the boundaries of a state. South Carolina was to do so in 1832, when it nullified the Tariff of 1828. The

Virginia and Kentucky Resolves had no immediate effect, but they had spelled out the theoretical position that those advocating states' rights could, and ultimately did, take.

The Alien and Sedition Acts took their place among a growing list of grievances against the Federalist Party. The Alien Act expired in 1800 and the Sedition Act in the following year. The Naturalization Act was repealed by the Republican-controlled Congress in 1802. The only tangible effect of these measures was to contribute to the defeat of Federalism in 1800. However, the mood that led to their passage was to return in later days.

—John G. Clark, updated by Edward R. Crowther

ADDITIONAL READING:

Elkins, Stanley, and Eric McKitrick. *The Age of Federalism: The Early American Republic, 1788-1800.* New York: Oxford University Press, 1993. Chapter 15 of this gracefully written document captures the motives and mentalities of the principals responsible for the acts.

McCoy, Drew R. *The Elusive Republic: Political Economy in Jefferson's America.* Chapel Hill: University of North Carolina Press, 1980. Contains an excellent discussion of the competing theories of society and government bantered about by Federalists and Republicans.

Miller, John C. *Crisis in Freedom: The Alien and Sedition Acts.* Boston: Little, Brown, 1951. A thorough and judicious narrative of the passage of and response to the Alien and Sedition Acts.

Sharp, James Roger. *American Politics in the Early Republic: The New Nation in Crisis.* New Haven, Conn.: Yale University Press, 1993. Places the Alien and Sedition Acts in the context of paranoid politics during the 1790's.

Smith, James Morton. *Freedom's Fetters: The Alien and Sedition Laws and American Civil Liberties.* Ithaca, N.Y.: Cornell University Press, 1966. Contains the best discussion of the congressional debates over the passage of these laws.

SEE ALSO: 1790's, First U.S. Political Parties; 1797, XYZ Affair; 1801, Jefferson Is Elected President.

1799 ■ CODE OF HANDSOME LAKE:

Native American and Christian traditions merge to create the Longhouse religion, aimed at reviving indigenous cultures

DATE: 1799
LOCALE: Western New York State
CATEGORIES: Native American history; Religion
KEY FIGURES:

Cornplanter, also known as *John O'Bail* (c. 1732-1836), principal Seneca chief during the American Revolution, half brother of Handsome Lake

Louis Hall, also known as *Karoniaktajeh* (c. 1920-1993), Mohawk leader of Warrior Society; twentieth century critic of Handsome Lake

Handsome Lake, also known as *Ganeodiyo* (c. 1735-1815), Seneca founder of the Code of Handsome Lake

Arthur Parker (1881-1955), Seneca, ethnologist and historian of Handsome Lake's life and religion

Red Jacket, also known as *Sagoyewatha* (1751?-1830), principal Seneca chief; nephew of Handsome Lake

SUMMARY OF EVENT. The Code of Handsome Lake was one of several Native American religions that evolved in reaction to European colonization. These religions often combined traditional Native American beliefs and rituals with the introduction of a Christian-style savior who was said to be able to recapture for Native Americans the better days they had known before colonization. One well-known example of this fusion was the Ghost Dance religion, which was begun by the prophet Wovoka, who had been raised with both Native American and Christian influences. Tenskwatawa (also known as the Delaware Prophet) also formulated a religion that combined both traditions during the eighteenth century.

Handsome Lake was born at Conawagus, a Seneca village near contemporary Avon, New York, on the Genesee River. He was a member of the Seneca nation, one of the five nations that had joined together as the Iroquois Confederacy. His personal name was Ganeodiyo; Handsome Lake, a reference to Lake Ontario, is one of the fifty chieftainship lines of the Iroquois Confederacy, a title bestowed on him by clan mothers. He was a half brother of the Seneca chief Cornplanter and an uncle of Red Jacket. Handsome Lake and many other Senecas sided with the British in the French and Indian War and the American Revolution. George Washington and his subcommanders, principally General John Sullivan, were merciless with Native Americans who supported the British. During the late stages of the revolution, many Seneca communities were laid waste by scorched-earth marches that destroyed crops, livestock, and homes.

After that war, many Iroquois and other Native Americans who had supported the British were forced into Canada, principally to lands secured by Joseph Brant at Grand River. Others fled westward to join other Native Americans who were still free. Those who remained in their homelands were forced onto small, impoverished reservations, and repeated attempts were made to force them out. It is estimated that by 1794, the Iroquois population had shrunk to approximately four thousand people.

Handsome Lake's revival occurred in an atmosphere of dissension within a fractured Iroquois Confederacy. The course of his life reflected the devastation of his people. Born into a prominent family of the Turtle Clan, Handsome Lake distinguished himself as a leader as a young man, before the American Revolution, when Iroquois society was still largely intact. Handsome Lake's decline began after his birthplace was taken by whites, and he was forced to move to the Allegheny Seneca reservation. The Seneca ethnologist Arthur Parker characterized Handsome Lake as a middle-sized man, unhealthy looking, dissolute, and an alcoholic. After four years lying ill in a small cabin under the care of a daughter, Handsome Lake began having a series of visions. Later, he used these visions to rally the Iroquois at a time when some of them were selling their entire winter harvest of furs for hard liquor, turning traditional ceremonies into drunken brawls, and in winter, often dying of exposure in drunken stupors.

Handsome Lake experienced considerable remorse over his alcoholism, but did not stop drinking until he was nearly dead. In 1799, Handsome Lake experienced a number of visions in which he was taken on a great journey to the sky. During this journey, he was shown a number of personages and events from the past, present, and future. In one of his visions, Handsome Lake met George Washington, who had died that year, and heard him confirm the sovereignty of the Iroquois.

After this series of visions, Handsome Lake stopped his heavy drinking and later committed his code to writing. He persuaded many other Iroquois to stop drinking and to reconstruct their lives. During his own lifetime, Handsome Lake achieved some political influence among the Senecas, but his popularity was limited because of his ideological rigidity. In 1801 and 1802, he traveled to Washington, D.C., with a delegation of Senecas to meet with President Thomas Jefferson and resist the reduction of Iroquois landholdings.

The Code of Handsome Lake combines European religious influences (especially those practiced by the Quakers, which Handsome Lake had studied) with a traditional Iroquois emphasis on family, community, and the centrality of the land to the maintenance of culture. Handsome Lake's largest following came after his death. Adherents to his code rejected alcohol and accepted his concepts of social relationships, good, and evil, which closely resemble Quakerism. The Quaker creed appealed to many Iroquois because the Quakers had been persecuted before coming to America, they had no ornate temples, and they lived frugally and communally, doing their best to respect their Native American neighbors.

A nationalistic figure in a religious context, Handsome Lake also borrowed heavily from the Iroquois Great Law of Peace, popularizing concepts such as looking into the future for seven generations and regarding the earth as mother, ideas that became part of pan-Indian thought across North America and were incorporated into late twentieth century popular environmental symbolism. With its combination of Old and New World theologies, the Code of Handsome Lake sought to reconcile the gods of Europe and America. It was to be so successful that it both subsumed the ancient religion and halted the spread of Christianity among the Iroquois. The Code of Handsome Lake has continued to be widely followed in Iroquois country as the Longhouse religion. In the late twentieth century, roughly a third of the thirty thousand Iroquois in New York State attended Longhouse rites.

Although his code remained popular among many Iroquois, others accused Handsome Lake of having sold out to the Quakers and white religious interests in general. Louis Hall, ideological founder of the Warrior Society in Iroquois country, regarded the religion of Handsome Lake as a bastardized form of Christianity grafted onto native traditions. Hall called

Handsome Lake's visions "the hallucinations of a drunk." Opposition to these teachings is one plank in an intellectual platform that allows the Warriors to brand both the Mohawk Nation Council at Akwesasne and the Iroquois Confederacy Council as enemies of the people, and to claim that the Warriors are the true protectors of "Mohawk sovereignty." Hall, who died in 1993, regarded Handsome Lake's followers as traitors or "Tontos." Hall's Warriors split bitterly with followers of Handsome Lake over gambling and other issues, leading to violence at Akwesasne, which peaked in 1990 with the deaths of two Mohawks. —Bruce E. Johansen

ADDITIONAL READING:

Deardorff, Merle H. *The Religion of Handsome Lake: Its Origins and Development*. American Bureau of Ethnology Bulletin 149. Washington, D.C.: Smithsonian Institution Press, 1951. Presents a detailed analysis of the Handsome Lake religion from an ethnographic perspective.

Handsome Lake. *The Code of Handsome Lake, the Seneca Prophet*. New York State Museum Bulletin 163. Albany: University of the State of New York, 1913. Outlines the Handsome Lake religion and discusses the historical circumstances of its creation.

Johansen, Bruce E. *Life and Death in Mohawk Country*. Golden, Colo.: North American Press, 1993. Details conflicts involving followers of Handsome Lake's code and Louis Hall's Warriors at Akwesasne in the late twentieth century.

Parker, Arthur. *Parker on the Iroquois*. Edited by William Fenton. Syracuse, N.Y.: Syracuse University Press, 1968. A detailed description of the Handsome Lake religion by a noted Seneca ethnologist.

Wallace, Anthony F. C. *The Death and Rebirth of the Seneca*. New York: Alfred A. Knopf, 1970. A classic work on the history of the Seneca at the time of Handsome Lake.

Wright, Ronald. *Stolen Continents*. Boston: Houghton Mifflin, 1992. A wide-ranging study of North America since the voyages of Columbus. Contains extensive treatment of the Iroquois Confederacy; describes Handsome Lake and his religion in the general context of the subjugation of the confederacy after the Revolutionary War.

SEE ALSO: 1500, Iroquois Confederacy; 1776, Indian Delegation Meets with Congress; 1784, Fort Stanwix Treaty; 1808, Prophetstown Is Founded.

1801 ■ JEFFERSON IS ELECTED PRESIDENT: *a bloodless transfer of power from one political party to another signifies the success of the new two-party system*

DATE: February 17, 1801
LOCALE: United States
CATEGORY: Government and politics
KEY FIGURES:
John Adams (1735-1826), second president of the United States, 1797-1801

Thomas Jefferson, in a portrait by Thomas Sully. Jefferson's ascension to the presidency proved for the first time in the new republic's history that a peaceful transfer of power from one political party to another was possible under the Constitution. (Library of Congress)

James A. Bayard (1767-1815), Federalist congressman from
Delaware

Aaron Burr (1756-1836), Republican vice presidential
candidate in 1800

Alexander Hamilton (1755-1804), Federalist leader in New
York

Thomas Jefferson (1743-1826), third president of the United
States, 1801-1809

Charles Cotesworth Pinckney (1746-1825), Federalist vice
presidential candidate in 1800

SUMMARY OF EVENT. The presidential campaign of 1800
pitted President John Adams against Vice President Thomas
Jefferson, an old adversary and an older friend. Adams had
defeated Jefferson in 1796 by the slim margin of three electoral
votes. New England seemed to be solidly Federalist and the
South seemed to be solidly Republican. The critical states were
Pennsylvania and New York. Jefferson had carried Pennsylvania in 1796; he hoped to maintain his position there and to win
New York to his side. South Carolina was also an important
state, for the Federalists enjoyed strong support there.

Deteriorating relations with France dominated the Adams
Administration, coming to a showdown over the XYZ affair—a
diplomatic incident in which corrupt French officials surreptitiously demanded an apology, a large loan, and bribes from the
United States. The Federalists were able to parlay U.S. indignation over the XYZ affair into strong political support for their
program. Many Federalists—including Adams, for a time, in
1798-1799—were willing to declare war or force a declaration
of war from France. Influential, well-to-do Federalist political
activists (called High Federalists) who often distrusted President Adams, a Federalist himself, realized that their continued
popularity depended on maintaining public opinion at a high
emotional level against the French. For a time, in 1799, it
seemed that the Republicans, damned by their opponents as
pro-French, were out of the running in 1800. However, as the
popular mood changed, as the war fever declined, as opposition to the military program and taxes increased, and as Adams
himself became less aggressive, Republican chances propor-
tionately improved. When the president suddenly decided to
send a new peace mission to France, the High Federalists realized that they were doomed. Peace was now the major theme.
The Republicans had been committed to peace all along.

Adams' peace policy split the Federalist Party. Alexander
Hamilton attacked the president directly and schemed to replace him. The Republicans, united behind Jefferson, applied
themselves diligently to capturing the critical middle states,
such as New York and Pennsylvania. As the outcome proved,
the Republicans were more efficiently organized than the Federalists.

In 1800, the popular vote occurred in the states at various
times during October and November. In the majority of states,
the state legislatures, not the voters, selected the presidential
electors. Significantly, while the Federalists maintained control over the national government, in 1800 the Republicans
controlled a majority of the state governments.

In New York, for example, Aaron Burr was the Republican
leader and Hamilton directed the opposition. At stake was the
composition of the state legislature. The party that captured
this body would control the twelve electoral votes cast by New
York. Burr completely outmaneuvered Hamilton, and the Republicans captured a majority in the lower house, thus giving
them a majority of one in the combined vote of both houses.
This defeat deflated the hopes of the Federalists. The Republicans staved off an energetic Federalist campaign in South
Carolina and brought Jefferson home the victor by eight electoral votes. This margin was not particularly impressive, but it
did represent a significant shift of party strength in the crucial
middle states. The Republican Party did not penetrate New
England, but John Adams did improve his position in some
Southern states. President Adams, in spite of a serious split in
his own party, looked stronger in 1800 than he had in 1796.

The Federalist Party had a second opportunity to prevent
the election of the "atheistic, Jacobinic, democratic" Jefferson.
In 1800, the electors did not distinguish between the president
and the vice president in casting their votes. The man who
received the highest number of votes became president, and
the runner-up became vice president. In a display of party
unity, each Republican elector cast a vote for Jefferson and a
vote for Burr, the vice presidential candidate on the Republican ticket. The resulting tie meant that the decision would be
made in the House of Representatives, with each state casting
one vote. A sufficient number of Federalists preferred Burr so
as to make Jefferson's election dubious.

Hamilton, whose dislike of the devious Burr later caused
the famous duel in which Hamilton lost his life, preferred and
supported Jefferson in the House. The Federalist Party ignored
Hamilton's advice, in the hope that a prolonged contest would
damage the Republican Party and perhaps postpone the transfer of power. The Federalists also sought some guarantees
from both candidates regarding their plans for the future, but
neither Jefferson nor Burr would commit himself. Finally,
after thirty-five ballots, James Bayard, the lone representative
from Delaware, decided to switch this vote, and thus his state's
support, to Jefferson. Finally, on February 17, 1801, the nation
had a president-elect.

Jefferson considered the election of 1800 "as real a revolution in the principles of our government as that of 1776 was in
its form." Jefferson's view was supported by some Federalists.
Many High Federalists were positive that Jefferson would lead
the nation into chaos and anarchy. However, Jefferson, in his
inaugural address, spoke of conciliation and moderation rather
than revolution.

The most concrete issue separating Adams from Jefferson's
policy toward France evaporated when Adams came out for
peace. Jefferson, in later days, charged Adams with monarchist
and antirepublican tendencies. There was little substance to
those charges. Jefferson did articulate a greater confidence in
popular government than did Adams, and the former was more
suspicious of centralist tendencies in government. Both men
were nationalists, however, devoted to representative govern-

ment, determined to disengage the United States from European politics, and convinced of the future greatness of the republic. In 1800, although Adams did lose to Jefferson, he also defeated the High Federalists in his own party. In so doing, Adams closed the already narrow gap between him and Jefferson.

Historians consider the political campaign and election of 1800 to be highly significant. The election ushered in the basic strategies of modern electoral campaigning. Jefferson, in particular, was instrumental in clearly defining the principles and objectives of Republicanism. He and his associates effectively used the press and pamphleteers to disseminate their appeals to farmers, laborers, and townsfolk.

More important, the election of 1800 demonstrated that the peaceful transfer of political power between rival ideologies was possible without bloodshed or revolution. The Federalists—the party that favored a strong centralized government and served the needs of rich merchants, speculators, and landed gentry—gave way to Republicans, later called Democratic Republicans and the forerunner of the modern Democratic Party.

Under the Republican banner, Jefferson campaigned in 1800 on a platform calling for change: promoting individual and political liberties, safeguarding states' rights against an encroaching central government, protecting the freedoms of press and religion, ensuring the right to dissent and criticize government, and encouraging free trade abroad but avoiding inappropriate alliances with European powers. During his two-term administration, Jefferson tried to keep those campaign promises. —*John G. Clark, updated by Richard Whitworth*

ADDITIONAL READING:

Cunningham, Noble E. *In Pursuit of Reason: The Life of Thomas Jefferson.* Baton Rouge: Louisiana State University Press, 1987. Details Jefferson's public carer. Provides critical resources on Jefferson's faith in human reason, progress, and education.

Elkins, Stanley, and Eric McKitrick. *The Age of Federalism.* New York: Oxford University Press, 1993. Re-creates the political climate in the 1790's, leading up the election of 1800. Focuses on the conflicting visions of Alexander Hamilton and Thomas Jefferson.

Mayer, David N. *The Constitutional Thought of Thomas Jefferson.* Charlottesville: University Press of Virginia, 1994. Shows how Jefferson's constitutional thinking evolved from Whig to Federalist to Republican. Scholarly but highly readable.

Peterson, Merrill D. *Thomas Jefferson and the New Nation: A Biography.* New York: Oxford University Press, 1970. A basic narrative of Jefferson's life. Sections 8 and 9 provide useful information on the election of 1800. Numerous illustrations, diagrams, and portraits.

Randall, Willard S. *Thomas Jefferson: A Life.* New York: Henry Holt, 1993. Challenges the assumptions offered by earlier scholars on the influences of Jefferson's revolutionary political thinking.

Risjord, Norman K. *Thomas Jefferson.* Madison, Wis.: Madison House, 1994. A concise bundling of existing scholarship on Jefferson's evolving political philosophy, along with Risjord's own view that Jefferson never successfully developed a coherent ideology.

Tucker, Robert, and David Hendrickson. *Empire of Liberty: The Statecraft of Thomas Jefferson.* New York: Oxford University Press, 1990. Examines Jefferson's ideas, and his impact on U.S. foreign policy. Useful in understanding the United States response to the world at large.

SEE ALSO: 1790's, First U.S. Political Parties; 1797, XYZ Affair; 1798, Alien and Sedition Acts.

1802 ■ U.S. Military Academy Is Established: *the first military academy and the nation's first engineering school helps erode Federalist domination of the army officer corps*

DATE: March 16, 1802
LOCALE: West Point, New York
CATEGORIES: Education; Organizations and institutions
KEY FIGURES:
John Adams (1735-1826), second president of the United States, 1797-1801
Henry Dearborn (1751-1829), secretary of war under President Jefferson
Alexander Hamilton (1757-1804), Federalist and leading proponent of a military academy
Thomas Jefferson (1743-1826), third president of the United States, 1801-1809
Henry Knox (1750-1806), General Washington's chief of artillery and the first secretary of war
James McHenry (1753-1816), secretary of war under President John Adams
George Washington (1732-1799), first president of the United States, 1789-1797, a persistent advocate of a military academy

SUMMARY OF EVENT. Even after emerging victorious from the Revolutionary War, the United States faced hostile forces from all directions. Monarchical European countries to the east were eager for the American experiment in democracy to collapse. Indians menaced settlement and further advancement in the American West. British Canada occupied the territory to the north and Spain the land to the south and southwest. The new nation obviously needed a system of national defense. Yet a traditional, strong suspicion of standing armies dated back to England's civil war in the seventeenth century. A large number of Americans feared an aristocracy as the most formidable threat to their democracy; aristocracies, they believed, had their roots in standing armies. Some Americans thought an army of citizen-soldiers led by a trained officer corps might be the answer. The disloyal actions by Continental Army officers at Newburgh in the winter of 1782-1783 and the elitist, self-perpetuating, and politically dangerous Society of Cincinnati formed by Colonel Henry Knox, George Washington's chief of artillery, and other army officers at the end of the Revolutionary War underscored concerns of those who feared the creation of a military officer class.

Knox was one of the first advocates of a military academy. In 1783, Washington had called for the establishment of one or more academies for instruction in the military arts. No action was taken, and by 1785, the army had dwindled to fewer than one hundred officers and men. In 1790, the government purchased the fort of West Point on the Hudson River for $11,085, at a time when the United States seemed to be once again on the brink of becoming involved in war. France, the United States' ally, was at war with Great Britain and Spain, and it was apparent that the United States would have to bolster its national defenses in order to remain neutral. On May 7, 1794, Congress authorized an increase in the Corps of Artillerists and Engineers at West Point. Congress also established the rank of cadet for junior officers assigned to West Point to be trained in the arts of war. With other duties absorbing most of their time, however, the cadets received little training. The war in Europe continued to mount, bringing pressures not only to enlarge the army drastically but also to found a military academy. On July 16, 1798, Congress empowered President John Adams to appoint four teachers for the purpose of instructing the cadets and young officers in the Corps of Artillerists and Engineers, but no qualified teachers were found.

At this juncture, after years of failure, Federalist leader Alexander Hamilton informed the secretary of war, James McHenry, that the United States needed a system of military education, including a school at West Point, another for artillerists and engineers, a third for cavalry and infantry, and a fourth for the navy. Students would attend West Point for two years and then spend two more years at one of the other schools. Washington echoed this sentiment, writing shortly before his death that "the Establishment of an Institution of this kind . . . has ever been considered by me as an Object of primary importance to this Country." McHenry received further advice in the form of a memorandum prepared by Louis de Tousard, a major in the First Regiment of Artillerists and Engineers. In January, 1800, McHenry consolidated the recommendations of Hamilton and Major Tousard; President Adams sent this plan to Congress. Congress again did nothing, chiefly because of the real fear among Republicans that a trained corps of officers would threaten democracy. The use of federal troops in Pennsylvania during the so-called Fries Rebellion in 1799 had underscored Thomas Jefferson's opposition to the enlarged army Congress had authorized in 1798 and its potential to act as a domestic "spanking army."

Some historians believe that the final impetus for the establishment of the United States Military Academy was the desire for a national university emphasizing science over the classics. Thomas Jefferson, who became president in 1801, was a leading advocate of more empirical courses in higher education.

He believed that a military academy could fill this role and might also be supported by those who would oppose the idea of a national university. More important, Jefferson was concerned deeply with the domination of the army officer corps by Federalists and saw a military academy as a way to break Federalist power within the military by the appointment of politically reliable (Republican) candidates into the army officer corps.

On March 16, 1802, Congress passed the Military Peace Establishment Act, which enabled the president to establish a corps of engineers stationed at West Point and constituting a military academy. After years of efforts by Knox, Washington, Hamilton, and others, a law had finally been enacted that acknowledged the need for such a civilian-controlled academy emphasizing training in the military arts.

In concert with his secretary of war, Henry Dearborn, Jefferson attempted to purge the officer corps of Federalists by restructuring and initially reducing the size of the officer corps. It was rebuilt with Antifederalist cadets drawn from Republican stock and trained at the U.S. Military Academy.

—*William M. Tuttle, updated by William M. McBride*

ADDITIONAL READING:

Ambrose, Stephen. *Duty, Honor, Country: A History of West Point*. Baltimore: The Johns Hopkins University Press, 1966. A comprehensive, readable account of the history of the U.S. Military Academy prior to the Vietnam War.

Crackel, Theodore J. *Mr. Jefferson's Army: Political and Social Reform of the Military Establishment, 1801-1809*. New York: New York University Press, 1987. A well-argued, well-documented study of Jefferson's attempts to "republicanize" the army officer corps.

Dupuy, R. Ernest. *Men of West Point: The First 150 Years of the United States Military Academy*. New York: William Sloan Associates, 1951. A sesquicentennial tribute to the U.S. Military Academy.

Forman, Sidney. *West Point: A History of the United States Military Academy*. New York: Columbia University Press, 1950. A history of West Point from its beginnings as a fortification on the Hudson River to its transition to a military academy.

Kohn, Richard H. *Eagle and Sword: The Federalists and the Creation of the Military Establishment in America, 1783-1802*. New York: Free Press, 1975. A contextual study useful for understanding the founding of West Point.

SEE ALSO: 1790's, First U.S. Political Parties.

1803 ■ MARBURY V. MADISON: *the U.S. Supreme Court establishes the right of judicial review*

DATE: February 24, 1803
LOCALE: Washington, D.C.
CATEGORIES: Court cases; Government and politics

KEY FIGURES:

John Adams (1735-1826), second president of the United States, 1797-1801

Thomas Jefferson (1743-1826), third president of the United States, 1801-1809

James Madison (1751-1836), secretary of state, who was ordered by Thomas Jefferson to withhold Marbury's commission

William Marbury (1761?-1835), man appointed justice of the peace by John Adams, whose commission James Madison refused to deliver

John Marshall (1755-1835), chief justice of the United States

SUMMARY OF EVENT. Although it has been a fundamental principle of constitutional interpretation, the power of judicial review is not mentioned explicitly in the Constitution. The first clear case in which the Supreme Court, guided by the spirit of the Constitution's provisions, declared a congressional act void was *Marbury v. Madison.*

To John Adams, in 1801, the transfer of presidential power to Thomas Jefferson signaled a virtual revolution in United States political life. The Jeffersonian Republican Party represented to Adams and the Federalists not just a different political party, which had opposed their stewardship of the federal government, but also the enemy of that government. The campaign of 1800 had been marked by almost hysterical appeals on both sides. The Federalists had identified themselves with government under the Constitution; the Republicans seemed to call for a radical change in the nature of that government. As the inauguration of Jefferson neared, the Federalists feared that their work of more than a decade in establishing a strong, viable government under the Constitution was in jeopardy, for Jefferson was sweeping into office a Republican Congress. The defeated John Adams attempted to maintain some of his party's power by appointing sixteen new circuit judges to strengthen the Federalist complexion of the federal bench.

Adams appointed and the Senate confirmed his secretary of state, John Marshall, to the vacant position of chief justice, while Congress reduced the size of the Supreme Court from six to five members upon the occasion of the next vacancy. Thus, Jefferson was presented with a court headed by a political enemy and a membership he might not be able to influence before the end of his term. Congress also authorized Adams to appoint up to fifty justices of the peace for the District of Columbia. Their appointments had been approved by the Senate, but Adams and Marshall did not have all the commissions delivered before the expiration of Adams' term on March 4, 1801, and the ensuing change of administration.

William Marbury, one of Adams' appointees, sued in the Supreme Court in December, 1801, for a writ of mandamus (an ancient common-law writ compelling a corporation, government official, or lower court to perform a particular duty required by law) requiring Jefferson's secretary of state, James Madison, to deliver his commission. Marbury cited Section 13 of the Judiciary Act of 1789, which compels the secretary of state to perform the office's duty under the law.

In its review of the case, Chief Justice Marshall, speaking for the Supreme Court, declared that Marbury indeed had a right to the commission that should be delivered to him, but that Marbury could not obtain from the Court a writ of mandamus ordering its delivery, because the Court did not have the power to issue such a writ. Section 13 of the Judiciary Act of 1789, which had added authority to the original jurisdiction of the Supreme Court, was void because it violated Article II of the Constitution. The original jurisdiction of the Supreme Court (when the Court acts as a trial court) was limited to cases "affecting ambassadors, other public ministers and consuls, and those in which a state is a party." Because Marbury was in none of those categories, and there was no mention of the authority to issue writs of mandamus at the trial level, the Court refused to assume jurisdiction over his case, despite the fact that Congress granted the Court such power is Section 13 of the Judiciary Act of 1789. In short, Marbury was requesting that the Court exercise an appellate function that was beyond its jurisdiction. Because the Judiciary Act of 1789 conflicted with the Constitution as the supreme law of the land, the former must be declared unconstitutional. Although Congress had passed a law, the Supreme Court had essentially reviewed and, in this case, rejected it. The principle of judicial review had been born.

The rule in *Marbury v. Madison* has been cited on countless occasions by the courts since 1803. To support his position that the Supreme Court could invalidate laws of Congress, Marshall relied heavily on the arguments of Alexander Hamilton in supporting the doctrines of judicial review as set forth in *The Federalist* No. 78. The argument stated that it is the duty of judges, where there is doubt, to say what the law in a particular case is. The Constitution is the supreme law. If, therefore, in the consideration of a case, the Supreme Court finds a conflict between the law as passed by Congress and the supreme law as stated in the Constitution, it must, under its constitutional oath, apply the supreme law. Although the Court would not exercise this power again until the case of *Dred Scott v. Sandford* in 1857, when the Court declared unconstitutional the Missouri Compromise Act of 1820, which excluded slaves from the territories, Marshall had succeeded in securing for the Court a preeminent position in the interpretation of the Constitution.

—Edward J. Maguire, updated by Marcia J. Weiss

ADDITIONAL READING:

Barber, Sotirios A. *On What the Constitution Means.* Baltimore: The Johns Hopkins University Press, 1984. A scholarly approach to the Constitution as an entire document interpreted as an expression of ideals and a commitment to ethics and morality in society.

Choper, Jesse, H. *Judicial Review and the National Political Process: A Functional Reconsideration of the Role of the Supreme Court.* Chicago: University of Chicago Press, 1980. Advances the thesis that, although judicial review is incompatible with democracy, the Supreme Court must exercise that power when individual rights need protection within the political process. Otherwise, the Court should decline to exercise its authority, thereby reducing conflict between majoritarian de-

James Madison. As secretary of state under the new President Jefferson, Madison was ordered not to deliver judicial commissions to several judges whom the outgoing president, John Adams, had appointed in order to preserve Federalist power in the government. When one of those appointees, William Marbury, sued for delivery of his commission by Madison in accordance with the Judiciary Act of 1789, the Supreme Court ruled that Marbury had a right to his commission but that it was unconstitutional for the Court to compel delivery of that commission, thereby establishing the principle of judicial review.
(Library of Congress)

mocracy and judicial review. Includes references to cases and secondary legal materials.

Clinton, Robert Lowry. *"Marbury v. Madison" and Judicial Review*. Lawrence: University Press of Kansas, 1989. A review of sources that this author believes have wrongly interpreted the principle of judicial review in *Marbury v. Madison*. Extensive notes and bibliography.

Corwin, Edward Samuel, and J. W. Peltason. *Corwin and Peltason's Understanding the Constitution*. 11th ed. New York: Holt, Rinehart and Winston, 1988. A succinct general overview of the Constitution emphasizing federalism, separation of powers, judicial review, and the Constitution's central structure and amendments.

Currie, David P. *The Constitution of the United States: A Primer for the People*. Chicago: University of Chicago Press, 1988. A well-documented resource, written for educated lay readers, with case references on central provisions of the Constitution.

Ely, John Hart. *Democracy and Distrust: A Theory of Judicial Review*. Cambridge, Mass.: Harvard University Press, 1980. Sets forth a new theory of constitutional interpretation based on principles of constitutional law. Detailed notes and citations.

Snowiss, Sylvia. *Judicial Review and the Law of the Constitution*. New Haven, Conn.: Yale University Press, 1990. A review of the historical intent and the debate surrounding judicial review, and the controversy concerning whether the Framers intended to establish judicial review.

Wolfe, Christopher. *The Rise of Modern Judicial Review: From Constitutional Interpretation to Judge-Made Law*. New York: Basic Books, 1986. Describes and documents the transformation of constitutional interpretation and judicial power, from its initial understanding by the Founders to a natural rights theory and, ultimately, to an expansive and discretionary approach. Includes references to secondary sources and case law.

SEE ALSO: 1789, Judiciary Act.

1803 ■ LOUISIANA PURCHASE: *the United States doubles its size and secures new western borders*

DATE: May 9, 1803
LOCALE: Paris, France, and Washington, D.C.
CATEGORIES: Expansion and land acquisition; Treaties and agreements
KEY FIGURES:
François de Barbé-Marbois (1745-1837), Napoleon's minister of finance
Thomas Jefferson (1743-1826), third president of the United States, 1801-1809
René Robert Cavelier, sieur de La Salle (1643-1687), French explorer of Louisiana, who claimed the area for France and named it

Robert R. Livingston (1746-1813), U.S. minister to France
James Madison (1751-1836), Jefferson's secretary of state
James Monroe (1758-1831), envoy whom Jefferson sent to Paris to assist Livingston in negotiating for the purchase
Juan Ventura Morales, Spanish intendant of Louisiana at New Orleans
Napoleon I, Bonaparte (1769-1821), First Consul of France
Pierre Dominique Toussaint L'Ouverture (1743-1803), leader of the slave revolt in Santo Domingo

SUMMARY OF EVENT. The first Europeans to explore Louisiana were the Spanish in the sixteenth century, but they failed to occupy the area effectively. In 1682, the French explorer René Robert Cavelier, sieur de La Salle, claimed the region for France and named it in honor of King Louis XIV. Louisiana remained French territory until near the end of the Seven Years' War (French and Indian War) in 1763, when France ceded it to Spain in return for its help in the war against Great Britain and its allies and to compensate Spain for the loss of the Floridas. In the late 1790's, France began to rebuild its empire in the Western Hemisphere, and by the secret Treaty of San Ildefonso of October 1, 1800, Spain ceded Louisiana back to France.

Reports of the transfer of Louisiana, and perhaps even the Floridas, from Spain to France began to reach the United States in the spring of 1801. The Jefferson Administration viewed this transfer with some alarm, because a powerful and aggressive Napoleonic France in control of the mouth of the Mississippi River would constitute a much graver threat to U.S. rights on that vital artery of commerce and communication than did weak and declining Spain's presence there.

Secretary of State James Madison instructed Robert R. Livingston, the U.S. minister to Paris, to investigate the continuing rumors. If they proved to be true, Livingston was to try to acquire the Floridas (or at least West Florida) if they were part of the cession. If Spain had not ceded them to France, the United States would attempt to obtain them from Spain. Livingston learned that France had acquired Louisiana and New Orleans, but not the Floridas. His discussions with the French government were otherwise inconclusive.

On October 16, 1802, the Spanish intendant of Louisiana at New Orleans, Juan Ventura Morales, issued a proclamation withdrawing from the United States the right to deposit goods at New Orleans, as the Pinckney Treaty of 1795 with Spain had provided. This meant that U.S. ships coming down the Mississippi River could no longer unload their goods at New Orleans for reloading aboard oceangoing vessels for shipment to the East Coast or to foreign ports. The United States blamed the French for this decision, although France had not yet taken possession of Louisiana.

When news of the suspension reached the Westerners, who depended on the Mississippi River and the use of the port of New Orleans as their commercial lifeline, they were greatly aroused, as were their spokespersons in Congress. There was a real possibility that Westerners might march on New Orleans and seize it. In response to their demands for action to protect

TERRITORY OF THE UNITED STATES IN 1803

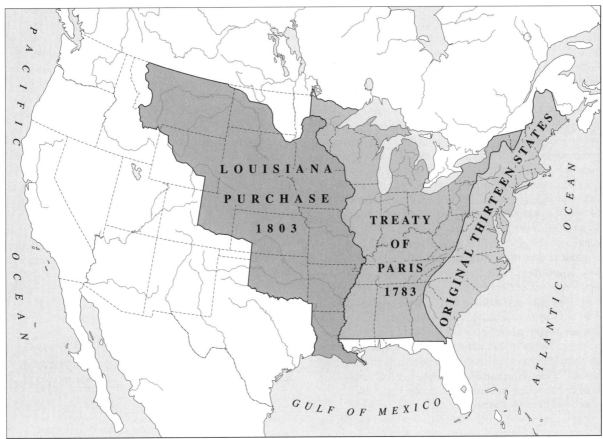

U.S. rights on the Mississippi River and at New Orleans, President Thomas Jefferson sent James Monroe as his envoy to France to help Livingston in the negotiations with the French government. Livingston and Monroe were supposed to try to acquire at most only New Orleans and the Floridas, should they belong to France, and the right of the free navigation of the Mississippi River.

Napoleon's plans for the restoration of the French empire in America depended on subjugation of the slaves on the West Indian island of Santo Domingo (Hispaniola) who were in revolt under the leadership of Pierre Dominique Toussaint L'Ouverture. The sugar, coffee, indigo, and cotton produced on this island were important to the French economy, and the island might serve as a staging ground for any projected French invasion of the North American continent. If the French could not control the island, Louisiana would be of little value to Napoleon. At the end of 1802, despite the expenditure of many lives, thousands of French troops, and enormous sums of money, the slaves were far from subdued, and Santo Domingo was in ruins. Napoleon decided to abandon it. As Louisiana would have been mainly a granary and supply region for that island, it would be of minimal worth to France. Napoleon, therefore, elected to sell Louisiana to the United States.

Napoleon had several other reasons for the sale. Determined to resume war against Great Britain and other European powers, Napoleon needed funds to restock his army after the military debacle in Santo Domingo. He feared that, in an international war, Great Britain might take Louisiana from France. He thought he could forestall the formation of an alliance between the United States and Great Britain, and even perhaps build up the United States as a rival that would check British expansion. He probably also was aware of the difficulties that Spain had had in dealing with the numerous Native American tribes in the region since 1762 and expected that France might have no better luck. Finally, he could avert a war with an expanding United States, set to empower the president to seize New Orleans.

On April 11, 1803, Napoleon ordered his minister of finance, the marquis de Barbé-Marbois, to negotiate the sale of the whole territory of Louisiana, not just New Orleans and its environs. Although they had no authorization to purchase all Louisiana, Livingston and Monroe entered into the bargaining and, after some haggling over price, came to terms. The negotiations ended by May 9, although the treaty and two conventions comprising the agreement bore the date April 30. The United States had acquired Louisiana, including New Orleans, but with its boundaries otherwise vaguely defined. In return, the United States would pay approximately $15 million, assume the debts that French citizens owed to the United States (roughly one quarter of the purchase price), and incorporate the inhabitants of Louisiana, except indigenous people and slaves, as citizens of the United States. The news reached the United States around July 4, adding extra jubilation to the patriotic mood on the nation's independence day.

Although Jefferson had some grave doubts about the constitutionality of the purchase, as the Constitution did not expressly grant the president or Congress the power to acquire foreign territory, he approved it. He mulled over the idea of proposing an amendment to legitimize the purchase and any future territorial acquisition. After further reflection—and the realization that, except for a few Federalists who worried that the nation would grow too large for an effective democracy, the majority of Congress and the people of the United States enthusiastically supported the purchase—Jefferson drew on a so-called Higher Laws doctrine and found enough constitutional justification in the Preamble. The Senate ratified the agreements on October 20, and the president proclaimed them to be in effect the next day. The transfer of the southern portion of the territory from Spain to France (despite the Treaty of San Ildefonso) occurred on November 30, 1803, and from France to the United States on December 20. The northern segment was transferred to the United States on March 10, 1804, the day after Spain had returned it to France. A little less than a year after Napoleon had proposed the sale, Louisiana was the property of the United States.

The acquisition of Louisiana virtually doubled the territorial extent of the United States, giving what seemed to be almost limitless room for expansion, and it made possible the later expansion to the Pacific Ocean. It set a precedent for obtaining foreign territory and peoples by treaty, and it increased nationalist feelings in the country and helped undercut secessionist intrigues in the West. It did not solve all the problems of the West, but it redirected their nature. Friction with New Spain, Mexico, and the various Great Plains and Texas Native Americans increased, but the French were no longer a factor. Within a few decades, the new territory would provoke major debates over the future expansion of slavery there and the removal of Native Americans to a newly created Indian Territory. In 1803, the purchase demarcated a reserve for Native Americans west of the Mississippi River and provided a place for the eventual relocation of most Eastern tribal peoples in the ensuing four decades.

—*John L. Loos, updated by Thomas L. Altherr*

ADDITIONAL READING:

Balleck, Barry J. "When the Ends Justify the Means: Thomas Jefferson and the Louisiana Purchase." *Presidential Studies Quarterly* 22, no. 4 (1992): 679-696. Argues that Jefferson's support of the purchase was consistent with his constitutional views.

Carson, David A. "The Role of Congress in the Acquisition of the Louisiana Territory." *Louisiana History* 26, no. 4

(1985): 369-383. Asserts that Napoleon was aware of unpassed congressional resolutions to authorize the president to employ force to take New Orleans.

Lyon, E. Wilson. *Louisiana in French Diplomacy, 1759-1804*. Norman: University of Oklahoma Press, 1934. The second half of the book gives a detailed account of French viewpoints leading to the sale of Louisiana.

Peterson, Merrill D. *Thomas Jefferson and the New Nation*. New York: Oxford University Press, 1970. This spirited interpretation demonstrates that Jefferson was more than a passive player in the negotiations to secure Louisiana.

Sheehan, Bernard W. *Seeds of Extinction: Jeffersonian Philanthropy and the American Indian*. Chapel Hill: University of North Carolina Press, 1973. Places the Louisiana Purchase within the context of Jeffersonian-era attitudes about removal of eastern Native Americans to the West.

Skolnik, Richard, comp. *1803: Jefferson's Decision: The United States Purchases Louisiana*. New York: Chelsea House, 1969. Reprints many of the primary sources pertinent to the purchase.

SEE ALSO: 1795, Pinckney's Treaty; 1804, Lewis and Clark Expedition.

1804 ■ FIRST BLACK CODES: *Ohio laws denying civil rights to African Americans discourage black immigration to that state*

DATE: January, 1804-January, 1807
LOCALE: Ohio
CATEGORIES: African American history; Civil rights; Laws and acts
KEY FIGURE:
Edward Tiffin (1766-1829), president of 1802 state constitutional convention and governor of Ohio

SUMMARY OF EVENT. The Northwest Territory was established in 1787 and ultimately became the states of Ohio, Indiana, Michigan, Illinois, and Wisconsin. In 1800, what was to become the state of Ohio separated from the rest of the territory. Two years later, Ohio elected delegates to a constitutional convention in preparation for a statehood petition, which was approved in 1803.

Although the Northwest Ordinance prohibited slavery in that territory, Ohio's constitutional convention debated the issue during its sessions. With the slaveholding states of Virginia on Ohio's eastern boundary and Kentucky on its southern boundary, there was considerable pressure for Ohio to recognize slavery. Many of the immigrants to Ohio came from slave states and saw nothing evil in the system. While many southern Ohioans did not object to slavery, persons in the northern part of the state were more likely to oppose it. Immigrants from New England, New York, and Pennsylvania tended to accept the concepts of the Enlightenment, as expressed in Thomas Paine's *The Rights of Man* (1791-1792) and the Declaration of Independence, which proclaimed the concepts of liberty and equality for all people. Northern Ohioans, many of whom had little contact with African Americans, usually opposed slavery from an idealistic perspective. Thus, a geographic division with regard to slavery existed within the state from the first.

Delegates at the 1802 constitutional convention debated several questions that focused on African Americans. Should slavery be permitted in Ohio? If slavery was prohibited, what about indentured servitude? Regardless of the outcome of those two discussions, the place of African Americans in the new state needed to be defined: Should they be allowed to vote? Should they be granted civil rights? Should they be encouraged to emigrate to Ohio? Should their immigration to the state be discouraged?

Edward Tiffin, from Virginia, was president of the convention. Before leaving Virginia, he had freed his slaves. He did not necessarily support the concept of equal rights for African Americans, however. When there was a tie in the vote on granting African Americans the right to vote, Tiffin cast the deciding ballot against it. There was no strong feeling for instituting slavery in Ohio; there was, however, strong opinion in favor of limited rights for African Americans. When the constitutional convention, held in Chillicothe, began on November 1, there were approximately five hundred African Americans in the Ohio territory, representing approximately 10 percent of the population. None of them was represented in the constitutional convention, however, because none could meet the property qualifications required for voting. After a major debate over allowing African Americans to vote, it was decided not to delete the word "white" from the qualifications for the franchise. Nevertheless, the African American population grew from five hundred in 1800 to nearly two thousand by 1810; it is probable that most of the growth occurred before the passage of the first Black Laws.

Former Southerners living in Ohio were responsible for the Black Laws. In 1804, the legislature debated and passed the first of these laws, "An Act to Regulate Black and Mulatto Persons." The intent of this legislation was clearly to discourage African Americans from moving into Ohio and to encourage those already there to leave. Many delegates from areas near Virginia and Kentucky undoubtedly acted based on their geographic location. Ohio shared a 375-mile border with those two states, and many legislators did not want to see a mass migration of African Americans to Ohio. Early Ohioans generally rejected slavery, but not strongly enough to protest against it. At the same time, they opposed African Americans living in Ohio as free citizens.

The law, which went into force in January, 1804, had several provisions designed to control African Americans. First, no African American or mulatto could settle in Ohio without a certificate of freedom from a United States court. African Americans or mulattoes already residing in Ohio had until June 1 to produce such a certificate. Certificates cost twelve and one-half cents each, and were required of children as well

as adults. It was a criminal offense for a white to employ, for more than one hour, an African American or mulatto who did not have the appropriate certificate. The fine was at least ten dollars but not more than fifty dollars for each offense, with half the money going to the informant. An additional fifty cents a day had to be paid to the African American's owner; the law assumed that a black or mulatto who did not have a certificate must be a slave. Penalties for aiding a fugitive from slavery remained the same, but the fine for assisting a fugitive slave attempting to escape from the state could be as much as one hundred dollars.

Again, the vote was split, with those in the northern half of the state opposed to the restrictions on African Americans and delegates from the south of Ohio supporting them. The bill passed in the House by a vote of nineteen to eight and in the Senate by a vote of nine to five, although the geographic lines in the Senate were not as clearly drawn as they were in the House.

A few years later, an even stronger bill to restrict African Americans was presented in the Senate. In its final version, it forbade African Americans from settling in Ohio unless they could present a five-hundred-dollar bond and an affidavit signed by two white men that attested to their good character. Fines for helping a fugitive slave were doubled. Finally, no African American could testify against a white in court. While there is no record of the vote in the Senate, the bill passed the House twenty to nine and became law in January, 1807.

However restrictive the original Black Codes were, the new law was far worse. African Americans were stripped of legal protection and placed at the mercy of whites. Whites did not need to fear being tried for offenses against African Americans unless there was a white witness who would testify. There is evidence of at least one African American being murdered by whites, with only African American witnesses to the crime. African American witnesses could not provide evidence against a white assailant. Even if a case went to court, it would be heard by an all-white jury before a white judge. African American victims could not testify on their own behalf, because of the restrictions against providing testimony against whites. Because they could not vote, African Americans could neither change nor protest these laws.

While the Black Codes of 1804 and 1807 were enforced only infrequently, they still were the law and were a constant reminder that African Americans in Ohio had only the barest minimum of human and civil rights, and that those rights existed only at the whim of white society. The laws fell into disuse and finally were repealed in 1849, long after the abolitionist movement, with its western center located in Oberlin, Ohio, was well under way, and long after the Underground Railroad had opened several stations in Ohio. —*Duncan R. Jamieson*

ADDITIONAL READING:
Bell, Howard H. "Some Reform Interests of the Negro During the 1850's As Reflected in State Conventions." *Phylon* 21, no. 2 (1960): 173-181. Includes information on Ohio's Black Codes.

Erickson, Leonard. "Politics and the Repeal of Ohio's Black Laws, 1837-1849." *Ohio History* 82, no. 3/4 (1973): 154-175. Discusses the movement to repeal Ohio's Black Codes beginning in the 1830's. Maps, tables, and notes.

Franklin, John Hope. *From Slavery to Freedom*. New York: McGraw-Hill, 1994. The standard history of African Americans, from the earliest days of slavery to the present.

Knepper, George W. *Ohio and Its People*. Kent, Ohio: Kent State University Press, 1989. A thorough history of Ohio, including a significant amount of material on African Americans.

Rodabaugh, James H. "The Negro in the Old Northwest." In *Trek of the Immigrants: Essays Presented to Carl Wittke*. Rock Island, Ill.: Augustana College Library, 1964. Discusses the antislavery movement among the New Englanders who settled in the Western Reserve, and the work of the Underground Railroad in bringing slaves into Ohio.

Wilson, Charles Jay. "The Negro in Early Ohio." *Ohio Archeological and Historical Quarterly* 39, no. 4 (1930). The most complete analysis of Ohio's Black Laws.

SEE ALSO: 1787, Northwest Ordinance; 1793, First Fugitive Slave Law; 1807, Congress Bans Importation of African Slaves; 1820, Missouri Compromise; 1850, Second Fugitive Slave Law; 1850, Underground Railroad.

1804 ■ LEWIS AND CLARK EXPEDITION: *the first federally sponsored transcontinental expedition opens the Louisiana Territory and reinforces U.S. claims to Oregon Country*

DATE: May 14, 1804-September 23, 1806
LOCALE: Trans-Mississippi West
CATEGORIES: Expansion and land acquisition; Exploration and discovery
KEY FIGURES:
Toussaint Charbonneau (born 1760?), French husband of Sacagawea and interpreter
William Clark (1770-1838), thirty-three-year-old co-leader of the expedition
George Drouillard (died 1809), expert hunter, sign language specialist, and interpreter for the expedition
Thomas Jefferson (1743-1826), third president of the United States, 1801-1809
Meriwether Lewis (1774-1809), twenty-nine-year-old co-leader of the expedition
Sacagawea (c. 1788-1812), sixteen-year-old Shoshoni woman whose presence with the expedition facilitated the Rocky Mountain portage
SUMMARY OF EVENT. Meriwether Lewis, William Clark, and their companions were the first Europeans to cross the western half of North America within the present limits of the United States. During their journeys, they traveled through the future

states of Missouri, Kansas, Nebraska, South Dakota, North Dakota, Montana, Idaho, Washington, and Oregon. Their exploration was the concluding act in the long and fruitless search for a water route through the continent—a Northwest Passage—that had begun soon after Columbus discovered the New World.

The instigator of the exploration was Thomas Jefferson, the third president of the United States. He had first thought of such an undertaking about the time the United States achieved independence in 1783, and during the succeeding decade he twice tried unsuccessfully to launch a transcontinental exploring party. Not until he assumed the presidency in 1801, however, was Jefferson in a position to have his plan implemented.

On January 18, 1803, the president asked Congress for authorization and for an appropriation of twenty-five hundred dollars to send a military expedition to explore along the Missouri River to its source in the Rocky Mountains, and then down the nearest westward-flowing streams to the Pacific Ocean. Jefferson gave two reasons for the proposed mission: to prepare the way for the extension of the American fur trade to the tribes throughout the area to be explored, and to advance geographical knowledge of the continent.

When he sent his message to Congress, none of the territory Jefferson wanted to be explored lay within the United States. The area between the Mississippi River and the Rocky Mountains, called Louisiana, belonged to France, while the Pacific Northwest was claimed by Great Britain, Spain, and Russia, as well as by the United States. While he was developing his plans for the transcontinental exploring expedition, however, the president also was conducting negotiations with the French government of Napoleon Bonaparte, which resulted in the purchase of Louisiana from France by a treaty signed on May 2, although antedated to April 30, 1803. Thus, in ascending the Missouri River, the expedition would be exploring U.S. territory, while by completing the journey to the Pacific Ocean, it would be strengthening the United States' claim to the region beyond the mountains.

To command the expedition, Jefferson chose his private secretary, Captain Meriwether Lewis. With the president's concurrence, Lewis then invited his longtime friend William Clark to be his co-leader. After making initial preparations in the East, Lewis traveled to Wood River, Illinois, opposite the mouth of the Missouri River. Clark and several recruits joined him on the way down the Ohio River. Lewis and Clark spent the winter of 1803-1804 at Camp Wood River recruiting and training their men, gathering additional supplies and equipment (including fourteen bales of trade goods), and collecting information about the Missouri River from traders and boatmen. The permanent party that was organized included twenty-seven young, unmarried soldiers; a mixed-blood hunter and interpreter named George Drouillard; Clark's black slave, York: and Lewis' big Newfoundland dog, Scammon. In addition, a corporal, five privates, and several French boatmen were to accompany the expedition during the first season and then return downriver with its records, sketches, and scientific specimens.

The Corps of Discovery began its historic journey on May 14, 1804. It started up the Missouri River in a fifty-five-foot keelboat and two pirogues, or dugout canoes. Averaging about fifteen miles a day, by the end of October, the corps had reached the villages of the Mandans and Minnatarees near the mouth of the Knife River in the future state of North Dakota. After ending their sixteen-hundred-mile trek, the explorers built a log stronghold called Fort Mandan and went into winter

Meriwether Lewis, private secretary to President Thomas Jefferson, at twenty-nine helped lead the expedition that took the first Europeans across North America within the current borders of the United States. (Library of Congress)

quarters. During the long, frigid winter, Lewis and Clark made copious notes in their journals, drew maps of their route, and counseled with numerous Native American visitors. From the Minnatarees, especially, they obtained invaluable information about the course of the Missouri River and the country through which it ran. The contributions of these and other Native Americans to the success of the exploration cannot be exaggerated.

On April 7, 1805, the expedition resumed its journey. The party now numbered only thirty-three persons. It included, besides the permanent detachment, interpreter Toussaint Charbonneau, his young Shoshoni wife Sacagawea, and her two-month-old son Jean Baptiste, nicknamed Pompey. On August 17, after passing through country never before visited by Europeans, the expedition reached the navigable limits of the Missouri River.

With Sacagawea's help, Lewis and Clark purchased horses from her brother Cameahwai of the Shoshoni tribe and began their journey through the Rocky Mountains. Sacagawea had been captured three years before by a Minnataree raiding party and carried back east to the prairies, where Charbonneau had purchased her for his wife. The chance meeting of Sacagawea and her brother, who had become the chief of their clan, was a convenient opportunity for the expedition. Along with the horses, Lewis and Clark were given travel instructions and lent a guide, called Toby, to assist them through the mountains. After crossing the mountains, the explorers descended the Clearwater, Snake, and Columbia Rivers to the Pacific, where they arrived in mid-November.

After a dreary winter at Fort Clatsop (named for a neighboring tribe) south of the Columbia River, the explorers started for home on March 23, 1806. Other than fighting to keep warm and searching for food, the highlight of their stay was a visit to the remains of a dead beached whale, from which they obtained three hundred pounds of blubber and oil. They were anxious to start back east, as they had only seen the sun six days during their stay at Fort Clatsop. En route, they divided temporarily; Lewis and a small party explored the Marias River, while Clark and the rest of the men descended the Yellowstone River. Reuniting below the mouth of the Yellowstone, they hurried on down the Missouri and arrived in St. Louis on September 23, 1806.

The Lewis and Clark expedition had accomplished its mission with remarkable success. During more than twenty-eight months, it covered more than eight thousand miles. On the entire journey, only one man, Sergeant Charles Floyd, lost his life, probably of a ruptured appendix. Although they met thousands of Native Americans, the explorers had only one violent encounter with them. This violence occurred while Lewis was high up the Marias River, and it resulted in the death of two Piegans, members of the Blackfoot Confederacy. The total expense of the undertaking, including the special congressional appropriation of $2,500, was $38,722.25. Charbonneau collected $500.33 and one-third cents for his and Sacagawea's services. At this small cost Lewis and Clark and their companions took the first giant step in opening the West to the American people.   —*John L. Loos, updated by Russell Hively*

ADDITIONAL READING:

Bakeless, John. *Lewis and Clark: Partners in Discovery.* New York: William Morrow, 1947. One of the most reliable sources on Meriwether Lewis and Williams Clark. Based on both of their journals.

Biddle, Nicholas, and Paul Allen, eds. *History of the Expedition Under the Command of Captains Lewis and Clark.* 2 vols. Philadelphia: J. B. Lippincott, 1961. Prepared by Biddle, a young Philadelphia lawyer, between 1810 and 1814, this work is based on both Lewis' and Clark's journals.

De Voto, Bernard. *The Journals of Lewis and Clark.* Boston: Houghton Mifflin, 1953. A one-volume condensation of the *Original Journals of Lewis and Clark Expedition.* Includes maps.

Dillon, Richard. *Meriwether Lewis: A Biography.* New York: Coward-McCann, 1965. A full-length study of Meriwether Lewis' life.

McGrath, Patrick. *The Lewis and Clark Expedition.* Morristown, N.J.: Silver Burdett, 1985. A simple but complete telling of the Lewis and Clark adventure for younger readers.

Salisbury, Albert, and Jane Salisbury. *Two Captains West.* Seattle: Superior Publishing, 1950. Descriptions of the Lewis and Clark trail, with maps and photographs. Designed for the lay reader.

Tourtellot, Jonathan B., ed. "Meriwether Lewis/William Clark." In *Into the Unknown: The Story of Exploration.* Washington, D.C.: National Geographic Society, 1987. A thirty-four-page chapter devoted to the Lewis and Clark expedition.

SEE ALSO: 1803, Louisiana Purchase; 1808, American Fur Company Is Chartered; 1810, Astorian Expeditions.

1804 ■ BURR'S CONSPIRACY: *an attempt to invade Mexico and detach the Mississippi Valley from the United States tests the unity of the new republic*

DATE: July 11, 1804-September 1, 1807
LOCALE: Ohio and Mississippi Valleys
CATEGORIES: Government and politics; Wars, uprisings, and civil unrest
KEY FIGURES:

Theodosia Burr Alston (1783-1813), Burr's daughter and only confidant

Harman Blennerhassett (1765-1831), Irish immigrant who supported Burr's expeditionary force

Aaron Burr (1756-1836), vice president of the United States, 1801-1805

Thomas Jefferson (1743-1826), third president of the United States, 1801-1809

John Marshall (1755-1835), chief justice of the United States and presiding judge at Burr's trial

Carlos Martínez de Yrujo y Tacón, Marqués de Casa Yrujo (1763-1824), Spanish minister to the United States from whom Burr solicited financial aid

Anthony Merry, British minister to the United States from whom Burr solicited financial and military assistance

James Wilkinson (1757-1825), commanding general of the U.S. Army and Burr's co-conspirator

SUMMARY OF EVENT. From 1804 through 1806, Aaron Burr promoted, organized, and led an expedition into the Mississippi Valley. Although his purpose remains unclear, he may have intended to invade Spanish Mexico, detach several western states from the Union, colonize in what is now Northwestern Louisiana, or some combination of these goals. In addition, he was accused of plotting to overthrow the United States government and seize Washington, D.C.

Burr had been prominent in the American Revolution and was a generally successful politician noted for ambition, elegance, womanizing, and opportunism. After he was rejected for a second term as vice president by Thomas Jefferson and the Republicans, he was defeated in a bid for governor of New York in 1804. Shortly thereafter, James Wilkinson, commanding general of the Army, requested a visit and surreptitiously spent the night at Burr's residence. What transpired is unclear, but it is thought they laid plans to conquer Texas and northern Mexico, and may have discussed separating the Western lands from the United States.

Burr, angered by Alexander Hamilton's derogatory personal remarks during the gubernatorial campaign, challenged him to a duel and killed him July 11, 1804. The election and duel effectively terminated Burr's political career. To escape arrest, Burr fled to Philadelphia, where he met Charles Williamson, an old friend and a British agent. He discussed his western plans with Williamson, who presented them to Anthony Merry, the British minister to the United States. Merry forwarded Burr's plan to detach the Western states and invade Mexico to his superiors in London, who were uninterested. Many historians believe Burr also met Wilkinson in Philadelphia and, at that time, concocted his conspiracy. Wilkinson's presence in Philadelphia, however, is unverified in public accounts. Burr resumed his vice presidential duties on November 4, 1804, in spite of outstanding indictments for murder in New York and New Jersey. Apparently furthering his plans, Burr influenced Jefferson to appoint Wilkinson governor of the northern part of the District of Louisiana at St. Louis.

On March 2, 1805, Burr withdrew from the Senate. He then met with Merry and offered to detach Louisiana (at that time, the huge region extending from the Great Lakes to the Gulf of Mexico, bordered on the east by the Mississippi River and on the west by the Great Plains) from the United States. His price for doing so would be one-half million dollars and British naval support in the Gulf of Mexico. Merry again wrote to his superiors on March 29, but received no response.

On April 23, Burr set out for Pittsburgh and the Ohio and Mississippi Valleys, seeking support and widely discussing his various plans. On his way down the Ohio River, he visited the estate of Harman Blennerhassett, a wealthy and idealistic Irish expatriate, who subsequently became one of Burr's principal supporters. He also met twice with Andrew Jackson at Nashville, Tennessee, enlisting his support for a campaign against the Spanish lands. He conferred with Wilkinson at Fort Massac, just below the junction of the Cumberland and Ohio Rivers on June 6, and probably matured a joint plan to invade Mexico. In New Orleans, he contacted the Mexican Associates, a group of Creoles (native-born Americans of French or Spanish descent) and the bishop of New Orleans, securing encouragement for an expedition against Mexico. On his return trip, Burr spent several days in September, 1805, with Wilkinson in St. Louis, and apparently made detailed plans for invading Mexico.

Returning to Washington in November, 1805, Burr and his associates unsuccessfully sought aid from Don Carlos Martínez de Yrujo y Tacón, Marqués de Casa Yrujo, the Spanish minister to the United States, to dismember the Union and establish an independent Western confederacy. In July, 1806, Burr purchased the Bastrop lands, about four hundred thousand acres on the Washita River in Northwestern Louisiana.

Burr then went west to recruit volunteers and support for a military expedition down the Mississippi River, planned for late fall. During this time, Jefferson ignored detailed reports of Burr's activities. On November 4, Burr was brought before a grand jury in Frankfort, Kentucky, for preparing a military expedition against Mexico but was declared innocent on November 5. In the meantime, Harman Blennerhassett converted his island estate on the Ohio River opposite what is now Parkersburg, West Virginia, into a supply depot and rendezvous site for Burr's recruits. This attracted the attention of the governor of Ohio, who sent the state militia to seize the island and most of Blennerhassett's supplies on December 5. Meanwhile, Burr went to Nashville, reassured Andrew Jackson, obtained boats from Jackson, and rejoined his group at the mouth of the Cumberland River on December 27. On December 29, accompanied by about sixty men, he appeared below Fort Massac, explaining that his purpose was to colonize the Bastrop lands.

Wilkinson apparently lost confidence in Burr's plan and informed Jefferson of the scheme to dismember the United States. Wilkinson also sent Jefferson a "cipher letter," purportedly from Burr, detailing Burr's plans; declared martial law in Louisiana; and arrested some of Burr's associates. Jefferson then ordered the arrest of anyone conspiring to attack Spanish territory. Learning of the president's order at Natchez, Burr attempted to flee to Spanish Florida. He was arrested near Mobile, brought to Richmond, Virginia, and arraigned on charges of treason for attempting to dismember the Union and of the misdemeanor of organizing an expedition against Spanish territory.

Chief Justice John Marshall, the presiding judge, narrowly interpreted the Constitution, ruling that an expressed intent to divide the Union did not constitute an overt act of treason. Government witnesses, some of whom were successfully contradicted, and the "cipher letter" failed to demonstrate overt acts of treason by Burr, so Marshall dismissed the charge of treason. The government was unable to prove that Burr's expedition had been military or had been directed against Spanish territory, so the misdemeanor charge was dropped as well. Marshall's decision preserved the right of Americans to voice opposition to the government without fear of being charged with treason and further defined the independent scope of the judicial and executive branches of government.

After his release, Burr spent four years in Europe lobbying the British and French governments to support his Mexican plans. Returning to the United States, he practiced law in New York. Wilkinson was investigated by Congress and court-martialed by the army but was cleared and retained his command.

Although Burr discussed his plans with hundreds of people, the true story of the conspiracy remains controversial. Until his death, he continued to promote diverse settlement schemes and expeditions into Spanish and Mexican territory. Surviving documents are wildly contradictory, unreliable, and incomplete. His daughter, Theodosia Burr Alston, the only person whom he fully trusted, was lost at sea with a large collection of his papers in 1813. Burr's personal papers, willed to Matthew L. Davis, a politician, journalist, and friend, were in part destroyed and lost.

Burr's alleged goals were by no means unique. Secession was repeatedly proposed to advance regional interests until the Civil War (1861-1865). Excursions into Spanish or Mexican territory persisted until after the Spanish American War (1898). A mature sense of national identity did not come to the United States until the late nineteenth and early twentieth centuries.

—*Ralph L. Langenheim, Jr.*

ADDITIONAL READING:

Adams, Henry. *History of the United States of America During the Administrations of Jefferson and Madison.* 9 vols. New York: Charles Scribner's Sons, 1889-1891. After examining English and Spanish archives, Adams concludes that Burr conspired to dismember the Union; his conclusion gained wide acceptance.

Brodie, Fawn M. *Thomas Jefferson: An Intimate History.* New York: Bantam, 1974. Concludes that Burr's many conflicting purported plots and unfounded claims resulted from mental imbalance.

Lomask, Milton. *Aaron Burr: The Conspiracy and Years of Exile: 1805-1806.* New York: Farrar, Straus, Giroux, 1982. Based on primary documents and scholarly analyses of older records, including a discrediting of Burr's purported "cipher letter" to Wilkinson.

Parmet, Herbert S., and Marie B. Hecht. *Aaron Burr: Portrait of an Ambitious Man.* New York: Macmillan, 1967. A well-documented biography.

Vidal, Gore. *Burr.* New York: Random House, 1973. A well-documented historical novel, in which fact and fiction are clearly separated. Re-creates the contemporary social and political environment. Author is remotely related to Burr.

SEE ALSO: 1803, Louisiana Purchase; 1815, Westward Migration; 1819, Adams-Onís Treaty.

1804 ■ Twelfth Amendment: *simplification of procedures for electing the president and vice president of the United States*

Date: September 25, 1804
Locale: Washington, D.C.
Categories: Government and politics; Laws and acts
Key figures:

John Adams (1735-1826), second president of the United States, 1797-1801

Aaron Burr (1756-1836), third vice president of the United States

Thomas Jefferson (1743-1826), third president of the United States, 1801-1809

James Madison (1751-1836), secretary of state in 1804

Thomas Pinckney (1750-1828), unsuccessful vice presidential candidate in 1796

John Taylor (1753-1824), senator from Virginia who advocated the Twelfth Amendment

Summary of event. The Twelfth Amendment to the United States Constitution was necessitated by a basic flaw in the original document. Article II, Section 1, clause 3 of the Constitution had established a most complicated and confusing procedure for electing the president and vice president. According to this procedure, the election was to be determined by the vote of an electoral college composed of electors from each of the states. Each state was entitled to the same number of electors as it had representatives in Congress. These electors, appointed in whatever manner the individual state legislatures chose, were to vote for two persons, presumably one for president and the other for vice president, although the ballots were not so labeled. The person receiving the highest number of votes, provided he received a majority of the electoral votes possible, was elected president. The person having the next highest number of votes was elected vice president.

If there are more than two major candidates for either the presidency or the vice presidency, it is possible that none will receive a clear majority of the electoral vote. In this situation, the House of Representatives elects the president from the top five candidates. Two-thirds of the members constitute a quorum for this purpose, and each state has one vote—a measure designed to ensure that the smaller states have equal weight. A simple majority vote in the House is required for election. If the same situation occurs in the vice presidential election, the Senate elects the vice president from the top two vote-getters by majority vote. Again, there is one vote for each Senator, and a quorum is two-thirds of the Senate. If the president should die or become disabled between the time of the popular election and determination of the electoral voter, the vice president would become president. This is similar to the case of the president's death during his or her term of office.

When the Constitution was written, it was presumed that many worthy candidates would receive votes from the various electors and that seldom, if ever, would anyone receive a majority of the electoral vote. The electoral college was intended to serve only as a nominating procedure to provide five good candidates for consideration by the House. The Founding Fathers did not anticipate the development of political parties, which began forming in the 1790's. The election of 1796 found Federalist John Adams, from Massachusetts, opposed by Republican Thomas Jefferson, from Virginia. Adams won the election, but his running mate, Thomas Pinckney, from South Carolina, finished in third place, nine votes behind Jefferson. This unusual election resulted in a situation in which presidential rivals, representing different political parties, were forced to serve four years together as president and vice president.

A different, but equally awkward, result came out of the electoral balloting in 1800. In this election, Jefferson and his vice presidential running mate, Aaron Burr, from New York, received the same number of votes. This election went into the House of Representatives, where Federalist opposition to Jefferson was strong. Although it was common knowledge that the electors who voted for Jefferson and Burr intended to place Jefferson in the top position, many die-hard Federalists were determined to thwart their intentions and to put Burr into the presidency. Moderate Federalists, influenced by Burr's home-state rival Alexander Hamilton, finally tipped the scales in favor of Jefferson. The Virginian was elected on the thirty-sixth ballot, dangerously close to Inauguration Day.

The somewhat bizarre results of the elections of 1796 and 1800 brought forth a demand for a change in the electoral system. John Taylor and other Jeffersonian Republicans prepared a series of resolutions suggesting an appropriate amendment to the Constitution. The resolutions were introduced into Congress, where support from several states was immediately evident. The major objection to changes in the electoral college came from smaller states and from the Federalists. The smaller states feared that their role in the presidential elections might be diminished if the electoral college was abandoned. The Federalists merely hoped to disrupt or confuse the election of 1804. After much debate, agreement was finally reached in Congress in December of 1803. An amendment was written and sent to the states for ratification. Within a year, the necessary number of states, thirteen out of seventeen, had ratified the amendment. On September 25, 1804, Secretary of State James Madison announced the adoption of the Twelfth Amendment in time for the election of 1804.

Although the Twelfth Amendment did not abolish the electoral college or radically change the method of electing the president and vice president, it did remedy some basic defects. Separate ballots were provided for the election of president and vice president, thus preventing the problem of 1796. Provision was also made for the vice president to take over as acting president if the House should delay too long in selecting a president, which almost occurred after the election of 1800. When no candidate received a majority vote in the electoral college, the House of Representatives was to choose a president from the three candidates who received the most votes, rather than from five. Equality among the states was maintained when presidential or vice presidential elections went into the House or the Senate. Twice in the history of the United States, a president has been elected despite having received a smaller percentage of the popular vote than an opponent. The first time, in 1876, Rutherford B. Hayes assumed the presidency after an election so close that ballots from at least four states were in dispute. A special commission was set up to decide the outcome. The second time, in 1888, Grover Cleveland had a majority of the vote but lost the presidency to Benjamin Harrison.

There has been, from time to time, discussion about amending the Twelfth Amendment to ensure that such a election cannot happen again. The usual proposal is that the electoral vote be counted in proportion to the popular vote. If there were two candidates for president and a state had ten electoral votes, a candidate who received 60 percent of the popular vote would receive six electoral votes, and the opponent would receive four electoral votes.

—*Edward J. Maguire, updated by Susan M. Taylor*

ADDITIONAL READING:

Hockett, Homer C. *The Constitutional History of the United States.* Vol. 1. New York: Macmillan, 1939. Contains pertinent information regarding the demand for and the adoption of the Twelfth Amendment.

Holder, Angela Roddey. *The Meaning of the Constitution.* New York: Barron's, 1987. Provides concise, comprehensive explanations of the significance of the words and clauses of the Constitution. Includes a good working bibliography.

Kuroda, Tadahisa. *The Origins of the Twelfth Amendment: The Electoral College in the Early Republic, 1787-1804.* Westport, Conn.: Greenwood Press, 1994. Outlines the election history of the United States and argues the need for a change in the electoral college.

Luttbeg, Norman R. *American Electoral Behavior, 1952-1992.* 2d ed. Itasca, Ill.: F. E. Peacock, 1995. Contrasts more recent electoral behavior with past electoral behavior. Includes some discussion of a possible amendment to the Twelfth Amendment.

Roseboom, Eugene H. *A Short History of Presidential Elections.* New York: Collier Books, 1967. Provides a brief account of the presidential elections from George Washington to Lyndon Johnson and explains the need for the Twelfth Amendment.

Rule, Wilma, and Joseph Zimmerman. *Electoral Systems in Comparative Perspective: Their Impact on Women and Minorities.* Westport, Conn.: Greenwood Press, 1994. Discusses elections and cross-cultural studies of the need for change.

Wright, Russell O. *Presidential Elections in the United States: A Statistical History, 1860-1992.* Jefferson, N.C.: McFarland Press, 1995. Discusses the history of the elections process and provides some interesting statistics.

SEE ALSO: 1790's, First U.S. Political Parties; 1801, Jefferson Is Elected President; 1877, Hayes Is Elected President.

1806 ■ PIKE'S SOUTHWEST EXPLORATIONS: *opening of the Santa Fe trade and creation of the "Great American Desert" myth*

DATE: July 15, 1806-July 1, 1807
LOCALE: Southwest
CATEGORIES: Economics; Expansion and land acquisition; Exploration and discovery
KEY FIGURES:

Facundo Melgares, Spanish lieutenant who led an expedition that nearly intercepted Pike
Zebulon Montgomery Pike (1779-1813), young army lieutenant who led the expedition
John Hamilton Robinson, Pike's civilian companion whose arrival in Santa Fe disclosed Pike's presence in New Mexico
James Wilkinson (1757-1825), commanding general of the Western Army of the United States, who ordered Pike to undertake the exploration

SUMMARY OF EVENT. On July 15, 1806, Lieutenant Zebulon Montgomery Pike of the Western Army of the United States set out from St. Louis with a party of twenty-two men with orders to locate and explore the headwaters of the Arkansas and Red Rivers. His plan was to ascend the Arkansas River, cross over to the Red River, and then descend that river to its junction with the Mississippi River. The boundary line between the United States and the Spanish Empire in the Southwest was as yet undetermined; the farther west Pike moved, the more likely he was to encounter trouble, as the Spanish furiously tried to protect their northern borderlands from encroachment. Already experienced in reconnaissance work, Pike had returned from a successful exploration to the upper Mississippi River, where he had negotiated land concessions from the Sioux and protested the presence of British fur posts in the Minnesota region. On this second, or Southwestern, expedition, Pike's first concern was to negotiate peace between the Osage and Pawnee tribes. He ascended the Missouri River and the Osage River to the Osage villages, where he obtained horses. Then he moved on to the Pawnee villages on the Republican River. There he found the Pawnees ready to resist further advances westward, because they had recently been visited by a much more impressive Spanish expedition sent out to defend New Spain's northern borders from U.S. encroachment. Don Facundo Melgares, leading a force of six hundred men and driving two thousand horses and mules, had distributed Spanish flags and medals among the Pawnees, captured U.S. traders in the region, and urged the Pawnees to turn back others who tried to head farther west. Contrary to long-standing legend, Melgares did not know that Pike was coming: He was hoping to deter the Lewis and Clark expedition to the north. It still seems that Spanish officials had been informed of the Pike expedition by Pike's commander, General James Wilkinson, who was also Special Agent Number 13 for the Spanish intelligence service. Whether and to

WESTERN EXPEDITIONS OF LEWIS AND CLARK (1804-1806) AND PIKE (1806-1807)

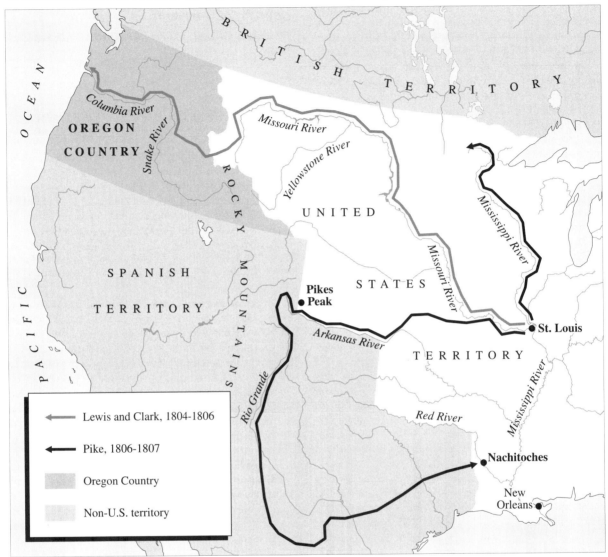

A new era in westward exploration and expansion of the United States followed the Louisiana Purchase of 1803. President Thomas Jefferson charged his private secretary, Meriwether Lewis, to undertake a northwestern reconnaissance expedition to explore the new lands. At about the same time, Zebulon Pike of the Western Army of the United States conducted several expeditions that led him deep into Spanish territory in the Southwest.

what degree Pike was involved in Wilkinson's intrigues in the Southwest has remained an area of fierce debate.

The near miss with Melgares proved to be a stroke of good fortune for Pike, who had moved so slowly that he had avoided an encounter with the superior Spanish detachment. After the Pawnees were pacified, he could follow Melgares' route into the Rockies. With a display of force, Pike's troops intimidated the Pawnees, then pressed on to the Big Bend of the Arkansas River. There six men descended the river in two canoes fashioned from cottonwood logs and buffalo skins and returned to the United States.

Following the return route of Melgares, Pike's trail led up the Arkansas River. In November, 1806, Pike's party spotted the Rockies for the first time. From an encampment near present-day Pueblo, Colorado, Pike and three companions set out to climb the peak now bearing his name. Armpit-deep snows and the lack of winter clothing prevented his making a successful ascent, but he wrote about this massive pinnacle of the Rockies, now called Pikes Peak, establishing his identification with it to this day. During the next two months, he explored the Colorado country, reaching the site of present-day Leadville, Colorado, hunting in vain for the headwaters of the

Red River. With several men in his band suffering from frost-bite, Pike established a winter camp at the Royal Gorge on the Arkansas River.

Leaving two men in a log shelter at this camp to guard the exhausted horses and a portion of the expedition's baggage, Pike and his few remaining men headed into the Wet Mountain Valley, crossed the rugged Sangre de Cristo Mountains into the San Luis Valley, and spied one of the wonders of Colorado, the massive dunes that today are part of the Sand Dunes National Park. Moving southwest, he stood at the foot of Mount Blanca and through his glass viewed a watercourse that he believed to be the Red River. What he had actually found was the Rio Grande. Pike headed south, crossed the river, and built a shelter near the confluence of the Rio Conejos and the Rio Grande, just south of the present-day hamlet of Sanford, Colorado. The weather was bitterly cold during this February journey, and the men waged a grim struggle with hunger. Although Pike did not know for sure where he was, he alleged that he was still on U.S. soil.

From the encampment on the Rio Grande, the enigmatic Dr. John H. Robinson, a civilian who had joined the expedition some time after its departure, set out for Santa Fe, professing to have a commission to collect a debt for a friend in Illinois. Robinson's arrival in Santa Fe made known Pike's presence in Spanish territory, and the Nyuutsiyu (Ute) Indians told the Spanish authorities of Pike's precise location. On February 26, 1807, one hundred Spanish troops appeared, took Pike and his men prisoner, and escorted them to the New Mexican capital. The Spanish were uncertain whether the explorers' presence was accidental or purposeful, and they were perplexed about what they should do with Pike and his men. They seized Pike's maps and papers, and after examining them became convinced that Pike was a spy. His party was escorted to Chihuahua City and detained there for several months. Nemesio Salcedo, who commanded the Spanish army in the northern provinces, finally decided to deport the group to the United States. Under escort, Pike and his men were taken by way of San Antonio, Texas, to Natchitoches, then a trading post on the Louisiana border, and there turned over to United States troops on July 1, 1807.

From the time he left Santa Fe, Pike took voluminous notes on the country through which he passed and concealed them skillfully to make certain that they would not be confiscated. Although he failed to carry out his assignment to locate the headwaters and descend the Red River, he incorporated the information he had obtained in a report he subsequently published in 1810, thereby adding to the U.S. knowledge of the Southwest. Pike gained national fame as a result of the publication; editions also appeared in French, German, and Dutch.

Pike was such a keen observer that when he returned to the United States, he was able to provide precise figures on the number and types of troops stationed in the northern provinces of the Spanish Empire, as well as information concerning the character and personality of the Spanish military officers. His reports showed Spain's New Mexico territory to be poorly defended and only adequately governed. In addition to this intelligence, Pike declared that the Great Plains were "sandy deserts" similar to those in Africa. Thus he originated the so-called "Great American Desert" myth. Finally, he pointed out in great detail the potential value of trade between the United States and Santa Fe.

—W. Turrentine Jackson, updated by Edward R. Crowther

ADDITIONAL READING:

Carter, Carrol Joe. *Pike in Colorado.* Fort Collins, Colo.: Old Army Press, 1978. An excellent, accurate study of Pike's passage through the Centennial State.

Cook, Warren L. *Flood Tide of Empire: Spain and the Pacific Northwest, 1543-1819.* New Haven, Conn.: Yale University Press, 1973. An outstanding account of the political, diplomatic, and economic conditions of the northern provinces of Spain's New World empire, including General Wilkinson's involvement in Spanish policy in the early nineteenth century.

Coues, Elliott, ed. *The Expeditions of Zebulon Montgomery Pike.* 3 vols. New York: Francis P. Harper, 1895. For many years, the standard edition of Pike's expedition journals.

Hollon, W. Eugene. *The Lost Pathfinder: Zebulon Montgomery Pike.* Norman: University of Oklahoma Press, 1949. An older but excellent full-scale biography of Pike.

Pike, Zebulon Montgomery. *Journals with Letters and Related Documents.* Edited by Donald Jackson. Norman: University of Oklahoma Press, 1966. The easiest to use of the many editions of Pike's journals.

SEE ALSO: 1803, Louisiana Purchase; 1804, Lewis and Clark Expedition; 1815, Westward Migration; 1820, Land Act of 1820; 1821, Santa Fe Trail Opens; 1823, Jedediah Smith Explores the Far West; 1846, Mormon Migration to Utah; 1846, Occupation of California and the Southwest; 1848, California Gold Rush.

1807 ■ CONGRESS BANS IMPORTATION OF AFRICAN SLAVES: *outlawing a two-century tradition fails to condemn slavery outright, reflecting the young nation's moral ambiguity*

DATE: March 2, 1807
LOCALE: Washington, D.C.
CATEGORIES: African American history; Economics
KEY FIGURES:
Stephen Row Bradley (1754-1830), Vermont senator who introduced the first bill on this subject
Barnabas Bidwell (1763-1833), Massachusetts representative who drafted anti-slave-trade legislation in the House of Representatives
Thomas Jefferson (1743-1826), third president of the United States, 1801-1809

SUMMARY OF EVENT. Because the essence of slavery is to regard human beings as property, the buying and selling of slaves is implicit in the institution; therefore, the slave trade is as old as slavery itself. In the ancient Mediterranean world, slaves were obtained from many locations, including North Africa. The Portuguese began importing African slaves as early as 1444, and at the end of the same century, Christopher Columbus took a few blacks born in Spain to Hispaniola, the first European New World colony. At first, the Spaniards intended to use Caribbean natives as slaves, but by the sixteenth century, most of these native populations had died from smallpox, syphilis, influenza, measles, and other diseases introduced by European contact. Those who remained proved rebellious, physically unsuitable for agricultural exploitation, and quick to disappear into familiar surrounding forests. Black African slaves were imported to work in the Spanish colonies beginning early in the sixteenth century.

The Netherlands and France also took up the practice in their New World possessions. By the seventeenth century, England began to gain ascendancy by developing the notorious "triangular trade," involving coastal Africa and the Caribbean. This trade had reached its peak at the time Great Britain's American colonies revolted and established the United States of America. Thus, by 1790, there were three-quarters of a million African Americans, almost nine-tenths of whom labored as slaves in the Southern states, with Virginia alone claiming three hundred thousand of them. About 28 percent of African Americans in the North were free, but only one American city, Boston, had no black slaves at all. The American struggle for political independence did not effect freedom for the slaves and their offspring.

Antislavery sentiment was growing at the time of the American Revolution but needed competent leadership to challenge the long-standing practice of people enslaving their fellow humans. The Society of Friends (Quakers), some of whose members had a long history of opposition to slavery, led the antislavery, or abolitionist, movement in Pennsylvania, beginning shortly before the outbreak of the American Revolution, and a few clergymen of other religious congregations in England and America took up the cause. Arguments against slavery at the Constitutional Convention of 1787 foundered on threats that delegates from South Carolina and Georgia would ratify no constitution that outlawed the slave trade.

Not all opposition to slavery was high-minded. The French

In 1807, Congress enacted a law specifying a twenty-thousand-dollar fine and forfeiture of ship and cargo for importing slaves, but enforcement proved weak. The slave trade continued as more Africans endured the trip from their native continent to North America during a period when the cotton gin and other technology increased the demand for labor. It is estimated that 1.9 million slaves were imported illegally between 1811 and 1870. (The Associated Publishers, Inc.)

Revolution of 1789 had led to African American efforts to end tyranny over blacks in the French colony of St. Dominque, or San Domingo, on Hispaniola (the island of the twentieth century Dominican Republic and Haiti). In the United States, fear of a similar uprising was probably a more powerful motive than democratic or humanitarian sentiments in the antislavery agitation of the 1790's.

Several states had outlawed slavery by that time, sometimes through legislation that instituted abolition gradually or at least banned traffic in slaves. Maryland, Massachusetts, Connecticut, New York, and New Jersey had all passed legislation in the 1780's, as did even South Carolina for a few years. Piecemeal legislation could not stop the trade in human beings, however, particularly after 1793, when Eli Whitney's invention of the cotton gin made cotton a more profitable crop by greatly increasing the speed at which seeds could be separated from the picked cotton, thus increasing plantation owners' desire for more cotton pickers. It has been said that slavery would have died out in the United States but for the New Englander's invention. Northern merchants, although not slave owners themselves, had few scruples against supplying new slaves for the cotton-growing states, and New England textile mill owners' delight over the burgeoning supply of cotton was not likely to make abolitionists of them. It has been estimated that no fewer than twenty thousand new slaves were imported in Georgia and South Carolina in 1803.

In December, 1805, Senator Stephen R. Bradley of Vermont introduced legislation that would prohibit the slave trade beginning in 1808, but the bill was stalled for some months. A similar bill was offered in the House of Representatives by Barnabas Bidwell of Massachusetts, again to no effect. Later that year, President Thomas Jefferson urged passage of the bill in his message to Congress. On March 2, 1807, Congress enacted a law specifying a twenty-thousand-dollar fine and forfeiture of ship and cargo for importing slaves, as well as other penalties for acts ranging from equipping a slave ship to knowingly buying an imported slave. The disposition of illegally imported slaves was left to the states, however. The law also prohibited coastal trade in slaves carried on in vessels smaller than forty tons. Enforcement of the law was delegated first to the secretary of the treasury and later to the secretary of the navy.

Antislavery forces rejoiced in this new and symbolically important law, but enforcement proved weak. An exhaustive census of the slave trade published in 1969 estimated that 1.9 million slaves were imported illegally between 1811 and 1870; more recent research has called that estimate low. Probably one-fifth of the Africans who became Americans involuntarily arrived after 1808, when the law took effect. Although more than one hundred slave vessels were seized and their officers arrested in the years between 1837 and 1862, and nearly as many cases were prosecuted, convictions were difficult to attain, and when they were attained, judges often pronounced light sentences. Furthermore, because of meager press coverage, few Americans were aware of the extent of the

violations. Just as white Americans for a century after the Civil War tended to regard African Americans as sharing in their own entitlement as citizens, most people in the decades following the 1807 law thought of slave importation as something of the past. Some people, particularly in the South, continued to sympathize with the slave trade.

Another weakness of the 1807 law was that it permitted the continuation of slave traffic between states. An owner could take his slaves into another slave state or, according to the Missouri Compromise of 1820, into a western territory south of 36°30', an area greatly increased by the annexation of Texas in 1845. Nor was a runaway slave out of danger in a "free" state. A half century after the 1807 law, according to the Fugitive Slave Act of 1850, anyone capturing a fugitive slave anywhere in the United States was legally obliged to return that slave to his or her owner.

It was morally important that Stephen Bradley and Barnabas Bidwell took initiatives to end the sanctioning of U.S. participation in the transatlantic slave trade, and that Thomas Jefferson, who owned slaves and whose ambiguous attitude toward slavery has continued to cause debate among historians, used his presidential influence to secure passage of the law. It was one step in the direction of a free society, and if not a highly effective step, it was a necessary one in a new nation that could not agree to condemn slavery outright at that nation's birth or in its early decades. Yet, the underlying problem with the law forbidding importation of slaves was the institution of slavery itself. As long as a person could be someone else's property, that person would inevitably be subject to slave trade of some sort. It was illogical to try to restrict the buying and selling of men, women, and children as long as slavery continued to be legal. Nothing better illustrates the problems of compromise between holders of diametrically opposed convictions than the long series of compromises over slavery. Ultimately, the nation could find no better solution for its ambiguous struggle with slavery than the bloody Civil War of 1861-1865.

—*Robert P. Ellis*

ADDITIONAL READING:

Blackburn, Robin. *The Overthrow of Colonial Slavery, 1776-1848.* New York: Verso, 1988. Chapter 7 treats the U.S. experience, with emphasis on politically expedient motives for containing the growth of slavery.

Davis, David Brion. *Slavery and Human Progress.* New York: Oxford University Press, 1984. In arguing that much of what is called progress rests on slavery and the slave trade, contends that abolitionists' most difficult opponents were progressives.

Eltis, David, and James Walvin, eds. *The Abolition of the Atlantic Slave Trade: Origins and Effects in Europe, Africa, and the Americas.* Madison: University of Wisconsin Press, 1981. Part 4, on "American Demographic and Cultural Responses," contains four essays, including one studying the effect of U.S. abolition on African American culture.

Franklin, John Hope. *From Slavery to Freedom: A History of Negro Americans.* 5th ed. New York: Alfred A. Knopf,

1980. A pioneering study by an African American historian, first published in 1947. Contains historical background and succinct summary of the enactment of the 1807 law and its aftermath.

Howard, Warren S. *American Slavers and the Federal Law: 1837-1862.* Berkeley: University of California Press, 1963. A copiously documented study of violations of the 1807 law during the quarter century before the outbreak of the Civil War.

Rawley, James A. *The Transatlantic Slave Trade: A History.* New York: W. W. Norton, 1981. Surveys the slave trade from its fifteenth century beginnings and places U.S. involvement in its international context. Revises upward previous estimates, but asserts that the U.S. slave trade was a small percentage of the whole.

SEE ALSO: 1793, Whitney Invents the Cotton Gin; 1793, First Fugitive Slave Law; 1820's, Social Reform Movement; 1820, Missouri Compromise; 1830, Proslavery Argument; 1831, Nat Turner's Insurrection; 1833, American Anti-Slavery Society Is Founded; 1839, Amistad Slave Revolt; 1850, Compromise of 1850; 1850, Second Fugitive Slave Law.

1807 ■ VOYAGE OF THE CLERMONT: *the first commercially successful steam-powered riverboat creates a flourishing trade*

DATE: August 17, 1807
LOCALE: Hudson (North) River, New York
CATEGORIES: Economics; Science and technology; Transportation
KEY FIGURES:
Oliver Evans (1755-1819), developer of the high-pressure steam engine
John Fitch (1743-1798), designer and builder of a steamboat on the Delaware River
Robert Fulton (1765-1815), designer and builder of the *Clermont*
Robert R. Livingston (1746-1813), Fulton's financial backer
Nicholas J. Roosevelt (1767-1854), Fulton's associate in developing riverboats
Henry Miller Shreve (1785-1851), developer of steamboats
Richard Wilson, African American cook on the *Clermont's* first voyage

SUMMARY OF EVENT. Robert R. Livingston, a wealthy and famous Hudson Valley landowner, persuaded the New York Legislature to grant him exclusive rights to operate steam-powered boats on the Hudson River (then known as the North River) from 1798 to 1818. Terms of this law required Livingston to produce within one year a boat that would run at four miles an hour. His attempts to satisfy this requirement failed, and he went to France as the United States minister. There he met Robert Fulton, a U.S. citizen who was studying and working on inventions in the areas of submarines and torpedoes.

Livingston persuaded Fulton to devote his efforts to designing and building a steamboat. Fulton's first attempt, on France's Seine River in 1803, was a failure. During a storm, the heavy engine and boilers broke through the bottom of the boat and sank it. Fulton learned much from this failure, and in 1806, he and Livingston decided to return to the United States and build a steamboat for the North River.

A steam engine ordered from the British firm of Boulton and Watt arrived in New York in November, 1806. The engine's cylinder was two feet in diameter, and the piston stroke was four feet. Fulton arrived from Europe the following month, but he seemed in no hurry to get on with building a boat in which to put the engine. Meanwhile, the legislature granted Livingston an extension of his monopoly.

The hull of the boat was built by Charles Brown at Corlears Hook on the East River. Fulton had the finished hull towed to Paulus Hook Ferry, where he set up his shop and began to install the machinery. There is some disagreement about the dimensions of the hull. Apparently it was about 130 feet long and 15 feet wide. The keel of the vessel rode three or four feet below the surface. At the bow and stern, the hull was sharply pointed. Its only deck was just a few feet above the waterline. Engine and boiler were installed on this deck, and the engine drove large paddle wheels on either side. These wheels were fifteen feet in diameter and four feet wide. As they rotated, the actual paddles dipped two feet into the water. Fulton was one of the first designers to use scientific methods. He successfully calculated that the Boulton and Watt engine, which produced twenty-four horsepower, could move the craft at about five miles per hour. Although modern theories give somewhat different results, his calculations were nearly correct.

Although some work remained to be completed, Fulton decided to make a short test voyage on Sunday, August 9, 1807. He set out from Brown's wharf and ran the boat about a mile up the East River to a point about even with what is now Houston Street. A speed of three miles per hour was achieved on this run, even though the paddle wheels were not complete. A week later, with paddle wheels fully equipped, Fulton moved the boat around the Battery to a wharf on the North River. Passengers during this short trip included U.S. Senator Samuel Latham Mitchill and Dr. William McNiven, dean of Ripon Cathedral in England.

At about one o'clock the next afternoon, the steamboat set out for Albany. The chief engineer was a Scot named George Jackson, and the captain was Davis Hunt. Food and drink had been brought on board, and Richard Wilson, an African American, served as the cook. Forty passengers, mostly members of the Livingston family, were on board. They reached Haverstraw Bay by nightfall and arrived at Livingston's estate above Kingston twenty-four hours after leaving New York. The distance covered was 110 miles. The name of this estate was Clermont, and the steamboat also became known by this name. Throughout his life, Fulton called his boat "The Steamboat" or "The North River Steamboat." The name *Clermont* seems to have been first used by Cadwallader D. Colden in his book *The Life of Robert Fulton* (1817), which was published two years after Fulton died.

The next morning, August 19, the steamboat set out from Clermont to cover the remaining forty miles to Albany, where she arrived just after 5:00 P.M. Although the governor of New York was among the welcoming crowd when the boat arrived, the event was not mentioned in the day's newspapers. Chief engineer Jackson got so drunk in Albany that Fulton fired him and placed his assistant, Charles Dyke, in charge for the return journey to New York.

A few paying passengers embarked for the return journey at a fare of seven dollars each, more than double what sailing vessels charged. Leaving Albany at 9:00 A.M. on Thursday, August 20, the steamboat arrived in New York at 4:00 P.M. Friday, August 21. There were some twenty newspapers in New York at the time, but only one, *The American Citizen*, took note of Fulton's accomplishment. After further improvements to cabins and decks, the steamboat entered full commercial service on September 2, 1807. The number of paying passengers grew rapidly. On October 1, there were sixty passengers going from Albany to New York; on October 2, ninety passengers went to Albany.

In 1824, the Supreme Court, in *Gibbons v. Ogden*, struck down state-sponsored monopolies such as Livingston's. This action fostered competition, which led to rapid improvements in technology and service. It is no exaggeration to say that Fulton's voyage was the beginning of an era. By the 1830's, the internal waterways of the United States were crowded with steamboats of various shapes and sizes. After the Erie Canal from Albany to Buffalo opened in 1825 and the Welland Canal between Lake Erie and Lake Ontario opened in 1833, a steamboat could sail from New York to ports on the Great Lakes.

Henry Shreve sailed from Wheeling, Virginia (now West Virginia), in his steamboat *Washington* on June 4, 1816, and went down the river to New Orleans. This was no great feat, since keelboats and flatboats had been doing it for years. However, he then sailed fifteen hundred miles *up* the river from New Orleans to Louisville, Kentucky, in twenty-four days. Keelboats powered by poles took four to six months to make this trip. Upriver voyages at reasonable speeds created a flourishing trade between New Orleans and cities such as Cincinnati, Louisville, and St. Louis.

Regular steamboat service from New York to Albany, which began in 1807, continued until 1948. On September 13 of that year, the steamboat *Robert Fulton* of the Hudson River Day Line made the last steamboat trip over this route.

—*Edwin G. Wiggins*

ADDITIONAL READING:

Buckman, D. L. *Old Steamboat Days on the Hudson River.* New York: Grafton Press, 1907. Written just one hundred years after the *Clermont* first ran, while steamboats still plied the Hudson. Black-and-white illustrations, index.

Dickinson, H. W. *Robert Fulton, Engineer and Artist: His Life and Works.* New York: John Lane, 1913. Written by a British scholar, this book takes a fairly skeptical view of Fulton's accomplishments. Black-and-white illustrations, index.

Donovan, Frank. *River Boats of America.* New York: Thomas Y. Crowell, 1966. Discusses the *Clermont* briefly; provides broad coverage of steam-powered riverboats throughout the United States. Black-and-white illustrations, bibliography, index.

Hutcheon, Wallace. *Robert Fulton, Pioneer of Undersea Warfare.* Annapolis, Md.: Naval Institute Press, 1981. Puts Fulton's steamboat in perspective with respect to his other inventions. Black-and-white illustrations, index.

Morgan, John S. *Robert Fulton.* New York: Mason/Charter, 1977. A biography covering all aspects of Fulton's life. Index.

Philip, Cynthia Owen. *Robert Fulton.* New York: Franklin Watts, 1985. Includes a full chapter about the *Clermont*. Extensive endnotes, index.

Ringwald, D. C. *Hudson River Day Line.* 2d ed. New York: Fordham University Press, 1990. A profusely illustrated, large-format book covering the Hudson River Day Line from the *Clermont* to the last Hudson River steamboat trip in 1948. Black-and-white illustrations, index, separate vessel index.

SEE ALSO: 1776, First Test of a Submarine in Warfare; 1824, *Gibbons v. Ogden*; 1825, Erie Canal Opens.

1808 ■ PROPHETSTOWN IS FOUNDED: *a Shawnee spiritual leader establishes the headquarters of Native Americans' renewed resistance to Anglo-American expansion*

DATE: April, 1808
LOCALE: Northwestern Indiana
CATEGORIES: Native American history; Settlements; Social reform
KEY FIGURES:
Main Poc (1760?-1816), Potawatomi shaman and war chief
Tecumseh (1768-1813), Shawnee war chief and diplomat
Tenskwatawa, also known as *the Prophet* (1768-1837),
    Shawnee spiritual leader

SUMMARY OF EVENT. At least since the 1730's, some native leaders west of the Appalachian Mountains advocated an alliance of tribes to resist the expanding British settlements and the powerful Iroquois Confederacy. Prophets preached a radical idea, beginning a new movement: All native peoples, despite their diverse languages and cultures and ancient tribal rivalries, were really one people, separate and distinct from the Europeans, and never meant to live with the Europeans or to adopt their ways.

By 1795, disagreements over strategy, factional strife within tribes, failing support from European allies, and military defeats disrupted the nativist movement. Tribal leaders willing to accept compromise signed treaties with the new United States government, surrendering millions of acres of land. In return, the U.S. government supported these so-called government chiefs, hoping that through them it could control the tribes and prevent organized resistance east of the Mississippi. Native people now faced a desperate struggle for survival.

Frontiersmen settling old grudges freely hunted and raided on tribal lands. Indians could not testify in U.S. courts and had no protection under U.S. law. Native people took their own form of revenge, escalating the violence. Anglo-American squatters crowded onto tribal lands, openly violating treaties. Displaced refugees fled to the remaining tribal lands, exhausting the already depleted game supply and farmlands. Most tribesmen had become dependent on the fur trade for the necessities of life. Cheap liquor was another basic fur trade commodity. By 1800, alcoholism had reached epidemic proportions among the northwestern tribes. European diseases, against which the native peoples had neither biological immunity nor medical remedies, ravaged tribes. For native peoples throughout the trans-Appalachian West, it was a time of despair, starvation, and social chaos.

In a Shawnee village, in April, 1805, an aging alcoholic called Lalawethika ("Rattle" or "Noisemaker" for his bragging and belligerent behavior) collapsed, apparently dead. Although of no use as a hunter or warrior, Lalawethika had studied with the noted doctor Penagashea. His teacher had died in 1804, however, and working alone, Lalawethika had failed to stop an epidemic that struck his village in early 1805. Now he too, it seemed, was dead.

Before Lalawethika's funeral could take place, he suddenly returned to life. He told his amazed neighbors that he was sent back from the spirit world with a mission. The alcoholic braggart was dead; he had been born again as Tenskwatawa, the "Open Door," to lead his people in a spiritual renewal. The use of alcohol and other vices must stop. Violence between neighbors and the greedy accumulation of material wealth must stop. The people must restore traditional communal values, living in peace with all other tribes. Native people were children of the Master of Life, but Europeans came from the Great Serpent, the Destroyer, and corrupted all they touched. The people must have nothing more to do with them or their goods. If the people purified themselves and faithfully performed the new rituals given in Tenkswatawa's visions, they would restore the spiritual power of the tribes, the earth would be renewed, and the white invaders would disappear forever.

News of the Shawnee Prophet spread among the tribes of the region. His message was believable, not only because Tenskwatawa seemed infused with magnetism and power but also because three generations of prophets among the tribes had reported similar visions. Followers gathered around Tenskwatawa in 1805, hoping that he might be able to make the promise of spiritual renewal finally a reality. In the summer of 1805, he established a new village at Greenville, Ohio, on the United States' side of a boundary line set by the 1795 Treaty of Greenville. The new site was not associated with any specific tribe; therefore, it would be easier to establish his great village of all tribes there. This new, independent village

would not be controlled by any of the government chiefs, and its location openly defied the hated treaty.

Through the fall and winter of 1805, Tenskwatawa met delegations from many tribes and cultivated alliances with Native American leaders throughout the region. Seven treaties signed by the government chiefs between 1804 and 1807 ceded millions of acres of tribal land to the United States and sent many angry, disillusioned tribesmen into Tenskwatawa's camp. Disciples and allied prophets carried his message throughout the Great Lakes region and to the tribes of the South. The powerful Potawatomi shaman and war chief Main Poc, probably the most influential native leader in the region, journeyed to Greenville in the fall of 1807 to confer with Tenskwatawa. Main Poc was in favor of the movement, although he planned a regional confederacy rather than a union of all native peoples. He firmly refused to give up his old blood feud with the Osage or his fondness for alcohol. On other crucial points, however, he and Tenkswatawa agreed and joined as allies.

Hundreds of people from a dozen tribes gathered at Greenville. Tenskwatawa, increasingly occupied with his duties as spiritual leader, delegated diplomatic missions to his older brother Tecumseh. Tecumseh was a gifted orator with a wide network of contacts among leaders of both northern and southern tribes. He was, moreover, a respected war chief and a confirmed nativist. Of intertribal heritage himself (his mother was Creek, his father Shawnee), Tecumseh had traveled widely among the tribes and knew their common problems and the need for a common solution. He opposed U.S. expansion; treaty land cessions in which he had no voice had cost him his home. His father and two brothers died fighting the Euro-Americans, and he made his reputation as a warrior in battle against that same enemy.

By 1807, Tecumseh had become his brother's adviser and representative abroad, while Tenskwatawa concentrated on the problems at Greenville. Relations with Shawnee government chief Black Hoof and his followers deteriorated rapidly, and a violent clash seemed likely. The small cornfields and depleted game around Greenville could not feed the village. The site was far from the northwestern tribes, now Tenskwatawa's strongest supporters. U.S. frontiersmen were alarmed by the rapidly growing village so near their settlements, and ugly incidents between individuals or small parties of natives and U.S. settlers escalated. Rumors spread of an impending military campaign against the village.

Main Poc urged Tenskwatawa to move the village to Potawatomi territory. The people would find better hunting and more land for their gardens. They would be farther from enemies and closer to friends. In January, 1808, Tenskwatawa agreed. Through February and March, his followers gathered supplies and prepared for the move. In the first week of April, they burned their old village and started west. Miami government chief Little Turtle, who claimed authority over the region to which Tenskwatawa was moving, attempted to prevent establishment of the new village. Tenskwatawa informed Little Turtle that the Master of Life had chosen the place. There, a great union of all native peoples would guard the boundary between Indian and U.S. lands and prevent further U.S. expansion.

While Tecumseh visited Canada to get supplies of food and ammunition from the British, Tenskwatawa supervised the construction of the new village. Called Prophetstown by the U.S. settlers, the village was situated on the northwest bank of the Wabash River, just below the mouth of the Tippecanoe River, in northwestern Indiana. The site quickly became a focal point for the nativist movement. With a population of more than four hundred in June, and more arriving daily, food and other supplies remained a pressing problem. While Tecumseh was persuading the British to help, Tenskwatawa tricked Indiana governor William Henry Harrison into supplying corn. The overconfident Harrison now believed he could control Tenskwatawa and his followers. The winter of 1808-1809 was unusually hard, and Prophetstown suffered severely from food shortages and a devastating epidemic. Many people went back to their old villages, bitterly disillusioned with Tenskwatawa. By summer, Harrison believed that the influence of the Prophet, as Tenskwatawa had become known, was broken and thought he could push another land cession on the tribes of the region. At the Treaty of Fort Wayne, September 30, 1809, government chiefs of the Miami, Potawatomi, and Lenni Lenape signed away millions of acres of land for about two cents an acre.

Members of Tenskwatawa's movement were outraged by the treaty. The widespread anger revitalized the movement, and people flocked again to Prophetstown. While Tenskwatawa remained the spiritual leader of the movement, Tecumseh emerged as the political and military leader. When Tecumseh traveled south to confer with the Creek, Choctaw, Chickasaw, and others, Harrison decided the time to strike had come. He burned Prophetstown after the Battle of Tippecanoe, November 7-8, 1811.   —*Mary Ellen Rowe*

ADDITIONAL READING:

Allen, Robert S. *His Majesty's Indian Allies*. Toronto: Dundurn Press, 1992. Presents material from British sources neglected by U.S. historians.

Dowd, Gregory Evans. *A Spirited Resistance*. Baltimore: The Johns Hopkins University Press, 1992. Traces the nativist movement from the 1730's, providing the ideological and historical context for Prophetstown.

Drake, Benjamin. *Life of Tecumseh*. 1858. Reprint. New York: Arno Press, 1969. Biography using primary documents and interviews with individuals who knew Tecumseh.

Edmunds, R. David. *The Shawnee Prophet*. Lincoln: University of Nebraska Press, 1983. Carefully researched and objective biography of Tenskwatawa.

_____. *Tecumseh and the Quest for Indian Leadership*. Boston: Little, Brown, 1984. Thorough research separates fact from fiction in this biography.

SEE ALSO: 1794, Battle of Fallen Timbers; 1799, Code of Handsome Lake; 1811, Battle of Tippecanoe; 1813, Creek War; 1813, Battle of the Thames.

1808 ■ AMERICAN FUR COMPANY IS CHARTERED: *the first American monopoly launches the American fur trade in the trans-Mississippi West*

DATE: April 6, 1808
LOCALE: Albany, New York
CATEGORIES: Business and labor; Economics; Expansion and land acquisition
KEY FIGURES:

John Jacob Astor (1763-1848), organizer of and principal stockholder in the American Fur Company
Ramsay Crook (1787-1859), Astor's chief assistant in the Western fur trade and president of the American Fur Company during its final days
Wilson Price Hunt (1783-1842), leader of the overland expedition to Astoria in 1811-1812
Thomas Jefferson (1743-1826), U.S. president who secured the Louisiana Purchase
Manuel Lisa (1772-1820), Missouri River explorer and founder of Missouri Fur Company
Robert Stuart (1785-1848), one of Astor's lieutenants in the fur trade

SUMMARY OF EVENT. On April 6, 1808, the New York state legislature granted a charter to the American Fur Company for a period of twenty-five years. The capital stock was not to exceed one million dollars until two years had passed, and thereafter it was not to exceed two million dollars. The sole stockholder was John Jacob Astor, who, in 1783, at the age of twenty, had come to the United States as an impoverished immigrant from Germany. After serving as an assistant to a fur merchant in New York City, Astor entered the business on his own account and soon began to trade with China and other areas of eastern Asia. By the early nineteenth century he had become one of the United States' richest and most powerful men.

By 1808, pondering the possibilities for a fur trade empire in the recently purchased Lousiana Territory and regions farther West, Astor decided to challenge Canada's North West Company and the Michilimackinac Company, which had long exploited the trade in those areas. Encouraged by the breakthrough efforts of St. Louis explorer and entrepreneur Manuel Lisa, who had built a trading post on the Missouri River at the mouth of the Big Horn River in 1807 and later a fort at Omaha, and who had created the Missouri Fur Company, Astor sensed that the time was ripe for aggressive American expansion up the Missouri.

Astor envisioned American control of the fur trade in the mountain regions of the Northwest all the way to the Pacific coast. He dreamed of extending that trade across the Pacific to China and other markets. His traders would take the furs to eastern Asia and trade for spices, silks, teas, and other commodities. Astor's scheme called for a huge company with trading posts along the shores of the Great Lakes and the Missouri and Columbia Rivers. First, however, Astor had to consolidate his holdings and obtain new capital, preferably with the blessings of the state or federal government. He therefore engineered the chartering of the American Fur Company in 1808 and similarly the creation of the Pacific Fur Company two years later. He controlled both companies and interchanged their resources so that the firms were virtually indistinguishable.

Once Astor had established the Pacific Fur Company, he made plans to dispatch two parties to the Columbia River. One party arrived by sea at the mouth of the Columbia in March, 1811. Work promptly began on a post called Astoria on the lower Columbia River. The second party, under the command of Wilson Price Hunt, departed overland from St. Louis in March, 1811. This group experienced terrible hardships along the way and the few who survived did not reach their objective until February, 1812. Uncertain about the viability of ocean trade routes, the Astorians sent Robert Stuart east to find an easier overland trail. The Astorians were winning their struggle for survival and had established trade with the local indigenous tribal peoples when the outbreak of war between the United States and Great Britain foiled their endeavors. In 1813 Astor, who feared a British seizure of his Columbia River post, elected to sell the project to the rival North West Company and abandoned his plans in the Pacific Northwest. The activities of his parties, however, had contributed greatly to Euro-American knowledge of the region, and had incidentally helped to reinforce American claims to the Oregon territory.

The War of 1812 also affected Astor's considerable operations in the Midwest. In 1811 the American Fur Company had merged with the North West and Michilimackinac Companies to form the South West Fur Company, which was to confine its activities to the Great Lakes south of the Canadian border. Although the war interrupted the operation, the company thrived later, and in 1817 Astor was able to buy out his partners. He established the Northern Department of the American Fur Company with headquarters at Michilimackinac, and because Congress excluded foreign traders from the territory the same year, Astor achieved a monopoly of the fur trade in the Great Lakes region.

He then moved to gain control of trade in the upper Missouri region. In 1817 he arranged a working agreement with powerful firms in St. Louis to set up the Western Department of the American Fur Company. In 1822, Congress abolished federally sponsored trading posts in tribal territories, part of the "factory system" in operation since 1796. Astor, using his considerable political influence, undercut this program.

Agents of the American Fur Company extended their sphere of influence in the upper Missouri area, crushing opposition ruthlessly. In 1827 Astor absorbed his greatest competitor, the Columbia Fur Company, and operated between the upper Mississippi and the upper Missouri as the Upper Missouri Outfit. By 1828, the American Fur Company commanded an overwhelming share of the fur trade on the northern plains and in the Northwest.

Mexican, French Canadian, and American trappers continued to maintain a brisk commerce in furs out of Taos, and a consortium of traders who would organize the Rocky Mountain Fur Company were consolidating control of trade in the central Rocky Mountains.

At the peak of his fortunes, Astor retired and his company split. One group included some ten stockholders of the Northern Department under Ramsay Crook, Astor's chief assistant. It assumed the name of the American Fur Company and became one of the first large American trusts. The company broke up in 1834 at the onset of the decline of the fur trade. Furs were becoming scarce as the "factors," the "mountain men" and trappers, overtrapped many of the furbearers' streams and ponds. In the late 1830's, the demand for fur garments also declined as fashions changed in Europe and the East. The American Fur Company, under Crook, survived the Panic of 1837 but lingered only as a much smaller concern in the 1840's. Small companies and free-lance trappers continued to mop up the shrinking trade in northern New Mexico, but for the most part they could only watch as new waves of settlers and miners arrived to exploit the agricultural and mineral resources of the trans-Mississippi West.

—James E. Fickle, updated by Thomas L. Altherr

ADDITIONAL READING:

Haeger, John D. *John Jacob Astor: Business and Finance in the Early Republic*. Detroit: Wayne State University Press, 1991. A detailed economic history of Astor's ventures in the Midwestern and Western fur trade and other businesses in the East.

Jones, Robert F., ed. *Astorian Adventure: The Journal of Alfred Seton, 1811-1815*. New York: Fordham University Press, 1993. A fascinating account of daily life at Astoria by one of the company's clerks.

Oglesby, Richard E. *Manuel Lisa and the Opening of the Missouri Fur Trade*. Norman: University of Oklahoma Press, 1963. This volume documents Lisa's importance in the expansion of American trade enterprises in the Upper Missouri River Valley.

Philips, Paul C. *The Fur Trade*. 2 vols. Norman: University of Oklahoma Press, 1961. A massive history of the North American fur trade from the beginning of the seventeenth century to the middle of the nineteenth, with Astor playing a leading role in the second volume.

Ronda, James P. *Astoria and Empire*. Lincoln: University of Nebraska Press, 1990. The most complete account of the founding of Astoria and its decline during the War of 1812; the book places Astor's efforts within an overall imperialist design.

Wishart, David J. *The Fur Trade of the American West 1807-1840*. Lincoln: University of Nebraska Press, 1992. This slender treatise examines the effects of Western geography on the process of establishing and expanding the fur trade.

SEE ALSO: 1803, Louisiana Purchase; 1804, Lewis and Clark Expedition; 1810, Astorian Expeditions; 1815, Westward Migration; 1823, Jedediah Smith Explores the Far West; 1846, Oregon Settlement.

1810 ■ FLETCHER V. PECK: *the U.S. Supreme Court expands the idea of the sanctity of contracts as expressed in the Constitution*

DATE: March 16, 1810

LOCALE: Washington, D.C.

CATEGORIES: Business and labor; Court cases; Expansion and land acquisition; Native American history

KEY FIGURES:

John Quincy Adams (1767-1848), son of president John Adams and future president of the United States, who represented Fletcher

Robert Fletcher, purchaser of the lands, who then demanded a refund, which Peck refused to grant

Gideon Granger (1767-1822), postmaster general under Jefferson, who advocated legislation to permit the United States to reimburse investors in the Yazoo lands

John Marshall (1755-1835), chief justice of the United States

Luther Martin (1748-1826), member of the Constitutional Convention and Peck's attorney

John Peck, seller of a small tract of the Yazoo lands

John Randolph (1773-1833), opponent of the United States paying investors in Yazoo lands

SUMMARY OF EVENT. While it is axiomatic that many of the cases from which great constitutional principles are derived have sordid backgrounds, few if any have emerged from such comic-opera corruption as *Fletcher v. Peck.* On January 7, 1795, the Georgia legislature passed a bill permitting the sale of some thirty-five million acres of fertile, well-watered land for five hundred thousand dollars, payable over a five-year period. The purchasers were four land companies that had been formed to speculate in Western lands. The fact that the state of Georgia did not have clear title to the lands apparently did not bother the legislature because, with one exception, every member of the legislature had been bribed. Nor did the problem of the title appear to inhibit Georgia's governor, who signed the legislation into law. To be sure, the action was not without some benefits to the state. It needed the money, and the problem of wresting the title to the land from the Native American tribes through action by the federal government now became the concern of the speculators. The state had sold a slightly smaller tract to other speculators six years earlier with the same clouded title and on inferior terms, and the electorate of the state had not been disturbed. In the interval, however, Eli Whitney had invented the cotton gin. Now these lands would be in great demand for the production of cotton, assuming that the Native Americans could be removed. The gross dishonesty of the whole transaction upset many conscientious citizens. As a consequence, in 1796, a new legislature was elected, with every member pledged to vote for the repeal of the act of sale. On February 13, the Rescinding Act was passed. So strong was the feeling in the state that a formal ceremony was held on the steps of the State House, during which the initial bill was formally burned. The fraud became known as the Yazoo affair.

Quick as the Georgia reaction to undo the fraudulent deal had been, it had not come in time to prevent the sale of certain of the lands to "innocent" third parties. It was over these titles that the legal and political battles took place. The land companies did not consider the Rescinding Act to be valid, and they continued to sell the land. Most of the purchasers lived in the Middle Atlantic and New England states, and they were greatly concerned as to the validity of their purchases. To defend their purchases, the New England-Mississippi Company had been formed to protect the rights of investors. The company sought an opinion from Alexander Hamilton concerning the legality of the land claims. Hamilton did not attempt to investigate the question of Georgia's title to the land but, in a pamphlet published in 1796, stated that if the title were valid, the Rescinding Act was void and in his opinion, the courts would so rule. Armed with an opinion from one of the country's most distinguished public servants, the company continued to offer its lands to both prospective settlers and speculators.

During the time that the New England-Mississippi Company was selling its lands, a proposal was made to Congress, with the full backing of the Jefferson Administration, that the United States should enter into an arrangement whereby Georgia would cede its claims to the lands in question to the federal government in return for compensation. In addition, the federal government would handle the claims to the area of the several Native American tribes and the Spanish government. This proposal became law. The report of the commissioners whom Jefferson appointed to study the problem proposed that five million acres of the lands be retained and the proceeds from their sale be used to indemnify the Yazoo land purchasers. Although the claims of the speculators, in the commissioners' opinion, could not be supported, they proposed the indemnity for them to ensure "the tranquility of those who may hereafter inhabit the territory," and argued that the federal government should enter into a compromise on reasonable terms. This move, however, caused a political fight of major proportions. When the commissioners' proposal reached the House floor, it was attacked by a wildly indignant John Randolph, who was determined to defeat it by any means possible. Randolph's motives were partly ideological and partly emotional. He had been in Georgia when the Rescinding Act had been passed and had been present at the burning ceremony; he undoubtedly felt that he understood the depths of the popular opposition to the grant in Georgia. He contended that Georgia had no initial right to make the sale, that the sale was firmly rooted in fraud and corruption so as to make it invalid, and that it was legally impossible to sell a third purchaser a better title. Randolph was opposed in the House by Gideon Granger, the postmaster general, who was lobbying with his considerable ability in favor of the measure. After four days of intensive debate, Randolph's eloquence won and the measure was defeated. The supporters of the legislation brought up the measure each year for several years, only to be defeated each time. Eventually, following the implicit advice given earlier by Alexander Hamilton, the purchasers sought relief through the courts.

The "friendly" suit of *Fletcher v. Peck* originated in the sale made by John Peck of Massachusetts to Robert Fletcher of New Hampshire of fifteen thousand acres of Yazoo lands. It was Fletcher's intention to test the legality of his purchase. Because the litigants lived in different states, the case was heard in the federal courts. After Justice William Cushing of the Supreme Court, acting in his capacity as a circuit judge, found for Peck in October, 1807, the case was appealed to the Supreme Court. Supreme Court justice William Johnson later said in a concurring opinion that the controversy had the appearance of a feigned case, but that his admiration for the attorneys involved in the case had induced him "to abandon [his] scruples, in the belief that they would never consent to impose a mere feigned case upon this Court." Luther Martin, Peck's attorney, contended that the several states were free, sovereign, and independent entities, and that "the sovereignty of each, not of the whole, was the principle of the Revolution." Consequently, Martin argued, the federal courts had no jurisdiction in the matter. John Quincy Adams, later replaced by Joseph Story, the future Supreme Court justice, based his case on Hamilton's old opinion that the grant was a contract, and under Article I, Section 10 of the Constitution, it could not be rescinded.

The issue in *Fletcher v. Peck* was essentially a question of public welfare versus public confidence in the sanctity of land grants. To refuse to allow the states the authority to repeal the land grant, especially in the context of an obvious fraud, would undermine the public welfare and invite land speculators to corrupt state legislatures. At the same time, to give the state legislature the right to revoke the land grant would jeopardize public confidence in all public grants, and in turn would discourage investment and the exploitation of land.

"That corruption," John Marshall wrote at the beginning of his opinion in *Fletcher v. Peck*, "should find its way into the governments of our infant republics and contaminate the very source of legislation . . . [is a circumstance] deeply to be to be deplored." Despite this, the Rescinding Act of the Georgia Legislature was still void.

Marshall did not clearly establish the reasons that the repeal of the land grant was constitutionally infirm. At one point in his opinion, he argued that the 1796 act of the Georgia legislature impaired the obligation of a contract in violation of Article I, Section 10 of the Constitution; elsewhere, he suggested that the Georgia act was a violation of the ex post facto clause of the same article and section. "The rescinding act," he wrote, "would have the effect of an ex post facto decision. It forfeits the estate of Fletcher for a crime not committed by himself, but from those from who he purchased." This argument had the defect of ignoring the fact that the ex post facto clause had been held applicable only to criminal cases in *Calder v. Bull* in 1698, and the law in *Fletcher* dealt solely with a civil subject.

Elsewhere in the opinion, following one of the arguments

of Alexander Hamilton, Marshall intimated that the Rescinding Act was invalid because it conflicted with the nature of society and government. At the conclusion of his opinion, Marshall said that "the state of Georgia was restrained by general principles which are common to our free institutions or by the particular provisions of the Constitution."

Despite the ambiguity of Marshall's opinion and its shortcomings, *Fletcher v. Peck* was the first clear precedent for the assertion by the Supreme Court of a power to declare state laws unconstitutional. Its immediate practical effect was negligible; Georgia no longer owned the Yazoo lands, as they had been ceded to the federal government. However, *Fletcher* did lay the foundations for using the contract clause of the Constitution to protect private property interests against the vagaries of state legislatures. As such, it is a reflection of the overall strategy of the Marshall Court to facilitate investment and energize the U.S. economy.

Although the speculators had won in the Supreme Court, they were not to secure a congressional, or monetary, victory until 1814, when Congress, after John Randolph's failure to win reelection, passed an appropriation of five million dollars to buy up their now untarnished titles.

—*Gustav L. Seligman, updated by David L. Sterling*

ADDITIONAL READING:

Beveridge, Albert J. *Conflict and Construction, 1800-1815.* Vol. 4 in *The Life of John Marshall.* Boston: Houghton Mifflin, 1919. This classic biography of Marshall devotes almost sixty pages to a discussion of *Fletcher v. Peck.*

Haines, Charles G. *The Role of the Supreme Court in American Government and Politics, 1789-1835.* Berkeley: University of California Press, 1944. A study of the Supreme Court in its formative period. Gives adequate coverage to *Fletcher v. Peck* and places it in the framework of the Court's development.

Hunting, Warren B. *The Obligation of Contracts Clause of the United States Constitution.* Baltimore: The Johns Hopkins University Press, 1919. Contains a technical discussion of an important phase of U.S. constitutional history. Detailed coverage of *Fletcher v. Peck.*

Newmyer, R. Kent. *Supreme Court Justice Joseph Story: Statesman of the Old Republic.* Chapel Hill: University of North Carolina Press, 1985. A comprehensive, analytical biography of Story, one of the lawyers in *Fletcher v. Peck* and a future associate of John Marshall.

White, G. Edward. *The Marshall Court and Cultural Change, 1815-1835.* Abridged ed. New York: Oxford University Press, 1991. Although abridged, this study of the record of the Marshall Court contains almost eight hundred pages of text and almost eighty pages on the contract clause cases.

Wright, Benjamin F., Jr. *The Contract Clause of the Constitution.* Cambridge, Mass.: Harvard University Press, 1938. A more detailed study of the contract clause than Hunting's and broader in scope.

SEE ALSO: 1793, Whitney Invents the Cotton Gin; 1813, Creek War; 1815, Westward Migration.

1810 ■ ASTORIAN EXPEDITIONS: *a new phase in the escalating American-British contest for control of the Northwest*

DATE: September 8, 1810-May, 1812
LOCALE: Pacific Northwest
CATEGORIES: Economics; Expansion and land acquisition; Exploration and discovery
KEY FIGURES:
John Jacob Astor (1763-1848), American entrepreneur and originator of the Astorian venture
Comcomly (1765?-1830), Chinook chief
Wilson Price Hunt (1783-1842), leader of the overland expedition
Duncan McDougall (1780?-1818) and
Robert Stuart, leaders of the sea expedition
David Mackenzie, first to arrive from the overland expedition
David Thompson (1770-1857), North West Company partner, explorer, and fur trader

SUMMARY OF EVENT. John Jacob Astor came to New York from Germany in 1784 to make his fortune in a new land. Beginning as a clerk in a furrier's shop, he eventually became a major fur dealer and one of the most successful entrepreneurs in the United States. By 1800, Astor realized that further expansion of his business would bring him into direct competition with the great British fur companies of Canada—the Hudson's Bay Company and the North West Company—and that much more than his personal fortune was at stake. Where the companies built their trading posts, the government of their nations would follow, establishing outposts and claiming the region. Over the next few years, Astor devised a plan to create a transcontinental U.S. company that could compete with British rivals, establish a fur trade monopoly across the center of the North American continent, and extend beyond to control trade with China and Russian Alaska. This company would not only make Astor a leader of the international fur industry but also establish the United States' sovereignty in the region and prevent British expansion from Canada.

In 1808, Astor incorporated the American Fur Company, then proceeded to set up subsidiary regional companies to carry out specific parts of his plan. One of these, the Pacific Fur Company, formally organized in the summer of 1810, was to establish a base of operations on America's northwest coast, explore and establish a trade monopoly in the rich fur regions west of the Rocky Mountains, manage a monopoly on trade with the Russian settlements in Alaska, and corner the market on the fur trade with China. To initiate this ambitious project, two expeditions of "Astorians" started out in 1810. One, led by Duncan McDougall and Robert Stuart, was to travel by sea around South America to the mouth of the Columbia River. Besides clerks, craftsmen, and laborers, the expedition would take the tools and supplies needed to build and maintain a trading post on the Columbia. The other expedition, led by Wilson Price Hunt, was to travel overland from St. Louis,

blazing a trail to the Columbia River and selecting sites for the network of trading posts that Astor intended to build across the continent.

McDougall and Stuart's expedition boarded the ship *Tonquin* and sailed from New York harbor on September 8, 1810. The voyage was plagued by bad luck, delays, and increasingly bitter quarrels between the *Tonquin*'s overbearing captain and the Astorians. In February, 1811, the *Tonquin* laid over in the Hawaiian Islands, taking on stores of food, water, and additional laborers and livestock to support the new trading post. After battling ocean storms and the sand bars, whirlpools, and treacherous currents at the river's mouth, the *Tonquin* finally found safe harbor in the Columbia River on March 24. McDougall and Stuart selected a site on the river's south bank, and the heavy work of clearing away the dense forest began. By April 19, actual construction on the new post of Astoria had commenced.

Hunt's party was delayed by recruiting and supply problems and did not leave St. Louis until October 21, 1810. Facing the onset of winter after a grueling trip up the Missouri River and uncertain about the best route west, the expedition went into camp on the Nodaway River, about five hundred miles above St. Louis. In March, 1811, the Astorians resumed their journey. Bad luck with weather, equipment, and travel routes exacerbated personnel problems and slowed their progress. A bit of good luck came from encounters with native people who proved helpful sources of food and geographical information.

Hunt followed native trade routes to the Rocky Mountains, crossing present-day South Dakota and Wyoming. West of the Continental Divide, the expedition got lost and suffered terribly from hunger, harsh weather, rough terrain, and the dangers of trying to navigate the wild Snake River. In late October, 1811, Hunt split the party into smaller groups to search for food and the best route to the Columbia River. A group led by Donald MacKenzie reached Astoria on January 18, 1812. Hunt and forty-five of the original sixty members of the main party, after an extremely difficult and dangerous overland journey during which Shoshoni Indians helped them, arrived on February 15. The remaining overlanders straggled in a few weeks later.

By that time, Astoria was a growing trading post with a large store, living quarters, a blacksmith shop, and storage sheds, all enclosed in a ninety-foot-square palisade. McDougall and the other Pacific Fur Company partners were planning to expand Astoria and establish satellite posts around the region. They, too, had been hampered by bad luck. Their lifeline to the outside world, the ship *Tonquin*, had left Astoria June 1, 1811, to trade with natives along the coast. By early July, rumors reached them that the people on Vancouver Island had destroyed the ship and its crew in revenge for the captain's insults to their chief. A lone survivor eventually reached Astoria to confirm the story.

Although tribes on the lower Columbia welcomed the traders, the Astorians remained nervous about their neighbors' intentions, particularly as they depended on the local people for food as well as furs. Although the newcomers immediately planted a garden at their post, it took time to learn how to grow crops in the unfamiliar climate and soil. Meanwhile, rations were short at Astoria. This situation suited the Chinook chief, Comcomly. As the most powerful native leader in the region, he claimed a monopoly on trade with Astoria. Through the traders' first year, Comcomly saw to it that they had enough food to survive and enough trade to keep them from leaving, but only enough to keep them dependent on him. Although the Astorians resented Comcomly's manipulation of their business, they could rarely outwit him and dared not oppose him openly.

To further Astor's grand plan and to break Comcomly's control, Hunt, McDougall, and the other partners planned expeditions to establish trading posts inland. Before they could act, however, a new challenge appeared. David Thompson, a North West Company partner, suddenly arrived at Astoria, July 15, 1811. Renowned as an explorer of the far Northwest, Thompson had discovered the source of the Columbia River in 1807. Now he was the first European to follow the river from its headwaters to its mouth. He had claimed the country he traversed for his company and Great Britain.

This unexpected appearance of an arch rival spurred the Astorians to action: One Astorian led an expedition up the Columbia River to hold the region against the North West Company. Other parties explored geography and trade prospects up the coast and up the Willamette River. In May, 1812, a long-overdue supply ship arrived with abundant supplies and more people. Operations expanded rapidly west of the Rockies, while Robert Stuart started eastward with a party to find a good overland express route to St. Louis. During their crossing, east of Jackson's Hole, they would discover the crucial South Pass through the Rockies, which would later open the floodgates to the settlement of the Oregon territory.

Fortune again turned against the Astorians, however. The United States declared war on Great Britain on June 18, 1812. In January, 1813, that news reached Astoria, with reports that the North West Company and the British navy planned joint expeditions to capture the U.S. outpost. Knowing that they could expect no help from Astor while the British controlled the seas, the partners began negotiations to sell Astoria to the North West Company before it was taken by force. The British sloop *Raccoon* arrived in November, 1813, and took possession of the post. In April, 1814, the Americans returned east. Most Astorians were Canadian, however, and many were former employees of the North West Company, who now went back to work for their old company. The North West Company took over Astoria, renamed Fort George, as its West Coast headquarters. Although Astor failed to establish his trade empire, he did provoke U.S. concern about British expansion in the Northwest. The U.S. government based future claims to the region in part on the U.S. occupation at Astoria. Returning Astorians brought back a wealth of information about the Far West; the route pioneered by Robert Stuart's 1812-1813 expedition would later become the famous Oregon Trail.

—Mary Ellen Rowe

ADDITIONAL READING:

Irving, Washington. *Astoria: Or, Anecdotes of an Enterprise Beyond the Rocky Mountains.* Philadelphia: Carey, Lea and Blanchard, 1836. Available in many modern editions, this history was written from interviews and diaries of participants by one of the United States' great authors.

Jaeger, John D. "Business Strategy and Practice in the Early Republic: John Jacob Astor and the American Fur Trade." *Western Historical Quarterly* 19, no. 2 (May, 1988): 183-202. Compares Astor's business strategy with modern business practices.

Lavender, David. *The Fist in the Wilderness.* Garden City, N.Y.: Doubleday, 1964. Examines the history of the American Fur Company and the Pacific Fur Company.

Rollins, Phillip A., ed. *The Discovery of the Oregon Trail: Robert Stuart's Narrative of His Overland Trip Eastward from Astoria in 1812-13.* New York: Edward Eberstadt & Sons, 1935. Contains the overland diaries of Hunt and Stuart and other useful material.

Ronda, James P. *Astoria and Empire.* Lincoln: University of Nebraska Press, 1990. Analyzes Astoria's role in the struggle for national sovereignty in the Northwest.

Ross, Alexander. *Adventures of the First Settlers on the Oregon or Columbia River, 1810-1813.* Lincoln: University of Nebraska Press, 1986. Ross, one of the original clerks at Astoria, gives a colorful firsthand account of the venture.

SEE ALSO: 1808, American Fur Company Is Chartered.

1810 ■ EL GRITO DE DOLORES: the Hidalgo revolt launches the opening salvos of the Mexican War of Independence

DATE: September 16, 1810
LOCALE: Dolores, Guanajuato, Mexico
CATEGORIES: Latino American history; Wars, uprisings, and civil unrest
KEY FIGURES:
Ignacio de Allende (1779-1811), army officer who led the movement to overthrow Spanish rule
Félix María Calleja del Rey (1759-1828), leader of the Spanish forces that fought the revolution
Miguel Hidalgo y Costilla (1753-1811), leader of the movement for Mexican independence from Spain
SUMMARY OF EVENT. Mexican society in 1810 reflected profound ethnic and caste distinctions. In a total population of six million, fifteen thousand *peninsulares* (Spaniards) monopolized the higher political and clerical positions in the colony. The 1,092,367 *criollos* (individuals of Spanish blood born in Mexico), although physically indistinguishable from *peninsulares*, were relegated to lower political offices or to the ranks of the lower to middle clergy. As a result, most *criollos* devoted themselves to economic pursuits. *Mestizos* (persons of mixed Spanish and American Indian or Spanish and African blood) numbered 1,328,706 and were, for the most part, so-

cioeconomically inferior to both *criollos* and *peninsulares*. Although Mexican Indians constituted the largest population group in the colony (3,676,281), they occupied the lower rungs of society and were subject to restrictions not applied to other groups.

As the largest and most economically significant of Spain's overseas possessions, Mexico entered the nineteenth century not unaffected by liberal and political currents in Europe. The Enlightenment, the American and French Revolutions, and the Napoleonic invasion of Spain had persuaded disaffected *criollos* to question Mexico's colonial status and, in some cases, to advocate Mexico's independence from Spain. Father Miguel Hidalgo y Costilla emerged as a principal leader of a nascent group espousing independence.

Born in 1753, Hidalgo began his religious studies at an early age, first under the Jesuits (until the order's expulsion from Mexico in 1767), then at the diocesan College of San Nicolás Obispo in Valladolid. Following a course of study in rhetoric, Latin, Thomistic theology, music, and Indian languages, Hidalgo took his bachelor's degree in 1774. He then began preparations for the priesthood and celebrated his ordination in 1778. Rising in his profession, Hidalgo became a rector at San Nicolás in 1790, only to resign his position two years later because of possible financial mismanagement of college funds, religious unorthodoxy, and charges of gambling and fornication. (Like many other Mexican curates of the time, Hidalgo had several relationships with women and fathered three illegitimate children during his career.) Although none of the charges was proven, Hidalgo subsequently held only rural curacies, culminating in his transfer to the small parish of Dolores in 1803. At Dolores, Hidalgo introduced industrial innovations in the production of pottery, olive oil, and other items, and made his residence a center for musical, literary, and intellectual gatherings.

While at Dolores, Hidalgo became acquainted with Ignacio de Allende, a captain of the queen's cavalry regiment, who brought the priest into the so-called Querétaro Conspiracy, a plot to overthrow Spanish rule and allow the *criollos* to take control of the country. Other conspirators included Juan de Aldama, Miguel Domínguez and his wife, Josefa Ortiz de Domínguez, and Mariano Galván. To offset Spanish superiority in arms, ammunition, and organization, the conspirators decided to appeal to the Indian and mestizo masses to join the revolt, set for December 8, 1810. Before this date, however, Galván betrayed the conspiracy and viceregal authorities began to make arrests. Forewarned of his impending arrest on September 16, Hidalgo decided to begin the revolt at once, ringing the bells of the Dolores church and summoning his parishioners.

Although the exact words Hidalgo used in his *grito* (literally "shout") are not known, it is generally believed that he launched the revolt in the name of King Ferdinand VII, then deposed by the French, and exhorted his Indian and mestizo followers to reclaim their lands, defend their rights and religion, and put an end to bad government. Already suffering

Father Miguel Hidalgo y Costilla launched a revolt that is considered the opening of the Mexican War of Independence which culminated a decade later. (The Institute of Texan Cultures, San Antonio, Texas)

from the effects of a bad corn harvest in 1809 and the economic dislocations that triggered in other areas of the economy, the people were predisposed to heed Hidalgo's words. Aroused, a force of between five hundred and eight hundred, led by Hidalgo and Allende, marched on San Miguel, a larger town in the vicinity and Allende's birthplace. Passing through the village of Atotonilco on the way, Hidalgo entered the church and took up a banner of Our Lady of Guadalupe, making the Indian Virgin the emblem of a revolt that would rely heavily on Indian and mestizo support.

An appeal to the disaffected masses added a social and ethnic dimension to the revolt that only became clear during the capture of San Miguel, when Hidalgo's forces degenerated into a destructive mob intent on sacking the city and persecuting its Spanish minority. Although Allende managed to reestablish order, the problem reasserted itself at the capture of Celaya, on September 21. The turmoil was seen even more dramatically at the important mining center of Guanajuato, where miners and the city's lower classes joined the rebels in storming the city's granary, where most of the local Spaniards had taken refuge. Breaching the walls, the rebels massacred the defenders before looting the city for two days.

By mid-October, Hidalgo's forces numbered between sixty and eighty thousand and the attack on Mexico City, the capital, began. Royalist forces met Hidalgo's army at Monte de las Cruces on October 30, 1810. Although vastly outnumbered, the highly disciplined and well-armed royalist forces inflicted severe casualties on Hidalgo's army before retreating back toward the city. Overruling Allende and other rebel leaders, Hidalgo forbade a final assault, possibly to recoup his losses and to avoid a repetition of Guanajuato on a much larger scale if the capital fell to the insurgents.

Retreating toward the northwest, the rebels reconstituted their forces at Guadalajara. Royalist forces under General Félix María Calleja del Rey met Hidalgo's new army on January 17, 1811. Although once more outnumbered, royalist forces under Calleja again demonstrated the organization and skill lacking in Hidalgo's army. Nevertheless, the issue was in doubt until a chance cannonball struck a rebel ammunition wagon. The resulting explosion and spreading fire created havoc and led to a general rout of Hidalgo's forces.

Fleeing northward, Hidalgo and other rebel leaders were eventually captured by royalist forces at Monclava, Coahuila. As a priest, Hidalgo avoided immediate execution and instead stood trial before the Inquisition. Hidalgo was found guilty of treason and heresy, and the court remanded him to the secular authorities. On July 30, 1811, Hidalgo met his death before a firing squad.

Hidalgo's death marked the end of the first phase of the Mexican War of Independence. Guerrilla forces fought on for much of the decade, but with little *criollo* support. Most of the *criollos* were disillusioned by the anarchy and racial conflict they perceived in Hidalgo's revolt and the inability or unwillingness of the Indian and mestizo insurgents to distinguish between Spaniard and *criollo*. The majority of the *criollos* were social conservatives and preferred an independence that would guarantee them political power. Only when they perceived that Spain suddenly was following a liberal course counter to their own did these *criollos* throw their support to independence in 1820-1821, supporting a political, if not a social, revolution.

Hidalgo's revolt is commemorated annually as part of Mexico's independence day celebrations, held September 15 and 16, with the Mexican president reenacting the Grito de Dolores.　—*Joseph C. Jastrzembski*

ADDITIONAL READING:
Hamill, Hugh M., Jr. "Caudillismo and Independence: A Symbiosis." In *The Independence of Mexico and the Creation of the New Nation*, edited by Jaime E. Rodriguez O. Los Angeles: University of California at Los Angeles, Latin American Center Publications, 1989. Contrasts the leadership styles and abilities of Hidalgo and Calleja.

_____. *The Hidalgo Revolt: Prelude to Mexican Independence*. Gainesville: University of Florida Press, 1966. The standard English-language account of the Hidalgo Revolt.

Lynch, John. *The Spanish American Revolutions, 1808-1826*. New York: W. W. Norton, 1973. Excellent overview of all the independence movements occurring in the Spanish American colonies. Highlights the social implications of the early Mexican movement.

Meyer, Michael C., and William L. Sherman. "The Wars for Independence." In *The Course of Mexican History*. 5th ed. New York: Oxford University Press, 1995. Highly readable account of the independence period. Contains suggestions for further reading. Illustrated.

Van Young, Eric. "Quetzalcóatl, King Ferdinand, and Ignacio Allende Go to the Seashore: Or, Messianism and Mystical Kingship in Mexico, 1800-1821." In *The Independence of Mexico and the Creation of the New Nation*, edited by Jaime E. Rodriguez O. Los Angeles: University of California at Los Angeles, Latin American Center Publications, 1989. Discusses how Indian messianism functioned as an element of popular ideology in the Mexican Revolution.

Villoro, Luis. "The Ideological Currents of the Epoch of Independence." In *Major Trends in Mexican Philosophy*. Notre Dame: University of Notre Dame Press, 1966. Surveys the intellectual underpinnings of the various Mexican independence phases.

SEE ALSO: 1821, Mexican War of Independence.

1811 ■ CONSTRUCTION OF THE NATIONAL ROAD: *the first federally financed interstate transportation project begins to link the states*

DATE: Beginning 1811
LOCALE: Cumberland, Maryland, to Wheeling, Virginia
CATEGORIES: Economics; Expansion and land acquisition; Transportation
KEY FIGURES:
Albert Gallatin (1761-1849), secretary of the Treasury under President Jefferson
Thomas Jefferson (1743-1826), third president of the United States, 1801-1809
David Shriver, Jr., first superintendent appointed by Congress to supervise construction of the road
Ebenezer Zane (1747-1812), pioneer road builder who laid out Zane's Trace, later part of the National Road

SUMMARY OF EVENT. As the United States expanded westward into the Ohio Valley, transportation became increasingly difficult. Much of the commerce of the Eastern seaboard relied upon rivers for transportation, but no water routes existed that cut through the Appalachian Mountains to the Northwest Territories. Roads were needed both for economic reasons and for military security. Recognizing the need for internal improvements, Congress in 1806 passed a bill authorizing the construction of a road from Cumberland, Maryland, to Ohio. The road reached Wheeling, Virginia, on the Ohio River in 1818; it was 130 miles long and cost, on the average, thirteen thousand dollars per mile. As the first federally mandated highway, it became known as the National Road. Construction continued intermittently until 1840, when the road reached Vandalia, Illinois. By then, railroads and canals had eclipsed turnpikes in transporting freight, and construction ended. The federal government did not become involved in road construction again until the twentieth century.

Construction of the National Road coincided with a report that Albert Gallatin, secretary of the Treasury under President Thomas Jefferson, submitted to Congress on the transportation needs of the nation. Gallatin recommended that the central government expend some twenty million dollars to develop a comprehensive and national transportation network. He was well aware that private or state capital, without the active financial aid of the federal government, could not accomplish such a vast undertaking. Gallatin recommended the construction of both roads and canal systems to link the expanding frontier with the more developed eastern states. Approval of the National Road project seemed to indicate that Gallatin's proposed system had taken the first momentous step.

Construction of the road from Cumberland, Maryland, a city located on the upper reaches of the Potomac River, to Wheeling, Virginia, a site on the Ohio River, would link the two river systems and make transportation of freight and people from the mid-Atlantic states to the interior of the growing country easier. Cutting through the ridges of the Appalachian Mountains would prove a daunting task. After five years of extensive surveys to determine the best route, road crews commenced preparing a sixty-six-foot-wide right-of-way. The thickly forested hills were cleared, and workers excavated a roadbed twelve to eighteen inches deep. The roadbed was filled with broken stone and then rolled to form a level surface. Stone and masonry bridges were constructed to cross the numerous streams and small rivers common in the mountains. In 1818, when the road reached Wheeling, it became a major trade route to the West. Large numbers of travelers left testimony to the economic importance of the road. Goods from Baltimore could now reach the Ohio River via wagon, at a considerable savings in freight. The road gave Baltimore, for a time, a decided advantage over its major competitor to the north, Philadelphia. Philadelphia was to feel increasingly pressed by its competitors, for in 1817, the state of New York authorized the construction of the Erie Canal. Thus, both Baltimore and New York City would be directly linked to the West. To maintain its commercial position, Philadelphia, with the aid of Pennsylvania, launched its own system of internal improvements in the direction of Pittsburgh.

Enormous quantities of goods and large numbers of people passed over the National Road. Cattle from the Ohio River Valley, Monongahela flour, and spiritous liquors passed over the road to market. Taverns and grazing stations sprang up along the road to serve the wagoners, drovers, and immigrants who moved along the route. Wheeling boomed, as did some of the towns located along the National Road. Supporters of the road wanted to extend it across Ohio, but the Panic of 1819 brought construction to a halt for seven years while Congress debated funding. Critics of federal involvement in internal

improvements felt the road had already served its purpose, and any additional improvements could be left to the states or private enterprise. In 1825, however, additional funds were allocated, and construction of the road proceeded across Ohio into Illinois. The road first followed and improved upon a crude public road developed by an Ohio pioneer, Ebenezer Zane, and then cleared a new path as it stretched toward the Mississippi River. It appeared to be a successful first step in federal efforts to link sections of the nation together.

The National Road was the last federal highway project for almost a century, as many people in the United States were convinced that the federal government lacked the constitutional authority to finance and build internal improvements. The constitutional barrier proved to be an obstacle that could not be overcome. Supporters of the National Road eventually were able to extend it a total of six hundred miles to a terminus at Vandalia, Illinois, but no other roads were funded. The states were thrown back on their own resources, as the federal government relinquished its responsibilities in this critical area.

Two specific actions, one occurring during the presidency of James Madison and the other during that of James Monroe, contributed to the federal government's assuming a passive and nondirective role in meeting the nation's transportation requirements. Both involved presidential vetoes.

The logistic problems of the War of 1812 and the rapid movement of population into the West aroused considerable support for federal activity in internal improvements. To meet the demand both of citizens and of national security, John C. Calhoun, representative from South Carolina, introduced the Bonus Bill into Congress in 1817. This bill was designed to provide a permanent fund for the construction of internal improvements, and it passed both Houses of Congress. President James Madison, who had publicly called for such a system, nevertheless vetoed the bill on strict constructionist grounds. He argued that the Constitution was one of enumerated powers, that federal activity in internal improvements was not one of those powers, and that to justify such activity under the "general welfare" clause was to make the government the judge of its own powers. Madison maintained that a constitutional amendment was required before the government could operate in the area of internal improvements. Five years later, President James Monroe vetoed a bill authorizing repair of the National Road to be financed by the collection of tolls. The general tenor of his veto message was similar to Madison's. These vetoes, coupled with the rising sectional antagonisms that eventually culminated in the Civil War, put an end to the hopes that the federal government would provide leadership and support in transportation.

In 1824, Congress passed the General Survey Act, which enabled the president to plot out a comprehensive system of roads and canals, but the battle was already lost. Nothing came of this legislation. The federal government thereafter confined itself to the granting of alternate sections of public lands along the route of intended canals and railroads. New York, as early as 1817, had anticipated this outcome and proceeded to construct the Erie Canal with state funds. State funds and private capital, both domestic and foreign, provided the financial support required to construct the canals and railroads that eventually bound the nation together. The National Road faded into obscurity, until the rise of bicycles and automobiles revived its usage. In 1926, the National Road became part of the U.S. Highway 40 and served as a major east-west artery until construction of Interstate 70.

—John G. Clark, updated by Nancy Farm Mannikko

ADDITIONAL READING:

Aitken, Thomas. *Albert Gallatin: Early America's Swiss-Born Statesman.* New York: Vantage Press, 1985. Biography of the secretary of the Treasury whose report on the transportation needs of the nation proved pivotal in planning the National Road.

Ierley, Merritt. *Traveling the National Road: Across the Centuries on America's First Highway.* Woodstock, N.Y.: Overlook Press, 1990. Interesting general history of the National Road.

Schneider, Norris F. *The National Road: Main Street of America.* Columbus: Ohio Historical Society, 1975. History of the National Road, emphasizing the role the highway played in Ohio's development.

Searight, Thomas B. *The Old Pike: A History of the National Road.* Berryville, Va.: Prince Maccus, 1983. Colorful history of the National Road with an emphasis on its early years.

Smith, Barry. *Cumberland Road.* Boston: Houghton Mifflin, 1989. History of U.S. Highway 40, with an emphasis on the portion of the highway that passed through Maryland and Virginia to the Ohio River.

SEE ALSO: 1815, Westward Migration; 1825, Erie Canal Opens; 1830, Baltimore and Ohio Railroad Begins Operation.

1811 ■ BATTLE OF TIPPECANOE: *a minor skirmish makes a hero of William Henry Harrison, later propelling him to the presidency*

DATE: November 7, 1811

LOCALE: Northwest Indiana

CATEGORIES: Government and politics; Wars, uprisings, and civil unrest

KEY FIGURES:

William Henry Harrison (1773-1841), governor of the Indiana Territory and later, ninth president of the United States, 1841

Tecumseh (1768-1813), political and military leader of the American Indian tribes of the Northwest

Tenskwatawa, also known as *the Prophet* (1768-1837), Shawnee spiritual leader and brother of Tecumseh

SUMMARY OF EVENT. William Henry Harrison, governor of the Indiana Territory, was determined to provoke a fight with the Native American tribes living within the territory recently ceded to the United States. The tribal leaders, Tecumseh and his brother, Tenskwatawa, the Prophet, hoped equally to avoid such a fight. They had established their capital, Prophetstown, at the village of Tippecanoe, eighty miles south of Lake Michigan near the confluence of the Tippecanoe and Wabash Rivers in present-day northwestern Indiana, and members of a growing Native American movement had flocked to the site. Despite a message of peace from the Prophet, Harrison moved up the Wabash River with a thousand troops on September 26, headed toward Prophetstown. On November 6, the U.S. troops encamped twelve miles from Tippecanoe.

Tecumseh and the Prophet had hoped to avoid bloodshed, but reckless members of the movement forced the issue. They attacked the U.S. forces in the predawn hours of November 7. Harrison, roused from his sleep, immediately moved to rally his men and reinforce his overrun flank. The forest and nearby river bottoms echoed with the sounds of screams, musket and rifle fire, shouted curses and commands, and the cries of frightened, wounded, and dying men and animals. Two of Harrison's close friends, Major Jo Daviess and Thomas Randolph, were among the dead. Harrison promised Randolph he would look after the dying man's young child, a promise he kept.

Harrison managed to hold his troops together, in time driving the attackers back. Two hours later, all was again relatively calm. Harrison's force surveyed its position and discovered nearly two hundred casualties, one-fifth of his force. More than sixty were dead or dying. The Native Americans, who had been driven back into the swamps and river bottoms, had left behind thirty-eight corpses. Two days later, they entered a deserted Tippecanoe, found food and British rifles, and burned the village. Such were the immediate results of the widely heralded Battle of Tippecanoe, which many historians consider to have been of fundamental importance in breaking Tecumseh's plan for a Western Indian confederation, speeding the outbreak of the War of 1812, and contributing to the election of William Henry Harrison to the U.S. presidency in 1840.

In broad terms, the clash at Tippecanoe was the inevitable result of two vastly different civilizations struggling for domination of the North American continent. In a more immediate sense, the conflict stemmed from the differing drives, personalities, and objectives of two significant Western leaders: the great Shawnee chieftain Tecumseh and the aspiring politician and military man William Henry Harrison.

The clash at Tippecanoe was a single episode in the long series of confrontations between natives and Europeans, going back to the early days of European colonization in North America. Conflict rather than cooperation between the races was the rule, and Tippecanoe represents one of the last stands east of the Mississippi River for the Native Americans as they were pushed farther and farther west by the encroachments of European civilization and institutions.

For the natives, Tippecanoe was one round in a long struggle in which they were poorly matched against the land-hungry and grasping white settlers. The natives were dependent on the whites for arms and ammunition; many had been weakened by addiction to alcohol obtained from frontier bootleggers; and they lacked organization and unity of purpose. Tecumseh, political and military leader of the tribes of the Northwest, and his brother, the Prophet, sought to overcome these weaknesses by calling on their people to reject the white man's culture, reassert their independence, and unite to drive the whites back across the Ohio. Since 1808, they had attempted to form a confederacy in response to movement of Europeans into the Ohio Valley; by 1811, only four thousand Native Americans remained in the region, as opposed to a hundred thousand white settlers. The attack at Tippecanoe had been intended to shatter the confederacy and the influence of the Prophet. In this, it was partially successful. The Prophet had promised immunity from the white man's bullets. Instead, the attack had meant death, and the Prophet's spell was broken. Tecumseh failed to rally the Sauk and Osage tribes to the south into his cause. Instead of terrifying Tecumseh, however, Harrison had stirred him to fury.

Despite the natives' defeat at Tippecanoe, the idea of confederation continued until Tecumseh, allied with the British in the War of 1812, was killed at the Battle of the Thames River, across Lake Erie on Canadian soil, in October, 1813. The natives had resisted white aggrandizement for a quarter of a century, but it was Tippecanoe that brought the Prophet's career into eclipse. He was never again trusted by his brother, and he drifted into obscurity.

Harrison's later career was largely built around the conflict at Tippecanoe. He was an ambitious man who extracted every ounce of glory that could be gained from his success in the battle. His version of the episode depicted the policies of the United States government toward the natives as enlightened and compassionate. U.S. settlers were admittedly encroaching on tribal lands, but those lands were legitimately acquired through treaties with the old village chiefs. Furthermore, Harrison argued, the settlers were making efforts to uplift and civilize the red men. If the natives, particularly Tecumseh and the Prophet, resisted these policies and the inevitable U.S. expansion, then it was because of their savage nature or, still worse, the result of British influence.

Harrison's views were not universally accepted by his own people, who heatedly debated everything about the Battle of Tippecanoe, but Harrison was so widely accepted as the Hero of Tippecanoe that he was given the opportunity of winning more military honors during the War of 1812, and he parlayed his military reputation into political offices, culminating in his election to the presidency.

The impact of the Battle of Tippecanoe on public sentiment was perhaps most important as a precursor to the War of 1812. Feelings between the United States and Great Britain were running high in 1811, and tempers were close to the breaking point. Many people in the United States believed, with some justification, that the British were stirring up trouble among the tribes. The discovery of British arms at the Battle of Tippecanoe was widely accepted as proof of a British-Native

American conspiracy that threatened U.S. security and violated the rights of the United States as a sovereign nation. The fact that the British had actually attempted to restrain Tecumseh and the Prophet was either unknown or ignored. The important fact is that many people in the United States were highly incensed by the Battle of Tippecanoe; that bad feeling became part of the package of western grievances and ambitions that helped to trigger the War of 1812.

—*James E. Fickle, updated by Richard Adler*

ADDITIONAL READING:

Berton, Pierre. *The Invasion of Canada, 1812-1813.* Boston: Little, Brown, 1980. First volume of a two-volume account of the War of 1812 from a Canadian perspective. An excellent description of the Battle of Tippecanoe and its long-term significance.

Cleaves, Freeman. *Old Tippecanoe: William Henry Harrison and His Time.* New York: Charles Scribner's Sons, 1939. One of the few major biographies of Harrison. Includes an excellent account of the Battle of Tippecanoe.

Dangerfield, George. *The Era of Good Feeling.* New York: Harcourt, Brace, and World, 1952. Pulitzer-Prize winning account of the early nineteenth century. Places the war and the Battle of Tippecanoe within the larger perspective.

Elting, John. *Amateurs to Arms! A Military History of the War of 1812.* New York: Da Capo Press, 1995. A detailed military view of an unpopular, badly fought, and arguably unnecessary war. Highlights the military campaigns.

Hickey, Donald. *The War of 1812.* Chicago: University of Illinois Press, 1990. An overview of the causes of the war. Concludes that the war was important in promoting nationalism and maintaining a sense of manifest destiny.

Klinck, Carl F. *Tecumseh: Fact and Fiction in Early Records.* Englewood Cliffs, N.J.: Prentice-Hall, 1961. A biographical sketch of Tecumseh based on relevant documentation.

Sugden, John. *Tecumseh's Last Stand.* Norman: University of Oklahoma Press, 1985. A straightforward account of Tecumseh's role in the War of 1812, emphasizing the period leading up to his death in battle.

SEE ALSO: 1808, Prophetstown Is Founded; 1812, War of 1812; 1813, Battle of the Thames; 1840, U.S. Election of 1840.

1812 ■ WAR OF 1812: *the first war waged by the United States under its new Constitution tests the republic's sovereignty and generates a sense of nationalism*

DATE: June 18, 1812-December 24, 1814
LOCALE: United States and Canada
CATEGORIES: Canadian history; Native American history; Wars, uprisings, and civil unrest

KEY FIGURES:

John Quincy Adams (1767-1848), sixth president of the United States, 1825-1829, and principal peace negotiator at Ghent

George Canning (1770-1827), foreign secretary of Great Britain

Henry Clay (1777-1852), Speaker of the House of Representatives in the Twelfth Congress and leader of the War Hawks

George Erskine, British minister to the United States

Thomas Jefferson (1743-1826), third president of the United States, 1801-1809

James Madison (1751-1836), fourth president of the United States, 1809-1817

Napoleon I (Bonaparte) (1769-1821), French emperor, 1804-1815

SUMMARY OF EVENT. The War of 1812 was a result of the Napoleonic Wars in Europe, during the first decade of the nineteenth century. Ever since war had broken out between France and Great Britain in 1793, the United States had tried, with some success, to follow a policy of neutrality toward both belligerents, avoiding a struggle with Great Britain by Jay's Treaty of 1794 and ending a war crisis with France in 1800 by the Convention of Mortefontaine.

In 1805, the Napoleonic War took a new turn, placing U.S. neutrality on a precarious basis. With Napoleon dominating the European continent and the British controlling the seas, the struggle turned into an economic squeeze, with the United States in the middle.

In an attempt to starve the other into submission, each side began to harass and seize U.S. ships. By the Order in Council of 1806, Great Britain declared a paper blockade of the European coast from Denmark to Brittany and required U.S. ships to be searched for contraband. France countered with the Berlin Decree, which authorized the seizure of any ship going to England before coming to a continental port. When Great Britain responded by issuing a second order in council requiring neutral vessels destined for a continental port to stop in England first, Napoleon issued the Milan Decree, ordering seizure of any neutral vessel that submitted to British search.

Because the British dominated the seas, their restrictions on U.S. shipping were more serious than those of France. Moreover, the British practice of impressing seamen under the U.S. flag, whom the British claimed were deserters from the Royal Navy, was an affront to the United States' honor and a challenge to its sovereignty. As a result, war almost erupted between the United States and Great Britain in the spring of 1807, when British seamen from HMS *Leopard* boarded the USS *Chesapeake*, after firing a broadside, and seized the alleged deserters on board. Outraged, President Thomas Jefferson barred British ships from U.S. waters and obtained another embargo, confining all U.S. shipping to port. By thus withholding needed supplies from the belligerents, he hoped to gain their recognition of U.S. neutrality.

The embargo was the first of a series of coercive economic measures adopted by the United States in an attempt to avoid war. Because the embargo seriously depressed the economy, which was dependent on the export trade, it was replaced in 1809 by the Non-Intercourse Act, which cut off shipping with Great Britain and France only. This measure was replaced the following year by Macon's Bill Number Two, restoring complete freedom of trade but providing that in case one of the belligerent nations should recognize the United States' neutral rights, nonintercourse would be revived against the other. When Napoleon pretended to revoke the Berlin and Milan decrees, President James Madison revived the policy of nonintercourse against Great Britain.

Despite U.S. efforts at economic coercion, the British refused to change their maritime policies. In 1809, an agreement was worked out between the British minister to the United States, George Erskine, and Secretary of State James Madison, whereby Great Britain would abandon its orders in council and the United States would suspend nonintercourse. However, Erskine was recalled from his post by George Canning, the foreign secretary of Great Britain, who pursued a hard line toward the United States. As a result of this diplomatic fiasco, relations between Great Britain and the United States deteriorated, each side feeling that it had been deceived by the other.

The failure of the Erskine agreement placed the United States firmly on the road to war. In 1810, a new Congress was elected that, when it took office at the end of 1811, brought into positions of leadership a group of young Republicans who were impatient with pacific responses to humiliation abroad. Angered by the British challenge on the seas to their country's sovereignty, these War Hawks, as they were known, also were incensed by news of secret British aid to the American Indians in the Northwest. Naming Henry Clay as Speaker of the House, the War Hawks passed a series of resolutions to increase the army and navy and arm the militia. In April, 1812, the Madison Administration boosted war sentiment in Congress by requesting a thirty-day embargo on U.S. shipping as a prelude to war. In June, Madison asked Congress to declare war against Great Britain. In a close vote that revealed sharp opposition to war, especially in the Northeast, Congress responded affirmatively.

In Great Britain, opposition to the orders in council had mounted sharply, and two days before war was declared, the British government announced its intention to repeal them. Even so, Madison refused to end the struggle as long as the issue of impressment remained unresolved.

Despite their bellicosity, the Jeffersonian Republicans had neglected their army and militia forces, which were unprepared for military operations. The war itself proved indecisive, and neither side was able to inflict a mortal blow on the other. The United States was able to control the Northern Great Lakes and Northwest for most of the war, but its strategy of invading Upper Canada proved a dismal failure. An army under General Stephen Van Rensselaer was forced to surrender

WAR OF 1812: BATTLES IN THE NORTH

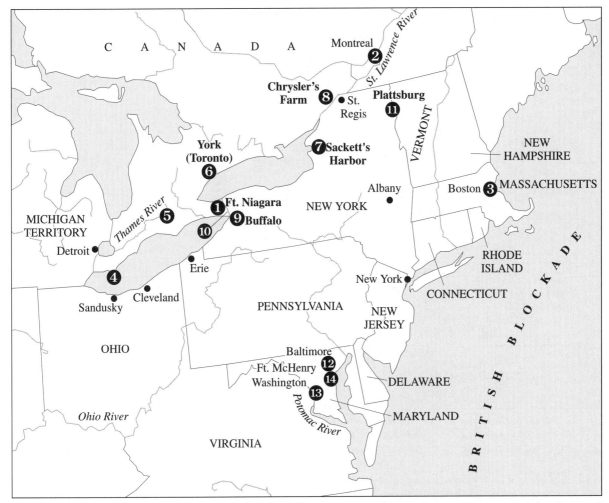

(1) Oct.-Nov., 1812: Niagara Campaign; U.S. defeat. (2) Nov., 1812: Montreal fiasco; U.S. troops refuse to fight. (3) June 1, 1813: Sinking of the USS Chesapeake. *(4) Sept. 10, 1813: Battle of Lake Erie at Put-In Bay; U.S. victory. (5) Oct. 5, 1813: Battle of the Thames; death of Tecumseh, British defeat. (6) Apr. 27, 1813: U.S. burning of York. (7) May 28-29, 1813: U.S. defense of Sackett's Harbor. (8) Nov. 11, 1813: Battle of Chrysler's Farm; U.S. defeat. (9) Dec. 29-30, 1813: British burning of Buffalo. (10) July, 1814: Battles of Chippewa, Lundy's Lane, and Ft. Erie; U.S. drive into Canada is repulsed. (11) Sept. 11, 1814: Battles of Lake Champlain and Plattsburg; British retreat to Canada. (12) Aug. 24, 1814: Battle of Bladensburg; U.S. defeat. (13) Aug. 24, 1814: British burn Washington, D.C. (14) Sept. 14, 1814: British siege of Ft. McHenry fails; Francis Scott Key writes "The Star-Spangled Banner"; British withdraw.*

to the British as Queenston Heights in 1812. The United States did invade Canada the following year, burning the provincial capital of York (now Toronto) and defeating a combined Indian and British force at the Battle of the Thames in 1813, but United States forces never established real control over Canadian soil.

By 1814, the performance of the United States Army had improved significantly. U.S. forces scored several hard-fought victories along the Niagara frontier, including at Chippewa, Lundy's Lane, and Fort Erie, but they lacked adequate resources to sustain the effort. Although the Navy won several

skirmishes, most notably the sinking of HMS *Guerriere* by the USS *Constitution*, the British were able to drive most U.S. shipping off the seas. They were far less successful in containing U.S. privateers, however, and these raided British commerce with impunity and much profit.

Napoleon's downfall and the subsequent reinforcement of Canada seriously jeopardized the United States' strategic position. Many members of Parliament began calling for punitive operations. However, the British strategy of launching a three-pronged attack against the United States also proved unsuccessful. In 1814, a British armada entered Chesapeake Bay

War of 1812: Battles in the South

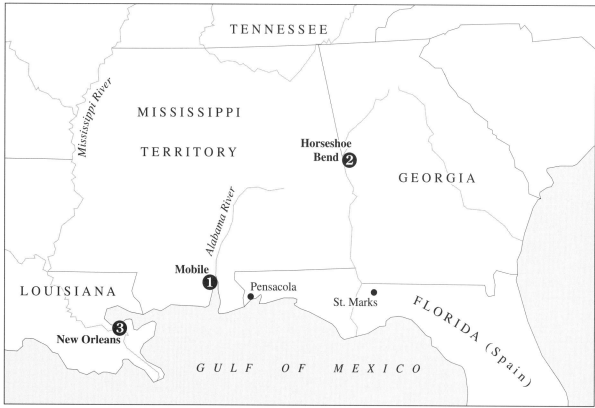

(1) Aug. 30, 1813: Creek War begins with massacre at Ft. Mims near Mobile; U.S. defeat prompts revenge against Indians by Andrew Jackson and Tennessee militiamen. (2) Mar. 27, 1814: Battle of Horseshoe Bend: Jackson defeats Creeks and seizes Creek lands. (3) Jan. 8, 1815: Battle of New Orleans; last battle of the war ends in British defeat.

and, in retaliation for the burning of York, burned Washington, D.C. The British forces failed in their second objective of taking Baltimore, despite an all-night bombardment of Fort McHenry in Baltimore Harbor. A second British drive across northern New York was repulsed at Plattsburg; a third British force suffered a major defeat at the Battle of New Orleans, as it tried to secure control of the Mississippi River. Ironically, this most bitter struggle of the war took place two weeks after peace had been concluded in Europe between the belligerent powers. By dint of skillful negotiating at Ghent in Belgium, the United States delegation under John Quincy Adams achieved their aim of preserving the conditions of *status quo ante bellum*, despite a position of weakness. The accord, signed on Christmas Eve, 1814, reflected both Adams' unwillingness to compromise the national interest and British preoccupation with European events.

When viewed against the backdrop of the Napoleonic conflict, the War of 1812 appears little more than a backwoods, frontier skirmish. Despite its inconclusive nature, however, this conflict exercised direct and salutary effects upon the development of North America. The United States had commenced the war in a fractured condition politically, yet emerged with a degree of consolidation and consensus it had not possessed before. The Federalists, by dint of their strident opposition, were thoroughly discredited and began a slide into obscurity. The prevailing nationalism also launched an entire generation of political leadership; at least three presidents—John Quincy Adams, Andrew Jackson, and William Henry Harrison—owed their elections, in part, to wartime activities. The army was drastically reformed during the postwar era and made great strides in proficiency and professionalism. The bitter legacy of defeats forced a Jeffersonian rapprochement with the military establishment and adoption of more rational defense policies.

The War of 1812 made indelible marks upon the inhabitants of Canada as well. Defeat of U.S. forces stimulated the Canadians' first surge of national consciousness and, abetted by patriotic organizations such as the United Empire Loyalists, Canadians undertook a political and cultural evolution entirely different from their southern neighbor. If the War of 1812 had any clear losers, they were the Native American peoples. Crushing defeats north and south presaged their ultimate removal and accelerated the pace of white expansion on the frontier. *—Emory M. Thomas, updated by John C. Fredriksen*

ADDITIONAL READING:

Elting, John R. *Amateurs to Arms! A Military History of the War of 1812.* Chapel Hill, N.C.: Algonquin Books, 1991. A revealing discussion of the factors surrounding U.S. military ineptitude; good coverage of obscure actions.

Hickey, Donald R. *The War of 1812: A Forgotten Conflict.* Urbana: University of Illinois Press, 1989. A broad synthesis of the political and diplomatic concerns that underscored U.S. political infighting.

Stagg, J. C. A. *Mr. Madison's War: Politics, Diplomacy and Warfare in the Early American Republic, 1783-1830.* Princeton, N.J.: Princeton University Press, 1983. Portrays the war as James Madison's ideological crusade to save republicanism; detailed notes and imaginative use of primary sources.

Stanley, George F. G. *The War of 1812: Land Operations.* Toronto: Macmillan of Canada in collaboration with the National Museum of Man, National Museums of Canada, 1983. Modern Canadian perspective on a variety of strategic and political considerations usually overlooked by U.S. scholars.

Watts, Steven. *The Republic Reborn: War and the Making of Liberal America, 1790-1820.* Baltimore: The Johns Hopkins University Press, 1987. Argues that the war and its aftermath were a reaffirmation of revolutionary principles and a factor in expanding them for posterity.

SEE ALSO: 1811, Battle of Tippecanoe; 1813, Creek War; 1813, Battle of the Thames; 1815, Battle of New Orleans; 1815, Treaty of Ghent.

1813 ■ CREEK WAR: *the destruction of the Creek nation opens Alabama to settlement and positions Andrew Jackson to win the War of 1812*

DATE: July 27, 1813-August 9, 1814
LOCALE: Alabama
CATEGORIES: Expansion and land acquisition; Native American history; Wars, uprisings, and civil unrest
KEY FIGURES:
Big Warrior (died 1825), mico of the Upper Creeks, leader of the progressive peace party
Andrew Jackson (1767-1845), major general of Tennessee militia, whose forces destroyed the Red Stick movement
Peter McQueen (died 1818), mixed-blood planter, mico, and a leader of the Red Stick faction
William Weatherford (c. 1780-1822), mixed-blood son of a Scots trader and a leader of the Red Stick faction
SUMMARY OF EVENT. Of all American Indian cultures, the Muscogee (called "Creeks" by the white populace) seemed the most likely to assimilate into the advancing white culture of the 1700's and early 1800's. Colonial deerskin traders from Charleston, South Carolina, married into this matrilineal native culture, establishing kinship ties with their wives' families

throughout the nation of Muscogee and siring mixed-blood children who became the nation's cultural and political elite. Alexander McGillivray—of Scottish, French, and Muscogee background—was educated in Charleston and became one of the most powerful and influential micos (chiefs) in the culture's history. William Weatherford, William McIntosh, and others born to both cultures remained influential in the tribe through and beyond the coming Creek War.

President George Washington appointed Revolutionary War veteran Benjamin Hawkins as Indian Agent to the Muscogee, and Hawkins attempted to teach the Muscogee modern, European-derived farming techniques. With well-established agricultural traditions of their own, the Muscogee took easily to the teachings of both Hawkins and their own mixed-blood people. The Muscogees established within their nation a subculture that featured frame houses, fenced fields, domesticated animals, the adoption of Anglo clothing and technology, and all the other vestments of the traditional frontier South, including cotton production with African American slave labor for the wealthy.

The transition was not smooth, however. One problem was the continued encroachment of advancing white civilization. So relentless were the demands of state governments for cessions of Muscogee lands that the natives named one Tennessee governor the Dirt King and gave a Georgia governor the name Always Asking for Land.

As buckskin breeches went out of fashion in Europe, the market for American deerskins evaporated. The Muscogee now found themselves with nothing to trade for the white man's clothing, weapons, household utensils, and other goods to which they had become accustomed. Continuing to buy these goods on credit, they fell deeply into debt to U.S. and British trading houses. The Jefferson Administration, through Hawkins, encouraged the paying off of these debts through cessions of land. The Muscogee strenuously objected to this plan, even when the U.S. government offered perpetual annuities to the tribe and bonuses to local micos who signed land treaties. The pressure on Muscogee hunting grounds intensified, and those micos who ceded land became enemies in the eyes of many of their kinsmen.

More sinister than the United States' insatiable land hunger was its innate distrust of American Indians and its general desire to eliminate rather than assimilate them. Some segment of the native population—Iroquois, Shawnee, Cherokee, Muscogee—seemed to be constantly at war with the frontiersmen. For whites, these violent clashes supported their belief that American Indians were dangerous savages in need of extermination. Another problem was the strength and depth of the Muscogees' own native culture. Their relationship to their environment and their tribal traditions had been deeply satisfying. Although white culture made life more comfortable, it did not resolve any life-threatening problem for the Muscogee. Thus, it was a luxury, not a necessity.

The pressure of encroaching white settlement continued to increase all along the U.S. frontier in the early 1800's, prompting the Shawnee chief Tecumseh to attempt an alliance of all Native American tribes so that, together, they might resist further white advances and save American Indian lands and culture. When Tecumseh and his brother, Tenskwatawa, known as the Prophet, visited the Muscogee tribal council to urge an alliance with the Shawnee, head mico Big Warrior rejected the idea and called for continued peace with white Americans. A movement—part spiritual, part political—was already growing among the Muscogee, however, calling for a return to the roots of Muscogee tradition and a rejection of the values and artifacts of white society.

The traditionalists were primarily young. Among their leaders were men who had successfully assimilated white culture—half-white cotton planters such as Peter McQueen, and such white traders' sons as William Weatherford and Josiah Francis. The leaders of the progressive, assimilationist wing were often older. Some, like William McIntosh, lived like white men. Others, like Big Warrior, maintained a traditional Muscogee lifestyle yet accepted the reality of progress.

On July 27, 1813, this cultural and political dispute broke into open warfare, a civil war within the nation over the direction the culture should take: toward the white man's style of life or back to the purity and spirituality of Muscogee life. The reactionary wing, led by a reluctant Weatherford, a vengeful Francis, and McQueen, became known, from the red color symbolic of war, as Red Sticks.

The war spilled over into white society with the killing of isolated settlers in southern Tennessee and the massacre of two large populations of whites, blacks, and Creeks at Forts Sinquefield and Mims in lower Alabama. These killings brought Major General Andrew Jackson into the conflict with an army of Mississippi, Georgia, and Tennessee militia, joined by progressive Muscogee, Choctaw, and Cherokee allies.

The early campaign was tedious and unsuccessful. With winter approaching, pay in arrears, little to eat, and enlistments expiring, many militiamen prepared to go home. Jackson branded them all mutineers and arrested and executed six leaders, cowing the frontiersmen into remaining to continue the fight. Through hard marching and sporadic fighting, the allied force of frontiersmen and progressive Native Americans chased and battled the Red Sticks across Alabama, finally cornering a large contingent at Tohopeka (Horseshoe Bend) on the Tallapoosa River. In this battle, more than five hundred Red Sticks were killed, destroying Red Stick resistance.

In the ensuing Treaty of Horseshoe Bend (August 9, 1814), Jackson took approximately twenty-five million acres of land from both Red Stick insurgents and his Muscogee, Choctaw, and Cherokee allies. The cession opened the land to immediate white and African American settlement and created the heart of the cotton South. The Creek Indian War left Andrew Jackson with a veteran and victorious army well-positioned to block the British invasion of New Orleans, giving the United States its most impressive land victory in the War of

1812 and opening the path to the White House for Andrew Jackson.

For the Muscogee, the defeat spelled the beginning of the end of their existence in their homeland. Within two decades, they and most other surviving members of the South's Five Civilized Tribes were banished to the Indian Territory, Oklahoma. —*Maurice Melton*

ADDITIONAL READING:

Braund, Kathryn E. Holland. *Deerskins and Duffels: The Creek Indian Trade with Anglo-America, 1685-1815.* Lincoln: University of Nebraska Press, 1993. Describes the competitors, pricing, credit policies, markets, and distribution of the Muscogee deerskin trade; provides a detailed look at Muscogee life.

George, Noah Jackson. *A Memorandum of the Creek Indian War.* Meredith, N.H.: R. Lothrop, 1815. 2d ed. Edited by W. Stanley Hoole. University, Ala: Confederate Publishing Company, 1986. Based on General Jackson's reports and correspondence, this pamphlet gives a battle-by-battle account of the campaign from the U.S. perspective. Written amid the passions of the War of 1812, it asserts that the Red Sticks were tools of the British.

Griffith, Benjamin W., Jr. *McIntosh and Weatherford, Creek Indian Leaders.* Tuscaloosa: University of Alabama Press, 1988. A highly readable account of the war. Argues that Weatherford was a most reluctant Red Stick, knowing from the outset that the movement was doomed.

Halbert, Henry Sale, and T. H. Ball. *The Creek War of 1813 and 1814.* Chicago: Donohue and Henneberry, 1895. Reprint with introduction and annotation by Frank L. Owsley, Jr. University: University of Alabama Press, 1969. Provides a lengthy discussion of the causes of the war, presenting it as an intertribal difference that would have been resolved had whites not interfered.

Hudson, Charles M. *The Southeastern Indians.* Knoxville: University of Tennessee Press, 1976. Places the Muscogee within the larger framework of the native population of the area. One of several excellent volumes on Southeastern American Indians by ethnologist Hudson.

Martin, Joel. *Sacred Revolt: The Muscogees' Struggle for a New World.* Boston: Beacon Press, 1991. Emphasizes the importance of spirituality in Muscogee life, in the evolution of the Red Sticks' back-to-our-culture campaign, and in their warmaking.

Woodward, Thomas S. *Woodward's Reminiscences of the Creek, or Muscogee Indians, Contained in Letters to Friends in Georgia and Alabama.* Tuscaloosa: Alabama Book Store, 1859. Reprint. Mobile, Ala.: Southern University Press, 1965. A veteran of the war, Woodward knew many Muscogee leaders and their culture. Although written with the wisdom and common sense of later years, this entertaining little volume has its errors and must be read with a critical eye.

SEE ALSO: 1808, Prophetstown Is Founded; 1811, Battle of Tippecanoe; 1812, War of 1812; 1815, Westward Migration; 1830, Indian Removal Act; 1830, Trail of Tears.

1813 ■ BATTLE OF THE THAMES: *U.S. victory in the Northwestern theater of the War of 1812 also sees the death of Tecumseh and the decline of his multitribal alliance*

DATE: October 5, 1813
LOCALE: Ontario, Canada
CATEGORIES: Canadian history; Native American history; Wars, uprisings, and civil unrest
KEY FIGURES:
William Henry Harrison (1773-1841), commander of U.S. forces at the battle
Richard Mentor Johnson (1780-1850), Kentucky congressman who was reputed to have killed Tecumseh
Henry Procter (1763-1822), commander of British forces at the battle
Tecumseh (1768-1813), Shawnee war chief

SUMMARY OF EVENT. The Battle of the Thames was an important United States victory in the Northwestern theater during the War of 1812 with Great Britain. The battle took place on the northern bank of the Thames River near Moraviantown in Upper Canada (southern Ontario Province). In the Battle of Put-In Bay (September 10, 1813), U.S. naval forces won control of Lake Erie. This prevented reinforcement and resupply of the British army at the lake's western end, in the vicinity of Detroit and Fort Malden.

When a superior U.S. force under William Henry Harrison crossed the lake on September 27, the British commander in Upper Canada, Major General Henry Procter, began withdrawing toward the east along the Thames River. Procter's native allies, who made up the bulk of his forces, angrily protested the abandonment of their homelands in Michigan. The Shawnee chief Tecumseh, leader of an alliance of warriors from many tribes, was reassured by Procter that a stand soon would be made against Harrison's advancing army. Procter's retreat up the Thames was mismanaged and slow, and most of his spare ammunition and other supplies were lost. Harrison's faster-moving army overtook the British on October 5, forcing Procter to turn and fight before he had reached a defensive position being prepared at Moraviantown.

The British force included five hundred warriors of Tecumseh's alliance. Besides Tecumseh's fellow Shawnees (then dwelling principally in Indiana), there were warriors from the Sac, Fox, Ottawa, Ojibwa, Wyandot, Potawatomi, Winnebago, Lenni Lenape, and Kickapoo nations, all from the Northwest Territory, and a small band of Creeks from the South. Their women and children accompanied the still-loyal warriors. Approximately a thousand of Tecumseh's followers, angered by Procter's retreat from Michigan, had abandoned the British. Procter's forces totaled more than a thousand, including 450 regulars of the Forty-first Regiment of Foot and a scattering of Canadian militia.

The U.S. army under Harrison numbered about three thousand troops. One hundred twenty of these were infantrymen from the regular army; the rest, Kentucky mounted militia volunteers. A thousand-soldier mounted militia regiment commanded by Colonel Richard Mentor Johnson played a decisive part in the battle. There were also 260 American Indians in Harrison's force, including about 40 Shawnees.

Procter's British and American Indian force, outnumbered three-to-one by the U.S. troops, took a position across a road that ran along the north bank of the Thames River. With the river protecting his left flank and a wooded swamp his right, Procter placed his British regulars in two parallel lines a hundred yards apart. On his left, commanding the road, Procter positioned his one cannon, a six-pounder. Tecumseh's warriors were placed in the swamp on the British right flank. The swamp slanted away at an angle that would enable the natives to fire into the left flank of U.S. troops advancing toward the British infantrymen. Because Procter expected Harrison to send his mounted units, as usual, against the Native Americans, he dispersed the two lines of British soldiers thinly, sheltering behind scattered trees in open order, several feet apart. Only when infantry were positioned almost shoulder-to-shoulder, however, could they effectively repel a cavalry charge. When Harrison noticed this inviting disposition, he sent Colonel Johnson's mounted regiment to attack the British infantry, while his other forces, dismounted as infantry, marched against the natives on the American left. The small force of regular U.S. infantry was assigned to rush the single British cannon.

Colonel Johnson's well-drilled mounted regiment, organized in columns, galloped through the two lines of thinly spread British infantry to their rear. The militiamen then dismounted and began to fire. The British, demoralized and hungry after not having eaten in more than fifty hours, surrendered. Each line of British soldiers seems to have fired a single volley and panicked. The crew of Procter's one cannon fled without even firing it. This part of the battle lasted less than five minutes.

The infantry units on the U.S. troops' left were having much less success against Tecumseh's warriors in the swamp. The poorly disciplined militia infantry, now on foot, were initially repulsed and driven back by the natives. The collapse of the main British position enabled Johnson to swing part of his regiment leftward to attack the Indians' flank. At this point, where his warriors joined the right of the British soldiers, Tecumseh and the Shawnees had taken their position. Led by Johnson and a small, select group that called itself the Forlorn Hope, Johnson's regiment dismounted and pushed into the woods. Heavy firing erupted, and most of the twenty men in the Forlorn Hope were killed or wounded. Colonel Johnson was hit by five bullets, his horse by seven. Early in this intense action, Tecumseh fell, killed by a shot near his heart.

With the death of their leader, the warriors in this part of the swamp (the natives' left) began to fall back. Demoralization spread, and this, coupled with the continuing advance of the

The Shawnee chief Tecumseh, leader of a confederation of Indian tribes and supporter of the British during the Battle of the Thames, lost his life to the Americans in that confrontation. With his death came the decline of the multitribal alliance that Tecumseh had fashioned and brilliantly led, dissolution of native support for the British, and victory for the colonists in the Northwestern theater of the War of 1812. (Library of Congress)

U.S. forces, brought an end to the fighting. Although Procter, the British commander, had fled after a brief effort to rally his troops, Tecumseh had stood his ground and died fighting, as he had sworn to do. The native warriors had fought on for more than thirty minutes after the British regulars had given up, but now they slipped away through the woods to find their families. The victory of Harrison's army was complete.

Because of mismanagement of the retreat and his poor handling of the battle, Major General Procter was court-martialed and publicly reprimanded. Harrison became a national hero, as did Colonel Johnson, widely credited with having shot Tecumseh. Of the British troops twelve were killed, twenty-two wounded, and six hundred one captured. Harrison reported a count of thirty-three warriors' bodies on the field. Contradictory records suggest that on the U.S. side, as many as twenty-five were killed or mortally injured, and thirty to fifty wounded.

The Battle of the Thames enabled the United States to regain control of territory in the Detroit area that had been lost in earlier defeats, ended any British threat at the western end

of Lake Erie, and greatly reduced the danger of tribal raids in the Northwest. An important result of the battle was the decline of the multitribal alliance that Tecumseh had fashioned and brilliantly led. Natives continued to take the field in support of British operations, but now this support was sporadic and ineffective. Tecumseh's strategy of protecting tribal lands through military cooperation with Great Britain had failed. On the northern shore of Lake Erie, the Canadian right flank, a stalemate developed. Harrison's army disintegrated as the enlistment of his militiamen expired, and they returned to Kentucky. The weakened U.S. troops were unable to advance eastward toward Burlington and York, or to threaten British-held Michilimackinac to the north. However, U.S. naval control of Lake Erie prevented fresh initiatives in the area by the British.

—*Bert M. Mutersbaugh*

ADDITIONAL READING:

Dowd, Gregory Evans. *A Spirited Resistance: The North American Indian Struggle for Unity, 1745-1815.* Baltimore: The Johns Hopkins University Press, 1992. Explains the Shawnee leaders' struggles as part of a larger pattern of cultural revitalization and military resistance. Maps, illustrations, and index.

Edmunds, R. David. *The Shawnee Prophet.* Lincoln: University of Nebraska Press, 1983. An insightful study of the Shawnee society that produced Tecumseh and his alliance. Argues that Tecumseh's brother, Tenskwatawa, the Prophet, originated the alliance, which Tecumseh took over as Tenskwatawa's influence faded. Maps, illustrations, and index.

_____. *Tecumseh and the Quest for Indian Leadership.* Boston: Little, Brown, 1984. A brief treatment that concentrates on the warrior brother. Map, illustrations, and index.

Gilpin, Alec R. *The War of 1812 in the Old Northwest.* East Lansing: Michigan State University Press, 1958. A scholarly, well-written study that puts Harrison's 1813 campaign and the Battle of the Thames into context of the entire war in the Northwestern theater. Maps, illustrations, and index.

Sugden, John. *Tecumseh's Last Stand.* Norman: University of Oklahoma Press, 1985. Detailed analysis of the battle and the campaign that preceded it. Examines the question of who killed Tecumseh. Maps, illustrations, and index.

SEE ALSO: 1808, Prophetstown Is Founded; 1811, Battle of Tippecanoe; 1812, War of 1812; 1813, Creek War.

1814 ■ NEW HARMONY AND THE COMMUNITARIAN MOVEMENT: *rapid modernization and industrialization encourage cooperative living experiments among those yearning for a simpler life*

DATE: Spring, 1814-1830
LOCALE: New Harmony, Indiana
CATEGORIES: Settlements; Social reform
KEY FIGURES:
William Maclure (1763-1840), an intellectual and partner of Robert Owen
Robert Owen (1771-1858), British industrialist, second owner of New Harmony
Robert Dale Owen (1801-1877), Robert's son, radical freethinker and later congressman and senator
George Rapp (1757-1847), founder of the Rappites and first owner of New Harmony
Thomas Say (1787-1834), entomologist and curator of the American Philosophical Society

SUMMARY OF EVENT. Founded in 1814, New Harmony, Indiana, was a small village located on the banks of the Wabash River in the southwestern part of the state. Its chief historical significance rests in the fact that it was the site of two experiments in communal living in the first part of the nineteenth century that reflected an important phase of U.S. social and cultural history during the pre-Civil War period. The town was founded by George Rapp, a German pietistic Lutheran and dissenter, a believer in communal life who sought a place in the American West where he might implement his social theo-

ries in detail. Having already developed a flourishing settlement of German immigrants like himself in Pennsylvania, Rapp sought a new abode that would be more spacious and closer to river transportation for the many goods his followers were producing for sale to the outside world. In the spring of 1814, he purchased more than twenty-four thousand acres of rich alluvial land near the Wabash River south of Vincennes, then the capital of Indiana Territory.

The hamlet of Harmonie, so named by Rapp after the town he and his followers were abandoning in Pennsylvania, flowered and prospered under the guiding hand of the industrious Germans. Within a few short years, the colony had placed under cultivation hundreds of acres of rich Indiana bottomlands that included large fruit orchards and an extensive grape vineyard as well as the usual farmlands. In addition, the colonists created an extensive system of small manufactures, including a gristmill, a tannery, a center for weaving, a distillery, and a cotton gin. The Rappites sold their products from farm and factory throughout the entire area and shipped quantities of goods by keelboat and flatboat down the Ohio and Mississippi Rivers to New Orleans. Private property was not allowed, and all property and profits were held in common, with all individuals sharing equal ownership.

The social practices of the community were as interesting as their economic life was successful. Rapp ruled with an iron hand, and his decisions served as the infallible guide to daily action within the town. Men and women lived in separate dormitories, which were constructed soon after the town was established, and celibacy was strictly enforced for everyone, even married couples. The concept of family was replaced by that of community. Regular churchgoing at the two churches in Harmonie, a flourishing school system, and weekly social activities, lectures, and intellectual discussions made life in the town busy and stimulating.

Although Harmonie prospered, evidence as early as 1821 suggests that Rapp was planning to relocate the community. Indiana was not as conducive to the experiment as he had hoped, because residents of the surrounding areas were uneducated, uncultured, and resistant to new ways. In his efforts to gain recognition for his communitarian movement, Rapp moved the experiment and founded Economy, Pennsylvania, in May, 1824. Earlier that year, Rapp had sent agents to England to seek out prospective buyers of the communal property in Indiana. Robert Owen, the famous Welsh-Scottish philanthropist, social reformer, and textile manufacturer, showed immediate interest in the site, viewing it as an opportunity to acquire a ready-made place to implement his personal theories for social reform. Owen was an atheist who believed that humankind was basically good and if removed from the corrupting influences of the modern world, might achieve perfection. He wanted to humanize, not reject, industry and had already created a small-scale model milltown in New Lanark, Scotland. Wanting to try his experiments on a larger scale, he personally inspected the lands in Indiana early in 1825 and purchased Harmonie for $95,000, complete with its twenty thousand acres of rich land and 180 buildings capable of providing places of business and housing for at least seven hundred people. Thereafter, the name of the town changed to New Harmony, by which it is best known to students of the communitarian movement in the United States.

Owen was a powerful propagandist—a man with a mission to bring reform, theoretical and practical, to the world. He wrote and traveled widely to disseminate his ideas; the purchase of New Harmony gave him a laboratory in which to experiment concretely with these theories. Within a relatively short time following the announcement of the transfer of ownership to Owen, people interested in participating in the new experiment in community living began to arrive in New Harmony. Hampered by overcrowding and by groups of people with a diversity of intentions and points of view, the New Harmony experiment struggled to keep afloat. Lacking the cohesiveness of the Germans who had preceded them, Owen and his supporters never experienced the economic success that had been accorded the Rappites. Only the commitment of Owen's considerable personal fortune to the enterprise prevented the operation from going under quickly. At

the same time, however, a substantive community life developed at New Harmony under the leadership of Owen and son Robert Dale. For a time, widely recognized intellectual leaders such as William Maclure, a famous geologist, philanthropist, and entomologist Thomas Say, curator of the American Philosophical Society, lived at New Harmony and participated enthusiastically in the bustling life of the experimental community.

After 1830, Robert Owen turned his attention to other reform projects. He had lost much of his fortune in financing the social experiment in Indiana, and his interest declined as debts piled up and small groups broke off from the main community of reformers. The reformist spirit symbolized by Owen continued in New Harmony long after the Welsh philanthropist personally abandoned his project. Experimental efforts in public education initiated by Maclure, and the continued residence in New Harmony throughout the 1830's and 1840's of various sons of the founder, served to remind the outside world of the significant heritage demanding basic changes in society that was emanating from this obscure village on the edge of the civilized world.

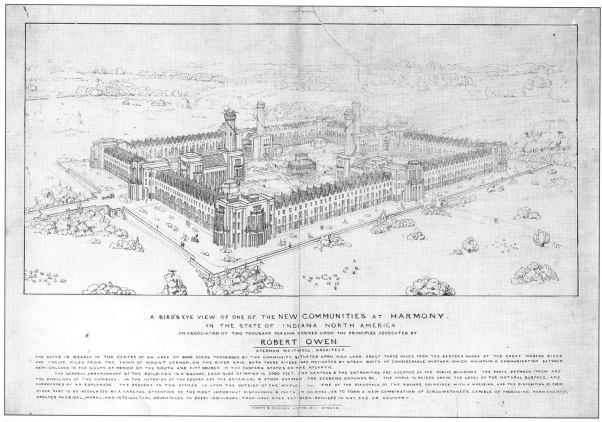

New Harmony was only one of the more elaborate of several early nineteenth century planned communities founded upon principles of social reform—in this case those promulgated by Robert Owen. The caption reads in part: "The disposition of every . . . part is so regulated by a careful attention to the most important discoveries & facts in science . . . capable of producing permanently, greater physical, moral, and intellectual advantages to every individual, than have ever yet been realized in any age or country." (Library of Congress)

New Harmony, both under Rapp and during the time of Robert Owen and his followers, was technically a community of social equals. A primitive form of socialism was attempted there under Owen's leadership, although it never functioned successfully. Still, this backwoods settlement was symbolic of efforts in many other parts of the United States in the pre-Civil War era to establish small, egalitarian communities that were to serve as beacon lights of reform for American society and for the Western world in general. Historians of this communitarian movement have identified almost one hundred of these small reformist societies that were established between 1825 and 1860, chiefly in the Midwest. New Harmony, then, clearly serves as a prototype for the entire movement. Communitarianism was collectivistic by nature, opposed to revolution, yet impatient with gradualism. The first purpose of the small experimental community was to implement apparently incompatible aims: to achieve immediate, root-and-branch reform by gradual, nonrevolutionary means. A second purpose was to serve as a model of peaceable change for the larger world. Microcosms of society could undergo drastic alterations, and then the rest of society could be depended upon to imitate these models, somewhat more slowly over a period of time, in achieving widespread and desirable social reform.

The two communitarian experiments at New Harmony also reflect the broad historical development of the communitarian ideal. It had its origins in the religious ideology of the radical Protestant sects that appeared at the time of the Reformation—attitudes that were transferred to the United States in the colonial and early national periods by immigrants much like George Rapp and his followers from Würtemberg, Germany. By the second quarter of the nineteenth century, however, the communitarian ideal was becoming rapidly secularized. Robert Owen, an atheist, symbolized this second phase in the development of the movement. Those attracted to New Harmony during his regime almost without exception were vitally interested in the social regeneration of humankind but saw no need to connect this concern to specific religious doctrines.

The communitarian ideal received the widespread attention it did in the four decades prior to the Civil War for a variety of reasons. The rapid westward expansion of the frontier during this period left the entire social structure of the country somewhat in flux. This movement seemed to give a special thrust to the work of social reformers, since their efforts might well serve as the basic institutional framework for the nation's foreseeable future as plastic institutions matured into permanence and the frontier era passed into history. The work of the communitarians also seemed attractive because alternative methods of social reform now were thought to be at a dead end. Rampant individualism seemed incapable of answering the need for some sort of collective action to deal with the ills of the nineteenth century. Remembering the bloodlettings of the period from 1789 to 1815 in Europe, observers suggested that revolution had revealed itself to be a dangerous two-edged sword. Moreover, the problems created by industrialization seemed already to have moved beyond gradualism as a means

of solving them. Drastic reform was necessary, but drastic reform without revolution. The communitarian approach seemed a model solution to the dilemmas posed by these attitudes. It was voluntaristic, genuinely experimental, deliberately planned, rational, and nonrevolutionary. All these characteristics were immensely appealing to reformers throughout the Western world in the first half of the nineteenth century.

These tendencies, and others, provided a special appeal in the United States during the same period. Faith in the idea that persons can remake their institutions by reasoned choice seemed normal, for that is what the United States had done during the period of constitution-making. The communitarians' belief in social harmony, not class warfare, was also a deeply held American attitude. The experimentation of the communitarians found a ready response in a nation of tinkers—a nation that was itself thought to be an experiment. Perhaps most important, the group procedure that was at the heart of the communitarian effort reflected a tendency that has revealed itself in many areas of American thought and activity. Perhaps as a product of the frontier experience and a deeply revered democratic tradition, the Americans have always placed great stress upon the development of voluntary associations. From the Mayflower Compact to the establishment of the Tennessee Valley Authority and the encouragement of grassroots community action programs, the belief in voluntary associations has asserted itself. The communitarian movement fits neatly into such an ideological framework.

—James F. Findlay, Jr., updated by Geralyn Strecker

ADDITIONAL READING:

Arndt, Karl J. R., ed. and comp. *A Documentary History of the Indiana Decade of the New Harmony Society, 1814-1824.* 2 vols. Indianapolis: Indiana Historical Society, 1975-1978. A vast, encyclopedic collection of letters, official documents, maps, and other records of the New Harmony Society taken from its archives. Volume 2 contains a large, detailed map of the community in 1832, with a key identifying buildings.

_____. *George Rapp's Harmony Society, 1785-1847.* Rev. ed. Rutherford, N.J.: Fairleigh Dickinson University Press, 1972. A comprehensive narrative using primary sources from the New Harmony Society's archives (see above) to let its members tell their own story. Previous historians of New Harmony did not have access to these sources; therefore, Arndt's work is far more accurate and comprehensive.

_____. *George Rapp's Successors and Material Heirs, 1847-1916.* Rutherford, N.J.: Fairleigh Dickinson University Press, 1971. Continues Arndt's volume that covered 1785-1847.

Bestor, Arthur E. *Backwoods Utopias: The Sectarian Origins and the Owenite Phase of Communitarian Socialism in America, 1663-1828.* 2d ed. Philadelphia: University of Pennsylvania Press. Situates New Harmony in the greater utopian and communal movement, paying special attention to Robert Owen's involvement with the group.

Lockwood, George B. *The New Harmony Movement.* New York: Augustus M. Kelley, 1970. An early yet still useful work covering the history and sociological implications of the movement through the nineteenth century.

Taylor, Anne. *Visions of Harmony: A Study in Nineteenth-Century Millenarianism*. New York: Oxford University Press, 1987. Offers speculative biographies of George Rapp and Robert Owen, drawing heavily from materials not included in Karl J. R. Arndt's work. Some of Taylor's assertions are not supported by fact, and the work does not provide as much information on Millenarianism as the title suggests.

SEE ALSO: 1790's, Second Great Awakening; 1815, Westward Migration; 1819, Unitarian Church Is Founded; 1820's, Social Reform Movement; 1836, Rise of Transcendentalism.

1814 ■ HARTFORD CONVENTION:
sectional divisions highlighted by the War of 1812 result in proposals to amend the U.S. Constitution and preserve the Union

DATE: December 15, 1814-January 5, 1815
LOCALE: Hartford, Connecticut
CATEGORY: Government and politics
KEY FIGURES:
George Cabot (1752-1823), Massachusetts Federalist
John "Jack" Lowell (1769-1840), radical member of the extremist faction in the Federalist Party
James Madison (1751-1836), fourth president of the United States, 1809-1817
Harrison Gray Otis (1765-1848), Massachusetts Federalist who conceived the idea of a New England convention
Caleb Strong (1745-1819), governor of Massachusetts and leader of the Federalist opposition to Madison's war policy
SUMMARY OF EVENT. The War of 1812 had never been popular among New England Federalists; they called it Mr. Madison's War. New Englanders as a whole recoiled from the war of conquest preached by Southerners and Westerners, and Federalists were eager to find fault with the Republicans' conduct of the war. By the fall of 1814, sectional and political feelings about the war had reached alarming proportions. The U.S. invasions of Canada had been abortive. British troops had burned Washington in August, 1814. The British army occupied eastern Maine, and enemy ships hovered about the New England coast. The Madison Administration collected war taxes and militia units in New England, but it appeared that a disproportionately small share of money and men was allotted to the defense of that section. New Englanders believed that they were carrying the dual burdens of defending themselves and also supporting the war effort of an incompetent national administration that showed no concern for them. New England had been the most fiercely anti-British part of the nation during the Revolutionary War. As the momentum of the nation had shifted to the Western states, New England had become more conservative in nature, sympathetic to the mercantile and business classes, much as the British had been. Although the

New England leaders who opposed the war had so far said or done nothing overtly treasonous, it was suspected by many that they were using the war as an excuse to consider some sort of reunion with Great Britain. Certainly this was what was hoped by the British press and public when they heard news of the Hartford Convention.

The bad situation threatened to become worse; Congress appeared to be ready to enact a national conscription act, which presumably would remove even more of New England's defenders. The U.S. commissioners at Ghent in Belgium were making no progress toward a negotiated peace, nor were they likely to do so as long as the British enjoyed military success. New England, with good reason, was alarmed.

Fear and frustration showed plainly in the results of the elections of 1814. The Federalists gained large majorities in both state and national offices, and the party leadership interpreted its success as a mandate for action against Mr. Madison's War. The activities of Governor Caleb Strong of Massachusetts demonstrated how extreme such action might become. In November, 1814, Strong offered thinly veiled hints of a separate peace and an alliance to General Sir John Sherbrooke, the British governor of Nova Scotia. Strong's overtures to the enemy came to nothing, but they served as an index of the desperation that infected Strong's section and his party.

This same mood of desperation moved Strong to call the Massachusetts General Court, or legislature, into special session in October, 1814. It responded to the crisis by calling for a convention of delegates from the New England states to meet at Hartford, Connecticut, on December 15. According to Harrison Gray Otis, the nephew of Revolutionary War agitator James Otis and the acknowledged author of the convention plan, the delegates were to discuss ways and means of sectional defense and to take steps to revise the United States Constitution to accord with sectional interests.

Three of the five New England states heeded Massachusetts' call. The legislatures of Connecticut and Rhode Island joined the Bay State in selecting delegations. Vermont and New Hampshire took no official action, but delegates chosen by local and county conventions in those states attended the Hartford sessions. Twenty-six men took part in the convention, and for the most part they were of a moderate temper. Extremists, such as Jack Lowell and former secretary of state Timothy Pickering, took no part in the proceedings and privately bewailed the convention's lack of "bold and ardent men." Well aware that a firm but fine line separated political opposition from treason in wartime, the Hartford delegates sought to play a positive, not negative, role.

This moderation was in part necessitated by the fact that New England, in political terms, was not monolithically Federalist at the time. Although the Federalists controlled the state legislatures of all five extant New England states (Maine still being a part of Massachusetts at that time), they did so by rather small margins. The national tide that had elected Thomas Jefferson and James Madison to the presidency had managed to elect a substantial minority of Democratic-Republican legislators to the New England state houses, and these, and the constituents they represented, surely would have opposed any more virulent antiwar or anti-Madison rhetoric.

The Hartford Convention, when assembled and organized, conducted most of its business in committees. George Cabot, the leader of the Massachusetts delegation who had explained that one of his objectives was to prevent "hot-heads from getting into mischief," was probably instrumental in stacking the committees with moderate men. Otis was apparently the guiding spirit of the committees and the author of the report adopted by the convention on January 3, 1815.

Otis' report, the product of the Hartford Convention, began by stating the mission of the convention, which was to provide for concerted sectional defense and to propose repairs to the Constitution. The report then discussed at length the circumstances that had given rise to the convention. It focused on the disaffection of extremists, and although it opposed radical solutions, such as dissolving the Union, it plainly implied that the Union was in peril. In effect, it contained a mild ultimatum to the Madison Administration to listen to the convention and its moderate solutions or be prepared to face the radicals and disunion. There followed a cataloging of the sins of Republican administrations past and present. Finally, the convention offered its solution in the form of a series of seven amendments to the Constitution providing that: the "three-fifths compromise," which allowed states to count a portion of their chattel population in determining proportionate representation in Congress and the Electoral College, be abolished; a two-thirds vote of both houses of Congress be required to admit new states into the Union; no embargo be imposed for more than sixty days; a two-thirds vote of both houses of Congress be required to adopt declarations of war; a two-thirds vote of both houses of Congress be required to adopt declarations of commercial nonintercourse acts; naturalized citizens be ineligible for federal office, elective or appointive; no president might succeed himself; and no successive presidents might be from the same state. All these provisions clearly exhibited New England's antagonism toward Southern and Western states and forecast the later sectional divisions that eventually were to lead to the Civil War.

The work of the convention reflected a mixture of sectional complaints and political rancor. Its enemies accused the assembly of treason, yet its temper was moderate. Although the convention addressed itself to some legitimate sectional grievances, it lapsed into the rhetoric of narrow partisanship. Perhaps no man came closer to the truth than John Adams, who described the Hartford delegates as "intelligent and honest men who had lost touch with reality."

The supreme irony was that even while the convention debated, U.S. arms won a great victory at New Orleans, and Great Britain and the United States made peace at Ghent. By the time representatives carrying the report of the Hartford Convention arrived in Washington, the country knew that peace had come. The Hartford Convention had, therefore, lost its point. Such circumstances blunted New England sectionalism, and the Federalist Party seemed treasonous, ludicrous, or both. Its demise was imminent.

—*Emory M. Thomas, updated by Nicholas Birns*

ADDITIONAL READING:

Banner, James M. *To the Hartford Convention: The Federalists and the Origins of Party Politics in Massachusetts, 1789-1815*. New York: Alfred A. Knopf, 1970. Places the convention in the context of Federalist Party history.

Elkins, Stanley M., and Eric McKitrick. *The Age of Federalism*. New York: Oxford University Press, 1993. Useful discussion of the mentality of Federalism.

Hickey, Donald. *The War of 1812: A Forgotten Conflict*. Urbana: University of Illinois Press, 1989. A reliable summary of the Hartford Convention.

Morison, Samuel Eliot. *Harrison Gray Otis: 1765-1848*. Boston: Houghton Mifflin, 1969. Presents a mildly sympathetic view of the Hartford Convention.

Stagg, J. C. A. *Mr. Madison's War: Politics, Diplomacy, and Warfare in the Early American Republic, 1783-1830*. Princeton, N.J.: Princeton University Press, 1983. Places the convention in the context of the War of 1812; takes a broad political overview.

Watts, Steven. *The Republic Reborn: War and the Making of Liberal America, 1790-1820*. Baltimore: The Johns Hopkins University Press, 1987. Argues that the Hartford Convention opposed the mainstream of U.S. political development.

SEE ALSO: 1790's, First U.S. Political Parties; 1812, War of 1812; 1813, Battle of the Thames; 1815, Treaty of Ghent.

1815 ■ WESTWARD MIGRATION: *early migration west of the Appalachian Mountains advances American industrialization, increases a growing sectionalism, and ultimately devastates Native American indigenous populations*

DATE: Beginning 1815
LOCALE: Old Northwest and the trans-Appalachian West
CATEGORIES: Expansion and land acquisition; Native American history; Science and technology; Transportation

SUMMARY OF EVENT. One of the great developments in the decade that followed the end of the War of 1812 was the mass migration of tens of thousands of Euro-Americans into the country west of the Appalachian Mountains. The West was not created overnight. Even before the American Revolution, American colonists had moved into the middle and upper Ohio River Valley. In 1775, Daniel Boone and thirty axmen blazed the Wilderness Road through the Cumberland Gap and founded the Kentucky settlement of Boonesborough. Settlers could follow the Great Valley Road down the Shenandoah Valley to a connection with Boone's route and from there,

Page. 245.

Captain Lewis shooting an Indian.

An illustration from Lewis and Clark's journal (published 1812) provides insight into the attitudes of at least some Euro-American settlers who were encroaching upon Native American lands in the trans-Mississippi West. (Library of Congress)

continue into Kentucky. To the north, routes such as Brad-dock's Road and Forbes' Road led to the forks of the Ohio River. By 1790, the population west of the mountains already totaled more than two hundred thousand, but the movement had only begun.

A number of factors stimulated men and women to under-take the arduous journey westward. Not the least of these were policies and programs pursued by the federal government. The Harrison Land Act of 1800, including subsequent amendments in 1804, reduced the minimum amount of land a settler could purchase to a quarter section (160 acres) and the minimum price to $1.64 an acre, thus allowing for more individual purchases. The act also granted credit for four years. Under this act, millions of acres of land were disposed of by the United States.

As important as a liberal land policy in encouraging west-ward migration in the late eighteenth century was the estab-lishment of security along the frontier. This was effected through both diplomatic and military measures. By treaties concluded with Great Britain in 1794 (Jay's Treaty) and Spain in 1795 (Pinckney's Treaty), Canadian and Floridian bounda-ries were settled. About the same time, U.S. military cam-paigns against the natives both north and south of the Ohio River led to a temporary lessening of tensions between Native

Americans and Euro-Americans. The Louisiana Purchase of 1803 and the Adams-Onís Treaty in 1819 gave the United States title to the Gulf Coast west of the Sabine River, while the campaigns of the War of 1812 crushed American Indian military power in the eastern Great Lakes region. With reason-able security thus obtained, the land proved more attractive to potential settlers.

Changes in technology were crucial to the movement west-ward. One technological development that stimulated western migration was the invention of the cotton gin in 1793. This device opened up most of the land in the South to the produc-tion of upland cotton, which found its major market in the enormous textile industry that had developed in England since the beginning of the nineteenth century. Cheap, fertile land to the west and depleted land to the east caused a great shift of cotton production into the trans-Appalachian area between 1815 and 1835.

Another major factor in westward migration was the im-provement in transportation methods. The construction of the Erie Canal, which was completed in 1825, reduced the cost of travel, particularly affecting the North. One factor that affected all sections was the invention and rapid exploitation of the steamboat. The steamboat enabled the rapid movement of people and goods, which significantly advanced westward expansion. The covered wagon made the movement of families easier, because household goods and farm tools could be transported more efficiently.

These factors and others gave rise to a new concept of the West. In 1790, about 95 percent of the total population resided east of the Appalachian Mountains and considered those mountains as the nation's western frontier; by 1820, the number was about 20 percent. Between 1790 and 1812, four Western states were admitted to the Union: Kentucky (1792), Tennessee (1796), Ohio (1803), and Louisiana (1812). Then admissions increased more rapidly—Indiana (1816), Mississippi (1817), Illinois (1818), Alabama (1819), and Missouri (1821). Michigan and Arkansas were organized into territories in 1805 and 1819, respectively. By 1820, the U.S. population was in a vast triangle with its base along the Atlantic Ocean and its apex roughly at the confluence of the Ohio and Missouri Rivers with the Mississippi River. Along both sides of the triangle, people were spilling over—north to the upper Great Lakes and south to the Gulf of Mexico.

This development had momentous social, political, and economic consequences for the nation. In terms of social disruption, both Native American and African American society was changed dramatically by the westward movement. By 1812, white settlers were encroaching upon much unceded Indian land. Eventually, several Native American tribes were relocated to Indian Territory west of the Mississippi River, thus changing the political and economic history of a large segment of the U.S. population. Many African American families were split when slaveholding whites moved westward with their slaves.

The political consequences included a geographically changed United States Congress and a growing sectionalism. For example, by 1820 eighteen new senators in Congress were from the West. No longer could the older regions operate in tandem or in opposition to each other without regarding Western interests. The West had become a political force and Westerners were not long in taking advantage of the fact that they were being courted by both the North and South. Politics in the United States assumed an increasingly sectional tone after 1815. This sectionalism made political parties even more important than earlier, because they were the sole vehicle through which national interests could contest with sectional interests. Between 1815 and 1830, there was little apparent difference between the objectives and needs of the Northwest and the Southwest. With the assimilation of the Southwest into a greater and solid South by about 1830, the Old Northwest became even more politically significant.

Economically, the early westward migration was of vast import. New land was brought into production, towns were developed, new market patterns were established, and new industries were created. The opening of the West to Euro-American settlement was an incentive to further movement westward, and wave after wave of migrants passed on, bringing with them newer needs and wants and establishing churches, schools, theaters, and prisons. Whatever was hap-pening politically, the flow into the West of Euro-American and foreign immigrants created that mass consumer demand upon which industry could thrive and out of which the beginnings of a national economy would develop.

—John G. Clark, updated by Judith Boyce DeMark

ADDITIONAL READING:

Billington, Ray A. *Westward Expansion: A History of the American Frontier*. New York: Macmillan, 1967. A classic overview of the migration westward, which includes a section on the early nineteenth century process. Focuses on Euro-American men as the most significant group in the westward migration.

Limerick, Patricia N. *The Legacy of Conquest: The Unbroken Past of the American West*. New York: W. W. Norton, 1987. A revisionist view of the migration west that includes the experience of minority groups and women in the migratory process.

Riley, Glenda. *The Female Frontier: A Comparative View of Women on the Prairie and the Plains*. Lawrence: University Press of Kansas, 1988. Analyzes the role of women in the westward movement by looking at several areas of frontier settlement, including the farm areas of the early westward migration.

Turner, Frederick Jackson. *Rise of the New West, 1819-1829*. 1906. Reprint. New York: Harper & Row, 1968. Remains the basis for study and discussion of the westward migration.

Wade, Richard C. *The Urban Frontier: The Rise of Western Cities, 1790-1830*. Cambridge, Mass.: Harvard University Press, 1959. One of the earliest and most widely read accounts of the significance of urbanization in the westward movement.

SEE ALSO: 1787, Northwest Ordinance; 1793, Whitney Invents the Cotton Gin; 1794, Jay's Treaty; 1795, Pinckney's Treaty; 1803, Louisiana Purchase; 1804, Lewis and Clark Expedition; 1806, Pike's Southwest Explorations; 1808, American Fur Company Is Chartered; 1810, Astorian Expeditions; 1811, Construction of the National Road; 1814, New Harmony and the Communitarian Movement; 1819, Adams-Onís Treaty; 1820, Land Act of 1820; 1821, Santa Fe Trail Opens; 1823, Jedediah Smith Explores the Far West; 1825, Erie Canal Opens; 1830, Baltimore and Ohio Railroad Begins Operation; 1830, Indian Removal Act.

1815 ■ BATTLE OF NEW ORLEANS: *defeat of the British by U.S. troops restores pride in the nation and launches Andrew Jackson toward the presidency*

DATE: January 8, 1815
LOCALE: New Orleans, Louisiana
CATEGORIES: Canadian history; Government and politics; Wars, uprisings, and civil unrest

KEY FIGURES:

Henry Bathurst, third Earl Bathurst (1762-1834), British secretary for war and the colonies

Alexander Forrester Inglis Cochrane (1758-1832), commander of the American Station of the Royal Navy and naval commander of the New Orleans expedition

Andrew Jackson (1767-1845), commander of the U.S. Military District Number Seven

John Keane, temporary commander of the British Army expeditionary force

Edward Michael Pakenham (1778-1815), general who succeeded Ross

Daniel T. Patterson, U.S. commander of the New Orleans Naval Station

Robert Ross (1766-1814), general appointed British commander of the New Orleans expedition, killed before assuming command

SUMMARY OF EVENT. For more than two years, Louisiana lay on the fringe of the Southern theater of the War of 1812. The campaigns were waged in Spanish Florida, where U.S. troops seized Mobile, and in the Mississippi Territory, where frontiersmen fought Creek Indians. The British blockade brought commerce to a standstill at New Orleans, but before late 1814, the war did not otherwise threaten its polyglot population. Engaged in a vast struggle with Napoleon's France, Great Britain could barely spare enough troops to defend Canada against U.S. attack, and the British War Ministry dismissed early proposals to capture New Orleans.

Napoleon's defeat at Leipzig in October, 1813, allowed the British to begin consideration of large-scale operations against the United States. When Napoleon's abdication in April, 1814, released substantial British forces from European commitments, preparations began in earnest to tighten the blockade of the United States, raid the Atlantic coast, and invade northern New York from Canada. In July, the War Ministry decided to attack New Orleans and subsequently appointed Admiral Sir Alexander Forrester Inglis Cochrane and Major General Robert Ross to command the expedition. The secretary for war, Earl Bathurst (Henry Bathurst), explained the purposes of the invasion to Ross in September: to obtain command of the mouth of the Mississippi River and deprive trans-Appalachian Americans of their link with the sea; and to occupy a valuable land possession whose restoration would improve the terms of peace for Great Britain, or whose cession by the United States could be exacted as the price of peace. Bathurst gave Cochrane and Ross discretion to strike at New Orleans directly from the Gulf of Mexico or overland from Mobile, and he instructed Ross to aid the Creoles if they desired to reattach themselves to Spain. At the time, Cochrane and Ross were raiding the Chesapeake Bay area, but New Orleans was their next target.

Cochrane believed that American Indians, slaves, and pirates who sheltered at Barataria, an island in the swamps off New Orleans, would assist a Gulf coast invasion directed against New Orleans. Operating under orders Cochrane issued before the War Ministry's decision, his subordinates occupied Spanish Pensacola in August and began to organize and arm natives and escaped slaves. In early September, the British made overtures to the Baratarians and prepared to attack Mobile, but their efforts came to nothing.

Andrew Jackson was major general of the Tennessee militia when he defeated the Creeks at Horseshoe Bend in March, 1814, and seriously weakened their ability to continue fighting. Two months later, Jackson was appointed federal commander of Military District Number Seven, which included the Mobile-New Orleans area, as well as the U.S. Army in the Southwest. Fully aware of British activities, he went south in August to strengthen Mobile's defenses, sever remaining British and Spanish connections with the Indians, and secure the coast against invasion. In mid-September, his forces defeated the British attempt on Mobile, which had been made without the Baratarians, who showed no signs of cooperating. In early November, Jackson expelled the British and Indians from Pensacola.

Ross's death near Baltimore in September dealt British fortunes another blow. The ship carrying Major General Sir Edward Michael Pakenham, Ross's successor, was slow in crossing the Atlantic. As a result, he was not with Cochrane's mighty invasion fleet when it sailed from its Jamaica rendezvous into the Gulf of Mexico in late November, nor when Cochrane's sailors overcame U.S. gunboats at the mouth of Lake Borgne, in December. Cochrane had decided to attack New Orleans from the Gulf of Mexico by sailing through Lake Borgne.

Jackson had arrived in New Orleans on December 1 and proceeded to block all invasion approaches, but through a subordinate's negligence, one approach was left open. On December 23, the vanguard of British troops landed, advanced along unprotected Bayou Bienvenue, and emerged from the swamps on the east bank of the Mississippi, fewer than ten miles below the city. Jackson responded quickly. That night, he attacked the British camp, inflicting large casualties and throwing the invaders off balance. When Pakenham arrived on Christmas Day, he found his army in *cul-de-sac*. On its right were cypress swamps; on its left were two U.S. warships and the Mississippi River; and in front, Jackson's small but growing army was constructing a mud and log breastwork on the narrow plain of Chalmett, barring the way to New Orleans.

Attempting to regain the advantage the British destroyed one of Commandant Daniel T. Patterson's ships on December 27. In the following days, they suffered serious reverses: the U.S. troops turned back a reconnaissance-in-force on December 28, 1814, and won an artillery duel on January 1, 1815, thwarting Pakenham's attempt to breach the breastwork. The only remaining alternative was a direct assault. Pakenham developed his plan: One large column would attack the U.S. center at the edge of the swamp; a smaller column would assault the U.S. right; a third would support one of the other two according to developments; a small force would attack the weak U.S. positions across the river; and the rest of his approximately ten thousand redcoats, some of whom were veterans of the Napoleonic Wars, would form the reserve.

At daybreak, on Sunday, January 8, Pakenham gave the signal to advance. Waiting for the attack was a heterogeneous collection of about five thousand defenders—Louisiana Acadians; Anglo-Saxons; Creoles; free men of color: Baratarians, Choctaw Indians, and French *émigrés*; Mississippi, Kentucky, and Tennessee militia; and United States Marines, regulars, and sailors. Only portions of the line were directly engaged, but the terrific fire from their artillery, muskets, and rifles cut down Pakenham's troops as they advanced through the mist across the rain-soaked field. Pakenham was killed while desperately urging his men on. Shortly afterward, his crippled army withdrew. The partially successful attack on the west bank came too late to affect the outcome of the great assault. American casualties totaled seventy-one (of whom only about a dozen were killed), while British losses in the fighting that Sunday were 2,057. In the campaign that was launched on December 23, British dead totaled more than twenty-four hundred.

Because of the apparent impregnability of Jackson's lines and a shortage of supplies, the British leaders decided to retreat. The withdrawal went unimpeded, as Jackson decided against allowing his relatively undisciplined and heterogeneous collection of troops to attack what was still a trained army; they remained behind their lines until the British had disappeared. Pakenham's forces moved through the swamp to Lake Borgne and then to Pea Island. On January 27, the remainder of the now half-starved British troops were gone from the Mississippi delta. In a face-saving move, Cochrane attempted to level Fort St. Philip near the Gulf; failing that, his fleet sailed away to attack Fort Bowyer at Mobile. After its fall, official news of the ratification of the Treaty of Ghent—concluded on December 24, 1814—reached the armies. In mid-March, the fleet returned to England.

On January 23, Jackson marched into the city of New Orleans with his troops, welcomed as a hero. However, he continued to maintain martial law until the middle of March and required the volunteers to remain under arms in the militia until he received official word of the signing of a treaty. As a consequence, the Louisiana Senate, when listing the officers to whom they extended official thanks, omitted Jackson's name.

The Battle of New Orleans, the last major battle in the War of 1812, constituted a British tragedy, inasmuch as it had taken place two weeks after the Treaty of Ghent had brought the war to a close. Despite the fact that the bloody engagement did not play a role in the outcome of the war, the Battle of New Orleans made Andrew Jackson a national hero.

The battle's consequences stretch beyond Jackson's role. One must address the question of British goals in a war that they certainly provoked, but that was started by the United States. First, the British aimed to limit U.S. settlement beyond the Appalachian Mountains. To do so, they wanted to create an American buffer state in the region beyond Ohio. Their second goal was to assuage the fear of U.S. aggression into Canada, a fear with some merit. Further, by annexing Louisiana, they could prevent communication of the west with the sea. Along with Spanish claims to Florida, this would serve to block U.S. expansion.

Pakenham arrived in the United States with instructions to "rescue" Louisiana; he brought with him a complete governmental staff, with himself appointed as governor. Although the Treaty of Ghent was signed, it was not to take effect until ratified by all concerned. In the meantime, Pakenham would have control of Louisiana, an eventuality interrupted by his defeat and death.—*Jeffrey Kimball, updated by Richard Adler*

ADDITIONAL READING:

Berton, Pierre. *The Invasion of Canada, 1812-1813*. Boston: Little, Brown, 1980. The first of two volumes on the War of 1812. A detailed, humanistic account with a British viewpoint.

_____. *The Invasion of Canada, 1813-1814*. Boston: Little, Brown, 1981. The second volume of Berton's vivid account of the war.

Brooks, Charles B. *The Siege of New Orleans*. Seattle: University of Washington Press, 1961. A detailed account of events leading up to the battle.

Coles, Harry L. *The War of 1812*. Chicago: University of Chicago Press, 1965. Remains a strong, concise history of the war.

McConnell, Roland C. *Negro Troops of Antebellum Louisiana: A History of the Battalion of Free Men of Color*. Baton Rouge: Louisiana State University Press, 1968. Contains an account of the role played by African Americans in the battle.

Remini, Robert V. *The Life of Andrew Jackson*. New York: Harper & Row, 1988. Condensation of the author's three-volume set. Among the best biographies written about Jackson.

SEE ALSO: 1811, Battle of Tippecanoe; 1812, War of 1812; 1813, Battle of the Thames; 1815, Treaty of Ghent.

1815 ■ TREATY OF GHENT: *the formal end to the War of 1812, the United States' "second war for independence"*

DATE: February 17, 1815
LOCALE: Ghent, Austrian Netherlands (now Belgium)
CATEGORIES: Canadian history; Diplomacy and international relations; Native American history; Treaties and agreements
KEY FIGURES:

John Quincy Adams (1767-1848), Republican nationalist from Massachusetts, who led the U.S. delegation

James A. Bayard (1767-1815), moderate Federalist from Delaware

Robert Stewart, Viscount Castlereagh (1769-1822), British foreign secretary

Henry Clay (1777-1852), Republican "war hawk" from Kentucky

Albert Gallatin (1761-1849), moderate Republican from Pennsylvania

James Madison (1751-1836), fourth president of the United
   States, 1809-1817

James Monroe (1758-1831), U.S. secretary of state

Jonathan Russell (1771-1832), "war hawk" from Rhode
   Island

SUMMARY OF EVENT. Chances of a negotiated, honorable
peace ending the War of 1812 appeared remote in the summer
of 1814. The United States ostensibly had gone to war to
protect its rights on the high seas. President James Madison
and Secretary of State James Monroe had repeatedly stated
that the recognition of such rights, and particularly an end to
the practice of impressing U.S. sailors into the British navy,
was essential to any settlement.

The British had refused to abandon impressment, and the
war continued. Militarily, the conflict had been inconclusive.
In many ways, the British were in the stronger position at the
outset of the talks. By the summer of 1814, they and their
allies had defeated Napoleon; now Great Britain could turn its
attention and energies to the war with its former colonies. With
France subdued and veteran troops available for North American duty, Great Britain seemed in a position to end the war by
military conquest. Moreover, the United States was divided
over "Mr. Madison's War." The Federalist Party and New
England generally had opposed the war from its beginning.
The Republican administration faced the unpleasant prospects
of political humiliation, military defeat, or both, should it
continue to pursue its war aims.

Such were the circumstances when U.S. and British commissioners met in Ghent on August 9, 1814. The British had
agreed to direct meetings as an alternative to mediation by
Alexander I, czar of Russia, and evinced no haste to deal with
the U.S. upstarts. Ghent was chosen as a convenient, easily
accessible site—a pleasant, neutral city in what was then the
Austrian Netherlands, soon to be part of the Kingdom of the
United Netherlands and a major city in Belgium after that
country's independence in 1830.

The United States government dispatched five commissioners, representing a broad spectrum of backgrounds. John
Quincy Adams, a Massachusetts Republican and nominally
the head of the delegation, was a staunch nationalist. Henry
Clay and Jonathan Russell were "war hawks" from Kentucky
and Rhode Island, respectively. James A. Bayard, a Delaware
Federalist, and Albert Gallatin, a Pennsylvania Republican,
were moderates; the latter, because of his role as peacemaker
among his colleagues, emerged as the functional leader of the
U.S. delegation at Ghent. The representatives from the United
States often quarreled among themselves, but they stood
firmly together in the face of their British counterparts.

Adams and Russell arrived in Ghent on June 23 and the
others, by July 6. Clearly, the talks were going to be protracted, and so the U.S. delegates moved out of their hotel
and into the Lovendeghem House in the heart of the city.
Far from being the "five lonely Americans" as they have been
often described, they became active in local intellectual and
cultural life.

Negotiations began in an atmosphere of distrust as a result
of a monthlong wait by the U.S. delegates for their British
counterparts. The British delegation included Admiralty lawyer
Dr. William Adams, Vice-Admiral Lord Gambier, and Henry
Goulburn of the Colonial Office. Accompanied by a secretary,
Anthony J. Baker, they took up residence in a former Carthu-
sian monastery at Meerhem. Their principal role was not so
much to negotiate as to act as the messengers of Viscount
Castlereagh (Robert Stewart), the British foreign secretary.

Although the United States had always posed as the injured
party in the conflict, the British dominated the early months of
the conference. They proposed the establishment of an American Indian buffer state in the American Northwest and asked
for a substantial cession of land along the border between
Canada and the United States. The U.S. representatives refused. The British, anticipating the capture of New Orleans,
then suggested that each party continue to occupy the territory
it held at the conclusion of hostilities (*uti possidetis*). Again,
the United States refused, holding to its principle of the restoration of territory as it was held prior to the outbreak of war
(*status quo ante bellum*).

Finally, the constancy and apparent unanimity of the U.S.
delegation bore fruit. Throughout the negotiations, the British
cabinet had debated whether to conquer or conciliate the
United States. Foreseeing greater good in Anglo-American
friendship than in lasting enmity between the kindred nations,
Castlereagh led the way toward compromise.

Several factors, some only vaguely relating to the war,
confirmed Castlereagh's judgment. The British were having
difficulties at the Congress of Vienna with their recent allies in
the Napoleonic Wars. It seemed for a time that war with Russia
was imminent. France was restive, portending Napoleon's return from Elba in 1815. At home, the British people were
war-weary and growing resentful of taxation. To make matters
worse, the United States won a timely victory at Plattsburg on
September 11, 1814. The architect of the victory over Napoleon, the duke of Wellington, estimated that a conquest of the
United States would come only at a heavy cost of men, money,
and time. At this juncture, the British decided to compromise.

The commissioners at Ghent still bargained hard, but the
stakes were no longer so great. On November 11, 1814, the
United States presented a proposal that would maintain prewar
boundaries. They agreed that the treaty would say nothing
about impressment, which would be unnecessary in a post-
Napoleonic Europe. The British abandoned their designs on
U.S. territory and their desire for a buffer state. They still
demanded the islands in Passamaquoddy Bay, the right of
navigation on the Mississippi River, and prohibitions on U.S.
rights to dry fish in Newfoundland.

In the end, the participants at Ghent delegated these matters
to commissions to resolve after peace had been concluded. The
Peace of Ghent provided for a return to the *status quo ante
bellum*. The two sides signed the treaty on Christmas Eve,
1814. Given the slow communications of the era, the treaty
only took effect on February 17, 1815, after ratification by the

governments of both sides. In the meantime, the British had suffered a humiliating defeat in the Battle of New Orleans on January 8, 1815.

Called America's second war for independence, the War of 1812 had several important results. Spawning a legacy of bad feeling between Great Britain and the United States, which persisted for many years, the war gave the U.S. people a greater feeling of national identity, simultaneously paving the way for the decimation of native populations. The war stimulated the growth of manufacturers and turned the U.S. people increasingly toward domestic matters and away from foreign affairs.

The treaty had a major impact on the United States' relationships with both Canada and the American Indian nations. Future war was averted by the Rush-Bagot Agreement of 1817, which limited armaments around the Great Lakes. Boundary commissions and subsequent treaties in 1818, 1842, and 1846 determined most of the border between the United States and British North America (Canada). The Red River Valley went to the United States; the borders of Alberta, Manitoba, and Saskatchewan were moved south to 49° north latitude. Oregon Territory (Oregon, Washington, and British Columbia) was to be jointly administered by Great Britain and the United States. The United States agreed to exact no retribution and to take no land from the American Indians who had fought for the British. However, the defeat of the British and their American Indian allies helped to open the Old Northwest and Southwest to the waves of settlement that would lead to white domination east of the Mississippi and eventually beyond.

At the time, the treaty was, in many ways, a victory for neither side. Yet for the United States, there was cause for rejoicing. The United States had stood firm against a great power. Castlereagh and the British had recognized U.S. military potential and decided to court instead of conquer. Most important, the peace that both sides wanted and needed was secure. The treaty provided a steady foundation for an Anglo-American relationship that, over a century, would transform the two nations' foreign policies from suspicious opposition to firm friendship.

—*Emory M. Thomas, updated by Randall Fegley*

ADDITIONAL READING:

Bemis, Samuel Flagg. *John Quincy Adams and the Foundations of American Foreign Policy*. New York: Alfred A. Knopf, 1949. A diplomatic historian presents Adams' role at Ghent as part of a larger triumph in statecraft.

Burt, A. L. *The United States, Great Britain, and British North America from the Revolution to the Establishment of Peace After the War of 1812*. New Haven, Conn.: Yale University Press, 1940. A judicious summary of early Anglo-American relations.

Coles, Harry. *The War of 1812*. Chicago: University of Chicago Press, 1965. This brief but incisive narrative of the war includes chapters on the treaty that provide a penetrating summary of the negotiations.

Dangerfield, George. *The Era of Good Feelings*. New York: Harcourt, Brace, 1952. Treats the Ghent negotiations in broad European perspective and regards them as contributing to the founding of U.S. nationalism.

Engelman, Fred. *The Peace of Christmas Eve*. New York: Harcourt, Brace, 1962. Written from a U.S. viewpoint, this excellent account of the negotiations and signing of the treaty contains much on the setting, personalities, and interaction related to the event.

Gallatin, James. *The Diary of James Gallatin*. New ed. Westport, Conn.: Greenwood Press, 1979. In this reprint of his diary, James Gallatin, secretary to and son of Albert Gallatin, observes the treaty negotiations from behind the scenes.

Horsman, Reginald. *The War of 1812*. New York: Alfred A. Knopf, 1969. A general history of the war that treats the treaty in its broader European context.

Perkins, Bradford. *Castlereagh and Adams: England and the United States, 1812-1823*. Berkeley: University of California Press, 1964. Part of a three-volume study of early Anglo-American diplomacy. More than half of this volume is devoted to the diplomacy surrounding the War of 1812.

Vannieuwenhuyse, Johan. *The Treaty of Ghent*. Ghent: Museum Arnold Vander Haeghen-Stadsarchief, 1989. This excellent, brief Belgian overview of the Treaty of Ghent presents details and sources frequently overlooked.

SEE ALSO: 1811, Battle of Tippecanoe; 1812, War of 1812; 1813, Battle of the Thames; 1815, Battle of New Orleans.

1815 ■ RED RIVER RAIDS: *a series of battles between native peoples and European settlers for the fur trade*

DATE: June, 1815-August, 1817
LOCALE: Red River Colony, Manitoba, Canada
CATEGORIES: Canadian history; Native American history; Wars, uprisings, and civil unrest
KEY FIGURES:
Thomas Douglas (1771-1820), fifth earl of Selkirk and founder of the Red River Colony
Miles Macdonell, first governor of Assiniboia
Robert Semple (1766-1816), second governor of Assiniboia
SUMMARY OF EVENT. In 1811, Thomas Douglas, fifth earl of Selkirk, bought a large number of shares in the Hudson's Bay Company, England's largest fur-trading company. In return, he received 116,000 square miles of land in the Red River Valley in what is now southern Manitoba, just north of the Dakota Territory of the United States. In this huge territory, he planned to build a community called Assiniboia. Colonists would grow food, mainly potatoes, for Hudson's Bay Company trappers but would not be allowed to trap or trade in furs. Selkirk hoped to recruit farmers suffering from an agricultural depression in his native Scotland to settle the land. He sent an advance party, led by Miles Macdonell, a retired army officer from Scotland,

to establish an initial base. Selkirk appointed Macdonell the colony's first governor. Macdonell's party of thirty-six Scottish and Irish farmers arrived on August 29, 1812. They settled near the junction of the Red and Assiniboine Rivers, in what is now Winnipeg. The settlement, called Point Douglas, was only a few miles from a North West Company post known as Fort Gibraltor.

Selkirk's original settlement had great difficulty surviving its first years on the prairie. Only help from fur traders and métis working for the North West Company, the Hudson's Bay Company's major rival for furs in the region, enabled Macdonell's group to survive. Metis, a French word meaning "mixed," was used to describe people of French-Indian, or English-Indian descent. (Sometimes these people were called the Bois Brulés.) Written with a small *m*, the word refers to all persons of mixed blood, but with a capital *M*, it signifies a distinct cultural and ethnic group living in the region of southern Manitoba. These Metis were descended from marriages between native women and European fishermen on Canada's Atlantic coast in the early 1600's. By 1810, the Metis had moved into buffalo country on the northern Great Plains. Many were employed as buffalo hunters by the North West Company to provide provisions for its trappers.

The second year, a group of eighty more immigrants arrived, which greatly increased the colony's chance for survival. They started growing wheat, barley, oats, and corn, although potatoes remained the principal crop. Some of the settlers also had brought sheep with them. Settlement took place during the War of 1812 with the United States, while another English army was engaging Napoleon's forces in Europe.

Macdonell proved to be an arrogant and unpopular governor, and engaged in major conflicts with North West Company trappers and Native Americans. With the population of his colony increasing to more than two hundred Europeans by 1814, he sought to prevent food shortages by prohibiting the export of pemmican from his lands. Buffalo hunters made pemmican—a key food source for trappers and métis—from dried strips of buffalo meat that they pounded into a powder, mixed with melted fat, and stored in buffalo skin bags. The governor angered local trappers and métis by prohibiting the export of pemmican from Assiniboia after January 8, 1814. This order made it difficult for employees of the North West Company to get food, since U.S. troops had recently recaptured the company's key trading post of Detroit, from which food supplies for trappers had been sent west. Now both sources of provisions, Assiniboia and Detroit, were cut off. The trappers for the North West Company saw the Pemmican Proclamation as part of a Hudson's Bay Company plot to destroy their business.

At a meeting in August, North West Company trappers decided to destroy the Red River colony and take back control of the region. To accomplish this goal, the company needed the support of the metis population of the upper Assiniboine River Valley.

Macdonell angered the Metis by prohibiting them from killing buffalo in his colony. The North West Company recognized the Metis as a new nation and accepted their title to lands occupied by Selkirk's colonists. Thus, the North West Company and the Metis came together to drive out the Assiniboia settlers. In 1815, agents of the North West Company arrested Governor Macdonell and brought him to Montreal for trial. He was charged with interfering with Native American rights in what the North West Company claimed was Indian Territory. While the governor stood trial in the east, the Metis attacked the colonists along the Red River, drove them from their homes, and burned their fields.

Only one colonist remained in the community after the attack, but he managed to save some of the wheat crop. When a few settlers, under the leadership of Colin Robertson, returned in the fall, they harvested enough grain to assure survival. A few weeks later, a relief party sent out by Lord Selkirk made it to the Red River. Led by the newly appointed governor, Robert Semple, the settlement began to rebuild. When news of this development reached the headquarters of the North West Company, orders were sent out to destroy the village again. Violence spread into the area again in the spring of 1816. Robertson led a force that took control of the North West Company's Fort Gibraltor in May, giving Assiniboians control of the river.

On June 1, Metis set out on the Assiniboine River in three boats filled with pemmican. When Robertson heard this news, he ordered the abandonment of Fort Gibraltor and left the colony for England. The Metis continued their journey and reached the Red River at Frog Plain, below the Hudson's Bay Company settlement. On June 19, Governor Semple set out with twenty-five colonists to intercept the Metis. At a point in the woods called Seven Oaks, the Metis confronted Semple's band. A Metis named Boucher rode out to talk with Semple, but after they exchanged a few words, a fight broke out between the two and a shot rang out. Firing began from all sides, but the colonists quickly were surrounded by a much larger force and twenty men, including Semple, were killed. The remaining six men escaped into the woods. Only one Metis was killed. The Massacre at Seven Oaks gave the North West Company control of the Red River territory once again.

Lord Selkirk did not give up on his colony, however, but hired a band of mercenaries to recapture control. Selkirk led the force himself and in June of 1817 returned to Assiniboia after destroying a North West Company outpost. He quickly signed a treaty with local Metis allowing resettlement of the region. Fields were restored, seeds were planted, and settlers brought in a small crop before winter arrived. New colonists from the Orkney Islands came in, along with a small group of French Canadians. Selkirk provided money for a school and a church, and Catholic and Presbyterian missionaries began work among the Cree and Assiniboin Indians living along the Red River. The colony seemed to be at peace at last.

The next summer brought further disaster, however. In August, a vast swarm of locusts attacked Assiniboia. Most of the potato crop was killed, forcing many farmers to abandon their land. Locusts came again in 1819 and devastated the entire prairie. No food or seed remained in the entire valley. Settlers had to send a party all the way into the Wisconsin Territory to buy seeds for a new potato crop. Lord Selkirk's death in 1820 was another major setback for the community, and it would be several years before farmers grew enough to feed the local population. Buffalo herds continued to provide subsistence during hard times. The Metis hunted the buffalo and sold their hides and meat to the farmers. Gradually, however, the native peoples and the new settlers learned to live together and end their hostilities.

While the Red River colony was becoming a permanent part of the landscape, the right for control of the fur trade was waged in the courts. Shortages of fur-bearing animals east of the Rocky Mountains brought economic problems to both companies. In 1821, the companies merged and ended their fighting. The Seven Oaks Massacre was the worst single incident in the great battle for control of Canada's fur trade.

—*Leslie V. Tischauser*

ADDITIONAL READING:

Brown, Jennifer S. *Strangers in Blood: Fur Trade Families in Indian Country*. Vancouver: University of British Columbia Press, 1980. Discusses the development of the Metis people in eastern Canada and the Great Plains from the 1600's to the twentieth century. Illustrations and index.

Davidson, Gordon Charles. *The North West Company*. New York: Russell & Russell, 1967. A history of the development and expansion of the second largest fur company in North America. Maps, illustrations, and index.

Morton, W. L. *Manitoba: A History*. Toronto: University of Toronto Press, 1967. One chapter is devoted to the importance of the Red River colony. Presents a decidedly old-fashioned view of the métis, referring to them as "halfbreeds" and "savages." Maps, illustrations, and index.

Pritchett, John Perry. *Red River Valley, 1811-1849: A Regional Study*. New Haven, Conn.: Yale University Press, 1942. Contains an almost minute-by-minute account of the Seven Oaks Massacre.

SEE ALSO: 1837, Rebellions in Canada; 1869, First Riel Rebellion; 1885, Second Riel Rebellion.

1816 ■ SECOND BANK OF THE UNITED STATES IS CHARTERED: *an effort to restore the monetary system to a gold standard leads to the creation of a central bank*

DATE: April, 1816
LOCALE: Washington, D.C.
CATEGORIES: Economics; Organizations and institutions
KEY FIGURES:
John Jacob Astor (1763-1848), New York merchant who was a major influence in creation of the Second Bank

Nicholas Biddle (1786-1844), director and third president of the Second Bank
Langdon Cheves (1776-1857), Speaker of the House of Representatives and second president of the Second Bank
Stephen Girard (1750-1831), powerful Philadelphia banker and largest subscriber to the Second Bank
William Jones (1760-1831), secretary of the navy and first president of the Second Bank
James Madison (1751-1836), fourth president of the United States, 1809-1817

SUMMARY OF EVENT. In April, 1816, President James Madison signed a bill authorizing the establishment of the Second Bank of the United States. In January, 1817, the bank commenced operations in Philadelphia in the same building that had housed the First Bank of the United States. The First Bank of the United States had been chartered in 1791 as part of the comprehensive financial program of Treasury Secretary Alexander Hamilton. One purpose in chartering the bank was to improve the market for the newly issued securities constituting the funded national debt, for these securities could be turned in to purchase stock in the new bank. In addition, the bank was expected to enlarge credit availability substantially. (There were only three commercial banks in existence in 1790.) The bank also would serve as a fiscal agent for the federal government, managing its checking account, helping issue and redeem government securities, and paying the interest on them. However, the First Bank failed to gain recharter in 1812, after a productive and efficient existence of twenty years.

In 1812, the United States went to war with Great Britain. As usual, government expenditures greatly increased, and most of the increase was financed by borrowing. The government borrowed extensively by selling securities to state-chartered banks, which numbered about eighty-eight in 1812. To pay for the securities, the banks expanded their notes and deposits, while their specie reserves declined. In 1814, when the British sailed up Chesapeake Bay and burned Washington, D.C., most banks outside New England suspended specie redemption of their liabilities. Suspension freed the banks to expand their credit with little restraint. As a result, many banknotes depreciated severely and commodity prices increased by about 50 percent from 1811 to 1814.

When the war ended in 1815, a movement to form a new Bank of the United States gained momentum. As in 1790, the government was burdened with a large public debt, much of it selling below face value. If the securities could be used to pay for the stock of a new bank, their market value probably would rise. Furthermore, Treasury officials needed competent help in managing their funds, having had bad experiences with state bank depositories. One of the most important motivations was to restore monetary order to the United States and halt the inflation process. Many businessmen, such as Stephen Girard and John Jacob Astor, believed that the banks needed to return to redeeming their notes and deposits in gold and silver on demand, as they had done before 1814. Girard and Astor also were large investors in government securities.

The new bank charter passed Congress in the spring of 1816. It specified the structure and operations of the bank but did not identify any public purpose it was to serve. The Second Bank of the United States resembled its predecessor in many respects, although its capitalization, at thirty-five million dollars, was larger. As before, the government took one-fifth of the stock. A new feature was that one-fifth of the directors were appointed by the government. The bank provided a depository for federal funds in every state where a branch was opened. Between 1817 and 1828, twenty-eight branches were established in the major commercial cities of the nation. It was through these branches that the Second Bank was enabled to exercise control over the rapidly increasing number of state banks. The bank transferred federal funds from place to place and paid public creditors without charge to the government. It was authorized to issue notes that were receivable at par in all payments to the government. The bank was authorized to lend money and to buy and sell bills of exchange. It became the manager of the Treasury's bank account and handled transactions involving issue, redemption, and interest payments on government securities.

The new bank was expected to lead the nation's banks back to specie redemption, aided by the Webster Resolution of 1816, which forbade the Treasury to accept notes of non-specie-paying banks. The banks nominally resumed specie payments in February, 1817, but their specie reserves were very small relative to their liabilities. The Second Bank tried to make their position easier by expanding its own credit rapidly. However, the bank was badly managed under its first president, William Jones, and made many bad loans.

In 1818, the country experienced a large international outflow of gold. Banks were called on to redeem notes and deposits in specie. As their reserves declined, they were obliged to reduce loans, and the resulting contraction of credit led to severe deflation and economic depression. The Second Bank reduced its loans from forty-three million dollars in early 1818 to thirty-one million dollars in September, 1819, during which time its note circulation fell from ten million dollars to four million dollars. Under fire for internal mismanagement and for the country's deflationary distress, Jones resigned as president in 1822. His successor, Langdon Cheves, concentrated on cleaning up the Second Bank's internal affairs without much concern for the nation's economy.

The Second Bank's role in the Panic of 1819 made it politically unpopular. In 1817, Maryland placed a tax upon the branch office in Baltimore. In 1819, after several other states had followed this example, Ohio and Kentucky imposed taxes of sixty thousand dollars and fifty thousand dollars, respectively, on the branches in those states. However, the landmark Supreme Court decision in *McCulloch v. Maryland* (1819) held that chartering the bank was within the constitutional authority of the Congress and that state taxes could not be imposed to block federal programs.

In 1823, Nicholas Biddle became president of the Second Bank. He developed many programs to expand its operation.

In particular, the bank became an extensive dealer in domestic exchange. The bank made loans secured by goods (such as cotton) produced in the interior and sent to Eastern cities for sale or export. These loans were repaid in the Eastern cities, but the bank's interior branches could sell drafts on those funds to local people needing to make payments to the East. The process yielded revenue for the bank and helped improve the country's interregional payments system. However, Biddle and the Second Bank had many political enemies. The number of state-chartered and private banks was increasing, and they and their customers resented the competition from the Second Bank and the restraints it imposed on them. Antagonism from President Andrew Jackson ultimately led him to block recharter of the Second Bank, and its federal charter expired in 1836.

—*John G. Clark, updated by Paul B. Trescott*

ADDITIONAL READING:

Govan, Thomas P. *Nicholas Biddle: Nationalist and Public Banker, 1786-1844.* Chicago: University of Chicago Press, 1959. This highly readable biography gives ample background on the evolution of the Second Bank and its political adventures.

Hammond, Bray. *Banks and Politics in America.* Princeton, N.J.: Princeton University Press, 1957. This breezy, entertaining book blends political and economic analysis. Criticizes the Jacksonian point of view.

Redlich, Fritz. *The Molding of American Banking: Men and Ideas.* 1951. Reprint. New York: Johnson Reprint, 1968. Emphasizes the role of businessmen in the initial chartering of the Second Bank, and assesses Biddle's innovations in both commercial and central banking.

Smith, Walter B. *Economic Aspects of the Second Bank of the United States.* Cambridge, Mass.: Harvard University Press, 1953. Presents considerable statistical data and objective analysis of the Second Bank's operations.

Timberlake, Richard H. *Monetary Policy in the United States: An Intellectual and Institutional History.* Chicago: University of Chicago Press, 1993. Chapter 3 depicts the Second Bank as a rather primitive central bank, constrained by its commitment to the gold standard.

SEE ALSO: 1790, Hamilton's *Report on Public Credit*; 1819, *McCulloch v. Maryland*; 1824, *Gibbons v. Ogden*; 1824, U.S. Election of 1824; 1832, Jackson vs. the Bank of the United States.

1816 ■ AME CHURCH IS FOUNDED: *a radically distinct denomination becomes an advocate for the cause of abolition and a bulwark of the African American community*

DATE: April 9, 1816
LOCALE: Philadelphia, Pennsylvania
CATEGORIES: African American history; Organizations and institutions; Religion

KEY FIGURES:

Richard Allen (1760-1831), founder and first bishop of the African Methodist Episcopal Church

Francis Asbury (1745-1816), leader of the Methodist Church in America in the eighteenth century

Absalom Jones (1746-1818), first priest of African descent in the U.S. Episcopal church

SUMMARY OF EVENT. Sixteen African Methodist delegates met in Philadelphia on April 9, 1816, to unite as the African Methodist Episcopal Church. Most delegates had gained their spiritual leadership skills through self-study and life struggles. From Philadelphia and Attleborough, Pennsylvania, delegates joined representatives from Baltimore, Wilmington, and Salem to elect a bishop. Accounts vary as to what happened next. Some reports indicate that the Reverend Daniel Coker, a Baltimore teacher and school founder, was elected bishop but declined the office the following day in deference to Richard Allen, who had organized the convention. Other records relate that both Allen and Coker were elected; Allen saw no need for two bishops and assumed the role of vice-chair. One account states that Coker's light skin made him unacceptable as the first head of a racially separate institution. Whatever the process, the outcome was the election of Richard Allen, who was consecrated as the first bishop of the African Methodist Episcopal Church on April 11, 1816. From the original sixteen delegates in 1816, membership grew to 7,257 by 1822.

Philadelphia provided a receptive haven for African American leaders. Before the American Revolution, manumissions had run high and a private school for African children had been founded. Following the Revolutionary War, city leaders such as Benjamin Franklin and Benjamin Rush established abolition societies, and the state legislature passed laws for the gradual emancipation of slaves.

Richard Allen, known as the father of African American religion, was born a slave in 1760 in Philadelphia. Sold to the Stokeley plantation near Dover, Delaware, Allen attended evangelical tent meetings and experienced a religious conversion when he was seventeen years of age. He joined the Methodist Society, which held classes in the forest under the leadership of a white man, Benjamin Wells. Allen became a convincing proselytizer, converting first his family and then his owner, who agreed to Allen's proposal to purchase his own freedom in 1777. Allen worked at many jobs and preached at his regular stops, developing broad contacts through his travels. As an aide to other itinerant preachers, he met Bishop Francis Asbury, who established the first General Conference of the Methodist Church in America in 1784. When Asbury asked Allen to accompany him on a southern trip, with the stipulation that Allen must not mingle with slaves and must accept segregated accommodations, Allen refused to accompany him and returned to Philadelphia in February, 1786.

Because the church was one of the only legal meeting places for African Americans, religion became a major focus of African American life. Allen joined such Philadelphia leaders as former slave clerk and handyman Absalom Jones, and

other members of the St. Thomas vestry: James Forten, free-born sailmaker, William White, Jacob Tapisco, and James Champion. Allen and Jones became lay preachers throughout the city—especially at St. George's Methodist Episcopal Church at early-morning and evening services. As African American attendance increased, racial conflict became apparent. In November, 1786, African Americans worshiping at St. George's were ordered to the gallery. After mistaking the section of the gallery assigned for their worship, Allen, Jones, and White were physically removed while praying at the Sunday morning worship service.

The humiliation of this incident led to a mass exodus of African Americans from this church and a movement to create a separate church as an organized act of self-determination. In the spring, these African American leaders established the Free African Society, the first mutual aid society established to serve their community. By 1791, they held regular Sunday services, assumed lay leadership positions, and made plans for construction of a church building. The effectiveness of the society's leadership and organization was demonstrated to white leaders during the yellow fever epidemic of 1793.

The leaders differed over the issue of church affiliation, with the majority voting to unite with the Episcopal church. On July 17, 1794, the St. Thomas African Church was dedicated as the first African church in Philadelphia, a Protestant Episcopal church with Absalom Jones as pastor. Jones became the first African American priest in 1804.

Jones and Allen favored Methodism, but only Allen withdrew from the Free African Society to form a separate church. Bishop Asbury of the Methodist Episcopal Church presided over the dedication of Allen's creation, the Bethel African Methodist Episcopal Church, on July 29, 1794. Allen declared the church independent in management but did not sever all relations with the Methodist Episcopal Church. The articles of incorporation ensured independence by allowing membership only to African Americans. Allen became the first African American to receive ordination from the Methodist Episcopal Church in the United States.

Such church independence helped African Americans resist the insults and subordination resulting from slavery and racial prejudice and reflected a growing role of the church in the community. Sermons underscored the need for the African American community to become self-reliant through the church, schools, and economic organizations in order to gain group solidarity and recognition. Christian character, in turn, depended upon Christian education. In the summer of 1795, Bethel cooperated with the Society for the Improving of the Condition of the Free Blacks by arranging for the arrival, temporary housing, and placement for newly emancipated slaves.

Church trustees petitioned the African school for free instruction. Bethel not only established the first Sunday school for African Americans but also set a precedent with the 1795 opening of the first day school established by African Americans for their children. The day school was soon followed by a night school for working people. In 1798, Allen and Jones

Richard Allen founded the first church for African Americans, Bethel African Methodist Episcopal (AME) Church in Philadelphia, Pennsylvania. (The Associated Publishers, Inc.)

gained permission from Prince Hall of Boston to set up the Second African (Masonic) Lodge in Philadelphia. Because music was an integral part of African American worship, Allen enhanced the cultural expression of his people by compiling a collection of sixty-four hymns for his congregation in 1801. As women experienced religious conversions and entered preaching, Allen supported their spiritual growth by allowing an Englishwoman, Dorothy Ripley, to speak to his congregation in 1803. In 1804, he established the Society of Free People of Color for Promoting the Instruction and School Education of Children of African Descent. In 1809, he helped James Forten and Absalom Jones organize the Society for the Suppression of Vice and Immorality in Philadelphia, to provide community supervision of the morality of African Americans and to establish means for their moral uplift. These leaders recruited three thousand members for the Black Legion during the War of 1812. The successful functions associated with African American churches led to greater membership. By 1813, St. Thomas had a membership of 560, while Bethel Church had 1,272 communicants.

Once the African Methodist Episcopal Church was established in 1816, the movement spread to other cities and along the seaboard states. Church leaders continued their pioneering efforts for group solidarity. In January, 1817, the First Negro Convention met at the Bethel Church to protest the plans of the American Colonization Society for emigration of free blacks to Africa. That same year, Allen's church supported the first female licensed worker of the African Methodist Episcopal Church, Jarena Lee. Also in 1817, Allen and Jacob Tapisco published the First Church Discipline as well as a book of hymns compiled by Allen, Daniel Coker, and James Champion. After the death of Absalom Jones, Allen served as Book Steward from 1818 to 1820, a position that served as the foundation for the church's twentieth century Book Concern, which continues to unite followers across the country.

The church continued to improve the conditions for African Americans. It supported the use of boycotts to protest the economic basis of slavery through the Free Produce Society of Philadelphia, which was organized at an assembly at Bethel Church on December 20, 1830, to advocate purchase only of produce grown by free labor. The First Annual Convention of the People of Color, convened in Philadelphia in 1831, elected Richard Allen as its leader shortly before his death on March 26, 1831. The African Methodist Episcopal Church has survived as an integral part of the African American community and continued its strong leadership role. —*Dorothy C. Salem*

ADDITIONAL READING:

Allen, Richard. "Letters of Richard Allen and Absalom Jones." *Journal of Negro History* 1, no. 4 (October, 1916): 436-443. The common concerns of the two leaders are expressed in their correspondence.

_____. *The Life, Experience, and Gospel Labors of the Right Reverent Richard Allen.* 1833. Reprint. Nashville, Tenn.: Abingdon Press, 1983. Presents an accounting of Allen's religious life.

Dvorak, Katharine L. *An African American Exodus.* Brooklyn, N.Y.: Carlson, 1991. Provides the history and theology of the nineteenth century African Methodist Episcopal Church.

George, Carol V. R. *Segregated Sabbaths: Richard Allen and the Rise of Independent Black Churches, 1760-1840.* New York: Oxford University Press, 1973. A standard account of the development of the independent churches.

Mwadilitu, Mwalimu I. [E. Curtis Alexander]. *Richard Allen: The First Exemplar of African American Education.* New York: ECA Associates, 1985. Examines Allen's educational leadership through the church.

Nash, Gary. "New Light on Richard Allen: The Early Years of Freedom." *William and Mary Quarterly* 46 (April, 1989): 332-340. Fills in biographical information about Allen's early life.

Wesley, Charles. *Richard Allen: Apostle of Freedom.* Washington, D.C.: Associated Publishers, 1935. The standard biography of Allen.

SEE ALSO: 1768, Methodist Church Is Established; 1775, Pennsylvania Society for the Abolition of Slavery Is Founded; 1784, Hall's Masonic Lodge Is Chartered; 1787, Free African Society Is Founded; 1789, Episcopal Church Is Established.

1817 ■ SEMINOLE WARS: *a continuation of the U.S. policy of containment and relocation of Native Americans east of the Mississippi*

DATE: November 21, 1817-March 27, 1858
LOCALE: Florida
CATEGORIES: Native American history; Wars, uprisings, and civil unrest
KEY FIGURES:
Arpeika, also known as *Sam Jones* (c. 1760-1860), Mikasuki shaman
Coacoochee, also known as *Wildcat* (c. 1810-1857),
Osceola, also known as *Billy Powell* (c. 1804-1838), and
Ote-emathla, also known as *Jumper*, Seminole war leaders
Holatamico, also known as *Billy Bowlegs* (c. 1810-1864)
Andrew Jackson (1767-1845), general, first U.S. governor of Florida, seventh president of the United States, 1829-1837
Thomas Sidney Jesup (1788-1860), commander of the army in Florida, 1836-1838
Micanopy (c. 1780-1849), Seminole chief
Zachary Taylor (1784-1850), commander of the army in Florida, 1838-1840

SUMMARY OF EVENT. The conflicts known as the First, Second, and Third Seminole Wars were never declared wars on the part of the U.S. government. The Seminole Wars were a continuation of U.S. policy to contain Native American populations east of the Mississippi and remove them to reservations west of the Mississippi, a policy that resulted in the Indian Removal Act of 1830. They also might be seen as early battles fought over the jurisdiction of runaway slaves that would eventually escalate into the Civil War.

The First Seminole War was preceded by years of border disputes along the Florida-Georgia border, climaxing in the destruction of Fort Negro on the Apalachicola River. Built by the British in 1815 and turned over to a band of runaway slaves on the British departure from Florida, Fort Negro proved an obstacle in the supply route to Fort Scott in Georgia. When a U.S. vessel was fired upon from the fort, Andrew Jackson ordered General Edmund Gaines to destroy the fort. A hot cannonball, fired from the expedition led by Lieutenant Colonel Duncan Clinch, landed in a powder magazine, blowing up the fort and killing 270 of its 344 occupants. Neamathla, village chief of Fowltown, reacted by warning General Gaines that if U.S. soldiers tried to cross the border into Florida, they would be annihilated. A gunfight between U.S. soldiers and Neamathla's Seminoles on November 21, 1817, is considered the opening salvo of the First Seminole War. This conflict, ending with Andrew Jackson's occupation of the city of Pensacola in May, 1818, led to the Adams-Onís Treaty of 1819, in which Spain ceded the territory of Florida to the United States.

The 1823 Moultrie Creek Treaty restricted Seminole settlements to a reservation of four million acres north of Charlotte Harbor and six small reservations for north Florida chiefs. The Seminoles agreed not to make the reservations a haven for escaped slaves. The 1830 enactment of the Indian Removal Act mandated that all Indians be encouraged to trade their eastern land for western land. If they failed to do so, they would lose the protection of the federal government.

In May, 1832, U.S. commissioner James Gadsden convened a meeting with the Seminole chiefs at Payne's Landing. What transpired at the meeting has been the subject of much political and scholarly controversy. All that is certain is that a treaty was signed on May 9, 1832, in which the chiefs agreed that a delegation would travel to inspect the lands in Oklahoma, and, if the lands were satisfactory, the Seminoles would agree to move west as a part of the Creek allocation. The ambiguity of who "they" were—the chiefs or their tribal councils—and the peculiar stipulation that the Seminoles would be absorbed by their longtime enemies, the Creeks, put the validity of the treaty into question. There have been allegations that bribery and coercion were used to get the Seminoles to sign the treaty. All of the chiefs whose names were on the treaty later repudiated it.

An exploratory party left for Oklahoma in October, 1832, and returned to Fort Gibson, Arkansas, in March, 1833, where they entered into a series of negotiations. Again, there have been allegations of coercion and forged marks on the Fort Gibson Treaty, by which the chiefs agreed that the Seminoles would move west within three years.

In October, 1834, Indian agent Wiley Thompson brought the chiefs together to discuss plans for a spring removal. The Seminoles gathered in their own council after Thompson's initial meeting, and strong opposition to migration emerged, especially from the Seminole war leader Osceola. Relations deteriorated and skirmishes increased between the government and Seminoles throughout 1835, culminating in the outbreak of war in December. The two most notable incidents occurred on December 28. Ote-emathla, also known as Jumper, and a warrior known as Alligator led 180 warriors in ambushing a relief column under the command of Major Francis Dade. Only 3 of the 108 soldiers escaped slaughter in the fierce battle that followed. Meanwhile, Osceola led sixty warriors in an attack on Fort King with the express purpose of killing Wiley Thompson, who had imprisoned Osceola in chains earlier in the year.

The army was in disarray during most of 1836. General Winfield Scott immediately began to feud with General Gaines. General Call was put in charge of the troops until November, when General Thomas S. Jesup arrived in Florida and assumed the command until 1839. Jesup's command in Florida was crucial for the outcome of the Seminole Wars. The general had persuaded a large number of chiefs and their tribes to emigrate on the condition that they would be accompanied by their African American allies and slaves. When opposition arose among landowners claiming that the Seminoles harbored runaway slaves, a compromise was reached: Only those blacks who had lived with the Seminoles before the outbreak of the war would be permitted to go. More than seven hundred Seminoles had gathered at Fort Brooke north of Tampa by the end of May, 1837. On the night of June 2, Osceola and the Mikasuki shaman Arpeika surrounded the camp with two hundred warriors and spirited away nearly the entire population.

The defection caused a drastic shift in Jesup's tactics; no longer did he feel any compunction about using trickery to gain his ends. In September, General Joseph Hernandez captured King Philip, Yuchi Billy, Coacoochee, and Blue Snake in the vicinity of St. Augustine and imprisoned them at Fort Marion. When Osceola and Coa Hadjo sent word to Hernandez that they were willing to negotiate, he set up a conference near Fort Peyton. Jesup ordered him to violate the truce and capture the Indians. News of Osceola's capture spread through the nation, and when he was transferred to Fort Moultrie in Georgia, George Catlin visited him and painted his portrait. His death on January 30, 1838, enshrined him as a martyr to the Indian cause.

Coacoochee, having escaped from Fort Marion on November 29, 1837, headed south to join bands led by Jumper, Arpeika, and Alligator. The largest and last pitched battle of the war was fought on the banks of Lake Okeechobee on December 25. Colonel Zachary Taylor commanded eleven hundred men against approximately four hundred Indians. The Indians finally retreated from the two-and-a-half-hour battle, leaving 26 killed and 112 wounded and having sustained 11 killed and 14 wounded.

In February, 1838, further treachery at Fort Jupiter netted more than five hundred Seminoles. Persuasion and mopping-up operations sent many of the remaining Seminole leaders, including Micanopy, the chief, on the westward migration. Jesup's tenure in Florida, which had resulted in the capture, migration, or death of more than twenty-four hundred Indians, ended in May, 1838, when General Zachary Taylor took over command of the Florida forces. Taylor remained in Florida for another two years, during which time operations were carried out against scattered bands of natives throughout the peninsula.

General Alexander MacComb, commanding general of the army, came to Florida in April, 1839, and declared the war over when he concluded an agreement with the Seminoles, who agreed to withdraw south of the Peace River by July 15, 1839, and remain there until further arrangements were made. Although a guarded trading post was set up on the Caloosahatchee River, the Indians learned that they were not to be allowed to stay in Florida. Chekika, chief of the Spanish Indians, led an attack and destroyed the post in July. After he led a raid on Indian Key in August, 1840, Chekika was surprised in the Everglades and executed.

The commands of General Walker K. Armistead and General William J. Worth saw the final years of the Second Seminole War. Following the successful policy of deceiving chiefs who came to negotiate, most notably Coacoochee, and through continuing guerrilla warfare, the army managed to remove all but about six hundred of Florida's Indians, who were restricted to a temporary reservation south of the Peace River because Congress refused to continue to fund any further campaigns in 1842. The Second Seminole War was more costly than all of the other Indian wars combined. Still, new settlers came to the interior of Florida, which had been made accessible by the mapping, exploration, and road-building entailed by the wars. The military had gained skill in guerrilla warfare and an understanding of the need for interservice cooperation, and the federal government learned to exercise its power to convert economic power into military strength.

Between 1842 and the outbreak of the Third Seminole War in 1855, the Seminoles kept to the reservation and followed the dictates of regulations imposed upon them. They remained adamant in their opposition to removal until Secretary of War Jefferson Davis declared that, if they did not leave voluntarily, the military would remove them by force.

In December, 1855, a patrol investigating Seminole settlements in the Big Cypress Swamp was attacked by a band of forty Seminoles led by Billy Bowlegs and Oscen Tustenuggee, marking the first skirmish of the war that was dubbed Billy Bowlegs' War. It was a war of skirmishes, raids, and harassment against small settlements, both white and Seminole. A treaty signed on August 7, 1856, that granted the Seminoles more than two million acres in Indian Territory separate from the Creek allotment, along with a generous financial settlement, was the catalyst to the end of the conflict in Florida. A government offer of money in return for removal was accepted on March 27, 1858. Bowlegs and his band left Florida in May, and two other bands left the following February. Only the Muskogee band led by Chipco, hidden north of Lake Okeechobee, and Arpeika's Mikasuki band, buried deep in the Everglades, a remnant of one hundred to three hundred persons, remained in relative peace in Florida, the ancestors of twentieth century Seminoles.

—*Jane Anderson Jones*

Additional reading:

Covington, James W. *The Seminoles of Florida*. Gainesville: University Press of Florida, 1993. The most thorough history of the Seminoles in Florida; devotes six chapters to the Seminole Wars.

Mahon, John K. *History of the Second Seminole War, 1835-1842*. Rev. ed. Gainesville: University Presses of Florida, 1985. Describes the battles and leaders, the problems of military organization and ordnance, and Seminole culture and history in the period of the Second Seminole War.

Tebeau, Charlton W. "The Wars of Indian Removal." In *A History of Florida*. Rev. ed. Coral Gables, Fla.: University of Miami Press, 1980. This chapter in a standard Florida history covers the Seminole Wars.

Wickman, Patricia R. *Osceola's Legacy*. Tuscaloosa: University of Alabama Press, 1991. A study of the life and myth of Osceola, based on a survey of artifacts and documents.

Wright, J. Leitch. *Creeks and Seminoles: The Destruction and Regeneration of the Muscogulge People*. Lincoln: University of Nebraska Press, 1986. An examination of the culture of the Creeks and Seminoles, and their Spanish, British, and African connections.

See also: 1813, Creek War; 1819, Adams-Onís Treaty; 1830, Indian Removal Act; 1830, Trail of Tears.

1819 ▪ UNITARIAN CHURCH IS FOUNDED:
the birth of a leading institution of religious and social reform during the nineteenth and twentieth centuries

DATE: 1819
LOCALE: Boston, Massachusetts
CATEGORIES: Organizations and institutions; Religion; Social reform
KEY FIGURES:
Hosea Ballou (1771-1852), Universalist minister of Portsmouth, New Hampshire
Lyman Beecher (1775-1863), pastor of Park Street Church, Boston
William Ellery Channing (1780-1842), known as the Apostle of Unitarianism, pastor of Federal Street Church, Boston
Charles Chauncy (1705-1787), pastor of First Church, Boston
Dorothea Lynde Dix (1802-1887), social reform leader
Ebenezer Gay (1696-1787), minister of a liberal church in Hingham, Massachusetts
Jonathan Mayhew (1720-1766), pastor of West Church, Boston
Jedidiah Morse (1761-1826), minister at Charlestown, Massachusetts, and founder of the *Panoplist*
Joseph Priestley (1733-1804), founder of the first Unitarian church in Philadelphia
Jared Sparks (1789-1866), Unitarian minister and editor of *The Unitarian*
Joseph Tuckerman (1778-1840), minister-at-large, Boston, Massachusetts
Henry Ware (1764-1845), liberal minister at First Church in Hingham, Massachusetts, and Hollis Professor of Divinity at Harvard College

SUMMARY OF EVENT. The roots of Unitarianism go back to sixteenth century Spain and the teachings of Michael Servetus (1511-1553). Unitarianism in the United States developed from an independent movement resulting from a split in the Congregationalist churches in Massachusetts in the nineteenth century.

In May, 1819, William Ellery Channing, pastor of the Federal Street Church in Boston, traveled to Baltimore to preach at the ordination of a Unitarian minister, Jared Sparks. His sermon, "Unitarian Christianity," was a landmark in the founding of the Unitarian church of the United States. Channing delivered his sermon in the midst of the Unitarian Controversy, a religious debate between liberal and orthodox Congregationalists, which had begun officially in 1805 when Henry Ware was appointed Hollis Professor of Divinity at Harvard College, but which reached back into the early eighteenth century. Religious liberalism, or Arminianism as it was called, emerged in the 1730's as a reaction against the rigorous Calvinism of men such as Jonathan Edwards and Samuel Hopkins. In the pre-revolutionary period, Charles Chauncy, pastor of First Church, Boston, and Jonathan Mayhew, pastor of West Church, Bos-

ton, were the foremost Arminian spokesmen, preaching anti-Trinitarianism, the benevolence of God, and human ability in salvation. Other denominations besides Congregationalists were affected by the liberal impulse. In the early 1780's, anti-Trinitarian views were heard in King's Chapel, which subsequently broke away from the Church of England. This established the first Universalist church in the United States in 1785; however, other ministers preached anti-Trinitarian views. One of the earliest was Ebenezer Gay, who passively expressed his views in church by simply omitting fundamental Calvinist beliefs from his sermons. Joseph Priestley, an early English Unitarian, began preaching in Philadelphia in 1794 after fleeing persecution in his homeland and established a Unitarian church in that city. Universalists, such as Hosea Ballou of Portsmouth, New Hampshire, also embraced the liberal theology.

Liberalism was particularly strong in Boston and among Congregationalists, and it was within that denomination that the Unitarian Controversy occurred. At the beginning of the nineteenth century, orthodox Congregationalists, led by such men as Jedidiah Morse, minister at Charlestown, Massachusetts, and Lyman Beecher, pastor of Park Street Church, Boston, tried to fight the tide of liberalism. Morse founded the *Panoplist* to proselytize "the faith once delivered to the saints" and succeeded in uniting Hopkinsians and Old Calvinists in a common front against the liberals. When the Hollis Chair of Divinity at Harvard College became vacant in 1803, orthodox Congregationalists attempted to get a moderate Calvinist appointed. When Ware was appointed, they gave up Harvard as lost to heterodoxy and founded their own seminary at Andover in 1808. Gaining the chair eventually led the Unitarians to take their first organizational step: the founding of the Harvard Divinity School.

In the decade following Ware's appointment at Harvard, the lines between orthodox and liberal Congregationalists hardened. Liberals—who preferred that title to the "Unitarian" label that their opponents had fastened on them—steadily gained strength, spreading their views by way of pulpit and press. The orthodox intensified their attack. In 1815, Morse distributed a pamphlet entitled *American Unitarianism*, a chapter from a British work that argued that New England liberals were Unitarians in the English sense, meaning that they avowed merely the humanity of Jesus. Morse also published a review of the pamphlet in the *Panoplist*, which denounced liberal Congregationalists as heretics secretly conspiring to overthrow the true faith and called for their expulsion from the Congregational church. As the leader of the Boston liberals, Channing answered the *Panoplist* attack by a public letter to Samuel C. Thacher, minister of the New South Church. This letter brought a reply from Samuel Worchester of Salem, who defended the review. A long pamphlet debate between Channing and Worchester followed, with the issue shifting from the *Panoplist* review to the more general question of the nature of Unitarianism. As the theological differences became clearer, liberals began to accept the once unpopular term Unitarian, although they expanded and elaborated on its meaning.

It was in this context of bitter theological debate that Channing decided in 1819 to deliver the now-famous Baltimore sermon, which laid the foundation for the Unitarian church in the United States. "Unitarian Christianity" provided a comprehensive statement of the beliefs of U.S. Unitarians, as well as an eloquent defense of their faith. Unitarians, Channing declared, interpreted the Scriptures by "the constant exercise of reason" and rejected any theological doctrines repugnant to reason and moral sense. Thus they believed in the unity of God, rejecting the "irrational and unscriptural doctrine of the Trinity." They also rejected the Calvinist God, worshiping instead a God who was "infinitely good, kind, and benevolent." Such a God offered salvation not to a few elect, but to all. Unitarians rejected doctrines of natural depravity and predestination, not only because of their "unspeakable cruelty" but also because such doctrines were adverse to God's "parental character." Channing concluded his sermon on a conciliatory note:

> We have embraced this system not hastily or lightly, but after much deliberation, and we hold it fast, not merely because we believe it to be true, but because we regard it as purifying truth, as a doctrine according to godliness, as able to "work mightily" and to "bring forth fruit" in them that believe. . . . We see nothing in our views to give offence, save their purity, and it is their purity which makes us seek and hope their extension through the world.

Despite its conciliatory tone, Channing's sermon made reconciliation between liberal and orthodox Congregationalists even less likely than before. Separation of Unitarians from Congregationalists and vice versa became commonplace, as one or the other group (usually the latter) within a church withdrew to form a new society. Unitarian organization was slow and met with resistance from within, but in May, 1825, the American Unitarian Association was founded "to diffuse the knowledge and promote the interests of pure Christianity." This was the final act of separation that divided Unitarians and Congregationalists into two denominations and ended the long theological conflict that had begun more than a quarter of a century earlier. In 1961, the denomination merged with the Universalist church to form the Unitarian Universalist Association.

The impact of Unitarianism reaches far beyond the splitting of the Congregationalist church. The Unitarians became leaders in promoting social progress. Dorothea Dix, one of Channing's own parishioners, spent most of her lifetime seeking to improve living conditions for the mentally ill. Joseph Tuckerman, a minister-at-large of Boston, not only brought Unitarian teachings to the city's poor but also worked hard to bring practical help to them through personal visits and counseling. Tuckerman's work generated similar endeavors in other cities. The examples of Dix, Tuckerman, and other early Unitarians sparked reforms in education, health, and women's rights.

—*Anne C. Loveland, updated by Pamela Hayes-Bohanan*

ADDITIONAL READING:

Buehrens, John, and F. Forrester Church. *Our Chosen Faith: An Introduction to Unitarian Universalism.* Boston: Beacon Press, 1989. Describes philosophies and histories of Unitarians and Universalists. Includes information on famous Unitarians and Universalists in history, and provides a chronology of the faith.

Elgin, Kathleen. *The Unitarians: The Unitarian Universalist Association.* New York: David McKay, 1971. Some background on Unitarian history in general, but mainly discusses Dorothea Dix and her work with the mentally ill.

Mead, Frank S. "Unitarian Universalist Association." In *Handbook of Denominations in the United States.* 7th ed. Nashville, Tenn.: Abingdon Press, 1983. Provides a brief history of Unitarian Universalism; discusses the church in the late twentieth century and its philosophies.

Robinson, David. *The Unitarians and the Universalists.* Westport, Conn.: Greenwood Press, 1985. Comprehensive history of Unitarian Universalism in the United States and its impact. Includes a biographical dictionary of Unitarian Universalist leaders.

Wright, Conrad. *The Beginnings of Unitarianism in America.* Boston: Starr King Press, 1955. Discusses the early roots of Unitarianism in America, from 1735 to 1805, and the events leading to the split in the Congregational churches.

SEE ALSO: 1650, Harvard College Is Established; 1730's, First Great Awakening; 1790's, Second Great Awakening; 1820's, Social Reform Movement; 1836, Rise of Transcendentalism.

1819 ■ ADAMS-ONÍS TREATY: *after Spain cedes Florida to the United States, a definitive western boundary for the Louisiana Purchase territory is established*

DATE: February 22, 1819
LOCALE: Washington, D.C., and Madrid, Spain
CATEGORIES: Expansion and land acquisition; Latino American history; Treaties and agreements
KEY FIGURES:
John Quincy Adams (1767-1848), Monroe's secretary of state
Ferdinand VII (1784-1833), king of Spain, 1814-1833
Andrew Jackson (1767-1845), commander of the military expedition into Florida in 1818
James Madison (1751-1836), fourth president of the United States, 1809-1817
James Monroe (1758-1831), Madison's secretary of state and fifth president of the United States, 1817-1825
Luis de Onís (1762-1827), Spanish minister to the United States, 1809-1819

SUMMARY OF EVENT. Following the end of the War of 1812, the United States intensified its efforts to resolve long-standing disputes with Spain. Spanish difficulties with the United States had entered a critical new phase during the undeclared naval war with France (1798-1800). As an ally of France at that time, Spain had permitted its ships to assist in ransacking U.S. commerce on the high seas and allowed the French to seize U.S.

ships in Spanish ports. The United States later demanded compensation from Spain for the loss of these vessels and cargoes. In 1802, the Spanish suspended the right of the United States to deposit and transfer goods at New Orleans, causing economic damage to the trans-Appalachian West. Although the Treaty of San Lorenzo of 1795 (known also as the Pinckney Treaty) between the United States and Spain had guaranteed U.S. deposit rights and prohibited privateering by either nation upon the other, the Spanish balked at paying compensation for its transgressions, leaving the issue deadlocked by 1805.

The United States' purchase of Louisiana from France in 1803 added serious complications to Spanish-American relations. The French had obtained the territory from Spain in the Treaty of San Ildefonso of 1800. By this agreement, France had pledged not to transfer Louisiana to another power without first offering to restore the territory to Spain. The Spanish thus considered the Louisiana Purchase to be illegal and continued to demand its return until 1818. The United States soon adopted an extensive definition of Louisiana's boundaries, which included two adjacent Spanish provinces—Texas and West Florida. U.S. claims to the latter territory were dubious at best, and Spanish rights to western and central Texas were solidly founded upon the chain of forts and missions established there by 1800. East Texas, however, was largely unsettled and would become the crux of the dispute after the War of 1812.

U.S. interest in Spanish territory also extended to areas to which the United States could make no plausible claim. East Florida was such an area, and the United States negotiated continuously for its purchase, beginning in the 1790's. U.S. leaders believed that possession of Florida would give their nation command of the Gulf of Mexico and would secure from foreign interference the trade that passed through the Mississippi River. After 1808, U.S. prospects for acquiring both West and East Florida improved greatly: Napoleon had invaded Spain, diverting that nation's resources to a life-or-death struggle against France.

In the summer of 1810, the United States colluded in the successful rebellion of settlers in the Baton Rouge region of West Florida. Later in the same year, the area was legally annexed to the United States up to the Pearl River, eventually becoming part of the state of Louisiana. After the United States went to war with Great Britain in 1812, the U.S. government came under domestic pressure to use the opportunity to expand at Spain's expense. In the spring of 1813, Congress authorized the occupation of Mobile, the principal port in the section of West Florida between the Pearl and Perdido Rivers. The Spanish responded to U.S. aggression by allowing the British to use Pensacola as a base, and by assisting the Creek Indians in their 1813-1814 war against the United States. The War of 1812 thus dramatically illustrated U.S. vulnerability: In the hands of Spain, Florida had become a yawning gap in the United States' coastal defenses—a highway through which the interior of the country could be penetrated easily.

After peace with Great Britain was concluded in early 1815, the acquisition of East Florida became the prime goal of U.S.

foreign policy. Spain recognized that it had only two choices to avoid a shameful abandonment of the region: to gain the support of a European ally, or to attain a semblance of honor in the affair by winning from the United States favorable territorial concessions west of the Mississippi. At first, the Spanish were successful in securing the support of the British, who warned the United States against further encroachments on their neighbors. Bolstered by Britain's encouragement, Spain's minister to the United States, Luis de Onís, successfully sparred with his counterpart, Secretary of State James Monroe, throughout 1815 and 1816. The Spaniard demanded the return of Louisiana and West Florida and protested against the United States' supplying of Spain's rebelling Latin American colonists and the privateers operating out of Baltimore against Spanish shipping. Soon, Spain had developed its own list of financial claims against the United States and was demanding compensation. President James Madison declined to intensify the diplomatic struggle, because delay only aided the United States, which would grow stronger in the future while Spain progressively weakened.

The inauguration of James Monroe as president in March, 1817, placed the negotiations in impatient, decisive hands. Monroe was determined to push the Spanish to an agreement and appointed a secretary of state, John Quincy Adams, who shared his views. In the fall of 1817, the U.S. cabinet decided to adopt a new attitude toward Spain, a decision that resulted in the dispatch of an army under the command of Major General Andrew Jackson into Florida—ostensibly to pursue Seminoles who were raiding in retaliation for the destruction of one of their villages. Jackson's orders from Washington were ambiguous: He was authorized to enter Florida to punish the Seminoles, but forbidden to attack them if they sheltered under a Spanish fort. At the same time, he was also enjoined to adopt the measures necessary to end the conflict. Once Jackson was actually in Florida, he discovered evidence of Spanish aid to the Seminoles. Relying on the discretion allotted to him, he judged that only the capture of Spanish forts would end the conflict. Jackson accordingly adopted these "necessary measures" by seizing St. Marks and Pensacola, effectively wresting Florida from Spain.

Although the U.S. administration would later deny having intended that Jackson should take such extreme action, Adams used the military pressure to cajole the Spanish into retreating from their extreme negotiating positions. International conditions also encouraged Spain to accommodate U.S. demands. By early 1818, Great Britain had made it clear that it would not risk war with the United States by seeking to enforce mediation of Spanish-American disputes. European commitments and dangers had caused the British to reconsider their support for Spain and to seek détente with the United States. In the summer, Great Britain agreed to negotiate with the United States over all outstanding issues. These talks resulted in the Convention of 1818. Anglo-American rapprochement thus ended Spanish pretensions to power.

Negotiations between the United States and Spain resumed in the fall of 1818, after the United States had agreed to restore

TERRITORY OF THE UNITED STATES IN 1819

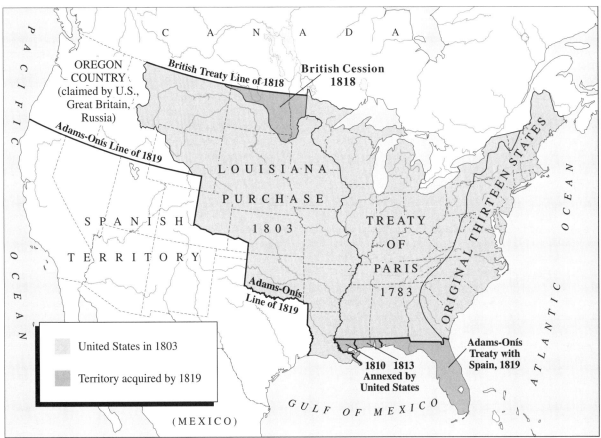

the forts to the Spanish. Near the end of the year, the two nations agreed upon a western boundary that went up the Sabine River from its mouth and continued north to the Red River, zigzagged westward along the Red and Arkansas Rivers, followed the crest of the Rocky Mountains to the forty-second parallel, and then turned westward to the Pacific Ocean. On February 22, 1819, Adams and Onís signed the treaty that bears their names. It embodied the compromise western boundary and resolved nearly all disputes between their two nations. The Spanish retained Texas but gave up claims to the Oregon Country. Spain ceded all territory east of the Mississippi to the United States. Both nations renounced their claims for damages, although the United States agreed to assume the claims of its citizens against Spain up to a maximum of five million dollars. Adams successfully avoided guaranteeing that the United States would not recognize the Latin American nations.

King Ferdinand VII of Spain initially refused to ratify the treaty because the United States had failed to provide such guarantees. In January, 1820, a revolution in Spain brought to power a liberal regime whose leaders were inclined to accommodate the United States. France and Russia, who feared that the Spanish-American quarrel threatened world peace, pressured the new government to settle. Spain finally ratified the

treaty in October, 1820, and the Adams-Onís Treaty (also known as the Transcontinental Treaty) became effective on February 22, 1821.

This agreement was crucial to determining the course of North American history. It signified the decay of Spanish power in the New World and provided conclusive evidence of British acquiescence in limited United States expansion. The acquisition of Florida strengthened the United States materially and enhanced its national security by closing a gap in its coastal defenses. Spain's recognition of U.S. rights in Oregon signaled the beginning of the United States' role as a global power. Resolving problems with Spain largely freed the United States from European entanglements for several decades. The treaty was also the decisive event in modern Seminole history. By replacing stagnant Spanish rule with that of a demographically and economically expanding United States, the treaty ensured that the Seminoles could not long remain in possession of their lands. Their removal westward inevitably followed during the 1830's.   —*Michael S. Fitzgerald*

ADDITIONAL READING:

Bemis, Samuel F. *John Quincy Adams and the Foundations of American Foreign Policy.* New York: Alfred A. Knopf, 1949. Detailed examination of Adams' role in the treaty negotiations, strongly emphasizing the continentalism in his thinking.

Brooks, Philip C. *Diplomacy and the Borderlands: The Adams-Onís Treaty of 1819*. Berkeley: University of California Press, 1939. Highly detailed account of the negotiations. Overly legalistic approach obscures the role of power in determining the treaty's final shape.

Cox, Isaac J. *The West Florida Controversy, 1798-1813: A Study in American Diplomacy*. 1918. Reprint. Gloucester, Mass.: P. Smith, 1967. Although inadequate in several respects, provides an excellent summary of the development of Spanish-American disputes before 1815.

Griffin, Charles C. *The United States and the Disruption of the Spanish Empire, 1810-1822*. New York: Columbia University Press, 1937. Stresses the domestic and international context of the negotiations. Analysis of U.S. public opinion illuminates United States decision making.

Weeks, William E. *John Quincy Adams and American Global Empire*. Lexington: University Press of Kentucky, 1992. A balanced account of the treaty negotiations, which includes the role of U.S. expansionism and aggression. Unlike some earlier historians, Weeks does not regard the Florida cession as the inevitable result of Spanish decay.

SEE ALSO: 1794, Jay's Treaty; 1795, Pinckney's Treaty; 1797, XYZ Affair; 1803, Louisiana Purchase; 1804, Burr's Conspiracy; 1813, Creek War; 1815, Treaty of Ghent; 1817, Seminole Wars; 1820, Land Act of 1820; 1823, Monroe Doctrine; 1830, Indian Removal Act; 1830, Trail of Tears.

1819 ■ MCCULLOCH v. MARYLAND: *the U.S. Supreme Court recognizes the doctrine of implied powers, giving broad authority to the federal government over state governments*

DATE: March 6, 1819
LOCALE: Washington, D.C.
CATEGORIES: Court cases; Government and politics
KEY FIGURES:

James W. McCulloch, cashier in the Baltimore branch of the Second Bank of the United States

John Marshall (1755-1835), chief justice of the United States

Luther Martin (1748?-1826), attorney general of Maryland and chief counsel for Maryland

William Pinkney (1764-1822), counsel for McCulloch and the Second Bank

Daniel Webster (1782-1852), senator and counsel for McCulloch and the Second Bank

William Wirt (1772-1834), U.S. attorney general and counsel for the Second Bank

SUMMARY OF EVENT. From its inception, the Constitution of 1787 has stirred controversy as to the nature of the Union that it created and the extent of federal authority. The Civil War would in 1865 settle certain outstanding questions as to the

nature of the Union, but a more articulate consideration of the problem was provided by the Supreme Court of the United States in 1819 in the landmark case of *McCulloch v. Maryland*.

The arguments surrounding the case were as old as the Constitution itself. Although the Constitutional Convention of 1787 had considered and rejected the proposal that Congress be empowered to charter corporations, a classic constitutional debate took place during the first administration of President George Washington over the question of chartering the First Bank of the United States. In their memoranda written at the president's request, Secretary of the Treasury Alexander Hamilton and Secretary of State Thomas Jefferson presented diametrically opposed advice on the question of whether the president should approve the bill chartering the First Bank of the United States. Hamilton urged a broad interpretation of the "necessary and proper" clause, contending that Congress had the power to make all laws that it considered expedient or convenient; Jefferson insisted on a strict interpretation and urged that the clause authorized Congress to pass only those laws that were necessary to give effect to its delegated powers.

Washington took Hamilton's advice, and the bank was chartered in 1791. The charter expired in 1811, and the adverse economic impact of the War of 1812, coupled with the abuses and irresponsibility of state-chartered banks, led to the chartering in 1816 of the Second Bank of the United States. The chartering of the First Bank of the United States had prompted a movement in favor of a constitutional amendment to restrict Congress' powers under the "necessary and proper" clause, and the chartering of the Second Bank of the United States led many states to adopt laws designed to suppress the bank's operations. The hostility toward the bank rested on a number of factors: It was regarded as a Federalist-controlled enterprise; much of the stock was held by foreign investors; the operations of the First Bank of the United States had tended to undercut the success of the state banks; and many blamed the bleak economic conditions following the War of 1812 on the policies of the First Bank of the United States. Champions of the bank regarded renewal of its charter as the only hope of improving economic conditions.

In certain states, antibank sentiment was rampant. Indiana, Illinois, Tennessee, Georgia, North Carolina, Kentucky, Ohio, and Maryland adopted laws designed to curtail or prohibit the operation of the bank. The momentum of the antibank movement was encouraged by the mismanagement and fraud of the managers of the Second Bank of the United States. The growing anxiety over the deteriorating state of the economy made an appeal to the courts an attractive way of settling the question of the legitimacy of the state burdens that were being imposed on the bank's operations. This was the immediate motivation for the litigation that resulted in *McCulloch v. Maryland*.

An agent of the state of Maryland, John James, called on James W. McCulloch, the cashier of the Baltimore, Maryland, branch of the bank, and demanded that McCulloch comply with the state law. The Maryland law, adopted in February, 1818, required all banks chartered outside Maryland to pay a tax of one hundred dollars on all notes issued or, alternatively, to pay an annual sum of fifteen thousand dollars into the state's treasury. McCulloch refused to comply with this prohibitive state law, and when he was prosecuted for his refusal, the Maryland courts ruled against him. In September, 1818, the case was appealed to the United States Supreme Court.

The Supreme Court heard arguments for nine days. Appearing on behalf of the bank were Attorney General William Wirt, William Pinkney, and Daniel Webster; Luther Martin, the fiery attorney general of Maryland who had expedited the bringing of the case to the Supreme Court, Joseph Hopkinson, and Walter Jones were the lawyers appearing for Maryland.

The Supreme Court handed down its decision on March 6, 1819, only three days after completion of arguments and while there was much activity in Congress aimed at revoking the bank's charter. The opinion by Chief Justice John Marshall is regarded by most scholars as his most important pronouncement in constitutional law and the one most important to the future of the United States. The Constitution, said Marshall, established a truly national government that "is emphatically and truly a government of the people. In form and in substance it emanates from them, its powers are granted by them, and are to be exercised directly on them, and for their benefit." Much of the remainder of his opinion is an extension and application of this "national" theory of the Constitution's foundations. Sovereignty is divided between federal and state governments. When state power conflicts with national power, the former must yield because national sovereignty is supreme. The judiciary, Marshall wrote, is constitutionally required to construe Congress' enumerated powers broadly. The "necessary and proper" clause, sometimes called the "elastic" clause, was designed to empower Congress to exercise its delegated powers by any convenient and expedient methods not prohibited by the Constitution itself. Marshall found that the "necessary and proper" clause gave rise to what has come to be called "implied powers."

A constitution, to contain an accurate detail of all the subdivisions of which its great powers will admit, and all of the means by which they may be carried into execution, would partake of the prolixity of a legal code, and could scarcely be embraced by the human mind. It would probably never be understood by the public. Its nature, therefore, requires that only its great outlines should be marked, its important objects designated, and the minor ingredients which compose those objects be deduced from the nature of the objects themselves.

By focusing on the ends sought to be achieved by the Constitution's framers, Marshall ensured that Congress neither overstepped its bounds nor was denied any powers involved with its responsibilities. That flexible approach allowed Congress to select the means by which to implement its powers. Both the spirit and the language of the Constitution supported this view; the Framers had "omitted to use any restrictive term which might prevent its receiving a fair and just interpretation. In considering this question, then, we must never forget, that it is a constitution we are expounding."

Twentieth century Supreme Court justice Felix Frankfurter asserted that those words were the most important ever uttered by a United States judge, acknowledging an expansive source of power and an extension of that power beyond those expressly named sources. "Let the end be legitimate, let it be within the scope of the Constitution, and all means are appropriate, which are plainly adopted to that end, which are not prohibited, but consist with the letter of the Constitution, are constitutional. . . ." As precedent for future assertions of national authority, the opinion asserted that legitimate uses of national power took priority over state authority and that the "necessary and proper" clause was a broad grant of national authority.

Luther Martin had insisted in his argument that even if Congress had the authority to establish the bank, the state could still levy the tax in question. Marshall rejected this argument and laid down the general principle that the central government had constitutional power to "withdraw any subject from the action" of the states. "The power to tax," he declared, "involves the power to destroy." To permit Maryland to tax the bank's operations would place all federal programs at the mercy of the states. This facet of the *McCulloch* opinion gave rise to the doctrine of intergovernmental tax immunity.

The "necessary and proper" clause rationale of *McCulloch v. Maryland* was used as late as 1966 in *South Carolina v. Katzenbach* to strike down the use of literacy tests as a means of racial discrimination barring African Americans and Hispanics from participation in government by denying them voting rights as guaranteed by the Fifteenth Amendment.

—*James J. Bolner, updated by Marcia J. Weiss*

ADDITIONAL READING:

Barron, Jerome A., and C. Thomas Dienes. *Constitutional Law in a Nutshell*. 2d ed. St. Paul, Minn.: West, 1991. A compact reference on the law for those with a legal or political science background.

Cox, Archibald. *The Court and the Constitution*. Boston: Houghton Mifflin, 1987. The former U.S. solicitor general and Watergate special prosecutor chronicles issues and debates in each era of constitutional history.

Gunther, Gerald, ed. *John Marshall's Defense of McCulloch v. Maryland*. Stanford, Calif.: Stanford University Press, 1969. A compilation of the debates surrounding Marshall's decision. Contains the newspaper battle with ideological opponents of the Supreme Court, as well as Marshall's replies. Introduction by the editor.

McCloskey, Robert G. *The American Supreme Court*. 2d ed. Revised by Sanford Levinson. Chicago: University of Chicago Press, 1994. A detailed treatment of the Marshall Court. Contains additional resources in a bibliographical essay.

Newmyer, R. Kent. *The Supreme Court Under Marshall and Taney*. Arlington Heights, Ill.: Harlan Davidson, 1968. Contains detailed information and presents Marshall's philosophy.

SEE ALSO: 1789, Judiciary Act; 1790's, First U.S. Political Parties; 1790, Hamilton's *Report on Public Credit*; 1803, *Marbury v. Madison*; 1810, *Fletcher v. Peck*; 1816, Second Bank of the United States Is Chartered.

GREAT EVENTS FROM HISTORY
NORTH AMERICAN SERIES

KEY WORD INDEX

CATEGORY LIST

NOTE: The entries in this publication are listed below under all categories that apply. The chronological order under each category corresponds to the chronological order of the entries in these volumes.

AFRICAN AMERICAN HISTORY

1619, Africans Arrive in Virginia
1641, Massachusetts Recognizes Slavery
1661, Virginia Slave Codes
1712, New York City Slave Revolt
1739, Stono Rebellion
1773, African American Baptist Church Is Founded
1775, Pennsylvania Society for the Abolition of Slavery Is Founded
1777, Northeast States Abolish Slavery
1784, Hall's Masonic Lodge Is Chartered
1787, Free African Society Is Founded
1787, Northwest Ordinance
1791, Haitian Independence
1793, Whitney Invents the Cotton Gin
1793, First Fugitive Slave Law
1804, First Black Codes
1807, Congress Bans Importation of African Slaves
1816, AME Church Is Founded
1820's, Social Reform Movement
1820, Missouri Compromise
1830, Proslavery Argument
1830, Webster-Hayne Debate
1831, *The Liberator* Begins Publication
1831, Nat Turner's Insurrection
1833, American Anti-Slavery Society Is Founded
1839, Amistad Slave Revolt
1847, *The North Star* Begins Publication
1850, Underground Railroad
1850, Compromise of 1850
1850, Second Fugitive Slave Law
1853, National Council of Colored People Is Founded
1854, Kansas-Nebraska Act
1856, Bleeding Kansas
1857, First African American University
1857, *Dred Scott v. Sandford*
1858, Lincoln-Douglas Debates
1859, Last Slave Ship Docks at Mobile
1859, John Brown's Raid on Harpers Ferry
1863, Emancipation Proclamation
1863, Reconstruction
1865, Freedmen's Bureau Is Established

1865, New Black Codes
1865, Thirteenth Amendment
1866, Rise of the Ku Klux Klan
1866, Civil Rights Act of 1866
1866, Race Riots in the South
1868, Fourteenth Amendment
1890, Mississippi Disfranchisement Laws
1895, Booker T. Washington's Atlanta Exposition Address
1896, *Plessy v. Ferguson*
1909, National Association for the Advancement of Colored People Is Founded
1910, Great Northern Migration
1917, Universal Negro Improvement Association Is Established
1930, Nation of Islam Is Founded
1931, Scottsboro Trials
1941, Executive Order 8802
1942, Congress of Racial Equality Is Founded
1944, *Smith v. Allwright*
1954, *Brown v. Board of Education*
1955, Montgomery Bus Boycott
1957, Southern Christian Leadership Conference Is Founded
1957, Little Rock School Desegregation Crisis
1960, Civil Rights Act of 1960
1962, Meredith Registers at "Ole Miss"
1963, King Delivers His "I Have a Dream" Speech
1964, Civil Rights Act of 1964
1965, Assassination of Malcolm X
1965, Voting Rights Act
1965, Watts Riot
1965, Expansion of Affirmative Action
1967, Long, Hot Summer
1968, Assassinations of King and Kennedy
1968, Fair Housing Act
1971, *Swann v. Charlotte-Mecklenberg Board of Education*
1972, Equal Employment Opportunity Act
1980, Miami Riots
1983, Jackson Becomes First Major African American Candidate for President

ASIAN AMERICAN HISTORY

1849, Chinese Immigration
1854, Perry Opens Trade with Japan
1868, Burlingame Treaty
1875, Page Law
1882, Chinese Exclusion Act
1882, Rise of the Chinese Six Companies
1892, Yellow Peril Campaign
1895, Chinese American Citizens Alliance Is Founded
1898, *United States v. Wong Kim Ark*
1899, Philippine Insurrection
1899, Hay's "Open Door Notes"
1901, Insular Cases
1907, Gentlemen's Agreement
1913, Alien Land Laws
1917, Immigration Act of 1917
1922, *Ozawa v. United States*
1930, Japanese American Citizens League Is Founded
1934, Tydings-McDuffie Act
1942, Censorship and Japanese Internment
1943, Magnuson Act
1959, Alaska and Hawaii Gain Statehood
1968, Bilingual Education Act
1974, *Lau v. Nichols*
1992, Asian Pacific American Labor Alliance

BUSINESS AND LABOR

1790, Slater's Spinning Mill
1793, Whitney Invents the Cotton Gin
1808, American Fur Company Is Chartered
1810, *Fletcher v. Peck*
1825, Erie Canal Opens
1833, Rise of the Penny Press
1842, *Commonwealth v. Hunt*
1842, Dorr Rebellion
1846, Howe's Sewing Machine
1859, First Commercial Oil Well
1882, Standard Oil Trust Is Organized
1886, American Federation of Labor Is Founded
1887, Interstate Commerce Act
1890, Sherman Antitrust Act
1894, Pullman Strike

1869, Rise of Woman Suffrage
Associations
1869, Western States Grant Woman
Suffrage
1872, Susan B. Anthony Is Arrested
1874, *Minor v. Happersett*
1876, Declaration of the Rights of
Women
1883, Civil Rights Cases
1890, Mississippi Disfranchisement Laws
1895, Booker T. Washington's Atlanta
Exposition Address
1896, *Plessy v. Ferguson*
1898, *United States v. Wong Kim Ark*
1902, Expansion of Direct Democracy
1909, National Association for the
Advancement of Colored People
Is Founded
1913, Alien Land Laws
1917, Propaganda and Civil Liberties in
World War I
1917, Espionage and Sedition Acts
1917, Canadian Women Gain the Vote
1919, Red Scare
1920, U.S. Women Gain the Vote
1922, Cable Act
1923, Proposal of the Equal Rights
Amendment
1929, League of United Latin American
Citizens Is Founded
1941, Executive Order 8802
1942, Censorship and Japanese
Internment
1942, Congress of Racial Equality Is
Founded
1944, *Smith v. Allwright*
1951, McCarthy Hearings
1954, *Brown v. Board of Education*
1955, Montgomery Bus Boycott
1957, Southern Christian Leadership
Conference Is Founded
1957, Little Rock School
Desegregation Crisis
1960, Civil Rights Act of 1960
1962, Meredith Registers at "Ole Miss"
1963, *Gideon v. Wainwright*
1963, Equal Pay Act
1963, King Delivers His "I Have a
Dream" Speech
1964, Twenty-fourth Amendment
1964, Civil Rights Act of 1964
1964, Berkeley Free Speech Movement
1965, Assassination of Malcolm X
1965, *Griswold v. Connecticut*
1965, Voting Rights Act

1965, Expansion of Affirmative Action
1967, Long, Hot Summer
1967, Freedom of Information Act
1968, Assassinations of King and
Kennedy
1968, Indian Civil Rights Act
1968, Fair Housing Act
1969, Stonewall Inn Riots
1970, Kent State Massacre
1970, October Crisis
1971, *Swann v. Charlotte-Mecklenberg
Board of Education*
1971, U.S. Voting Age Is Lowered to
Eighteen
1971, Attica State Prison Riots
1972, Equal Employment Opportunity
Act
1973, *Roe v. Wade*
1975, Equal Credit Opportunity Act
1976, *Gregg v. Georgia*
1977, Canada's Human Rights Act
1978, Pregnancy Discrimination Act
1978, *Regents of the University of
California v. Bakke*
1978, American Indian Religious
Freedom Act
1982, *Plyler v. Doe*
1988, Civil Rights Restoration Act
1990, Americans with Disabilities Act
1991, Civil Rights Act of 1991
1993, Family and Medical Leave Act
1993, Branch Davidians' Compound
Burns

COMMUNICATIONS

1828, *Cherokee Phoenix* Begins
Publication
1831, *The Liberator* Begins Publication
1833, Rise of the Penny Press
1844, First Telegraph Message
1847, *The North Star* Begins
Publication
1858, First Transatlantic Cable
1860, Pony Express
1861, Transcontinental Telegraph Is
Completed
1866, Suffragists Protest the Fourteenth
Amendment
1876, Bell Demonstrates the Telephone
1900, Teletype Is Developed
1939, Debut of Commercial Television
1947, Invention of the Transistor
1981, IBM Markets the Personal
Computer
1990's, Rise of the Internet

COURT CASES

1734, Trial of John Peter Zenger
1803, *Marbury v. Madison*
1810, *Fletcher v. Peck*
1819, *McCulloch v. Maryland*
1824, *Gibbons v. Ogden*
1831, Cherokee Cases
1842, *Commonwealth v. Hunt*
1857, *Dred Scott v. Sandford*
1874, *Minor v. Happersett*
1883, Civil Rights Cases
1896, *Plessy v. Ferguson*
1898, *United States v. Wong Kim Ark*
1901, Insular Cases
1903, *Lone Wolf v. Hitchcock*
1908, *Muller v. Oregon*
1922, *Ozawa v. United States*
1925, Scopes Trial
1927, Sacco and Vanzetti Are Executed
1931, Scottsboro Trials
1935, Black Monday
1954, *Brown v. Board of Education*
1962, Reapportionment Cases
1963, *Gideon v. Wainwright*
1963, *Abington School District v.
Schempp*
1965, *Griswold v. Connecticut*
1971, *Swann v. Charlotte-Mecklenberg
Board of Education*
1973, *Roe v. Wade*
1974, *Lau v. Nichols*
1976, *Gregg v. Georgia*
1978, *Regents of the University of
California v. Bakke*
1982, *Plyler v. Doe*

**CULTURAL AND INTELLECTUAL
HISTORY**

1776, Declaration of Independence
1787, *Federalist* Papers Are Published
1820's, Free Public School Movement
1828, *Cherokee Phoenix* Begins
Publication
1828, Webster's *American Dictionary
of the English Language*
1831, *The Liberator* Begins Publication
1831, Tocqueville Visits America
1833, Rise of the Penny Press
1836, Rise of Transcendentalism
1846, Smithsonian Institution Is
Founded
1847, *The North Star* Begins
Publication
1871, Barnum's Circus Forms
1893, World's Columbian Exposition

1918, Demobilization After World War I
1924, Dawes Plan
1929, Stock Market Crash
1929, Great Depression
1930's, Mass Deportations of Mexicans
1930, Baltimore and Ohio Railroad
  Begins Operation
1931, Empire State Building Opens
1932, Reconstruction Finance
  Corporation Is Created
1932, Ottawa Agreements
1932, Bonus March
1933, The Hundred Days
1933, Tennessee Valley Authority Is
  Established
1933, National Industrial Recovery Act
1934, Tydings-McDuffie Act
1934, The Dust Bowl
1935, Works Progress Administration Is
  Established
1935, Black Monday
1935, National Labor Relations Act
1935, Social Security Act
1936, Reciprocity Treaty
1939, Mobilization for World War II
1941, 6.6 Million Women Enter the
  U.S. Labor Force
1942, Bracero Program
1943, Inflation and Labor Unrest
1943, Urban Race Riots
1946, Employment Act
1955, AFL and CIO Merge
1959, St. Lawrence Seaway Opens
1961, Peace Corps Is Established
1967, Long, Hot Summer
1971, Devaluation of the Dollar
1973, Arab Oil Embargo and Energy
  Crisis
1974, Construction of the Alaska Pipeline
1981, Reagan's Budget and Tax Reform
1988, Indian Gaming Regulatory Act
1989, Lincoln Savings and Loan
  Declares Bankruptcy
1993, North American Free Trade
  Agreement
1994, General Agreement on Tariffs
  and Trade

EDUCATION
1650, Harvard College Is Established
1785, Beginnings of State Universities
1802, U.S. Military Academy Is
  Established
1820's, Free Public School Movement
1820's, Social Reform Movement

1823, Hartford Female Seminary Is
  Founded
1833, Oberlin College Is Established
1837, Mt. Holyoke Seminary Is
  Founded
1857, First African American University
1862, Morrill Land Grant Act
1865, Vassar College Is Founded
1867, Office of Education Is Created
1912, U.S. Public Health Service Is
  Established
1925, Scopes Trial
1929, League of United Latin American
  Citizens Is Founded
1944, G.I. Bill
1954, *Brown v. Board of Education*
1957, Little Rock School
  Desegregation Crisis
1962, Meredith Registers at "Ole Miss"
1963, *Abington School District v.
  Schempp*
1964, Berkeley Free Speech Movement
1965, Expansion of Affirmative Action
1968, Bilingual Education Act
1971, *Swann v. Charlotte-Mecklenberg
  Board of Education*
1974, *Lau v. Nichols*
1978, *Regents of the University of
  California v. Bakke*
1982, *Plyler v. Doe*

ENVIRONMENT
1872, Great American Bison Slaughter
1908, White House Conservation
  Conference
1916, National Park Service Is Created
1924, Halibut Treaty
1934, The Dust Bowl
1978, Toxic Waste at Love Canal
1979, Three Mile Island Accident
1981, Ozone Hole Is Discovered
1989, *Exxon Valdez* Oil Spill

**EXPANSION AND LAND
  ACQUISITION**
1626, Algonquians "Sell" Manhattan
  Island
1670, Hudson's Bay Company Is
  Chartered
1673, French Explore the Mississippi
  Valley
1702, Queen Anne's War
1711, Tuscarora War
1728, Russian Voyages to Alaska
1737, Walking Purchase

1754, French and Indian War
1763, Proclamation of 1763
1763, Paxton Boys' Massacres
1769, Rise of the California Missions
1774, Lord Dunmore's War
1774, Quebec Act
1784, Fort Stanwix Treaty
1785, Ordinance of 1785
1787, Northwest Ordinance
1790, Nootka Sound Convention
1790, Little Turtle's War
1793, Mackenzie Reaches the Arctic
  Ocean
1794, Battle of Fallen Timbers
1794, Jay's Treaty
1795, Pinckney's Treaty
1803, Louisiana Purchase
1804, Lewis and Clark Expedition
1806, Pike's Southwest Explorations
1808, American Fur Company Is
  Chartered
1810, *Fletcher v. Peck*
1810, Astorian Expeditions
1811, Construction of the National Road
1813, Creek War
1815, Westward Migration
1819, Adams-Onís Treaty
1820, Land Act of 1820
1821, Santa Fe Trail Opens
1823, Jedediah Smith Explores the Far
  West
1830, Webster-Hayne Debate
1830, Indian Removal Act
1830, Trail of Tears
1835, Texas Revolution
1840's, "Old" Immigration
1841, Preemption Act
1842, Frémont's Expeditions
1842, Webster-Ashburton Treaty
1846, Mormon Migration to Utah
1846, Mexican War
1846, Oregon Settlement
1846, Occupation of California and the
  Southwest
1848, California Gold Rush
1850, Compromise of 1850
1853, Pacific Railroad Surveys
1853, Gadsden Purchase
1858, Fraser River Gold Rush
1862, Homestead Act
1864, Sand Creek Massacre
1866, Chisholm Trail Opens
1867, Purchase of Alaska
1872, Great American Bison Slaughter

1952, Eisenhower Is Elected President
1957, Diefenbaker Era in Canada
1960, Quebec Sovereignist Movement
1960, Kennedy Is Elected President
1961, Peace Corps Is Established
1962, Reapportionment Cases
1963, Pearson Becomes Canada's Prime Minister
1963, Assassination of President Kennedy
1964, Twenty-fourth Amendment
1964, Johnson Is Elected President
1968, Assassinations of King and Kennedy
1968, Trudeau Era in Canada
1968, Chicago Riots
1968, Nixon Is Elected President
1969, Alcatraz Occupation
1972, Rapprochement with China
1972, Watergate Affair
1974, Nixon Resigns
1976, Carter Is Elected President
1979, Clark Elected Canada's Prime Minister
1980, Abscam Affair
1980, Reagan Is Elected President
1982, Canada's Constitution Act
1983, Jackson Becomes First Major African American Candidate for President
1984, Mulroney Era in Canada
1986, Iran-Contra Scandal
1988, Bush Is Elected President
1990, Bloc Québécois Forms
1992, Clinton Is Elected President
1993, Campbell Becomes Canada's First Woman Prime Minister
1994, Republicans Return to Congress

HEALTH AND MEDICINE
1846, Surgical Anesthesia Is Safely Demonstrated
1857, New York Infirmary for Indigent Women and Children Opens
1900, Suppression of Yellow Fever
1912, U.S. Public Health Service Is Established
1921, Sheppard-Towner Act
1952, Development of a Polio Vaccine
1960, FDA Approves the Birth Control Pill
1978, Toxic Waste at Love Canal
1981, First AIDS Cases Are Reported
1982, *Plyler v. Doe*

1989, Human Genome Project
1993, Family and Medical Leave Act

IMMIGRATION
1798, Alien and Sedition Acts
1840's, "Old" Immigration
1844, Anti-Irish Riots
1848, California Gold Rush
1849, Chinese Immigration
1868, Burlingame Treaty
1882, Chinese Exclusion Act
1882, Rise of the Chinese Six Companies
1892, Yellow Peril Campaign
1892, "New" Immigration
1895, Chinese American Citizens Alliance Is Founded
1898, *United States v. Wong Kim Ark*
1907, Gentlemen's Agreement
1913, Anti-Defamation League Is Founded
1917, Immigration Act of 1917
1919, Red Scare
1922, Cable Act
1922, *Ozawa v. United States*
1924, Immigration Act of 1924
1927, Sacco and Vanzetti Are Executed
1930's, Mass Deportations of Mexicans
1942, Bracero Program
1943, Magnuson Act
1945, War Brides Act
1952, McCarran-Walter Act
1953, Refugee Relief Act
1954, Operation Wetback
1965, Immigration and Nationality Act
1978, Canada's Immigration Act of 1976
1980, Mariel Boat Lift
1980, Miami Riots
1982, *Plyler v. Doe*
1986, Immigration Reform and Control Act

JEWISH AMERICAN HISTORY
1654, First Jewish Settlers
1913, Anti-Defamation League Is Founded

LATINO AMERICAN HISTORY
A.D. 200, Mayan Civilization
A.D. 700, Zapotec Civilization
1428, Aztec Empire
1492, Columbus' Voyages
1519, Cortés Enters Tenochtitlán

1528, Narváez's and Cabeza de Vaca's Expeditions
1540, Coronado's Expedition
1542, Settlement of Alta California
1598, Oñate's New Mexico Expedition
1632, Zuñi Rebellion
1810, El Grito de Dolores
1819, Adams-Onís Treaty
1821, Mexican War of Independence
1823, Monroe Doctrine
1835, Texas Revolution
1839, Amistad Slave Revolt
1846, Mexican War
1846, Occupation of California and the Southwest
1848, Treaty of Guadalupe Hidalgo
1850, Bloody Island Massacre
1853, Gadsden Purchase
1857, Cart War
1877, Salt Wars
1889, First Pan-American Congress
1895, Hearst-Pulitzer Circulation War
1898, Spanish-American War
1903, Platt Amendment
1910, Mexican Revolution
1912, Intervention in Nicaragua
1916, Pershing Expedition
1917, Jones Act
1929, League of United Latin American Citizens Is Founded
1930's, Mass Deportations of Mexicans
1933, Good Neighbor Policy
1942, Bracero Program
1948, Organization of American States Is Founded
1952, Puerto Rico Becomes a Commonwealth
1954, Operation Wetback
1956, Cuban Revolution
1962, Cuban Missile Crisis
1965, Delano Grape Strike
1968, Bilingual Education Act
1972, United Farm Workers Joins with AFL-CIO
1974, *Lau v. Nichols*
1978, Panama Canal Treaties
1980, Mariel Boat Lift
1980, Miami Riots
1983, United States Invades Grenada

LAWS AND ACTS
1641, Massachusetts Recognizes Slavery
1649, Maryland Act of Toleration
1660, British Navigation Acts

1790, Little Turtle's War
1793, Mackenzie Reaches the Arctic Ocean
1794, Battle of Fallen Timbers
1799, Code of Handsome Lake
1808, Prophetstown Is Founded
1810, *Fletcher v. Peck*
1812, War of 1812
1813, Creek War
1813, Battle of the Thames
1815, Westward Migration
1815, Treaty of Ghent
1815, Red River Raids
1817, Seminole Wars
1821, Santa Fe Trail Opens
1828, *Cherokee Phoenix* Begins Publication
1830, Indian Removal Act
1830, Trail of Tears
1831, Cherokee Cases
1837, Rebellions in Canada
1847, Taos Rebellion
1861, Stand Watie Fights for the South
1861, Apache Wars
1862, Great Sioux War
1863, Long Walk of the Navajos
1864, Sand Creek Massacre
1866, Bozeman Trail War
1867, Medicine Lodge Creek Treaty
1868, Washita River Massacre
1869, First Riel Rebellion
1871, Indian Appropriation Act
1872, Great American Bison Slaughter
1874, Red River War
1876, Canada's Indian Act
1876, Battle of the Little Bighorn
1877, Nez Perce Exile
1885, Second Riel Rebellion
1887, General Allotment Act
1890, Closing of the Frontier
1890, Battle of Wounded Knee
1903, *Lone Wolf v. Hitchcock*
1924, Indian Citizenship Act
1934, Indian Reorganization Act
1953, Termination Resolution
1959, Alaska and Hawaii Gain Statehood
1965, Voting Rights Act
1968, Indian Civil Rights Act
1969, Alcatraz Occupation
1971, Alaska Native Claims Settlement Act
1972, Trail of Broken Treaties
1973, Wounded Knee Occupation

1978, American Indian Religious Freedom Act
1988, Indian Gaming Regulatory Act

ORGANIZATIONS AND INSTITUTIONS

1627, Company of New France Is Chartered
1650, Harvard College Is Established
1670, Hudson's Bay Company Is Chartered
1768, Methodist Church Is Established
1775, Pennsylvania Society for the Abolition of Slavery Is Founded
1784, Hall's Masonic Lodge Is Chartered
1785, Beginnings of State Universities
1787, Free African Society Is Founded
1789, Episcopal Church Is Established
1790's, First U.S. Political Parties
1802, U.S. Military Academy Is Established
1816, Second Bank of the United States Is Chartered
1816, AME Church Is Founded
1819, Unitarian Church Is Founded
1823, Hartford Female Seminary Is Founded
1833, American Anti-Slavery Society Is Founded
1833, Oberlin College Is Established
1834, Birth of the Whig Party
1837, Mt. Holyoke Seminary Is Founded
1846, Independent Treasury Is Established
1846, Smithsonian Institution Is Founded
1853, National Council of Colored People Is Founded
1854, Birth of the Republican Party
1857, New York Infirmary for Indigent Women and Children Opens
1865, Freedmen's Bureau Is Established
1866, Rise of the Ku Klux Klan
1867, Office of Education Is Created
1867, National Grange of the Patrons of Husbandry Forms
1869, Rise of Woman Suffrage Associations
1871, Barnum's Circus Forms
1875, Supreme Court of Canada Is Established
1886, American Federation of Labor Is Founded

1889, Hull House Opens
1890, Women's Rights Associations Unite
1895, Chinese American Citizens Alliance Is Founded
1905, Industrial Workers of the World Is Founded
1905, Niagara Movement
1913, Anti-Defamation League Is Founded
1916, National Woman's Party Is Founded
1916, National Park Service Is Created
1917, Universal Negro Improvement Association Is Established
1918, Republican Resurgence
1919, Black Sox Scandal
1920, League of Women Voters Is Founded
1929, League of United Latin American Citizens Is Founded
1930, Nation of Islam Is Founded
1930, Japanese American Citizens League Is Founded
1935, Works Progress Administration Is Established
1935, Congress of Industrial Organizations Is Founded
1942, Congress of Racial Equality Is Founded
1955, AFL and CIO Merge
1957, Southern Christian Leadership Conference Is Founded
1960, Quebec Sovereignist Movement
1966, National Organization for Women Is Founded
1968, Chicago Riots

PREHISTORY AND ANCIENT CULTURES

15,000 B.C., Bering Strait Migrations
1500 B.C., Olmec Civilization
700 B.C., Ohio Mound Builders
300 B.C., Hohokam Culture
A.D. 200, Mayan Civilization
A.D. 200, Anasazi Civilization
A.D. 700, Zapotec Civilization
A.D. 750, Mogollon Culture
A.D. 750, Mississippian Culture
1428, Aztec Empire

RELIGION

1620, Pilgrims Land at Plymouth
1630, Great Puritan Migration
1632, Settlement of Connecticut

TRANSPORTATION
1807, Voyage of the *Clermont*
1811, Construction of the National Road
1815, Westward Migration
1821, Santa Fe Trail Opens
1823, Jedediah Smith Explores the Far West
1825, Erie Canal Opens
1845, Era of the Clipper Ships
1853, Pacific Railroad Surveys
1860, Pony Express
1866, Chisholm Trail Opens
1869, Transcontinental Railroad Is Completed
1887, Interstate Commerce Act
1903, Acquisition of the Panama Canal Zone
1903, Wright Brothers' First Flight
1913, Ford Assembly Line Begins Operation
1927, Lindbergh's Transatlantic Flight
1930, Baltimore and Ohio Railroad Begins Operation
1959, St. Lawrence Seaway Opens
1973, Arab Oil Embargo and Energy Crisis
1978, Panama Canal Treaties

TREATIES AND AGREEMENTS
1778, Franco-American Treaties
1783, Treaty of Paris
1784, Fort Stanwix Treaty
1790, Nootka Sound Convention
1794, Jay's Treaty
1795, Pinckney's Treaty
1803, Louisiana Purchase
1815, Treaty of Ghent
1819, Adams-Onís Treaty
1842, Webster-Ashburton Treaty
1848, Treaty of Guadalupe Hidalgo
1853, Gadsden Purchase
1867, Purchase of Alaska
1867, Medicine Lodge Creek Treaty
1868, Burlingame Treaty
1871, Treaty of Washington
1907, Gentlemen's Agreement
1919, Treaty of Versailles
1921, Washington Disarmament Conference
1924, Halibut Treaty
1928, Kellogg-Briand Pact
1932, Ottawa Agreements
1936, Reciprocity Treaty
1940, Ogdensburg Agreement
1942, Bracero Program

1948, Organization of American States Is Founded
1949, North Atlantic Treaty
1978, Panama Canal Treaties
1979, SALT II Is Signed
1987, INF Treaty Is Signed
1993, START II Is Signed
1993, North American Free Trade Agreement
1994, U.S.-North Korea Pact
1994, General Agreement on Tariffs and Trade

WARS, UPRISINGS, AND CIVIL UNREST
1495, West Indian Uprisings
1598, Oñate's New Mexico Expedition
1622, Powhatan Wars
1632, Zuñi Rebellion
1636, Pequot War
1642, Beaver Wars
1664, British Conquest of New Netherland
1675, Metacom's War
1676, Bacon's Rebellion
1680, Pueblo Revolt
1702, Queen Anne's War
1711, Tuscarora War
1712, New York City Slave Revolt
1714, Fox Wars
1739, Stono Rebellion
1739, King George's War
1754, French and Indian War
1759, Cherokee War
1763, Pontiac's Resistance
1763, Paxton Boys' Massacres
1765, Stamp Act Crisis
1767, Townshend Crisis
1768, Carolina Regulator Movements
1770, Boston Massacre
1773, Boston Tea Party
1774, Lord Dunmore's War
1775, Battle of Lexington and Concord
1775, Second Continental Congress
1776, Indian Delegation Meets with Congress
1776, First Test of a Submarine in Warfare
1777, Battle of Oriskany Creek
1777, Battle of Saratoga
1781, Cornwallis Surrenders at Yorktown
1790, Little Turtle's War
1791, Haitian Independence
1793, Whiskey Rebellion

1794, Battle of Fallen Timbers
1797, XYZ Affair
1804, Burr's Conspiracy
1810, El Grito de Dolores
1811, Battle of Tippecanoe
1812, War of 1812
1813, Creek War
1813, Battle of the Thames
1815, Battle of New Orleans
1815, Red River Raids
1817, Seminole Wars
1821, Mexican War of Independence
1831, Nat Turner's Insurrection
1835, Texas Revolution
1837, Rebellions in Canada
1839, Amistad Slave Revolt
1842, Dorr Rebellion
1844, Anti-Irish Riots
1846, Mexican War
1846, Occupation of California and the Southwest
1847, Taos Rebellion
1850, Bloody Island Massacre
1857, Cart War
1859, John Brown's Raid on Harpers Ferry
1860, Confederate States Secede from the Union
1861, Stand Watie Fights for the South
1861, Apache Wars
1861, First Battle of Bull Run
1862, *Monitor* vs. *Virginia*
1862, Great Sioux War
1863, First National Draft Law
1863, Battles of Gettysburg, Vicksburg, and Chattanooga
1864, Sherman's March to the Sea
1864, Sand Creek Massacre
1865, Surrender at Appomattox and Assassination of Lincoln
1866, Race Riots in the South
1866, Bozeman Trail War
1868, Washita River Massacre
1869, First Riel Rebellion
1874, Red River War
1876, Battle of the Little Bighorn
1877, Nez Perce Exile
1877, Salt Wars
1885, Second Riel Rebellion
1890, Battle of Wounded Knee
1898, Spanish-American War
1899, Philippine Insurrection
1910, Mexican Revolution
1912, Intervention in Nicaragua
1916, Pershing Expedition